Apple® IIGS™ Technical Reference

Michael Fischer

Osborne **McGraw-Hill**
Berkeley, California

Osborne **McGraw-Hill**
2600 Tenth Street
Berkeley, California 94710
U.S.A.

For information on translations and book distributors outside of the U.S.A., please write to Osborne **McGraw-Hill** at the above address.

A complete list of trademarks appears on page 681.

Apple® IIGS™ Technical Reference

34567890 DODO 8987

ISBN 0-07-881009-4

Apple® IIGS™ Technical Reference

C O N T E N T S

ACKNOWLEDGMENTS

Obviously a book like this one could not have been written without the active support and encouragement of Apple Computer, Inc. An organization is represented by its people, and many Apple employees were kind enough to guide me through some of the more obscure (to me) portions of the IIGS. Others provided equipment and documentation. There always seemed to be someone at Apple who could refer me to someone else who could answer what must have seemed the most arcane or inane questions.

In any attempt to list the many helpful people at Apple, I surely would fail to include some who deserve mention. But I would be remiss in not thanking Martha Steffen and Neal Amsden for their continuing assistance.

I have been blessed in this project with as fine a technical reviewer and philosophical critic as any author could have. Jim Mensch, of Apple Computer, Inc., has done his best to keep me honest—both technically and philosophically. Jim is responsible for much of the merit of this book.

In addition to technical accuracy, careful attention to style, grammar, and production is essential for a quality book. Kevin Shafer has been of inestimable assistance in guiding me through the snares of the English language, and he has been supportive throughout the production process.

The folks at Osborne/McGraw-Hill have demonstrated once again what makes their company the finest publisher one could want. Cindy Hudson has been supportive and encouraging, keeping me more or less on an impossible schedule. Lyn Cordell has handled the production with organization and a sense of humor, particularly important qualities when page proof time rolls around.

I also wish to thank the Osborne/McGraw-Hill art department, and particularly Pamela Webster, not only for designing a good looking product, but for working with the many tables in this book to make them both usable and attractive.

Finally, I would like to thank Jon Erickson, formerly with Osborne/McGraw-Hill and now with BYTE Magazine. Jon originally piqued my interest in this undertaking. Now that the project is drawing to a close, I am grateful to him for believing in and encouraging me.

MF

INTRODUCTION

The Apple IIGS computer acts as a bridge between the Apple II and the Macintosh. It links the diverse worlds of these two earlier machines in a number of areas, including

- □ Programming philosophy
- □ Peripheral interchangeability
- □ User interface
- □ Computing power
- □ Toolbox availability

For Apple II owners and programmers, the switch to the Apple IIGS can be daunting, notwithstanding the fact that the IIGS can run nearly all 8-bit Apple II software. Some people may have difficulty learning to use that plastic offshoot of the rodent species, the mouse. Others may resist menus and the human interface that is supposed to make using computers easier.

Especially challenging for the Apple II programmer are the needs to learn a new philosophy of programming, a new programming environment, and a drastically increased set of programming aids. The Apple IIGS toolbox is massive—so large that it does not fit within the confines of the 128K of ROM in the IIGS. Nor does a complete description of it fit within the confines of a single Apple technical manual.

The IIGS is a change for the Macintosh programmer, too. That programmer knows about human interface guidelines, about the toolbox, and about mice, but doesn't know how to work with registers that have a maximum size of 16 bits, with a segmented memory space, or with a tool function locator. Most importantly, the Macintosh programmer has not dealt with the possibility of several different display modes, with color, with a text-only mode, or with an Apple II user who fancies herself or himself different from "those Macintosh people."

In spite of all these considerations, the IIGS is ideal programming territory for both Apple II and Macintosh programmers. It provides a great deal that both have been asking for.

One big problem anyone who is trying to master the IIGS will encounter is the massive amount of official documentation available for the computer from Apple. There are thirteen different manuals for the IIGS, two with their own pocket reference. The product even has two technical introduction manuals.

The purpose of this book is to incorporate in one reference most of the relevant material about the Apple IIGS in a form useful to people with some technical interest in the machine. Care has been taken to provide an overview as well as substantial coverage of the various technical aspects of the IIGS. Of course, to keep within the confines of a single volume, not every technical subject has been covered exhaustively. What is covered is the information that is essential or especially helpful to programmers or interested users, those who have made the Apple II family of computers legendary.

This book provides facts about the differences between the IIGS and the earlier members of the Apple II family. Such information will be useful to the current Apple II owner who is considering upgrading to a IIGS, as well as to the Apple II programmer interested in programming for the IIGS.

This book also compares the programming and user environments of the IIGS with those of the Macintosh. This comparison will be of use to the Macintosh programmer wishing to migrate programs into the color environment of the IIGS.

The sample program segments in this book all were written in 65816 assembly language, using the macro libraries available in the Apple IIGS Programmer's Workshop Assembler. Because of the nature of the macro calls, much of the information in the listings should be understandable, not only to 65816 and 6502 assembly language programmers, but also to 68000 assembly language programmers, and even to those who are not experienced assembly language programmmers on any chip.

PART I

Overview

CHAPTER 1

Comparison and Compatibility

As a computer, the Apple IIGS is part Apple II, part Macintosh—and all new. This chapter compares the IIGS with its siblings, the 8-bit Apple IIs and the Macintosh. In name and by heritage and lineage, the Apple IIGS is a member of the Apple II family of computers. It resembles both an Apple IIe and an Apple IIc. But there are also important differences.

MICROPROCESSORS

The Mega II custom chip is the base of the compatibility between the Apple IIe, Apple IIc, and the Apple IIGS. It contains the elements of much of the support circuitry on the earlier Apple II's for such purposes as timing and control, including memory management (main and auxiliary memory, language cards) and video-display modes (40- and 80-column text; low-, high-, and double-high-resolution graphics).

The memory of the IIGS is arranged for maximum compatibility with Apple IIe-Apple IIc operation. Certain Apple IIe-Apple IIc operations must occur at certain speeds. To understand this concept, we first need to understand how processor speed affects the operation of the computer.

The 65C02 in the Apple IIe and Apple IIc runs at a speed of 1 MHz—that is, it can perform 1 million operation cycles each second. Each actual command takes between two and eight cycles. The 65816 in the IIGS performs 2.8 million operation cycles per second. Some of these cycles are used in servicing the various support circuitry in the IIGS, reducing the effective speed of the IIGS to 2.5 million cycles.

Some programs are speed-dependent—that is, they expect that particular operations will take a certain period of time. This type of program either will not function reliably or may not function at all if the speed of the processor or of the memory is not what it needs. Examples of speed-dependent applications include disk operating systems during input and output (and most other input and output routines) and music programs. In addition, certain games will be unplayable if they run at a speed 2 1/2 times faster than expected.

The solution in the IIGS is to provide two types of memory. All of the expansion RAM, and 128K of the IIGS's built-in RAM, run at the faster speed of 2.5 MHz. The other 128K runs at 1 MHz. The Mega II and Fast Processor Interface custom chips provide the necessary support circuitry to enable this dual-speed memory to work.

The IIGS also differs from its predecessors in terms of the microprocessor used in the machine. The Apple IIe and Apple IIc uses a 65C02 microprocessor. This chip has a 16-bit program counter and the following 8-bit registers: accumulator, X, Y, stack pointer, and processor status. The stack must operate from $0100-01FF. Direct page operations, known as zero page on the 65C02, must occur from $0000-00FF. The chip may directly address 64 kilobytes of memory, so all these addresses are on the equivalent of bank $00 of the IIGS.

The Apple IIGS uses a 65816 microprocessor, which has a 16-bit program counter and two 8-bit auxiliary addressing registers (program and data bank registers). This chip also has 16-bit registers for all but the processor status register, whereas the 65C02 has 8-bit registers. That is, the 65816 has a 16-bit accumulator, stack pointer, and direct and X and Y index registers. The stack may operate anywhere in bank zero and be any size. Direct page operations, while restricted to 256 bytes, can occur anywhere in bank zero. The chip may directly address 16 megabytes of memory.

The 65816 is a very different microprocessor from the 68000 chip found in the Macintosh. While both chips evolved from the Motorola 6800, their evolutionary paths have parted to the extent that the two chips now bear little resemblance to each other in architecture and instruction sets. It is not even possible to compare machine speeds directly. (For a fuller listing of the instruction set similarities and the differences between the two processors, see Fischer, *65816 Assembly Language Programming,* Osborne/McGraw-Hill, 1986.)

PORTS

The IIGS has most of the slots of the Apple IIe. The numbered expansion slots (1-7) exist on both machines and are essentially identical. (See the discussion in Chapter 3 for the minor difference.) The IIGS has a memory expansion slot not available on the IIe. And the IIe Aux slot, used for 80-column display and memory expansion, is not available on the IIGS. The IIc and Macintosh do not have slots, except for a relatively hard-to-access memory expansion slot on the IIc.

Table 1-1 lists the IIe hardware products (some of which are attached to slots in the IIGS and IIe) that work on the IIGS. Table 1-2 lists those hardware products that work only if the IIGS is operating at normal (1 MHz) speed. Table 1-3 lists hardware products that require an upgrade to the support software in order to work on the IIGS.

The IIGS also has ports similar to those on the Apple IIc. It has two serial ports, mapped to Slots 1 and 2, which resemble those on the IIc. The ports are firmware-compatible with those on the IIc, although a different controller is used. The 6551 ACIA (Asynchronous Communications Interface Adapter) is used on the IIc and the Super Serial Card, and the 8530 SCC (Serial Communications Controller) is used on the IIGS. Because different hardware is used for these ports, direct hardware commands

Product	Company	Notes
100 Robotic Modem	Visionary	
7710 Serial Card	Cal. Computer Systems	
Apple IIc Monitor (monochrome)	Apple Computer	
Apple Color Monitor IIc	Apple Computer	
Apple Color Monitor IIe	Apple Computer	
Apple Color Plotter	Apple Computer	
Apple Daisy Wheel Printer	Apple Computer	
Apple Dot Matrix Printer	Apple Computer	
Apple Graphics Tablet	Apple Computer	
Apple Hand Controller II	Apple Computer	
Apple Joystick II	Apple Computer	
Apple Modem 300/1200	Apple Computer	
Apple Monitor II Monochrome	Apple Computer	
Apple Mouse	Apple Computer	Note 1
Apple Mouse Card	Apple Computer	Note 1
Apple IIe Numeric Keypad	Apple Computer	Note 2
Apple Personal Modem	Apple Computer	
Auto Dial 212A Modem	US Robotics	
Cat 300 Baud Modem	Novation	
Centronics Parallel Printer	Centronics	
Champion Parallel Card	Cietech	
Constellation II Network	Corvus	
Corvus Multiplexer Network	Corvus	
Decillionix DX-1	Decillionix	
Disk Controller: Disk II	Apple Computer	
Disk Controller: DuoDisk	Apple Computer	
Disk Controller: UniDisk 3.5	Apple Computer	
Disk II	Apple Computer	
DuoDisk	Apple Computer	Note 3
Elite One 5.25	Rana Systems	
Fourth Dimension 5.25	Fourth Dimension	
FX-80 Dot Matrix Printer	Epson	
Gold Card 192K	Digital Research	
Graph Writer Printer Card	MPC	
Grappler+ Parallel Interface	Orange Micro	
Grappler+ Serial Interface	Orange Micro	
Grappler Serial Interface	Orange Micro	
HitachiVM 129U Monitor	Hitachi	
HR 15 Dot Matrix Printer	Brother	

Table 1-1

Apple IIe Hardware Products Reported to Work with Apple IIGS

Product	Company	Notes
IEEE-488 Card	Apple Computer	
ImageWriter I	Apple Computer	
ImageWriter II	Apple Computer	
IQS 401LX Spectrum Analyzer	IQS	Note 4
Keys-1 Parallel Interface	Syntauri	
Koala + Pad	Koala Technologies	
Kurzweil Reading Machine	Kurzweil	
Listner 1000 v 2.0	MicroMint	
Lobo 5.25 Disk Drive	Lobo	
M&R Enterprises Monitor	M&R Enterprises	
MD212 Modem	Ven-Tel	
MD212-3E Modem	Ven-Tel	
Micom Instalink 460 Modem	Micom	
Micromodem IIe	Hayes	Note 4
Microstore Hard Disk	ATS	
Microtek Parallel Interface	Microtek	
Mikron ADC 4000 (RS232)	Mikron	
Model A-2 Modem	Micro SCI	
Mountain Music Card	Mountain Computer	
Muppet Learning Keys	Koala Technologies	
MX-80 F/T Dot Matrix Printer	Epson	
Novation Cat Modem	Novation	
Novation Series 4000 Modem	Novation	
Orange Parallel Card	Orange Micro	
Pansonic Omni Monitor	Pansonic	
Parallel Interface Card	Apple Computer	
PJ-1080A Printer	Canon	
PKASO/U Interface	PKASO/U Interact	
Power Pad	Chalk Board	
QC 10 HD	Quark	
Quick 20 HD	CMC Computer Systems	
Qume Sprint 5 Printer	Qume Corp	
Rx-80 Printer	Epson	
Sanyo DM5012 CX Monitor	Sanyo	
Sanyo VM 4209 Monitor	Sanyo	
Scribe Printer	Apple Computer	
Seiko Watch Data Terminal	CPU	
Sider II 10 Mb HD	First Class Peripherals	
Sider II 20 Md HD	First Class Peripherals	

Table 1-1

Apple IIe Hardware Products Reported to Work with Apple IIGS (continued)

Product	Company	Notes
Silentype Printer	Apple Computer	
SmartHome	Cyberlynx	
Smartmodem 2400	Hayes	
Softcard CATS Rev.A	Microsoft	
Super Serial Card	Apple Computer	
Super Serial Interface 7711	Apple Computer	
Swyftcard	Information Appliance	
Telmac LDD-1 Modem	Telmac	
Telmac Modem	Telmac	
Think Jet Printer	Hewlett-Packard	
Thunderclock Plus	Thunderware	
US Robotics Password Modem	US Robotics	
Ufonic Voice System	Borg Warner	
UniDisk 3.5	Apple Computer	
UniDisk (5.25)	Apple Computer	
Volksmodem	Volksmodem	

Notes:

1. Old Apple Mouse and Mouse Card (in Slot 4) works similarly to the built-in IIGS ADB mouse.
2. Only works on the IIGS that is an upgrade of a IIe.
3. Must remove one resistor on drive card.
4. 40 columns only.

Table 1-1

Apple IIe Hardware Products Reported to Work with Apple IIGS (continued)

Product	Company
Corvus 20Mb H D	Corvus
Echo +	Street Electronics
Micro Music DAC Board	Temporal Acuity
Z-Engine	Advanced Logic Systems
Z80 Plus	Applied Engineering

Table 1-2

Apple IIe Hardware Products Reported to Work on Apple IIGS Only at Normal Speed

Product	Company
Microsoft Softcard II System	Microsoft
Passport MIDI Interface Card	Passport Designs
Syntech MIDI Interface Card	Syntech

Table 1-3

Apple IIe Hardware Products Reported to Require Software Upgrades to Work on Apple IIGS

that work on the IIc do not work on the IIGS. The 8530 SCC is also used on the Macintosh.

The AppleTalk circuitry is part of the IIc, the IIGS, and the Macintosh. The IIc serial ports use DIN-5 connectors. Those on the Macintosh use DB-9 connectors, and the IIGS and the Macintosh Plus use mini-circular-8.

The Diskport on the IIGS is similar to that on the IIc. The IIc has a built-in drive, mapped to slot 6. The IIGS has no built-in drive; 3.5-inch drives are mapped to slot 5, and 5.25-inch drives are mapped to slot 6, in a manner similar to that on the IIc. The difference is that the firmware on the IIGS supports extended commands from anywhere in memory, and supports more devices than the port on the IIc (see discussion in Chapter 21). The Macintosh, likc the IIGS and the IIc, uses the IWM controller for the disk drives. The IIe has no built-in disk controller circuitry.

The Apple IIGS uses Apple 5.25 disk devices (like the IIe and IIc), UniDisk 3.5 devices (like the IIe and IIc), or AppleDisk 3.5 devices (like the Macintosh).

The IIc, the Macintosh, and the IIGS have built-in mouse connectors. The connector on the IIc doubles as the game input/output port and uses a DB-9 connector. The connector on the IIGS is a part of the Apple Desktop Bus (discussed in Chapter 15). It uses a mini-circular-4 connector. The mouse in the IIc relies on the 65C02 in the IIc for its operation. The mouse in the IIGS uses the ADB microcontroller.

The Apple IIc has a special DB-15 video connector, which was designed for RGB output, as well as a flat display screen. The RGB output requires support circuitry that is not built in. The Apple IIGS has a DB-15 RGB video connector that outputs analog RGB signals. It connects directly to an analog RGB monitor without the need for other support circuitry. The Macintosh has a built-in video display screen.

The Apple IIc has a sound output jack (mini-stereo wired together) with a volume control. The IIGS and Macintosh have a similar sound output jack, but without a volume control. The volume control is handled by the Control Panel (discussed in Chapter 3) for the IIGS. In the case of the IIc and the Macintosh, the internal speaker is disabled when the output jack is being used.

The quality of the sound is significantly different in the IIGS. Both the Apple IIe and IIc have single-voice sound output under software control. The Macintosh sound system has a four-voice capability with a 185-byte sound buffer. The Apple IIGS has a 15-voice, 32-oscillator sound system using several custom chips, the Ensoniq synthesizer chip, and 64K of dedicated memory. Of course, the IIGS also contains the ability to simulate the single-voice sound used in the earlier Apple II's.

All three Apple II machines—the Apple IIGS, IIe, and IIc—have an NTSC-compatible, composite-video output that can be connected to a monochrome or color composite monitor. The connector is an RCA phono jack.

The Apple IIe, like the Apple II and II Plus before it, has a cassette input and output port, which initially used standard cassette tape to transfer data and programs to and from other cassette tapes. Later uses of these ports, particularly with the faster mass-storage devices like the disk drive, included music output. These ports are not found on the Apple IIGS, the IIc, or the Macintosh.

The IIGS has both a nine-pin (DB-9) game port, like the IIe and IIc, and a 16-pin game connector, like the IIe. These connectors are essentially unchanged from the IIe version, which itself was unchanged from the Apple II. The Macintosh has no game controller connectors.

VIDEO DISPLAY AND KEYBOARD

The video display output choices available on the IIGS correspond to all the modes available on the IIe and IIc, with the addition of significant new modes and some additional features. Both 40- and 80-column text display, as well as low-, high-, and double-high-resolution graphics, are built in as they are on the IIc. (On the IIe, an 80-column display card is necessary for 80-column text and an extended 80-column display card is necessary for double-high-resolution graphics.) In the Apple IIGS (but not on the Apple

IIe or IIc) the text, background, and border can be displayed in any of 16 different user-selected colors on an analog RGB monitor.

On the IIGS, the IIe and IIc graphics display modes are complemented by two new super-high-resolution display modes. These modes enable a screen display of either 320 or 640 pixels across by 200 pixels down. Colors are selected from among 4096 choices. The graphics display modes are summarized in Table 1-4 together with the Macintosh display mode.

Neither the Apple IIe nor the Apple IIc comes with a built-in real-time clock, although a clock may be added to either unit. The Apple IIGS and Macintosh come with a built-in real-time clock with a battery backup that keeps the clock accurate even when the computer is turned off.

Mode Name	Pixels Down	Pixels Across	Number of Colors Per Line	Number of Colors On Screen	Palette Size	Found On
Low-resolution	40	48	16	16	16	All
Double-low-resolution	80	48	16	16	16	All but 64K IIe
High-resolution	256	192	6*	6	6	All
Double-high-resolution	512	192	16	16	16	All but 64K IIe
320 Super-high-resolution	320	200	16	256	4096	IIGS
640 Super-high-resolution	640	200	16/4**	256/64**	4096	IIGS
Macintosh	512	342	2***	2***	2***	Macintosh

Notes:

* Certain restrictions apply as to which colors can appear in which column and which colors can appear next to each other.

** In 640 mode with four colors per line (64 per screen), each of the colors can be displayed anywhere on the line. In 640 modes with 16 colors per line (256 per screen), certain restrictions apply as to which colors can appear in which column. (See discussion in Chapter 9.)

*** The two Macintosh colors are black (off) and white (on).

Table 1-4

Summary of Apple II Family Graphics Display Modes

The keyboard on the IIGS has a numeric keypad in addition to the keys found on the Apple IIe and IIc keyboards. The names of several keys have changed from the traditional Apple II names. The solid or closed Apple key has been renamed OPTION, while the outline or open Apple key has been renamed APPLE. The Apple symbol shares the keycap with the cloverleaf command symbol found on the Macintosh. The keyboard is similar to the Macintosh Plus keyboard, except that the IIGS keyboard has CONTROL and ESCAPE keys and has an ENTER key only on the numeric pad. In addition it has only one OPTION key.

FIRMWARE AND SOFTWARE

The ROM firmware on the IIGS is significantly expanded over that in the IIe and IIc. The IIe and the IIc have 32K ROM. By comparison, the IIGS has 128K of ROM, similar to that of the Macintosh Plus and 512K Enhanced. The IIGS ROM includes Applesoft (basically unchanged from the Apple IIe and IIc), a system monitor expanded for the 65816 processor (discussed in Chapter 7), a toolbox based on the Macintosh Toolbox, extensive diagnostics, and device drivers. The toolbox is too large for the ROM and some of it is disk-based and must be loaded into RAM when used.

The various steps taken in the design and implementation of the IIGS have resulted in significant compatibility between it and the IIe and IIc. As a result, much software written from the IIe and IIc works without modification on the IIGS. Table 1-5 is a list of IIe software that is reported to work on the IIGS together with a list of conditions applicable to some of the software. Because it uses a processor that is incompatible with the 68000 in the Macintosh, the IIGS cannot run programs written for the Macintosh, nor can the Macintosh run programs written for the IIGS.

The main disk for the IIGS is the double-sided 800K 3.5 disk. This disk is the same used in the UniDisk 3.5 and in the double-sided Macintosh drives. The format of the disk is that used with the UniDisk 3.5, although with proper software, a IIGS disk can be read by a Macintosh and a Macintosh disk can be read by a IIGS.

In terms of philosophy of operation, the IIGS resembles a Macintosh with a desktop graphics display, mouse selection, and event-driven applications. But it still is an Apple II. This relationship is made most apparent by the availability of classic desk accessories for the IIGS, which can run with much Apple II 8-bit software so long as the Control Panel is accessible

Product	Company	Notes
Adv. Business Accountant	Manzanita Software	Note 1
Algebra 1-6, vols 1-6	Edu-Ware	
Algebra Arcade	Wadsworth	
Alien Action	DLM	
Alien Addition	DLM	
Alligator Alley	DLM	
Alligator Mix	DLM	
Alphabet Zoo	Spinnaker	
Alphabetic Keyboard	Southwestern	
Amazon	Telarium	Note 1
Anagrams Hispanomericanos	Gessler	
Animal Photo Fun	DLM	
Annam	Educational Action	
Apple Access II	Apple Computer	Notes 1,2,3
Apple at Play	Apple Computer	Notes 1,2,4,5
Apple at Work 40/80	Apple Computer	Note 1
Apple Education Classics	Apple Computer	Notes 1,4,5
Apple FORTRAN	Apple Computer	Note 1
Apple II Instant Pascal	Apple Computer	
Apple II Pascal 1.1	Apple Computer	Note 1
Apple II Quickfile	Apple Computer	Note 1
Apple Logo (64K)	Apple Computer	Note 1
Apple Logo II (128K)	Apple Computer	Note 1
Apple Logo Classroom Kit	Apple Computer	
Apple Pascal 1.3	Apple Computer	Note 1
Apple Presents Apple Logo	Apple Computer	Note 1
Apple Super Co-PILOT	Apple Computer	Note 1
Apple SuperPILOT Log	Apple Computer	Note 1
AppleWorks 1.3	Apple Computer	Note 1
AppleWriter II (ProDOS)	Apple Computer	Note 1
Arcade Machine	Broderbund	Note 1
ASCII Express (ProDOS)	United Software	Note 3
Astronomy: Stars for All	Educational Action	Note 6

Table 1-5

Apple IIe-Apple IIc Software Products Reported to Work on Apple IIGS

Product	Company	Notes
Back to Basics Accounting	Peachtree Software	Note 7
Backup II	Apple Computer	Note 1
Bank Street Speller	Scholastic	
Bank Street Storybook	Mindscape	
Bank Street Writer	Broderbund	Notes 8,9
Baron	Blue Chip Software	
BASIC Programming with ProDOS	Apple Computer	Note 1
Blazing Paddles	Baudville	
Body in Focus	CBS	Note 10
Body Transparent, The	Designware	
BPI Accounts Payable	BPI	Note 1
BPI Accounts Receivable	BPI	Note 1
BPI Business Analyst	BPI	
BPI General Accounting	BPI	Note 1
BPI Inventory Control	BPI	Note 1
BPI Payroll	BPI	Note 1
Build-A-Book About You	Scarborough Systems	
Bumble Plot	Learning Company	
Business Works	Manzanita	Note 1
Capitalization Plus	Microcomputer	
Cartels & Cutthroats	Strategic Simulations	
Cavern Creatures	Data Most	
Charles Goren Bridge	CBS	
Charlie Brown's ABC	Random House	
Choplifter	Broderbund	Note 8
Coast to Coast America	CBS	
Code Quest	Sunburst	
Color Keys	Sunburst	
Color Me	Mindscape	
Comp-U-Solve	Educational Action	Note 5
Compassion Kitchen	DLM	
Copy II+	Central Point	

Table 1-5

Apple IIe-Apple IIc Software Products Reported to Work on Apple IIGS (continued)

Product	Company	Notes
Crossword Magic	Mindscape	
Crypto Cube	DesignWare	
Cut & Paste	Electronic Arts	Note 11
Dinosaur Dig	CBS	Note 10
Dollars & Sense	Monogram	Note 11
DOS 3.3 System Master	Apple Computer	
Dragon Mix	DLM	
Early Games for Young Children	Springboard	
Elementary Mathematics	MECC	
Elementary, My Dear Apple	Apple Computer	
English Achievement I-V	Microcomputer	
Ernie's Quiz	CTW	
Exploring Logo	Apple Computer	Note 1
Explorer Metros	Sunburst	
Factory, The	Sunburst	
FantaVision	Broderbund	
Fahrenheit 451	Telarium	
Fay, That Math Woman	Dida Tech Software	
Fish Scales	DLM	
Flash Spell Helicopter	M W	
FlashCalc	Paladin Software	Note 1
Flight Simulator II	SubLogic	Note 8
French Achievement I-II	M W	
Galaxy Math Facts Game	Random House	
Game of the States	Milton Bradley	
Geometry Concepts	Ventura	
Gertrude's Puzzles	Learning Co.	
Gertrude's Secrets	Learning Co.	
Getting Down to BASIC	Apple Computer	Note 1
Golf Classic & Compubar	Edufun	
Grammar Examiner	DesignWare	
Grandma's House	Spinnaker	

Table 1-5

Apple IIe-Apple IIc Software Products Reported to Work on Apple IIGS (continued)

Product	Company	Notes
Graphics Magician	Penguin	
GraphWorks	PBI Software	Note 1
Great Maine to Calif. Race	Hayden	
Home Accountant Expanded	Continental Software	
Idea Invasion	DLM	
Incredible Labratory, The	Sunburst	
Inside Story, The	Apple Computer	Note 9
Instant Zoo	CTW	
Jane	Arktronics	Note 8
Jenny of the Prairie	Addison-Wesley	
Juggle's Rainbow	Learning Co.	Note 10
Karel the Robot	Krell	
La Corrida de Toros	Gessler	
La Guillotine	Gessler	
LISA V 2.6	Laserware	
Magic Office System	Artsci	
Magic Spells	Learning Co.	
Management Edge	Human Edge Software	
Master Match	Advanced Ideas	
Mastering the SAT	CBS	
Mastertype	Scarborough	
Math Blaster!	Davidson & Associates	
MegaWorks	Megahaus	
Memory—a First Step	Sunburst	
Memory Myth	Micro Power & Light	
Meteor Mission	DLM	
Meteor Multiplication	DLM	
Microtype Paws	Southwestern	
Microzine	Scholastic	
Millionaire	Blue Chip	
Minus Mission	DLM	
Mix & Match	CTW	
Monkey Math	Artwork Software	

Table 1-5

Apple IIe-Apple IIc Software Products Reported to Work on Apple IIGS (continued)

Product	Company	Notes
Moptown	Learning Co.	
Moptown Hotel	Learning Co.	Note 1
Moptown Parade	Learning Co.	Note 1
Mouse Budget	International Solutions	
MouseDesk	International Solutions	
MouseDesk Selector	International Solutions	
MousePaint	Apple Computer	Note 1
MouseWrite	Roger Wagner	
Multiplan	Microsoft	
Muppet Learning Keys	Koala	
Murder by the Dozen	CBS	Note 1
Music Construction Set	Electronic Arts	
Newsroom, The	Springboard	Notes 1,12
Oh, Deer!	MECC	
Operation: Frog	Scholastic	
Pascal Profile Manager	Apple Computer	Note 1
Personal Tax Planner	McGraw-Hill	
pfs:FILE	Software Publishing	
pfs:Graph	Software Publishing	Note 6
pfs:Plan	Software Publishing	Note 1
pfs:Report	Software Publishing	
pfs:Write	Software Publishing	Note 1
Pic.Builder	Xerox Education Publishing	
Pinball Construction Set	Electronic Arts	
Poker Parat (German)	Gessler	
Pond, The	Sunburst	
President Elect	Strategic Simulations	
Print Shop, The	Broderbund	
ProDOS Assembler Tools	Apple Computer	Note 1
ProDOS Users Disk	Apple Computer	
Projectiles II	Vernier Software	
Quizagon	Springboard	

Table 1-5
Apple IIe-Apple IIc Software Products Reported to Work on Apple IIGS (continued)

Product	Company	Notes
Reader Rabbit	Learning Co.	
Remember!	Designware	
ReportWorks	Megahaus	
Robot Odyssey I	Learning Co.	
Robotwar	Muse	Note 12
Rocky's Boots	Learning Co.	Note 11
Run Robot Run	Edu Teach Aids	
SAT Preparation Course	EduTech	
Secrets of Science Island	Grolier	Note 1
Sensible Speller IV DOS	Sensible Software	Note 1
Sensible Speller ProDOS	Sensible Software	
Shell Games, The	Apple Computer	
Songwriter	Scarborough	
Space Math	Learning Well	
Spanish Achievement I	Microcomputer	
Spanish Grammar Review	Gessler	
Speed Reader II	Davidson & Associates	
Spell It!	Davidson & Associates	
Spellicopter	Designware	
Spelling Wiz	DLM	
Spot Light	CTW	
Star Search	Earthware	
State of the Art Accounting	State of the Art	
States & Traits	DesignWare	
Stickeybear ABC's	Xerox	
Stickeybear Basket Bounce	Xerox	
Stickeybear Bop	Xerox	
Stickeybear Numbers	Xerox	
Stickeybear Opposites	Xerox	
Stickeybear Reading	Xerox	
Stickeybear Shapes	Xerox	
Stickeybear Town Builder	Xerox	

Table 1-5
Apple IIe-Apple IIc Software Products Reported to Work on Apple IIGS (continued)

Product	Company	Notes
Story Maker	Sierra on Line	Notes 9,11
Story Tree	Scholastic	
Success with Math	CBS	
SuperCalc3a	Computer Associates	Notes 6,12
Survival Math:Simulations	Sunburst	
Swyftcard	Information Appliance	Notes 1,8,9
Talk Back	Russ Systems	
Teach Yourself Essentials	Addison-Wesley	Note 1
Terrapin Logo	Terrapin	Notes 1,6
Terrapin Logo Utilities	Terrapin	
The Visible Computer:6502	Software Masters	
Trains	Spinnaker	
Treasure Hunter	Grolier	
Turbo Pascal	Borland	Note 1
Turtle Tracks	Scholastic	Notes 1,6
Typing Tudor III	Kriya Systems	
Verb Viper	DLM	
Versaform	Applied Software	Note 1
Volcanos	Earthware	
Welcome Aboard!	Broderbund	
Where in the World is Carmen Sandiego	Broderbund	
Wiz Works	DLM	
Wizard of Words	Advanced Ideas	
Word Attack!	Davidson & Associates	
Word Invasion	DLM	
Word Master	DLM	
Word Radar	DLM	
Word Spinner	Learning Co.	
Your Personal Net Worth	Scarborough	Note 5
Zaxxon	Datasoft	Note 8
Zoom Grafix	Phoenix Software	Notes 1,12

Table 1-5

Apple IIe-Apple IIc Software Products Reported to Work on Apple IIGS (continued)

Notes:

1. Cannot use Control panel
2. Works with AppleMouse but not with Apple Desktop Bus Mouse
3. Cannot use modem port; requires card
4. Not usable with Page 2 of text
5. Must set alternate display mode
6. Display is different
7. Does not work with UniDisk
8. Works in 40-column mode only
9. Documentation wrong for IIGS
10. Keyboard overlay works only with IIe keyboard (available only on IIGS upgrade of IIe)
11. Does not work with mouse; works with keyboard
12. Cannot use printer port; requires card

Table 1-5
Apple IIe-Apple IIc Software Products Reported to Work on Apple IIGS (continued)

from the program. Classic desk accessories are discussed in Chapter 24.

Applications written for the IIGS using full IIGS mode, including the desktop, mouse, and windows, resemble in format Macintosh applications. In fact, the same set of user-interface guidelines are now used for both machines. These guidelines and programming format are discussed in Chapter 2.

CHAPTER 2

Programming the IIGS

Most computer program applications are linear in nature — they begin at a specified point, go through a variety of different operations (with either one or two potential operations usually following on the first), potentially loop back to some other part of the application code, and eventually end up with a termination routine (see Figure 2-1). This organization usually results in

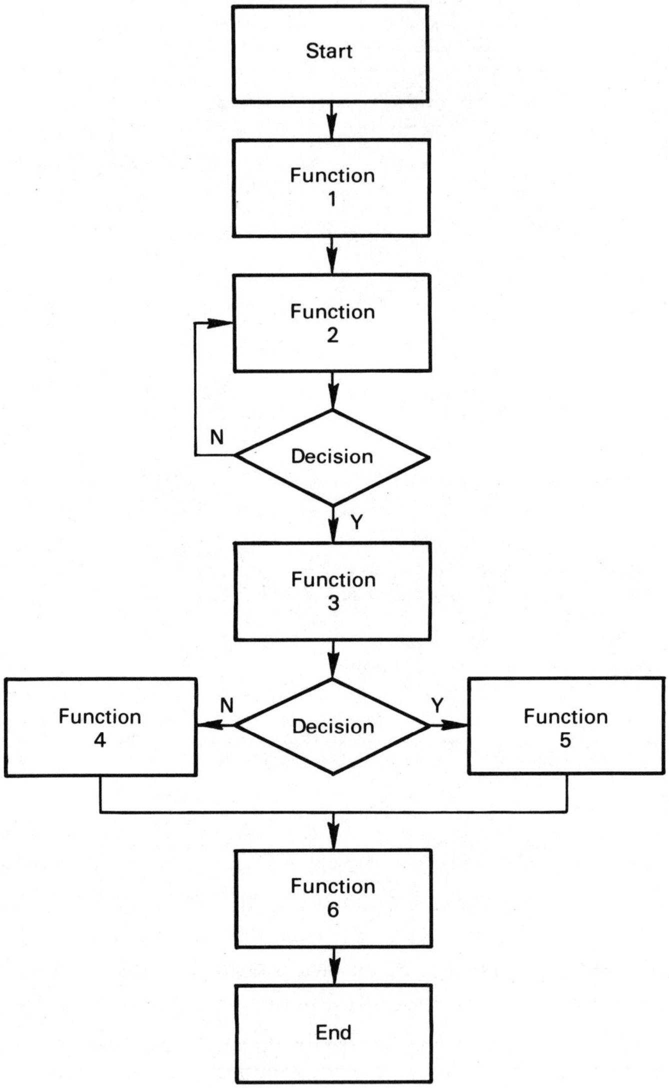

Figure 2-1

Linear nature of computer program

typical computer applications in which the user moves from one group of choices to another in a variety of different modes that cause different actions to occur.

The real power of the IIGS, like that of the Macintosh, is not in linear programming; however, by ignoring most of the toolbox routines discussed in this chapter, you can still make it work linearly. The IIGS, in 8-bit Apple II mode, is more easily programmed in this manner because, without special techniques, the toolbox routines are not accessible in 8-bit Apple II mode.

The method of programming at which the IIGS shines is known as *circular programming*, although its image is really more a circle with a line at either end. This method of programming begins with an initialization section and ends with a termination section. In between, the program consists of a giant loop during which the computer keeps checking what the user wants to do and responds to it, continuing this technique until a quit request comes in (see Figure 2-2).

As discussed later in this chapter in the "Human Interface Guidelines" section, circular programs are much more easily used by humans—the human operator is in charge and can handle the various requests (known as *events* in the IIGS world) as they come in. Another name for this type of program is event-driven because the user requests, or events, not the linear program code, determine what the program will do.

THE CONCEPT OF MANAGERS—THE IIGS TOOLBOX

The problem with writing event-driven programs is the large amount of code necessary to provide the various utilities the user needs—menus for commands, windows to display the information, mouse (or other pointing device) for pointing and selecting, controls for adjusting the environment, dialogs for interaction with the user, and events for reporting the choices. In addition, the best environment for an event-driven application is a graphics one, with all the various parts (including text) being displayed in graphics.

If you had to write individual code for all these functions, you would be loath to write software except for a large and very expensive application. Fortunately, the Apple IIGS comes with many of these utilities already

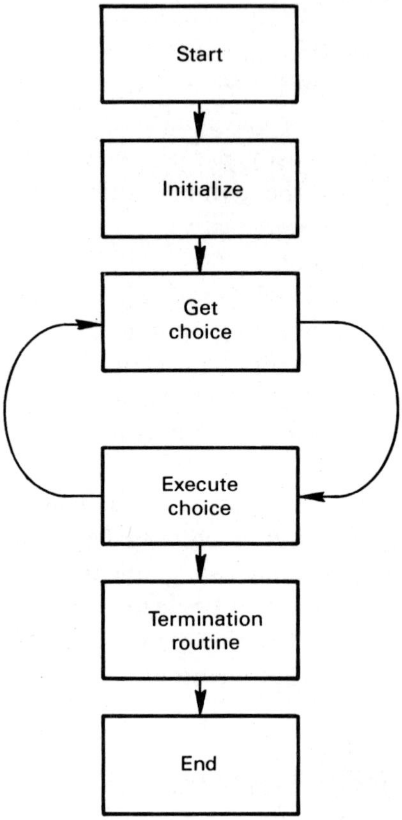

Figure 2-2
Circular programming

done for you and ready to use. Some of these routines are found in ROM code, comprising a great deal of the 128K found in the IIGS ROM. The remaining routines are in files found on the IIGS system disk and application disks. These routines are loaded into RAM when requested by the application.

These routines, called *tools*, are divided into logical groupings that are known alternatively as *tool sets* or *managers*. The entire collection of tool

Set	Name	RAM	ROM
1	Tool Locator	-	x
2	Memory Manager	-	x
3	Miscellaneous Tools	-	x
4	Quickdraw II	x	x
5	Desk Manager	-	x
6	Event Manager	-	x
7	Scheduler	-	x
8	Sound Manager	-	x
9	Apple Desktop Bus Tools	-	x
10	SANE Tools	-	x
11	Integer Math Tools	-	x
12	Text Tools	-	x
13	Reserved for System Use		
14	Window Manager	x	-
15	Menu Manager	x	-
16	Control Manager	x	-
17	Loader	x	-
18	High-Level Printer Driver	x	-
19	Low-Level Printer Driver	x	-
20	Line Edit	x	-
21	Dialog Manager	x	-
22	Scrap Manager	x	-
23	Standard File Tools	x	-
24	Disk Utilities	x	-
25	Note Synthesizer	x	-
26	Note Sequencer	x	-

Table 2-1
Number and Location of Tool Sets

sets or managers is considered the *toolbox*. A list of the tool sets, the number assigned to each, and the place of implementation—in ROM, in RAM, or in both—are given in Table 2-1.

The various managers get their name from the fact that each contains a set of routines that manages one aspect of the IIGS. Thus the Memory Manager manages most of the RAM of the IIGS, parceling it out among applications, other managers, and desk accessories, and ensuring that no two portions of code are placed in the same memory location or use the same memory location (unless they both, knowingly, wish to access the same data).

The toolbox routines are designed to be usable by any application running in native IIGS mode. They provide the background of utilities needed to program in an event-driven, graphic-oriented environment. Much of the remainder of this book is concerned with the toolbox routines.

These routines can function as a black box — all the programmer really needs to know is what inputs the routine requires, what results it outputs, and what other effects it causes when it operates. The exact form of the code need not be known, nor is it published by Apple.

Each of the toolbox routines is called in the same manner as the other toolbox routines. The tools themselves shift into full native mode (E, M, and X flags all = 0) and put you back where you came from. You begin by pushing space for any output onto the stack. This is a departure from the practice of most Apple II assembly language programmers. The reason for this requirement is the need with multiple subroutine calls (both long and short) to be sure that the stack is not corrupted. If the routine always knows that space for the returned value has to be pushed on the stack, it always knows where in the stack to place the value using the 65816 stack relative addressing modes. This measure prevents writing over the return address. The requirement of pushing space for the result on the stack is also consistent with the method employed by Pascal programmers.

Following the space for the return values, if any, the application should push the input parameters expected by the routine in the order expected by the routine. This book, as well as the Apple IIGS *Toolbox Reference Manuals*, list the parameters for each routine in the order in which they should be pushed on the stack if you are programming in assembly language.

Next you set the X register so that the value of the lower byte is set to the tool set number, and the value of the high byte is set to the function number you wish to call within the tool set. Finally you issue a JSL (jump to subroutine long) to the Tool Locator assembly language dispatch address (which is $E1/0000).

The IIGS Programmer's Workshop Assembler comes with a list of macros for each tool function. These are arranged in libraries, each library containing the functions for one tool set. Typically each macro takes the following form:

```
       MACRO
&lab   _FunctionName
&lab   LDX #<Set number>+256*<Function number>
       JSL $E10000
       MEND
```

Note that the macro contains the code, not only for properly setting the X register, but also for the JSL to the proper Tool Locator dispatch point. Your application, therefore, can call the macro simply by using the macro name as a pseudo op code. Not only does this result in less chance for error in setting up the X register and calling the Tool Locator, it also makes for more readable and understandable code. Thus, while use of the macro libraries is not required, it is highly recommended.

The IIGS Programmer's Workshop Assembler also comes with a set of other macros that make programming with the IIGS toolbox much easier. Some of these macros are used in the listings in this book including:

□ *Movelong Source, Dest.* Moves a long-word (32-bit) value from the Source Address to the Destination Address.

□ *Pushword Value.* If value starts with a #, it pushes the word (16-bit) length value on the stack. Otherwise it pushes on the stack the word value found at the address of value.

□ *Pushlong Value.* If value starts with a #, it pushes the long-word (32-bit) length value on the stack. Otherwise it pushes on the stack the long-word value found at the address of value.

After the tool function is complete, control of the IIGS returns to your application. Upon return, the carry flag and accumulator show the status of the function call. A clear carry flag (C=0) and a zero accumulator indicate no error, while a set flag (C=1) indicates an error with the accumulator holding the error code. Note that a few functions may not support error codes and, in that case, may return a value in the accumulator even if there is no error. Table 2-2 gives a list of the effect of a tool function call on each 65816 processor status flag and register.

Flag	Effect
N	May be changed by function
V	May be changed by function
M	Unchanged (must be 0)
X	Unchanged (must be 0)
D	Set to 0 by function
I	Unchanged
Z	May be changed by function
C	Set by function to indicate error status
E	Unchanged (must be 0)

Register	Effect
A	Set by function to indicate error code (0= no error)
X	May be changed by function
Y	May be changed by function
S	Changed by function when input parameters removed from stack
D	Unchanged
P	See flags
B	Unchanged
K	Unchanged
PC	Changed to point to address following call

Table 2-2
Effect of Tool Function Call on 65816 Registers and Flags

Error codes returned by the tools are a word value in which the higher byte is the tool set number reporting the error and the lower byte is the actual error reported by the function. The use of the tool set number in the error code is helpful because a function in one tool set may call a function in another tool set, and that later function may return the error. Error codes with a tool set number of $00 are *system death* errors—they are returned by the system and result in a termination of the application and

Code	Meaning
$0001	ProDOS/16—unclaimed interrupt
$0004	Attempt to divide by zero
$000A	ProDOS/16—volume control block unusable
$000B	ProDOS/16—file control block unusable
$000C	ProDOS/16—block zero allocated illegally
$000D	ProDOS/16—interrupt occurred when $C000 area shadowing was off
$0015	Segment loader error
$0017-24	Can't load a package
$0025	Out of memory
$0026	Segment loader error
$0027	File map destroyed
$0028	Stack overflow error
$0030	File manager alert to insert disk
$0032-53	Memory manager error
$0100	Can't mount system startup volume

Table 2-3
System Death Error Codes

the need to reboot. (System death is discussed in Chapter 25.) A list of the system death codes is given in Table 2-3.

When calling a tool from a higher-level language, such as the IIGS Programmer's Workshop (compiled) C, you first include the source code for the particular tool set macro library in your code. With C this would be done with the "#include" statement.

The macro code typically contains a short interface routine that takes the parameters to be input to the routine (and space for the output) and passes them to a "glue" routine, so called because it glues the assembly language and higher language routines together. This routine places the parameters on the stack, sets the X register as required (a difficult if not impossible task in most higher-level languages), and calls the Tool Locator higher-level language dispatch point. It is necessary to have this alternate entry point because there is an extra return address (3 bytes) on the stack when the toolbox routine is called from a higher-level language (the return address back to the code from the glue routine).

With the proper include library, any toolbox routine may be used by calling the macro (using the name of the routine) with the parameters in the proper format for macro calls in that particular language.

THE TOOL LOCATOR AND CUSTOMIZED TOOLS

If you are writing your own tools, or patches or extensions to existing tools, or if you are using any of the many RAM-based tools (such as the Menu, Window, or Control Manager), you need to know how to load these tools. Loading tools is one of the functions of the Tool Locator.

The Tool Locator will load any RAM-based tool sets, either those that come with the IIGS or those that you write yourself. A loader file for each desired tool set must be located in the tools subdirectory of the system director on the boot disk. The file type in the ProDOS/16 operating system is $BA. Each file name begins with the word *TOOL* and is followed by a three-digit decimal number specifying the tool set number. If the number has only two digits, a leading zero should be used in the file name. The tool loader files begin with a "Function Pointer Table" (discussed later in this chapter), followed by the code for each tool function.

The easiest way to load the RAM tools your program needs is to place in memory a tool table that lists the desired tools in the following form:

```
ToolTable       DC I'NumToolsRequired'
                DC I'ToolNum1,Version1'
                . . .
                DC I'ToolNumN,VersionN'
```

This tool table lists each desired RAM-based tool by its tool set number, followed by the lowest acceptable version number of that tool set.

Version numbers for each tool consist of a word value. Bits 0-7 of the word contain the minor revision number, beginning with zero. Bits 8-14 contain the major revision number, beginning with one. Bit 15 is set (=1) if the version is a prototype, and is clear (=0) if the version is a released version. Thus $90 is version 1.0 prototype, $12 is version 1.2 official release, and so on.

After the tool table is in memory, you issue a call to the Tool Locator LoadTools routine with a pointer to the tool table. This would take the following code:

```
PushLong #ToolTable ;Pointer to tool table
_LoadTools          ;Invoke macro
```

If the boot disk is no longer in one of the IIGS drives, the ProDOS/16 system will return a "volume not found" error (discussed in Chapter 23) through the Tool Locator. Because of the various potential display modes the IIGS can be in when a load-tools call is made, the Tool Locator does not automatically issue a command to place the boot disk in the appropriate drive. Your application must do this.

The Tool Locator provides two routines that can assist your application in telling the user to insert the boot disk. If the application is using the super-high-resolution display mode, your application should call TLMountVolume. This routine places a pseudo-dialog box on the screen, first saving the screen contents. (Dialogs are discussed in Chapter 19.) Your application specifies the location of the box, the two lines of text that will appear in the dialog, and the titles for the two buttons appearing in the dialog box.

Note that TLMountVolume does not use either the Dialog Manager or the Control Manager (discussed in Chapter 18) in performing this function. These two managers are RAM-based tools and may not yet have been loaded into memory. The standard title for button 1 in the pseudo-dialog is "OK." This button is selected either with the mouse or by pressing the RETURN key. The standard title for button 2 is "Cancel" and is selected either with the mouse or by pressing the ESCAPE key.

If the application is using the 8-bit Apple II mode text screen, it should call the TLTextMountVolume routine. This works similarly to the TLMountVolume routine with the following exceptions:

- The text screen, not the super-high-resolution screen, is used for the display.
- Buttons are not drawn, but are simulated using text.

- A button can be selected not with the mouse but only with the RETURN (button 1) or ESCAPE (button 2) keys.

If you have only one RAM-based tool to load, you may use a shorter method that does not require setting up a tool table in memory. This is the LoadOneTool command. It takes two inputs, the tool number and minimum version, similar to the two entries for each tool in the tool table.

Any RAM-based tool in memory can be removed by your application by using the UnloadOneTool routine. This routine requires an input parameter of the number of the tool set to be removed. Removal of a tool set from memory should be done rarely. If you have a custom-designed tool set that is used for a specific part of an application and will not be used again, you may be justified in removing it from memory. Repeated loading and unloading of tool sets from memory is not recommended for the following reasons:

- The time required to reload tool sets will result in a serious degradation of performance of the application.
- The user either will be required to keep the boot disk in a drive during the entire application or will risk being prompted to reinsert the disk.
- Many of the RAM-based tools call other RAM-based tools. You will have to program carefully to avoid removing from RAM a tool set that is needed by another tool set.

If you are planning to write your own tools, or to patch existing tools, you may use additional functions in the Tool Locator, and you will need to know additional information about the structure of tools.

A tool function should have the following characteristics to function properly:

- The 65816 processor must be operating in full native mode (meaning the E, M, and X flags are all cleared to 0).
- The function must be written using position-independent code techniques, although you may assume that a code segment will not extend over a bank boundary. (For a discussion of writing position-independent code using the 65816, see Fischer, *65816/65802 Assembly Language Programming*, Chapter 14, Osborne/McGraw-Hill, 1986.)

- All workspace needed by the tool must be obtained from the Memory Manager, preferably by the application initializing the tool set.
- A function must either be reentrant (discussed in Fischer, *65816/65802 Assembly Language Programming*, Chapter 13, Osborne/McGraw-Hill, 1986) or it must disable interrupts during its execution. (See discussion of interrupts and the restrictions on disabling them in Chapter 25 of this book.)
- The applications execution environment must be saved upon entry to the function, and restored upon exit from it.
- The user should not assume that any particular operating system is active.
- The first six functions of any new tool set must be used for specific functions as shown in Table 2-4. Functions 7 and 8 must be reserved and do nothing.

TOOL RECORDS

The IIGS maintains a table with every active tool listed in it. This table is called the Tool Pointer Table (TPT). Initially the TPT is located in ROM and lists the various ROM tools. A single RAM long-word pointer location, maintained in bank $E1, points to the TPT. The system startup code moves the ROM-based pointer to the ROM TPT into RAM. It also initializes three other long-word pointers, discussed later in this chapter. The system startup then calls the Tool Locator Boot initialization routine, which initializes not only the Tool Locator but all the other ROM-based tool sets by calling their boot initialization routines.

When a RAM-based tool set is loaded, or when RAM patches are made to ROM-based tools, the TPT is copied to RAM with all its entries, the master pointer adjusted to point to the RAM location of the TPT, and modifications are made to the TPT as appropriate.

The TPT structure is a series of long-word values. The first value is equal to the total number of tool sets in the table plus one. Each other value is a pointer to a particular tool set's Function Pointer Table (FPT) in numerical order for the tools.

There are actually two different types of tool sets and, consequently,

Function	Purpose
1	Boot initialization function. Designed to be executed once either by the system startup code or when the tool is installed into RAM. Performs any necessary system initialization functions.
2	Application startup function. Called by each application once before using the tool set. Should check that tool was properly shut down by the previous application or that a satisfactory beginning environment for the tool set exists. Should check that tool not already initialized and return an "already initialized" error when appropriate.
3	Application shutdown function. Called by each application before it terminates. Releases any memory allocated to the tool set and performs other appropriate shutdown functions.
4	Version information function. Returns the version number of the tool set as a word with the following value: Bits 0-7 — Minor release number (beginning with 0) Bits 8-14 — Major release number (beginning with 1) Bit 15 — Set (= 1) if a prototype version
5	Reset function. Called when a reset occurs. Does whatever is appropriate for a reset. If the tool is unable to continue after the reset, it should return a cannot reset error code. (A system death call will be forced by the Tool Locator if any tool returns an error on reset.)
6	Status function. Returns whether the particular tool is presently active.

Table 2-4
Specified Tool Functions

two different TPTs. System tools are those designed for general use and are usually made available by Apple as part of the IIGS ROM or system disks. System tools are numbered beginning at $01 up through, potentially, $7F (127). In order to allow the use of user-created tools without conflict, the IIGS maintains a separate table for user-created tools that are numbered with the high bit of the value set (from $81 through $FF).

Each tool set has a Function Pointer Table (FPT). That tool set's entry in the Tool Pointer Table points to the location of the tool's FPT. ROM-based tools have their FPT in ROM unless the tool set has been patched. RAM-based tools, of course, have their FPT in RAM.

The format of the FPT is similar to the TPT. It also consists of long-word values. The first value is equal to the highest numbered function in the tool set plus one. Following that value are a series of long-word values, each of which is a pointer to the actual code for that particular function number.

Each tool set may need memory for data storage. If it needs nonmovable memory in bank zero, the application is supposed to pass to the tool set the address it may use for bank zero memory. This is done as part of the startup call from the application to the tool set. Of course the application should first request allocation of the memory from the Memory Manager.

If an application does not need memory in bank zero, it may request the memory itself from the Memory Manager as part of its initialization code.

The requirement that a tool set must get bank zero memory from the application using it is a suggested convention, not an actual requirement. In many cases your tool set could obtain the bank zero memory itself without dire consequences, but you face an increased risk of fragmentation of bank zero memory space and the chance that you will run out of that special memory if your tool set does not follow the convention.

The IIGS Tool Locator maintains a table showing the data memory used by each tool set. This is known as the Work Area Pointer Table (WAPT). This table consists of long-word pointers to the data or work area memory for each tool set. A zero value indicates that the tool set either does not use a work area or has not had one allocated to it. In a manner similar to the TPT, there are actually two WAPTs, one for system tool sets and one for user tool sets.

The Tool Locator maintains in bank $E1 a series of four long-word pointers that point to the active system TPT (either RAM- or ROM-based), the user TPT, the system WAPT, and the user WAPT.

The Tool Locator has several routines that aid in the utilization of the tool records. GetTSPtr returns the value of the pointer to the FPT for a specified tool set. The two parameters passed to it consist of either the value $0000, if the application wants system tool set information, or the value $8000, if the application wants user tool set information, and the tool set number. The value returned is obtained from the appropriate TPT. If you wish to change this value to point to a modified FPT for that tool set, you should call the SetTSPtr routine.

The actual address of any tool routine can be determined by passing the appropriate information to the GetFuncPtr routine. Note that this routine obtains the value from the specified tool set's FPT. There is no matching SetFuncPtr routine. The manner of changing an entry in the FPT for a tool consists of either modifying the RAM record directly (after obtaining its address using GetTSPtr) or moving the ROM record to RAM and modifying it. In the latter case, your application should be sure to report

Function Name	**Function Number**	**FPTPtr**	**TSNumber**	**WAPtr**	**but1Ptr**	**but2Ptr**	**funcNumber**	**funcPtr**
Parameter Size		L	W	L	L	L	W	L
Parameter Type		P	V	P	P	P	V	P
TLBootInit	1							
TLStartUp	2							
TLShutDown	3							
TLVersion	4							
TLReset	5							
GetTSPtr	9	O1	I2					
SetTSPtr	10	I3	I2					
GetFuncPtr	11		I2				I3	O1
GetWAP	12		I2	O1				
SetWAP	13		I2	I3				
LoadTools	14							
LoadOneTool	15							
UnloadOneTool	16							
TLMountVolume	17				I5	I6		
TLTextMountVolume	18				I3	I4		

Notes:

Parameter size
- L = Long-word (32 bits)
- W = Word (16 bits)

Parameter type
- P = Pointer
- V = Value
- 1 = $0000 (system) or $8000 (user)
- 2 = 1 or 2

Table 2-5

Tool Locator Functions and Parameters

the changed address of the FPT via SetTSPtr so that TPT will be modified appropriately.

The WAPT is not designed to be directly accessible using the Tool Locator. Rather, the function GetWAP will return the pointer to the specified tool set's work area while the function SetWAP will change the

	line1Ptr	line2Ptr	minVersion	systemOrUser	toolNumber	toolTablePtr	versionInfo	whereX	whereY	whichButton
	L	L	W	W	W	L	W	W	W	W
	P	P	V	1	V	P	V	V	V	2
							O1			
				I1						
				I1						
				I1						
				I1						
				I1						
						I1				
			I2		I1					
					I1					
	I3	I4						I1	I2	O1
	I1	I2								O1

pointer to the specified tool set's work area to the value passed to the routine.

A summary of all the Tool Locator commands and the parameters expected by each routine are given in Table 2-5.

CODING A TOOL

Whenever a tool function is called by your application (through the Tool Locator), the Tool Locator ensures that the X register contains the value of the function and tool set numbers, the accumulator contains the lower word of the Work Area Pointer Table entry, and the Y register contains the upper word of the WAPT. Your tool should expect these values and use them appropriately. It should also save the value of the direct register and data bank register so they can be restored upon exit. In addition, the value of the I (interrupt disable) bit should be restored on exit.

The stack will contain a long return from subroutine address (3 bytes) as its first three values down from the top of stack, a second long return from subroutine address (3 bytes), and the parameters. Thus, the parameters for the routine should begin at an offset of 7 bytes from the top of the stack and can be accessed by the stack relative addressing mode with an offset value of seven.

There are two 3-byte return addresses on the stack, when the tool is active, because the Tool Locator is called with a long jump to subroutine (JSL $E10000), which in turn uses another JSL to call the actual tool function.

The following routine would be used by a tool that as part of its startup routine, reserves $100 bytes of memory anywhere. It requires, as an input parameter, the Memory Manager identification number passed to the application.

```
Startup         Begin
RTL1            EQU 1
RTL2            EQU RTL1+3
IDNum           EQU RTL2+3
*First check that tool set has not been previously initialized
                CMP #$0000          ;Is lower word of WAPT zero?
                BEQ OKLow           ;Yes - check upper word
                LDX #DblInit        ;No - error code to show already initialized
                BRL InitErr         ;and branch around operation
OKLow           CPY #$0000          ;Is upper word of WAPT zero?
                BEQ NotInit         ;Yes - not previously initialized
                LDX #DblInit        ;No - error code to show already initialized
                BRL InitErr         ;and branch around operation
```

```
NotInit         LDX #$0000            ;Show no error
                Pushlong #$00000000 ;Long-word space for returned handle
                Pushlong #$00000100 ;Want to reserve $100 bytes
                Pushword IDNum,S      ;Get identification number passed
                PEA $0000             ;No special attributes needed
                Pushword #$0000       ;No specified starting location
                _NewHandle            ;Memory Manager call (See Chapter 5)
*Handle is now on stack; set up for call to SetWAP routine
                PEA $8000             ;User toolset indicator
                Pushword #TSNum       ;Toolset number on stack
                Pushword 5,S          ;Get actual pointer to memory onto stack
                Pushword 9,S          ;Get second half of pointer also
*Note - since there was additional stack activity between the
*two loads, the second offset is 9 bytes, not 7.
                _SetWAP               ;and set the Work Area Pointer Table entry
                PLA                   ;Remove memory handle from stack
                PLA                   ;It's a long-word value
*We no longer need the ID number word and should remove it from the stack.
*This is done by moving up  in the stack the 6 bytes of return address
*information.  Moving it up one word overwrites the ID number, leaving
*one garbage word at the top of the stack.  If there is an already
*initialized error, the function will branch to this point where it
*removes the ID number from the stack.
InitErr         LDA $05,S             ;These functions can also
                STA $07,S             ;be handled by a macro
                LDA $03,S
                STA $05,S
                LDA $01,S
                STA $03,S
*Finally we remove the garbage word
                PLA
                TXA                   ;Set the accumulator with the error status
                CMP #$0001            ;This will clear the carry if the accumulator
*has a zero value, showing a no error status, and set it otherwise
                RTL                   ;and exit
```

This routine should give you an idea of how to program tool set functions. The following suggestions might prove helpful, depending on the need in a particular situation:

□ If your toolbox has workspace in bank zero (in effect, its own direct page), you should save the current direct register and then use the bank zero values passed in the accumulator by the Tool Locator dispatcher. The following code fragment accomplishes this.

```
PHD                       ;Save current direct register
TCD                       ;and set to your direct page
```

□ In some cases, particularly if the application passes pointers to your routine, it is helpful to set the stack itself as a direct page. In this case, you must be certain to set the stack offsets properly, including the room for saving the original value of the direct register on the stack prior to resetting the direct register. The following code fragment shows how this is done:

```
*Assume that the function is to move 3 words from the address in Pointer1
*to the address in Pointer2
DrctSave        EQU 1             ;Top of stack to be old direct register
```

```
Return1         EQU DrctSave+2  ;First return address
Return2         EQU Return1+3   ;Second return address
Pointer1        EQU Return2+3   ;First pointer passed by the call
Pointer2        EQU Pointer1+4  ;and second one
                PHD             ;Save direct register
                TSC             ;Take stack pointer
                TCD             ;And convert it to direct page
                LDY #$0003      ;Move three words
Loop            LDA [Pointer1],Y
                STA [Pointer2],Y
                DEY             ;Three words moved?
                BNE Loop        ;No - continue
                PHD             ;Reset direct register
*Rest of function code goes here
```

□ If there is more than one parameter on the stack that needs to be removed at the end of the routine, the movement of the return address will be over a greater distance. In addition, rather than adjusting the stack pointer by means of a PLA, you may have to perform addition directly to it for proper adjustment. The following code fragment shows the adjustment of the stack for the previously listed routine that put two long-word pointers on the stack.

```
                LDA $05,S
                STA $0D,S       ;Move up 2 long words, 8 bytes
                LDA $03,S
                STA $0B,S
                LDA $01,S
                STA $09,S
*Now we must adjust the stack pointer back by the same 8 bytes
*we move up the return addresses
                TSC             ;Get stack pointer
*Stack pointer is adjusted by adding to it because it starts high
*and builds the stack down into memory
                CLC
                ADC #$0008
                TCS
                LDA #$0000      ;Show no error by a zero accumulator
                CLC             ;and a clear carry
                RTL             ;and exit
```

HUMAN INTERFACE GUIDELINES

Apple's strong belief in consistent, understandable, user-controlled applications has resulted in a publication called *Human Interface Guidelines.* These guidelines (available from Apple) consist of a number of suggestions, both general and detailed, about the proper method of presenting an application program.

The human interface guidelines first became well known with the appearance of the Macintosh, which was designed with 64K of ROM tools to aid in the development of an application consistent with the guidelines. Apple II family guidelines have also existed for some time, although in a significantly different form. This difference resulted from (1) the lack of significant, consistent routines available to all Apple II programmers, (2) the inability of the 6502 or 65C02 microprocessor in the Apple II machines to access more than 64K of memory at one time, and (3) the relative coarseness of the Apple II graphics display.

With the appearance of the IIGS, Apple has settled on one set of human interface guidelines, used in both the Macintosh and IIGS environments. The guidelines are just that—they are not requirements for your application to run properly, nor are they required for your application to be commercially successful. But they are well-thought-out and will help ensure that any application you produce will be easy to use and learn.

An additional benefit to adhering to the guidelines is that it will quite likely make an application written for the IIGS, using the IIGS toolbox, more portable to the Macintosh. Using the guidelines will have the same effect on a program being moved from the Macintosh to the IIGS.

GUIDELINE PRINCIPLES

The human interface guidelines consist of five basic principles, which are presented here. Their effect on specific programming techniques is discussed later in this chapter.

The user is in control of the application. This principle, which is the prime principle of the guidelines, provides that the user tells the application what to do, rather than the application telling the user what can be done. Many programs written for other computers are not guided by such a rule. As previously discussed in this chapter, this principle is responsible for the event-driven or circular nature of IIGS programs.

Putting the user in control of the application results in a preference for what is known as a *modeless application.* Many "standard" computer programs move the user from one operation to another, often through a series of choices presented on the screen. In each operation, known as a *mode,* the user can perform only those functions permitted by that mode.

By contrast the IIGS user has available a wide selection of choices through a series of menu titles that always appear at the top of the screen (see Figure 2-3). And even in those cases when some of the choices in the menu are not available, the user can still view the choices without leaving the current operation.

Modelessness is the ideal in a IIGS application. There are some cases where it cannot be accomplished and others where it would be undesirable. But it should be used as much as possible.

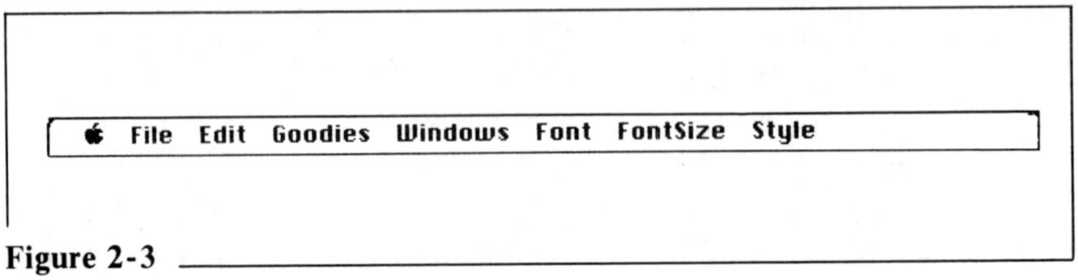

Figure 2-3
Menu titles

Putting the user in control is accomplished by permitting the user to give commands to the application by means of a noun-verb sequence. The noun represents the thing (file, word, graphic object, and so forth) on which the particular operation is to be performed. The verb represents the particular operation. The noun-verb sequence requires that the user first select the object and then choose the operation.

This order of noun and then verb is not an arbitrary one. Most computer operations, including those on the IIGS, usually take place when the computer has both the noun and verb it needs. Anyone who has used a computer for word processing knows the anguish of entering delete mode and then deleting too much text. If the operation were reversed (first selecting the text and then selecting delete), this potential problem would be minimized.

The noun-verb sequence on the IIGS is usually initiated by the user selecting the object by clicking on it or dragging through it with the mouse. Then the user manipulates the mouse to select an operation, usually from the menu.

Another aspect of putting the user in control is providing her or him with information about the selections being made and the action being taken. For example, if the user has attempted to save a file to a full disk, the application should respond with a message that the disk is full rather than merely beeping or refusing to save the file (or, worse yet, hanging). Even better, the application should suggest an alternative approach, such as saving the file on another disk.

Information should also be provided to the user whenever an action has been taken, letting the user know that the computer received and understood the action. If the requested action was not understood, the user should be told what the computer did not understand about the action. This information is known as *feedback*. In many cases feedback can be given simply by highlighting a selection (either noun or verb) made by the user, or by flashing to indicate completion of the selection. In other cases

Figure 2-4
Wristwatch icon signaling a long operation

feedback can be a confirmation to the user that an operation, which may take a long time, is continuing. The standard method of indicating continuation is to change the cursor icon to a wristwatch during somewhat long operations (see Figure 2-4) and to change the icon to a revolving ball during even longer operations.

Operations should be reversible and certain operations confirmed. Closely related to putting the user in control of the application is the notion that certain operations should be confirmed before they are carried out. Exactly what operations should be confirmed is left to the author of the application. This is not necessarily an easy choice.

Failing to seek confirmation of an operation can result in the user losing time or data. Yet seeking confirmation of too many operations can result in the user either getting frustrated with the application, or routinely (and unthinkingly) confirming each warning, thus destroying any value that confirmation has.

An integral part of the confirmation question is the issue of reversibility of operations. Whenever possible, your application should provide a means for the user to undo the previous operation (and to undo that undoing, known as *redo*). For a variety of reasons, usually the result of memory constraints, a particular operation may not be undoable. Nearly all such operations that are not undoable, particularly those involving large amounts of data, should be confirmed.

What you see is what you get. The principle of what you see is what you get, often known by its acronym *WYSIWYG* (pronounced "wizzy-wig"), originally appeared in word processing programs. A WYSIWYG word processing program is one in which the particular document appears on the screen with the same margins or line length as it will appear when printed by your printer.

In the IIGS world, WYSIWYG has an expanded meaning. The standard display mode of the IIGS is super-high-resolution graphics (discussed in Chapter 9). When a document is being displayed on the screen, it is shown in graphic form, even if it is a text document. And the various text sizes used in the document appear on the screen in the same display as they will appear when printed (if printed on a IIGS-compatible graphics printer such as the Imagewriter II). This capability is a significant change from the inability of earlier (and many contemporary) computers to display text in a variety of sizes even when the printer can print text in these sizes.

In addition, the IIGS integration of graphics with text results in a screen display of what will be printed even when a combined text and graphics document is created. With the previous exception of the Macintosh and Lisa, and a very few other machines, this ability in a machine resulted in a serious performance speed deterioration. The toolbox routines in the IIGS permit this expanded WYSIWYG display without any significant performance cost.

See and point. Most computer applications require the user to issue commands by typing them at the keyboard. Such a requirement usually means that the user must remember the commands. Indeed, many applications include as part of their documentation a command summary card. This card lets the user see what commands the application will accept and how to type in those commands. Of course, each command summary card is unique and uniquely organized. Some alphabetize the commands by name. Some sort them by the keys that invoke the command. And some arrange them by type, choosing one of the previous two methods to arrange commands within types.

"See and point" is an improvement over this method, but not merely because it provides a method for lessening the use of the keyboard. Unfortunately, no matter how well conceived the human interface guideline, the user will occasionally have to use the keyboard until a reliable, high-speed voice-recognition peripheral is available. "See and point" frees the user from having to remember commands or from having to remember where the command summary card is kept. When combined with a consistent menu structure, "see and point" also provides the user with an easy method of finding each command merely by pointing to it with the mouse.

One of the advantages of "see and point" is that you can always see what commands, or series of commands, are available. For example, if you want to know whether a program permits search and replace, you may have to look through the entire command summary card to see if it is used. Even then the card may have omitted the command, and it may be discussed

Figure 2-5

Key equivalent of menu operation and menu title

only in the 250-page manual.

To determine if search and replace is available in a "see and point" application, all you need do is pull down the appropriate menu, such as edit, and see if it is listed. All available functions are usually shown in menus. If it is not available, it is not listed.

A problem can arise if "see and point" is used with a keyboard-dependent application such as word or outline processing. While editing in such applications by means of "see and point" is usually at least as handy as "remember and type," changing operations in the middle of data entry can be quite difficult if you need to remove a hand from the keyboard to use the mouse. This detriment becomes more significant the more proficient you are as a touch-typist.

The human interface guidelines provide an alternative for "see and point" through the use of command keys. Various keys, when pressed in combination with the APPLE/COMMAND key (or sometimes in conjunction with other keys), perform the same function as a menu operation. Note that this facility is in addition to the menu operation, not a substitute for it. Further, the key equivalent of a menu operation is normally displayed with the menu title, reinforcing your ability to remember it (see Figure 2-5).

Consistency in approach. The human interface guidelines stress that applications should be consistent in how they treat particular operations, not only within a particular application, but also among applications. Thus programs that perform "cut and paste" should, whenever possible, work in the same manner as other programs that also do "cut and paste." This makes it much easier for a user to switch between applications. The user not only does not need to remember the commands between applications, but can be reasonably confident that the manner of performing the operation will remain constant.

IMPLEMENTATION GUIDELINES

The suggestion of consistency results in the significant detail in the human interface guidelines as to how particular operations and displays should be implemented. The detail can be found in the *Human Interface Guidelines Manual.* The remainder of this chapter summarizes some of these details. (Note that these recommended methods of handling user commands are not built into the IIGS toolbox, although the toolbox does provide a variety of operations that make it easier for you to implement these guidelines. It is up to your application to code the appropriate response and up to you to decide how much of the guidelines to implement.)

ARROW Keys

□ ARROW keys should be an alternative method of moving the text insertion point.

□ When text is selected, the ARROW key can be used to expand or shrink the particular selection.

□ An ARROW key in combination with the OPTION key can be used to expand or shrink the particular selection in the next higher unit. For example, if the ARROW key alone provides for letter movement, the ARROW-OPTION combination provides for word movement. (This use of the OPTION key is referred to as a *semantic modifier.*)

□ An ARROW key in combination with the APPLE/COMMAND key can be used to move the cursor to the appropriate window boundary or, if the cursor is already there, to scroll one screen in that direction.

Selecting an Object

□ Clicking once on an object selects it.

□ Dragging through a range of objects results in the range being selected.

□ Clicking with the SHIFT key depressed extends a selection range. If the objects are text or an ordered array, SHIFT-click extends the nearer end of the range to the point where the SHIFT-click occurred. If the objects are graphic objects, the item selected is included as a selected item even if there are intervening nonselected items.

□ Clicking with the APPLE/COMMAND key depressed extends a text or ordered array by including the object on which the APPLE-click occurred as a selected item even if there are intervening nonselected objects or text.

□ Double-clicking on text selects a word. A word is defined, in applications to be used in the United States and Canada, as a continuous string of the specified characters (see Table 2-6 for a list).

Letter
Digit
Nonbreaking space created by pressing APPLE/COMMAND in combination with the space bar
Currency symbol (dollar, cent, pound, or yen)
Percent sign
Comma if between digits
Period if before digits
Apostrophe if between letters or digits
Hyphen

Note: A minus sign, created by pressing APPLE/COMMAND in combination with a hyphen, and a dash, created by pressing SHIFT and APPLE/COMMAND in combination with a hyphen, are not considered hyphens for this purpose.

Table 2-6
Characters Constituting a Word

Text Editing

□ Text is inserted whenever typed, beginning at the current insertion point and pushing existing text toward the end of the document. An *insertion point* is shown in Figure 2-6. Word wraparound is always active.

□ Backspacing when text is selected results in the deletion of the text without saving it in the clipboard.

□ Typing when text is selected replaces the selected text with whatever is typed. The replaced text is not saved in the clipboard.

□ Intelligent "cut and paste" automatically adjusts for intervening spaces and lack of intervening spaces when cutting and pasting whole words.

Menus

□ Menu item names should be either verbs (showing what can be done) or adjectives (showing the attribute of an object). If a verb is selected, the program performs the operation and then returns to the main application loop. Selecting an adjective changes the attribute (and indicates the selection of the attribute by a checkmark next to the item in the menu).

□ Menu items should be arranged in descending order or frequency of use. Action items and attributive items in the same menu should be separately grouped and separated by a dividing line. Groups of attributes,

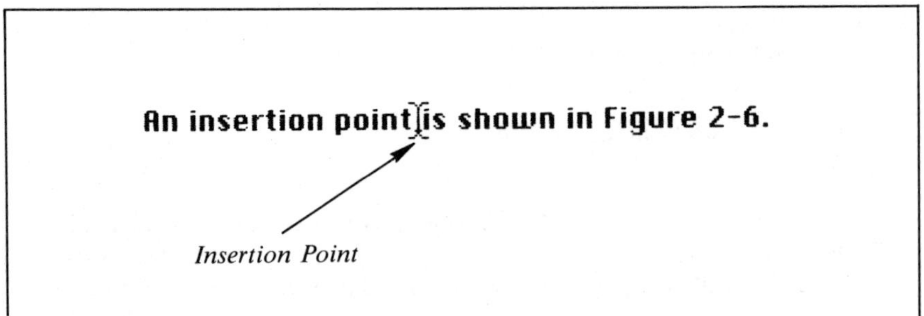

Figure 2-6
Insertion point

either related or mutually exclusive, should be arranged together and separated from other attributes by a dividing line.

- When selecting an item results in a dialog box seeking additional information (not merely warning or confirming the operation), the item title should be followed by an ellipsis (. . .).
- An item that cannot be chosen because of the current state of the program (for example, delete when no text has been selected) should be shown in dimmed type. Other type styles (such as bold or underscore) should be used only in menu item names as part of the Style menu.
- Certain command key equivalents (see discussion in Chapter 17) are reserved for specific functions in order to provide a consistency of use (see Table 2-7).

Apple Menu
/ or ? Help

File menu
N or n New file
O or o Open file
S or s Save file
Q or q Quit application

Edit menu
Z or z Undo or redo
X or x Cut
C or c Copy
V or v Paste

Style menu
P or p Plain text
B or b Bold text
I or i Italic text
U or u Underscore text

ESCAPE or APPLE/COMMAND with period (.) stops the current operation.
Note: All keys are pressed in combination with the APPLE/COMMAND key.

Table 2-7
Reserved Menu APPLE/COMMAND Key Equivalents

□ Particular standard menus should be used in all applications. They should be used for the purposes shown here and not changed for other purposes, although related functions can be added to these menus. (See Figure 2-7 for an extended illustration of all of these menus. Note that this illustration is whimsical; it is not possible for more than one menu to be pulled down at any one time.) Here are the standard items for each menu:

Apple menu

About. . .(displays a dialog box with the application version number, copyright information, and other optional information)

Help, if available

Desk accessories

File menu

New

Open

Close (should use the standard dialog box, shown in Figure 2-8, to check whether any changes should be saved)

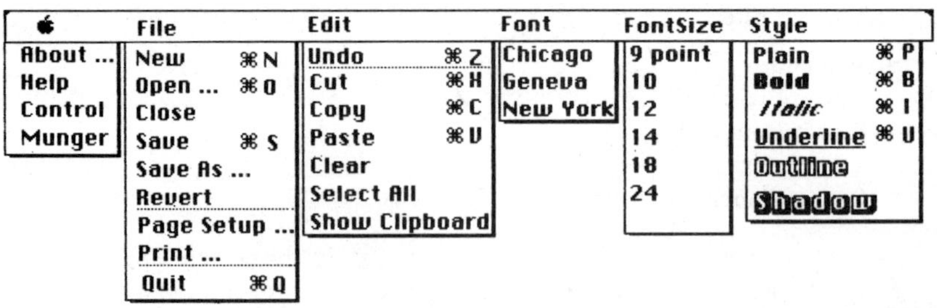

Figure 2-7

Standard menus

Save (dim when there have been no changes to the document)

Save as

Revert to saved

Page setup (the selected parameters should be saved with the document)

Print (the selected parameters should not be saved with the document)

Quit (with the same dialog box as in “close” if the document has been changed since last saved)

Edit menu

This menu and some of its options (Undo, Cut, Copy, Paste, and Clear) should always be present even if not used by a particular application. Desk accessories that require text editing do not produce this menu, but require it to be available from your application.

Undo (change to redo after an operation is undone)

Dotted separation line

Cut

Copy

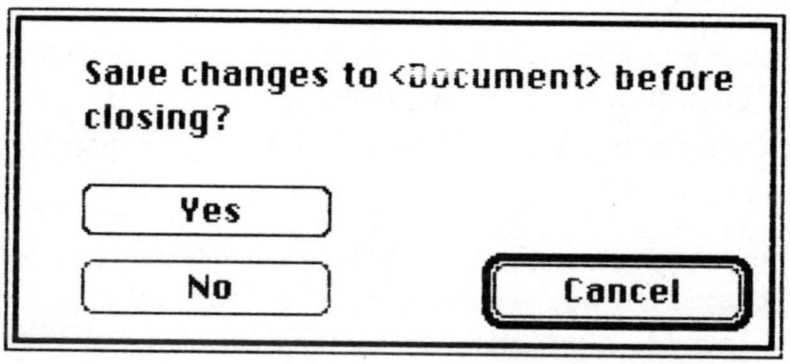

Figure 2-8
Standard close dialog box

Paste

Clear

Select all

Show/hide clipboard (the wording should change to reflect whether the clipboard is currently shown or hidden)

Font-related Menus

The Font menu lists the currently available fonts and has a checkmark beside the font currently in use.

The Font Size or Size menu lists the standard font sizes, shows in outline the currently available font sizes, and has a checkmark beside the currently selected size. If there is not room in the menu bar for both a Font Size and a Style menu, and your application needs both, you can place the font size items at the end of the Style menu.

The Style menu displays the available font styles and has a checkmark next to the style attribute(s) that have been selected.

Windows

- □ When first opened, a window should be in what is known as the *standard state.* This is the full size of the screen or the size and location best suited for working on the document. It is up to the application to set the standard window state properly. When the user has changed the window size and location, the application should retain the user settings for future use with that window.
- □ A window can be split into *panes* by the user. Panes are either horizontal or vertical divisions of the window, or are both horizontal and vertical divisions (see Figure 2-9). Panes provide separate views of the same data area and format.
- □ The application can display a window in *panels.* Panels are similar to panes, except that they are selected by the application rather than the user and provide alternative characterization of the same data. An example is a window that has one panel showing a column of a spreadsheet and another panel showing a graph of that column. As an alternative to panels, an application can use separate windows for the alternative characterizations. Use of panels results in less memory being

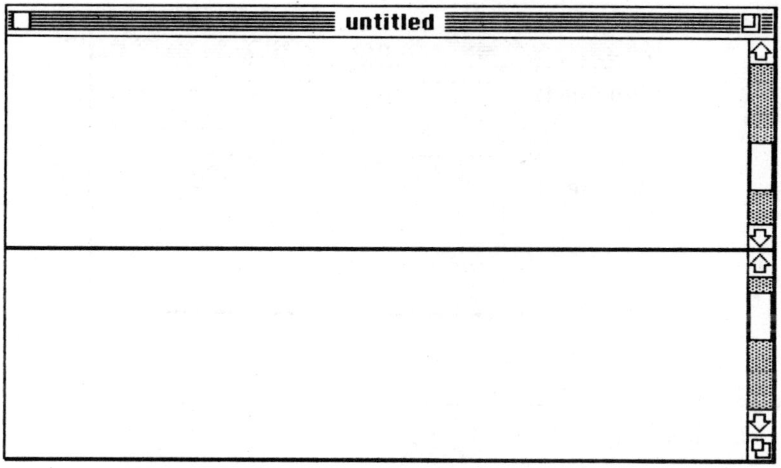

Figure 2-9
Window panes

required, although the panels of a window must be handled as a unit. Separate windows do not need to be so handled.

Controls

□ Button labels (pushbuttons, checkboxes, and radio buttons) should have a label that refers to the result of pressing the button.

Dialogs

□ All dialogs should be in a rectangular window.

□ Dialog windows may have text explanations, controls, and icons. Some of the text should show which command resulted in this dialog and what the function of the dialog is.

□ Controls and text fill-in fields should be set to the most likely or last used values as a default.

□ The first text field, if it has a default value, should be highlighted so that the user can erase it easily.

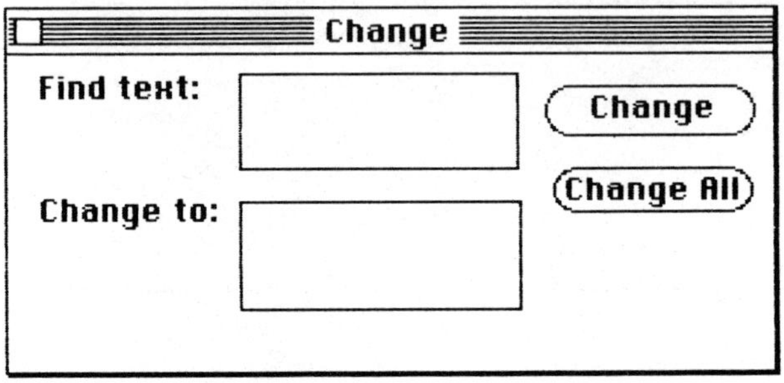

Figure 2-10
Modeless dialog box

- □ The TAB key should move between items.
- □ *Modal dialogs* (dialogs that the user must dismiss before continuing with the program—see Figure 2-8) should meet several criteria: they should be sparingly and intelligently used; they should contain at least an OK button (either called OK or something equally descriptive) and a Cancel button (always called Cancel); they should offer a default button, with a bold outline, selected by pressing the RETURN or ENTER key. This key should be the safest or most likely choice of the user.
- □ A modeless dialog box should not be closed except explicitly (that is, merely selecting OK or Cancel will not close the box, just affect the operation associated with OK or Cancel). A typical modeless dialog box is shown in Figure 2-10.

Alerts
- □ A beep of the speaker should be used for a minor, immediately obvious error.
- □ A more serious error, or a repeat error, should result in an alert box. An alert box should resemble a modal dialog box except that it is narrower and lower on the screen. The user should acknowledge the alert either

by clicking on the pushbutton or pressing ENTER or RETURN. There should be no text fields, radio buttons, checkboxes, dials, or other types of controls except the pushbutton (although there should be a text message in the alert box).

□ There are four types of alert boxes:

Note	shows a minor mistake with no serious consequences.
Caution	shows there may be potential undesirable results and gives the user a choice to continue with the operation.
Stop	is used for a serious problem. It usually requires remedial action by the user or termination of the application.
Talk	is used for a spoken alert.

CHAPTER 3

Slots, Ports, and Other Options: Making Your Choice

The Apple IIGS comes with seven expansion slots, designed to have peripheral cards or interfaces plugged in; these slots are nearly equivalent to those on the Apple IIe. (See Figure 3-1 for a display of the connections on these slots.) The main difference between Apple IIGS and Apple IIe slots is pin 39. On the Apple IIe this pin is PSYNCH. On the IIGS this pin is referred to as /M2SEL.

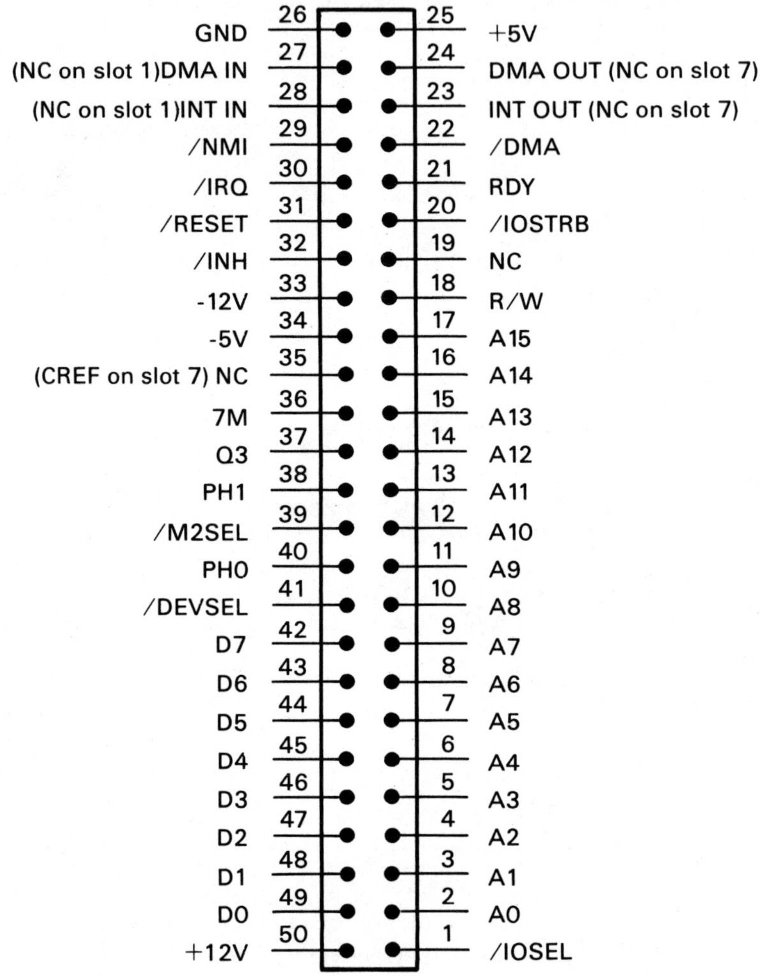

Figure 3-1
Expansion slot connector

As discussed in Chapter 5, memory banks $E0 and E1 are the only two banks in the IIGS that operate at 1 MHz. The remainder of the RAM operates at 2.5 MHz. When a peripheral card is performing input or output, the IIGS must use the RAM in banks $E0 or E1 so that the input and output will be placed at the proper locations of addresses $C000-CFFF in those banks.

The 65816 in the IIGS uses 24-bit addressing to permit it to address 16 MB. It uses a bank register of 8 bits to determine which of 256 different banks is being addressed and a 16-bit address bus within each bank to determine the location within the 64K of each bank.

A problem arises from the fact that the address bus on the input/output slots contains only 16 lines, permitting addressing of 64K. If the IIGS is currently set to address bank $E0 or E1, there is no problem in using the address over these lines because it properly refers to the input/output area of memory. But if the bank currently being referenced is any other bank, the value in these lines is erroneous.

The solution is the /M2SEL line. This line goes high (=1) when the addressing references bank $E0 or E1. A card that does not use one of the input/output enable lines should be sure to check this line to see if it has been selected before doing address decoding.

MEMORY EXPANSION SLOT

The IIGS has a memory expansion slot that is different from previous Apple II slots. The slot is a distant cousin to the Aux slot on the Apple IIe in that both are special-purpose slots and both are used for memory expansion. But the slots are very different electronically and logically.

The memory expansion slot is used for adding either RAM, ROM, or both. (Expansion RAM is discussed in Chapter 5, while expansion ROM is discussed in Chapter 6.) The memory expansion slot has 44 connectors, as compared to the 50 connectors on the IIGS peripheral expansion slots. These connectors are shown in Figure 3-2.

PERIPHERAL PORTS

The IIGS also has ports to which peripheral devices can be attached, much like those of the IIc. These ports are mapped to specific slots and, when active, operate just like a peripheral card plugged into its respective slot. The Control Panel, discussed later in this chapter, is the means for determining when the port is active. In current operating systems, the associated slot cannot be active. A list of the various ports and the slots to

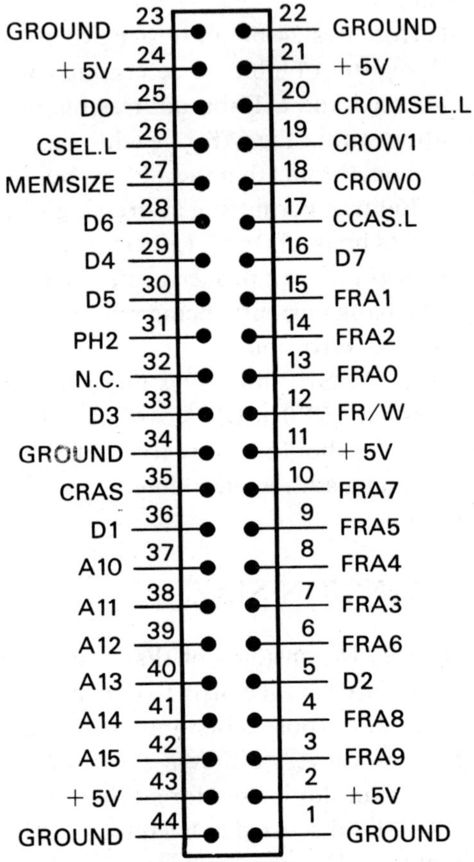

Figure 3-2
Memory expansion connector

which they are mapped is shown in Table 3-1. The design of the various ports of the back panel of the IIGS is shown in Figure 3-3.

Port	Mapped to Slot
Serial port 1 (Printer)	1
Serial port 2 (Modem)	2
80-column text display	3
Mouse interface	4
Smartport	
3.5″ drives	5
5.25″ drives	6
AppleTalk	7

Table 3-1

List of Ports and Applicable Slots

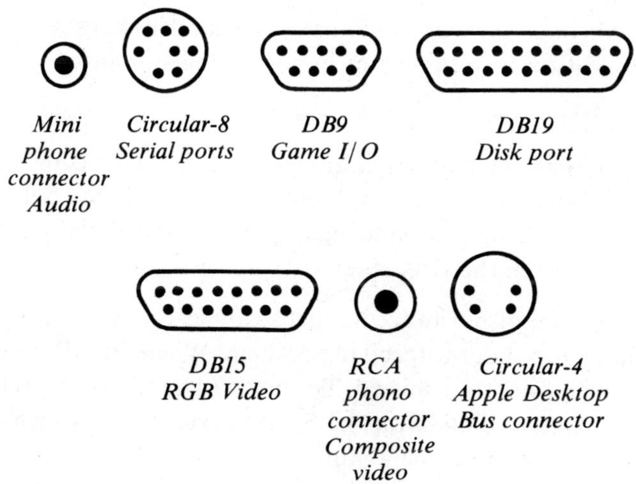

Figure 3-3

IIGS back panel connectors

Serial Ports

The Apple IIGS contains a SCC8530 (Serial Controller Chip) to manage the two serial ports. This is the same chip used on the Macintosh computer. It differs from the ACIA6551 (Asynchronous Communications Interface Adapter) that is used on the Super Serial Card for the Apple IIe and from the similar circuitry in the Apple IIc.

The connectors on the serial ports on the IIGS are Circular-8 Mini sockets, identical to those used on the Macintosh Plus. This socket contains eight pins and is shown in Figure 3-4. The use for each of the eight pins is shown in Table 3-2. Also shown in Table 3-2 is the direction of the data flow on each of the pins, depending on whether the connected peripheral is Data Terminal Equipment (DTE) or Data Communication Equipment (DCE). Certain connectors are used by AppleTalk, and the use made by AppleTalk is also shown in Table 3-2.

The serial ports will support input/output buffering in an application-specified buffer of up to 65K and a default size of 128 bytes. They also support background printing. Both are done on an interrupt basis.

There are three forms of handshaking supported by the serial ports and generally set through the Control Panel. (The handshaking can also be set by your application.) The types of handshaking supported include the following:

- *DTR/DSR*. This form of hardware handshaking results in characters transmitted only when the input handshaking line (Data Set Ready—pin 2) is high. The output handshaking line (Data Terminal Ready—pin 1) is high when the IIGS is ready to accept data.
- *DCD*. This form of hardware handshaking affects only the transmitting of characters, not the receiving of them. When the GPline (pin 7) is high, characters are transmitted. This form of handshaking is included to provide compatibility with the Super Serial Card, which uses the GPline for hardware handshaking.
- *XON/XOFF*. This is generally referred to as software handshaking. When the receiving device wishes to stop receiving information, it sends over the data line what is known as an XOFF signal to the transmitting device. The XOFF signal is normally a CONTROL-S (ASCII code $13) but can be changed depending on the application. When the receiving

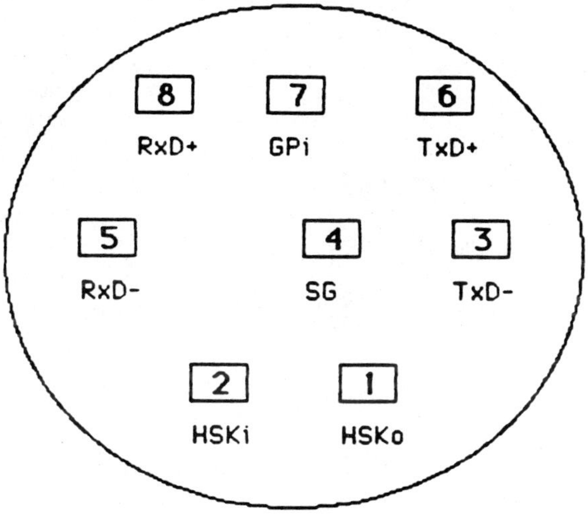

1. Handshake Out (HSKo)
2. Handshake In (HSKi)
3. Transmit Data Minus (TxD-)
4. Signal Ground (SG)
5. Receive Data Minus (RxD-)
6. Transmit Data Plus (TxD+)
7. Goes to DCD input on SCC (GPi)
8. Receive Data Plus (Rxd+)

Figure 3-4
Serial port connectors (courtesy of Apple Computer, Inc.)

device wishes to start receiving information again, it sends an XON signal, normally a CONTROL-Q (ASCII code $11). This handshaking method is referred to as software handshaking because the data line, rather than a separate line, is used to send the signal and it is a series of

Pin	Name	General Purpose	DTE	DCE	AppleTalk Use
1	HSKo	Handshake signal output	FROM	TO	
2	HSKi	Handshake signal input	TO	FROM	Handshake
3	TxD–	Transmit Data Minus	FROM	TO	Transmit Data Minus
4	SG	Signal Ground			
5	RxD–	Receive Data Minus	TO	FROM	Receive Data Minus
6	TxD+	Transmit Data Plus			Transmit Data Plus
7	GPi	GPinout (DCD handshake)	TO	FROM	
8	RxD+	Receive Data Plus	TO	FROM	Receive Data Plus

Table 3-2
Serial Port Connectors

bits representing an ASCII character, not simply setting the line to a high or low voltage state.

Because the Apple IIGS uses the SCC8530, not the ACIA6551 used in the Apple IIe and IIc, some incompatibility may exist for some programs that use the serial ports. The firmware commands for the SCC (discussed later in this chapter) are the same as those for the Apple IIe and IIc. Programs that use the firmware, notably printer programs, work on either machine. But telecommunications software generally make direct calls to the hardware. These programs will not work on the IIGS without modification.

Programming the serial port consists of finding its dispatch address and performing a 65816 emulation mode JSR to that address. That address is located by finding the value at $E0/C112 (for port 1) or $E0/C212 (for port 2). The same information also resides at $E1/C112 and $E1/C212. The byte value at that location is added to $E0/C100 (for port 1) or $E0/C200 (for port 2). These locations can also be shadowed into bank $00 (see discussion in Chapter 5).

For example, to find the Dispatch point for serial port 1, you could use the following code segment:

```
        LDA #%00011110   ;Get shadowing for I/O
        STA $E0C035      ;to Shadow register
        SEC
        XCE              ;Emulation mode
        PHA              ;Save data bank register
        LDA $C112        ;Dispatch value location
        STA Dispatch     ;Store on direct page
        LDA #$C1         ;And get higher byte
        STA Dispatch+1   ;And store it as well
*From this point, a routine needs only to perform a JSR (Dispatch,X)
* with X set to $00 in order to use the routine.
```

One problem with this code is that the X register must be set to zero, or the Dispatch address adjusted accordingly, if it is to be used. As discussed later, the X register is used to pass part of the address of the command list. Therefore, if its value is not $00, the Dispatch address must be adjusted, as per the following code:

```
*Assumes Xreg memory location contains value that will be in
*X register
        LDA Dispatch
        SEC              ;Prepare to subtract
        SBC Xreg         ;And subtract it
        STA Dispatch
        LDA Dispatch+1   ;Process higher byte
        SBC #$00
        STA Dispatch+1
```

A command list, located anywhere in memory, passes the data to the routine. The command list address is passed to the Dispatch routine by placing its lowest byte (bits 0-7) in the accumulator, the middle byte (bits 8-15) in the X register, and the highest byte (bits 16-23) in the Y register.

The command list starts with a 1-byte parameter count that lists the number of parameters (not bytes) that follow. Next comes the command number (byte value) and space for a result code (word value). Following the result code is space for the other output values and, finally, input parameters.

Table 3-3 lists the various serial port commands by name and function. Table 3-4 lists the parameters expected by the different commands. Some of the parameters in Table 3-4 require further explanation. These are given in Tables 3-5 to 3-8. Note that use of the hardware control calls will likely render your application incompatible with a revision to the Apple II line, which does not use the SCC controller, as well as to the Apple IIc and IIe using a Super Serial Card.

Mode Control Codes	
GetModeBits	Returns a bit array with information about the status of some of the operational modes of the port. The meaning of each bit in the Mode Bit Image is shown in Table 3-5.
SetModeBits	Alters the value of any of the bits that control the status of some of the port's operational modes. The mean ing of each bit in the Mode Bit Image is shown in Table 3-5. Bits marked with an * in the table should not be changed; they are for information (using GetModeBits) only.
Buffer Management Calls	
GetInBuffer	Returns the address and length of the current input buffer.
GetOutBuffer	Returns the address and length of the current output buffer.
SetInBuffer	Specifies the address and length of the input buffer. The buffer must not be moved while buffering is active, although the buffer may span a bank boundary.
SetOutBuffer	Specifies the address and length of the output buffer. The buffer must not be moved while buffering is active although the buffer may span a bank boundary.
FlushInQueue	Removes all characters from the input queue.
FlushOutQueue	Removes all characters from the output queue.
InQStatus	Returns the number of characters in the input queue and, if the Heartbeat Interrupt System has been turned on (see Chapter 25), the number of ticks (one tick = 1/30 second) since the last character was queued.
OutQStatus	Returns the number of characters that can be placed in the output queue without a queue overflow.
SendQueue	Used to perform background printing. The output buffer address must have been set and the data desired to be printed must be in the output buffer. The Recharge address is the address of the subroutine to be called by the firmware when all data have been printed.

Table 3-3
Functions of Serial Port Commands

Hardware Control Calls	
GetPortStat	Returns the hardware level status of the serial channel in the form of a bit array. The meaning of each bit is shown in Table 3-6.
GetSCC	Returns the value in the specified SCC register.
SetSCC	Sets the specified SCC register to the specified value.
GetDTR	Returns the value of the DTR output handshake line.
SetDTR	Sets the value of the DTR output handshake line.
GetIntInfo	Returns the type of interrupt that caused the completion routine to be called. The value of the InterruptSetting parameter that corresponds to each type of interrupt is shown in Table 3-7.
SetIntInfo	Sets the types of interrupts that will be handled by the completion routine and the address of the completion routine. The types of interrupts are part of a word length bit array. The meaning of each bit in that value is shown in Table 3-8.

Table 3-3

Functions of Serial Port Commands (continued)

	Command Code	BufferAddress	BufferLength	CharsUntilOverflow	CompletionAddress	DataLength	DTRState	InterruptSetting	ModeBitImage	PortStatusInfo	ReceiveQueueChars	RechargeAddress	Register Value	Reserved	SCCRegister	TimeSinceLastQueue
Parameter Size		L	W	W	L	W	W	W	L	W	W	L	B	W	B	W
Parameter Type		A	V	V	A	V	B	BA	BA	BA	V	A	V	-	V	T
FlushInQueue	$14															
FlushOutQueue	$15															
GetDTR	$0A						O1									
GetInBuffer	$10	O1	O2													
GetIntInfo	$0C							O1								
GetModeBits	$00								O1							
GetOutBuffer	$11	O1	O2													
GetPortStat	$06									O1						
GetSCC	$08												O1		I1	
InQStatus	$16										O1					O2
OutQStatus	$17			O1										O2		
SendQueue	$18					I1						I2				
SetDTR	$0B						I1									
SetInBuffer	$12	I1	I2													
SetIntInfo	$0D				I2			I1								
SetModeBits	$03								I1							
SetOutBuffer	$13	I1	I2													
SetSCC	$09												I2		I1	

Notes:

Size:
- B = Byte (8 bits)
- W = Word (16 bits)
- L = Long-word (32 bits)

Type:
- A = Address
- B = Boolean (only bit 7 significant)
- BA = Bit array
- T = Heartbeat ticks (1/30 seconds)
- V = Value

Table 3-4
Parameters of Serial Port Commands

Bit	Meaning
0*	1=modem mode; 0=printer mode
1*	1=awaiting XON character
2	1=DTR/DSR handshaking enabled
3	0=Delete line feed after carriage return
4	1=accept keyboard input
5	1=XON/XOFF handshaking active
6	1=Generate line feed after carriage return
7	1=Echo input to the video screen
8*	1=background printing in progress
9*	1=output flow halted
10*	1=input flow halted
11	1=generate carriage return at end of line
12	Reserved
13	1=DCD handshaking enabled
14*	1=I/O buffering enabled
15-19	Reserved
20	1=parity error has occurred
21	Reserved
22	1=framing error has occurred
23	1=ignore commands in output flow
24-31	Reserved

Note: Bits marked with an asterisk should not be modified.

Table 3-5

Meaning of Bits in Mode Bit Image

Bit	Name	Function
0	Rx Char Avail	=1 when a character is available to be read
1	Reserved	
2	Tx Buff Empty	=1 when ready to transmit the next character
3	DCD	Shows state of general purpose input line
4	Reserved	
5	DSR	Shows state of input handshake line
6	Tx Underrun	=1 when a transmission underrun occurs
7	Break/Abort	=1 when a break sequence occurs
8-15	Reserved	

Table 3-6

Port Status Value

Value	Type of Interrupt
$0001	Character available to receive
$0004	Transmission register empty
$0008	Transition (high to low or low to high) on general-purpose input line
$0020	Transition (high to low or low to high) on DRS line
$0040	Transmission underrun detected
$0080	Break sequence detected

Table 3-7

Interrupt Setting Values

Bit	Name	Purpose
0	Rx	Character available
1	Reserved	
2	Tx	Transmission register empty
3	DCD	Transition on general-purpose input line
4	Reserved	
5	CTS	Transition on input handshake line (Clear To Send)
6	Tx Underrun	Transmission underrun detected
7	Break/Abort	Break sequence detected
8-15	Reserved	Must be set to zero

Table 3-8

Interrupt Handler Value

Other Peripheral Ports

Information about the other peripheral ports can be found in other chapters of this book. The 80-column text display, mapped to Slot 3, is discussed in Chapter 8. The mouse connector, mapped to Slot 4, is discussed in Chapter 15. The disk connector, mapped to Slots 5 and 6, is discussed in Chapter 21. AppleTalk shares one of the serial port connectors but is mapped to Slot 7.

Other Connectors

The back panel of the IIGS, as well as the motherboard, contain other connectors, some of which are unchanged from the IIe or IIc and some of which are new.

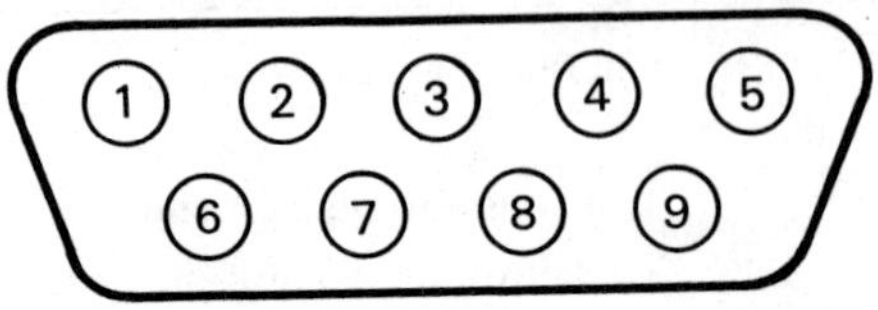

Pin	Use	Pin	Use
1	PB0	6	PB2
2	+5 volts	7	PB1
3	Ground	8	PDL1
4	PDL2	9	PDL3
5	PDL0		

Figure 3-5
Game I/O connector

The game port 9-pin connector is the same as that on the IIe and IIc (except that the connector on the IIc also doubles as a mouse connector). The arrangement of the pins on this connector is shown in Figure 3-5. The use made of each pin is shown in Table 3-9.

The IIGS also has a 16-pin DIP (dual in-line package) game connector on the motherboard. This is the same as the connector found on the Apple IIe, II Plus, and II.

The audio mini-headphone or speaker connector (9-mm miniature stereophone jack with its channels connected together) is similar to that on the Apple IIc. On the IIc there is a volume-control knob, while on the IIGS volume is controlled through the setting in the Control Panel.

The composite-video output connector (RCA phono jack type) is similar to that found on all Apple II's. It is used to connect a color composite or monochrome monitor to the IIGS. Composite-video output is discussed in greater detail later in this chapter. There are connection pins for a radio frequency modulator on the RGB connector similar to those on the Apple IIc.

Pin	Name	Use
1	PB0	Button 0 input
2	+5V	5 volt output
3	GND	Ground
4	PDL2	Paddle 2 input
5	PDL0	Paddle 0 input
6	PB2	Button 2 input
7	PB1	Button 1 input
8	PDL1	Paddle 1 input
9	PDL3	Paddle 3 input

Table 3-9
Nine-Pin Game Connector

The analog RGB connector (DB-15) is new with the IIGS. It is used to connect an analog RGB monitor to the IIGS. RGB output is discussed in greater detail later in this chapter. Previously, add-on RGB for the Apple II was digital.

The Apple Desktop Bus connector is used to connect the keyboard to the IIGS central unit. The mouse, in turn, is connected to bus via the keyboard. The keyboard, mouse, and Apple Desktop Bus are discussed in Chapter 15.

THE CLOCK

The IIGS comes with a built-in real-time clock. This clock, once set, maintains the current time and date, even when the IIGS is not turned on, by means of a battery.

The clock is compatible with the new 8- and 16-bit versions of ProDOS available for the IIGS and, with a properly installed driver, is also compatible with the earlier versions of ProDOS written for the Apple IIe and IIc. The clock is not the same as the ThunderClock, which previously was the "standard" ProDOS clock. All versions of ProDOS support *time and date* stamping of files—that is, whenever information is written to a particular file on disk, the date and time the information was written are stored in the directory entry for that file.

The IIGS Miscellaneous Tool set permits several operations involving the clock. While the user can always set the clock using the Control Panel, the WriteTimeHex (function 14) routine permits an application to set the clock time. This routine is called with the various byte-length (8-bit) values on the stack in the order as shown in Table 3-10. Note the restrictions that apply to each value. Thus, to set the clock to 5:00 A.M., Monday, September 15, 1986 (the date of the press release announcing the IIGS), you would use the following code:

```
SEP #$30            ;8-bit mode
LDA #09-1           ;September
PHA
LDA #15-1           ;15th day
PHA
LDA #1986-1900      ;Year
PHA
LDA #5-1            ;Hour - 5 AM in 24-hour format
PHA
LDA #00             ;Minutes and seconds
PHA
PHA
_WriteTimeHex       ;And set the clock
```

There are two routines that read the value of the clock. One returns hexadecimal values for each part of the time and date. The other returns the time and date in an ASCII format depending on the setting of certain format values in the Control Panel.

Name	Range	Meaning
Month	0-11	January = 0; December = 11
Day	0-30	The first of the month is 0
Year	—	Current year minus 1900
Hour	0-23	24-hour clock format
Minute	0-59	
Second	0-59	

Note: All values are 1 byte (8 bits).

Table 3-10

Order of Values Passed to WriteTimeHex

ReadTimeHex (function 13) returns values in the order specified in Table 3-11. The values are all one byte in length and are given in order from the top of stack down.

ReadASCIITime (function 15) returns the time in the form of an ASCII string. Your application places a long-word (32-bit) value on the stack specifying the address of a 20-byte buffer where the string should be

Item	Meaning/Range
Second	0-59
Minute	0-59
Hour	0-23 - 24-hour format
Year	Year minus 1900
Day	0-30 - day minus 1
Month	0-11 - January=0; December=11
Null	Space filler
Day of Week	0-6 - 0=Sunday; 6=Saturday

Table 3-11

Values Returned by ReadTimeHex

Date Format	Time Format	Output
0	0	mm/dd/yy HH:MM:SS AM/PM
1	0	dd/mm/yy HH:MM:SS AM/PM
2	0	yy/mm/dd HH:MM:SS AM/PM
0	1	mm/dd/yy HH:MM:SS
1	1	dd/mm/yy HH:MM:SS
2	1	yy/mm/dd HH:MM:SS

Table 3-12

Variations of Date/Time Format

placed. The string is placed into memory, lowest character first, and is in one of the formats shown in Table 3-12, depending on the setting of the date and time format in BatteryRAM. The string is padded to the right with blanks if a 24-hour time format is used. The high bit of each character is set to 1 (that is, negative ASCII values are used). This function, unlike ReadHexTime, does not return a day-of-the-week value.

The clock also makes use of a small buffer in memory at $E1/03E0-03FF. This memory is for internal use of the clock.

BATTERYRAM AND THE CONTROL PANEL

The same battery that keeps the clock running when the IIGS is turned off maintains an area of special memory, consisting of 256 bytes, known as the battery backed-up RAM, or BatteryRAM. Because the battery maintains power to this area of memory even when the IIGS's main power is off, the values stored in this area of memory are preserved. The values stored in the BatteryRAM consist of configuration information about the Apple IIGS, much of which is set by means of the Control Panel.

The values in the BatteryRAM are also stored, on system startup, in a buffer at $E1/02C0-03BF. When the Control Panel is called, it ensures that the current BatteryRAM values are placed in the buffer. Changes made by the user in the Control Panel are made to the values in the buffer. When you quit the Control Panel, the changes are stored in the BatteryRAM.

Table 3-13 shows the use of the BatteryRAM. That table lists the standard value and the range of permissible values for each item.

The Miscellaneous Tool Set contains four routines that assist in manipulation of the BatteryRAM. ReadBRam (function 10) reads the 256 bytes of BatteryRAM into a buffer whose address, as a long-word, has been placed on the stack. The correlative routine, WriteBRam, writes the 256-byte block of data at the specified address to the BatteryRAM.

Note that one of the parts of a BatteryRAM is a checksum.The checksum is computed when the system is started up and compared with the stored value. If the two values do not match, the IIGS presumes the BatteryRAM has been corrupted, possibly as a result of a changed battery. It resets the BatteryRAM to the standard or default parameters, destroying any modifications you may have made.

Byte	Function	Std.	Range
0 ($00)	Port 1 Function	$00	$00-01
1 ($01)	Port 1 Line length	$00	$00-04
2 ($02)	Port 1 Delete line feed after carriage return	$00	$00-01
3 ($03)	Port 1 Add line feed after carriage return	$01	$00-01
4 ($04)	Port 1 Echo	$00	$00-01
5 ($05)	Port 1 Buffer	$00	$00-01
6 ($06)	Port 1 Baud rate	$0D	$00-0E
7 ($07)	Port 1 Number of Data/Stop bits	$06	$00-07
8 ($08)	Port 1 Parity	$02	$00-02
9 ($09)	Port 1 DCD handshake	$01	$00-01
10 ($0A)	Port 1 DSR handshake	$01	$00-01
11 ($0B)	Port 1 XON/XOFF handshake	$00	$00-01
12 ($0C)	Port 2 Function	$01	$00-01
13 ($0D)	Port 2 Line length	$00	$00-04
14 ($0E)	Port 2 Delete line feed after carriage return	$00	$00-01
15 ($0F)	Port 2 Add line feed after carriage return	$00	$00-01
16 ($10)	Port 2 Echo	$00	$00-01
17 ($11)	Port 2 Buffer	$00	$00-01
18 ($12)	Port 2 Baud rate	$07	$00-0E
19 ($13)	Port 2 Number of Data/Stop bits	$06	$00-07
20 ($14)	Port 2 Parity	$02	$00-02
21 ($15)	Port 2 DCD handshake	$01	$00-01
22 ($16)	Port 2 DSR handshake	$01	$00-01
23 ($17)	Port 2 XON/XOFF handshake	$00	$00-01
24 ($18)	Display color/monochrome	$00	$00-01
25 ($19)	Display 40/80-column text	$00	$00-01
26 ($1A)	Color for text	$0F	$00-0F
27 ($1B)	Color for background	$06	$00-0F
28 ($1C)	Color for border	$06	$00-0F
29 ($1D)	50/60 Hz operation	——	$00-01
30 ($1E)	Speaker volume	$06	$00-0E
31 ($1F)	Speaker pitch	$07	$00-0E
32 ($20)	System speed	$00	$00-01

Table 3-13

BatteryRAM Memory Map

Byte	Function	Std.	Range
33 ($21)	Slot 1 use	$00	$00-01
34 ($22)	Slot 2 use	$00	$00-01
35 ($23)	Slot 3 use	$00	$00-01
36 ($24)	Slot 4 use	$00	$00-01
37 ($25)	Slot 5 use	$00	$00-01
38 ($26)	Slot 6 use	$00	$00-01
39 ($27)	Slot 7 use	$01	$00-01
40 ($28)	Startup slot	$00	$00-09
41 ($29)	Text display language	$00	$00-1F
42 ($2A)	Keyboard language	$00	$00-1F
43 ($2B)	Keyboard buffering	$00	$00-01
44 ($2C)	Keyboard repeat speed	$03	$00-07
45 ($2D)	Keyboard repeat delay	$02	$00-04
46 ($2E)	Double-click time	$02	$00-04
47 ($2F)	Flash rate	$02	$00-04
48 ($30)	Shift Caps/Lowercase	$00	$00-01
49 ($31)	Fast Space/Delete Keys	$00	$00-01
50 ($32)	Dual Speed	$00	$00-01
51 ($33)	High-mouse resolution	$00	$00-01
52 ($34)	Date format	$00	$00-02
53 ($35)	Time format	$00	$00-01
54 ($36)	RAMDisk minimum space	$00	$00-20
55 ($37)	RAMDisk maximum space	$00	$00-20
56-64 ($38-40)	List of available display languages		
65-81 ($41-51)	List of available keyboard layouts		
82-127 ($52-7F)	Reserved		
128 ($80)	AppleTalk node number		

Table 3-13
BatteryRAM Memory Map (continued)

Byte	Function	Std.	Range
129-161 ($81-A1)	Operating system variables		
162-251 ($A2-FB)	Reserved		
252-255 ($FC-FF)	Checksum		

Table 3-13
BatteryRAM Memory Map (continued)

Apple stresses that changes to the BatteryRAM should be made only through the Control Panel or through the Miscellaneous Tool calls. These functions properly compute the checksum and store it in the BatteryRAM whenever a write operation occurs. An attempt to modify the BatteryRAM directly would most likely result in faulty checksum and, therefore, a resetting of the BatteryRAM on the next system startup.

Changes to the entire BatteryRAM, made with WriteBRam, should be handled with caution. Note that certain values in the BatteryRAM are not user-created configuration values but rather system values. Specifically, values above address 55 ($37) should not be modified. If your application is planning to do wholesale modification to the BatteryRAM, it should first read in the entire 256 bytes using ReadBRam and then perform its modification only to the lower 56 bytes.

In addition to the commands that read or write the entire BatteryRAM, you can have your application check or change any of the values in the BatteryRAM. WriteBParam (function 11) writes a 1-byte value to the specified location in BatteryRAM. Calling the function is done like this:

```
*Routine to place a one-byte value, stored in memory
*location called "Value," into specified address of
*BatteryRAM, stored in memory location called "BRLoc"
     LDA Value         ;Only lower byte of word is significant
     PHA               ;Even though full word gets pushed
     LDA BRLoc         ;Address is between 0 and 255
     PHA               ;Upper byte should be zero
     _WriteBParam
```

ReadBParam (function 12) provides the correlative ability to read a specific byte of the BatteryRAM. It is used in the following manner:

```
*Routine to read a specified byte of the BatteryRAM, whose
*address is stored in the memory location called "BRLoc "
*At exit, the word on top of the stack will contain the
*value in its lower byte
      PushWord #$0000       ;Space for result goes on stack
      PushWord BRLoc        ;Address of location to be read
      _ReadBParam           ;Get the value
      PLA                   ;It's on the stack
      STA ParamValue        ;and save it
```

Modifying the BatteryRAM — the Control Panel

The easiest method for the user to modify any of the configuration settings in the BatteryRAM is by means of the Control Panel. This part of this chapter will discuss the modification of BatteryRAM based on the Control Panel screens. In addition, each of the modifiable parameters discussed will also show the address of the parameter in BatteryRAM and the meaning of the various values which that parameter can have. For the range and default value for each value, consult Table 3-13.

The default value is significant in the following ways:

□ It is the setting of the item placed in the BatteryRAM when you first purchase the IIGS and when the battery for the BatteryRAM and clock is replaced.

□ It is the setting of the item when the BatteryRAM has been corrupted and the IIGS resets it to standard values.

□ It is the setting of the item when you tell the Control Panel to set the parameters to the system standards.

□ It is the setting of the item that causes a checkmark to appear next to the item in the Control Panel screen.

The Control Panel is called in several ways. It can be directly called by pressing the OPTION key when turning on the IIGS or by pressing the OPTION key in conjunction with the CONTROL and RESET keys. It can also be selected from the Classic Desk Accessory menu, which can be reached

1=Enter Control Panel.

2=Set system standards and 60 hertz.

3=Set system standards and 50 hertz.

4=Continue restarting the system.

Press 1,2,3 or 4 to continue.

Options for this screen:

1. Press 1 to enter the control panel.
2. Press 2 to set Apple standard system parameters with 60 hertz selected.
3. Press 3 to set Apple standard system parameters with 50 hertz selected.
4. Press 4 to enter normal startup sequence.

Figure 3-6

Option-Control-Reset entry screen (Courtesy of Apple Computer, Inc.)

by pressing APPLE/COMMAND-SHIFT-ESCAPE from any application (in either 8-bit Apple II mode or 16-bit mode) that has not disabled interrupts.

Upon first entry to the Control Panel you are shown four choices (see Figure 3-6) if you have entered via the CONTROL-RESET method. The fourth choice is used if you have entered the Control Panel by mistake. The second and third choices set the various items in the Control Panel to standard settings. The second choice is used if the electrical power in your area is 60 Hz (60 alternating current cycles per second). This is the standard electrical current in the United States. The third choice is used if your electrical power is 50 Hz. No harm will result to your IIGS from selecting the wrong number of hertz, although the system clock may run incorrectly and the display screen may roll. These two choices are the only means of changing the hertz rating for your IIGS. There is no way to change the setting without resetting the IIGS to its standard configuration. The hertz selection made is shown on a display selection screen of the Control Panel, although it cannot be changed on that screen. The second and third choices also are the easiest way to reset the Control Panel to its default setting if you have hopelessly messed it up.

When you enter the Control Panel (the first choice), you are given a screenful of options plus a display of the current time and date as shown in Figure 3-7.

The display options, shown in Figure 3-8, determine how the text output of the IIGS will appear. The Standards option is not maintained as an item in BatteryRAM. Rather, it is a quick method to reset the display items to the system standards.

Selecting Monochrome (value = $01) rather than Color (value = $00) displays graphics and text in monochrome through the NTSC (composite video) port by means of a gray scale.

The effect of the selection of different colors for text, background, and border is immediately shown as you rotate through the various choices. The background and text colors are not allowed to be the same, but the border can be the same color as either the text or background.

The colors selected for display correspond to the 16 double high resolution colors in the Apple IIe and IIc. Table 3-14 gives a value for each color when chosen for the Control Panel.

The IIGS has the built-in capability to display text in either 40 or 80 characters across the screen (known as 40- and 80-column text). The 40/80-column text display option does not affect the display when set by a

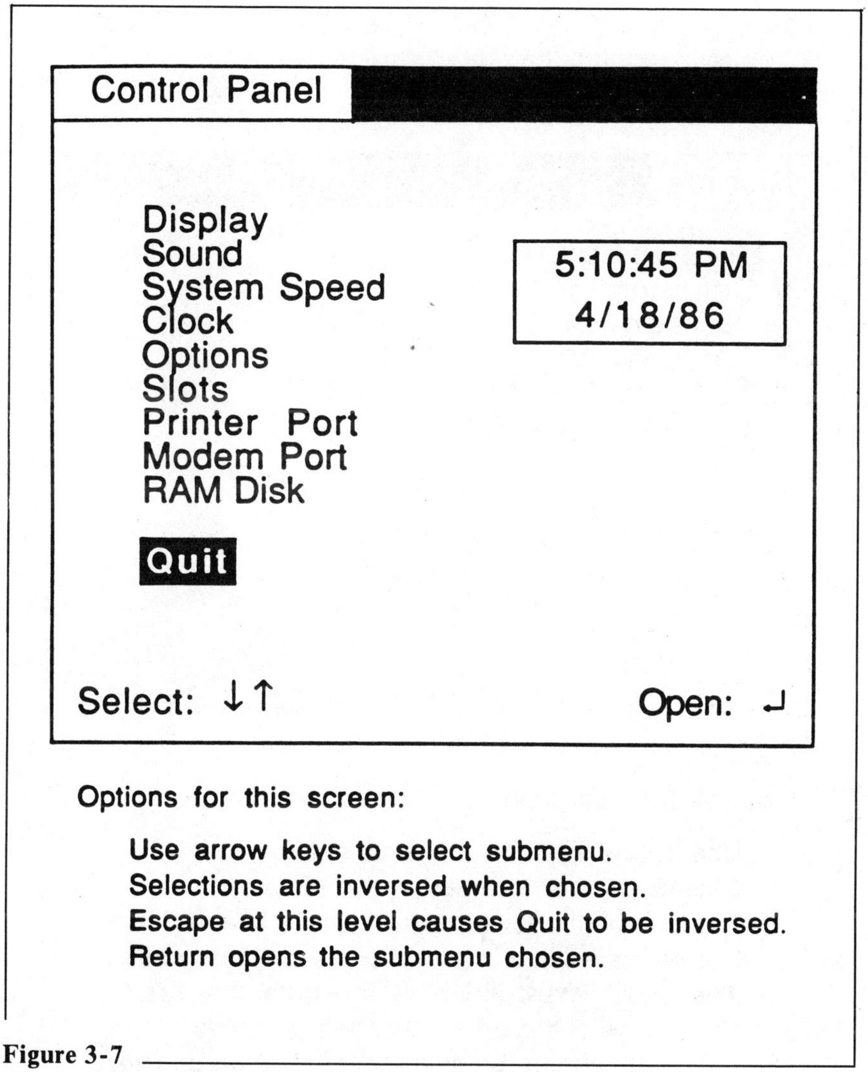

Figure 3-7
Main menu screen (Courtesy of Apple Computer, Inc.)

particular program. Either 40 or 80 columns will be used as set by that program. This option, which is used in several cases, uses a value of $00 indicating 40-column text and avalue of $01 indicating 80-column text.

```
Control Panel

Display

√ Type: Color
√ Columns: 40
  -Screen  Colors-
√ Text: White
√ Background: Medium Blue
√ Border: Medium Blue
√ Standards: Yes

  -Hertz:  60-

Select: ← → ↓ ↑    Cancel: Esc    Save: ↵
```

Options for this screen:

Use arrow keys to make selection.
Selections are inversed when chosen.
Escape at this level causes return to main menu.
Return saves the users choices on this screen.
The check mark indicates the default value.
Standards restores the standard colors.
'No' cannot be selected on Standards line.
Standards options change automatically as user changes text, backgound, and border colors.

Figure 3-8

Display screen (Courtesy of Apple Computer, Inc.)

Color Name	Control Panel number
Black	$00
Deep red	$01
Dark blue	$02
Purple	$03
Dark green	$04
Dark gray	$05
Medium blue	$06
Light blue	$07
Brown	$08
Orange	$09
Light gray	$0A
Pink	$0B
Light green	$0C
Yellow	$0D
Aquamarine	$0E
White	$0F

Table 3-14

Values of Colors Used in Control Panel Text Settings

The Control Panel and System Monitor displays use this setting for determining whether to use the 40- or 80-column screen. If you wish, your application can read this setting and set display for 40- or 80-columns as desired. The following code will read the value:

```
      Pushword #$0000       ;Space for data
      Pushword #$0019       ;Read 40/80-column text location
      _ReadBParam
      PLA                   ;Get returned value
      AND #$00FF            ;Isolate lower byte
      BEQ Do40Col           ;Set for 40 columns so set up code for 40 columns
*Code to set up for 80 columns goes here
```

The Sound screen (Figure 3-9) permits you, by means of a sliding asterisk, to select the volume and pitch given as the beep by the built-in speaker. There are 15 different selections for both volume and pitch with the lowest selection shown on the left. The lowest value for either selection

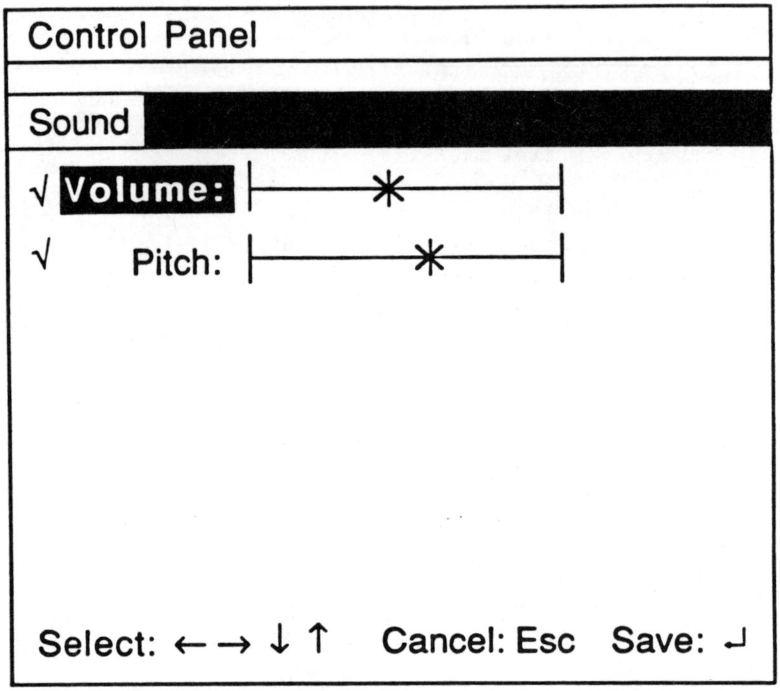

Options for this screen:

Use arrow keys to make selection.
Selections are inversed when chosen.
Escape at this level causes return to main menu.
Return saves the users choices on this screen.
The check mark indicates the default value.
Each time the left or right arrows are pressed
the bell routine is called so the user can
hear the new volume and pitch chosen.

Figure 3-9
Sound screen (Courtesy of Apple Computer, Inc.)

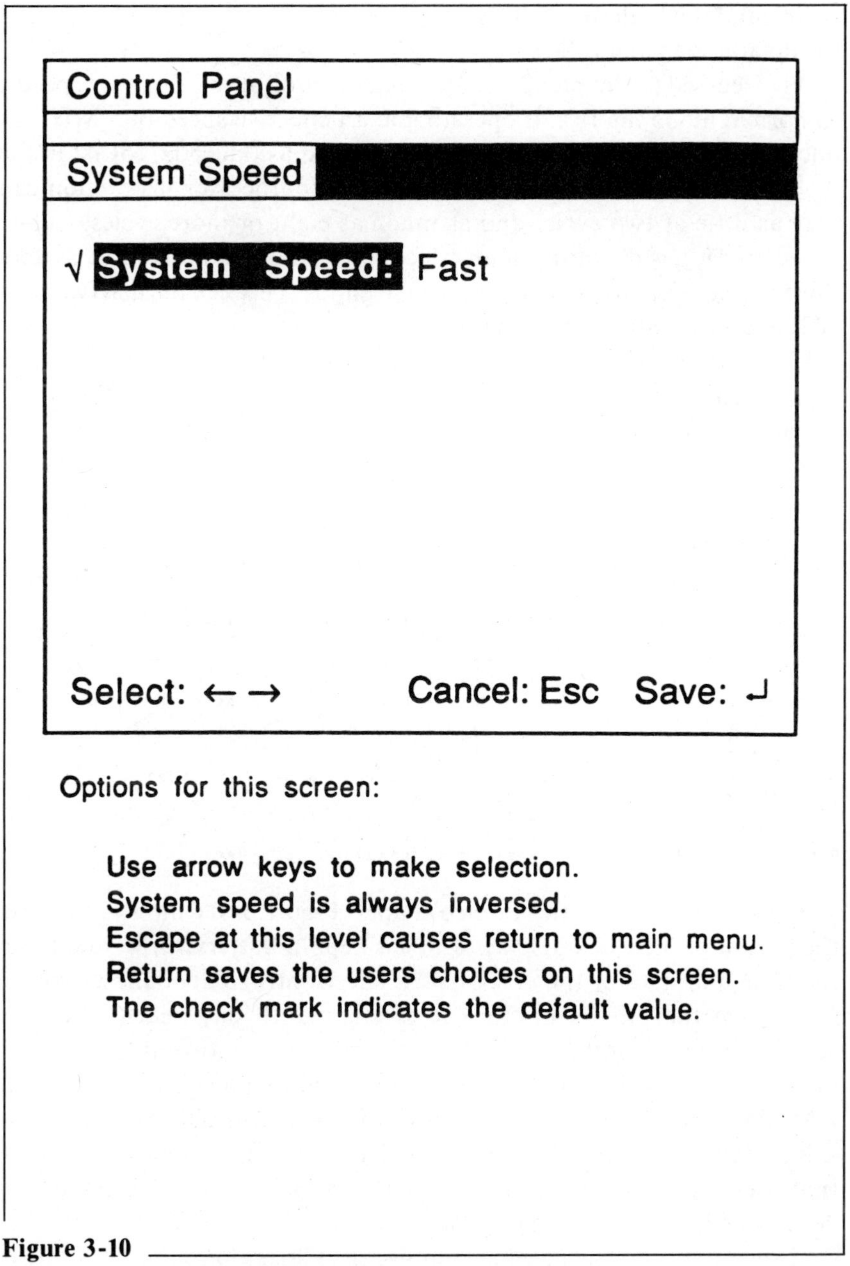

Figure 3-10

System speed screen (Courtesy of Apple Computer, Inc.)

is $00, and the highest is $0E. The default for volume is $06 (step 6), and the default for pitch is $07.

As discussed in Chapter 2, the IIGS can function at two different speeds. In normal mode the IIGS is operating at an effective speed of 1 MHz, or one million cycles per second, the same speed as the 6502/65C02 in the Apple II, II Plus, IIe, and IIc. A single microprocessor instruction can take as little as two cycles and as much as eight or more cycles. In fast mode the IIGS is operating at an effective speed of 2.5 MHz. The System Speed screen (Figure 3-10) allows you to choose between normal (value of $00) and fast (value of $01) speed.

If written specifically for the IIGS, your application may set the system speed itself, irrespective of the user setting. Be sure that the speed is reset to its earlier value after the program ends. The following code accomplishes this:

```
        PEA $0000               ;Result space
        PEA $0020               ;Want system speed parameter
        _ReadBParam             ;Get value
        PLA                     ;returned on stack
        AND #$00FF              ;Mask off high byte
        STA OldSpeed            ;Save the value
        BNE ItsFast             ;Skip rest if already fast speed
        PEA $0001               ;Set it to fast speed
        PEA $0020               ;System speed parameter
        _WriteBParam            ;And change it
ItsFast . . .                   ;Rest of main program code here

*At end of program reset speed as follows
        LDA OldSpeed            ;Get old speed
        BNE Done                ;If it's not zero, no need to reset
        PHA                     ;Normal speed
        PEA $0020               ;System speed parameter
        _WriteBParam            ;and reset it
Done . . .                      ;Rest of termination code here
```

The Clock screen in the Control Panel (Figure 3-11) allows you to set the format of the clock display, which is kept in BatteryRAM, and to set the time and date of the clock itself. The Control Panel allows you to specify whether the format for the date is month/day/year (value $00, standard), day/month/year (value $01), or year/month/day (value $02). You can also specify whether the hours should be displayed in 12-hour AM/PM format (value $00, standard) or 24-hour format ($01).

The date-setting mechanism is intelligent. It won't let you enter a date that does not exist, and it properly calculates leap year for all years except 2000 (which will not be a leap year).

A snag that may occur when you use the Clock option in the Control Panel merely to change time or date format is that you may inadvertently

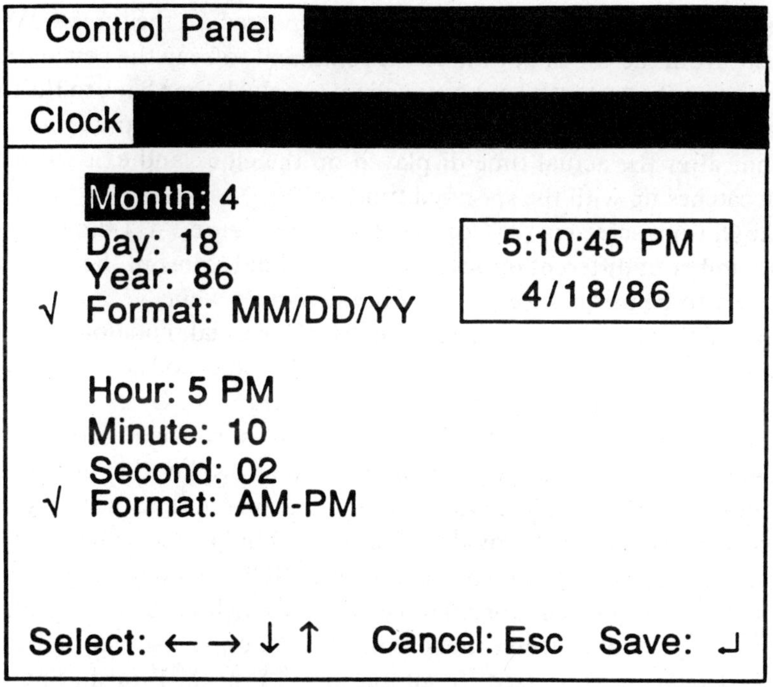

Options for this screen:

Use arrow keys to make selection.
Selections are inversed when chosen.
Escape at this level returns to main menu.
Formats change in clock display whenever
the user changes them. They revert back
to the previous setting is user presses Esc
to cancel the last change.
Default arrows only available for Format options.

Figure 3-11

Clock screen (Courtesy of Apple Computer, Inc.)

reset the clock erroneously. When you enter the clock-setting screen, it shows the current clock values for date and time. While you are using the screen, however, the date and time are not updated on the screen. When you exit from the Clock option with a command to keep the new settings (by pressing the RETURN key), you will set the clock time back to the time it was when you entered the option. To avoid this, set the time for a few seconds after the actual time displayed on the clock and exit when the clock catches up with the specified time.

The Options screen in the Control Panel (see Figure 3-12) allows you to set a number of different options for the Cortland. Most of these choices are likely to be made once or only once in a great while.

The display language changes, at most, the special, nonalphanumeric character displayed for ten different ASCII character codes. These codes, and their representation in the U.S.A., U.K., French, German, Danish, Spanish, Italian, and Swedish display sets is shown in Figure 3-13. It should be noted that if a special character can be displayed in inverse and flashing, as well as normal, in the U.S.A. character set, the other language-corresponding character can also be displayed in inverse or flashing.

The changed keyboard layout affects the ASCII code generated when a particular key is pressed. For example, with a French keyboard layout, the letter Q is generated when the key marked A on the standard U.S.A. QWERTY layout is pressed. In all, the U.K., French, Danish, Spanish, Italian, German, Swedish, and French Canadian keyboard layouts affect 27 of the 48 character-generating keys on the keyboard in a manner different from the U.S.A. layout. (The layout of the characters on the numeric keypad is unaffected by the keyboard layout selection.) The Dvorak keyboard layout affects 34 of the 48 keys.

A chart showing the more commonly available keyboard layouts is given in Appendix A.

The codes assigned to the potential keyboard and display languages are shown in Table 3-15. The actual language choices available are determined by the particular ROM in your system's keyboard. A list of the values of the available languages is stored by the system in BatteryRAM. There are 8 potential display languages and 16 potential keyboard layouts.

A certain amount of keyboard buffering is accomplished by the keyboard microcontroller unit (see discussion in Chapter 15). Further buffering can be accomplished by setting the Buffering option to "Yes" in the Control Panel. With this option, a nearly unlimited number of keystrokes

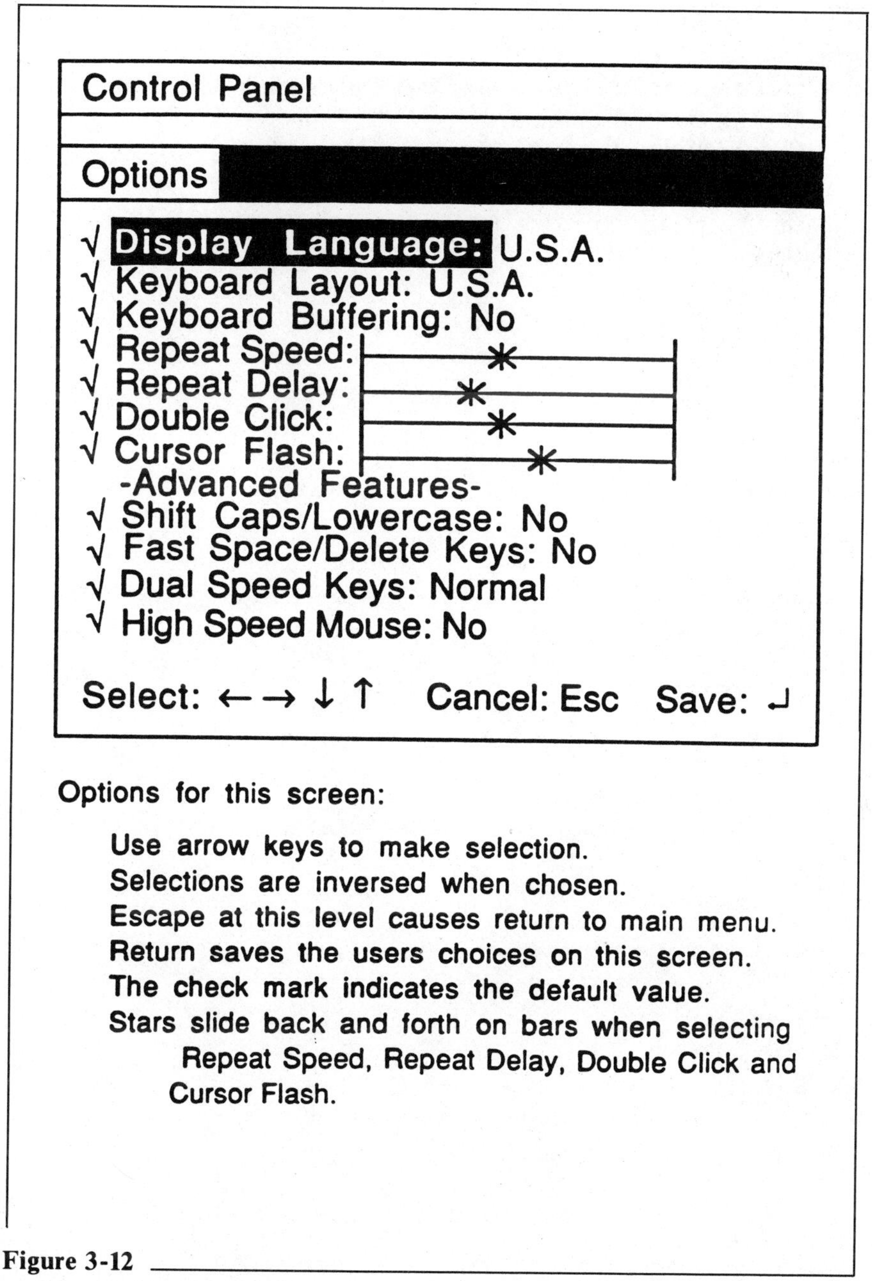

Figure 3-12

Options screen (Courtesy of Apple Computer, Inc.)

<table>
<tr><th colspan="2">ASCII Value</th><th></th><th></th><th></th><th></th><th></th><th></th><th></th><th></th></tr>
<tr><th>Hex.</th><th>Dec.</th><th>USA</th><th>UK</th><th>France</th><th>Germany</th><th>Denmark</th><th>Spain</th><th>Italy</th><th>Sweden</th></tr>
<tr><td>23</td><td>35</td><td>#</td><td>£</td><td>£</td><td>#</td><td>#</td><td>£</td><td>£</td><td>#</td></tr>
<tr><td>40</td><td>64</td><td>@</td><td>@</td><td>à</td><td>§</td><td>@</td><td>§</td><td>§</td><td>@</td></tr>
<tr><td>5B</td><td>91</td><td>[</td><td>[</td><td>^</td><td>Ä</td><td>Æ</td><td>¡</td><td>^</td><td>Ä</td></tr>
<tr><td>5C</td><td>92</td><td>\</td><td>\</td><td>ç</td><td>Ö</td><td>Ø</td><td>Ñ</td><td>ç</td><td>Ö</td></tr>
<tr><td>5D</td><td>93</td><td>]</td><td>]</td><td>§</td><td>Ü</td><td>Å</td><td>¿</td><td>é</td><td>Å</td></tr>
<tr><td>60</td><td>96</td><td>`</td><td>`</td><td>`</td><td>`</td><td>`</td><td>`</td><td>ù</td><td>`</td></tr>
<tr><td>7B</td><td>123</td><td>{</td><td>{</td><td>é</td><td>ä</td><td>æ</td><td>°</td><td>à</td><td>ä</td></tr>
<tr><td>7C</td><td>124</td><td>|</td><td>|</td><td>ù</td><td>ö</td><td>ø</td><td>ñ</td><td>ò</td><td>ö</td></tr>
<tr><td>7D</td><td>125</td><td>}</td><td>}</td><td>è</td><td>ü</td><td>å</td><td>ç</td><td>è</td><td>å</td></tr>
<tr><td>7E</td><td>126</td><td>~</td><td>~</td><td>¨</td><td>ß</td><td>~</td><td>~</td><td>ì</td><td>~</td></tr>
</table>

Figure 3-13

Alternative country display sets

Language	Value
English (U.S.A.)	$00
English (U.K.)	$01
French	$02
Danish	$03
Spanish	$04
Italian	$05
German	$06
Swedish	$07
Dvorak	$08
French Canadian	$09
Flemish	$0A
Hebrew	$0B
Japanese	$0C
Arabic	$0D
Greek	$0E
Turkish	$0F
Finnish	$10
Portuguese	$11
Tamil	$12
Hindi	$13
Reserved	$14-1F

Table 3-15

Language Values

can be saved and processed by the IIGS without losing keys pressed while other functions are occurring.

Keyboard buffering is not always desired. Certain programs, particularly game programs, may not work properly when buffering is enabled. In addition, it is easy to get lost in some programs if you do not have a currently updated screen while buffering is occurring. A value of $01 shows buffering is active while $00 shows it is disabled.

The Repeat Speed, Repeat Delay, Double-click, and Cursor-flash options are all given as points on a sliding bar with the slower choices on the left side of the bar and the faster choices on the right side, except for the Repeat Delay. The various stops on the bar correspond to a given value, each of which is given in Table 3-16. Note that the Repeat Delay is backward from the other slide bars, and that the farthest right Repeat Delay is a value of infinite delay (no repeat).

Double-click and Cursor-flash are given not in seconds but in ticks. A tick refers to approximately 1/60 of a second.

The four advanced features values are each $00 if off and $01 if on.

Shift Caps/Lowercase works only if the CAPS LOCK key is engaged. If CAPS LOCK is engaged and Shift Caps/Lowercase is on, every letter key pressed with the SHIFT key up results in a capital letter and every key pressed with the SHIFT key down results in a lowercase letter. Number and symbol keys are unaffected.

Fast Space/Delete Keys permits you to alter the repeat speed behavior of the space bar and DELETE key. If this option is on, the space bar and DELETE key will repeat at the normal speed if held down alone; they will repeat at a faster speed if held down in conjunction with the CONTROL key. This behavior, called *Dual Speed,* is not restricted to the space bar and CONTROL key but also applies, without any setting in the Control Panel, to the arrow keys.

The Dual Speed setting permits you to alter the faster speed at which the dual speed keys (including space bar and DELETE if activated) repeat. The normal setting causes the higher repeat speed (that is, with the CONTROL key held down) to be relative to the normal repeat speed as set in the Control Panel. The fast setting makes the higher repeat speed always the fastest speed, irrespective of the repeat speed setting in the Control Panel. The standard repeat speed (that is, the CONTROL key is not held down) is not affected by this setting.

High Speed Mouse changes the effect of mouse movement when the user moves the mouse at a high speed. Under normal operation (high speed = "No"), moving the mouse the same distance, at whatever speed, results in the same value of distance being passed to the application. Under high

Repeat Speed Values

Characters per Second	Value
4	0
8	1
11	2
15	3
20	4
24	5
30	6
40	7

Repeat Delay

Delay Time	Value
.25 second	0
.50 second	1
.75 second	2
1 second	3
No repeat	4

Double-click time

Number of Ticks	Value
50	0
40	1
30	2
20	3
10	4

Cursor-Flash Time

Number of Ticks	Value
0	0
60	1
30	2
15	3
10	4

Table 3-16

Options Screen Slide Bar Settings

speed operation (high speed = "Yes"), moving the mouse the same distance at a high speed, rather than a low speed, results in a larger value being passed to the application.

The Slots screen (see Figure 3-14) allows the user to select whether a peripheral card in a particular slot is active or whether the built-in port mapped to that slot is active. The selection will not take effect until ProDOS is booted. A zero as the particular value shows that the built-in port is active and a one shows that the peripheral card for that slot is active. Note that the printer port and modem port cannot both be active if AppleTalk is also active.

The IIGS checks to see if there is a disk drive attached to the startup slot and, if there is, boots the drive attached to the peripheral card in that slot or to the port mapped to that slot. The meanings of the various values for this parameter are given in Table 3-17. The Slot options 1-7 are self-explanatory. RAM disks are discussed in this chapter and ROM disks are discussed in Chapter 6. The Standard Scan option will start with Slot 7, looking for a disk drive, and work down through Slot 1, following with a check for a RAM disk or a ROM disk.

The printer port and modem port screens (see Figure 3-15) are identical except for the port number to which each applies and certain default values. The values for the connected device are zero for a printer and one for a modem. *Line length* refers to the number of characters the port will transmit or receive before adding a carriage return. The available options and the value assigned to each option are given in Table 3-18.

Some computers, interfaces, modems, and printers add a line feed (ASCII $0A) and then send a carriage return (ASCII $0D). Others do not. This can result in a problem if the sending device is not coordinated with the receiving device. Text that is sent single-spaced can either be double- or triple-spaced when received. Text spaced properly when sent can be received so that each line prints on top of the previous one. Neither situation is desirable.

The IIGS serial ports permit you to specify either that a line feed following a carriage return should be removed (Delete first LF after CR) or that a line feed should be added after a carriage return (Add LF after CR). In both cases the "No" setting is shown by a value of zero and the "Yes" setting by a value of one.

Echo refers to the fact that every character sent out the serial port is also displayed on the screen. *Buffering* refers to the ability of the port to hold characters when the IIGS itself is handling other details. In both of these cases, a "No" is indicated by a zero value and a "Yes" by a one value.

```
Control Panel

Slots

√ Slot 1: Printer Port
√ Slot 2: Modem Port
√ Slot 3: Built-in Text Display
√ Slot 4: Mouse Port
√ Slot 5: Smart Port
√ Slot 6: Disk Port
√ Slot 7: Your Card

√ Startup Slot: Scan

Select: ← → ↓ ↑    Cancel: Esc   Save: ↵
```

Options for this screen:

Use arrow keys to make selection.
Selections are inversed when chosen.
Escape at this level causes return to main menu.
Return saves the users choices on this screen.
The check mark indicates the default value.
If Printer Port, Modem Port and Built-in AppleTalk are selected at the same time the message 'WARNING: Printer / Modem / AppleTalk cannot be active at the same time!!! ' appears. At that point the user must change one of them to continue or press Esc.

Figure 3-14

Slots screen (Courtesy of Apple Computer, Inc.)

Value	Meaning
0	Scan
1	Boot slot 1
2	Boot slot 2
3	Boot slot 3
4	Boot slot 4
5	Boot slot 5
6	Boot slot 6
7	Boot slot 7
8	Boot RAM disk
9	Boot ROM disk

Table 3-17
Startup Slot

Baud refers to the rate at which a serial port transmits data. A baud is a bit per second. The standard character contains eight data bits, one start bit, and one stop bit for a total of ten bits. Thus, a transmission rate of 1200 baud is 120 characters per second. The number of characters per second can vary if each character has a greater or lesser number of bits (because of a variable number of data bits and stop bits and the presence or absence of a parity bit). The values for the baud rates are listed in Table 3-19.

Each character transmitted can vary in number of data bits between 5 (for Baudot code or any code with values between 0 and 31) and 8 (for extended ASCII or EBCIDIC or any code with values between 0 and 255) and can have either one or two bits indicating the end of a character. The values assigned to the various combinations of data and stop bits are shown in Table 3-20.

Parity is a low-level method of detecting errors in data transmission. When parity is used, the number of bits set to one in each character is counted. If parity is odd and the number of set bits is odd, the parity bit is set to zero. If parity is odd and the number of set bits is even, the parity bit is set to one to make an odd number of set bits. Treatment of each character is similar if even parity is used. If no parity is used, there is no parity bit. The value for odd parity is zero, for even parity is one, and for no parity is two.

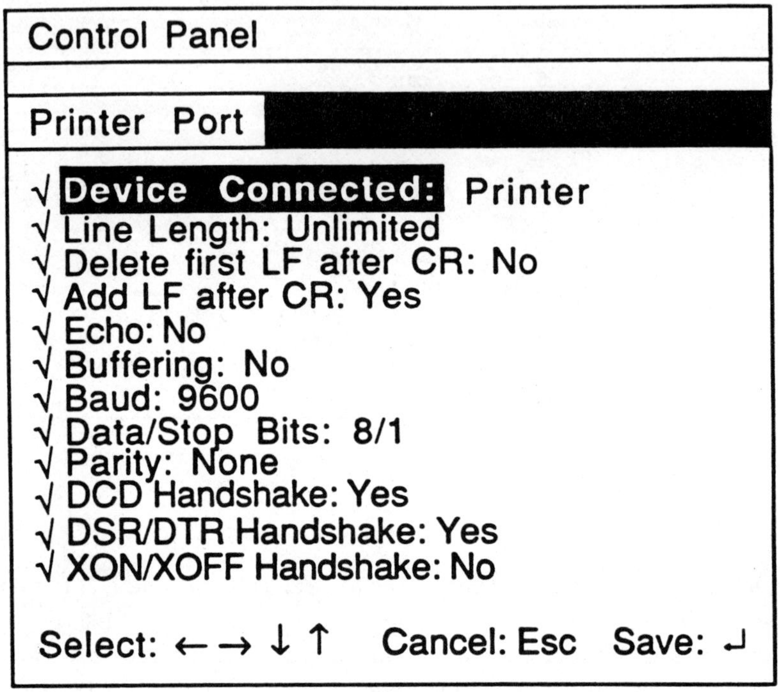

Options for this screen:

Use arrow keys to make selection.
Selections are inversed when chosen.
Escape at this level causes return to main menu.
Return saves the users choices on this screen.
The check mark indicates the default value.

Figure 3-15

Printer/modem port screen (Courtesy of Apple Computer, Inc.)

Value	Line Length
0	Unlimited
1	40 characters
2	72 characters
3	80 characters
4	132 characters

Table 3-18
Line Length Values

Value	Baud Rate
$00	50
$01	75
$02	110
$03	134.5
$04	150
$05	300
$06	600
$07	1200
$08	1800
$09	2400
$0A	3600
$0B	4800
$0C	7200
$0D	9600
$0E	19200

Table 3-19
Baud Rate Values

Value	Data Bits	Stop Bits
0	5	1
1	5	2
2	6	1
3	6	2
4	7	1
5	7	2
6	8	1
7	8	2

Table 3-20
Data/Stop Bit Values

The RAM Disk screen (see Figure 3-16) gives you the ability to set up a RAM disk. The largest selectable RAM disk is determined by the system based on the amount of available RAM in your IIGS. Within these limits you can determine the minimum and maximum sizes for a RAM disk. The increments by which you can change the minimum and maximum sizes are 1/32 of the largest selected RAM disk. A value of $00 indicates no RAM disk, while a value of $20 indicates a RAM disk equal to the largest selectable size.

The remaining values on the RAM disk screen are for information only. The system obtains them from the Memory Manager (discussed in Chapter 5). These values are not stored in BatteryRAM.

VIDEO OUTPUT

The IIGS has two video-output ports. The composite-video output, which requires an RCA phono jack, is identical to the one that has existed in the Apple II family since the beginning. In a IIGS manufactured for the United States market, this output conforms to the NTSC (National Television

```
Control Panel

RAM Disk

√ Minimum RAM Disk Size:              0K
√ Maximum RAM Disk Size:              0K
  -Largest Selectable:             1024K-

  -RAM Status-
  RAM Disk Size:                      50K
  Total RAM in Use:                   85K
  Total Free RAM:                   1194K

Select: ← → ↓ ↑    Cancel: Esc   Save: ↵
```

Options for this screen:

Use arrow keys to make selection.
Selections are inversed when chosen.
Escape at this level causes return to main menu.
Return saves the users choices on this screen.
The check mark indicates the default value.

Figure 3-16
RAM Disk screen (Courtesy of Apple Computer, Inc.)

Signal	Voltage Level (Approximate)
White	2.00 volts
Black	0.75 volts
Sync	0.00 volts

Table 3-21
Composite-Video Signal Voltage Levels

Pin	Signal
1	Ground
2	Red analog video
3	Composite sync
4	Not connected
5	Green analog video
6	Ground
7	-5 volts
8	+12 volts
9	Blue analog video
10	Not connected
11	Sound
12	Composite video (NTSC, PAL, or SECAM)
13	Ground
14	Not connected
15	Not connected

Table 3-22
RGB Output Signals

Systems Committee) standard. It will thus work with a variety of different models, depending on your country.

The composite-video output has the signal at the tip of the connector, while the shield is the ground. The impedance is 75 ohms. The signal voltage levels are given in Table 3-21.

The RGB output is a 15-pin, DB-15 miniature D-type connector. The output signal is analog RGB, not digital RGB. The AppleColor 100 RGB monitor is not compatible with this output. The AppleColor RGB monitor is designed to be used with this output. Table 3-22 shows the signals available for the various pins on this connector.

When running in 8-bit Apple II mode, using one of the older Apple II display modes, the output is modified to reflect properly the composite nature of that color output. The Super Resolution display modes provide true analog RGB output without the artificial color and boundary restrictions that affected earlier Apple II RGB.

The IIGS has a custom chip that provides most of the circuitry and signals needed for proper display of the previously existing and new displays. The chip is called the VGC (Video Graphics Controller). It provides the connection between the display output and the IIGS as well as providing certain interrupt-handling capabilities required by the display modes. In addition, it provides an interface to the Mega II chip and the clock chip.

CHAPTER 4

The IIGS and the 65816 Microprocessor

This chapter is not meant as a comprehensive treatment of the 65816 microprocessor and the mechanics of programming it. Likewise, it is not an introduction to assembly language programming. Readers wishing a more complete treatment of the 65816 should consult *65816/65802 Assembly Language Programming* from Osborne/McGraw-Hill. The following text will, in fact, presume a rudimentary understanding of assembly language programming, either in the 6502 or 68000 world.

The microprocessor in the Apple IIGS is a 65SC816, (65816) designed by Western Design Center. The chip is a version of the 4 MHz chip and operates at two speeds—2.8 MHz and 1 MHz. As discussed in Chapter 5, some of the IIGS functions must occur at 1 MHz for compatibility with earlier 8-bit Apple II software or peripherals. Other operations can take place at the faster speed. The effective rate at the faster speed is actually 2.5 MHz, since a certain number of machine cycles are used to service interrupt polling routines and similar housekeeping tasks.

This chip is an upwardly compatible member of the 65xxx family of microprocessors including the 6502 (used in the Apple II, II Plus, and earlier models of the Apple IIe standard) and the 65C02 (used in the Apple IIc and later models of the Apple IIe enhanced). Because the chip is upwardly compatible, it can, almost always, run programs written for the 6502 or 65C02.

The chip is not downwardly compatible with the 6502/65C02. These earlier chips will not run programs written to take advantage of the enhanced operating capabilities of the 65816.

The 65816 is a microprocessor with a 24-bit addressing capability. It has a total of 8 data lines and 16 address lines. It can use either 16- or 24-bit addresses. When it uses 16-bit addressing, it uses the standard 16 address lines. When it uses 24-bit addressing, it uses the 8 data lines. This use of the data line for both data and addressing is called *multiplexing.*

Internally the 65816 handles data in either 8-bit bytes or 16-bit words. Since there are only 8 data lines, though, data are handled externally in 8-bit bytes. When 16-bit data are being moved from memory to the 65816, or from the 65816 to memory, the operation takes place in two cycles. During the first cycle, the 65816 reads or writes the lower 8 bits of the value. During the second cycle it reads or writes the upper 8 bits of the value. The lower 8 bits are thus always stored in the lower memory location.

When reading or writing an address, the 65816 also takes in the data in bytes, beginning with the lowest byte. A 24-bit address is handled with the lowest byte first, followed by the middle byte, and ending with the highest byte. Thus, whether a 2- or 3-byte value is being used, the 65816 always starts working with the lowest value, or the value at the lowest memory address. This is consistent with the way multibyte values are generally treated in the 65xxx world.

The 65816 has two modes of operation. In emulation mode the chip responds to commands more or less as the 65C02 works. In native mode it handles commands using 16-bit data and 24-bit addressing. The internal configuration of the 65816 also varies depending upon whether it is in native or emulation mode.

REGISTERS

The 65816 has a number of internal *registers,* locations where it stores data. These registers serve various functions.

Accumulator

The workhorse register is the accumulator. It is where most data are added, subtracted, modified, or compared. With few exceptions, values stored in memory can only be modified through the accumulator.

In native mode the accumulator is treated in a variety of different ways. It is a 16-bit register, which can also be considered as two 8-bit registers. As a 16-bit register it is referred to as the A or the C register. The two 8-bit registers are referred to as the A (lower 8 bits) and B (upper 8 bits) registers.

Switching between one 16-bit accumulator and two 8-bit registers is accomplished by the setting of a single bit in the processor status register (discussed later). When this bit, referred to as the m (for memory bit), is set to 0, the 65816 uses a 16-bit accumulator. When the m bit is set to 1, the 65816 uses two 8-bit registers.

The setting of the M bit also affects how the 65816 treats memory. When the M bit is set to 0, the 65816 treats memory in most commands as 2-byte chunks. When the M bit is set to 1, memory is handled in single 8-bit bytes.

In emulation mode the accumulator is considered to be an 8-bit register, referred to as the A register. The B register is used only as a temporary storage area and is not directly accessible except with the XBA command.

Index Registers

The 65816, like the 6502 and 65C02 before it, has two index registers, known as the X and Y registers. These registers are either 8 or 16 bits wide, depending on several factors.

In native mode the setting of the X bit in the processor status register determines the width of the index registers. If the X bit is set to 1, the two registers are only 8 bits wide. If the X bit is set to 0, the two registers are 16 bits wide.

In emulation mode the X and Y registers are permanently set to the 8-bit width.

Unlike the treatment of the B register when the 65816 is in 8-bit accumulator mode, the upper 8 bits of the X and Y register are not accessible when the 65816 is in 8-bit index register mode. You can rely on the value in the upper 8 bits of these registers remaining between a switch to 8-bit index mode and back to 16-bit mode, provided you do not also switch to emulation mode.

Stack Pointer

One significant change in the 65816 from the 65C02/6502 is the increase in the width of the stack pointer from 8 to 16 bits. This permits the stack to be located anywhere in bank $00 and allows it to extend, theoretically, to 64K. The 16-bit stack is available, though, only when the 65816 is in native mode. When the microprocessor is in 8-bit mode, the upper 8 bits of the 16-bit stack pointer are permanently set to $01, resulting in a 256-byte stack from $00/01FF to $00/0100, the same as with the 65C02.

Switching from native to emulation mode, thus, results in the high byte of the stack pointer being changed. Unless special care is take to preserve the stack pointer on the switch, the previous native mode value of the stack pointer is lost when the 65816 is switched back to native mode.

The following code shows how to switch from native mode to emulation mode. It presumes that the emulation mode stack pointer was previously saved in a memory location with the label SaveStck.

```
*This code assumes the 65816 is in full 16-bit mode.  If it is not,
*the code should begin with a REP #$30 to set full 16-bit mode.
         TSC              ;Place stack pointer in accumulator
         TSX              ;and in X register as well
         SEP #$20         ;Switch to 8-bit accumulator
         XBA              ;So we can check what page stack was on
         DEC A            ;Was it Page 1 - if so DEC will result in zero value
         BEQ OnPage1      ;Yes - don't need to reset emulation stack pointer
         LDA #$01         ;No - set top byte of pointer to Page 1
         XBA              ;Move lower byte (now $01) to upper byte
         LDA Emulstack    ;Get the emulation bank stack pointer (lower byte)
         TCS              ;and set it
OnPage1  PHX              ;Save 16-bit native stack pointer in X register
         SEC              ;and move to emulation mode
         XCE
*Rest of code goes here
```

When switching back from emulation mode to native mode, your application should perform the following action to restore the stack pointer properly:

```
*This code presumes that the stack was not corrupted while in
*emulation mode; that is, any data placed on the stack was removed
*from the stack and the values on the stack when the 65816 went into
*emulation mode were left unchanged.
          CLC
          XCE        ;Get into native mode
          REP #$30   ;Full 16-bit operation
          PLX        ;Retrieve native mode stack pointer
          TXS        ;and give it to the stack pointer.
```

The code could also use a PLA instruction in place of the PLX and a TCS in place of the TXS. In the latter case the previous value in the accumulator would be scrambled. In the case of the listed code the previous value in the X register would be scrambled.

Program Counter and Addressing Bank Registers

The Program Counter in the 65816 is 16 bits wide, the same size as that in the 65C02/6502. This results in the ability to address 64K of memory.

With the 65C02/6502 the 64K of addressable memory is an absolute limit, absent the use of a technique like bank switching. The 65816, however, has the ability to address considerably more memory than this.

As discussed earlier in this chapter, the 65816 can address up to 16 MB of memory using 24 addressing lines. Yet the Program Counter is only 16 bits wide. The ability to use the other addressing lines, when reading in program code, is gained by means of another register in the 65816—the program bank register. When a code-related 24-bit address is used, as in the JSL or JML instruction, the upper 8 bits of the address are placed in the program bank register. Whenever the 65816 seeks a new instruction, it uses the full 24 bits, including the value in the program bank register.

The following are certain idiosyncrasies with the program bank register:

- When the 65816 obtains an address at the end of a 64K bank, such as a 3-byte instruction beginning at $00/FFFF, the first byte will come from $00/FFFF while the second and third bytes will come from $00/0000 and $00/0001 rather than from the same locations in bank $01. This is because the program bank register is not incremented whenever the Program Counter recycles from top ($FFFF) to bottom ($0000).

- The program bank register can be saved on the stack (PHK), but it cannot be restored from the stack—there is no correlative PLK instruction.
- Only a few instructions directly set a value in the program bank register. These instructions are listed in Table 4-1. Several hardware operations also affect the program bank register. These are the various forms of hardware interrupts including ABORT, IRQ (interrupt request), NMI (nonmaskable interrupt), and RES (reset).

Because of these idiosyncrasies it is extremely difficult, and very risky, to write code that will span a bank boundary.

When the 65816 accesses data, it can obtain the data in a number of ways. In some cases the address of the data is directly or indirectly included in the addressing information. These addressing modes are known as the long modes and are listed in Table 4-2.

Other addressing modes provide information about the lower 16 bits of the address, have the value in another register in the 65816 (the data bank

Op Code	Addressing Mode	Effect
BRK	N/A	Resets register to $00 after first pushing its value on the stack
COP	N/A	Resets register to $00 after first pushing its value on the stack
JML	[aabb] absolute indirect	Sets register to value found at aabb+2
JML	aabbcc absolute long	Sets register to aa
JSL	aabbcc absolute long	Sets register to aa
RTI	N/A	Sets register to fourth byte on stack
RTL	N/A	Sets register to third byte on stack

Table 4-1

Instructions That Affect the Program Bank Register

register), and specify the upper 8 bits (or bank number) of the address. These modes are listed in Table 4-3.

A pair of commands places the value of the data bank register on the stack (PHB) and retrieves it from the stack (PLB). In addition, the value of the data bank register is changed by the MVN and MVP commands. In these two commands the data bank register contains the value of the destination bank following the execution of the command.

Mode	Location of Bank Number
Absolute Long LDA aabbcc	aa
Direct Indirect Long Indexed LDA [aabb],y	value in aabb + 2
Absolute Long Indexed with X LDA aabbcc,x	aa
Direct Indirect Long LDA [aabb]	value in aabb + 2

Table 4-2
65816 Long Addressing Modes

Mode Name	Example
Absolute	LDA aabb
Direct Indirect Indexed	LDA (aa),y
Direct Indexed Indirect	LDA (aa,x)
Absolute Indexed with X	LDA aabbcc,x
Absolute Indexed with Y	LDA aabbcc,y
Direct Indirect	LDA (aa)
Stack Relative Indexed Indirect	LDA (aa,s),y

Table 4-3
Addressing Modes That Use the Data Bank Register

Direct Register

The 65816 has a register, not available on the 65C02/6502, that permits it to have what is known as a *relocatable zero page*. In the 65C02 world, zero page is that area of memory from $00/0000-00FF. Several different addressing modes permit addressing the memory area in a manner that is considerably faster than addressing other memory.

The direct register in the 65816 permits this page of memory to be located in any 256-byte area of bank zero, from $00/0000 to $00/FFFF. This relocatable zero page is called the *direct page*. It differs from the zero page in the 65C02 world only in that the value in the direct register is added to the specified address to obtain the actual address.

The direct register also affects the use of zero page addressing mode when the 65816 is operating in emulation mode as follows:

- If the direct register is set to $0000, the operation is the same as in the 65C02/6502, except with the PEI instruction and direct indirect long and direct indirect long indexed addressing modes. These exceptions, if used with an effective address of $00/00FE or $00/00FF, will obtain the third, or second and third, bytes of information from $00/0100 and $00/0101 rather than from $00/0000 and $00/0001 as do the other instructions and addressing modes.
- If the upper byte of the direct register does not equal $00 while the lower byte does, the 65816 treats the page whose value is in the upper byte of the direct register as though it were zero page.
- If the lower byte of the direct register is not $00, the 65816 treats direct page commands the same as though they were native mode commands. Thus all applicable instructions and addressing modes do not fold back when they reach the top of the page.

The ability to relocate the direct page with the 65816 is widely used in the IIGS. Many of the tool sets require use of a direct page and the various tool set setup commands permit the application to specify a separate direct page for each of the sets.

Processor Status Register

The processor status register in the 65816 is somewhat expanded from the one in the 65C02. There are two different status registers depending on whether the 65816 is in native or emulation mode.

In emulation mode the status register is identical to that in the 65C02 and 6502 with the exception of the e or emulation bit. This bit hides behind the carry bit and is only accessible through the carry bit (and the XCE instruction). The emulation bit is 1 when the 65816 is in emulation mode and 0 when it is in native mode.

The other bits present in the 65816 emulation mode status register are shown in Table 4-4. Those present in native mode are shown in Table 4-5.

Bit	Description
B	Break bit
C	Carry bit
D	Decimal mode bit
I	Interrupt disable bit
N	Negative bit
V	Overflow bit
Z	Zero bit

Table 4-4
Emulation Mode Status Register

Bit	Description
C	Carry bit
D	Decimal mode bit
I	Interrupt disable bit
M	Accumulator/memory width bit
N	Negative bit
V	Overflow bit
X	Index register width bit
Z	Zero bit

Table 4-5
Native Mode Status Register

COMPARISON OF 65816 WITH 65C02, 6502, AND 68000

The microprocessors used in all Apple computers have been those microprocessors that evolved from the Motorola 6800. This includes the 6502 used in the Apple II, II Plus, and earlier models of the IIe, the 65C02 used in the Apple IIc and later models of the IIe, the 65816 used in the Apple IIGS, and the 68000 used in the Macintosh and Macintosh Plus. As would be expected with microprocessors with a common ancestor, these chips are very similar. Table 4-6 is a list of instructions found on the 65816

65816	6502	65C02	68000
ADC	ADC	ADC	ABCD ADD ADDA ADDI ADDQ ADDX
AND	AND	AND	AND ANDI
ASL	ASL	ASL	ASL ASR
BCC/BLT	BCC/BLT	BCC/BLT	BCC
BCS/BGE	BCS/BGE	BCS/BGE	BCS BGE
BEQ	BEQ	BEQ	BEQ
BIT	BIT	BIT	——
BMI	BMI	BMI	BMI
BNE	BNE	BNE	BNE
BPL	BPL	BPL	BPL
BRA	——	BRA	BRA BSR
BRK	BRK	BRK	——
BRL	——	——	——
BVC	BVC	BVC	BVC
BVS	BVS	BVS	BVS
CLC	CLC	CLC	——
CLD	CLD	CLD	——
CLI	CLI	CLI	——
CLV	CLV	CLV	——
CMP	CMP	CMP	CMP CMPI CMPM

Table 4-6

Comparison of 65816 Instructions with 6502, 65C02, and 68000

65816	6502	65C02	68000
COP	——	——	——
CPX	CPX	CPX	CMPA
CPY	CPY	CPY	CMPA
DEC	DEC	DEC	——
DEX	DEX	DEX	——
DEY	DEY	DEY	——
EOR	EOR	EOR	EOR EORI
INC	INC	INC	——
INX	INX	INX	——
INY	INY	INY	——
JML	——	——	——
JMP	JMP	JMP	JMP
JSL	——	——	——
JSR	JSR	JSR	JSR
LDA	LDA	LDA	MOVE MOVEA MOVEM MOVEP MOVEQ
LDX	LDX	LDX	MOVE MOVEA MOVEM MOVEP MOVEQ
LDY	LDY	LDY	MOVE MOVEA MOVEM MOVEP MOVEQ
LSR	LSR	LSR	LSL LSR
MVN	——	——	——
MVP	——	——	——
NOP	NOP	NOP	NOP
ORA	ORA	ORA	OR ORI
PEA	——	——	——
PEI	——	——	——
PER	——	——	——
PHA	PHA	PHA	——
PHB	——	——	——
PHD	——	——	——
PHK	——	——	——
PHP	PHP	PHP	——
PHX	——	PHX	——

Table 4-6

Comparison of 65816 Instructions with 6502, 65C02, and 68000 (continued)

65816	6502	65C02	68000
PHX	——	PHX	——
PHY	——	PHY	——
PLA	PLA	PLA	——
PLB	——	——	——
PLD	——	——	——
PLP	PLP	PLP	——
PLX	——	PLX	——
PLY	——	PLY	——
REP	——	——	——
ROL	ROL	ROL	ROL ROXL
ROR	ROR	ROR	ROR ROXR
RTI	RTI	RTI	RTE
RTL	——	——	——
RTS	RTS	RTS	RTS
SBC	SBC	SBC	SBCD SUB SUBA SUBI SUBQ SUBX
SEC	SEC	SEC	MOVE CCR
SED	SED	SED	MOVE CCR
SEI	SEI	SEI	MOVE CCR
SEP	——	——	MOVE CCR
STA	STA	STA	MOVE MOVEA MOVEM MOVEP MOVEQ
STP	——	STP*	——
STX	STX	STX	——
STY	STY	STY	——
STZ	——	STZ	CLR
TAX	TAX	TAX	——
TAY	TAY	TAY	——
TCD	——	——	——
TCS	——	——	——
TDC	——	——	——
TRB	——	TRB	——
TSB	——	TSB	TAS
TSC	——	TSC	——

Table 4-6

Comparison of 65816 Instructions with 6502, 65C02, and 68000 (continued)

65816	6502	65C02	68000
TSX	TSX	TSX	——
TXA	TXA	TXA	——
TXS	TXS	TXS	——
TXY	——	——	——
TYA	TYA	TYA	——
TYX	——	——	——
WAI	——	WAI*	——
WDM	——	——	——
XBA	——	——	EXG
XCE	——	——	SWAP

*Found on the Western Design Center version of the 65C02 only.

Table 4-6
Comparison of 65816 Instructions with 6502, 65C02, and 68000 (continued)

and any related instructions on the 6502, 65C02, and 68000. Table 4-7 is a list of the op codes for each 65816 instruction and a brief description of that command.

Instruction	Meaning
ADC	ADD with carry
AND	And accumulator with memory
ASL	Arithmetic shift left
BCC/BLT	Branch if carry is clear (if value compared is less than other value)
BCS/BGE	Branch if carry is set (if value compared is greater than or equal to other value)

Table 4-7
65816 Instructions

Instruction	Meaning
BEQ	Branch if two values are equal or if result is equal to zero
BIT	Bit test
BMI	Branch if result is minus
BNE	Branch if two values are not equal or if result is not equal to zero
BPL	Branch if result is plus
BRA	Branch always
BRK	Software interrupt break
BRL	Branch always long
BVC	Branch if no overflow
BVS	Branch if overflow
CLC	Clear carry flag
CLD	Clear decimal flag
CLI	Clear interrupt disable flag
CLV	Clear overflow flag
CMP	Compare accumulator with memory
COP	Co-processor latch
CPX	Compare X register with memory
CPY	Compare Y register with memory
DEC	Decrement memory or accumulator
DEX	Decrement X register
DEY	Decrement Y register
EOR	Exclusive OR between accumulator and memory
INC	Increment memory or accumulator
INX	Increment X register
INY	Increment Y register
JML	Jump long
JMP	Jump
JSL	Jump to subroutine long
JSR	Jump to subroutine
LDA	Load accumulator
LDX	Load X register
LDY	Load Y register

Table 4-7

65816 Instructions (continued)

Instruction	Meaning
LSR	Logical shift right
MVN	Move block negative
MVP	Move block positive
NOP	No operation
ORA	OR between accumulator and memory
PEA	Push effective address or immediate data
PEI	Push effective indirect address
PER	Push program counter relative address
PHA	Push accumulator
PHB	Push data bank register
PHD	Push direct register
PHK	Push program bank register
PHP	Push processor status register
PHX	Push X register
PHY	Push Y register
PLA	Pull accumulator
PLB	Pull data bank register
PLD	Pull direct register
PLP	Pull processor status register
PLX	Pull X register
PLY	Pull Y register
REP	Reset processor status bits
ROL	Rotate left
ROR	Rotate right
RTI	Return from interrupt
RTL	Return from subroutine long
RTS	Return from subroutine
SBC	Subtract with carry
SEC	Set carry bit
SED	Set decimal bit
SEI	Set interrupt disable bit
SEP	Set processor status bits
STA	Store accumulator
STP	Stop the processor

Table 4-6

65816 Instructions (continued)

Instruction	Meaning
STX	Store the X register
STY	Store the Y register
STZ	Store zero
TAX	Transfer accumulator to X register
TAY	Transfer accumulator to Y register
TCD	Transfer accumulator to direct register
TCS	Transfer accumulator to stack pointer
TDC	Transfer direct register to accumulator
TRB	Test and reset bits
TSB	Test and set bits
TSC	Transfer stack pointer to accumulator
TSX	Transfer stack pointer to X register
TXA	Transfer X register to accumulator
TXS	Transfer X register to stack pointer
TXY	Transfer X register to Y register
TYA	Transfer Y register to accumulator
TYX	Transfer Y register to X register
WAI	Wait for interrupt
WDM	Reserved
XBA	Exchange A and B registers
XCE	Exchange carry and emulation bits

Table 4-7
65816 Instruction (continued)

Because the 68000 is a more powerful chip than the 65816, it has a number of instructions not found on the 65816. Table 4-8 is a listing of those instructions. Note that all 6502 and 65C02 instructions are found on the 65816.

Another aspect to the instruction set of each microprocessor is the available *addressing modes,* the methods by which the microprocessor determines the address of the data to be used. Table 4-9 is a list of each

BCHG	DBGT	LEA	SGT
BCLR	DBHI	LINK	SHI
BGT	DBLE	MULS	SLE
BHI	DBLS	MULU	SLS
BLE	DBLT	NBCD	SLT
BLS	DBMI	NEG	SMI
BLT	DBNE	NEGX	SNE
BSET	DBPL	NOT	SPL
BTST	DBRA	RESET	ST
CHK	DBT	RTS	SVC
DBCC	DBVC	SCC	SVS
DBCS	DBVS	SCS	TRAP
DBEQ	DIVS	SEQ	TRAPV
DBF	DIVU	SF	TST
DBGE	EXT	SGE	UNLK

Table 4-8

68000 Instruction Not Found on 65816

65816	6502	65C02	68000
Absolute	Absolute	Absolute	Absolute
Absolute indexed indirect		Indexed absolute indirect	
Absolute indexed with X	Absolute indexed with X	Absolute indexed with X	
Absolute indexed with Y	Absolute indexed with Y	Absolute indexed with Y	
Absolute indirect	Absolute indirect	Absolute indirect	
Absolute long			
Accumulator	Accumulator	Accumulator	Inherent
Block			

Table 4-9

Comparison of 65816 Addressing Modes with 6502, 65C02, and 68000

65816	6502	65C02	68000
Direct	Zero page	Zero page	
Direct indirect indexed	Indirect indexed	Indirect indexed	Absolute register
Direct indirect long indexed			
Direct indexed indirect	Indexed indirect	Indexed indirect	
Direct indexed with X	Zero page indexed with X	Zero page indexed with X	
Direct indexed with Y	Zero page indexed with Y	Zero page indexed with Y	
Direct indirect		Zero page indirect	
Direct indirect long			
Immediate	Immediate	Immediate	Immediate
Implied	Implied	Implied	Inherent
Program counter relative	Program counter relative	Program counter relative	Program counter relative with displacement
Program counter relative long			
Stack			
Stack relative			
Stack relative indexed indirect			

Table 4-9

Comparison of 65816 Addressing Modes with 6502, 65C02, and 68000 (continued)

addressing mode available on the 65816 and any related addressing modes on the 6502, 65C02, and 68000. Table 4-10 is a listing of those addressing modes found on the 68000 and not on the 65816. All 6502 and 65C02 addressing modes are found on the 65816.

Address register indirect with displacement
Address register indirect with post-increment
Address register indirect with decrement
Address register indirect with placement
Program counter relative with index and displacement

Table 4-10

68000 Addressing Modes Not Available on the 65816

PART II

Memory

CHAPTER 5

RAM Organization and Management

RAM in the IIGS is designed both to mimic that in the Apple IIe and IIc and to be available for the nearly contiguous memory usage permitted by the 65816 microprocessor in the IIGS.

IIe-IIc 128K BANKS

The Apple IIe with an extended 80-column display card has at least 128K of RAM, as does the standard Apple IIc.

In both machines this RAM is not arranged contiguously from addresses $0000 to $1FFFF because the 65C02 in these two machines cannot address more than 64K of memory at one time (addresses $0000 to $FFFF). In addition, the 65C02 must not only be able to address the 128K of RAM, it must also be able to address 32K of ROM and 4K of input/output locations.

In the Apple IIe and IIc the ability to address up to 164K of memory with only 64K of addressing space is accomplished by a technique called bank switching. *Bank* in this terminology does not refer to a 64K block of memory ending in $FFFF, which is the standard meaning in the 65816 world. Rather, it means any chunk of memory that can be moved in and out of a specific address location upon a signal from the computer.

This book will not discuss the mechanics of bank switching and how it works in the Apple IIe or IIc. The user who wishes more information about this topic should consult the Apple IIe or IIc *Technical Reference Manual.*

On the IIGS, the Apple IIe-IIc 128K RAM area is mapped into banks $00 and $01 (from $00/0000-01/FFFF), as well as banks $E0 and $E1 (from $E0/0000-E1/FFFF). The reason for using two different 128K memory blocks is discussed later in this chapter under the section "Memory Shadowing." The IIGS, when operating in 8-bit Apple II mode, switches between these two alternative 64K memory banks. The 64K in banks $00 and $E0 is called main memory and that in banks $01 and $E1 is called auxiliary memory. This conforms to Apple IIe and IIc terminology.

Each 64K bank includes not only the actual 64K of RAM but also the input/output locations at $C000-CFFF. The use of memory addresses $C000-CFFF by the firmware of the peripheral expansion slots and other input and output hardware means that these addresses are not available to use for RAM storage. Therefore the address for RAM in each of these banks is $0000-BFFF and $D000-FFFF. The extra 4K of RAM, which would normally be mapped at $C000-CFFF, is mapped instead to $D000-DFFF. As a result, two 4K blocks of memory share the locations $D000-DFFF. This conforms to the memory organization in the Apple IIe and IIc. These double blocks are referred to as language card bank 1 and bank 2 (or sometimes, bank 0 and bank 1). These two 4K banks are switched in a manner similar to the switching of main and auxiliary memory banks. The term *language card* refers to a peripheral found on the Apple II and II Plus. The terminology remains with us.

The arrangement of memory in the IIGS is necessary for maximum compatibility with existing Apple IIe and IIc programs. But it does create a few problems for the following reasons:

- The Apple IIe and IIc use part of their main and alternate memory for text and low-resolution graphics video display ($0400-0BFF) and high-resolution graphics video display ($2000-5FFF).
- The IIGS needs to provide contiguous memory beginning at bank $00, extended to the maximum RAM, at the fast operating speed on the IIGS of 2.5 MHz.
- The programming for input/output and video display has to be in RAM with an operating speed of 1 MHz for timing and compatibility considerations.

MEMORY SHADOWING

The solution to this problem is to have a 128K chunk of normal speed memory (residing at addresses $E0/0000-E1/FFFF) that handles the true input/output, and to provide for automatic transfer of values placed in certain locations in banks $00 and $01 to the same places in banks $E0 and $E1. This technique is referred to as *shadowing*.

Shadowing can occur in different parts of memory from $00/0000 to $01/FFFF. The various shadowed areas and the name given to each particular area are listed in Table 5-1.

The current shadowing status is called the *quagmire state*. A quagmire is an area of swampy or shaky land, an appropriate metaphor for shadowed memory, which can actually be changed by changing the value in another location. The quagmire state is stored in memory location $E0/C035. It is a 1-byte value that indicates the state of six areas of memory shadowing plus the state of the machine speed. The remaining bit in the quagmire state is unassigned but always must be set to zero. The bit associated with each factor included in the quagmire state is also indicated in Table 5-1.

Memory shadowing causes a reduction of the operating speed of the

Shadowed Area	Name	Quagmire State Bit Number
0400-07FF	Text Page 1	0
2000-3FFF	Hires Page 1	1
4000-5FFF	Hires Page 2	2
2000-9FFF	Super hires	3
2000-3FFF*	Auxiliary memory hires	4
— — — —	Reserved	5**
C000-DFFF	I/O and language card	6
N/A	Speed	7

*Bank $01 location

** Must be set to zero

Notes:

Text Page 2 shadowing is accomplished by accessing a toggle at $FF/F962 or selecting turn on alternate display mode from the Desk Accessory Manager Screen.

Bits are set to 1 to indicate shadowing, except for bit 6, which is set to 0 to indicate shadowing.

Bit 7 is set to 1 to indicate high speed.

Table 5-1
Shadowing and the Quagmire State

IIGS to 1 MHz only when there is a write operation to the shadowed memory. This reduction results from the need to transfer the value written from the fast memory to the normal, 1 MHz speed memory as part of the shadowing procedure. There is no need for transfer of values when a read operation occurs—thus reads of shadowed memory take place at the faster speed.

When banks $00-01 are being used in 8-bit Apple II mode, they are arranged just like in the Apple IIe and IIc. The memory map layout of these two banks in 8-bit Apple II mode is shown in Figure 5-1. In IIGS 16-bit mode, banks $00-01 are nearly fully available for program use. Special use in banks $00-01 in IIGS 16-bit mode is restricted to (optional,

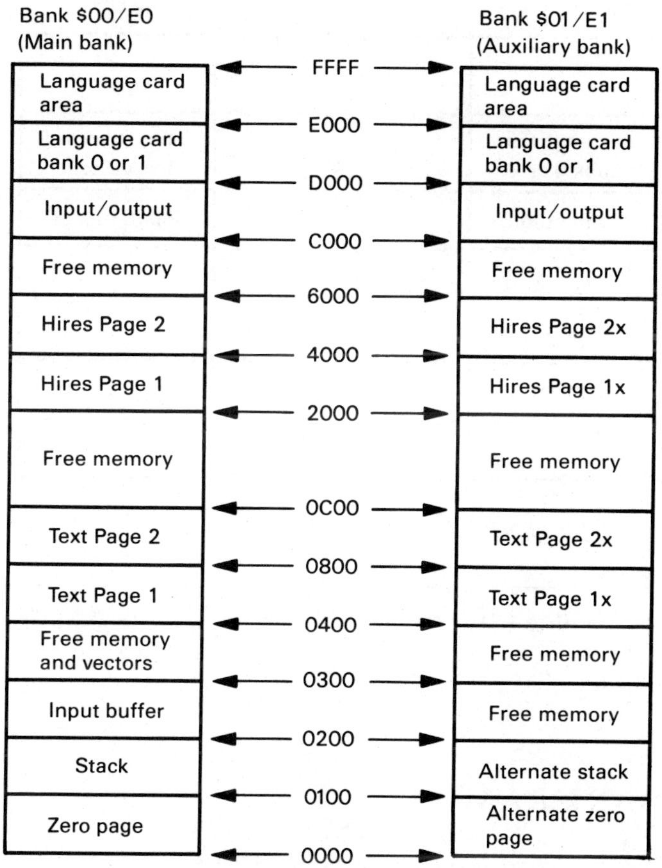

Figure 5-1

Memory map for 8-bit Apple II mode

shadowed) text and low-resolution graphics video display, input/output routines, and language card banks, as shown in Figure 5-2.

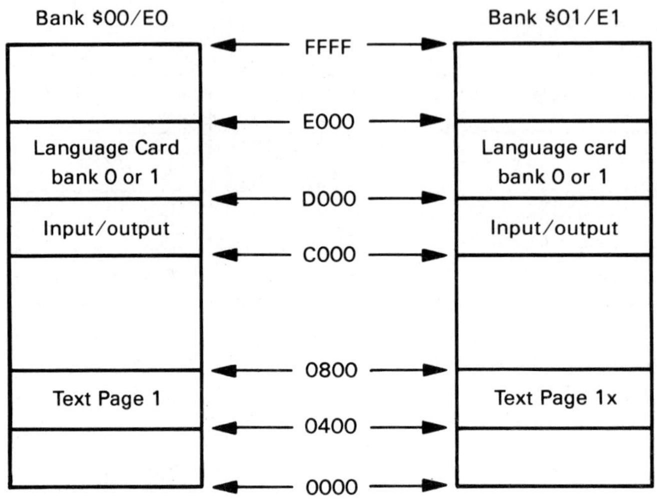

Figure 5-2
Memory map in 16-bit IIGS mode

FIRMWARE RAM

Built-in, motherboard-resident RAM in the IIGS resides at memory locations $00/0000-01/FFFF and $E0/0000-E1/FFFF. The memory in banks $E0 and $E1 is known as firmware RAM, system RAM, or normal speed RAM. It operates at a speed of 1 MHz in comparison to the faster 2.5-MHz speed of the remainder of the memory in the IIGS.

These two memory banks are used for a variety of special purposes by the operating system. Some of this memory is free for your use, although how much is available depends on what video display modes are being used by your application or any coresident applications such as desk accessories.

Memory in bank $E0 includes $6000-BFFF (24K) that is always available for use and is managed by the Memory Manager. If you are not using single- or double-high-resolution graphics you can also use the memory taken by those display areas ($2000-5FFF or 16K). The Memory Manager considers this memory as special, although available for use. Similarly, Text Page 2 ($0800-0BFF or 1K) is available if not used by your application, although the Memory Manager does not manage this area (you will have to allocate and keep track of it yourself).

Two other areas in bank $E0 are also available, but are not recommended for use. The first is 0.75K from $0000-02FF, which is reserved by Apple for future expansion of the IIGS. If you use this area of memory, you run a significant risk that a revision to the IIGS will destroy your program. If your application does not use Text Page 1 ($0400-07FF or 1K), you may be able to get away with using that area of memory, although it is possible that a coresident program such as a desk accessory will use it, and some firmware may use the screen holes.

The remaining part of bank $E0 is used for a variety of system uses. Table 5-2 gives a listing of the 12 categories of system usage and the use of banks $E0 and $E1 made by each. Figure 5-3 is a detailed memory map of bank $E0, showing the specific use made of each portion of that bank.

Memory in bank $E1 (always available for use) includes $A000-BFFF (8K), which is managed by the Memory Manager. If you are not using super-high-resolution graphics, you can use the memory at $6000-9FFF (16K), although this memory is considered special by the Memory Manager. If you are not using either super-high-resolution graphics or double-high-resolution graphics Page 2, you can use the memory at $4000-5FFF (8K). Very few double-high-resolution programs use Page 2. If you are not using any double-high-resolution graphics, you can also use the memory at $2000-3FFF (8K).

The memory used for 80-column display of Text Page 1 (1K at $0400-07FF) or Text Page 2 (1K at $0800-0BFF) can be used subject to the restriction concerning bank $E0 discussed previously.

Other areas of bank $E1 that can be used (with some potential danger) include

- □ $19B8-1DAF (approximately 1K), which is reserved for expansion and thus may result in a future program incompatibility.
- □ $1000-14E1 (approximately 1.25K), which is reserved for AppleTalk

Category	Number of Bytes	E0 Usage	E1 Usage
1. Firmware permanent storage	0F6E		0000-03BF 03E0-03FF 0C00-0FCF 0FFC-0FFF 1000-1549 158A-15A9 15C1-15CC 1DB0-1DCF 1DD8-1FFF
2. Desk accessory data area	1300	0300-03FF 0C00-1DFF	
3. Operating system expansion usage	4000	D000-DFFF E000-FFFF	
4. Memory Manager	03BA		15FE-19B7
5. Future use	0729	0000-02FF	15CD-15FD 19B8-1DAF
6. Tool locator use	0010		03C0-03CF
7. Front Desk Bus use	0076		03D0-03DF 0FD6-0FFB 154A-158A
8. AppleTalk higher level routines	4000		D000-DFFF E000-FFFF
9. Quickdraw II Vectors	0200	1E00-1FFF	
10. Miscellaneous and Text Tools use	0025		0FD0-0FD5 15AA-15C0 1DD0-1DD7
11. Video display	D000	0400-0BFF 2000-5FFF	0400-0BFF 2000-9FFF
12. Input/output	2000	C000-CFFF	C000-CFFF

Notes: Area at D000-DFFF consists of two blocks (called banks 0 and 1) of "Language Card."

All values and addresses are hexadecimal.

Table 5-2

Banks $E0-E1 — System Usage Categories

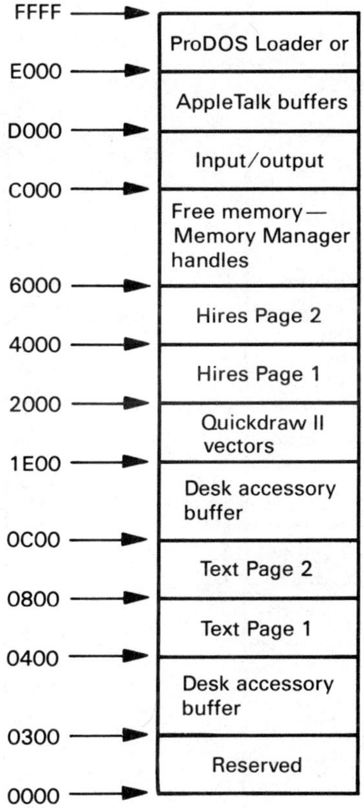

Figure 5-3
Detailed memory map of bank $E0

use this area, but a coresident desk accessory using AppleTalk may cause some problems.

Figure 5-4 is a detailed memory map of bank $E1, similar to that for bank $E0, showing the specific use made of each portion of that bank.

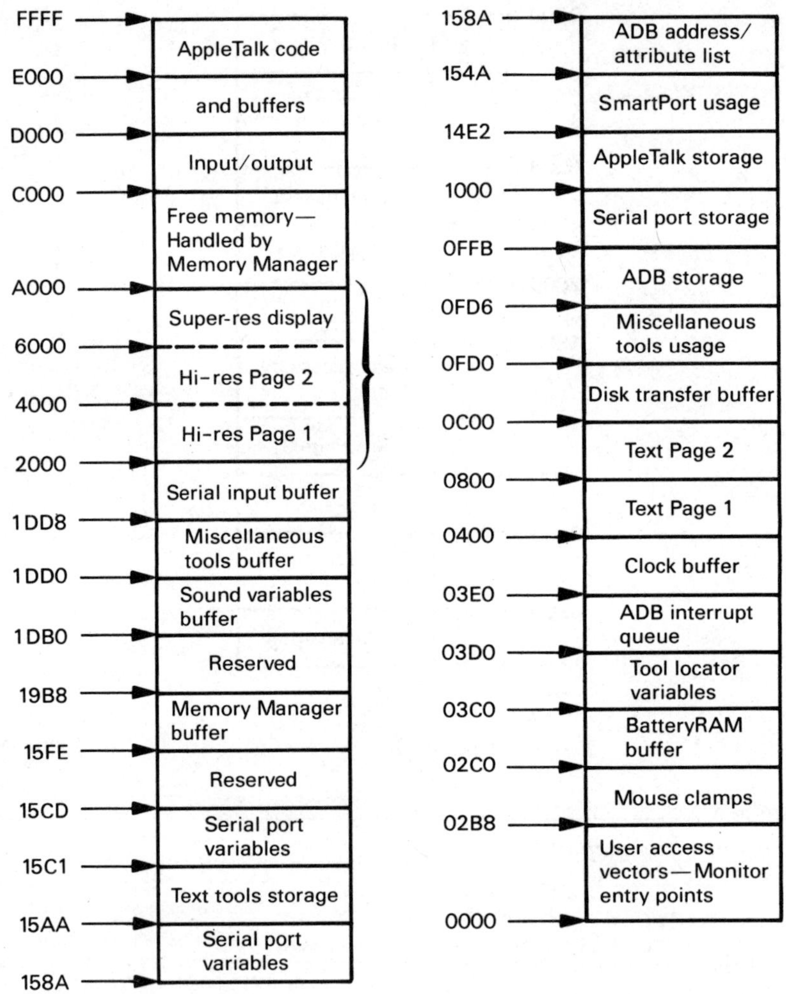

Figure 5-4

Detailed memory map of bank $E1

EXPANSION RAM

Banks \$00-01 and \$E0-E1 are built into every Apple IIGS. A special memory expansion slot is used to add memory to the IIGS. Cards can be plugged into this slot, expanding the RAM of the IIGS into banks \$02 through \$79, permitting a fast RAM of 8 MB and a total RAM of 8.125 MB. When the Memory Manager is first initialized, it determines all available RAM and keeps a record of it. Any memory plugged into the memory expansion slot is available to your native mode application through the Memory Manager. In 8-bit Apple II mode this memory is not available to your application, although ProDOS/8 treats it as a RAM disk with the name /RAM5/.

MEMORY MANAGER

The IIGS comes with a minimum of 256K of RAM and can be expanded up to 8.25 MB. The configuration of the machine also permits the near-concurrent running of several programs. While these programs do not technically run at the same time, one program can interrupt another and then return control of the machine back to the original program.

The possibility of multiple programs in the IIGS's memory at one time, each with its own data and some with multiple segments of program code, could easily create chaos if an efficient method of managing the memory were not available. The IIGS does not leave the memory management task to each individual program. Rather, it has a Memory Manager, mostly implemented in ROM, that each program must call for memory as desired.

In 8-bit Apple II mode, the ProDOS/8 operating system provides for some rudimentary memory management. When running in Apple IIGS 16-bit mode, the Memory Manager handles the tasks of determining which portions of memory are in use by which application and which parts of memory are free. As a programmer, you need only to have your application call one of the routines in the Memory Manager to get memory, release memory, or perform other operations on memory.

When a program is to be loaded into memory, the loader asks the Memory Manager to allocate a block of memory needed to load the program. This information is contained in the directory entry of the program. The program must then ask the Memory Manager to allocate memory for its data space and other code segments as needed. Most IIGS

16-bit programs are relocatable when loaded, but they are not necessarily position-dependent.

This method of obtaining memory should be compared to that used by the major 8-bit Apple II operating systems, ProDOS/8 and DOS 3.3. Machine-language programs or code segments in those systems are stored with the memory address at which the program or segment must be loaded in order to run. Unless the code is position-independent, it must be placed at that address to run properly. Neither Pro-DOS/8 nor DOS 3.3 has the capacity to relocate code segments. Therefore, two code segments that have been designed to operate at the same address cannot be both in memory and able to be run at the same time, even though there are sufficient memory blocks for each segment.

The Memory Manager uses the concept of a handle to refer to allocated memory blocks. When a program (either a loader program or an application program) calls the Memory Manager to allocate a block of memory, the Memory Manager responds with a handle to that memory.

A *pointer* is a location in the IIGS's memory that holds a 32-bit value. This value is the address of the actual data (see Figure 5-5). The first address (the pointer) points to the second address.

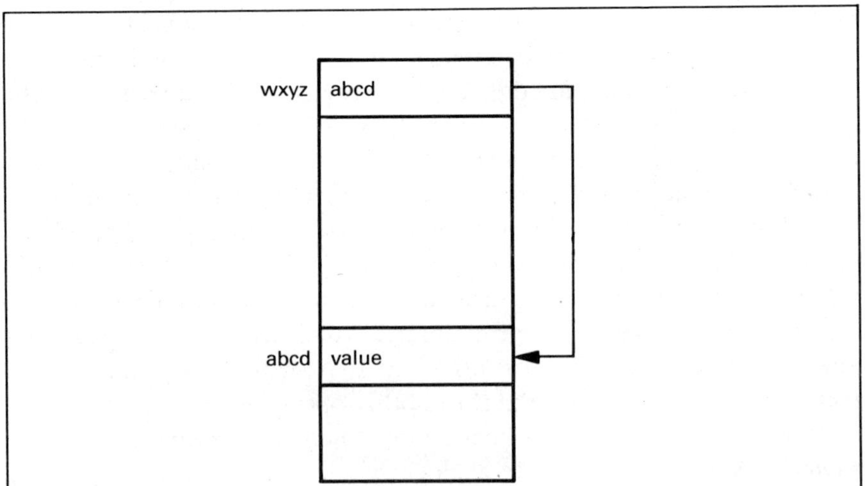

Figure 5-5
Use of a pointer

A *handle* can be thought of as a double pointer, or a pointer to a pointer. It is a memory location that holds a 32-bit value. This value is the address of another memory location. The second location also holds a 32-bit value. This latter value is the address of the actual data (see Figure 5-6).

The use of a handle was not designed to make programming the IIGS more difficult or esoteric. The Memory Manager maintains a set of memory addresses that it uses as pointers to the various allocated blocks. These pointers are always in a specific, fixed location. When the Memory Manager needs to move a block, it needs only to change the address in the pointer—and it always knows where the pointer is.

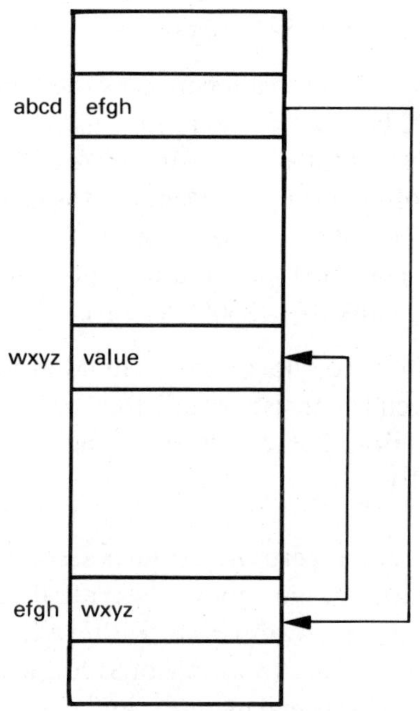

Figure 5-6
Use of a handle

If the address of the memory block were given directly to the application program, the Memory Manager would then need to remember which program has which block. It would also need to remember where the memory location that held the address to the block was within the program. The double indirection of a handle ensures that the Memory Manager needs only to change addresses in fixed locations whenever it moves blocks. It guarantees, too, that the program always knows exactly where to look to find the address of the needed memory block.

The Memory Manager operates only on RAM in the IIGS—ROM is already fixed in location and contents. The IIGS's RAM, for purposes of the Memory Manager, is divided into the following three classes:

- Some of the RAM is off-limits to the Memory Manager. This unmanaged, or reserved, memory consists of certain blocks in banks $00, $01, $E0, and $E1 of the IIGS. These banks are those present in every IIGS of whatever memory configuration, and contain many locations that serve specialized functions. Table 5-3 contains a list of these locations.
- Some of the RAM is subject to allocation by the Memory Manager but is considered special because of alternative uses for this memory. This memory includes: (1) all the memory in banks $00 and $01, except for the memory that is off-limits to the Memory Manager; (2) that memory in banks $E0 and $E1 that comprises high-resolution graphics screens 1 and 2 ($2000-5FFF); and (3) the remaining portion of the super-high-resolution screen in bank $E1 ($6000-9FFF).
- Memory that is subject to allocation by the Memory Manager, and is not considered special, consists of all the remaining memory. In a minimum-configuration, 256K IIGS this consists of $E0/6000-BFFF and $E1/A000-BFFF.

Each block of memory has certain attributes associated with it that help determine its location and permanency. These attributes include whether the block must reside at a fixed address or within a fixed bank, whether it must begin on a page boundary (multiple of $100), whether it may span a bank boundary or reside in special memory, and whether the block may be moved or purged. These attributes are all part of a 16-bit word associated with the memory block. The location of each attribute within the attribute's word is shown in Table 5-4. All the attributes, except the locked and

Banks $00 and a $01	
$0000-00FF	"Zero page" and alternate zero page
$0100-01FF	8-bit Apple II mode stack and alternate stack
$0200-02FF	8-bit Apple II mode input buffer
$0300-03FF	8-bit Apple II vectors and special use
$0400-07FF	Text Page 1 and Text Page 1x
$C000-CFFF	Input/output locations (shadowed)
$D000-DFFF	"Banks" 0 and 1 of bank-switched memory
$E000-FFFF	Language card

Bank $E0	
$0000-02FF	Reserved
$0300-03FF	Desk accessory buffer storage
$0400-07FF	Text Page 1
$0800-0BFF	Text Page 2
$0C00-1DFF	Desk accessory buffer
$1E00-1FFF	Quickdraw II vectors
$C000-CFFF	Input/output locations
$D000-DFFF	"Banks" 0 and 1 of bank-switched memory
$E000-FFFF	Language card

Note: $D000-FFFF used for ProDOS system loader and AppleTalk buffers when not switched out for ROM addresses.

Bank $E1	
$0000-0287	User access vectors/new entry points/monitor
$0288-02BF	Mouse clamps
$02C0-03BF	BatteryRAM buffer
$03C0-03CF	Tool locator variable storage
$03D0-03DF	ADB interrupt queue
$03E0-03FF	Clock buffer
$0400-07FF	Text Page 1x
$0800-0BFF	Text Page 2x
$0C00-0FCF	Disk transfer buffer
$0FD0-0FD5	Miscellaneous tool storage
$0FD6-0FFB	Apple Desk Bus storage

(continued on next page)

Table 5-3

List of Unmanaged and Reserved Memory Locations

Bank $E1	
$0FFC-0FFF	Serial port storage
$1000-14E1	AppleTalk storage
$14E2-1549	Disk port storage
$154A-1589	ADB address/attribute list
$158A-15A9	Serial port storage
$15AA-15C0	Text tools storage
$15C1-15C8	Serial port storage
$15C9-15FD	Reserved
$15FE-1987	Memory Manager storage
$1988-1DAF	Reserved for expansion
$1DB0-1DCF	Sound storage
$1DD0-1DD7	Miscellaneous tools storage
$1DD8-1FFF	Serial input buffer
$C000-CFFF	Input/output locations
$D000-DFFF	"Banks" 0 and 1 of bank-switched memory
$E000-FFFF	Language card

Note: $D000-FFFF used for AppleTalk code and buffers when not switched out for ROM addresses.

Table 5-3
List of Unmanaged and Reserved Memory Locations (continued)

purge-level attributes, are fixed upon block allocation and cannot be modified later.

Be careful in setting any of the attributes true, because each can restrict the Memory Manager both in allocating the block and in compacting existing allocated blocks. Potential reasons for setting the various attributes true include

- *Fixed.* A program code block that is not position-independent has to be fixed in memory. The loader will properly place a relocatable, but position-dependent, code segment in a variety of memory locations initially, but it will not allow subsequent movement of the code.
- *Within one bank.* Unless special and normally nonrecommended programming techniques are followed, a segment of program code should be contained all within a single bank.

Bit Number	Attribute
15	Locked (modifiable attribute)
14	Fixed (not movable once located)
13	Reserved
12	Reserved
11	Reserved
10	Reserved
9	Purge level (modifiable attribute)
8	Purge level (modifiable attribute)
7	Reserved
6	Reserved
5	Reserved
4	May not cross bank boundary
3	May not use special memory
2	Must be aligned on a page boundary
1	Must be at specified address
0	Must be in specified bank

Note: Purge level is a 2-bit value between 0 and 3.

Table 5-4

Memory Block Attributes Word Arrangement

- *Page aligned.* Certain 65816 instructions in certain addressing modes require extra cycles to operate when they cross page boundaries. These are listed in Table 5-5. When a program uses these modes and codes, and requires a specified number of machine cycles to operate, the memory block containing the data used may need to be page-aligned. Another timing-related reason for requiring page-aligned data is that it may be required for data that is to be accessed by one of the direct addressing modes (such as data in bank zero). If the low byte of the direct register is not $00, an extra cycle is used to access the data.
- *Fixed address.* Certain memory in the IIGS is considered special. If you are using the super-high-resolution graphics screen and want to prevent other applications from using this area for code or data storage, you should allocate this area for your program's use.
- *Fixed bank.* The 65816 permits the direct page to be any 256-byte portion of bank zero. The stack can also begin in any location within

Op Code	Direct Indirect Indexed	Absolute,X	Absolute,Y
ADC	x	x	x
AND	x	x	x
ASL		x	
BIT		x	
CMP	x	x	x
DEC		x	
EOR	x	x	x
INC		x	
LDA	x	x	x
LDX			x
LDY		x	
LSR		x	
ORA	x	x	x
ROL		x	
ROR		x	
SBC	x	x	x
STA	x	x	x
STZ		x	

Table 5-5

65816 Op Code and Addressing Modes Using Extra Cycles When Crossing Page Boundaries

bank zero. If you are allocating direct page or stack memory for your application, you need to specify that it is located in bank zero.

□ *Use of special memory.* For most applications it would be desirable to restrict memory usage to those areas not encompassing special memory (in order to save special memory for those uses that it and it alone can use). Unfortunately, no allocation call exists that asks for nonspecial memory if available and for special memory if not. The following code segment, however, first asks for nonspecial memory. If a "memory full" error is returned, indicating the memory is not available in nonspecial memory, special memory is then allocated as follows:

```
Pushlong #$00000000          ;Space for handle returned
Pushlong #Blocksize          ;Size of block desired
LDA Owner                    ;ID assigned to program
PHA
Pushword #Atrributes         ;Bit 3 set - may not use special memory
Pushlong #$00000000          ;Location zero; block not fixed
_NewHandle                   ;Allocate block
BCC Gotit
CMP #$0201                   ;Memory full error?
BNE Error_Routine            ;No - handle as error
Pushlong #$00000000          ;Yes - try using special memory
Pushlong #Blocksize          ;Size of block desired
LDA Owner                    ;ID assigned to program
PHA
LDA #Attributes
AND #%1111 1111 1111 0111 ;Turn off bit 3 - may use special memory
PHA                          ;Place on stack
Pushlong #$00000000          ;Location zero; block not fixed
_NewHandle                   ;Allocate block
BCC Gotit
BRA Error_Routine
```

The program segment assumes these things about your source code:

- Using the EQU pseudo op code, you have defined in your source code the size of the block you want and the attributes you want the handle to have. If you have instead used a label to define the address at which the values are stored, you must make the following substitutions:

  ```
  Pushlong Blocksize
  ```

  for

  ```
  Pushlong #Blocksize
  ```

  and

  ```
  Pushword Attributes
  ```

  for

  ```
  Pushword #Attributes
  ```

  Note, however, that the Owner value (identification number) is stored in a memory location, not defined with the EQU pseudo op code. This value is not known at assembly time—it is assigned to the program when it makes the MMAppInit call to the Memory Manager.

- You have defined a routine to handle Memory Manager errors and included it in your source code with the label Error_Routine.

The Memory Manager has a number of routines in it. Table 5-6 lists each routine with a short description of the purpose of the routine and any additional useful information.

Routine	Description
MMBootInit	This call is made at boot time by the system. It should not be made by an application since it destroys any allocated blocks.
MMAppInit	This call is the first Memory Manager call made by your application. It returns the identification number to be used in identifying your application.
MMAppQuit	Your application should make this call when it is through. It releases all memory allocated by your application.
MMGetVersion	This call returns the version number of the Memory Manager.
MMReset	This call is made at reset time by the system. It should not be made by an application since it destroys any allocated blocks.
MMStatus	This call is made to determine if the Memory Manager is active. It always returns true because the Memory Manager is always active. It is included to provide compatibility with other tools.
NewHandle	This call is made to allocate memory for use by your application. It is the most common call made by applications.
ReallocHandle	This call reallocates a block that was previously purged.
RestoreHandle	This call works like ReallocHandle, except that the attributes, owner, and size of block are the same as in the original purged block. May not be a fixed address or fixed bank block.
DisposHandle	This call purges a specified block. The memory area is free for other uses. The block must be unlocked, but purge level is irrelevant.
DisposAll	This call is similar to DisposHandle, except that all blocks belonging to the specified application will be purged.

Table 5-6
Memory Manager Routines Description

PurgeHandle	This call is similar to DisposHandle, except that the handle of the block is changed to NIL, indicating an allocated block of zero size.
PurgeAll	This call is similar to PurgeHandle, except that the handles of all blocks belonging to the specified application will be set to NIL.
GetHandleSize	This call returns the size of the block with the specified handle.
SetHandleSize	This call is made to increase or decrease the size of the specified block. If the block is locked and the size is to be increased, the Memory Manager may not be able to allocate sufficient space contiguous to the existing block.
FindHandle	This returns the handle of the block of allocated memory that contains the address specified when calling the routine. It returns NIL if the address is not part of any allocated memory.
FreeMem	This routine tells your application the amount of free bytes in memory, without couunting any purgeable memory. This figure represents the total free memory, not the largest allocatable block.
MaxBlock	This routine tells your application the largest free block in memory. Since it does not perform a CompactMem routine, your application may want to do so. It also does not count any memory that can be freed up by purging.
TotalMem	This routine tells your application the total amount of RAM in the IIGS, including RAM not under the control of the Memory Manager.
CheckHandle	This determines if the handle is a valid Memory Manager error, returning a HandleErr if not. Mainly a debugging aid.
CompactMem	This routine moves any unlocked blocks as needed to create the largest possible block of free memory.
HLock	This routine locks a specified block so that it is nonmovable. Locking a block unnecessarily can result in excessive fragmentation of memory. When memory is too fragmented, you may not be able to allocate a block of memory to perform a particular function or to use a desk accessory.

Table 5-6

Memory Manager Routines Description (continued)

HLockAll	This routine works just like HLock, but it affects all blocks belonging to the calling application.
HUnlock	This routine unlocks a specified block so that it can be moved or relocated. When memory is compacted, the Memory Manager attempts to move allocated blocks together so that the available memory space is not fragmented. An unlocked block can be moved during this compaction process.
HUnlockAll	This routine works just like HUnlock, but it affects all blocks belonging to the calling application.
SetPurge	This routine sets the purge level for a specified block. Purge level is a value between 0 (unpurged block) and 3 (first block to be purged).
SetPurgeAll	This routine works like SetPurge, but it affects all blocks belonging to the calling application.
PtrtoHand	This routine moves a block of memory from location specified by pointer to location specified by pointer.
HandtoPtr	This routine moves a block of memory from location specified by handle to location specified by pointer.
HandtoHand	This routine moves a block of memory from one location to another, both specified by handles.
BlockMove	This routine moves a block of memory from one location to another. It works with overlapping blocks and across bank boundaries. It is a potentially dangerous routine since it does no checking before moving. Allocated block can be written over.

Table 5-6
Memory Manager Routines Description (continued)

Table 5-7 shows, for each routine, the function number, input and output parameters, and potential error codes.

Table 5-8 lists the potential Memory Manager error codes and the meaning of each code.

Table 5-9 compares the IIGS Memory Manager routines with those of the Macintosh Memory Manager.

Function Name	Function Number	Version	Status	NewSize	NewPLevel	TheHandle	BlockSize	Owner	Attributes	Location	Size	Source	Dest	Count
Parameter Size		W	W	L	W	L	L	W	W	L	L	L	L	L
Parameter Type		V	B	V	1	H	V	V	BA	A	V	2	2	V
MMBootInit	01													
MMAppInit	02							O1						
MMAppQuit	03							I1						
MMGetVersion	04	O1												
MMReset	05													
MMStatus	06		O1											
NewHandle	09					O1	I1	I2	I3	I4				
ReallocHandle	0A					I1	I2	I3	I4	I5				
RestoreHandle	0B					I1								
DisposHandle	10					I1								
DisposAll	11							I1						
PurgeHandle	12					I1								
PurgeAll	13							I1						
GetHandleSize	18					I1					O1			
SetHandleSize	19			I1		I2								
FindHandle	1A					O1				I1				
FreeMem	1B										O1			
MaxBlock	1C										O1			
TotalMem	1D										O1			
CheckHandle	1E					I1								
CompactMem	1F													
HLock	20					I1								
HLockAll	21							I1						
HUnlock	22					I1								
HUnlockAll	23							I1						
SetPurge	24				I1	I2								
SetPurgeAll	25				I1			I2						

Table 5-7

Memory Manager Function Calls

Function Name	Function Number	Version	Status	NewSize	NewPLevel	TheHandle	BlockSize	Owner	Attributes	Location	Size	Source	Dest	Count
PtrtoHand	28											I1	I2	I3
HandtoPtr	29											I1	I2	I3
HandtoHand	2A											I1	I2	I3
BlockMove	2B											I1	I2	I3

Notes:

Size:

L = long-word (32 bits)
W = word (16 bits)

Type:

A = Address
B = Boolean
BA = Bit array
H = Handle
V = Value
1 = 0-3
2 = Handle or pointer based on function

Table 5-7

Memory Manager Function Calls (continued)

Code	Meaning
$0201	MemErr — Memory full error; not enough memory available to allocate given the required parameters
$0202	Empty-Err — Illegal operation on an Empty handle
$0203	NonEmptyErr — Empty handle expected for routine
$0204	LockErr — Illegal operation on a locked or immovable block
$0205	PurgeErr — Attempt to purge an unpurgeable block
$0206	HandleErr — Invalid handle given
$0207	IDErr — Invalid owner identification number given
$0208	AttrErr — Operation not allowed on block with specified attributes

Table 5-8

Memory Manager Error Codes (Returned in Accumulator)

Function Name	Macintosh	IIGS
ApplicZone	x	
BlockMove	x	x
CheckHandle		x
CompactMem	x	x
DisposAll		x
DisposHandle	x	x
DisposePtr	x	
FindHandle		x
FreeMem	x	x
GetApplLimit	x	

Table 5-9

Comparison of IIGS and Macintosh Memory Manager Functions

Function Name	Macintosh	IIGS
GetHandleSize	x	x
GetPtrSize	x	
GetZone	x	
GZSaveHnd	x	
HandleZone	x	
HandtoHand		x
HandtoPtr		x
HLockAll		x
HUnlockAll		x
HLock	x	x
HNoPurge	x	
HPurge	x	
HUnlock	x	x
InitApplZone	x	
InitZone	x	
MaxApplZone	x	
MaxBlock (MaxMem)	x	x
MemError	x	
MMAppInit		x
MMAppQuit		x
MMBootInit		x
MMGetVersion		x
MMReset		x
MMStatus		x
MoreMasters	x	
MoveHHi	x	
MyGrowZone	x	
NewHandle	x	x
NewPtr	x	
PtrZone	x	
PtrtoHand		x
PurgeAll		x

Table 5-9

Comparison of IIGS and Macintosh Memory Manager Functions (continued)

Function Name	Macintosh	IIGS
PurgeHandle (EmptyHandle)	x	x
PurgeMem	x	
ReallocHandle	x	x
RecoverHandle	x	
ReservMem	x	
RestoreHandle		x
SetApplBase	x	
SetApplLimit	x	
SetGrowZone	x	
SetHandleSize	x	x
SetPtrSize	x	
SetPurge		x
SetPurgeAll		x
SetZone	x	
SystemZone	x	
TopMem	x	
TotalMem		x

Table 5-9

Comparison of IIGS and Macintosh Memory Manager Functions (continued)

CHAPTER 6

ROM and Softswitches

The Apple IIGS comes with the most built-in ROM of any Apple II. It also has an increased number of softswitches and status registers to handle the greater capabilities of the IIGS. Finally the IIGS has provision for expansion ROM that can be used either for tool expansion or for a ROM disk.

This chapter discusses the various aspects of the expanded ROM of the IIGS. It does not, however, discuss the various aspects of the IIGS ROM and softswitches that are unchanged from the Apple IIe and IIc. If you wish additional information about these functions, consult the *Apple IIe Technical Reference Manual* (Addison-Wesley, 1985) and the *Apple IIc Technical Reference Manual* (Addison-Wesley, 1985).

BUILT-IN ROM

The Apple IIGS has 128K of built-in ROM. The built-in ROM is located in banks $FE and $FF. The Apple IIe and IIc have 32K of ROM. The ROM on the Apple IIe consists of video firmware, the system monitor, diagnostics routines, and the Applesoft interpreter. The Apple IIc ROM also has Protocol Converter and AppleTalk firmware.

The IIGS has all of these functions as well as a portion of the IIGS toolbox. Table 6-1 is a listing of the Function Pointer Tables (discussed in Chapter 2) of the ROM-based tools. Each of these Function Pointer Tables contains, for the particular toolset involved, a pointer to each of the tool functions. Tables 6-2 through 6-13 contain the locations of functions for each of the ROM-based tools.

The ROM-based functions should not be called by the addresses shown in Table 6-2 through 6-13. Instead, they should be called through the Tool Locator discussed in Chapter 2. The addresses are listed for ease in inspecting and disassembling the code, which will aid you in writing your own tool functions or patching ROM-based tools.

There are at least two reasons you should not call tools directly. None of the tools are guaranteed to be immovable. Any tool called directly may no longer be in the same place and the call will fail. In addition, a tool is called with certain information passed to it in registers by the Tool Locator and with certain information on the stack. This information is missing if you call a tool directly, and the stack is different as well.

SOFTSWITCHES AND STATUS REGISTERS

Table 6-14 is a list of the publicly supported softswitches and status registers in the Apple IIGS. Not all of these softswitches are new to the IIGS. The new locations are indicated by an asterisk (*) in the table.

Tool Set Number	Name	Location of Function Pointer Table
1	Tool Locator	$FE/01C3
2	Memory Manager	$FF/0000
3	Miscellaneous Tools	$FE/905F
4	QuickDraw II	$FE/0BBE
5	Desk Manager	$FE/AEA6
6	Event Manager	$FE/BB3C
7	Scheduler	$FE/C80D
8	Sound Manager	$FF/3E00
9	ADB Tools	$FF/8000
10	SANE Tools	$FE/CEFC
11	Integer Math Tools	$FE/C8F3
12	Text Tools	$FE/A7D2

Table 6-1
Function Pointer Tables for ROM-Based Tools

Set Number	Function Number	Name	Location
1	1	TLBootInit	$FE/0203
1	2	TLStartUp	$FE/0301
1	3	TLShutDown	$FE/0307
1	4	TLVersion	$FE/030D
1	5	TLReset	$FE/0315
1	6	TLStatus	$FE/036E
1	7	———	$FE/0933
1	8	———	$FE/0933
1	9	GetTSPtr	$FE/0416
1	10	SetTSPtr	$FE/044B
1	11	GetFuncPtr	$FE/068A
1	12	GetWAP	$FE/06EF
1	13	SetWAP	$FE/0724

Table 6-2
Location of Tool Locator Functions

Set Number	Function Number	Name	Location
2	1	MMBootInit	$FF/01EB
2	2	MMAppInit	$FF/0464
2	3	MMAppQuit	$FF/0107
2	4	MMGetVersion	$FF/04B0
2	5	MMReset	$FF/04C0
2	6	MMStatus	$FF/04CA
2	7	———	$FF/0107
2	8	———	$FF/0107
2	9	NewHandle	$FF/04D2
2	10	ReallocHandle	$FF/052D
2	11	RestoreHandle	$FF/058B
2	12	———	$FF/0107
2	13	———	$FF/0107
2	14	———	$FF/0107
2	15	———	$FF/0107
2	16	DisposHandle	$FF/05C1
2	17	DisposAll	$FF/05D2
2	18	PurgeHandle	$FF/05FE
2	19	PurgeAll	$FF/060C
2	20	———	$FF/0107
2	21	———	$FF/0107
2	22	———	$FF/0107
2	23	———	$FF/0107
2	24	GetHandleSize	$FF/0646
2	25	SetHandleSize	$FF/065E
2	26	FindHandle	$FF/0767
2	27	FreeMem	$FF/0799
2	28	MaxBlock	$FF/07C5
2	29	TotalMem	$FF/07F0
2	30	CheckHandle	$FF/0801
2	31	CompactMem	$FF/080C
2	32	HLock	$FF/0820
2	33	HLockAll	$FF/0835
2	34	HUnlock	$FF/0883
2	35	HUnlockAll	$FF/0898
2	36	SetPurge	$FF/08B8
2	37	SetPurgeAll	$FF/08D7
2	38	———	$FF/0107

Table 6-3

Location of Memory Manager Functions

Set Number	Function Number	Name	Location
2	39	———	$FF/0107
2	40	PtrtoHand	$FF/0901
2	41	HandtoPtr	$FF/093E
2	42	HandtoHand	$FF/097B
2	43	BlockMove	$FF/09C7
2	44	———	$FF/0107
2	45	———	$FF/0107
2	46	———	$FF/0107
2	47	———	$FF/0107

Table 6-3
Location of Memory Manager Functions (continued)

Set Number	Function Number	Name	Location
3	1	MTBootInit	$FE/910F
3	2	MTStartUp	$FE/9171
3	3	MTShutDown	$FE/9171
3	4	MTVersion	$FE/918F
3	5	MTReset	$FE/9174
3	6	MTStatus	$FE/9197
3	7	———	$FE/9171
3	8	———	$FE/9171
3	9	WriteBRam	$FE/91B9
3	10	ReadBRam	$FE/91EC
3	11	WriteBParam	$FE/921B
3	12	ReadBParam	$FE/9235
3	13	ReadTimeHex	$FE/9251
3	14	WriteTimeHex	$FE/9402
3	15	ReadASCIITime	$FE/95C2

Table 6-4
Location of Miscellaneous Tools Functions

Set Number	Function Number	Name	Location
3	16	SetVector	$FE/96F6
3	17	GetVector	$FE/971E
3	18	SetHeartBeat	$FE/9743
3	19	DelHeartBeat	$FE/9823
3	20	ClrHeartBeat	$FE/98E0
3	21	SysDeathMgr	$FE/9974
3	22	GetAddr	$FE/9983
3	23	ReadMouse	$FE/990A
3	24	InitMouse	$FE/98CD
3	25	SetMouse	$FE/9A18
3	26	HomeMouse	$FE/9BBD
3	27	ClearMouse	$FE/9BAC
3	28	ClampMouse	$FE/9A2E
3	29	GetMouseClamp	$FE/9AEB
3	30	PosMouse	$FE/9A99
3	31	ServeMouse	$FE/9ACB
3	32	GetNewID	$FE/9DC8
3	33	DeleteID	$FE/9EE9
3	34	StatusID	$FE/9FB6
3	35	IntSource	$FE/A033
3	36	FWentry	$FE/A175
3	37	GetTick	$FE/A163
3	38	PackBytes	$FE/A19F
3	39	UnPackBytes	$FE/A403
3	40	Munger	$FE/A563
3	41	GetIRQenble	$FE/A75D
3	42	SetAbsClamp	$FE/A799
3	43	GetAbsClamp	$FE/A7B7

Table 6-4

Location of Miscellaneous Tools Functions (continued)

Set Number	Function Number	Name	Location
4	1	QDBootInit	$FE/0939
4	2	QDStartUp	$FE/0965
4	3	QDShutDown	$FE/0AEC
4	4	QDVersion	$FE/0B6F
4	5	QDReset	$FE/0B7C
4	6	QDStatus	$FE/0B86
4	7	———	$FE/07A2
4	8	———	$FE/07A2
4	9	GetAddress	$FE/1090
4	10	GrafOn	$FE/1377
4	11	GrafOff	$FE/1388
4	12	GetStandardSCB	$FE/1399
4	13	InitColorTable	$FE/13A1
4	14	SetColorTable	$FE/13D0
4	15	GetColorTable	$FE/13FF
4	16	SetColorEntry	$FE/142E
4	17	GetColorEntry	$FE/1465
4	18	SetSCB	$FE/149C
4	19	GetSCB	$FE/14BC
4	20	SetAllSCBs	$FE/14DC
4	21	ClearScreen	$FE/14EF
4	22	SetMasterSCB	$FE/1516
4	23	GetMasterSCB	$FE/1525
4	24	OpenPort	$FE/1534
4	25	InitPort	$FE/157E
4	26	ClosePort	$FE/160F
4	27	SetPort	$FE/163F
4	28	GetPort	$FE/1652
4	29	SetPortLoc	$FE/1665
4	30	GetPortLoc	$FE/1683
4	31	SetPortRect	$FE/16A1
4	32	GetPortRect	$FE/16C7
4	33	SetPortSize	$FE/16ED
4	34	MovePortTo	$FE/170E
4	35	SetOrigin	$FE/173D
4	36	SetClip	$FE/17AD
4	37	GetClip	$FE/17D2

Table 6-5

Location of Quickdraw II Functions

Set Number	Function Number	Name	Location
4	38	ClipRect	$FE/17F7
4	39	HidePen	$FE/1866
4	40	ShowPen	$FE/1879
4	41	GetPen	$FE/188C
4	42	SetPenState	$FE/18D5
4	43	GetPenState	$FE/18AF
4	44	SetPenSize	$FE/1A11
4	45	GetPenSize	$FE/1A29
4	46	SetPenMode	$FE/18FB
4	47	GetPenMode	$FE/1901
4	48	SetPenPat	$FE/1907
4	49	GetPenPat	$FE/191A
4	50	SetPenMask	$FE/1944
4	51	GetPenMask	$FE/1957
4	52	SetBackPat	$FE/196A
4	53	GetBackPat	$FE/197D
4	54	PenNormal	$FE/1A4C
4	55	SetSolidPenPat	$FE/192D
4	56	SetSolidBackPat	$FE/1990
4	57	SolidPattern	$FE/19A7
4	58	MoveTo	$FE/1A6C
4	59	Move	$FE/1A84
4	60	LineTo	$FE/2861
4	61	Line	$FE/2883
4	62	SetPicSave	$FE/1B3E
4	63	GetPicSave	$FE/1B44
4	64	SetRgnSave	$FE/1B4A
4	65	GetRgnSave	$FE/1B50
4	66	SetPolySave	$FE/1B56
4	67	GetPolySave	$FE/1B5C
4	68	SetGrafProcs	$FE/1B62
4	69	GetGrafProcs	$FE/1B68
4	70	SetUserField	$FE/1B6E
4	71	GetUserField	$FE/1B74
4	72	SetSysField	$FE/1B7A
4	73	GetSysField	$FE/1B80
4	74	SetRect	$FE/1E64
4	75	OffsetRect	$FE/1E81
4	76	InsetRect	$FE/1EA1

Table 6-5

Location of Quickdraw II Functions (continued)

Set Number	Function Number	Name	Location
4	77	SectRect	$FE/1ECA
4	78	UnionRect	$FE/1F1C
4	79	PtInRect	$FE/1F47
4	80	Pt2Rect	$FE/1F73
4	81	EqualRect	$FE/1F91
4	82	EmptyRect	$FE/1FAE
4	83	FrameRect	$FE/255C
4	84	PaintRect	$FE/2572
4	85	EraseRect	$FE/2588
4	86	InvertRect	$FE/259E
4	87	FillRect	$FE/25B4
4	88	FrameOval	$FE/88CA
4	89	PaintOval	$FE/88E0
4	90	EraseOval	$FE/88F6
4	91	InvertOval	$FE/890C
4	92	FillOval	$FE/8922
4	93	FrameRRect	$FE/8A75
4	94	PaintRRect	$FE/8A96
4	95	EraseRRect	$FE/8AB7
4	96	InvertRRect	$FE/8AD8
4	97	FillRRect	$FE/8AF9
4	98	FrameArc	$FE/89A6
4	99	PaintArc	$FE/89C7
4	100	EraseArc	$FE/89E8
4	101	InvertArc	$FE/8A09
4	102	FillArc	$FE/8A2A
4	103	NewRgn	$FE/4A0B
4	104	DisposeRgn	$FE/4A54
4	105	CopyRgn	$FE/4B4F
4	106	SetEmptyRgn	$FE/4A6E
4	107	SetRectRgn	$FE/4AAA
4	108	RectRgn	$FE/4B0D
4	109	OpenRgn	$FE/62E1
4	110	CloseRgn	$FE/6334
4	111	OffsetRgn	$FE/6B20
4	112	InsetRgn	$FE/69E2
4	113	SectRgn	$FE/6832
4	114	UnionRgn	$FE/6840
4	115	DiffRgn	$FE/684E

Table 6-5
Location of Quickdraw II Functions (continued)

Set Number	Function Number	Name	Location
4	116	XorRgn	$FE/685C
4	117	PtInRgn	$FE/58EF
4	118	RectInRgn	$FE/5981
4	119	EqualRgn	$FE/4B9A
4	120	EmptyRgn	$FE/4BDE
4	121	FrameRgn	$FE/4712
4	122	PaintRgn	$FE/4728
4	123	EraseRgn	$FE/473E
4	124	InvertRgn	$FE/4754
4	125	FillRgn	$FE/476A
4	126	ScrollRect	$FE/3A49
4	127	PaintPixels	$FE/3695
4	128	AddPt	$FE/2078
4	129	SubPt	$FE/208C
4	130	SetPt	$FE/20A0
4	131	EqualPt	$FE/20B1
4	132	LocalToGlobal	$FE/20CE
4	133	GlobalToLocal	$FE/20FA
4	134	Random	$FE/1FD2
4	135	SetRandSeed	$FE/2062
4	136	GetPixel	$FE/2126
4	137	ScalePt	$FE/218F
4	138	MapPt	$FE/6E26
4	139	MapRect	$FE/6E01
4	140	MapRgn	$FE/6BA0
4	141	SetStdProcs	$FE/106C
4	142	SetCursor	$FE/40B4
4	143	GetCursorAdr	$FE/41A3
4	144	HideCursor	$FE/41DA
4	145	ShowCursor	$FE/41BA
4	146	ObscureCursor	$FE/41F6
4	147	SetMouseLoc	$FE/42B9
4	148	SetFont	$FE/1AA2
4	149	GetFont	$FE/1AC6
4	150	GetFontInfo	$FE/72F5

Table 6-5

Location of Quickdraw II Functions (continued)

Set Number	Function Number	Name	Location
4	151	GetFontGlobals	$FE/7335
4	152	SetFontFlags	$FE/1AEA
4	153	GetFontFlags	$FE/1AF0
4	154	SetTextFace	$FE/1AF6
4	155	GetTextFace	$FE/1AFC
4	156	SetTextMode	$FE/1B02
4	157	GetTextMode	$FE/1B08
4	158	SetSpaceExtra	$FE/1B0E
4	159	GetSpaceExtra	$FE/1B14
4	160	SetForeColor	$FE/1B26
4	161	GetForeColor	$FE/1B2C
4	162	SetBackColor	$FE/1B32
4	163	GetBackColor	$FE/1B38
4	164	DrawChar	$FE/6F2C
4	165	DrawString	$FE/6F42
4	166	DrawCString	$FE/6F87
4	167	DrawText	$FE/6F69
4	168	CharWidth	$FE/6E45
4	169	StringWidth	$FE/6E5F
4	170	CStringWidth	$FE/6EAC
4	171	TextWidth	$FE/6E8A
4	172	CharBounds	$FE/710F
4	173	StringBounds	$FE/712D
4	174	CStringBounds	$FE/7182
4	175	TextBounds	$FE/715C
4	176	SetArcRot	$FE/8B7C
4	177	GetArcRot	$FE/8B82
4	178	SetSysFont	$FE/10B7
4	179	GetSysFont	$FE/10CB
4	180	SetVisRgn	$FE/181C
4	181	GetVisRgn	$FE/1841
4	182	SetIntUse	$FE/42EA
4	183	OpenPicture	$FE/1F00
4	184	PicComment	$FE/1F04
4	185	ClosePicture	$FE/1F08

Table 6-5
Location of Quickdraw II Functions (continued)

Set Number	Function Number	Name	Location
4	186	DrawPicture	$FE/1F0C
4	187	KillPicture	$FE/1F10
4	188	FramePoly	$FE/8B88
4	189	PaintPoly	$FE/8B9E
4	190	ErasePoly	$FE/8BB4
4	191	InvertPoly	$FE/8BCA
4	192	FillPoly	$FE/8BE0
4	193	OpenPoly	$FE/8DC5
4	194	ClosePoly	$FE/8E3F
4	195	KillPoly	$FE/8EF0
4	196	OffsetPoly	$FE/8F08
4	197	MapPoly	$FE/8F3B
4	198	SetClipHandle	$FE/1B86
4	199	GetClipHandle	$FE/1B8C
4	200	SetVisHandle	$FE/1B92
4	201	GetVisHandle	$FE/1B98
4	202	InitCursor	$FE/3FA1
4	203	SetBufDims	$FE/10E1
4	204	ForceBufDims	$FE/111E
4	205	SaveBufDims	$FE/112D
4	206	RestoreBufDims	$FE/115A
4	207	GetFGSize	$FE/73AE
4	208	SetFontID	$FE/1ACC
4	209	GetFontID	$FE/1AD8
4	210	SetTextSize	$FE/1ADE
4	211	GetTextSize	$FE/1AE4
4	212	SetCharExtra	$FE/1B1A
4	213	GetCharExtra	$FE/1B20

Table 6-5

Location of Quickdraw II Functions (continued)

Set Number	Function Number	Name	Location
5	1	DeskBootInit	$FE/AD54
5	2	DeskStartUp	$FE/AE83
5	3	DeskShutDown	$FE/AE86
5	4	DeskVersion	$FE/AE89
5	5	DeskReset	$FE/AE91
5	6	DeskStatus	$FE/AE91
5	7	———	$FE/07A2
5	8	———	$FE/07A2
5	9	SaveScrn	$FE/AF16
5	10	RestScrn	$FE/AF51
5	11	SaveAll	$FE/B004
5	12	RestAll	$FE/B280
5	13	———	$FE/07A2
5	14	InstallNDA	$FE/07A2
5	15	InstallCDA	$FE/B890
5	16	———	$FE/07A2
5	17	ChooseCDA	$FE/B51D
5	18	———	$FE/07A2
5	19	SetDAStrPtr	$FE/BA73
5	20	GetDAStrPtr	$FE/BAD0
5	21	OpenNDA	$FE/07A2
5	22	CloseNDA	$FE/07A2
5	23	SystemClick	$FE/07A2
5	24	SystemEdit	$FE/07A2
5	25	SystemTask	$FE/07A2
5	26	SystemEvent	$FE/B3F7
5	27	GetNumNDAs	$FE/07A2

Table 6-6

Location of Desk Manager Functions

Set Number	Function Number	Name	Location
6	1	EMBootInit	$FE/BBA4
6	2	EMStartUp	$FE/BBA7
6	3	EMShutDown	$FE/BE6D
6	4	EMVersion	$FE/BF3E
6	5	EMReset	$FE/BF46
6	6	EMStatus	$FE/BF54
6	7	———	$FE/07A2
6	8	———	$FE/07A2
6	9	DoWindows	$FE/BF59
6	10	GetNextEvent	$FE/BF6D
6	11	EventAvail	$FE/C0D2
6	12	GetMouse	$FE/C0DF
6	13	Button	$FE/C11E
6	14	StillDown	$FE/C15E
6	15	WaitMouseUp	$FE/C1B7
6	16	TickCount	$FE/C208
6	17	GetDblTime	$FE/C238
6	18	GetCaretTime	$FE/C265
6	19	SetSwitch	$FE/C292
6	20	PostEvent	$FE/C2A4
6	21	FlushEvents	$FE/C324
6	22	GetOSEvent	$FE/C381
6	23	OSEventAvail	$FE/C444
6	24	SetEventMask	$FE/C451
6	25	FakeMouse	$FE/C462

Table 6-7

Location of Event Manager Functions

Set Number	Function Number	Name	Location
7	1	SchBootInit	$FE/C7B9
7	2	SchStartUp	$FE/C7E6
7	3	SchShutDown	$FE/C7E9
7	4	SchVersion	$FE/C7EC
7	5	SchReset	$FE/C7F4
7	6	SchStatus	$FE/C805
7	7	———	$FE/07A2
7	8	———	$FE/07A2
7	9	SchAddTask	$FE/C839
7	10	SchFlush	$FE/C870

Table 6-8

Location of Scheduler Functions

Set Number	Function Number	Name	Location
8	1	SoundBootInit	$FF/3E8B
8	2	SoundStartUp	$FF/3F3B
8	3	SoundShutDown	$FF/3FE4
8	4	SoundVersion	$FF/4026
8	5	SoundReset	$FF/4031
8	6	SoundToolStatus	$FF/4291
8	7	———	$FF/3EAE
8	8	———	$FF/3EAE
8	9	WriteRamBlock	$FF/413A
8	10	ReadRamBlock	$FF/40E8
8	11	GetTableAddress	$FF/403E
8	12	GetSoundVolume	$FF/41B1
8	13	SetSoundVolume	$FF/4188
8	14	FFStartSound	$FF/4359
8	15	FFStopSound	$FF/41F0
8	16	FFSoundStatus	$FF/42A3
8	17	FFGeneratorStatus	$FF/42AF
8	18	SetSoundMIRQV	$FF/42EA
8	19	SetUserSoundIRQV	$FF/431C
8	20	FFSoundDOneStatus	$FF/46C0

Table 6-9

Location of Sound Manager Functions

Set Number	Function Number	Name	Location
9	1	ADBBootInit	$FF/805C
9	2	ADBStartUp	$FF/8097
9	3	ADBShutDown	$FF/8097
9	4	ADBVersion	$FF/8099
9	5	ADBReset	$FF/8097
9	6	ADBStatus	$FF/809F
9	7	———	$FF/8097
9	8	———	$FF/8097
9	9	Send	$FF/82A6
9	10	RCV	$FF/82CC
9	11	RDmem	$FF/82E9
9	12	———	$FF/850B
9	13	ADBpoll	$FF/8322
9	14	ADBrcv	$FF/836C
9	15	ABSOn	$FF/80A5
9	16	ABSOff	$FF/80B3
9	17	RdAbs	$FF/80C1
9	18	Scale	$FF/80EC
9	19	RdScale	$FF/80D8
9	20	SRQPl	$FF/8104
9	21	SRQRmv	$FF/8246
9	22	ClrSRQTbl	$FF/8299

Table 6-10

Location of Apple Desktop Bus Tool Functions

Set Number	Function Number	Name	Location
10	1	SANEBootInit	$FE/CF2C
10	2	SANEStartUp	$FE/CF2F
10	3	SANEShutDown	$FE/CF4E
10	4	SANEVersion	$FE/CF64
10	5	SANEReset	$FE/CF6C
10	6	SANEStatus	$FE/CF6F
10	7	———	$FE/CF6F
10	8	———	$FE/CF6F
10	9	FPNum	$FE/CFFB
10	10	DecStrNum	$FE/E56E
10	11	ElemNum	$FE/EB3C

Table 6-11
Location of SANE Tool Set Functions

Set Number	Function Number	Name	Location
11	1	IMBootInit	$FE/07A2
11	2	IMStartUp	$FE/07A2
11	3	IMShutDown	$FE/07A2
11	4	IMVersion	$FE/09A5
11	5	IMReset	$FE/07A2
11	6	IMStatus	$FE/C9AD
11	7	———	$FE/07A2
11	8	———	$FE/07A2
11	9	Multiply	$FE/C9B5
11	10	SDivide	$FE/C9E7
11	11	UDivide	$FE/C9D5
11	12	LongMul	$FE/CA4D
11	13	LongDivide	$FE/CA7D

Table 6-12
Location of Integer Math Functions

Set Number	Function Number	Name	Location
11	1	IMBootInit	$FE/07A2
11	14	FixRatio	$FE/CAC1
11	15	FixMul	$FE/CB33
11	16	FracMul	$FE/C97F
11	17	FixDiv	$FE/C99F
11	18	FracDiv	$FE/C99F
11	19	FixRound	$FE/C99F
11	20	FracSqrt	$FE/C99F
11	21	FracCos	$FE/C99F
11	22	FracSin	$FE/C99F
11	23	FixATan2	$FE/C99F
11	24	HiWord	$FE/C99F
11	25	LoWord	$FE/C99F
11	26	Long2Fix	$FE/C99F
11	27	Fix2Long	$FE/C99F
11	28	Fix2Frac	$FE/C99F
11	29	Frac2Fix	$FE/C99F
11	30	Fix2X	$FE/C99F
11	31	Frac2X	$FE/C99F
11	32	X2Fix	$FE/C99F
11	33	X2Frac	$FE/C99F
11	34	Int2Hex	$FE/CB5C
11	35	Long2Hex	$FE/CB79
11	36	Hex2Int	$FE/CB44
11	37	Hex2Long	$FE/CBF6
11	38	Int2Dec	$FE/CC8D
11	39	Long2Dec	$FE/CD0A
11	40	Dec2Int	$FE/CD98
11	41	Dec2Long	$FE/CDD8
11	42	HexIt	$FE/CEBF

Table 6-12
Location of Integer Math Functions (continued)

Set Number	Function Number	Name	Location
12	1	TextBootInit	$FE/A866
12	2	TextStartUp	$FE/A892
12	3	TextShutDown	$FE/A892
12	4	TextVersion	$FE/A895
12	5	TextReset	$FE/A866
12	6	TextStatus	$FE/A89D
12	7	———	$FE/A892
12	8	———	$FE/A892
12	9	SetInGlobals	$FE/A8A5
12	10	SetOutGlobals	$FE/A8C3
12	11	SetErrGlobals	$FE/A8C8
12	12	GetInGlobals	$FE/A8CD
12	13	GetOutGlobals	$FE/A8EB
12	14	GetErrGlobals	$FE/A8F0
12	15	SetInputDevice	$FE/A8F5
12	16	SetOutputDevice	$FE/A914
12	17	SetErrorDevice	$FE/A921
12	18	GetInputDevice	$FE/A926
12	19	GetOutputDevice	$FE/A94D
12	20	GetErrorDevice	$FE/A952
12	21	InitTextDev	$FE/A957
12	22	CtrlTextDev	$FE/A9A7
12	23	StatusTextDev	$FE/A9DA
12	24	WriteChar	$FE/AA03
12	25	ErrWriteChar	$FE/AA06
12	26	WriteLine	$FE/AA50
12	27	ErrWriteLine	$FE/AA53
12	28	WriteString	$FF/AA76
12	29	ErrWriteString	$FF/AA79
12	30	WriteBlock	$FF/AAA6
12	31	ErrWriteBlock	$FF/AAA9
12	32	WriteCString	$FF/AAD0
12	33	ErrWriteCString	$FF/AAD3
12	34	ReadChar	$FF/AAF2
12	35	ReadBlock	$FF/AB3A
12	36	ReadLine	$FF/AB86

Table 6-13

Location of Text Tools Functions

Location	Name/Use
C000	Keyboard Data and Strobe
C000	80Store Off—Page2 selects main RAM page 2
C001	80Store On—Page 2 selects auxiliary memory RAM
C002	RAMRD main
C003	RAMRD auxiliary
C004	RAMWRT main
C005	RAMWRT auxiliary
C006	SlotCXRom enable slot ROM
C007	SlotCXRom enable internal ROM
C008	Altzp Off—use main bank pages 0 and 1
C009	Altzp On—use auxiliary bank pages 0 and 1
C00A	SlotC3Rom enable internal ROM
C00B	SlotC3Rom enable slot ROM
C00C	80Col Off—display 40 columns
C00D	80Col On—display 80 columns
C00E	Altchar Off—use primary character set
C00F	Altchar On—use alternate character set
C010	Any Key Down and Clear Keyboard Strobe
C011	Read whether LC bank 1 or bank 2
C012	Check if reading RAM or ROM
C013	Read RAMRD switch
C014	Read RAMWRT switch
C015	Read SlotCXRom switch
C016	Read Altzp switch
C017	Read SlotC3Rom switch
C018	Read 80Store switch
C019	VBL—read vertical blanking
C01A	Read Text switch
C01B	Read Mixed switch
C01C	Read Page2 switch
C01D	Read Hires switch
C01E	Read Altchar switch
C01F	Read 80Col switch
*C021	Monochrome/Color Register
*C022	Screen Color Register
*C023	VGC Interrupt Register
*C024	Mouse Data Register
*C025	Modifier Key Register
*C026	Command/Status Register
*C027	System Status Register

Table 6-14

Softswitches and Status Registers

Location	Name/Use
*C029	Video Control Register
*C02B	Language Select Register
*C02D	Slot Select Register
C030	Speaker
*C031	Disk Interface Register
*C032	VGC Interrupt Clear Register
*C033	Real-Time Clock Data Register
*C034	Real-Time Clock and Border Color Control Register
*C035	Shadow Register
*C03C	Sound Control Register
C040	Strobe Output Signal
C050	Text Off—display graphics
C051	Text On—display text
C052	Mixed Off—display only text or only graphics
C053	Mixed On—display mixed text and graphics if Text Off
C054	Page2 Off—select page 1
C055	Page2 On—select page 2 or auxiliary memory RAM
C056	Hires Off—Display low-res graphics if Text Off
C057	Hires On—Display hi-res or double-hi-res if Text Off
C058	Annunciator 0 Offn
C059	Annunciator 0 Onn
C05A	Annunciator 1 Offn
C05B	Annunciator 1 Onn
C05C	Annunciator 2 Offn
C05D	Annunciator 2 Onn
C05E	Annunciator 3 Offn
C05E	DHires On—turn on double-hi-res
C05F	Annunciator 3 Onn
C05F	DHires Off—turn off double-hi-res
C061	Switch 0 (Apple)
C062	Switch 1 (Option)
C063	Switch 2
C064	Paddle 0
C065	Paddle 1
C066	Paddle 2
C067	Paddle 3
*C068	State Register
C070	Analog Paddle Input Reset
C080	Read RAM, use LC bank 2
C081	Read ROM, write RAM, use LC bank 2

Table 6-14

Softswitches and Status Registers (continued)

Location	Name/Use
C082	Read ROMk, use LC bank 2
C083	Read and write RAM, use LC bank 2
C088	Read RAM, use LC bank 1
C089	Read ROM, write RAM, use LC bank 1
C08A	Read ROM, use LC bank 1
C08B	Read and write RAM, use LC bank 1
*C0C8	Slot 4 Motor Off
*C0C9	Slot 4 Motor On
*C0D8	Slot 5 Motor Off
*C0D9	Slot 5 Motor On
*C0E0	Disk stepper motor phase 0 low
*C0E1	Disk stepper motor phase 0 high
*C0E2	Disk stepper motor phase 1 low
*C0E3	Disk stepper motor phase 1 high
*C0E4	Disk stepper motor phase 2 low
*C0E5	Disk stepper motor phase 2 high
*C0E6	Disk stepper motor phase 3 low
*C0E7	Disk stepper motor phase 3 high
*C0E8	Disk spindle motor enabled
*C0E9	Disk spindle motor disabled
*C0EA	Drive 0 select
*C0EB	Drive 1 select
*C0EC	Disk Q6 (IWM) select bit low
*C0ED	Disk Q6 (IWM) select bit high
*C0EE	Disk Q7 (IWM) select bit low
*C0EF	Disk Q7 (IWM) select bit high
*C0F8	Slot 7 Motor Off
*C0F9	Slot 7 Motor On
*C0xx	Keyboard GLU Status Register

Note: * indicates softswitch/status register that is new with the IIGS

Table 6-14

Softswitches and Status Registers (continued)

The addresses for the softswitches listed in the table are 16-bit addresses. Each address is in bank $E0 and, depending on the shadow state, may be mapped into other banks.

One of the largest categories of new softswitches are those that involve the various video display modes available on the IIGS. The enhanced text display mode on the IIGS (discussed in Chapter 8) provides for displaying text in 1 of 16 colors, on a background of 1 of 16 colors, and with a border of 1 of 16 colors. The RGB signal for the text is always in color. The composite video signal for text is black and white.

The monochrome/color register, at $C021, uses bit 7 to determine whether composite output is color (0) or gray scale (1). Bits 0-6 in this register are not used and must be set to 0.

The screen color register, at $C022, contains the color for text in the high nibble (bits 4-7) and the color for the background in the low nibble (bits 0-3). The border color is determined by the low nibble (bits 0-3) of the combined register at $C034.

The upper nibble of this register is used in connection with the built-in clock using the clock data register at $C033. This register makes it possible for your application to read from and write to the clock chip directly. If you are not careful, though, you can corrupt the clock chip. The IIGS provides toolbox routines for reading the clock chip in either ASCII or numeric form. As discussed in Chapter 3, the use of these routines is easier than the direct access routines discussed here.

In order to transfer data between the clock chip and memory, your application must first set bit 6 of the clock data register to either 1 for a read or to 0 for a write. Your application must then set bit 5 to 0. Bit 7 will become a 1 at that time and will be reset to 0 by the clock chip when the data have been either read from the data register ($C033) or written to it. Subsequent data bytes can be obtained by continuing to place a 0 in bit 5. Your application should write a 1 to bit 5 after the last byte is transferred in order to avoid data corruption in the clock chip.

Two interrupts are also controlled by the IIGS Video Graphics Controller. These are the scan-line interrupt and the one-second interrupt. Scan-line interrupts are enabled by writing a 1 to bit 1 of the VGC Interrupt Register at $C023, and disabled by writing a 0. One-second interrupts are similarly controlled by bit 2. Your application can determine if a scan-line interrupt has occurred by checking for a 1 in bit 5 of this register; the occurrence of a one-second interrupt can be determined by checking for a 1 in bit 6.

Bits 5 and 6 of the VGC interrupt register are read-only bits—your application cannot directly change the value in these bits. If they are set, though, they can be cleared by using the VGC interrupt clear register. To clear the scan-line interrupt status bit of the VGC interrupt register, your application should write a 0 to bit 5 of the VGC interrupt clear register at $C032. To clear the one-second interrupt status bit of the VGC interrupt register, your application should write a 0 to bit 6 of the VGC interrupt clear register.

The Video Control Register affects certain aspects of the video display of the IIGS. Bit 7 is set to 1 to enable super-high-resolution graphics. Bit 6 is set to enable linear mapping of the memory used in the super-high-resolution graphics display. Bit 5 is set to inhibit the display of color in standard 8-bit Apple II video modes. Bits 1-4 are reserved. Bit 0 is used by the system to latch data to the auxiliary memory, or as specified by other softswitches in the system.

The language select register, located at $C02B, affects certain input and output operations of the IIGS. Bits 5-7 form a 3-bit code that determines which language display set and keyboard mapping will be used. Each code refers to a primary and secondary language (see Table 6-15). The primary language is used if bit 3 is 1, and the secondary language is used if bit 3 is 0. Bit 4 determines the number of scan lines for the video output. If it is a 0, there are 262 scan lines (as in NTSC video), and if it is a 1, there are 312 scan lines (as in PAL video). Bits 0-2 are reserved and must be 0.

As discussed in Chapter 5, the Apple IIGS has increased memory as compared with the Apple IIe and Apple IIc. It also has both slots and

Bit Pattern	Primary Language	Secondary Language
000	English—USA	Dvorak
001	English—UK	English—USA
010	French	English—USA
011	Danish	English—USA
100	Spanish	English—USA
101	Italian	English—USA
110	German	English—USA
111	Swedish	English—USA

Table 6-15

Language Select Bits

built-in ports for peripheral expansion. Various softswitches and status registers control aspects of the IIGS memory and peripheral expansion.

The slot register, located at $C02D, determines whether the internal ROM (for the built-in port) or the slot-card ROM (for a specified slot) is active. The bit value is 0 to select the internal ROM and 1 to select the slot-card ROM. Each slot is controlled by its own bit number—thus slot 2 is controlled by bit 2, slot 6 by bit 6, and so forth. The two exceptions are bits 0 and 3. Bit 0 is reserved because there is no slot 0; it should always be a zero. Bit 3 is reserved because the internal ROM for slot 3 (80-column display) is always selected; the value here should always be a zero.

Some of the memory bank softswitches available on the Apple IIe and Apple IIc are collected in one register on the IIGS. This register is the state register at $C068. The meaning of each bit in this register is shown in Table 6-16. This register provides a quick method of reading the status of many different softswitches. The state register can also be used to write new softswitch settings, although this use of the register can result in a momentarily slowed system.

The state of some memory shadowing (discussed in Chapter 5) as well as some other memory bank operations, is controlled by the shadow register

Bit Number	Use
0	SLOTCxROM—selects whether internal or slot card ROM is used from $C100-C7FF
1	ROMBANK—selects ROM bank
2	BANK2—selects auxiliary RAM bank
3	RDROM—reads from ROM
4	RAMWRT—writes to RAM
5	RAMRD—reads from RAM
6	PAGE2—uses alternate text page
7	ALTZP—selects the alternate zero page

Table 6-16

Bit Meaning in State Register

Bit Number	Use
0	Write a 0 to enable shadowing for text page 1 and auxiliary text page 1 ($0400-07FF).
1	Write a 0 to enable shadowing for hi-res page 1 and, unless bit 4 is 1, auxiliary hi-res page 1 ($2000-3FFF).
2	Write a 0 to enable shadowing for hi-res page 2 and, unless bit 4 is 1, auxiliary hi-res page 2 ($4000-5FFF).
3	Write a 0 to enable shadowing for the 32K video buffer ($2000-9FFF).
4	Write a 1 to inhibit shadowing auxiliary hi-res display (that is, the odd-numbered banks).
5	Reserved—must be zero.
6	Write a 0 to enable input/output in $C000-CFFF, transferring the RAM area for $C000-CFFF into language card area bank 2 ($D000-DFFF). Write a 1 to enable contiguous RAM from $0000-FFFF.
7	Reserved—must be zero.

Table 6-17
Bit Meaning in Shadow Register

at $C035. The meaning of each bit in this register is shown in Table 6-17.

The Apple Desktop Bus also has several operations and settings that are controlled by some softswitch locations. The use of these registers is discussed in Chapter 15. The use of the sound control register is discussed in Chapter 14.

EXPANSION ROM

The Apple IIGS has banks $F0-FD reserved for use as expansion ROM. This allows for as much as 896 kilobytes of ROM. Eight of these banks, $F0-F7, are for user expansion and the rest, $F8-FD, are reserved for use by Apple. There are no sockets on the IIGS motherboard for this expansion ROM. Any ROM must be included on a memory card that is inserted into the memory expansion slot of the IIGS.

Two uses can be made of the expansion ROM. Either custom tool sets or patches to existing tool sets can be created and placed in ROM if they are installed by your initialization routine through proper calls to the Tool Locator described in Chapter 2. Because ROM/PROM/EPROM is not easily changed, it should not be used for either custom tools or patches. The disadvantages of such uses are that you also would have to customize your bootup routines, and you cannot easily modify the code further.

A ROM disk provides a method of permanently storing commonly used applications where they are always available for your use. A ROM disk must start at $F0/0000, and the first 7 bits must contain the word *ROMDISK* in uppercase letters with the most significant bit set (that is, negative ASCII). The following code segment would create the proper ROM disk header that could be burned into a ROM:

```
ROMDisk         START
* Most significant bit, by default, is on; but ensure that it is on
                MSB ON          ;just in case
                DC C'ROMDISK'   ;Must be all uppercase
                . . .           ;Rest of ROMdisk goes here
```

When the Smartport initializes devices in the chain (discussed in Chapter 21), it checks at location $F0/0000 for the word *ROMDISK*. If the Smartport finds ROMDISK, it places the ROM disk in the Smartport device chain.

CHAPTER 7

Working with Memory: Using the Monitor

The IIGS system monitor is a set of subroutines located in ROM that aid you in keeping track of, regulating, or controlling the IIGS. The system monitor in the IIGS is derived from that in the original Apple II, present since the introduction of the first Apple II. This monitor, written by Steve Wozniak and Alan Baum, has been modified over the years to add new commands and to support features added by the Apple II Plus, IIe, and IIc. Over the same years, several features have also been dropped.

As can be expected, the IIGS system monitor is significantly changed from the existing Apple II system monitors, most notably to provide support for the additional registers, new operating modes, and increased memory-addressing capabilities of the 65816 microprocessor.

The system monitor consists of several parts, each providing a distinct function. Some routines perform low-level input/output operations, such as reading input from the keyboard or game port and sending output to the screen or speaker. In the earlier Apple II system monitors these functions were a significant part of the monitor—programs would often call the monitor subroutines to perform their input/output functions.

As discussed in Chapter 2, the IIGS has ROM routines that are four to eight times the size of the ROM routines in the previous Apple II's. This greatly expanded ROM contains highly sophisticated routines aiding in many aspects of input/output, not merely the low-level routines found in the Apple II system monitor. These new routines, called *tools* and *managers*, are discussed in other chapters of this book.

The low-level routines of the traditional Apple II system monitor exist, for the most part, in the IIGS system monitor. They are required for compatibility with existing Apple II software. Table 7-1 is a list of each of these routines and its location in the ROM. For more information on these functions, see the Apple IIe or IIc *Technical Reference Manual.*

The Miscellaneous Tool Set contains one function that aids in the use of these monitor routines from the IIGS 16-bit mode. FWentry, which is function $24, takes as input the accumulator, X register, and Y register values passed to the routine (as the low bytes in three different word values) followed by the 16-bit address of the entry point as shown in Table 7-1. Values returned by the function include the processor status, accumulator, and X and Y registers as the low bytes in four different word values.

The second aspect of the system monitor is a program that is run whenever you enter the monitor through its main entry point ($FF/FF69). These routines provide a method of determining and changing the values in various places in the IIGS memory or the 65816 processor, running machine-language programs, and performing mathematical or other functions. These functions have been greatly expanded from those available on the Apple IIe and IIc. They are discussed later in this chapter.

A third function of the system monitor is providing a means to write, on a simplified level, assembly-language programs. This is a function that is

Address	Name	Description
F800	PLOT	Plot on the low-resolution graphics screen
F80E	PLOT1	Modify low-resolution byte on the screen
F819	HLINE	Draw low-resolution horizontal line
F828	VLINE	Draw low-resolution vertical line
F832	CLRSCR	Clear the low-resolution screen
F836	CLRTOP	Clear the low-resolution screen in mixed mode
F847	GBASCALC	Calculate base address for low-resolution screen
F85F	NXTCOL	Increment low-resolution color by three
F864	SETCOL	Set the low-resolution color
F871	SCRN	Determine low-resolution screen color
F88C	INSDS1.2	LDA (PCL,X) and go to INSDS2
F88E	INSDS2	Set up indexes for op code in accumulator
F890	GET816LEN	Return 65816 instruction length in $2F
F8D0	INSTDSP	Display disassembled instruction
F8D9	SPATFNS	Applesoft call for HLIN
F93A	GETAN3STATUS	Transfer AN3 status to accumulator bit 7
F940	PRNTYX	Print values of X and Y registers in hex
F941	PRNTAX	Print values of accumulator and X register in hex
F944	PRNTX	Print value of X register in hex
F94B	PRBLNK	Print three spaces
F94A	PRBL2	Print X register number of spaces
F953	PCADJ	Adjust program counter
F962	TEXT2COPY	Enable/disable Text Page 2 copy
FA40	IRQ	Interrupt request handler
FA4C	BREAK	Break handler
FA59	OLDBRK	Print 65816 BRK printout
FA62	RESET	Reset handler
FA68	FBBYTE	$FB required here for some code
FAA6	PWRUP	System coldstart
FABA	SLOOP	Disk controller slot search loop

Table 7-1

List of System Monitor Routines

Address	Name	Description
FABF		Match $00 at FAFF
FAD7	REGDSP	Display contents of register
FAFF		$00 must appear here
FB05	APPLEMSG	'Apple II' must appear here
FB19	RTBL	Register names table
FB1E	PREAD	Read a hand controller (paddle)
F821	PREAD4	Timeout paddle and call PREAD
F82F	INIT	Initialize system
FB39	SETTXT	Place system in text mode
FB40	SETGR	Place system in graphics mode
FB4B	SETWND	Set text window
FB51	SETWND2	Set window size
FB5B	TABV	Vertical tab
FB60	APPLEII	Print machine type
FB6F	SETPWRC	Create a power-up byte
FB78	VIDWAIT	Wait for CONTROL-S
FB83	KBDWAIT	Wait for key press
FBB3	VERSION	Monitor ROM identification byte
FBBF	ZIDBYTE2	Monitor ROM sub identification byte #2
FBC0	ZIDBYTE	Monitor ROM sub identification byte #1
FBC1	BASCALC	Text base address calculator
FBDD	BELL1	Generate user-selected tone
FBE2	BELL1.2	Branch to BELL1
FBE4	BELL2	Branch to BELL1
FBF0	STORADV	Place a printable character on screen
FBF4	ADVANCE	Increment the cursor position
FBFD	VIDOUT	Place a character on the screen
FC10	BS	Back space
FC1A	UP	Move cursor up a line
FC22	VTAB	Vertical tab
FC24	VTAB2	Vertical tab (alternate entry)
FC42	CLREOF	Clear to end of page
FC58	HOME	Home cursor and clear screen

Table 7-1
List of System Monitor Routines (continued)

Address	Name	Description
FC62	CR	Carriage return — begin a new line
FC66	LF	Line feed
FC70	SCROLL	Scroll the screen
FC9C	CLREOL	Clear to end of line
FC9E	CLEOLZ	Clear to end of line for BASL position
FCAB	WAIT	Delay
FCB4	NXTA4	Increment pointer A4
FCBA	NXTA1	Increment pointer A1
FCC9	HEADR	Write header to cassette tape. Cassette port not available
FD0C	RDKEY	Inverse flash cursor and get input character
FD0C	RDKEY	Inverse flash cursor and get input character
FD10		BASIC.SYSTEM uses for input
FD18	RDKEY1	Get an input character
FD1B	KEYIN	Read the keyboard input
FD35	RDCHAR	Get an input character of ESCape code
FD67	GETLNZ	Get an input line
FD6A	GETLN	Get an input line after prompt
FD6C	GETLN0	Alternate entry for GETLN
FD6F	GETLN1	Get an input line without prompt
FD8B	CROUT1	Print a carriage return and clear to end of line
FD8E	CROUT	Print a carriage return
FD92	PRA1	Print carriage return and A1 in hex
FDDA	PRBTYE	Print value of accumulator in hex
FDE3	PRHEX	Print low nibble of accumulator in hex
FDED	COUT	Output a character through the output hooks
FDF0	COUT1	Output a character to the screen
FDF6	COUTZ	Output a character to the screen
FE1F	NEWID	New system identification routine
FE20	MOVE	Move a block of memory
FE80	SETINV	Set inverse text mode
FE84	SETNORM	Set normal text mode
FE89	SETKBD	Reset input to keyboard

Table 7-1

List of System Monitor Routines (continued)

Address	Name	Description
FE8B	INPORT	Reset input to slot
FE95	OUTPORT	Reset output to slot
FEB6	GO	Begin code execution
FECD	WRITE	Write a record to cassette
FEFD	READ	Read a record from cassette
FF2D	PRERR	Print ERR and sound beep
FF3A	BELL	Call BELL1 to generate beep
FF3F	RESTORE	Restore all registers from stored locations
FF4A	SAVE	Save all registers in set locations
FF58	IORTS	Known RTS ($60) for peripheral card use
FF59	OLDRST	Old entry point to enter monitor
FF65	MON	Standard monitor entry point with beep
FF69	MONZ	Standard monitor entry point
FF6C	MONZ2	Monitor entry point—registers intact
FF70	MONZ4	Act on command in input buffer ($200-2FF)
FF8A	DIG	Shift hexadecimal digit into A2
FFA7	GETNUM	Transfer hexadecimal input into A2
FFAD	NXTCHR	Translate next character
FFBE	TOSUB	Execute command pointed to by Y register
FFC7	ZMODE	Clear mode and set Y register to 0
FFCB	PRODOSRTS	RTS ($60) used by ProDOS
FFD0	DOSEF	DOS use
FFF6	CHKSUM TWEAK+1	Tweaked to make checksum = $1234

Table 7-1
List of System Monitor Routines (continued)

implemented by the Mini-Assembler, a program that has existed since the original Apple II. The Mini-Assembler is discussed later in this chapter.

The fourth major function of the IIGS system monitor is a series of diagnostic routines. Built-in diagnostic routines appeared in the Apple IIe, disappeared in the Apple IIc and reappeared in 32K ROM in the Apple IIc.

On the Apple IIe and IIc, the routines tested the main and auxiliary RAM (64K each) as well as the softswitches in the Memory Management and Input/Output units. The diagnostics in the IIGS are discussed later in this chapter.

A final function of the system monitor is providing what are referred to as *video-support routines*—methods by which the user or a program can adjust the video display of the computer. The IIGS monitor video-support routines handle the display when in the text and low-resolution modes. The Quickdraw II and related tools handle the video-output display when operating in super-resolution graphics, the default IIGS native operating mode (see Chapters 10-13 for a discussion of these routines). The system monitor Apple II mode video-support routines are basically unchanged from the later Apple IIe and 32K ROM in the IIc. Information about them can be found in the Apple IIe and IIc *Technical Reference Manuals.*

The IIGS system monitor resides in bank $FF of memory, beginning at location $FF69. It is shadowed onto bank 0 when it is called from 8-bit Apple II mode by a CALL-151 command in Applesoft BASIC.

COMMANDS

One of the main functions of the system monitor is to provide a means of examining, modifying, and otherwise overseeing the operation of the IIGS. These functions are supported by a variety of commands that you can give to the monitor. The commands can be divided into six different categories.

These different commands, for the most part, also exist in the IIGS Programmer's Workshop Debugger. Indeed, in many cases, the debugger commands are more sophisticated and more integrated than the monitor routines. However, the monitor comes with every IIGS. The debugger is available only if you have purchased the Programmer's Workshop.

Before giving a command to the system monitor, you must first place the IIGS in the system monitor level operating mode. The mode is indicated by the use of the asterisk (*) for a prompt character. To enter the system monitor you must call the entry routine, which is located at $FF/FF69. From Applesoft BASIC this can be accomplished by CALL-151.

Address locations in the IIGS monitor are given in hexadecimal notation. The address consists of two parts, a 1-byte bank number separated with a slash (/) from a 2-byte bank address. In most cases, if the bank number is not used, the last-accessed bank is assumed.

Values can be entered in the monitor in several different ways:

- Addresses and bank numbers must be entered as hexadecimal numbers without the $ prefix that normally signifies a hex value. If fewer than two digits for a 1-byte value or four digits for a 2-byte value are entered, the value is padded on the left with one or more 0's (for example, the 2-byte value 3E2 is interpreted as 03E2).
- Except for addresses and bank numbers, hexadecimal values of up to 8 bytes in length can be entered. Multiple values can be entered on the same line if separated by a space. If the total number of digits entered is an odd number, a 0 is added on to the left end. The hexadecimal values of bytes entered without spaces are flipped when the value is stored so that the least-significant byte is placed in memory first. Thus, the value 34F41E is placed into memory with 1E in the lowest address, F4 in the next address, and 34 in the highest address.
- In some cases an ASCII character can be used in place of a hexadecimal number. Two forms of ASCII input—literal and flipped—are supported. In both cases the negative ASCII value (that is, high-bit set) of the character is placed into memory after it is ANDed with the ASCII filter mask.

Literal ASCII, which is delimited by quotation marks ("), is placed into memory in the order entered (that is, the value of the leftmost character is placed in the lowest memory address). The maximum length of a literal ASCII entry is restricted only by the maximum input length of 255 characters.

Flipped ASCII, which is delimited by single quotation marks ('), is placed into memory in the reverse order of entry (that is, the value of the rightmost character is placed in the lowest memory address). The maximum length of a flipped ASCII entry is four characters. If more than four characters are entered, the monitor uses the last four entered.

The Apple IIe and Apple IIc monitors do not support flipped hex or ASCII input. Literal ASCII input is restricted to single character values and the character has to be preceded by a single quotation mark ('). There is no AND mask and the high bit of the value is always set.

Examining the System

Seven different commands examine the status of either memory or a 65816 register on the IIGS (see Table 7-2 for a listing). Memory examination commands make use of the concept of the last opened location, which is the last memory location examined. Simply pressing the RETURN key at the monitor prompt will display the contents of up to 16 consecutive memory locations, starting just after the last opened location.

The exact number of locations displayed by pressing the RETURN key depends on whether the IIGS is in 40- or 80-column text mode and what the last opened location was. In 40-column mode the IIGS displays up to eight values, ending with an address whose last digit is either \$7 or \$F. In 80-column mode the IIGS displays up to 16 values, ending with an address whose last digit is \$F. At the end of a bank (\$xx/FFFF), the display will wrap around to the beginning of the same bank (\$xx/0000) and not span the bank boundary (to \$xx+1/0000).

The memory display, which is illustrated in Figure 7-1, consists of three

Command	Explanation
BAddress.EAddress	Displays memory from BAddress to EAddress
<Return>	Displays next 8 (in 40-column mode) or 16 (in 80-column mode) memory locations
Add1S<Add2S.Add2EV	Verify if block of memory from Add2S to Add2E is the same as that block beginning at Add1S
\Pattern \<RangeS.RangeE	Search for pattern in range beginning at RangeS and ending at RangeE
L	List (disassemble) assembly language code
CONTROL-E	Examine 65816 and IIGS registers
=T	Display system time and date

Table 7-2

Monitor Memory Examination Commands

```
#FF/3C90:04 D0 85 C2 30 A2 84 00-.P5B0"..
```

Address — *1-byte hexadecimal values* — *ASCII code values*

Figure 7-1
Memory display

parts. The beginning address location, which is one number higher than the last opened location, is displayed with a 1-byte bank number, a slash (/) as a separator character, a 2-byte address, and a colon (:). Following the address are 1-byte hexadecimal values (two digits) for each memory location, separated by spaces. After the last value is a dash followed by the one-character ASCII representation of each of the memory locations. Values not having a printable ASCII character representation will display a period.

To display memory at a specific location other than the last opened location, you merely enter the address and press the RETURN key. To display a specific range of addresses, enter the beginning address, a period (.), and the ending address. Addresses are entered as either a 1-byte bank number, a slash (/), and a 2-byte value, or just as a 2-byte value (in which case the current bank number is assumed). The hex prefix symbol ($) should not be entered. The range must all be within the same bank. If the ending range value has a bank number different from the beginning bank number, the ending bank number is ignored.

If you have entered a display range with a large number of values and wish to interrupt the display, you can enter a CONTROL-X to stop the display. A CONTROL-S will temporarily freeze the display until another key is pressed.

The behavior of the memory display function on the IIGS monitor parallels that of the Apple IIe and IIc except for the addition of the bank address value and the display of 16 values in 80-column mode. The ASCII display was added in the Apple IIc and later Apple IIe monitors.

The V (for verify) command determines if the contents of two different memory ranges are the same. Its form is

```
{Address 1 Start}{<Address 2 Start}.{Address 2 End}V
```

This command compares the values in the range specified by Address 2 Start and Address 2 End with the correlative values in the range beginning with Address 1 Start.

If the two ranges have the same values, the monitor prompt (*) value returns without any other output. If there are differences between the two ranges, the locations with different values are displayed as {Address 1 Location}-{Address 1 Value} ({Address 2 Value}).

Assume that the following command is given:

```
*E0/3456<E1/2356.E1/2456V
```

and the values in the two ranges are identical except that E0/3458 contains a 4F while E1/2358 contains a 3C. The result of the command would be

```
*E0/3458-4F (3C)
```

The V command displays the all nonmatching locations.

The V command is identical to the V command on the Apple IIe and IIc except for the bank part of the address.

A close relative to the verify command is the P (for pattern) command, which determines if a specified pattern is present in a given range of memory. The pattern can be up to 236 bytes long and consist of either hexadecimal numbers, literal ASCII, or flipped ASCII. If the pattern is not found, the computer returns you to the monitor prompt (*) without any message. If the pattern is found, each starting address for the pattern is displayed on the screen. The format for the command is

```
\{pattern}\{range start}.{range.end}P
```

The search range is restricted to a single bank.

Assume you want to determine if the pattern 49 49 47 53 (which is the ASCII code for "IIGS") is in bank $01 of your IIGS. To do this you would enter the command

```
\49 49 47 53\01/0000.FFFFP
```

or you could enter the equivalent command

```
\"IIGS"\01/0000.FFFFP
```

If the pattern exists starting at 01/279C and at 01/342D, the monitor response to this command is

```
*01/279C
*01/342D
```

On the later Apple IIe and IIc the pattern command is known as the S (for search) command. It is restricted to a 2-byte hexadecimal value that is always flipped. The command is not available on the earlier models of the Apple IIe and IIc.

The contents of memory on the IIGS, as on most computers, can be interpreted in several different ways. It can be considered a number, an ASCII character, or a part of a program. The display command (discussed previously) shows the alternative interpretation of the contents of each memory location as a number and as an ASCII character. The L (for list) command interprets memory contents as part of a machine-language program.

The process of taking an assembly-language source listing and converting it to a machine-language code is called *assembly.* The process of taking machine-language code and converting it to an assembly-language source listing is called *disassembly.*

The L command in the IIGS system monitor takes the contents of memory beginning at the location you specify and processes enough bytes to produce sufficient assembly-language lines to fill the current window. Each line of disassembly is up to 40 characters across, and the disassembly display consists of a header line showing the machine state, a blank separator line, up to 20 lines of disassembly, another blank separator, and the monitor prompt character at the bottom of the screen (see Figure 7-2). If the screen window is less than 24 lines, the number of lines of disassembly listing is decreased accordingly.

Each line of the main disassembly consists of three parts (see Figure 7-3). The address consists of a bank number separated from the address by a slash (/). A colon and a space follow the address. Next comes the

Machine state	0=m 0=x 1=LC bank (0/1)
Separator	
Disassembly listing	FF/3C90:04D0 TSB D0 (19 more lines go here)
Separator	
Monitor prompt	*

Figure 7-2
Disassembly screen display

FF/3C94:	30 A2	BMI 3C38	(−5E)
Address	*Machine language code*	*Disassembled code*	*Branch offset (if applicable)*

Figure 7-3
Disassembled line

machine-language code that is from 1 to 4 hexadecimal bytes with a space between each byte. The disassembled source code, starting in column 16, consists of an operation code and, where applicable, an operand. The op codes and operands follow standard 65816 format with the following exceptions:

□ No $ prefix is used to denote hexadecimal values. All values are presumed to be hexadecimal values.

- Following a branch instruction is the amount of the offset in parentheses.
- The ProDOS/8 machine-language interface call (which is a JSR $BF00 command when in bank zero) is displayed on three lines as follows, only when the instruction is found in bank zero:

JSR BF00	ProDOS/8 MLI call
00	Command number
1234	Pointer to parameter table

- The ProDOS/16 machine-language interface call (which is a JSL $E100A8 from any bank) is displayed on three lines as follows:

JSL E100A8	ProDOS/16 MLI call
0456	Command word
005FD321	Double-word pointer to parameter table

A complete list of 65816 op code and addressing mode formats appears in Appendix B.

The L command differs from the L command in the Apple IIe and IIc monitor in the following respects:

- The bank number is part of the address.
- A colon follows the address rather than a dash.
- Up to 4 bytes per command are used (10 if the ProDOS/16 call is involved).
- The full 65816 command set is supported.
- The offset follows branch locations.
- There is no $ hexadecimal prefix.
- Shorter vertical text windows are automatically accommodated.
- The ProDOS/8 and ProDOS/16 MLI calls are specially displayed.

It is important to be able to check the values in the various 65816 registers as well as the values in the memory locations of the IIGS. The examine registers command, CONTROL-E, displays the contents of all the 65816 registers as well as several IIGS softswitch settings. The display occupies one screen line in 80-column mode and two lines in 40-column mode. Figure 7-4 shows how the registers are displayed in 80-column mode; the registers and registers' widths shown are the same in both emulation and native mode and with both 8- and 16-bit accumulator and index registers.

```
A=BF6F X=86FF Y=0000 S=86FB D=0000 P=81 B=00 K=00 M=0C Q=80 L=1 m=0 x=0 e=0
```

Figure 7-4
Display of registers in 80-column mode

The meaning of the register labels is given in Table 7-3. Note that the program counter is not displayed by the examine command.

The examine command in the Apple IIe and IIc monitor displays only the registers available on the 6502/65C02—namely, A, X, Y, P, and S. Each register is only 8 bits wide. The command also permits changing the values in the registers. A discussion of how to change the 65816 registers using the IIGS monitor appears in the next section.

Label	Register
A	Accumulator
B	Data bank register
D	Direct register
e	Emulation bit
K	Program bank register
L	Language card bank
M	Machine state
m	Memory width bit
P	Processor status register
Q	Quagmire state
S	Stack pointer
X	X register
x	Index register width bit
Y	Y register

Table 7-3
Register Labels Used by CONTROL-E Command

As discussed in Chapter 3, the IIGS has a built-in real-time clock. The display time (=T) command displays the current system date and time as follows:

Time = MM/DD/YY HH:MM:SS AM

Since the Apple IIe and IIc do not have a built-in real-time clock, there is no Apple IIe or IIc monitor command relating to time.

Modifying Memory

Memory modification commands, which allow you to change the values in memory locations or 65816 registers, are a second major category of commands.

Like the main memory examination command, the main memory modification command uses the concept of the last opened location, also known as the next changeable location. Entering a colon followed by values will insert those values in the IIGS's memory beginning with the next changeable location. The values may be either hexadecimal, flipped hexadecimal, literal ASCII, or flipped ASCII. If multiple values are to be entered, they should be separated by spaces. Multiple flipped hexadecimal or ASCII can be entered if each 4 bytes are separated by a space.

If you wish to enter values at a location other than the next changeable location, or if you do not know what the next changeable location is, you can specify a starting location for the insertion of values. To do this, you enter an address in the standard IIGS monitor format, a colon, and the values to be entered.

Another way to change memory values is by the M (for move) command. Technically speaking, this command performs not a move but a copy. A move deletes the existing data after it transfers it to a new location. A copy leaves the data in the old location as well as transferring it to the new location. This distinction is quite fuzzy in the 65816 world because the 65816 MVN and MVP commands, which copy blocks of memory, are called move commands by the 65816 literature.

The format of the move command is

```
{destination.start}<{source.start}.{source.end}M
```

When given this command, the monitor takes the byte at source.start and copies it to destination.start. It then takes the next higher byte from the source block and copies it to the next location in the destination block, continuing until it reaches source.end.

A useful method of remembering where the source and the destination addresses go in the command is to think of the < as an arrowhead pointing to the direction of movement of the values.

The move command can be used to place a repeating pattern in memory. To do this, place the pattern in memory, using the store (:) command, beginning with the first location in which the pattern is to appear. Issue the move command using the location in which the next repetition of the pattern is to appear as the destination.start. The place where you put the start of the pattern is the source.start address. To compute the source.end location, multiply the number of bytes in the pattern by the number of times you wish the pattern to repeat less one, subtract one, and add the result to the destination.start location.

By way of illustration, to place the 4-byte pattern 02 ED 4F 37 into memory beginning at location 01/3459 for a total of eight times, you would do the following:

1. Enter

   ```
   *10/3459:374FED02
   ```

   (Place bytes in memory. Multibyte hexadecimal input is flipped.)

2. Compute values as follows:

   Destination.start = 01/345D (3459 + 4)
   Source.start = 01/3459
   Source.end = 01/3474 (7 repetitions (8−1) times 4 bytes = \$1C bytes \$1C − 1 = 1B. \$345D + 1B = 3474)

3. Then enter

   ```
   *01/345D<3459.3474M
   ```

The move command can both copy memory from one location to another and create a repeating pattern in memory. Where the repeating pattern consists of a single byte value, there is another method of placing that byte in memory. The Z (for zap) command places a 1-byte value throughout a specified memory block. The format of the command is

```
{val}<{block.start}.{block.end}Z
```

The value in any of the 65816 registers may be modified by using the appropriate monitor command. Other items that can be changed through similar commands include some of the IIGS softswitches, memory shadowing, machine speed, language card bank, ASCII filter mask, and three status registers bits—m (accumulator/memory width), x (index register width), and e (emulation or native mode switch). The basic format of these commands is

```
{val}={register.symbol}
```

Table 7-4 gives a listing of the various register symbols and indicates for each whether the value should be 1 or 2 bytes.

As mentioned, the setting of certain softswitch state indicators, in addition to the 65816 registers, can be modified. The machine state is a 1-byte value that indicates the state of eight different IIGS softswitches. The

Label	Register
A	Accumulator (1 or 2 bytes)
B	Data bank register (1 byte)
D	Direct register (2 bytes)
e	Emulation bit (0 or 1)
K	Program bank register (1 byte)
L	Language card bank (0 or 1)
M	Machine state (1 byte)
m	Memory width bit (0 or 1)
P	Processor status register (1 byte)
Q	Quagmire state (1 byte)
S	Stack pointer (1 or 2 bytes)
X	X register (1 or 2 bytes)
x	Index register width bit (0 or 1)
Y	Y register (1 or 2 bytes)

Table 7-4

Labels Used to Set Various Registers

purpose of each bit is shown in Table 7-5. The machine state value is modified by

```
{val}=M
```

The softswitch determining which of the two 4K language card or D000 RAM banks are active is controlled by the L or language card bank value. A 0 indicates the first bank (sometimes called bank zero and sometimes called bank one) is active. A 1 indicates the second bank (sometimes called bank one and sometimes called bank two) is active. See Chapter 5 for a discussion of the IIGS RAM including bank-switched RAM. (Note that when used in this context, *bank* refers to a 4K range of memory mapped to $E0/D000 or $E1/D000 through $DFFF. It does not mean a 64K range of memory that is the common usage of bank in 65816 terminology.) The language card state is set by

```
{value}=L
```

Value should be either 0 or 1. If not, then it takes the value of the least significant bit of that value.

The quagmire state, discussed in Chapter 5, can be changed by the following command:

```
{val}=Q
```

Bit #	Meaning
0	INTXCROM active if set
1	Alternate ROMBANK active if set
2	Language card bank 2 active if set
3	RDLCROM active (for read only) if set
4	RAMWRT active if set
5	RAMRD active if set
6	Page 2 active if set
7	Alternative zero page active if set

Table 7-5

Meaning of Bits in Machine-State Byte

The purpose of the 1-byte ASCII filter mask was examined earlier in this chapter in the discussion of ASCII input. Its value is changed by

```
{val}=F
```

The status of three processor status register bits can also be individually modified. (The =P command modifies all eight status bits.) The value passed to the command must be either 0 or 1 or it is ignored. The general format of the command is

```
{value}={bit symbol}
```

The symbol used for each bit, and the meaning of that symbol, are given in Table 7-6.

The various registers, machine state, and similar values discussed previously are not immediately changed when the change command is given. The monitor itself requires certain values in the registers and certain machine states. A change in these values could either crash the monitor or cause it to perform erratically. Instead, the change commands modify the values that are stored in certain reserved RAM locations. Apple has not made these locations public. When one of the various monitor run commands is given, these values are placed in the 65816 registers and appropriate changes are made to machine states before control is passed to the called program. These stored values—especially the m and x bits, language card value, quagmire state, and machine state—are also used by the disassembly command and the display memory commands.

Symbol	Meaning
e	Emulation bit in 65816 processor
m	Memory width bit in 65816 processor
x	Index register width bit in 65816 processor

Table 7-6
Meaning of Bit-State Symbols

The various values stored for register and status change can be reset to the standard monitor configuration by the use of the CONTROL-R (for restore) command. This sets the values to those in existence upon entrance to the monitor. These values are listed in Table 7-7.

The setting of the IIGS's real-time clock can be changed either by use of the control panel (see Chapter 3) or by use of the time-setting command from the monitor. The format of the command is

```
=T=mon/day/year hour:minute:second
```

Any delimiter except a single quotation mark may be used between the values entered. The range for the various time values is given in Table 7-8.

The standard cursor shape in the IIGS monitor is a checkerboard in 40-column mode without the 80-column firmware active and a solid

Register	Value
A	0000
B	00
D	0000
e	1
K	00
L	1
M	0C
m	1
P	00
Q	00
S	01F2
X	0000
x	1
Y	0000

Table 7-7
Standard Configuration Given by CONTROL—R Command

Item	Range
Hour	00-23
Minute	00-59
Second	00-59
Month	1-12
Day	1-31
Year	00-99

Table 7-8
Range for Time Command Values

square in either 40- or 80-column mode with the 80-column firmware active. This character can be changed to a character you specify by entering a CONTROL-^ (pressing and holding CONTROL and SHIFT and then pressing the ^ key) followed by the character you wish the cursor to be. To change back to the standard cursor, enter CONTROL-^ followed by the DELETE key.

Running a Routine

The IIGS monitor comes with three related commands that will run a machine-language routine in the computer's memory. These three commands all take the basic form of the starting address of the routine followed by the letter R, G, or X. In all three cases the monitor sets the IIGS environment according to the stored locations of the 65816 registers, softswitches, and memory shadowing.

In the case of the R (for run) command, the monitor performs a jump to the routine via the 65816 JML command. At the end of the routine there should be a jump to the location where control should be passed.

If the command is the G (for go) command, the monitor performs a jump to subroutine via the 65816 JSR command. Because the monitor works as though it were in bank zero (see discussion on shadowing in Chapter 5), the routine called must be in bank zero and end with an RTS (return from subroutine) so that it can return to the monitor in bank zero.

If the command is the X (for eXtended go) command, the monitor performs a jump to subroutine long via the 65816 JSL command. The routine called can be anyplace in memory and should end with an RTL (return from subroutine long) instruction. If the routine is in bank zero and ends with an RTS instruction, it will also work, although it will leave the bank number on the stack (potentially corrupting the stack).

Two other monitor commands perform a run operation similar to that done by the R, G, and X commands, but they do so in a manner that is most useful for program debugging and testing. These are the step and trace commands. The command consists of the starting address of the routine to be tested followed by either an S (for step) or a T (for trace).

The step and trace commands are not implemented in ROM on the IIGS. Instead, they provide a hook for your own step or trace routine.

Another way to run a program you have created is to use the CONTROL-Y or user command. When you press CONTROL-Y, the IIGS monitor begins to execute a program beginning at location $00/03F8. Unless you have modified this location, it contains the code for a JMP $FF65.

The monitor only reserves the 3 bytes from $00/03F8-03FA to contain instructions for the user command. Memory locations beginning at $00/03FB are used for other purposes. Obviously you are not expected to write an assembly-language routine in just 3 bytes. Rather, you store a jump to your actual program, start at that location, and store your actual program elsewhere.

For example, assume you want to have a program that prints the word "IIGS" on the screen every time you press CONTROL-Y. Assume that the program will be placed into memory starting at location $00/0300 using the following command:

```
*00/0300:..........
```

You then need to place the code for the JMP $0300 instruction (4C 00 03) at location $00/03F8 with the following command:

```
*00/03F8:03004C
```

or its equivalent, unflipped format:

```
*00/03F8:4C 00 03
```

After that, each time you press CONTROL-Y the monitor will jump to your routine, which will print the word "IIGS" and then return control to the monitor.

The final program call command in the IIGS monitor is the U (for utility) command. This permits you to call a function in a tool, pass parameters to the tool function, and receive parameters back from the tool function. Its format is

```
\{parameter bytes to function) {parameter bytes from function)
{parameter byte 1} ... {parameter byte n) {function #} {tool #}\U
```

The theories and operations of tools are discussed in Chapter 2. A list of available tool numbers and function numbers, the parameters passed to and from the function, and the size of each parameter is given in the chapters discussing each tool set.

When the U command is given, the monitor places the various parameters onto the stack in the order given in the command (which must be in the same order required by the function). Each multibyte parameter must be entered as separate single bytes or single ASCII characters. A 4-byte address is entered as 4 separate bytes beginning with the null byte (00) space holder as the highest byte, followed by bank number, high byte of 16-bit address, and low byte of 16-bit address.

Note that each value (parameter bytes to or from function, parameter bytes, and function/tool number) given in the U command must be separated from other values by a space.

Following the return from the utility call, the error code returned by the tool function in the accumulator is printed together with the parameters returned by the tool function. The format is

```
Tool error-> ####
```

If the error code is $0000, the tool call was successful. If the error code is $000F or less, the bytes pushed on the stack will be displayed. If the error code is greater than $000F, no parameters will be displayed because none is left on the stack. Lists of tool error codes and their meanings are given in chapters that discuss the individual tool sets.

Assume you are in the monitor and want to move a 200-byte block of memory using the Memory Manager BlockMove routine. This routine, discussed in Chapter 5, requires the following inputs:

□ Source	long word pointer	4 bytes
□ Destination	long word pointer	4 bytes
□ Count	long word value	4 bytes

The total bytes in the input parameters are 12, and no output parameter bytes are generated. The tool set number of the Memory Manager is $02 and the function number is $2B. This results in the entry of the following values:

Parameter bytes to function	0C
Parameter bytes from function	00
Source parameter ($00013410)	00
	01
	34
	10
Destination parameter ($00006429)	00
	00
	64
	29
Count (in hexadecimal) (200 = $C8)	00
	00
	00
	C8
Function number	2B
Tool number	02

To perform this routine, enter the following while in the monitor:

```
\0C 00 00 01 34 10 00 00 64 29 00 00 00 C8 2B 02\U
```

Base Conversion and Computation Commands

The IIGS monitor comes with a built-in decimal-to-hexadecimal and hexadecimal-to-decimal converter. It will convert up to an eight-digit hexadecimal number to its signed and unsigned decimal equivalents (which differ only for negative numbers) and will convert up to a ten-digit signed or unsigned decimal number into its hexadecimal equivalent.

Number conversion represents an exception to the IIGS monitor treatment of flipping multiple byte values when entered. Thus entering the value $1DED will result in the conversion of the value $1DED to decimal 7661, and not the conversion of the flipped value $ED1D (decimal 60701 / −4835).

The format for converting from hexadecimal to decimal is

```
{hexadecimal value}=
```

The monitor will respond, beginning on the next line, with

```
Decimal -> unsigned decimal value (signed decimal value)
```

The format for converting from decimal to hexadecimal is

```
= {signed or unsigned decimal value}
```

The monitor will respond, beginning on the next line, with

```
${hexadecimal value}
```

Note that this is one of the few cases in which the IIGS monitor uses the hexadecimal prefix $ to indicate a hexadecimal value.

Base conversion commands are not available in the Apple IIe and IIc monitors.

The IIGS monitor will perform addition, subtraction, multiplication, and division on values up to 32 bits (4 bytes) in length. The input and results are all treated as unsigned values. The result in addition and subtraction is expressed as a 32-bit value. The multiplication result is expressed as a 64-bit product. The division result is expressed as a 32-bit remainder (prefixed by an "R->") followed by a 32-bit quotient (prefixed by a "Q->"). Any bank information is ignored such that 01/1234+03/2366 results in a sum of 359A.

The symbols used for math functions are + (addition), − (subtraction), * (multiplication), and _ (division). The result is printed on the next line prefixed by a ->. Several sample arithmetic computation samples are shown in Figure 7-5.

The Apple IIc and IIe monitors permit 1-byte (8-bit) unsigned addition and subtraction only.

```
*12ED3456+43DE
-> $12ED7834

*345D2E3-43BF
-> $034196E5

*38D214*34BBBFE
-> $0000BB4581B10BD8

*93612DEF_34DE
R-> $00002E3F Q-> $0002C9A8
```

Figure 7-5
Sample arithmetic computations

Miscellaneous Commands

On system boot, the IIGS monitor is set to expect input from the keyboard through the hardware directly, through the KEYIN routine, or through the event manager (if it is active) and to send output to the video-display screen.

If you want output sent to another device, you must redirect output to that device. The monitor CONTROL-P (for print) command performs this function. It takes the form

```
*{Slot #}Control-P
```

Following this command, all output will be directed either to the port configured as slot # (by means of the Control Panel) or through the peripheral card in slot #.

Redirecting input is similar, except that it uses the CONTROL-K (for keyboard) command. The syntax and effect are the same.

To send output to the built-in 80-column IIGS display, assuming it (as opposed to whatever card is plugged into slot 3) has been set as active by means of the Control Panel, use the following command:

```
3<Control-P>
```

Do not use 0<CONTROL-P> to return to normal 40-column video from 80-column video. That command disconnects the enhanced 80-column firmware but leaves some of the softswitches displaying 80 columns. The correct method to disable 80-column video from the keyboard is

```
<Escape><Control-Q>
```

The CONTROL-P and CONTROL-K commands work by changing what is known as the *input* and *output link* locations. Whenever a character is to be input, the IIGS monitor calls RDKEY (at $FF/FD0C), which performs a JMP indirect to location $00/0038. That location, on bootup, contains the address of the KEYIN routine ($FF/FD1B) shadowed to bank $00. When a CONTROL-K command is executed, the monitor substitutes the entry location for the firmware associated with the slot number ($Cs00) for the previous address in $00/0038-39. Location $00/0038 is known as KSWL (for Keyboard SWitch Low byte) and $00/0039 is known as KSWH (for Keyboard SWitch High byte).

With output and the CONTROL-P command, the same theory applies except that the output routine is known as COUT (Character OUTput) located at $FF/FDED. The indirect jump address location is at $00/0036-37 and is known as CSWL and CSWH (Character SWitch Low and High). It is set at bootup to point to the routine called COUT1 (Character OUTput 1), located at $FF/FDF0, and points to the routine called BASICOUT, located at $FF/C307, when the 80-column firmware is active.

The keyboard switch also is known as the input link or hook. The character switch also is known as the output link or hook.

The CONTROL-P and CONTROL-K routines are basically unchanged from the Apple IIe and IIc monitors.

Two monitor commands are used to switch the text video display between normal (with a monochrome monitor—white, green, or amber text on a black background) and inverse (with a monochrome monitor—black text on a white, green, or amber background) modes. The N command makes subsequent display in normal mode, and the I command makes subsequent display in inverse mode.

If you are using a color RGB monitor (which permits the use of color text and background), the I command changes the display so that the background color becomes the text color and the text color becomes the background color.

The N command is also used to aid in the placing of multiple commands on a single line. Multiple monitor commands can be placed on a single line subject to the following rules:

- □ The total number of characters on the line cannot exceed 254.
- □ Commands must be separated by spaces, except for adjacent single-letter commands.
- □ The values in a store (:) command must be followed by a letter command before another address is entered.

The N command is used to separate the store command from subsequent address commands because it is a letter command. But, if video display is already normal, the command will have no effect except to act as the needed separator.

At bootup in IIGS mode, the display is set to text display using the text page. The text displayed is the same as though Text Page 1 was being used. Setting various softswitches can result in the current display screen being either another text page, or a graphics page in graphics mode. To switch the screen display back to Text Page 1 while in the monitor, you enter the CONTROL-T (for text) command.

This command does not exist on the Apple IIe or Apple IIc monitor.

Leaving the Monitor

Three built-in monitor commands provide a means to leave the monitor and enter either Applesoft BASIC or the current operating system.

The Q (for quit) command performs a jump to the operating system (normally ProDOS/16) warm-start entry vector at memory location \$00/03D0. This is the same as the \$3D0G command used in the Apple IIe and IIc monitors. The advantages to the Q command are the ease of remembering it and the saving of three keystrokes.

To enter Applesoft BASIC without an active disk operating system, you can type CONTROL-B to jump to the cold-start entry location (equivalent to a \$FF/E000G), or type CONTROL-C to jump to the warm-start entry location (equivalent to a \$FF/E003G). A warm start reenters Applesoft in such a way that any of the programs and variables that were present when you exited are still intact (unless they have been changed in the monitor). A cold start clears any program from memory and initializes all variables to 0 or the null string. In both cases the hooks connecting any disk operating system to Applesoft are disconnected when BASIC is started or restarted.

The CONTROL-B and CONTROL-C commands are present in the Apple IIe and IIc monitors.

THE MINI-ASSEMBLER

A series of bytes instructing the 65816 in the IIGS to perform a function or group of functions is known as a *program.* The 65816, like all microprocessors, understands only a limited number of commands, each of which is represented by a hexadecimal byte, known as the *operation code* (op code). In many cases the op code is followed by 1 to 3 bytes of addressing information, known as the *operand.*

These programs, known as *machine-language code,* can be difficult and tedious to enter into the memory of the IIGS. The solution is to invent a programming language that is more like English, and to create a program that can translate this language into the machine code the 65816 needs.

The programming language that is closest to machine code is known as *assembly language,* and the program that translates assembly language code into machine-language code is known as an *assembler.*

For many assembly-language programming purposes a full-featured assembler—which supports labels, conditional assembly, and macros—is desirable or even essential. The IIGS Programmer's Workshop Assembler, derived from the Orca/M Assembler from Byte Works, is perhaps the most powerful and full-featured of all the 65816 assemblers. It also requires an investment of both money and time to learn, and it must be booted from disk to use.

Built into the IIGS monitor, however, is a Mini-Assembler. This program does not support labels, computation in the operands, conditional assembly, or macros. It does, however, provide a quick method of entering simple programs. Steve Wozniak is reputed to have written Integer BASIC for the original Apple II using just the Mini-Assembler for that machine.

To enter the Mini-Assembler you merely press the EXCLAMATION key (SHIFT-1) and the RETURN key. This changes the prompt from the monitor prompt (*) to the Mini-Assembler prompt (!). You can then begin to enter assembly-language instructions. As you enter each instruction and press the RETURN key, you get an instant translation of the instruction and an indication of any errors in the code.

The first instruction entered in the Mini-Assembler must be preceded by an address and a colon, followed by the op code and the operand. See Appendix D for a list of valid op codes, an indication of the acceptable addressing modes for each, and the proper format for each type of addressing mode. All subsequent instructions need only be preceded by a space.

After you press RETURN to confirm an instruction entry, the Mini-Assembler replaces what you typed in with a display of the address at which the instruction was placed, a colon and a space as a separator, the machine-language bytes representing the instruction, and the assembly-language instruction. The display is the same as that produced by the disassembler discussed earlier in this chapter.

Errors in entry are flagged by a beep sound and a redisplay of the erroneous input line with a caret (^) under the source of the error (see Figure 7-6). Common errors include misspelled op codes, incorrectly formatted operands, no space before an instruction line without an address, or a branch that is out of the permissible range for the branch (+/− 127 bytes) or branch long (+/− 32767 bytes) instruction.

Direct value entry is permitted in the Mini-Assembler, either as flipped hexadecimal values of up to eight values (prefix the values with a : as the character in column 1) or as unflipped ASCII text (prefix the values with a " as the character in column 1). Any ASCII text value is ANDed with the ASCII filter before being placed into memory.

```
! 01/8000:LAD #3456
```

Figure 7-6

Mini-Assembler errors

Assume you want to enter a short simple program that prints the letter A using the COUT routine. The code for this program, on bank zero, is

```
COUT    EQU     $FDED   ;Shadowed on bank 0
        SEP     #$30    ;8-bit mode
        LDA     #'A
        JSR     COUT
        RTS
```

When you enter this in the IIGS using the Mini-Assembler, you must first make two changes—namely, substitute JSR $FDED for JSR COUT because the Mini-Assembler does not support labels, and remove the comments because they are not allowed by the Mini-Assembler. The following shows lines as entered by you and as changed by the Mini-Assembler:

```
!00/0300:SEP #$30
```

becomes

```
*00/0300: E2 30        SEP #30
```

```
! LDA #'A
```

becomes

```
00/0302: A9 C1         LDA #C1
```

```
! JSR $FDED
```

becomes

```
00/0304: 20 ED FD      JSR FDED
```

```
! RTS
```

becomes

```
00/0307: 60            RTS
```

One area of ambiguity with 65816 assemblers is the immediate addressing mode. (This ambiguity does not exit with the REP and SEP commands, which always take an 8-bit immediate value, and with the PEA command, which always takes a 16-bit immediate value.) In this mode, if the particular register being accessed is in 8-bit mode (m or x bit = 1), an 8-bit or 1-byte value is needed by the program. If the register is in 16-bit mode (m or x bit = 0), a 16-bit (2 bytes or one word) value is needed.

Most 65816 assemblers use a pseudo op code assembler instruction to tell the assembler whether it is in 8- or 16-bit mode. A few use a special form of the direct addressing mode (such as ## instead of #) to indicate 16-bit immediate mode values. The Mini-Assembler uses neither form but expects you to place properly either an 8- or 16-bit value in the immediate mode operand. If you place a 16-bit value in the operand, a 16-bit operand will be generated. But if the 65816 is in 8-bit mode when the program is run, the program won't run properly.

The use of the hexadecimal prefix $ is optional when using the Mini-Assembler (in the operand field) because all values, except ASCII text, are considered to be hexadecimal. You can enter the Mini-Assembler and give it the first command in one line by typing an exclamation (!) followed immediately by the first address location, a colon, and the first op code and operand.

Programmers experienced with the 6502 or 65C02 should be aware of a change in handling of the BRK op code by both the 65816 and the Mini-Assembler. The 65816 treats the BRK instruction (as well as the related COP command) as a 2-byte instruction and the Mini-Assembler will treat a BRK instruction without a 1-byte operand as an error.

The later Apple IIe and 32K ROM IIc monitors have a Mini-Assembler that only accepts 6502 codes (not 65C02). It lacks the direct hexadecimal and ASCII input modes and permits only hexadecimal values, not ASCII, as part of the operand.

DIAGNOSTIC TESTS

The Apple IIGS, like the Apple IIe and the 32K ROM Apple IIc, has a series of diagnostic tests built in as part of its ROM. These tests are performed whenever the user holds the APPLE/COMMAND and the OPTION keys down (or the equivalent joystick buttons 0 and 1) either on power up or when the user also presses CONTROL and RESET. The tests are actually a subset of the various tests performed during the manufacturing process of the IIGS.

A total of 11 different tests are conducted. The time for running the entire series is 47 seconds. These tests, their test number, and the ROM location where each test is found are listed in Table 7-9.

Number	Test Name	Memory Location of Routine
1	ROM checksum	$FF/7CAE
2	RAM 1—Moving Inversions	$FF/776C
3	Softswitches and status reg.	$FF/7A58
4	RAM addressing	$FF/7F54
5	Speed (FPI)	$FF/7AF7
6	Serial tests	$FF/7902
7	Clock	$FF/7CFA
8	BatteryRAM	$FF/7DD3
9	Apple Desk Bus	$FF/7EC9
A	Shadow register	$FF/7D5F
B	Interrupts	$FF/7B3C

Table 7-9
Diagnostic Test

Just before each test is run, its test number is displayed on the screen as a long integer value. The first byte is the test number and the remainder of this value is zero. Because of the nature of the tests, and the length of time some of them take, the only visible test numbers displayed are tests 1, 4, 6, 7, 8, 9, and B. Tests 1 and 7 display for only a short time.

At the successful conclusion of the tests the speaker sounds a 1-KHz tone for 1 second and displays the phrase "System Good" at the bottom of the screen. If a test fails, the speaker sounds a 6-KHz tone for 1 second, displays the phrase "System Bad" on the bottom of the screen with a long integer value. This value is also displayed on the upper portion of the screen. The reason for displaying the error value twice is to permit display of the value even when part of the RAM screen display area is bad.

The routines also send the error value, preceded by a prompt (*) to the printer port (serial port 1), ignoring any user setting and using the default settings except that the baud rate is 1200 baud. This alternate output of the error value is provided in case the entire video display is not working.

The first byte of the error code is the test number. The remaining portion of the value is the error type. The various error codes that can occur with each test are discussed with that test. Note that an error code that indicates test number $FF shows a likely problem with the Mega II chip. That test number is only used during manufacturing testing.

The first test is the ROM checksum. This routine checks the contents of the system ROM (banks $FE-FF), performing an exclusive OR with each byte. It then compares this value with the specified value for the checksum. In addition to printing the error number and the faulty checksum error (as the second byte of error code), it prints "RM" (for ROM) at the top of the screen. This latter feature occurs because there is a good chance of a system crash occurring before the printing of the error code in the event of a ROM checksum error.

The second and longest test is the RAM-1 or Moving Inversions test, which is characterized by a series of high-resolution and super-high-resolution patterns displayed on the screen. It checks banks $00, $01, $E0, and $E1. In each bank it tests pages 0-4 without destroying the contents of those pages and the remaining pages by writing over the previous contents. If it finds an error, it displays the address of the faulty RAM as the second and third bytes of the error code.

The third test checks the softswitches by setting them, testing them, and then clearing them and testing them. The equivalent bits in the status register for eight of these softswitches are also tested. The second byte of the error code indicates the status register bit, if any. The third byte of the error code indicates the softswitch read address.

The fourth test checks the unique addressing capability of the RAM both within a bank and between banks. The second byte of the error code shows the faulty bank number, and the third byte indicates the faulty bit.

The fifth test determines if the Fast Processor Interface (FPI) is functioning correctly. It compares the speed of the video counters to the system speed in both fast and normal speed modes. It ensures that the FPI causes the system to function in normal speed when accessing the Mega II chip. The second byte is 1 if the system is stuck in normal speed and 2 if the system is stuck in fast speed.

The sixth test verifies the SCC registers for read and write functions and also performs an internal loop back test. The value of the second byte of the error code changes depending on the type of error. The various settings of this byte are given in Table 7-10.

The seventh test performs a read/write test on the long-word clock register. It saves the previous value of the clock and restores it following

Number	Meaning
1	Register read/write error
4	Transmit buffer empty status
5	Transmit buffer empty failure
6	All sent status failure
7	Receive character available
8	Bad data

Table 7-10
Serial Test Error Types

the test. The setting of the clock loses about one second during this test. The only use made of the lower three bytes of the error code is to set the lowest byte to 1 if a fatal error occurred during the test, requiring abandonment of the test.

The eighth test checks the 256 bytes Battery RAM. It first checks for address uniqueness and then performs a pattern test. The values in the BatteryRAM are saved and restored following the test. If an address uniqueness error occurs, the second byte of the error code is set to 1 and the third byte is set to the faulty address. If a pattern test error occurs, the second byte of the error code is set to 2, the third byte is set to the pattern value, and the fourth byte is set to the fault address.

The ninth test performs a checksum on the Apple Desk Bus ROM. The second and third bytes of the error code show the bad checksum value determined, the fourth byte, if set to 1, indicates no checksum was computed because of a fatal error.

The tenth test verifies that the shadow register is functioning.

The eleventh test verifies that the Mega II and Video Graphics Controller chip are able to generate the required interrupts. The second byte of the error code indicates the type of interrupt that could not be generated. The meaning of this value is shown in Table 7-11.

When running the diagnostic tests, you should be careful not to interrupt the running of the tests (by pressing CONTROL-RESET) after the RAM-1 or Moving Inversions test. To do so could result in a corrupted BatteryRAM (including the clock values).

Number	Meaning
1	VBL interrupt timeout
2	VBL IRQ status failed
3	1/4 second interrupt
4	1/4 second interrupt
6	VGC IRQ
7	Scan line

Table 7-11

Interrupt Test Error Types

Individual diagnostic routines can be individually called by performing a JSL to their address. Upon return from the routine the carry bit is clear (=0) if there was no error, and the carry bit is set (=1) if there is an error. In the event of an error, the IIGS uses five RAM locations at $00/0315-0319 to store the applicable error codes. Your calling routine should be sure to clear these locations before calling the particular diagnostic routine.

When calling any of these routines, the 65816 should be in native mode (e=0) but with 8-bit wide memory, accumulator, and index registers (m=1 and x=1). The data bank register should be set to $00. On exit the 65816 will be in native mode (e=0). The values of the m and x bits and of the DBR are unknown. The tests, except for the RAM tests, use memory locations $00/0000-1FFF.

PART III

Output: Visual and Aural

CHAPTER 8

Text Display

DISPLAY MODES

The Apple IIGS provides a variety of methods for exhibiting information on the video display screen. The primary display mode of the IIGS is super-resolution graphics, which has either 320 or 640 pixels across by 200 pixels down, and has up to 256 colors out of a total palette of 4096 colors. The technical details of super-resolution graphics are given in Chapter 9, and Chapters 10 to 13 offer information about the Quickdraw II tool set designed for using this display mode.

This chapter discusses the Apple IIGS's 8-bit Apple II text display mode, which also is found on earlier Apple II computers. The 8-bit Apple II graphics display modes—low-resolution graphics (48 × 40 in 16 colors), high-resolution (or hi-res) graphics (280 × 192 in limited 6 colors), and double-high-resolution graphics (280 × 192 in full 16 colors or 560 × 192 in black and white)—are discussed in the Apple IIe *Technical Reference Manual* and the Apple IIc *Technical Reference Manual.* The double-high-resolution graphics memory area overlays the super-resolution graphics display screen memory area in bank $E1 (see Chapter 5).

The Apple IIGS, like every Apple II before it, is capable of displaying what is known as 40-column text—up to 40 characters per line across the screen with 24 lines. The IIGS also supports 80-column text with up to 80 characters per line. This mode of text display is also supported in the Apple IIe with an 80-column display card and in the Apple IIc. On both the IIGS and the IIc this 80-column display is completely built into the machine.

All the display modes on the Apple IIGS use *memory-mapped video.* That is, the values stored in certain locations of the IIGS's memory directly affect what is displayed on the screen. Replacing a value in one of these "video memory" areas results in a change in the video display.

In 40-column display mode, the area of memory assigned for text display is found in $E0/0400-07FF. If memory shadowing is enabled, this memory is shadowed at $00/0400-07FF. The values for text display are, by and large, the ASCII code for the particular characters.

The text display memory is not used consecutively. You cannot start at the beginning of $E0/0400 and find the value for each text character across and down the screen. The 40 characters in each line do appear consecutively, although the place each line begins is not consecutive. Table 8-1 gives the line number for each of the 24 lines and the beginning location of that line in the video display memory. That location and the next 39 bytes contain the text characters for that line.

A careful checking of Table 8-1 will show that not all the memory from $E0/0400-07FF is given to video display. These "unused" memory locations are known as *screen holes.* They are traditionally reserved as

Starting Location		
Line Number	**Hex**	**Decimal**
0	$0400	1024
1	$0480	1152
2	$0500	1280
3	$0580	1408
4	$0600	1536
5	$0680	1664
6	$0700	1792
7	$0780	1920
8	$0428	1064
9	$04A8	1192
10	$0528	1320
11	$05A8	1448
12	$0628	1576
13	$06A8	1704
14	$0728	1832
15	$07A8	1960
16	$0450	1104
17	$04D0	1232
18	$0550	1360
19	$05D0	1488
20	$0650	1616
21	$06D0	1744
22	$0750	1872
23	$07D0	2000

Table 8-1

Starting Memory Location of Each Text Line

scratchpad locations for peripheral cards in each of the expansion slots. Table 8-2 lists the various screen holes and the use made of each.

Displaying text in 80 columns on the IIGS is similar to 40-column text display. The same memory in bank $E0 is required and, in addition, memory in bank $E1 from $0400-07FF is also used. The same mapping of screen lines is used in bank $E1 as bank $E0. The zero character in the line (and all even column number characters) is stored in bank $E1, and all the odd column number characters are stored in bank $E0.

Slot	Allocated to Locations							
	$0478	04F8	0578	05F8	0678	06F8	0778	07F8
1	$0479	04F9	0579	05F9	0679	06F9	0779	07F9
2	$047A	04FA	057A	05FA	067A	06FA	077A	07FA
3	$047B	04FB	057B	05FB	067B	06FB	077B	07FB
4	$047C	04FC	057C	05FC	067C	06FC	077C	07FC
5	$047D	04FD	057D	05FD	067D	06FD	077D	07FD
6	$047E	04FE	057E	05FE	067E	06FE	077E	07FE
7	$047F	04FF	057F	05FF	067F	06FF	077F	07FF

Table 8-2
Screen Holes

To determine the exact location of any particular character, divide its column number (with the first column being 0) by 2 (ignoring any remainder). Add this number to the base address for that line in Table 8-1. If the original column number is odd, the character is found in bank $E0. Otherwise the character is found in bank $E1. For example, to find the location of column 55 in line 12, do the following:

55/2 = 27 (dropping the remainder)
Base address for line 12 = $0628
27 (decimal) = $1B
$0628 + 001B = $0643
Column number is odd, bank is $E0
Character address is $E0/0643

Previously we mentioned that the value representation of video display text is basically the ASCII character set. The Apple IIGS actually has two text-character display sets, referred to as the *primary* and *alternative character sets.* These two sets are the same except for the treatment of values $40-7F. Table 8-3 shows the characters displayed for each value using the primary character set. The alternative character set is shown in Table 8-4.

The alternative character set is available only if the built-in 80-column firmware has been activated, as discussed later in this chapter. The actual text display does not necessarily have to be in 80 columns.

The primary character set is capable of displaying the uppercase letters, numbers, and most of the symbols in inverse and flashing mode, as well as the full 96 standard displayable characters in normal mode. The alternative character set is capable of displaying the full 96 standard displayable characters in normal and inverse mode, as well as the special MouseText characters. These latter characters are designed for implementing a human-interface-type program, using the mouse for selection purposes, but on the text screen instead of the graphics screen. Figure 8-1 shows the various MouseText characters and the value associated with each symbol.

Displaying text on the text screen generally requires the use of character device drivers, which are present in the Apple IIGS and which are basically unchanged from the text device drivers in the Apple IIe and IIc. Writing to the text screen, in its simplest form, consists of placing the ASCII code of the character to be displayed in the accumulator and calling the COUT (Character OUTput) routine located at $FF/FDED. This routine uses the output hooks CSWL and CSWH (discussed in Chapter 7) to determine the actual character output routine to use. If the Apple IIGS is in 40-column text mode (that is, the 80-column built-in firmware is not active), the output routine used is located at $FF/FDFO (COUT1). If the 80-column firmware is active, the output routine used is located at $FF/C307 (C3COUT1, sometimes referred to as BASICOUT).

All of these output routines need to be called with the 65816 in emulation mode (and with the direct register set to $0000). This requirement can make it difficult to use text display when running the IIGS with the 65816 in native mode. Accordingly, a tool set is used to make it easier to call the text drivers while the 65816 is in native mode.

TEXTTOOLS

TextTools is a ROM-based tool set ($0C) that takes care of saving the current state of the 65816, switching to emulation mode, switching to bank zero, and calling the appropriate routine. The routines are designed to use any character device driver as long as it either complies with the BASIC or Pascal 1.1 standards or is a RAM-based driver.

Unlike most of the IIGS tool sets, TextTools does not need to be started up by your application. TextTools supports two kinds of output—regular text and error messages—and one kind of input. It also has two masks for

Higher Nibble	0	1	2	3	4	5	6	7	8	9	A	B	C	D	E	F	Format
0	@	A	B	C	D	E	F	G	H	I	J	K	L	M	N	O	Inverse
1	P	Q	R	S	T	U	V	W	X	Y	Z	[	\	]	^	_	Inverse
2		!	"	#	$	%	&	'	(	)	*	+	,	-	.	/	Inverse
3	0	1	2	3	4	5	6	7	8	9	:	;	<	=	>	?	Inverse
4	@	A	B	C	D	E	F	G	H	I	J	K	L	M	N	O	Flashing
5	P	Q	R	S	T	U	V	W	X	Y	Z	[	\	]	^	_	Flashing
6		!	"	#	$	%	&	'	(	)	*	+	,	-	.	/	Flashing
7	0	1	2	3	4	5	6	7	8	9	:	;	<	=	>	?	Flashing
8	@	A	B	C	D	E	F	G	H	I	J	K	L	M	N	O	Normal
9	P	Q	R	S	T	U	V	W	X	Y	Z	[	\	]	^	_	Normal
A		!	"	#	$	%	&	'	(	)	*	+	,	-	.	/	Normal
B	0	1	2	3	4	5	6	7	8	9	:	;	<	=	>	?	Normal
C	@	A	B	C	D	E	F	G	H	I	J	K	L	M	N	O	Normal
D	P	Q	R	S	T	U	V	W	X	Y	Z	[	\	]	^	_	Normal
E	`	a	b	c	d	e	f	g	h	i	j	k	l	m	n	o	Normal
F	p	q	r	s	t	u	v	w	x	y	z	{	¦	}	~		Normal

Table 8-3

Primary Character Set Display

each type of input or output—the AND mask and the OR mask. Each character is ANDed with the appropriate AND mask (to turn off specified bits) and ORed with the appropriate OR mask (to turn on specified bits) before it is input or output. The text tools are set, on bootup, with an AND mask of $FF (no masking) and an OR mask of $80 (set the high bit of each byte). This tool set is also set by default to use BASIC drivers and to expect both the input and output device in Slot 3. This results in the IIGS using the C3COUT character output routine unless modified.

Routines exist for changing the AND or OR mask for input (SetInGlobals), output (SetOutGlobals), and error output (SetErrGlobals). The tool set can also obtain the current value of these masks (GetInGlobals, GetOutGlobals, and GetErrGlobals).

Higher Nibble	0	1	2	3	4	5	6	7	8	9	A	B	C	D	E	F	Format
	Lower Nibble																
0	@	A	B	C	D	E	F	G	H	I	J	K	L	M	N	O	Inverse
1	P	Q	R	S	T	U	V	W	X	Y	Z	[	\	]	^	_	Inverse
2		!	"	#	$	%	&	'	(	)	*	+	,	-	.	/	Inverse
3	0	1	2	3	4	5	6	7	8	9	:	;	<	=	>	?	Inverse
4	(MouseText characters — see Figure 8-1)																
5	(MouseText characters — see Figure 8-1)																
6	`	a	b	c	d	e	f	g	h	i	j	k	l	m	n	o	Inverse
7	p	q	r	s	t	u	v	w	x	y	z	{	¦	}	~		Inverse
8	@	A	B	C	D	E	F	G	H	I	J	K	L	M	N	O	Normal
9	P	Q	R	S	T	U	V	W	X	Y	Z	[	\	]	^	_	Normal
A		!	"	#	$	%	&	'	(	)	*	+	,	-	.	/	Normal
B	0	1	2	3	4	5	6	7	8	9	:	;	<	=	>	?	Normal
C	@	A	B	C	D	E	F	G	H	I	J	K	L	M	N	O	Normal
D	P	Q	R	S	T	U	V	W	X	Y	Z	[	\	]	^		Normal
E	'	a	b	c	d	e	f	g	h	i	j	k	l	m	n	o	Normal
F	p	q	r	s	t	u	v	w	x	y	z	{	¦	}	~		Normal

Table 8-4

Alternative Character Set Display

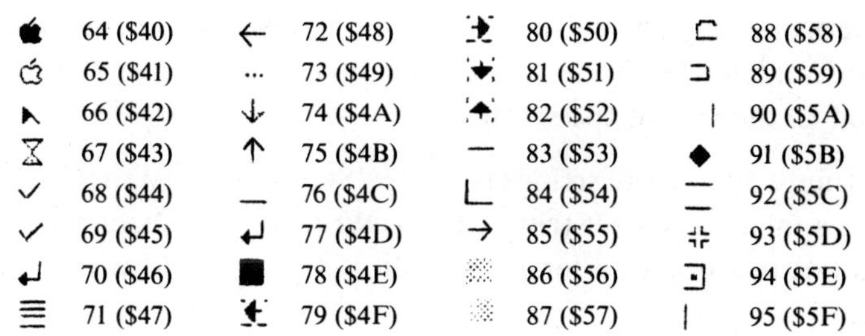

Figure 8-1

Mouse Text characters and symbol values

TextTools makes it easy to change the current input (SetInputDevice), output (SetOutputDevice), or error device (SetErrorDevice). Each of these routines is passed two parameters. The first is a word value that must be between 0 and 2. A value of 0 is used for a BASIC driver, a value of 1 is used for a Pascal driver, and a value of 2 is used for a RAM-based driver. The second parameter is a long-word value that is the slot number for a BASIC- or Pascal-type driver and the initialization entry point for a RAM-based driver.

Routines for obtaining the current set drivers are GetInputDevice (input driver), GetOutputDevice (output driver), and GetErrorDevice (error driver).

The primary text output tool functions come in pairs—one for the standard output device and the other for the error output device. The following are the five pairs:

1. To write a specified character (after processing it with the AND and OR masks), call WriteChar or ErrWriteChar.

2. To write a line (after processing it with the AND and OR masks), call WriteLine or ErrWriteLine. This call expects the character string to be in a specified memory address (passed to the function) with the first byte containing the length of the string. A carriage return is added to the end of the string. A Pascal driver also adds a line feed to the string.

3. To write a string (after processing it with the AND and OR masks), call WriteString or ErrWriteString. This call expects the character string to be in a specified memory address (passed to the function) with the first byte containing the length of the string. However, this call differs from WriteLine and ErrWriteLine in that no carriage return or line feed is added to the end of the string.

4. Another way to write strings is WriteCString or ErrWriteCString. This call is similar to WriteString and ErrWriteString except that the string does not begin with a length byte but is terminated with a null ($00) byte.

5. To write a block of text (after processing it with the AND and OR masks), call WriteBlock or ErrWriteBlock. These functions expect a pointer to the start of the block, an offset to the actual start within that block (use $0000 for the beginning of the block), and the length of the text to be written.

TextTools gives you many alternative methods of writing a *string of text*—a group of characters that are to be printed without a terminating carriage return or line feed. The following shows three alternative methods of displaying a text message on the screen.

```
*Program segment to display a text message on the text screen
*Three alternative methods used
*
*Method 1 uses a string with its length in the first byte
Message1  DATA
          DC H'TEnd+1-Text'       ;Length byte for message
Text      DC C'Apple IIGS'        ;Actual message
TEnd      Anop
          END
String    START
          PushLong Message1       ;Starting location of message
          _WriteString            ;Write the message
          END
*
*Method 2 uses a string with a terminating zero
Message2  DATA
          DC C'Apple IIGS'        ;Actual message
          DC H'00'                ;Terminating character
          END
CString   START
          PushLong Message2       ;Starting location of message
          _WriteCString           ;Write the message
          END
*
*Method 3 uses a block
Block     DATA
Forever   DC C'Apple II Forever'
GS        DC C'Apple IIGS'
BlockEnd  ANOP
          END
DoBlock   START
          PushLong Block          ;Starting location of block
          Pushword GS+1-Forever   ;Offset to start of actual text
          Pushword BlockEnd+1-GS  ;Length of text
          _WriteBlock             ;Write the message
          END
```

Your choice of the actual method of programming the application depends in large part on how the strings are generated. If you wish to have a large number of strings in one data section, you may find the block write routines most useful. If you intend to have just one message, and its text is known at assembly or compilation time, you should use a string with a length byte—with the length being figured by the assembler as shown in the previous example. If you intend to have a message whose text is not known at assembly time, you should add a $00 to the end of the string when created and use the CString routine. This precaution eliminates the need for performing a computation to determine the string length during the running of the program.

Function Name	Function Number	ANDMask	BlockPtr	Character	ControlCode	Count	DeviceKind	DeviceType	Offset	ORMask	RequestCode	Slot or Ptr	Status	StrPtr	Version
Parameter Size		W	L	W	W	W	W	W	W	W	W	L	W	L	W
Parameter Type		By	P	By	By	V	K	T	V	By	By	V	B	P	V
CtrlTextDev	16				I2		I1								
ErrWriteBlock	1F		I1			I3			I2						
ErrWriteChar	19			I1											
ErrWriteCString	21													I1	
ErrWriteLine	1B													I1	
ErrWriteString	1D													I1	
GetErrGlobals	E	O1								O2					
GetErrorDevice	14							O1				O2			
GetOutGlobals	D	O1								O2					
GetOutputDevice	13							O1				O2			
InitTextDev	15						I1								
SetErrGlobals	B	I1								I2					
SetErrorDevice	11							I1				I2			
SetOutGlobals	A	I1								I2					
SetOutputDevice	10							I1				I2			
StatusTDev	17						I1				I2				
TextBootInit	1														
TextReset	5														
TextShutDown	3														
TextStartUp	2														
TextStatus	6												O1		
TextVersion	4														O1
WriteBlock	1E		I1			I3			I2						
WriteChar	18			I1											
WriteCString	20													I1	
WriteLine	1A													I1	
WriteString	1C													I1	

Notes:

Size codes:
- L Long-word (32 bits)
- W Word (16 bits)

Type codes:
- B Boolean ($0000 = false; $FFFF = true)
- By Byte value — only lower 8 bits significant
- K Kind of device (0=input; 1=output; 2=error)
- P Pointer
- T Type of device (0=BASIC; 1=Pascal; 2=RAM)
- V Value

Table 8-5

TextTool Character Output Routines

The various TextTool output functions and the parameters expected by each are summarized in Table 8-5.

Sending certain ASCII codes to the character driver results in certain actions other than the display of a character. These codes are called *control codes* because they are often generated from the keyboard in conjunction with the CONTROL key. Some are used whether COUT1 or C3COUT1 is active, and some are valid only when C3COUT1 is active. These codes are listed in Table 8-6.

Beside COUT, COUT1, and C3COUT1, several other text character drivers are available on the IIGS. These routines are used for specific purposes. All these routines, including the three already discussed, are

ASCII Value	Key (with Control)	Purpose	Also used with COUT1
87	G	Bell	Yes
88	H	Backspace	Yes
8A	J	Line feed	Yes
8B	K	Clear to end of screen	No
8C	L	Home and clear	No
8D	M	Carriage return	Yes
8E	N	Normal video display	No
8F	O	Inverse video display	No
91	Q	40-column display	No
92	R	80-column display	No
93	S	Stop display	No
95	U	End 80-column firmware	No
96	V	Scroll down	No
97	W	Scroll up	No
98	X	Mouse characters off	No
99	Y	Home	No
9A	Z	Clear line	No
9B	[	Mouse characters on	No
9C	\	Forward cursor	No
9D	]	Clear to end of line	No
9F	_	Cursor up	No

Table 8-6.
C3COUT1 Control Codes

listed in Table 8-7. Note, however, that the locations given in Table 8-7, while correct, should not be accessed except in 8-bit Apple IIe mode with the monitor ROM locations shadowed into bank $00, or through a text tool set.

Location	Name	Description
FF/C307	C3COUT1	Displays character on screen via 80-column firmware
FF/FC9C	CLREOL	Clears from current cursor position to end of line
FF/FC9E	CLEOLZ	Clears from cursor position based on Y register to end of line
FF/FC42	CLREOP	Clears to bottom of screen
FF/FDED	COUT	Displays character via output routine stored in CSW
FF/FDFO	COUT1	Displays a character on the screen
FF/FD8E	CROUT	Generates a carriage return
FF/FD8B	CROUT1	Clears from cursor position to end of line and then prints a carriage return
FF/FC58	HOME	Clears the screen and places cursor in upper-left corner (home position)
FF/F948	PRBLNK	Print three blank spaces
FF/F94A	PRBL2	Prints from 1-256 blanks depending on value in 8-bit X register (256 if X=0)
FF/FDDA	PRBYTE	Display contents of A register in hexadecimal
FF/FF2D	PRERR	Prints the word ERR and a bell
FF/FDE3	PRHEX	Prints lower nibble of A register in hexadecimal
FF/F941	PRTAX	Prints the A and X registers (8 bits each) as a 2-byte value
FF/FE80	SETINV	Change to inverse display mode
FF/FE84	SETNORM	Change to normal display mode

Table 8-7

Text Character Monitor Output Routines

The Pascal 1.1 firmware protocol, as discussed previously, is one of the supported character output devices. This is generally a printer or modem interface card, although it can also be a terminal or other device. These devices support at least four functions: PINIT, PREAD, PWRITE, and PSTATUS. The PWRITE and PSTATUS functions are useful in text character output.

PWRITE requires a character with its high bit (bit 7) clear. To do this, the AND mask should be set to %01111111 or $7F. The Pascal devices recognize several control codes, which are listed in Table 8-8.

PSTATUS requires a request code. A code of $00 inquires whether the device is ready for output, and a code of $01 inquires whether the device

CONTROL Key	Function
E or e	Enable cursor display
F or f	Disable cursor display
G or g	Bell
H or h	Backspace
J or j	Line feed
K or k	Clear to end of screen
L or l	Clear screen and home cursor
M or m	Carriage return
N or n	Switch to normal video display
O or o	Switch to inverse video display
V or v	Scroll up one line
W or w	Scroll down one line
Y or y	Home cursor
Z or z	Clear cursor line
¦ or \	Move cursor right
} or]	Clear to end of line
^ or 6	Go to xy sequence. Next two characters are considered to be cursor position x+32 and y+32
—	Move up one line if not at top of screen

Table 8-8

Pascal-Type Devices Control Codes

has any input. The carry bit is set (=1) if the answer is "yes" and cleared if the answer is "no."

Four different areas are actually used for 8-bit Apple II text display on the IIGS. The 40-column text is displayed either on Text Page 1 ($E0/0400-07FF) or Text Page 2 ($E0/0800-10BFF). The 80-column display uses either the 40-column Text Page 1 or Text Page 2 screen memory area, as well as the corresponding area in bank $E1. The text memory areas are also used for display of low-resolution graphics.

Several softswitches in the IIGS provide a facility for switching between these various modes and determining the setting of a particular switch. Table 8-9 lists each softswitch affecting text display in groups of three. The switches that turn on or turn off the function can be activated by writing only to that location (indicated by a W), or by reading or writing to that location (indicated by an R). The status location for the switch is obtained by reading the location. If bit 7 is set (=1), the switch is on.

Name	Off Address	On Address	Status Address	Purpose
80COL	C00C W	C00D W	C01F	Display 80 columns of text
80STORE	C000 W	C001 W	C018	PAGE2 switches main (Page 1 and 2) instead of main (bank $E0) and auxiliary (bank $E1) RAM areas
ALTCHAR	C00E W	C00F W	C01E	Use alternate character set in place of primary character set
MIXED	C052 R/W	C053 R/W	01B	If text off, display mixed text and graphics
PAGE2	C054 R/W	C055 R/W	C01C	If on, use either page 2 of text or auxiliary bank display area depending on setting of 80STORE switch
TEXT	C050 R/W	C051 R/W	C01A	Display text rather than either graphics or mixed text and graphics

Table 8-9
Text Softswitch Locations

CHAPTER 9

Super-Resolution Graphics

The Apple IIGS super-resolution graphics (super-res) can display either 320 or 640 pixels across the screen and 200 lines down the screen. Each horizontal line of pixels is known as a scan line.

Bit Number	Use
0-3	Color table number (0 to 15)
4	Reserved (must be 0)
5	Fill mode (1 = on; 0 = off)
6	Interrupts (1 = generated; 0 = not generated)
7	Number of pixels (0 = 320; 1 = 640)

Table 9-1
Scanline Control Byte (SCB) Structure

Four characteristics affect the whole of each scan line:

1. Whether the line displays 320 or 640 pixels
2. Which color table is used to determine pixel colors for the line
3. Whether an interrupt will be generated when the line is refreshed
4. Whether fill mode is active for the line

The characteristics of each scan line are contained in the scanline control byte (SCB) for each line. The structure of this byte is shown in Table 9-1.

The SCB for each line is stored in memory in bank $E1, beginning at $E1/9D00 for the first line, and extends through $E1/9DC7. The area from $E1/9DC8 through $E1/9DFF is reserved and must be filled with zeros.

The pixel data for each scan line are stored in memory beginning at $E1/2000. Each scan line requires 160 bytes ($A0) for its pixel data. For each scan line, Table 9-2 shows the location of the scanline control byte and the beginning location of the pixel data. All addresses are in bank $E1 and are given in hexadecimal values. Scan lines are given in decimal values.

Line Number	SCB Location	Pixel Data
1	9D00	2000
2	9D01	20A0
3	9D02	2140
4	9D03	21E0
5	9D04	2280
6	9D05	2320
7	9D06	23C0
8	9D07	2460
9	9D08	2500
10	9D09	25A0
11	9D0A	2640
12	9D0B	26E0
13	9D0C	2780
14	9D0D	2820
15	9D0E	28C0
16	9D0F	2960
17	9D10	2A00
18	9D11	2AA0
19	9D12	2B40
20	9D13	2BE0
21	9D14	2C80
22	9D15	2D20
23	9D16	2DC0
24	9D17	2E60
25	9D18	2F00
26	9D19	2FA0
27	9D1A	3040
28	9D1B	30E0
29	9D1C	3180
30	9D1D	3220
31	9D1E	32C0
32	9D1F	3360
33	9D20	3400
34	9D21	34A0

Table 9-2

Scanline Control Byte Storage Areas

Line Number	SCB Location	Pixel Data
35	9D22	3540
36	9D23	35E0
37	9D24	3680
38	9D25	3720
39	9D26	37C0
40	9D27	3860
41	9D28	3900
42	9D29	39A0
43	9D2A	3A40
44	9D2B	3AE0
45	9D2C	3B80
46	9D2D	3C20
47	9D2E	3CC0
48	9D2F	3D60
49	9D30	3E00
50	9D31	3EA0
51	9D32	3F40
52	9D33	3FE0
53	9D34	4080
54	9D35	4120
55	9D36	41C0
56	9D37	4260
57	9D38	4300
58	9D39	43A0
59	9D3A	4440
60	9D3B	44E0
61	9D3C	4580
62	9D3D	4620
63	9D3E	46C0
64	9D3F	4760
65	9D40	4800
66	9D41	48A0
67	9D42	4940
68	9D43	49E0
69	9D44	4A80
70	9D45	4B20
71	9D46	4BC0
72	9D47	4C60

Table 9-2
Scanline Control Byte Storage Areas (continued)

Line Number	SCB Location	Pixel Data
73	9D48	4D00
74	9D49	4DA0
75	9D4A	4E40
76	9D4B	4EE0
77	9D4C	4F80
78	9D4D	5020
79	9D4E	50C0
80	9D4F	5160
81	9D50	5200
82	9D51	52A0
83	9D52	5340
84	9D53	53E0
85	9D54	5480
86	9D55	5520
87	9D56	55C0
88	9D57	5660
89	9D58	5700
90	9D59	57A0
91	9D5A	5840
92	9D5B	58E0
93	9D5C	5980
94	9D5D	5A20
95	9D5E	5AC0
96	9D5F	5B60
97	9D60	5C00
98	9D61	5CA0
99	9D62	5D40
100	9D63	5DE0
101	9D64	5E80
102	9D65	5F20
103	9D66	5FC0
104	9D67	6060
105	9D68	6100
106	9D69	61A0
107	9D6A	6240
108	9D6B	62E0
109	9D6C	6380
110	9D6D	6420

Table 9-2

Scanline Control Byte Storage Areas (continued)

Line Number	SCB Location	Pixel Data
111	9D6E	64C0
112	9D6F	6560
113	9D70	6600
114	9D71	66A0
115	9D72	6740
116	9D73	67E0
117	9D74	6880
118	9D75	6920
119	9D76	69C0
120	9D77	6A60
121	9D78	6B00
122	9D79	6BA0
123	9D7A	6C40
124	9D7B	6CE0
125	9D7C	6D80
126	9D7D	6E20
127	9D7E	6EC0
128	9D7F	6F60
129	9D80	7000
130	9D81	70A0
131	9D82	7140
132	9D83	71E0
133	9D84	7280
134	9D85	7320
135	9D86	73C0
136	9D87	7460
137	9D88	7500
138	9D89	75A0
139	9D8A	7640
140	9D8B	76E0
141	9D8C	7780
142	9D8D	7820
143	9D8E	78C0
144	9D8F	7960
145	9D90	7A00
146	9D91	7AA0
147	9D92	7B40
148	9D93	7BE0

Table 9-2
Scanline Control Byte Storage Areas (continued)

Line Number	SCB Location	Pixel Data
149	9D94	7C80
150	9D95	7D20
151	9D96	7DC0
152	9D97	7E60
153	9D98	7F00
154	9D99	7FA0
155	9D9A	8040
156	9D9B	80E0
157	9D9C	8180
158	9D9D	8220
159	9D9E	82C0
160	9D9F	8360
161	9DA0	8400
162	9DA1	84A0
163	9DA2	8540
164	9DA3	85E0
165	9DA4	8680
166	9DA5	8720
167	9DA6	87C0
168	9DA7	8860
169	9DA8	8900
170	9DA9	89A0
171	9DAA	8A40
172	9DAB	8AE0
173	9DAC	8B80
174	9DAD	8C20
175	9DAE	8CC0
176	9DAF	8D60
177	9DB0	8E00
178	9DB1	8EA0
179	9DB2	8F40
180	9DB3	8FE0
181	9DB4	9080
182	9DB5	9120
183	9DB6	91C0
184	9DB7	9260
185	9DB8	9300
186	9DB9	93A0

Table 9-2

Scanline Control Byte Storage Areas (continued)

Line Number	SCB Location	Pixel Data
187	9DBA	9440
187	9DBA	9440
188	9DBB	94E0
189	9DBC	9580
190	9DBD	9620
191	9DBE	96C0
192	9DBF	9760
193	9DC0	9800
194	9DC1	98A0
195	9DC2	9940
196	9DC3	99E0
197	9DC4	9A80
198	9DC5	9B20
199	9DC6	9BC0
200	9DC7	9C60

Table 9-2
Scanline Control Byte Storage Areas (continued)

320 OR 640 MODE

The pixel data vary depending on whether the particular scan line is in 320 or 640 mode. A pixel in 320 mode is 4 bits wide, representing a value between 0 and 15. This value refers to the number of a color in the color table associated with that scan line.

A pixel in 640 mode is only 2 bits wide, representing a value between 0 and 3. The color that this value refers to depends on the position of the particular pixel in the byte. The pixel in the highest two bits (6-7) of the byte refers to the first four colors (0-3) in the color table. The pixel in the next two bits (4-5) refers to the next four colors (4-7) in the color table. The pixel in the third two bits (2-3) refers to the next four colors (8-11). The pixel in the lowest two bits (0-1) refers to the highest four colors (12-15). This information is summarized in Table 9-3.

Bit Numbers	Colors Referred to
0-1	12-15
2-3	8-11
4-5	4-7
6-7	0-3

Table 9-3
Color Reference in 640 Mode

Super-res can display 16 colors in each line even in 640 mode, although it cannot display each of the 16 colors in each pixel position. Rather it can display only one of four colors in each particular position. If your application needs 16 colors per line in 640 mode super-res, you must be prepared to accept that some colors cannot be displayed in some locations. You can, however, create the effect of multiple colors on a line through the use of *dithering*. This technique alternates the color values of adjacent pixels to create the illusion of intermediate colors.

COLOR TABLES

The standard method of handling colors in 640 super-res mode is to restrict each line to four colors and to construct the color table with four colors repeated throughout the table. This technique is used by Quickdraw II (discussed in Chapters 10-13) when in 640 mode.

Sixteen different color tables can be in memory at one time. Each SCB refers to a color table value between 0 and 15. A color table consists of 16 word-length (16-bit) entries for a total of 32 bytes for each table. The location of color tables is shown in Table 9-4.

The word-length entry for each color contains three 4-bit (nybble) values representing the intensity of the colors blue, green, and red (beginning with the lowest nybble). The highest nybble in the word is reserved and must be set to 0. The format of each color entry is shown in Table 9-5.

Table Number	Location
0	9E00
1	9E20
2	9E40
3	9E60
4	9E80
5	9EA0
6	9EC0
7	9EE0
8	9F00
9	9F20
10	9F40
11	9F60
12	9F80
13	9FA0
14	9FC0
15	9FE0

Table 9-4

Location of Color Tables in Bank $E1

Bits	Meaning
0-3	Intensity of blue color
4-7	Intensity of green color
8-11	Intensity of red color
12-15	Reserved (must be 0)

Table 9-5

Color Table Entry Format

INTERRUPTS

Special effects can be achieved with the use of scan line interrupts. If bit 6 in the SCB for a particular line is on (=1), an interrupt is generated each time that scan line is refreshed. Your application can plan to change the pixels in the line only after each interrupt to avoid changing a pixel as it is being drawn. In most applications, however, this is not necessary, particularly in view of the need to have additional code to synchronize the drawing with the interrupt.

FILL MODE

If a scan line enables fill mode by having bit 5 of the SCB set to 1, that line has only 15 active colors. The 0th color in the table is inactive. Instead, a pixel with a 0 color value is a signal to the super-res circuitry that that pixel should be displayed in the same color as the previous pixel on that line. Thus, a scan line with fill mode enabled, and with the values

3 0 0 4 5 7 0 0 0 5 0 8 0 1 0 0 3 4 5 6 7 8

is the equivalent of

3 3 3 4 5 7 7 7 7 5 5 8 8 1 1 1 3 4 5 6 7 8

and will display in the same way. Fill mode is most useful, obviously, in drawing filled shapes. It is not compatible with 640 super-res display mode and may produce unpredictable results.

The area occupied in memory by the super-res display ($E1/2000-9FFF) is also used, in part, by the double hi-res display. The video register softswitch, shadowed into $C029 in banks $E0 and $E1, determines whether super-res or normal hi-res graphics is displayed. Bit 7 of that softswitch is set to 1 to enable super-res graphics display, and bit 6 is set to 1 to enable the super-res pixel display to be linear mapped (that is, each scan line pixel image follows the previous one in memory).

The screen memory for the super-res display area can be shadowed into bank $01 if bit 3 of the shadow register (located at $C035) is set to 1. If shadowing is on, your application can write to the display space in fast memory in bank $01. (Shadowing is discussed in Chapter 5.) If your application is using the Quickdraw II routines for super-res drawing, shadowing should be off as the Quickdraw II routines write directly to bank $E1.

The Quickdraw II tool set also properly sets the softswitches for super-res display and linear mapping when it is first initialized. In fact, the various Quickdraw II routines handle nearly all the drawing and manipulating of the pixels. These routines are discussed in the next four chapters.

CHAPTER 10

Quickdraw II: Introduction and Record Structure

The Apple IIGS comes with a set of routines that aid in drawing and manipulating the super-resolution graphics display. These routines are based, as are many of the IIGS tool sets, on the analogous tool set in the Macintosh. The Macintosh graphics tool set is known as Quickdraw; accordingly, the tool set in the Apple IIGS is called Quickdraw II.

FrameOval	FrameArc
PaintOval	PaintArc
EraseOval	EraseArc
InvertOval	InvertArc
FillOval	FillArc
FrameRoundRect	OpenPicture
PaintRoundRect	PicComment
EraseRoundRect	ClosePicture
InvertRoundRect	DrawPicture
FillRoundRect	KillPicture

Table 10-1
Quickdraw II Functions Located in RAM

Because of the significance of the super-resolution graphics in particular, and graphics as an integral part of the IIGS, the Quickdraw II tool set is quite large. It contains 213 different routines; many of these are in ROM, although some are in RAM. Table 10-1 shows which of the tool functions are in RAM. The remainder are in ROM, at least in version 1.0 of Quickdraw II. Mainly the drawing functions involving curved lines or pictures are implemented in RAM.

The basic purpose of Quickdraw II is to provide a quick and relatively simple method of manipulating graphic objects and displaying them on the IIGS screen. This chapter examines the basic concepts behind Quickdraw II and looks at the data records used by this tool set, particularly the Grafport. Chapter 11 describes some of the tools used in drawing with Quickdraw II—pens and patterns—and explains how the basic drawing routines are done. Chapter 12 looks at various shapes that can be drawn—known in the Quickdraw II world as *primitive objects*—including rectangles, regions, polygons, rounded rectangles, ovals, and arcs. Chapter 12 also examines a special object—the cursor.

One of the uses made of the super-resolution graphics screen, particularly in text-oriented applications, is to display text in the particular font and style in which it will be printed. The Quickdraw II tool set contains a series of routines that make it easier for you to program an application to use text on the super-resolution graphics screen. The Quickdraw II text functions are discussed in Chapter 13.

The Quickdraw II tool set is too massive to be completely covered in this book. The next four chapters will provide you with the means of doing the more common functions, some of which are quite intricate. Readers interested in the less-used functions should consult the Apple IIGS *Toolbox Reference Manual.*

PIXEL MAPS

All drawing in Quickdraw II takes place on a two-dimensional grid with a center point of 0,0 and borders 16,383 pixels from that center point (see Figure 10-1). However, Quickdraw II does not check to see if you are within the proper bounds when you draw. It will happily draw outside the limits if commanded to do so. The results of this action are unpredictable—

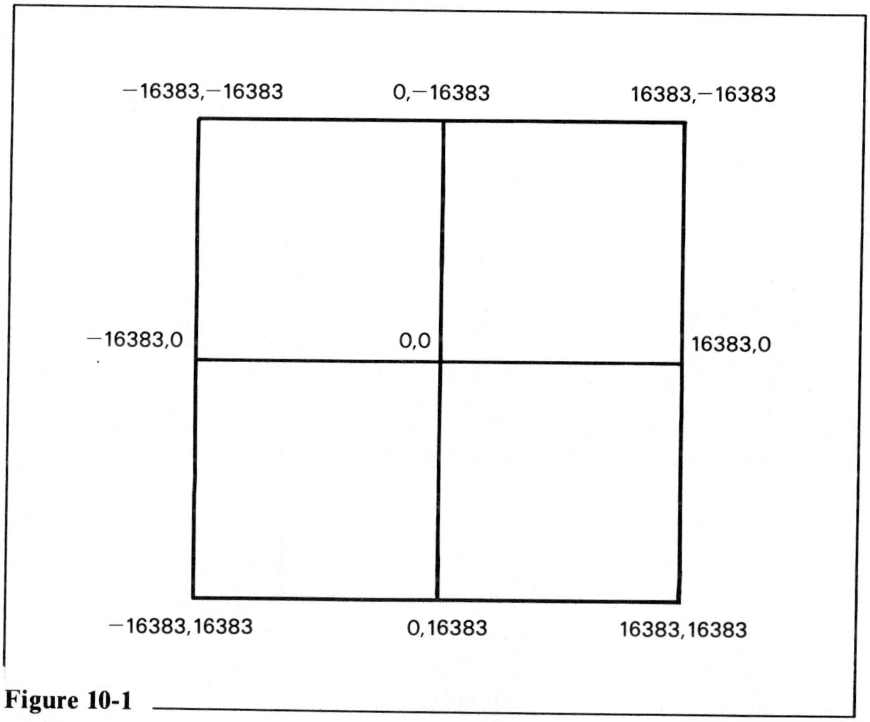

Figure 10-1
Two-dimensional grid for drawing in Quickdraw II

it may do nothing except not produce the image you expected, or it may write over either program code or data.

The grid on which drawing takes place consists of a number of points, numbered from the center point, along the X and Y axes. Note that, unlike standard graphing convention, movement down the Y axis results in a more positive value, and movement up results in a more negative value.

The pixels on the drawing grid do not fall directly on the point. Instead the points are considered to be the space between the pixels. Each pixel is given a number value equivalent to the point with which it is associated. This point is immediately above and to the left of the pixel (see Figure 10-2).

The set of pixels consists of a graphic image that is known as a *pixel map.* (On the Macintosh the term is *Bit Image.*) This pixel map can be anywhere in memory when manipulated by the various Quickdraw II routines. It is enclosed by a rectangle, known as the BoundsRect.

This entire pixel map is not, however, necessarily manipulated by

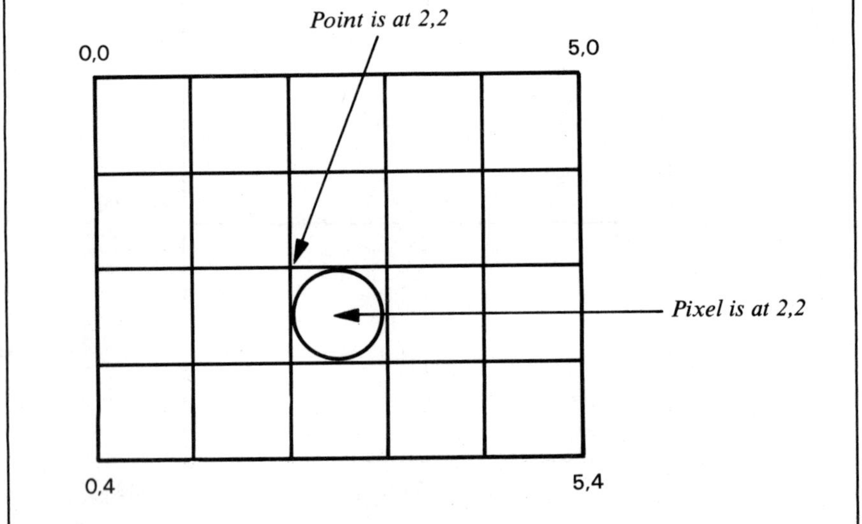

Figure 10-2

Example of number value assigned to pixel

Quickdraw II, nor is it necessarily displayed on the super-resolution graphics screen. The active region of the pixel map is a rectangular area within that map called the PortRect. It is the only part of the pixel map in which drawing can take place. If your application instructs Quickdraw II to draw in an inactive part of the pixel map (that is, outside the PortRect), Quickdraw II will simply ignore the part of the command that would result in drawing outside the PortRect. Note that if the PortRect is not entirely within the BoundRect, the actual active drawing area is that rectangle formed by the intersection of the BoundsRect and the PortRect (see Figure 10-3).

The display of the pixel map on the screen depends on another structure, known as the VisRgn (for visible region). This area is generally maintained by the Window Manager (discussed in Chapter 16). By default, VisRgn is set to the PortRect, although it can (and usually does) change during the process of an application to handle overlapping windows and other events.

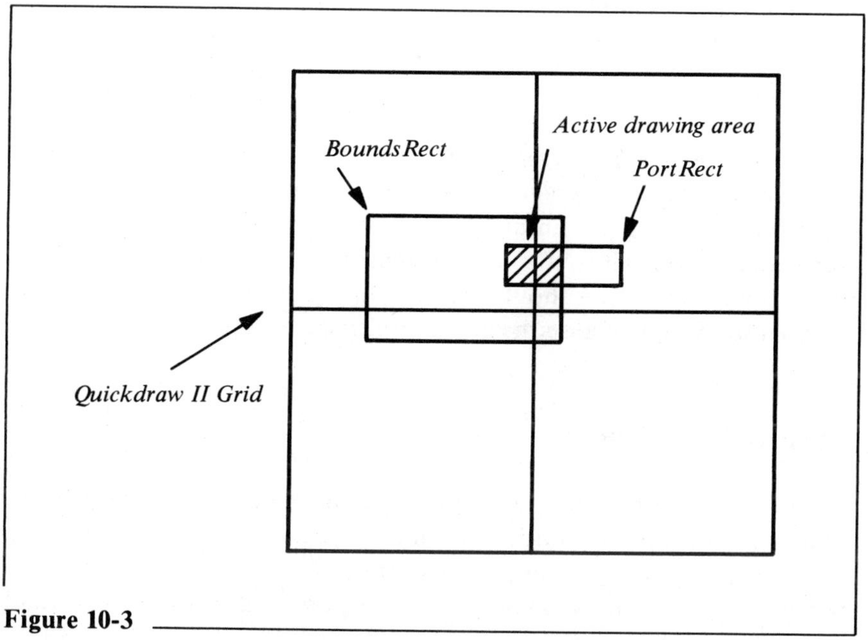

Figure 10-3

Actual active drawing area rectangle (intersection of BoundsRect and PortRect)

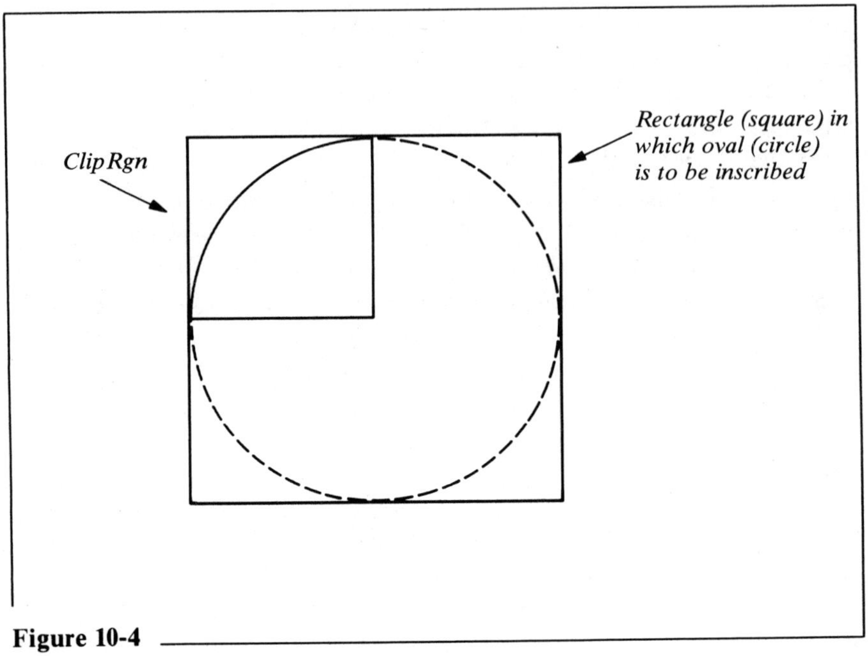

Figure 10-4
Drawing a quarter-circle

Drawing does not necessarily occur within all parts of the PortRect. Quickdraw II supports a *clipping region* (ClipRgn), which prevents drawing from occurring within any portion of the PortRect not within the particular region. Thus, if you want to provide for drawing of a quarter-circle, your application should set the ClipRgn to be one-quarter of the square that would enclose the entire circle (see Figure 10-4).

THE GRAFPORT

One of the means by which Quickdraw II manages to draw many different objects on the super-resolution graphics screen, and to do so quickly, is by keeping a record of the drawing environment for each area (normally each window). This record is known as a Grafport, and drawing commands within Quickdraw II usually require a reference to the current active Grafport so that it knows which drawing environment to use.

The Grafport is considered a private record—that is, access to it should be made only through the Quickdraw procedures that either change a portion of the record or that read data from the record. Attempts to modify the record directly can cause unpredictable results.

The reason for keeping the Grafport record as a private structure is to permit modifications to Quickdraw II and the Grafport record structure. If modifications are made, an application that uses the Quickdraw II functions to change a value in the record still works because Quickdraw II knows where the value is in the revised record. An application that attempts to modify a modified structure directly may change a different value than was intended.

The Macintosh Grafport record is not considered a private record, although Apple does discourage direct access to that record structure. Future modification to the Macintosh Quickdraw routines are likely to result in a private structure.

The structure of the Grafport record is shown in Table 10-2. (The structure is shown here for purposes of discussion of the Grafport and to aid in program debugging. The structure discussed is that used in Quickdraw II versions 1.0 and 1.1. If you are working with a later version of Quickdraw II, you should not assume that the structure has remained static.)

The PortInfo, which uses the LocInfo record structure discussed in Table 10-3, lets Quickdraw II know which area of memory it should use with its drawing commands and the characteristics of that area. The first part of this information is contained in a single byte value known as a *scanline control byte* (SCB). The structure of the SCB is shown in Table 10-4. It contains the following information:

- *Chunkiness* refers to whether each pixel is 2 bits wide (640 mode) or 4 bits wide (320 mode). The chunkiness of the pixel map is shown by bit 7 of the PortSCB.
- An interrupt is generated when the scan line is refreshed if bit 6 is set.
- Fill mode (see Chapter 9) is active if bit 5 is set.
- The number of the master color palette (0 to 15) is shown by bits 0 to 3.

Byte Offset	Length	Name	Type
0	16	PortInfo	LocInfo
16	8	PortRect	Rectangle
24	4	ClipRgn	Handle
28	4	VisRgn	Handle
32	32	BkPat	Pattern
64	4	PnLoc	Point
68	4	PnSize	Point
72	2	PnMode	Word
74	32	PnPat	Pattern
106	8	PnMask	Mask
114	2	PnVis	Word
116	4	FontHandle	Handle
120	4	FontID	Long-word
124	2	FontFlags	Word
126	2	TxSize	Word
128	2	TxFace	Style
130	2	TxMode	Word
132	4	SpExtra	Fixed point
136	4	ChExtra	Fixed point
140	2	FgColor	Word
142	2	BgColor	Word
144	4	PicSave	Handle
148	4	RgnSave	Handle
152	4	PolySave	Handle
156	4	GrafProcs	Pointer
160	2	ArcRot	Word
162	4	UserField	Long-word
166	4	SysField	Long-word

Explanation of types:

Fixed point—long-word value with a 16-bit integer represented by the higher word and an unsigned fraction represented by the lower word.

Handle—long-word pointer to a long-word pointer.

LocInfo—see Table 10-3 for structure.

Long word—32-bit value.

Mask—an array with 64 bits (8 bytes).

Table 10-2

Grafport Record Structure (Quickdraw II Versions 1.0 and 1.1)

Explanation of types (*continued*):

Pattern — in 320-mode, an array with 64 nibbles (4 bits, 0 to 15). In 640-mode, an array with 64 2-bit (0 to 4) values and padded with 0's for remaining bytes.

Point — two words representing the vertical position followed by the horizontal position.

Pointer — long-word value specifying an address where the data will be found.

Rectangle — four words representing vertical-top, horizontal-left, vertical-bottom, and horizontal-right positions.

Style — word value with bits set to indicate style is on: bit 0 is bold, 1 is italic, and 2 is underline.

Word — 16-bit value.

Table 10-2

Grafport Record Structure (Quickdraw II Versions 1.0 and 1.1) (continued)

Byte Offset	Length	Name	Type
0	1	PortSCB	an SCB*
1	1	Reserved	byte**
2	4	PointerToPixelImage	pointer
6	2	Width	word
8	8	BoundsRect	rectangle

*Structure of an SCB is shown in Table 10-4.
**Byte is an 8-bit value.

Table 10-3

LocInfo Structure

Bit	Purpose
0-3	Color table number
4	Reserved
5	0 = fill off; 1 = fill on
6	0 = interrupt off; 1 = interrupt on
7	0 = 320 resolution mode; 1 = 640 resolution mode

Table 10-4
Structure of an SCB

The remainder of the PortInfo record contains the following information:

- □ The address of the pixel map is shown by the PointerToPixelImage.
- □ The width of the pixel map is shown by Width. Width refers to the number of bytes in each row of pixels in the pixel map. This number, called rowBytes on the Macintosh, must be a multiple of 8.
- □ The BoundsRect shows how large the pixel map actually is. The width is the true value, not the padded value shown by Width. This rectangle also imposes a local coordinate system on the pixel map with its top-left corner being 0,0.

The PortRect portion of the Grafport describes the rectangle part of the pixel map that is active (that is, the portion in which drawing may occur).

The ClipRgn is a handle to a region that further restricts drawing with the particular Grafport. Unless the ClipRgn is set to enclose the entire PortRect, drawing can occur only in the area that is within both the PortRect and the ClipRgn.

The VisRgn represents the portion of the pixel map that is visible (that is, it is shown on the super-resolution graphics screen). This region is maintained and manipulated by the Window Manager, not by your application. It handles overlapping windows.

The BkPat represents a pattern that is used to draw the background of the picture. When performing an erase operation, Quickdraw II replaces the portion of the image being erased with the background pattern. A pattern is an 8-pixel × 8-pixel square with each pixel (2 to 4 bits, depending on the graphics mode—320 or 640) representing a particular color. Patterns are discussed further in Chapter 11.

The Grafport also maintains various information about the drawing pen, including:

- □ The current location in the pixel map of the pen point (PnLoc).
- □ The width and height of the pen point (PnSize).
- □ The transfer mode used when drawing a horizontal line with the fill pattern (PnMode).
- □ The pattern used when drawing an object with the pen (PnPat).
- □ The drawing mask used during pattern drawing with the pen, which modifies the pattern actually drawn by the pen (PnMask).
- □ Whether the pen will actually draw or just move when given a drawing command (PnVis). The use of the graphics pen in Quickdraw II is discussed further in Chapter 11.

The Grafport also contains much information about the text aspects of the drawing environment. These text aspects, which are discussed in greater detail in Chapter 13, include the following:

- □ The handle of the system or default font, which will be used for text in the absence of font specification, is given in FontHandle.
- □ The long-word identification number assigned to the font is found in FontID.
- □ The FontFlags field is presently (version 1.1) used only to differentiate between fixed and proportionally spaced fonts.
- □ TxSize represents the size of the font, in points, from the top of the tallest character to the bottom of the character with the longest descender.
- □ TxFace represents a bit array with the various type styles. Style is bold if bit 0 is set and underlined if bit 1 is set.
- □ TxMode specifies which of eight different methods of transferring the text character to the pixel map is used.

- SpExtra is the average number of pixels that should be added to each space character in a line in order to expand it for fill justification.
- ChExtra is the amount of space to be added to each character when a particular font is to be drawn in a particular style. This field can be used to help adjust a font that needs extra space when characters are drawn in bold or italic style.

Two fields in the Grafport hold the colors used in drawing with that Grafport. FgColor is the foreground color value, and BgColor is the background color value.

The PicSave, RgnSave, and PolySave fields are handles used by Quickdraw II when it is creating a picture, region, or polygon. (See discussion of these shapes in Chapter 12.) These values should not be modified by your application. The various Quickdraw II routines that permit changing these values are meant as internal calls.

GrafProcs contains the pointer to the GrafProcs record, which contains a series of pointers to the various routines that perform standard, low-level, object, and text drawing. This value should be changed only if you are installing customized standard routines. (The object routines are discussed further in Chapter 12, and the text routine is discussed in Chapter 13.)

The GrafProc also contains two fields that can be used for saving long-word values for a variety of purposes. The UserField is designed for use by your application and can hold a pointer to a specialized routine or any other value you wish. The SysField is reserved for use by Quickdraw II and should not be changed by your application.

Because Apple intends the Grafport record to be a private data structure not directly accessible by the application, it has provided a method to access and change the various portions of the Grafport record by means of Quickdraw II commands. Table 10-5 lists each portion of the Grafport record. The table shows the Quickdraw II function that determines the current setting of that portion of the record, as well as the Quickdraw II function that modifies that portion of the record.

The various Quickdraw II functions that work with the Grafport record structure, as well as those involved with Quickdraw II initialization and setup, are listed in Table 10-6 with a short description of their uses. Table 10-7 shows the standard color table values used in Quickdraw II. Table 10-8 lists each of the Quickdraw II functions with the parameters expected by each.

Record Part	Accessing Function	Modifying Function
PortInfo	GetPortLoc	SetPortLoc
PortSCB	GetMasterSCB	SetMasterSCB
PointerToPixelImage		
Width		
BoundsRect		
PortRect	GetPortRect	SetPortRect
		SetPortSize
		MovePortTo
ClipRgn	GetClip	SetClip
	GetClipHandle	ClipRect
		SetClipHandle
VisRgn	GetVisRgn	SetVisRgn
	GetVisHandle	SetVisHandle
BkPat	GetPenState	SetPenState
	GetBackPat	SetBackPat
		SetSolidBackPat
PnLoc	GetPen	SetPenState
	GetPenState	MoveTo
		Move
PnSize	GetPenState	SetPenState
	GetPenSize	SetPenSize
		PenNormal
PnMode	GetPenState	SetPenState
	GetPenMode	SetPenMode
		PenNormal
PnPat	GetPenState	SetPenState
	GetPenPat	SetPenPat
		SetSolidPenPat
		PenNormal
PnMask	GetPenState	SetPenState
	GetPenMask	SetPenMask
		PenNormal
PnVis		HidePen
		ShowPen
FontHandle	GetSysFont	SetSysFont
	GetFont	SetFont
FontID	GetFontID	SetFontID
FontFlags	GetFontFlags	SetFontFlags

Table 10-5

Quickdraw II Functions Directly Accessing or Modifying the Grafport Record

Record Part	Accessing Function	Modifying Function
TxSize		
TxFace	GetTextFace	SetTextFace
TxMode	GetTextMode	SetTextMode
SpExtra	GetSpaceExtra	SetSpaceExtra
ChExtra	GetCharExtra	SetCharExtra
FgColor	GetForeColor	SetForeColor
BgColor	GetBackColor	SetBackColor
PicSave	GetPicSave	SetPicSave
RgnSave	GetRgnSave	SetRgnSave
PolySave	GetPolySave	SetPolySave
GrafProcs	GetGrafProcs	SetGrafProcs
ArcRot		
UserField	GetUserField	SetUserField
SysField	GetSysField	SetSysField

Table 10-5

Quickdraw II Functions Directly Accessing or Modifying the Grafport Record (continued)

QDBootInit	Boot-time initialization of Quickdraw II. Called by the system. Should not be called by your application.
QDStartup	Run-time initialization of Quickdraw II. Creates a standard port, sets the current port to be this standard port, and clears the screen. The routine needs to be passed a starting address of $300 bytes in bank zero among other parameters. If the maximum width passed is 0, the pixel map is set to the screen width.
QDShutDown	Shuts down Quickdraw II and frees any memory that was allocated by it.
QDVersion	Returns the version number of Quickdraw II.
QDStatus	Returns true if Quickdraw II is active and false if not.
GetStandardSCB	Low byte of value is the standard screen control byte (color table 0, fill and interrupt off, 320 mode).

Table 10-6

List of Functions Concerning Record Structure, Initialization, and Setup

SetMasterSCB	Changes value used to set the default screen control byte value when a new port is initialized.
GetMasterSCB	Returns value used to set the default screen control byte value when a new port is initialized.
InitColorTable	Fills the specified color table with the standard values. The standard values are shown in Table 10-7.
SetColorTable	Transfers a set of values to the proper location for the specified table number.
GetColorTable	Transfers a set of color values from a color table to a specified memory location.
SetColorEntry	Changes the color value for a specified entry in a specified color table.
GetColor Entry	Returns the color value of a specified entry in a specified color table.
SetSCB	Sets the scanline control byte for the specified scan line to the specified value.
GetSCB	Returns the value of the scanline control byte for the specified scan line.
SetAllSCBs	Sets all 200 scanline control bytes to the specified value.
ClearScreen	Clears the screen to the specified color word passed by placing that word in each location of screen memory. Unless all pixels are the same color value, this does not result in a screen cleared to a solid color.
GrafOn	Turns on super-resolution graphics display without affecting linearization.
GrafOff	Turns off super-resolution graphics display without affecting linearization.
OpenPort	Creates a new Grafport using the specified memory location as a data area and using standard values. Allocates a new visible and clip region.
InitPort	Creates a new Grafport using the specified memory location as a data area and using standard values. Does not allocate a new visible and clip region.
ClosePort	Deallocates a port and the memory associated with it. Should not be called set to the current port.
SetPort	Makes the specified port the current port.
GetPort	Returns the handle to the current port.

Table 10-6

List of Functions Concerning Record Structure, Initialization, and Setup (continued)

Function	Description
SetPortLoc	Changes the PortInfo field of the current Grafport to the values in the location pointed to.
GetPortLoc	Copies the current Grafport's PortInfo field to the address specified.
SetPortRect	Changes the port rectangle of the current Grafport to the values specified in the location pointed to.
GetPortRect	Copies the values of the port rectangle of the current Grafport to the address specified.
SetPortSize	Changes the size of the port rectangle of the current Grafport to the specified values.
MovePortTo	Changes the location of the port rectangle of the current Grafport to the specified location.
SetOrigin	Adjusts the contents of both the port rectangle and the bounds rectangle so that the upper-left corner (origin) of the port rectangle is set to the specified point. The visible region is changed accordingly. The pen position does not change nor does the clip region.
SetPicSave	Changes the PicSave field of the Grafport. Should not be used by an application.
GetPicSave	Returns the value of the PicSave field of the Grafport.
SetRgnSave	Changes the RgnSave field of the Grafport. Should not be used by an application.
GetRgnSave	Returns the value of the RgnSave field of the Grafport.
SetPolySave	Changes the PolySave field of the Grafport. Should not be used by an application.
GetPolySave	Returns the value of the PolySave field of the Grafport.
SetGrafProcs	Changes the GrafProcs field of the Grafport. Only used for customized use of Quickdraw II (discussed more in Chapter 12).
GetGrafProcs	Returns the value of the GrafProcs field of the Grafport.
SetUserField	Changes the User Field value in the Grafport.
GetUserField	Returns the value of the User Field in the Grafport.
SetSysField	Changes the System Field value in the Grafport. Should not be used by an application.
GetSysField	Returns the value of the System Field in the Grafport.
LocalToGlobal	Converts a point from local coordinates (based on 0,0 as the upper-left corner of the bounds rectangle) to global

Table 10-6

List of Functions Concerning Record Structure, Initialization, and Setup (continued)

	coordinates (based on 0,0 as the upper-left corner of the pixel image).
GlobalToLocal	Converts a point from global coordinates (based on 0,0 as the upper left corner of the pixel image) to local coordinates (based on 0,0 as the upper left corner of the bounds rectangle).
SetStdProcs	Passes to Quickdraw II the pointer to a record containing the addresses of the standard, low-level Quickdraw II procedures. This is a procedure normally used in customizing certain aspects of Quickdraw II.
SetIntUse	Tells Quickdraw II whether to use scanline interrupts for drawing a cursor without flicker (default) or leave scanline interrupts alone so that the application can use them.

Table 10-6

List of Functions Concerning Record Structure, Initialization, and Setup (continued)

	320 Mode		640 Mode	
Number	**Value**	**Name**	**Value**	**Name**
0	000	Black	000	Black
1	777	Dark Gray	F00	Red
2	841	Brown	0F0	Green
3	72C	Purple	FFF	White
4	00F	Blue	000	Black
5	080	Dark Green	00F	Blue
6	F70	Orange	FF0	Yellow
7	D00	Red	FFF	White
8	FA9	Flesh	000	Black
9	FF0	Yellow	F00	Red
A	0E0	Green	0F0	Green
B	4DF	Light Blue	FFF	White
C	DAF	Lilac	000	Black
D	78F	Periwinkle Blue	00F	Blue
E	CCC	Light Gray	FF0	Yellow
F	FFF	White	FFF	White

Table 10-7

Standard Color Tables

Function Name	Function Number	Color	ColorTPtr	ColorWord	EntryNum	GrafProcsPtr	H	Height	LocInfoPtr	MasterSCB	MaxWidth
Parameter Size		W	L	W	W	L	W	W	L	W	W
Parameter Type		V	P	V	V	P	V	V	P	BA	V
ClearScreen	21			I1							
ClosePort	26										
GetColorEntry	17	O1			I2						
GetColorTable	15		I2								
GetGrafProcs	69					O1					
GetMasterSCB	23								O1		
GetPicSave	63										
GetPolySave	67										
GetPort	28										
GetPortLoc	30								I1		
GetPortRect	32										
GetRgnSave	65										
GetSCB	19										
GetStandard SCB	12										
GetSysField	73										
GetUserField	71										
GlobalToLocal	133										
GrafOff	11										
GrafOn	10										
InitColorTable	13		I1								
InitPort	25										
LocalToGlobal	132										
MovePortTo	34							I1			
OpenPort	24										
QDBootInit	1										
QDShutDown	3										
QDStartup	2									I2	I3
QDStatus	6										
QDVersion	4										
SetAllSCBs	20										
SetColorEntry	16	I3			I2						
SetColorTable	14		I2								

Table 10-8

List of Quickdraw II Record and Initialization Commands

PointPtr	PortPtr	ProgramID	RectPtr	SaveValue	ScanLineNum	SCB	Status	StdProcsPtr	SysFieldValue	TableNum	UseInt	UserFieldValue	V	Version	Width	ZeroPageLoc
L	L	W	L	L	W	W	W	L	L	W	W	L	W	W	W	W
P	P	V	P	P	V	BA	V	P	V	V	B	V	V	V	V	A
	I1															
										I1						
										I1						
				O1												
				O1												
	O1															
			I1													
				O1												
					I1	O1										
						O1										
									O1							
												O1				
I1																
	I1															
I1																
														I2		
	I1															
		I4														I1
							O1									
														O1		
						I1										
										I1						
										I1						

Function Name	Function Number	Color	ColorTPtr	ColorWord	EntryNum	GrafProcsPtr	H	Height	LocInfoPtr	MasterSCB	MaxWidth
Parameter Size		W	L	W	W	L	W	W	L	W	W
Parameter Type		V	P	V	V	P	V	V	P	BA	V
SetGrafProcs	68					I1					
SetIntUse	182										
SetMasterSCB	22								I1		
SetOrigin	35						I1				
SetPicSave	62										
SetPolySave	66										
SetPort	27										
SetPortLoc	29								I1		
SetPortRect	31										
SetPortSize	33							I2			
SetRgnSave	64										
SetSCB	18										
SetStdProcs	141										
SetSysField	72										
SetUserField	70										

Table 10-8

List of Quickdraw II Record and Initialization Commands (continued)

Note that some of the functions in Quickdraw II are available for you to use in your application, although there is normally little need for them. For example, OpenPort permits you to initialize a Grafport with standard values in a memory location specified by you. (InitPort provides the same function without allocating handles for the visible and clip regions.) In actual practice this command is rarely used directly, because the Window Manager, when it creates a window, creates a Grafport for that window by calling OpenPort. All drawing by your application within that window is done by referring to that window's Grafport, not to a separate Grafport.

PointPtr	PortPtr	ProgramID	RectPtr	SaveValue	ScanLineNum	SCB	Status	StdProcsPtr	SysFieldValue	TableNum	UseInt	UserFieldValue	V	Version	Width	ZeroPageLoc
L	L	W	L	L	W	W	W	L	L	W	W	L	W	W	W	W
P	P	V	P	P	V	BA	V	P	V	V	B	V	V	V	V	A
											I1					
														I2		
				I1												
				I1												
	I1															
			I1													
															I1	
				I1												
					I1	I2										
								I1								
									I1							
												I1				

The Quickdraw II startup function (QDStartup) also provides a port, known as the *system* or *standard port.* The startup function makes this port the current port. Even if your application does not use the Window Manager, it can still use the system port for its drawing.

Note that once a Grafport has been created, either by the Window Manager or Quickdraw II, your application may need to customize it. OpenPort, whether called directly or by another manager, uses standard values when creating a Grafport. It sets the SCB for the port to the value of the master SCB. This SCB is the value of the standard SCB unless it has

Bit	Meaning	Setting	Meaning of Setting
0-3	Color Table	%0000	Color Table 0
4	Reserved	%0	
5	Fill	%0	Fill off
6	Interrupts	%0	Interrupts off
7	Color mode	%0	320 mode

Table 10-9
Standard Scanline Control Byte (SCB)

been changed. The values in the standard SCB are shown in Table 10-9. This value can be obtained by using the GetStandardSCB function. The value of the master SCB can also be changed using the SetMasterSCB function, and the current setting can be obtained using GetMasterSCB.

For example, the following program segment checks to see if the IIGS is in 640 resolution mode and, if not, changes to that mode.

```
*Program segment to check whether the IIGS is in 640 resolution
*mode and, if not, changes to that mode
        . . .
        PEA $0000                   ;Space for result
        _GetMasterSCB               ;Get the master scanline control byte
        PLA                         ;from the stack
        TAY                         ;Temporarily save value
        AND #%0000000010000000      ;Mask off bit 7
        BNE Its640                  ;If bit 7 is set, resolution is already 640
        TYA                         ;Get back original value of SCB
        ORA #%0000000010000000      ;Set bit 7
        PHA
        _SetMasterSCB
        . . .                       ;Other adjustments for 640 mode go here
Its640  . . .                       ;Rest of code goes here
```

The program checks to see if the IIGS is in 640 mode, rather than just setting 640 mode, because certain other managers (particularly the Window and Menu Manager) need to be readjusted if the pixel resolution mode is switched between 320 and 640. See Chapters 16 and 17 for further discussion.

If your application has several Grafports in existence at once, it needs to make the Grafport in which it wants to draw the current or active port. The SetPort function permits your application to pass a pointer to the Grafport that it wants to make active. Since this Grafport is usually a window, the application passes the pointer to the window's Grafport when the Window Manager creates the window.

The Grafport record also contains a special, application-defined field known as the *User Field.* This is a long-word (32-bit) value that can contain any data your program needs. If more than a long-word of data is needed, the application can store a pointer to the data area here. The value is set by thc SetUserField function and can be obtained by the GetUser-Field function.

Each point in a Grafport has two values, based on two different coordinate systems. *Global coordinates* are determined based on the upper-left corner of the pixel image being 0,0. *Local coordinates* are determined based on the upper-left corner of the current BoundsRect (see Figure 10-5). The GlobalToLocal function converts the global coordinates

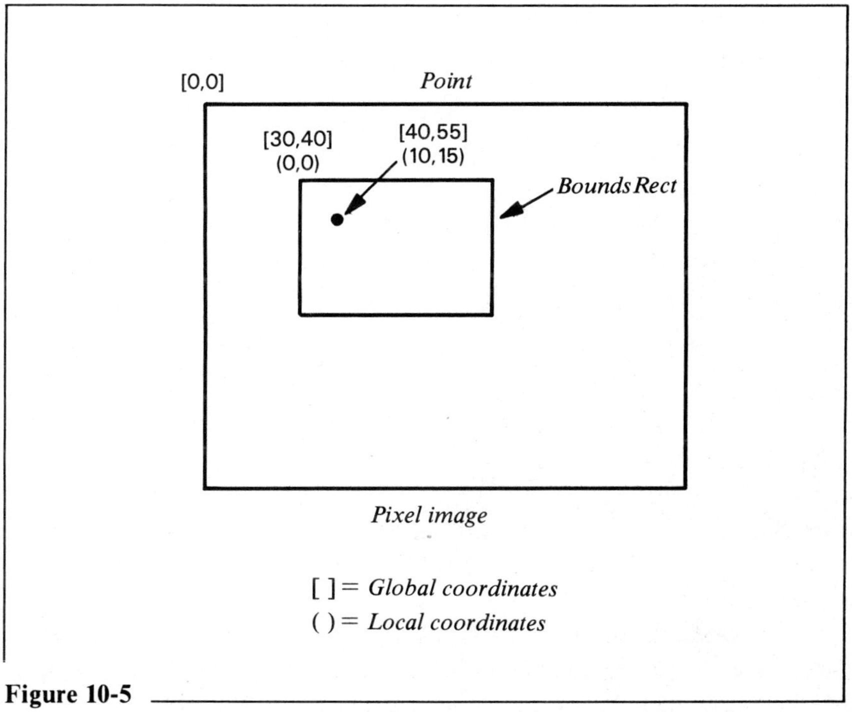

Figure 10-5
Determination of local coordinates

of a point to local coordinates, and the LocalToGlobal function performs the conversion in the opposite direction. These conversions are often needed by the various drawing commands that are discussed in Chapters 11 to 13.

CHAPTER 11

Quickdraw II: Pens, Patterns, and Drawing

There are many different ways to place an image into a pixel image in Quickdraw II. This chapter discusses the base-level methods of drawing with a pen, use of patterns, and the effects of clipping. Chapter 12 discusses drawing with shapes (including cursors), and Chapter 13 deals with drawing with text.

DRAWING WITH A PEN

The easiest method of drawing in Quickdraw II uses the *pen*, a mythical instrument controlled by various Quickdraw II commands. Moving the pen can, if circumstances are right, result in an image of its moving point appearing on the super-resolution graphics screen.

The Quickdraw II pen has several different aspects. Six of these aspects make up the pen state, a specific record structure used in Quickdraw II. The layout of this record structure is given in Table 11-1.

The entire pen state record can be placed into a memory location by the GetPenState function. Note that this function, like many of the Quickdraw II "get" functions, does not return its values on the stack. Rather, the input to the function includes a pointer to the location of the pen state record in memory. When the function is called, it transfers the various values of the pen state record from the Grafport into the pen state record location specified by the input.

A stored (or stored-and-modified) pen state can also be restored in the Grafport by means of the SetPenState function. This restoration permits fast shuffling between different types of pens using the same Grafport.

The pen location refers to the place of the pen point (upper-left corner of a point that is more than one pixel in size) in the current pixel image, using local coordinates. As in all Quickdraw II coordinates, the pen point is below and to the right of the coordinate location rather than exactly on it. The current pen location can be obtained by means of the GetPen function. There is no corresponding SetPen function. Instead the pen location is explicitly moved by the MoveTo and Move commands discussed later in this chapter.

Byte offset	Type	Purpose
0	Point	Pen location
4	Point	Pen size
8	Word	Transfer mode
10	Pattern	Pen pattern
42	Pattern	Drawing mask
74	Pattern	Background pattern

Table 11-1

Pen State Record

The pen size is the height and width of the pen point. A point can be multiple pixels in width or height—theoretically up to the maximum dimensions of the pixel image. The location used for determining the location of the pen point, in a multiple-pixel pen point, is the upper-leftmost pixel. The current pen size can be obtained by the GetPenSize function and modified by the SetPenSize function.

When drawing takes place with the pen point, pixels in the pixel image are changed according to the transfer mode (as well as other factors). There are eight different transfer modes, each of which affects the destination or pixel map image differently depending on the pen and pixel setting. The drawing mode affects individual bits in the pixel image, not just pixels themselves. This is a change from the Macintosh transfer modes, and is made necessary by the fact that pixels in the IIGS are 2 to 4 bits in width, while they are all uniformly 1 bit in the Macintosh.

There are actually 16 different transfer modes available in Quickdraw II, but 8 of them apply only to text transfer. These modes are discussed in Chapter 13. The modes available for pen, shape, and pixel transfers are listed in Table 11-2.

Mode	Value	Use
BIC	$0003	Expressly clears individual bits (BIC = BIt Clear). Often done prior to overlaying another image.
COPY	$0000	Typically copies image to the pixel image.
notBIC	$8003	Displays the intersection of two images by performing a reverse bit clear.
notCOPY	$8000	Copies inverse of image to the pixel image.
notOR	$8001	Copies inverse of a new image on top of an existing image nondestructively.
notXOR	$8002	Draws inverse of an image and erases it by redrawing.
OR	$0001	Overlays a new image on top of an existing image nondestructively.
XOR	$0002	Draws image and erases it by redrawing.

Table 11-2
Pen Transfer Modes

The effect of a particular transfer mode on the bit in the pixel image depends on whether that bit and the corresponding bit in the pen point image are set or clear. For each transfer mode, a truth table shows the final value of the bit in the pixel image based on that bit's initial value and the value of the bit in the pen point. These truth tables are listed in Tables 11-3 to 11-10. The current pen mode can be obtained by the GetPenMode function and changed by the SetPenMode function.

		Pen 0	Pen 1
Initial Pixel Image	0	0	0
	1	1	0

Table 11-3
BIC Truth Table

		Pen 0	Pen 1
Initial Pixel Image	0	0	1
	1	0	1

Table 11-4
COPY Truth Table

		Pen 0	Pen 1
Initial Pixel Image	0	0	0
	1	1	0

Table 11-5
notBIC Truth Table

		Pen 0	Pen 1
Initial Pixel Image	0	1	0
	1	1	0

Table 11-6
notCOPY Truth Table

		Pen 0	Pen 1
Initial Pixel Image	0	1	0
	1	1	1

Table 11-7
notOR Truth Table

		Pen 0	Pen 1
Initial Pixel Image	0	1	0
	1	0	1

Table 11-8
notXOR Truth Table

		Pen 0	Pen 1
Initial Pixel Image	0	0	1
	1	1	1

Table 11-9
OR Truth Table

		Pen 0	Pen 1
Initial Pixel Image	0	0	1
	1	1	0

Table 11-10
XOR Truth Table

Pixel Value	Color Name
0	Black ($0000)
1	Dark gray ($0777)
2	Brown ($0841)
3	Purple ($072C)
4	Blue ($000F)
5	Dark green ($0080)
6	Orange ($0F70)
7	Red ($0D00)
8	Flesh ($0FA9)
9	Yellow ($0FF0)
A	Green ($00E0)
B	Light blue ($04DF)
C	Lilac ($0DAF)
D	Periwinkle blue ($078F)
E	Light gray ($0CCC)
F	White ($0FFF)

Table 11-11
Standard Color Table

USE OF PATTERNS

To understand the use of transfer modes, assume the IIGS is in 320 super-resolution mode using the standard color table as shown in Table 11-11. A 6×6-pixel area of the screen has a pattern consisting of alternating red, orange, and yellow in a three-line offset pattern as follows:

Red	Orange	Yellow	Red	Orange	Yellow
Orange	Yellow	Red	Orange	Yellow	Red
Yellow	Red	Orange	Yellow	Red	Orange
Red	Orange	Yellow	Red	Orange	Yellow
Orange	Yellow	Red	Orange	Yellow	Red
Yellow	Red	Orange	Yellow	Red	Orange

This pattern results in pixel values as follows:

7	6	9	7	6	9
6	9	7	6	9	7
9	7	6	9	7	6
7	6	9	7	6	9
6	9	7	6	9	7
9	7	6	9	7	6

Or, in binary format, the pattern is as follows:

0111	0110	1001	0111	0110	1001
0110	1001	0111	0110	1001	0111
1001	0111	0110	1001	0111	0110
0111	0110	1001	0111	0110	1001
0110	1001	0111	0110	1001	0111
1001	0111	0110	1001	0111	0110

Further assume that the pen-drawing pattern is alternating green (color \$A) and purple (color \$3) lines with a point size of 2 pixels high × 2 pixels wide, and assume that it is being moved beginning from point 3,3. The bit image of the pen point, thus, looks like this:

1010	1010	2 pixels of green (\$A)
0011	0011	2 pixels of purple (\$3)

In OR mode the following takes place at the initial pen location:

PenPoint 1,1	OR	Screen 3,3 = 1010	OR	0110 = 1110
PenPoint 1,2	OR	Screen 3,4 = 1010	OR	1001 = 1011
PenPoint 2,1	OR	Screen 4,3 = 0011	OR	1001 = 1011
PenPoint 2,2	OR	Screen 4,4 = 0011	OR	0111 = 0111

The screen image is thus changed as follows:

0111	0110	1001	0111	0110	1001
0110	1001	0111	0110	1001	0111
1001	0111	1110	1011	0111	0110
0111	0110	1011	0111	0110	1001
0110	1001	0111	0110	1001	0111
1001	0111	0110	1001	0111	0110

Or, in hexadecimal, the screen image is as follows:

7	6	9	7	6	9
6	9	7	6	9	7
9	7	E	B	7	6
7	6	B	7	6	9
6	9	7	6	9	7
9	7	6	9	7	6

This pattern represents the following pixel colors:

Red	Orange	Yellow	Red	Orange	Yellow
Orange	Yellow	Red	Orange	Yellow	Red
Yellow	Red	L. Gray	L. Blue	Red	Orange
Red	Orange	L. Blue	Red	Orange	Yellow
Orange	Yellow	Red	Orange	Yellow	Red
Yellow	Red	Orange	Yellow	Red	Orange

This example shows the importance (if your application will use a transfer mode other than COPY) of carefully choosing the location of the colors in the color table. Colors that are opposite should be certain to have opposite values in the color table (that is, color %0110 should be the opposite color to color %1001).

A *pattern* is an array of bits representing an 8×8 square of pixels. When the pen draws in the pixel image, it always uses the pen pattern to do its drawing. This pattern is pixel-aligned so that it forms a continuous, unbroken pattern in all areas in which it appears. This means that pixel number 1 of the pattern always appears in pixel number 1 of the image (and pixel number 9, 17, 25, and so forth). Pixel number 2 of the pattern always appears in pixel number 2 of the image, and so on. The example assumes that screen location 3,3 is actually a pixel image location in which pixel 1,1 of the pen point appears.

A pattern is expressed as 64 pixels with each pixel being 2 bits in 640 mode and 4 bits in 320 mode. The various pattern functions require that your application place this pattern in memory and then pass the routines a pointer to this memory location. The pixels must be placed in memory with the first row followed by the second row, and so forth.

Two different patterns, each with a different use, are kept for the pen. The pen pattern, as discussed previously, is used by the pen in drawing. It can be obtained by the GetPenPat function and modified by the SetPen-Pat function.

The SetSolidPenPat function also sets the pen pattern, but by a different method. The input to this function consists of a color table number (4 bits in 320 mode and 2 bits in 640 mode) that consists of the lower 2 or 4 bits of a word value. Note that in 640 mode this instruction will cause a solid color pattern only if the color is repeated every fourth position in the color table. (See the discussion of color tables and pixel values in Chapter 9.) Otherwise this command will result in a vertical-striped pattern.

The other pattern used by the pen—the background pattern—erases anything in the pixel image. It has a related set of three functions that manipulate its value in the same manner as the pen pattern. These are GetBackPat, SetBackPat, and SetSolidBackPat.

A command also exists for changing either the pen pattern or background pattern into a solid pattern. To use this function, you first move the appropriate pattern from the Grafport to a specified memory location and then call the SolidPattern function. The following code segment sets the background pattern to the first color in the background pattern:

```
Pattern   DATA
          DS '32'                ;32 bytes for a pattern in 320 mode
          END
          . . .
Solid1    START
          Pushlong #Pattern      ;Pointer to pattern storage
          _GetBackPat            ;Get background pattern
          Pushlong #Pattern      ;Pointer to background pattern
          Pushword Pattern       ;Get first color from pattern
          _SolidPattern          ;Make it solid color
          Pushword #Pattern      ;Pointer to now solid background pattern
          _SetBackPat            ;Moved into Grafport background pattern
          . . .
```

An alternative method of this code, using SetSolidBackPat, is

```
Pattern   DATA
          DS '32'                ;32 bytes for a pattern in 320 mode
          END
          . . .
Solid2    START
          Pushlong #Pattern      ;Pointer to pattern storage
          _GetBackPat            ;Get background pattern
          Pushword Pattern       ;Get first color from pattern
          _SetSolidBackPat       ;And make it solid
```

Note that the second code example is much more efficient. The first example is given mainly to show use of the SolidPattern function.

The solid pattern functions—SolidPattern, SetSolidPenPat, and SetSolidBackPat—take a word (16-bit) value as the color, but do not use all 16 bits. Instead they use either the lowest 2 bits (if the Port SCB indicates 640 mode) or the lowest 4 bits (if the Port SCB indicates 320 mode).

Drawing a pixel onto the screen is not simply a matter of matching the bits in the pen point and the pixel images using the appropriate transfer mode. Before that task can be undertaken, Quickdraw II must determine whether the particular pen pixel is allowed to be drawn. For that task it consults the drawing mask.

The *drawing mask* is a pattern that is conceptually much like the pen pattern and background pattern. It is 8 pixels × 8 pixels. But the mask consists of single-bit pixels, either 1 (on) or 0 (off). If the pen point pixel at a particular point is to be drawn to the screen, the particular bit in the 8-bit × 8-bit mask must be set to 1. Otherwise the pixel image pixel at that point remains unchanged.

The drawing mask record is an 8-byte (4-word) array of bits. Each byte in the record represents one of the eight rows of the mask. The mask is set by the SetPenMask command, and the current value of the mask is obtained by the GetPenMask command. For example, your application would use the following code to provide for a drawing mask with a checkerboard shape as shown in Figure 11-1.

```
Mask      DATA             ;Storage for drawing mask
          DS '8'
          END
Checker   START
          LDA #$AA55       ;=%1010 1010 0101 0101
          LDX #$0007       ;Store in 4 words
Loop      STA Mask,X
          DEX
          DEX              ;Decrement twice for storing words
          BPL Loop         ;If not done, continue
          Pushlong #Mask   ;Address of mask onto stack
          _SetPenMask      ;And set mask
          . . .
          END
```

When manipulating the various parts of the pen state record, you may wind up with an unknown pen state. The PenNormal command is made just for situations like this. It sets a portion of the pen state record to default values as shown in Table 11-12.

One of the advantages of moving the entire pen state record into and out of the Grafport with a single command is the ability to change quickly

Figure 11-1
Drawing mask with checkerboard shape

Field	Value
PnLoc	Unchanged
PnSize	$0001,0001
PnMode	$0000
PnPat	Black (color 0)
PnMask	$FFFFFFFFFFFFFFFF (No effective mask)
BkPat	Unchanged

Table 11-12
Normal Setting of Pen State by PenNormal

between separate pens while drawing. For example, assume you want four pens in a Grafport: one that draws in COPY mode with a one-square pixel point, one that draws in COPY mode with a two-square pixel point, one that draws in XOR mode with a one-square pixel point, and one that draws in XOR mode with a two-square pixel point. In addition, the two-square pixel pens draw with a pattern of alternating colors (numbers 3 and 5), while the one-square pixel pens draw with color 2.

The following code would work to perform the necessary switching. The code assumes that the Y register contains the value of the pens that should be used (the four pens are numbered 0-3), and it assumes that the pen number currently in use is stored in the memory-variable PenNum.

```
Pens         Data
Pen1         DS '4'                ;Pen location storage
PSize1       DC I'1,1'             ;Size of 1 by 1
PMode1       DC I'0000'            ;Copy mode
PPat1        DC 32I1'22'           ;Pattern of color #2
PMask1       DC 8I1'FF'            ;Mask = all 1's
BPat1        DS '32'               ;Storage for background pattern
Pen2         DS '4'                ;Pen location storage
PSize2       DC I'2,2'             ;Size of 2 by 2
PMode2       DC I'0000'            ;Copy mode
PPat2        DC 32I1'35'           ;Pattern of colors 3 and 5
PMask2       DC 8I1'FF'            ;Mask = all 1's
BPat2        DS '32'               ;Storage for background pattern
Pen3         DS '4'                ;Pen location storage
PSize3       DC I'1,1'             ;Size of 1 by 1
PMode3       DC I'0002'            ;XOR mode
PPat3        DC 32I1'22'           ;Pattern of color #2
PMask3       DC 8I1'FF'            ;Mask = all 1's
BPat3        DS '32'               ;Storage for background pattern
Pen4         DS '4'                ;Pen location storage
PSize4       DC I'2,2'             ;Size of 2 by 2
PMode4       DC I'0002'            ;XOR mode
PPat4        DC 32I1'35'           ;Pattern of colors 3 and 5
PMask4       DC 8I1'FF'            ;Mask = all 1's
BPat4        DS '32'               ;Storage for background pattern
             END
PenSwitch    START
             JMP Begin
SwitchTable DC I2'P1J,P2J,P3J,P4J'
SaveTable    DC I2'P1S,P2S,P3S,P4S'
Begin        LDA PenNum            ;Get current pen number
             ASL A                 ;Double to use as index
             TAX
             JSR (SaveTable,X)     ;Save existing pen state
             STY PenNum            ;Save new pen number
             TYA                   ;Pen number in accumulator
             ASL A                 ;Doubled for index
             TAX
             JSR (SwitchTable,X)   ;Set pen state to new setting
             . . .
P1J          PushLong #Pen1        ;Pointer to pen state record
              _SetPenState
             RTS
P2J          PushLong #Pen2        ;Pointer to pen state record
              _SetPenState
             RTS
P3J          PushLong #Pen3        ;Pointer to pen state record
              _SetPenState
             RTS
P4J          PushLong #Pen4        ;Pointer to pen state record
              _SetPenState
             RTS
P1S          PushLong #Pen1        ;Pointer to current pen state record
```

```
               _GetPenState            ;Save it before changing
               RTS
P2S            PushLong #Pen2          ;Pointer to current pen state record
               _GetPenState            ;Save it before changing
               RTS
P3S            PushLong #Pen3          ;Pointer to current pen state record
               _GetPenState            ;Save it before changing
               RTS
P4S            PushLong #Pen4          ;Pointer to current pen state record
               _GetPenState            ;Save it before changing
               RTS
               END
```

One aspect of the pen that is saved in the Grafport but not in the pen state record is the visibility level of the pen. When the Grafport is first created, the pen is given a *visibility level* of zero, which means that any drawing with the pen appears on the screen if the area in which the drawing occurs is otherwise visible and active. A pen visibility of less than zero results in no effect from drawing commands (except for the movement of the pen).

There is no command for accessing the pen visibility except directly from the Grafport itself. No GetPenVis command exists. Similarly there is no command to set the pen visibility directly to a certain level. Instead two commands modify pen visibility. HidePen decrements the pen visibility level by one, while ShowPen increments the pen visibility level by one. These two commands are misnamed because neither necessarily works to either hide or show the pen. Instead they may cause that particular effect depending on the present pen visibility level.

When coding an application, be sure to balance HidePen and ShowPen commands. If a subroutine calls one of these routines, it should also call the other routine before returning to the main program loop. Otherwise your application may end up either with a pen that will draw when it should not or with a pen that will not draw when it should. The one exception to this rule concerns the initial setting of the visibility level. If you want the pen invisible in your application except when explicitly made visible, then your application can have an initial, unbalanced HidePen command at the beginning.

Quickdraw II provides two commands for moving the pen around the pixel image. Both of these commands perform the pen movement without any drawing, notwithstanding the visibility level of the pen. The MoveTo command moves the pen to a specified absolute point in the pixel image, using local coordinates. Your application merely passes the horizontal and vertical coordinates to which the pen should be moved. The Move command causes the pen to move relative to its current location. Both a horizontal and vertical displacement are passed to the routine. A positive displacement moves the pen down (if vertical) or to the left (if horizontal). A negative displacement moves the pen up (if vertical) or to the right (if horizontal).

For example, assume the pen is currently located at coordinates 12,171 and is to be moved to coordinates 26,130. To perform this movement using the MoveTo function, issue the following series of commands:

```
PEA $001A      ;$1A=26 decimal (horizontal location)
PEA $0082      ;$82=139 decimal (vertical location)
_MoveTo
```

The same result occurs using the following code in conjunction with the Move function:

```
PEA $000E      ;Positive horizontal displacement of 14
PEA $FFD6      ;Two's complement of 41, negative vertical movement
_Move
```

Two drawing commands that use the pen function in the same manner as the two move commands are LineTo and Line. LineTo draws a line from the current location of the pen to the point specified in the parameters passed to the function. Line performs the same action, except that the parameters passed to it consist of displacement values, not absolute coordinates.

Both the LineTo and Line commands perform the actual drawing only if the pen visibility level is not negative. The pen is also moved to the end point of the line by these functions, even if the drawing does not occur. These two commands also contribute to the definition of a polygon or a region if either of these functions are active. (See discussion of the OpenPoly and OpenRgn commands in Chapter 12.)

EFFECTS OF CLIPPING

All drawing done by the Grafport pen does not necessarily appear on the IIGS's display screen. As discussed in Chapter 10, the BoundsRect is a portion of the PortInfo of the Grafport. It is a rectangle around that portion of the entire theoretical drawing space that is the pixel map of that

Grafport. The PortRect, another part of the Grafport, is a rectangle that describes the active area of the drawing space. That part of the drawing space present in both the BoundsRect and PortRect is normally the only area in which drawing can occur.

The intersection of the BoundsRect and PortRect is not necessarily displayed on the IIGS super-resolution graphics screen. That image can be further restricted by the *clip region* and the *vis region*.

As discussed in Chapter 12, a *region* is an area of the pixel image that can be any size and shape. It does not need to be contiguous and may have holes within itself. For an image to be displayed on the screen, it must be within both the clip region and the vis region. These two regions are both set, upon Grafport initialization, to be a rectangle the size of the pixel image, thereby not causing any restriction on the visible image. Further action can result in the image being restricted by a contracting of one or both of these regions.

The final displayed image, then, consists of that part of the pixel image that is within the BoundsRect, PortRect, ClipRgn, and VisRgn (see Figure 11-2).

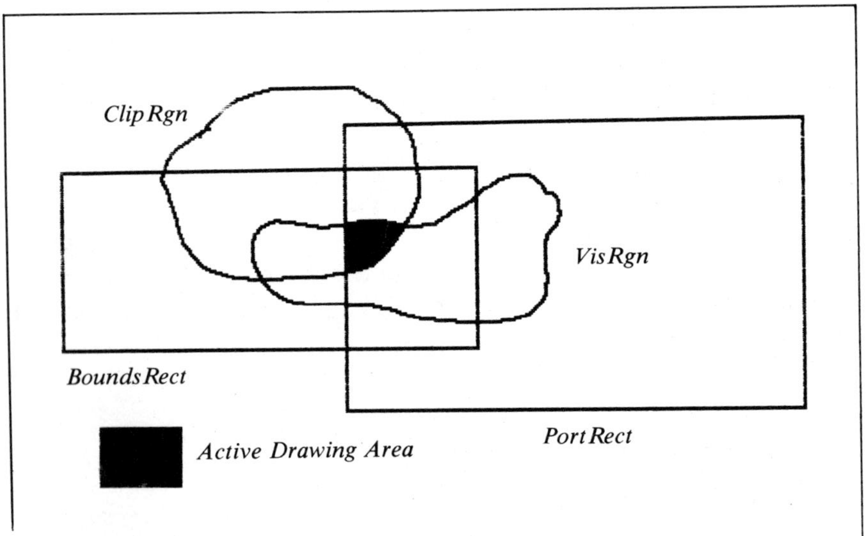

Figure 11-2
Portion of pixel image in BoundsRect, PortRect, ClipRgn, and VisRgn

The clip region is designed for use by your application. SetClip copies a region specified by your application to the clip region, resulting in that screen image being clipped accordingly. GetClip copies the current clip region to a specified area.

Another method of changing the clip region is to change its handle, which is maintained as part of the Grafport record. GetClipHandle returns the handle to the current clip region, while SetClipHandle changes the handle of the clip region to the input data.

The vis region is created for use by the system, primarily by the Window Manager. Under ordinary circumstances, your application should not use this region for clipping or other manipulation—the clip region should be used instead. But there may be a reason for your application to use the vis region in some cases, such as the use of custom windows or custom Window Manager routines. Quickdraw II provides for routines that permit an application to manipulate the vis region in the same manner as the clip region. The relationship between the clip region and vis region routines is shown in Table 11-13.

Table 11-14 is a listing of the various Quickdraw II functions that affect the pen, the clip region, or the vis region, together with the various parameters each function requires. Table 11-15 is a comparison of these Quickdraw II functions with the similar Quickdraw functions available on the Macintosh.

Clip Region Routine	Vis Region Routine
ClipRect	n/a
GetClip	GetVisRgn
GetClipHandle	GetVisHandle
SetClip	SetVisRgn
SetClipHandle	SetVisHandle

Table 11-13

Comparable Routines for Manipulating the Vis and Clip Regions

Function Name	Function Number	ColorNum	dH	dV	H	Height	MaskPtr	PatternPtr	PenMode	PenStatePtr	PointPtr	RectPtr	RgnHandle	V	Width
Parameter Size		W	W	W	W	W	L	L	W	L	L	L	L	W	W
Parameter Type		V	V	V	V	V	P	P	V	P	P	P	H	V	V
ClipRect	38											I1			
GetBackPat	53							I1							
GetClip	37												I1		
GetClipHandle	199												O1		
GetPen	44										I1				
GetPenMask	51						I1								
GetPenMode	47								O1						
GetPenPat	49							I1							
GetPenSize	45										I1				
GetPenState	43									I1					
GetVisHandle	201												O1		
GetVisRgn	181												I1		
HidePen	39														
Line	61		I1	I2											
LineTo	60				I1									I2	
Move	59		I1	I2											
MoveTo	58				I1									I2	
PenNormal	54														
SetBackPat	52							I1							
SetClip	36												I1		
SetClipHandle	198												I1		
SetPenMask	50						I1								
SetPenMode	46								I1						
SetPenPat	48							I1							
SetPenSize	44					I2									I1
SetPenState	42									I1					
SetSolidBackPat	56	I1													
SetSolidPenPat	55	I1													
SetVisHandle	200												I1		
SetVisRgn	180												I1		
ShowPen	40														
SolidPattern	57	I2						I1							

Table 11-14

Quickdraw II Commands Involving the Pen, VisRgn, or ClipRgn

Notes:

Parameter sizes:

L	long-word (32-bit) value
W	word (16-bit) value

Parameter types:

H	handle
P	pointer
V	value

Table 11-14

Quickdraw II Commands Involving the Pen, VisRgn, or ClipRgn (continued)

Command	Quickdraw II (Apple IIGS)	Quickdraw (Apple Macintosh)
ClipRect	X	X
GetBackPat	X	
GetClip	X	X
GetClipHandle	X	
GetPen	X	X
GetPenMask	X	
GetPenMode	X	
GetPenPat	X	
GetPenSize	X	
GetPenState	X	X
GetVisHandle	X	
GetVisRgn	X	
HidePen	X	X
Line	X	X
LineTo	X	X
Move	X	X
MoveTo	X	X
PenNormal	X	X
SetBackPat	X	X (BackPat)

Table 11-15

Comparison of Selected Quickdraw II and Quickdraw Commands

Command	Quickdraw II (Apple IIGS)	Quickdraw (Apple Macintosh)
ClipRect	X	X
SetClip	X	X
SetClipHandle	X	
SetPenMask	X	
SetPenMode	X	X (PenMode)
SetPenPat	X	X (PenPat)
SetPenSize	X	X (PenSize)
SetPenState	X	X
SetSolidBackPat	X	
SetSolidPenPat	X	
SetVisHandle	X	
SetVisRgn	X	
ShowPen	X	X
SolidPattern	X	

Table 11-15

Comparison of Selected Quickdraw II and Quickdraw Commands (continued)

CHAPTER 12

Shapes and the Cursor

One of the major sources of Quickdraw II's power is its ability to *draw* and *calculate* with shapes. Drawing with a shape involves placing some part of its image on the display screen. Calculating means altering the shape or determining certain attributes about it.

SHAPES

Quickdraw II works with many different shapes. For instance, the rectangle, previously discussed in Chapters 10 and 11, may be the most important shape used by Quickdraw II. It is the foundation for many other shapes and aspects of Quickdraw II (including the active area of a Grafport).

A rectangle is defined geometrically as a four-sided object with parallel sides and a right (90-degree) angle where the sides meet. In the Quickdraw environment the rectangle has infinitely thin sides that lie between pixels. The rectangle encloses all pixels that are below and to the right of its top-left corner, and that are to the left and above its bottom-right corner (see Figure 12-1 for an example). As is generally true of pixels and coordinates in Quickdraw II, the actual pixels for any coordinate point lie below and to the right of the point.

A rectangle can be placed within a pixel image based on the coordinates at which it exists. In the Quickdraw II environment the four coordinates to a rectangle represent, in order, the left, top, right, and bottom sides of the rectangle (see Figure 12-2).

In Quickdraw II, a *point record* consists of a vertical location followed by a horizontal location. A *rectangle record* includes a left (vertical)

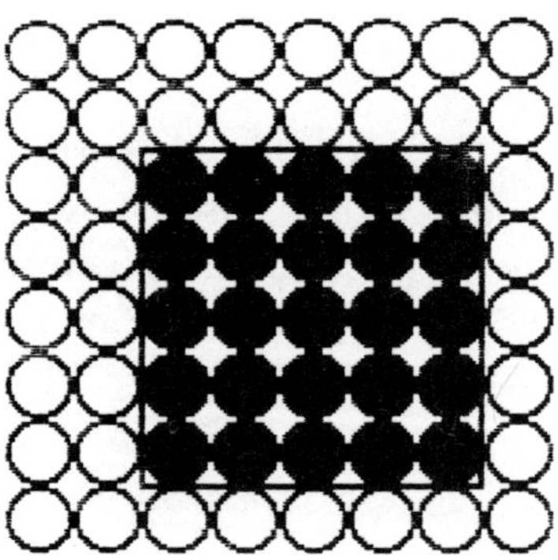

Figure 12-1

Pixels and enclosing rectangle

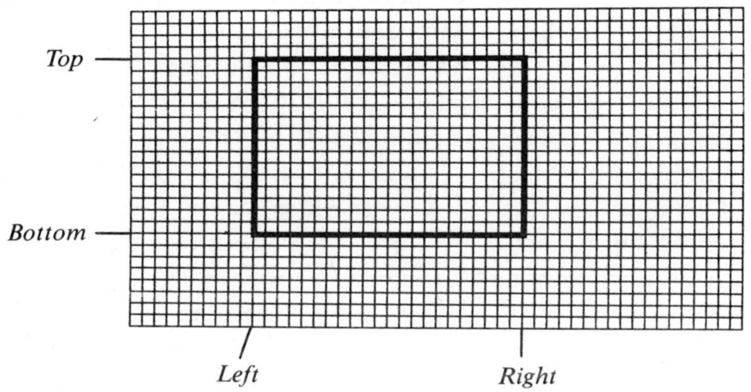

Figure 12-2
Coordinates representing a rectangle

location, a top (horizontal) location, a right (vertical) location, and a bottom (horizontal) location. Thus the rectangle can be considered either as four values defining the location of the four sides of the rectangle or as a pair of points defining the top-left (left first) and bottom-right (right first) points of the rectangle (see Figure 12-3).

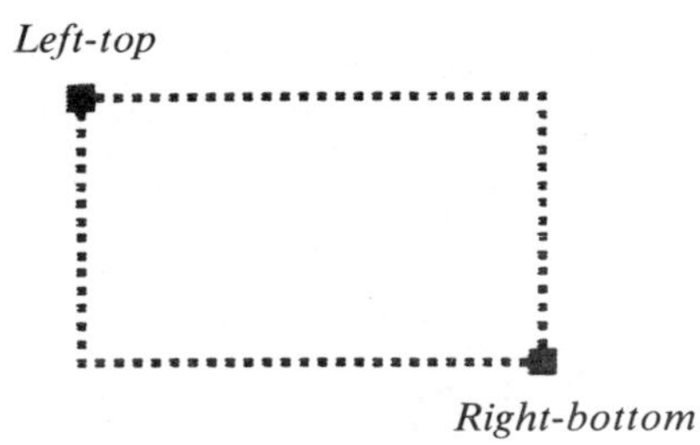

Figure 12-3
Pair of points defining a rectangle

In geometry a square is defined as a rectangle with equal sides. Quickdraw II has no shape called a square, although if a rectangle has equal sides, it is automatically a square. You cannot, however, easily determine what constitutes equal sides in a rectangle. On the Macintosh, each screen pixel is square-shaped. Thus, a line that is 10 pixels in length appears on the screen as the same size whether it is displayed horizontally or vertically. With the Apple IIGS, a pixel is not square—it is longer vertically than horizontally by a factor of 8 to 7 in 320 mode and 16 to 7 in 640 mode. This relationship results in a 10-pixel line appearing longer when displayed vertically than when it is displayed horizontally (see Figure 12-4).

The simple solution is to adjust the measurements to account for this difference in pixel dimensions. Thus, a rectangle appears square on the screen if it is 8 pixels horizontally by 7 pixels vertically in 320 mode (and 16 × 7 in 640 mode). If your application only displays shapes on the screen (that is, it does not print them), you can use this method.

A more significant problem exists if your application also prints the square on a printer. The Apple Imagewriter II printer prints circular dots when it prints. Thus a rectangle printed on the Imagewriter II that is 10 dots × 10 dots appears square. Adjustment can be made in some cases although not in all cases because pixels for a nonsquare object also have to be adjusted, and these cannot always be adjusted in even pixel amounts. In

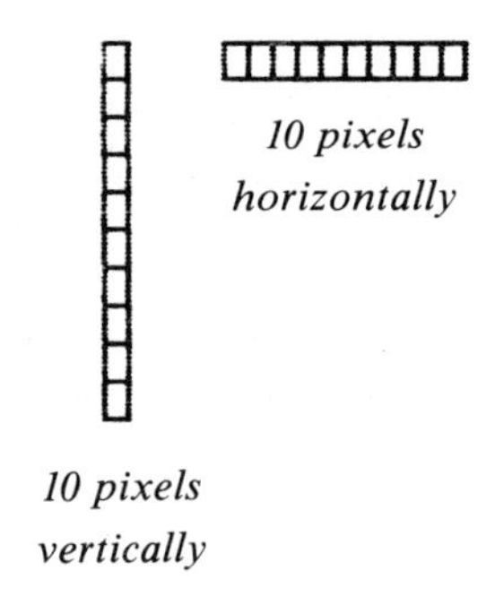

Figure 12-4

A 10-pixel line appearing longer when displayed vertically than when displayed horizontally

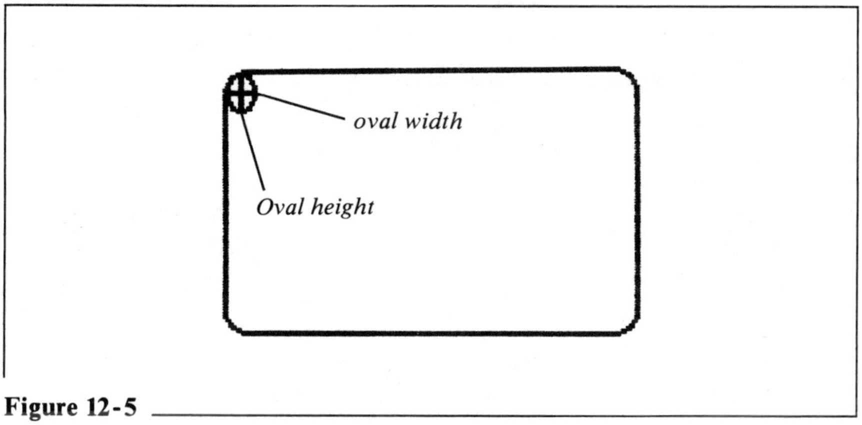

Figure 12-5
Oval width and height used for corners of roundrect

any event the screen image does not exactly match the printed image.

The rectangle forms the basis for many other shapes in Quickdraw II. The *oval* is a curved object inscribed within a rectangle. Like the geometric oval, it has two axes around which the arcs constituting the oval are inscribed. In the case of a *circle,* which is an oval inscribed within a square, these two axes are in the same location. The outer edges of the oval are never outside the edges of the rectangle, although in at least four locations they are identical with the edges.

A *roundrect* is a rectangle with rounded corners. When your application draws a roundrect, by calling the appropriate Quickdraw II command, it also specifies the degree of rounding of the corners. The application does this by specifying an oval width and height to use for the corners (see Figure 12-5).

An *arc* is a part of the outside or circular aspect of an oval. Quickdraw II also uses the name arc to refer to an enclosed geometric shape more properly known as a *wedge.* A wedge consists of an arc with a line from each end point of the arc extending to the middle of the rectangle in which the arc is inscribed (see Figure 12-6).

An arc is defined in terms of a rectangle (that encloses the oval of which the arc is a part), a *starting angle,* and an *arc angle.* The arc begins at the starting angle and extends for arc angle degrees along the oval. If the arc angle is positive, the arc extends in a clockwise direction. If the arc angle is negative, the arc extends in a counter clockwise direction.

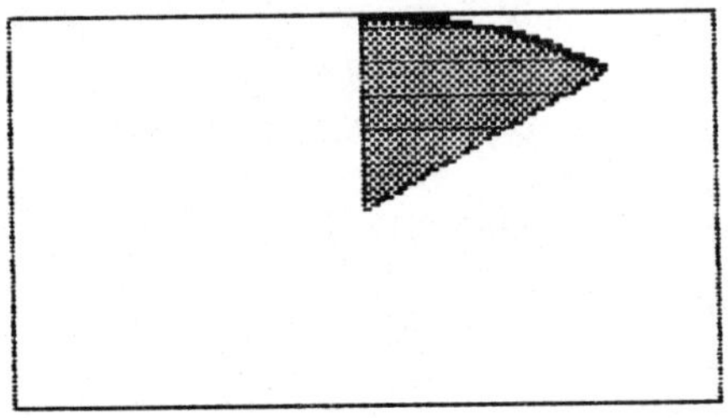

Figure 12-6
Example of a wedge (or arc)

The angle degrees are not always true geometric circular arc degrees. The 0, 90, 180, and 270 degree points are based on geometric degrees, corresponding to straight up, right, down, and left. The other degrees are based on the rectangle, so that 45, 135, 225, and 315 represent angles going through the four corners of the rectangle (see Figure 12-7).

In addition to the simple shapes of rectangle, roundrect, oval, and arc, all of which are based on an enclosing rectangle, Quickdraw II has more complex shapes—a *polygon* and a *region.* A polygon consists of any

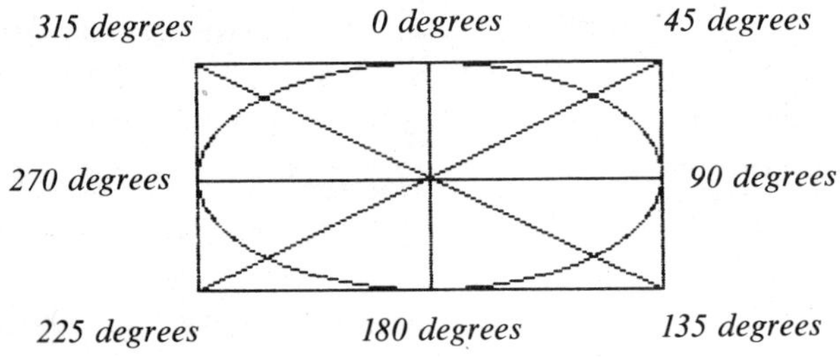

Figure 12-7
Angles going through four corners of a rectangle

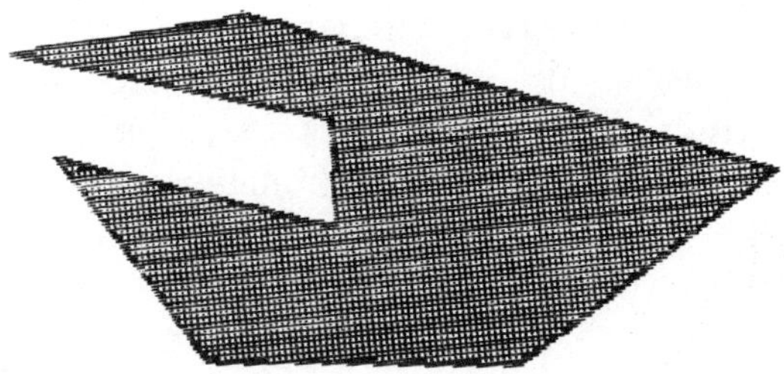

Figure 12-8
Example of a polygon

number of different lines that are drawn with the Line or LineTo commands discussed in Chapter 11. A polygon must be an enclosed shape—that is, the end point of its last line must be at the same location as the beginning of the first line. If it is not, the command closing the definition of the polygon places this extra line in the definition (see Figure 12-8).

A region, which is an even more complex shape than a polygon, can be any shape and may consist of noncontiguous areas. It is created out of lines and framed shapes, including polygons (see Figure 12-9).

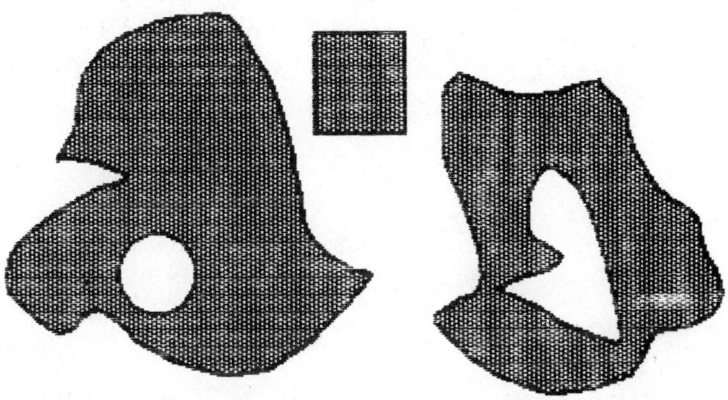

Figure 12-9
Example of a region

Defining Shapes

Quickdraw II has two different commands that can define a rectangle. In each case you must set up a space in memory for an 8-byte rectangle record. The SetRect command must be passed a pointer to this address as the first value, together with four additional values consisting of the left, top, right, and bottom coordinates of the rectangle. The following code creates a rectangle with the coordinates of 0 (left), 0 (top), 10 (right), and 30 (bottom).

```
Shapes    DATA
Rect1     DS '8'                 ;Storage for rectangle record
          . . .
          END
DefRect1  START
          Pushlong #Rect1        ;Pointer to rectangle storage area
          PEA $0000              ;Left coordinate of rectangle
          PEA $0000              ;Top coordinate of rectangle
          PEA $000A              ;Right coordinate of rectangle
          PEA $001E              ;Bottom coordinate of rectangle
          _SetRect               ;Creates the rectangle
          END
```

Note that this listing only creates the rectangle in memory. It does not draw it on the screen or any place else in the pixel image.

A rectangle may also be defined in terms of two points—the first representing the upper-left corner of the rectangle and the second representing the bottom-right corner. The Pt2Rect command then converts these points to a rectangle. The parameters passed to this routine consist of pointers to two-point records and a pointer to the rectangle record. Unlike the SetRect command, Pt2Rect requires the rectangle pointer be the last, not the first, parameter passed to the routine. The following code creates a rectangle identical to the one in the previous listing. This code also uses the SetPt command, which creates a point record from various parameters.

```
Shapes    DATA
Rect1     DS '8'                 ;Storage for rectangle record
Point1    DS '4'                 ;Storage for first point record
Point2    DS '4'                 ;Storage for second point record
          . . .
          END
DefRect2  START
          Pushlong #Point1       ;Pointer to first point record
          PEA $0000              ;Horizontal coordinate of point
          PEA $0000              ;Vertical coordinate of point
```

```
_SetPt                  ;Create first point
Pushlong #Point2        ;Pointer to second point record
PEA $000A               ;Horizontal coordinate of point
PEA $001E               ;Vertical coordinate of point
_SetPt                  ;Create second point
Pushlong #Point1        ;Upper-left corner of rectangle
Pushlong #Point2        ;Lower-right corner of rectangle
Pushlong #Rect1         ;Pointer to rectangle record
_Pt2Rect                ;Create the rectangle
END
```

A polygon is created by a combination of commands. The first command is OpenPoly. This command returns a handle to the polygon record. Following the OpenPoly command, all Line and LineTo commands add another line to the polygon. The polygon definition is completed with the ClosePoly command. For example, the following code creates a right isosceles triangle with the equal sides being 11 pixels in length, beginning at coordinates 0,0 in the pixel image:

```
Triangle START
         _MoveTo 0,0            ;Place pen at starting point
         Pushlong #$0000000     ;Space for polygon handle
         _OpenPoly              ;Begin the polygon definition
         PLA                    ;Get returned handle
         STA PHandle            ;into memory location
         PLA                    ;It's a long word
         STA PHandle+2
         PEA $0000              ;No horizontal displacement
         PEA $000B              ;11-pixel vertical displacement
         _Line                  ;And draw the first line
         PEA $000B              ;11-pixel horizontal displacement
         PEA $0000              ;No vertical displacement
         _Line                  ;And draw the second line
         PEA $0000              ;Horizontal coordinate
         PEA $0000              ;Vertical coordinate
         _LineTo                ;And draw back to beginning
         _ClosePoly             ;End the polygon definition
         END
```

Note that the drawing commands used to create a polygon ignore the current pen point, pattern, and mode settings. The Line and LineTo commands do not result in any drawing on the screen until the polygon is finished and FramePoly is called.

A region can be created in much the same fashion as a polygon but with many more defining commands. The first requirement for creating a region, no matter what defining commands are to be used, is to allocate the space for the region. The NewRgn command allocates space for the region, initializes the region to the empty region, and returns a handle to the region for future use.

Once space for the region has been allocated, any of the following commands changes the region as indicated:

- □ CopyRgn makes the destination region the same as the source region.
- □ SetEmptyRgn makes the specified region empty, just like the region was when first allocated.
- □ SetRectRgn makes the region a rectangle according to the rectangle coordinates passed to the routine.
- □ RectRgn works likes SetRectRgn, except a pointer to an existing rectangle record, rather than the coordinates of the rectangle, is passed.
- □ OpenRgn acts much like OpenPoly. All Line, LineTo, and frame commands (except FrameArc) add the specified line or shape to the region. When your application is finished defining a region, the CloseRgn command should be given.

Table 12-1 shows the various shape-definition commands and the parameters used by each. This table also indicates whether a similar command exists in Quickdraw on the Macintosh.

Drawing Shapes

Each of the six shapes discussed previously may be drawn on the Apple IIGS screen in one of five different ways. The simplest method of displaying a shape is by means of the frame commands. The frame commands always draw in the current pen pattern and pen size.

For FrameRect and FrameOval, the only values passed to the routine are a pointer to the memory area in which the enclosing rectangle record is located. Thus the following code draws an oval that fits inside an existing rectangle. Note that the rectangle exists in memory but does not necessarily exist on the display screen unless it has also been drawn with the FrameRect command.

```
DoOval    START
          Pushlong #Rect       ;Pointer to existing rectangle
          _FrameOval
          END
```

Function Name	Function Number	Bottom	DestRgnHandle	H	Left	Point1Ptr	Point2Ptr	PolyHandle	RectPtr	RgnHandle	Right	SrcPtPtr	SrcRgnHandle	Top	V	Macintosh?
Parameter Size		W	L	W	W	L	L	L	L	L	W	L	L	W	W	
Parameter Type		V	H	V	V	P	P	H	P	H	V	P	H	V	V	
ClosePoly	194															Y
CloseRgn	110									I1						Y
CopyRgn	105		I2										I1			Y
NewRgn	103									O1						Y
OpenPoly	193							I1								Y
OpenRgn	109															Y
Pt2Rect	80					I1	I2		I3							Y
RectRgn	108								I2	I1						Y
SetEmptyRgn	106									I1						Y
SetPt	130			I2								I1			I3	Y
SetRect	74	I5			I2				I1		I4			I3		Y
SetRectRgn	107	I5			I2					I1	I4			I3		Y

Notes:

Parameter sizes:
- L long-word (32-bit) value
- W word (16-bit) value

Parameter types:
- H handle
- P pointer
- V value

Table 12-1

Commands Involving Shape Definition

Framing a polygon or a region is as easy as framing a rectangle or oval. The application must first pass the handle of the polygon (as returned by OpenPoly) or region (as returned by NewRgn) to the appropriate frame routine, either FramePoly or FrameRgn.

To frame a roundrect, the application must be passed three parameters—

the rectangle itself, and the width and height of the oval that forms the corners of the roundrect. This framing has already been illustrated in Figure 12-5. Framing an arc requires that the frame command be passed the rectangle, the starting angle, and the arc angle.

Most of the remaining drawing commands applicable to each of the shapes take the same parameters as the frame commands. The difference is in the effect of the command on the pixel image. In the arc commands a wedge, not just the arc line, is actually displayed.

The paint commands draw the shape and then fill it with the current pen pattern. The erase commands draw the shape and fill it with the background pattern. The invert commands change each pixel in the interior of the shape into its inverse. This command changes the pixel pattern so that each 1 in each pixel becomes a 0 and each 0 becomes a 1. In 320 mode, if a pixel consisted of %0110 (color number 6), it would be changed into %1001 (color number 9).

The fill commands require one additional parameter—a pointer to the pattern to be used as the fill pattern. The fill commands fill the specified shape with the specified pattern. They differ from the paint commands in that the paint commands always use the current pen pattern, while the fill commands always use the specified pattern passed to the command.

The ScrollRect command performs a scrolling operation on the specified rectangle. It actually works only on the intersection of the specified rectangle, VisRgn, ClipRgn, PortRect, and BoundsRect. Each pixel in this area is shifted a specified number of pixels horizontally (negative values to the left and positive values to the right) and vertically (negative values up and positive values down). All pixels that are shifted out of the active scrolling area are lost. The area opened up is made into a region and placed in the update region.The update region is initially filled with the background pattern. ScrollRect is designed for use in responding to scroll bars. (See discussion of windows and scrolling in Chapter 16 and description of controls in Chapter 18.)

The final two drawing commands in version 1.1 of Quickdraw II are PaintPixels and PPToPort. Both transfer pixels from a source rectangle to a destination rectangle using one of the transfer modes applicable to pen drawing (discussed in Chapter 11). In Quickdraw II versions 1.0 and 1.1, the pixels are transferred without stretching or shrinking. Thus only the upper-left corner of the destination rectangle, not the entire rectangle, is used. In both transfer commands the source and destination rectangles must have the same "chunkiness"—that is, they must both be in 320 mode or both in 640 mode.

Byte Offset	Length	Function
0	Long-word	Pointer to LocInfo record for source rectangle
4	Long-word	Pointer to LocInfo record for destination rectangle
8	Long-word	Pointer to source rectangle
12	Long-word	Pointer to destination rectangle
16	Word	Transfer mode
18	Long-word	Handle for clipping region

Table 12-2
PaintParameter Record Structure

PaintPixels is passed one parameter, a pointer to a record structure known as PaintParameters. The contents of that record are shown in Table 12-2. Note that the transfer of pixels is handled without regard to the current Grafport.

In PPToPort, the transfer takes place in regard to the current Grafport. This port automatically handles the clipping. No clipping region need be specified. PPToPort requires five parameters, shown in Table 12-3.

Length	Type	Function
Long-word	Pointer	Pointer to LocInfo record for source rectangle
Long-word	Pointer	Pointer to source rectangle
Word	Value	Horizontal location of upper-left corner of transfer location
Word	Value	Vertical location of upper-left corner of transfer location
Word	Value	Transfer mode

Table 12-3
PPToPort Parameters

Table 12-4 is a list of the various drawing commands and the parameters expected by each. The final column in the table shows whether a similar command exists in Quickdraw on the Macintosh.

Calculating with Shapes

Quickdraw II comes with a number of different commands that allow calculation with several of the different shapes—rectangles, regions, and polygons, as well as points. The offset commands work on rectangles, regions, and polygons. They move a shape (in memory, not on the screen unless the offset command is followed by a drawing command) a specified number of pixels horizontally (positive values to the right and negative

Function Name	Function Number	ArcAngle	DestX	DestY	dH	dV	OvalHeight	OvalWidth	PaintParamPtr	PatternPtr	PolyHandle	RectPtr	RgnHandle	SrcLocPtr	SrcRect	StartAngle	TransferMode	UpdateRgnHandle	Macintosh?
Parameter Size		W	W	W	W	W	W	W	L	L	L	L	L	L	L	W	W	L	
Parameter Type		V	V	V	V	V	V	V	P	P	H	P	H	P	P	V	V	H	
EraseArc	100	I3										I1				I2			Y
EraseOval	90											I1							Y
ErasePoly	190										I1								Y
EraseRect	85											I1							Y
EraseRgn	123												I1						Y
EraseRRect	95						I3	I2				I1							Y
FillArc	102	I3								I4		I1				I2			Y
FillOval	92									I2		I1							Y
FillPoly	192									I2	I1								Y
FillRect	87									I2		I1							Y
FillRgn	125									I2			I1						Y
FillRRect	97						I3	I2		I4		I1							Y

Table 12-4

Quickdraw II Drawing Commands

Function Name	Function Number	ArcAngle	DestX	DestY	dH	dV	OvalHeight	OvalWidth	PaintParamPtr	PatternPtr	PolyHandle	RectPtr	RgnHandle	SrcLocPtr	SrcRect	StartAngle	TransferMode	UpdateRgnHandle	Macintosh?
Parameter Size		W	W	W	W	W	W	W	L	L	L	L	L	L	L	W	W	L	
Parameter Type		V	V	V	V	V	V	V	P	P	H	P	H	P	P	V	V	H	
FrameArc	98	I3										I1				I2			Y
FrameOval	88											I1							Y
FramePoly	188										I1								Y
FrameRect	83											I1							Y
FrameRgn	121												I1						Y
FrameRRect	93						I3	I2				I1							Y
InvertArc	101	I3										I1				I2			Y
InvertOval	91											I1							Y
InvertPoly	191										I1								Y
InvertRect	86											I1							Y
InvertRgn	124												I1						Y
InvertRRect	96						I3	I2				I1							Y
PaintArc	99	I3										I1				I2			Y
PaintOval	89											I1							Y
PaintPixels	127								I1										Y*
PaintPoly	189										I1								Y
PaintRect	84											I1							Y
PaintRgn	122												I1						Y
PaintRRect	94						I3	I2				I1							Y
PPToPort	214		I3	I4										I1	I2		I5		N
ScrollRect	126				I2	I3						I1						I4	Y

Notes:

Parameter sizes:

L long-word (32-bit) value
W word (16-bit) value

Parameter types:

H handle
P pointer
V value

* Name in Macintosh is CopyBits

Table 12-4

Quickdraw II Drawing Commands (continued)

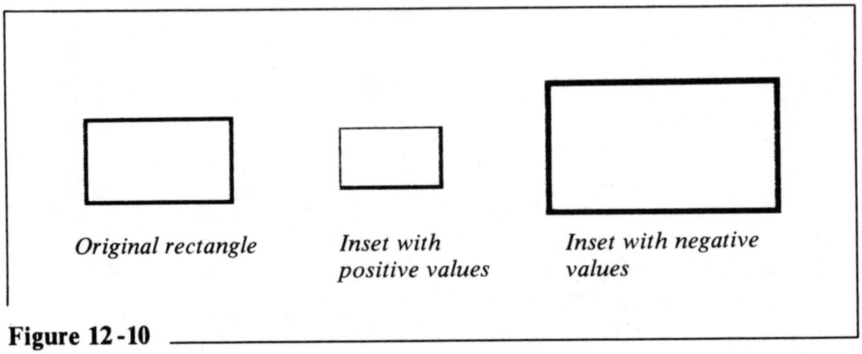

Figure 12-10
Effect of an insert command on a rectangle

values to the left) and vertically (positive values down and negative values up). These commands do not, however, change the size or shape of the object.

The inset commands, which work on rectangles or regions, move the edges of the particular shape either in toward the center (positive values) or out from the center (negative values). Figure 12-10 shows the effect of an inset command, using both positive and negative values, on a rectangle.

The intersection of two shapes is defined as those pixels that are present in both shapes. Figure 12-11 shows the intersection of two shapes. The first

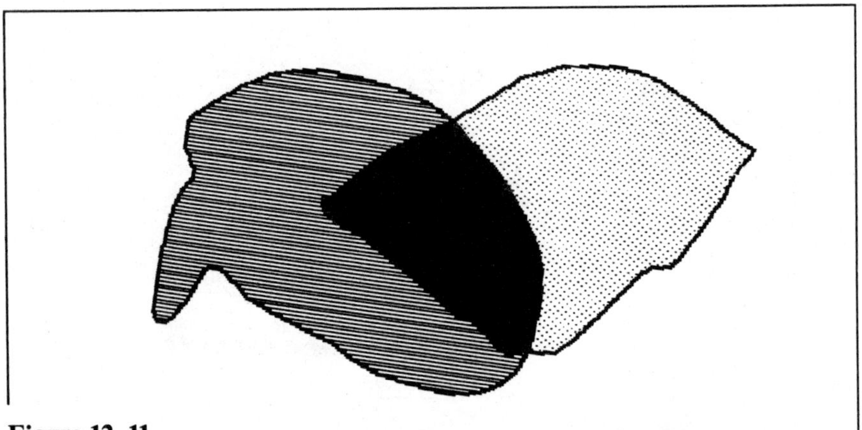

Figure 12-11
Intersection of two shapes

shape has a line pattern and the second shape a dot pattern. The solid black portion is the intersection of the two shapes. The two "sect" commands function similarly. SectRect sets the third rectangle equal to the intersection of the first two rectangles, although the third rectangle may be the same as one of the first two. SectRgn functions the same. Both commands also set the third shape to empty if there is no intersection. SectRect also returns a flag, called EmptyFlag, which shows whether the intersection is empty. The flag shows true (not equal to zero) if the intersection is not empty.

The *union* of two shapes is defined as that shape (the same type as the first) that is just large enough to hold the two shapes (plus any extra area made necessary by the orientation of the two shapes). In the case of rectangles (see Figure 12-12) the union created by UnionRect is also a rectangle. The union of regions created by UnionRgn is also a region. As in the case of the intersection, the union shape that holds the result may be one of the two input shapes.

Two other commands involve calculations with regions. DiffRgn calculates Region 1 minus Region 2. It is that part of the first region not present in the second region. Unlike the SectRgn and UnionRgn commands, DiffRgn returns different results depending on which region is the first region and which is the second (see Figure 12-13).

XorRgn calculates the *exclusive OR* of the two regions. The exclusive

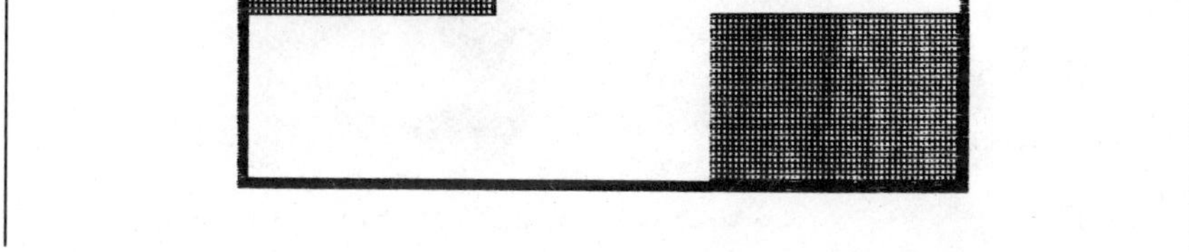

Figure 12-12
Union of rectangles

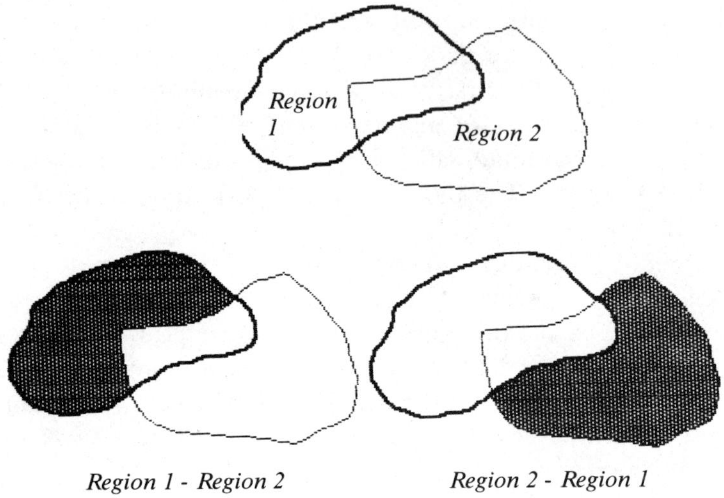

Figure 12-13
Calculation using DiffRgn

OR of two regions is defined both as the union of the two regions minus the intersection of the two regions, and as that part of the image that is present in one or the other of the regions but not both of them (see Figure 12-14).

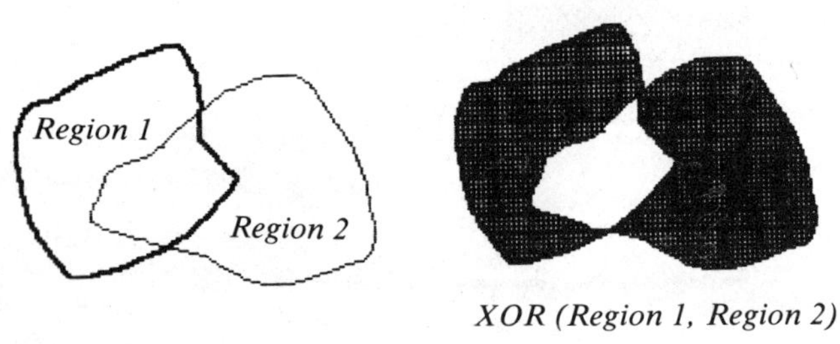

Figure 12-14
Calculation using XorRgn

Two different Quickdraw II commands also determine if a particular point is present in the shape. PtInRect and PtInRgn function the same and return a word result that is true (not equal to zero) if the specified point is in the specified shape; the word result is false (zero) if the specified point is not in the specified shape. Similarly, RectInRgn determines if a rectangle is included within a particular region.

Three Quickdraw II commands are used to determine if shapes are the same. EqualRect, EqualPt, and EqualRgn each return a true result if the two specified shapes are the same. Shapes are considered *equal* only if they are equal in shape, size, and location.

The two empty commands, EmptyRect and EmptyRgn, return a flag showing true if the specified shape is *empty*. A shape is empty if it encloses no pixels. For example, an empty rectangle is one whose bottom is higher than or equal to its top side, or whose left side is to the right of (or congruent with) its right side.

Points may be *added* or *subtracted* with AddPt and SubPt. The result is placed in the second point. Points are added by taking the two horizontal coordinates and adding them together, and taking the two vertical coordinates and adding them together. Subtraction works in a similar fashion.

Two of the more useful commands, particularly when comparing objects in different Grafports, are LocalToGlobal and GlobalToLocal. LocalToGlobal takes a point whose coordinates are expressed in coordinates local to the particular Grafport and changes them to global coordinates. GlobalToLocal converts the coordinates in the opposite direction.

Table 12-5 is a list of the various commands involving calculations with shapes, and includes the parameters expected by each. The final column in the table shows whether a similar command exists in the Quickdraw toolset on the Macintosh.

THE CURSOR

The cursor is a very specialized shape in Quickdraw II. Once the cursor is initialized, its shape appears on the screen (unless your application takes steps to hide it), and it follows the movement of the mouse. In most of its functions the Quickdraw II cursor follows that of the Macintosh.

One significant difference between the Apple IIGS cursor and the Macintosh cursor is the size. On the Macintosh, the cursor is a 16 × 16-pixel square. On the IIGS, the cursor size is not limited. Rather it is defined

Function Name	Function Number	DestPtPtr	DestRectPtr	DestRgnHandle	dH	dV	EmptyFlag	EqualFlag
Parameter Size		L	L	L	W	W	W	W
Parameter Type		P	P	H	V	V	B	B
AddPt	128	I2						
DiffRgn	115			I3				
DisposeRgn	104							
EqualPt	131	I2						O1
EqualRect	81							O1
EqualRgn	119							O1
EmptyRect	82						O1	
EmptyRgn	120						O1	
GlobalToLocal	133							
InsetRect	76				I2	I3		
InsetRgn	112				I2	I3		
KillPoly	195							
LocalToGlobal	132							
MapPoly	197		I3					
MapPt	138		I3					
MapRect	139		I3					
MapRgn	140		I3					
OffsetPoly	196				I2	I3		
OffsetRect	75				I2	I3		
OffsetRgn	111				I2	I3		
PtInRect	79							
PtInRgn	117							
RectInRgn	118							
ScalePt	137		I3					
SectRect	77						O1	
SectRgn	113			I3				
SubPt	129	I2						
UnionRect	78							
UnionRgn	114			I3				
XorRgn	116			I3				

Notes:

Parameter sizes:
L long-word (32-bit) value
W word (16-bit) value

Parameter types:
B boolean P pointer
H handle V value

Table 12-5

Quickdraw II Shape Calculation Commands

PointPtr	PolyHandle	RectPtr	Rect1Ptr	Rect2Ptr	Rect3Ptr	Result	Rgnhandle	Rgnhandle1	Rgnhandle2	SrcPtPtr	SrcRectPtr	Macintosh?
L	L	L	L	L	L	W	L	L	L	L	L	
P	H	P	P	P	P	B	H	H	H	P	P	
										I1		Y
								I1	I2			Y
							I1					Y
										I1		Y
			I1	I2								Y
								I1	I2			Y
		I1										Y
							I1					Y
I1												Y
		I1										Y
							I1					Y
	I1											Y
I1												Y
	I1										I2	Y
I1											I2	Y
		I1									I2	Y
							I1				I2	Y
	I1											Y
		I1										Y
							I1					Y
I1		I2				O1						Y
I1						O1	I2					Y
		I1				O1	I2					Y
I1											I2	Y
			I1	I2	I3							Y
								I1	I2			Y
										I1		Y
			I1	I2	I3							Y
								I1	I2			Y
								I1	I2			Y

by the cursor record. The various fields of this record are shown in Table 12-6. Note that the first two fields in this record consist of the cursor height (in pixels) and the cursor width (in 16-bit words). The last word in each cursor width line must be $0000.

The cursor is the one shape not displayed in color. Instead it is always black or white. The various bits in the cursor image and cursor mask arrays indicate which pixels are black, which are white, which are not displayed, and which are affected by the underlying screen pixel. The relationship of the pixel image and pixel mask bit to the actual screen bit is shown in Table 12-7.

Just six different commands affect the cursor. SetCursor is called after a cursor record has been set up in memory. Your application should pass a pointer to the cursor record when the call is made. The routine changes the shape of the cursor according to the cursor record. The inverse of SetCursor is GetCursorAdr. When your application calls this routine, the routine passes back the address of the currently active cursor record.

Whether the cursor is visible on the screen is a function of cursor level. When the level is zero, the cursor is displayed. When the level is less than zero, the cursor is not displayed. The cursor level can never be greater than zero. The two commands, HideCursor and ShowCursor, function in a manner similar to that of HidePen and ShowPen discussed in Chapter 11,

Field name	Size	Function
CursorHeight	Word	Value specifying the cursor height in pixels
CursorWidth	Word	Value specifying the cursor width in words
CursorImage	Array	Size of array is CursorHeight by CursorWidth words
CursorMask	Array	Size of array is CursorHeight by CursorWidth words
HotSpotY	Word	Vertical coordinate of active point of cursor
HotSpotX	Word	Horizontal coordinate of active point of cursor

Table 12-6

Cursor Record Structure

Cursor Image Bit Value	Cursor Mask Bit Value	Effect on Screen Pixel
0	1	White pixel
1	1	Black pixel
0	0	Unchanged
1	0	Inverse of screen pixel

Table 12-7

Effect of Cursor Image and Cursor Mask on Screen Display

except the cursor level is never greater than zero.

Each call to HideCursor decrements the cursor level. Since the cursor level can never be more than zero, a call to HideCursor will always hide the cursor. A call to ShowCursor increments the cursor level unless the level is already zero. When the cursor level reaches zero, the cursor is displayed.

Because of the interaction between ShowCursor and HideCursor, you need to be especially careful when programming with these commands. You not only need to be certain to balance a HideCursor with a ShowCursor, you also need to be aware that a ShowCursor with the cursor already visible followed by a HideCursor will result in a net decrementing of the cursor level. A HideCursor followed by a ShowCursor will result in the cursor level remaining the same. The order in which the commands are given, then, is quite important.

ObscureCursor temporarily hides the cursor until there is a movement of the mouse. The most traditional use for this command is to remove the cursor from the display while text typing is being performed.

The InitCursor routine is a way to reset the cursor to the standard arrow and make the cursor visible (that is, set the cursor level to 0). It is particularly useful in the following two circumstances:

1. When the cursor level is out of balance, resulting in a nondisplayed cursor when you want to display the cursor.
2. When the display mode has changed from 320 to 640, or vice versa.

Function Name	Function Number	CursorPtr
Parameter Size		L
Parameter Type		P
GetCursorAdr	143	O1
HideCursor	144	
InitCursor	202	
ObscureCursor	146	
SetCursor	142	I1
ShowCursor	145	

Table 12-8

Cursor-Handling Commands

Table 12-8 is a listing of the various cursor commands and the parameters expected by each. These commands all have a correlative and similarly named commands in Macintosh Quickdraw except for GetCursorAddr. This function is similar to the Macintosh Toolbox utility command GetCursor.

CHAPTER 13

Quickdraw II and Text

The Apple IIGS user interface—including the use of windows, dialogs, menus, and such—is central to the concept of the IIGS. One of the main purposes of the IIGS Toolbox is to make using this interface easier for the programmer. All activity using windows, dialogs, and menus takes place on the super-resolution graphics screen. Since this screen is pixel- and object-oriented, your application cannot simply write text on the screen by the 8-bit Apple II method of placing ASCII code in specific memory locations or having a built-in ROM routine do it. (See discussion in Chapter 8 of the 8-bit Apple II text display modes.)

Quickdraw II provides many different utilities to allow the display of text on the IIGS super-resolution graphics display screen, performing the conversion from characters to the proper pixel pattern for that character. And Quickdraw II permits this display in a variety of font sizes, shapes, and styles.

A *font* is a collection of up to 256 different characters that form a unified set for one purpose or another. It can be letters, symbols, and numbers in one particular style. But a font might also be a collection of icons or a mixed set of letters, symbols, numbers, and icons. The font could even be identified as a mixed collection in various sizes, shapes, and styles. Figure 13-1 shows characters from three fonts that originally appeared on the Macintosh and that can also be used, when converted, on the IIGS.

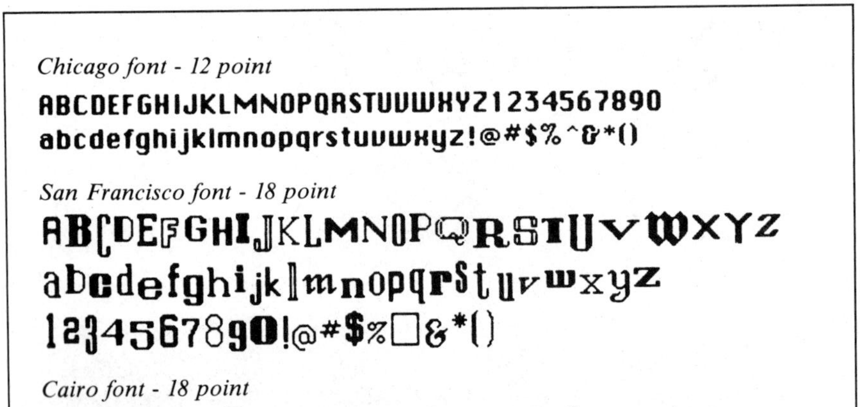

Figure 13-1

Macintosh fonts that can be moved to the IIGS

You do not generally need to know the various aspects of font layout to use text in a IIGS application. This chapter first discusses those aspects of text and fonts that are needed for the more common uses of text. Next the Quickdraw II text commands are discussed. Following that is a more detailed discussion of fonts and their structure.

TEXT AND FONTS

The Apple IIGS comes with a character font, known as the system font, built into ROM. Additional fonts come in the Font subdirectory in the System subdirectory in the System disk. Apple also has a Macintosh utility, known as Font Munger, that allows Macintosh fonts to be converted for use on the IIGS.

The system font can be changed by an application. The SetSysFont call changes the system font to the specified font. GetSysFont returns a handle to the current system font. Changing the system font is not necessary for changing the current font in use. In fact, Quickdraw II does not change the current font in use, but rather uses the system font for the following two purposes:

1. Setting the default font for a new Grafport
2. Determining what font to use for specialized drawing functions.

The Grafport record has several fields that refer to various aspects of text drawing. The FontHandle field refers to the current font. Its value can be determined by the GetFont call and it can be changed by the SetFont call. Each font also has a FontID, a long-integer value that identifies each font. The value of this field can be determined by the GetFontID call and changed by the SetFontID call.

FontHandle and FontID are not merely alternative methods of setting and changing the current font. They actually serve a different function. FontHandle identifies the font that will be used in most all text drawing commands. The exception is picture drawing. The picture-recording mechanism uses the FontID field to determine the desired font.

The FontFlags field is a word-length bit array. In Quickdraw version 1.1, the only flag defined is whether the font is a proportionally spaced or fixed-spaced font. If bit 0 is set, the font is fixed-spaced; otherwise, it is proportionally spaced. The current value of FontFlags can be determined using GetFontFlags and changed using SetFontFlags. Note that all bits except bit 0 are reserved and should be set to 0.

As discussed later in this chapter, there is a field within the font record itself that shows whether the font is proportionally spaced or fixed-spaced. This field is a vestige of the Macintosh fonts, and its setting is ignored by Quickdraw II. Of course, your application can read this value and set FontFlags accordingly. Quickdraw II, however, will not do this for you.

The point size of the current font record is maintained in the TxSize field in the Grafport record. This information is maintained for Quickdraw II and is not available for direct modification by your application. Each time your application changes the currently used font, Quickdraw II updates this field.

The TxFace field is a word-length bit array containing information about style modifications being made to the current font when it is displayed. Each bit in this word, if set to 1, modifies the font in a specified manner. In Quickdraw II version 1.1, two style modifications are supported—bold (bit 0) and underline (bit 2). Both of these are implemented in ROM.

When a character or a string is boldfaced, it is drawn with an added character width of one pixel for each width. The string is drawn in its normal position and then one pixel to the right. The two images are ORed together. This process is illustrated in Figure 13-2.

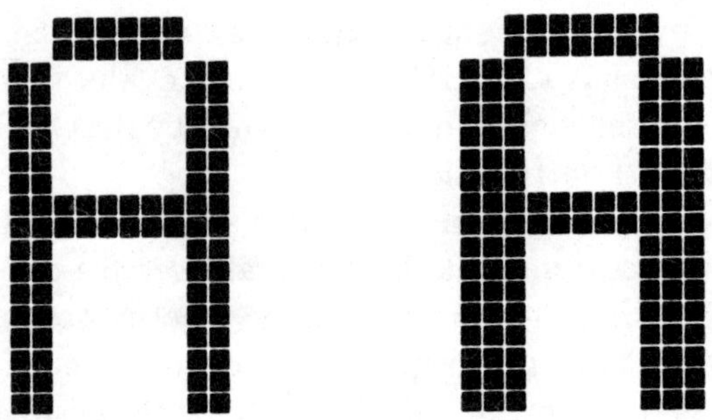

Figure 13-2
Bolding a character

A character or string is underlined using the following criteria:

- □ The font must have a descent greater than or equal to two.
- □ The underline is one pixel high.
- □ The underline is drawn two pixels under the base line.
- □ The underline is drawn the entire length of the characters or string.
- □ The underline is omitted if there is a foreground pixel immediately above, below, to the right, or to the left of the underline position.

The last criterion causes an underline to break around character descenders. This effect is illustrated in Figure 13-3. The grey portions of the line reflect where the underline would have been drawn except for a descender near it. The grey areas show when an underline would have been drawn over a descender. Figure 13-4 shows how the underlining looks normally and how it would look if the omission of underlining (to allow for descenders) was not implemented.

Future style types are anticipated in later versions of Quickdraw II. We can imagine what the style types are by taking a look at the style types that are provided for Quickdraw on the Macintosh. These styles are listed in Table 13-1.

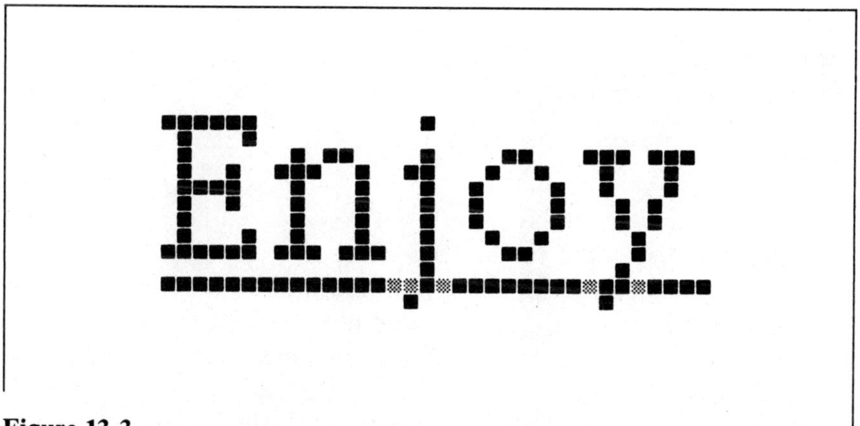

Figure 13-3

Underline breaking around character descenders

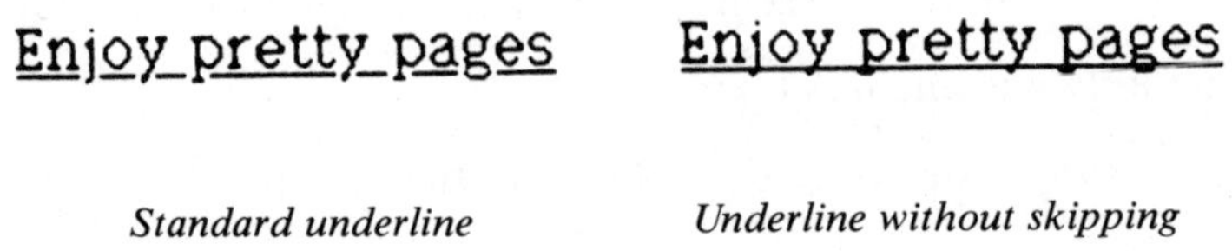

Figure 13-4
Normal underlining and underlining without omission around descenders

Bit	Style
0	Bold
1	Italic
2	Underline
3	Outline
5	Shadow
6	Extended
7	Condensed

Table 13-1
Macintosh Font Style Modifications

TxMode refers to the method by which text is transferred to the super-resolution graphics display screen. As discussed in Chapter 10, eight pixel-transfer modes are used only for text. These modes, and their meanings, are listed in Table 13-2. The current mode can be obtained by GetTextMode and changed with SetTextMode.

The text modes vary in the speed with which they work. The eight text-only modes generally are faster than their corresponding general modes. And the four standard text-only modes are generally faster than

Value	Mode	Meaning
$0004	foreCOPY	Copies the foreground pixels into the destination pixel map without altering the destination background pixels.
$0005	foreOR	ORs the foreground pixels into the destination pixel map without altering the destination background pixels.
$0006	foreXOR	XORs the foreground pixels into the destination pixel map without altering the destination background pixels.
$0007	foreBIC	BICs the foreground pixels into the destination pixel map without altering the destination background pixels.
$8004	notforeCOPY	Inverts the foreground pixels and then copies them into the destination pixel map without altering the destination background pixels.
$8005	notforeOR	Inverts the foreground pixels and then ORs them into the destination pixel map without altering the destination background pixels.
$8006	notforeXOR	Inverts the foreground pixels and then XORs them into the destination pixel map without altering the destination background pixels.
$8007	notforeBIC	Inverts the foreground pixels and then BICs them into the destination pixel map without altering the destination background pixels.

Note: See Chapter 10 for definitions of copy, OR, XOR, and BIC

Table 13-2
Special Text Transfer Modes

their corresponding inverted ("not") modes. Within the four standard text modes, the OR and XOR modes are the fastest, while BIC is nearly as fast.The copy mode is the slowest.

Some applications, particularly word processing and desktop publishing programs, need the capability of displaying text in fill justification style (that is, with even left and right margins). The spExtra field in the record is used for this purpose.

The spExtra value is a fixed-point long-word length value. The upper

15	14	13	12	11	10	9	8	7	*Bit number*
1/2	1/4	1/8	1/16	1/32	1/64	1/128	1/256	1/512	*Value*

6	5	4	3	2	1	0	*Bit number*
1/1024	1/2048	1/4096	1/8192	1/16384	1/32768	1/65536	*Value*

Figure 13-5
Binary fraction values

word is a signed integer value between −32768 and 32737. The lower word is a fraction with each bit representing a binary fraction whose value is shown in Figure 13-5. It represents the number of pixels to be added to each space character when printing text. This value can be modified by your application until the text length is the correct line length.

While the spExtra value has a fractional part, only whole pixels can be added to a space character. When it is drawing text, Quickdraw II keeps track of the fractional part of the value. The actual drawing uses rounded integer values, with 1/2 being rounded up. This arrangement results in a relatively even spreading of the added space values.

The spExtra value is added only to the space character, or only to a character with an ASCII value of 32 ($20). A nonbreaking space, included in some fonts, does not have the spExtra value added to it. The current value of spExtra can be obtained by calling GetSpaceExtra and modified by SetSpaceExtra.

The Quickdraw II Grafport also has a value known as chExtra. This value, like spExtra, is a long-word fixed-point value. It is added to the width of every character, not just the space character. This value is not available in Quickdraw on the Macintosh.

Some fonts look proper in 320 super-res mode, but are too tightly spaced in 640 mode. If that font were properly spaced for 640 mode, it would appear too widely spaced in 320 mode. The chExtra field can be

Byte	Field	Length
0	Ascent	Word
2	Descent	Word
4	WidMax	Word
6	Leading	Word

Table 13-3
FontInfo Record Structure

used to adjust the spacing, permitting the use of a font in both 320 and 640 modes. GetCharExtra returns the current setting of the chExtra field, and SetCharExtra changes that value.

A font character has many different values associated with it. Four of these values are included in a FontInfo record, which is a separate record structure from the Grafport. The structure of the FontInfo record is shown in Table 13-3.

Each font has a *base line,* or a line on which the base of all uppercase letters, as well as most other letters and characters, is normally drawn. Almost every character extends a number of pixels above the base line. This value is known as the *ascent* of the character. Some characters also extend some pixels below the base line (particularly letters such as *g, j,* and *y*). This value is known as the *descent* of the character. Each character is also a number of pixels wide, a value known as *character width.* The base line, ascent, descent, and character width are shown in Figure 13-6.

For each font there is a maximum ascent (the greatest ascent of any character), a maximum descent (the greatest descent of any character), and a maximum width (the greatest width of any character). A line of text can also be separated from the next line by any number of pixels (including a negative number, which results in characters being drawn on top of each other). The number of pixels between the maximum descent of the first line and the maximum ascent of the second line is called the *leading.*

The values given in the FontInfo record refer to the maximum ascent, descent, and width of any character in the font, and the leading used for that font. These values appear in the record of the particular font (discussed later in this chapter). This information may be obtained by the

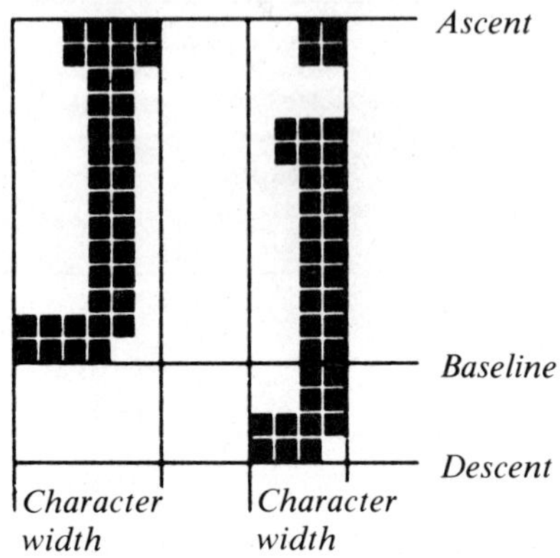

Figure 13-6
Base line, ascent, descent, and character width

GetFontInfo call. The information returned does not reflect any changes that have been made to these values by chExtra, spExtra, or style modifications. Note that there is no SetFontInfo call. Modifying these values could have bizarre results.

QUICKDRAW TEXT COMMANDS

Quickdraw II works with several types of text. It can draw one character, a group of text characters of a specified length, a ProDOS or Pascal string (called *string*) that consists of a length byte followed by the characters, and a *cstring* that consists of a group of characters with an ASCII null ($00) character indicating the end.

The four draw commands—DrawChar, DrawText, DrawString, and DrawCString—each draw the specified character or group of characters with the following conditions:

- □ The current font is used.
- □ The current pen position is the starting point.

- The current text mode is used.
- The current foreground color is used.
- The current background color is used.
- The pen is advanced the width of the drawn text.

If your application wants to know how far the pen would be advanced if a specified character, text, string, or cstring were drawn, it can determine this value without actually drawing the text. This capability would be useful in determining if specified text would fit in a given location, or in determining how much space should be allocated for the specified text.

The four calls—CharWidth, TextWidth, StringWidth, CStringWidth—each are called in a manner similar to the four draw commands. The major difference is that these four routines return an integer value equal to the width. The width value also reflects the effect of any specified chExtra, spExtra, and style modifications. The characters are not actually drawn, and the pen position is not moved.

FONTS AND FONT STRUCTURES

Character width is not always the width of a character. Each character has both a character width and an image width. The character width refers to the number of pixels the pen is to be advanced after the character has been drawn. The *image width* equals the number of pixels wide that the character actually is.

To appreciate the difference, we need to define a few other terms involving fonts (see Figure 13-7). The *character origin* of a font is the location from which the pen begins drawing the character. It can actually draw to the left or to the right (or both) from the origin. The character width is the number of pixels from the character origin to the next character origin.

In some cases a character can have a character width of 0. This size especially applies to certain accent marks like the circumflex or umlaut. If a character has a character width of 0, it will be drawn without moving the pen position. When the next character (presumably a vowel) is drawn, it will be placed under the accent.

A character can overlap the previous or the next character in the line, extending either to the left of its own origin or to the right of the next

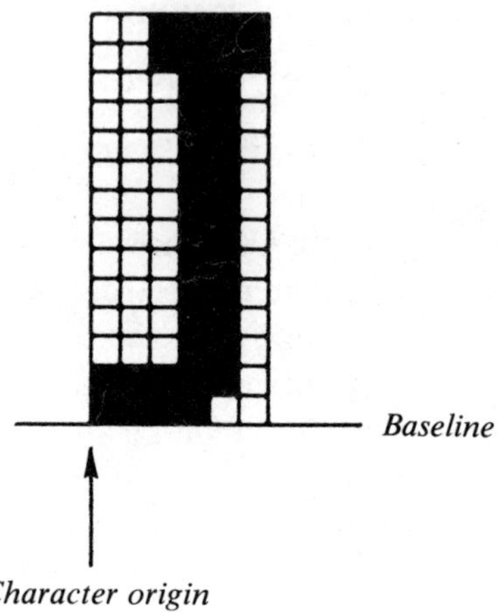

Figure 13-7
Additional font terms

character origin. If a character extends to the left of its origin, it is said to kern to the left. If it extends to the right of the next character origin, it is said to kern to the right. A character theoretically could kern both to the left and right. Kerning is used to allow certain characters, such as a stylized lowercase *f*, to be displayed without creating what appears to be uneven spacing between letters (see Figure 13-8).

The image width of a character is the number of horizontal pixels from the first foreground pixel of the character to the last foreground pixel. The bounds calls—CharBounds, TextBounds, StringBounds, CStringBounds—return the value of the smallest rectangle that encloses the specified character or text if the character or text were drawn at the current pen location. Expressed in local coordinates, the image width extends from the current pen position

- □ As high as the font ascent
- □ As low as the font descent
- □ As far left as either the current pen position or the leftmost kerning pixel, whichever is farther left

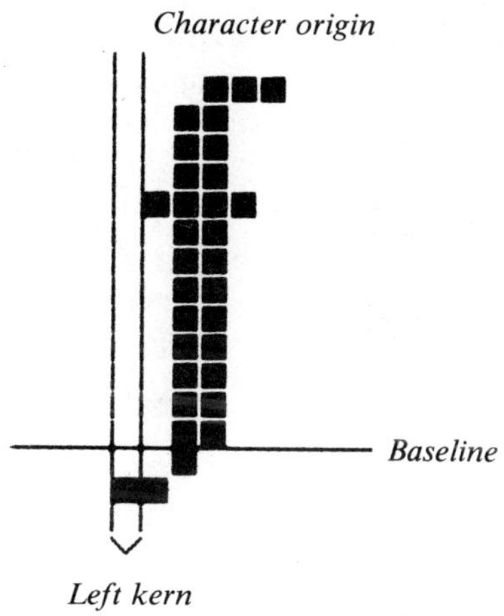

Figure 13-8
Kerning

□ As far right as the new pen position would be, or the rightmost kerning pixel, whichever is farther right

A font is a record that consists of a variable-length header and a Macintosh-type font record. The header is designed to provide information about the font that is handled on the Macintosh by the use of resources and a complete Font Manager.

The current font header (as of Quickdraw II version 1.1) is 12 bytes in length. Its structure is shown in Table 13-4. In order to provide for expansion of the font header, the first value is the length of the header. This setup provides a method for Quickdraw II to move quickly from the beginning of the font record to the Macintosh-type portion of the record. Such a relationship will allow various versions of Quickdraw II to use the font without needing a fixed-length font header. Examples of information that could be part of a future font header include thickness of underline and the degree of italicization.

The *style value* in the header is used to determine if the font was drawn in a particular style. It uses the standard method of style-word discussed earlier in this chapter. For example, a font may be drawn in a bold-faced

Byte	Field	Length	Use
0	offsetToMF	Word	Number of words to beginning of Macintosh-type font record (currently set to 6)
2	family	Word	Font family number
4	style	Word	Style with which font was designed
6	Size	Word	Size of font in points
8	Version	Word	Quickdraw II version number
10	fbrExtent	Word	Font bounds rectangle extent

Table 13-4
Font Header Structure

form. Your application can use this field to prevent the prebolded font from being further bolded when it is drawn.

The *size value* in the header is the size of the font in points, taking into account the maximum ascent and maximum descent.

The *version value* is the version number of Quickdraw II for which the font was designed. This designation allows a version of Quickdraw II that normally expects to find certain values in the font header to determine that the font it is using lacks these values. The application could then set these values to an appropriate default and still use the font.

The *font bounds rectangles extent value* is the maximum horizontal pixel distances from the character origin to any pixel of any character in the font.

Five of the six fields in the font record header are also part of another font record, the font globals. This record consists of nearly the same fields as in the font header. The exceptions are the following:

- □ The offset to the Macintosh-type font record is not included.
- □ The widMax value from the Macintosh-type font record is included, following the version number.

Since the information in the font globals record will increase as the information in the font header increases, Quickdraw II provides a routine, GetFGSize, that returns the size of the font globals record in bytes. The

Byte	Field	Length	Use
0	fontType	Word	Fixed or proportionally spaced
2	firstChar	Word	ASCII code of first defined character
4	lastChar	Word	ASCII code of last defined character
6	widMax	Word	Maximum character width
8	kernMax	Word	Maximum leftward kerning of any character
10	nDescent	Word	Negative of maximum font descent
12	fRectWidth	Word	Width of font rectangle
14	fRectHeight	Word	Height of font rectangle
16	owTLoc	Word	Number of words to offset/width table
18	ascent	Word	Maximum font ascent
20	descent	Word	Maximum font descent
22	leading	Word	Leading to be used by font
24	rowWords	Word	Number of words of width for bit image
28	bitImage	Variable*	Font strike
...	locTable	Variable*	Location table
...	owTable	Variable*	Offset/width table

*The bitImage is 2 (rowWords*fRectHeight) bytes in length.
The locTable and owTable are 2 (lastChar+2-firstChar+1) bytes in length.

Table 13-5

Structure of Macintosh-style Portion of IIGS Font Record

current font globals record can be obtained by the routine GetFontGlobals. There is no corresponding set function.

The Macintosh-style font record portion of the IIGS font record is not exactly like a Macintosh font. The Macintosh stores word-length integers with the highest byte first, while the IIGS stores them with the lowest byte first. Therefore, values that are integers in a Macintosh font record must have their bytes reversed in order. The bitImage, or font strike, being an array of pixels, does not need to have its bytes reversed. The structure of the Macintosh-style portion of the font record is shown in Table 13-5.

The fontType field is used in font records in the Macintosh to indicate whether the font is proportional ($9000) or fixed-width ($B000). The field is not used by Quickdraw II. Instead it uses the FontFlags value, stored in the Grafport, to convey this information. (FontFlags is discussed earlier in this chapter.)

The firstChar field contains the ASCII code for the first character that is defined in the font. The lastChar field contains the ASCII code for the last-defined character in the font. ASCII codes that are less than the first character or greater than the last character are undefined. In addition, certain characters within the font can also be undefined. The method of indicating defined or undefined is discussed later in this chapter.

The widMax field is the maximum character width of any character in the font, measured in pixels. Note that this is the pen movement while writing a character, not necessarily the actual image width of the character, which, as discussed previously, can be either greater or less.

KernMax is the largest number of pixels that any character kerns to the left. The value is 0 if no character kerns to the left. The value is negative if a character kerns to the left. The descent value made negative is nDescent. The *descent value* is the greatest number of pixels that any character extends below the base line.

The width and height of the font rectangle are fRectWidth and fRectHeight. This is the smallest rectangle that can enclose all the character rectangles laid on top of each other and aligned through their character origin points. The character rectangle for each character consists of a rectangle with a height of font height and a width of image width. Thus, fRectHeight is the same as font height. fRectWidth is not necessarily the same as the widest character width because the font rectangle is created by overlaying character rectangles through their character origin.

The offset to the offset/width table is owTLoc, discussed later in this chapter. The offset value is given from the owTLoc field, not from the beginning of the record. Ascent is the font ascent, while descent is the font descent, both expressed in pixels. Total font height is equal to ascent plus descent.

Leading is the number of pixels of horizontal space to skip between lines of the font. It is the spacing between the descent of the top line and the ascent of the bottom line.

The width of the font strike (bit image) in words is rowWords. The font strike uses one bit per pixel to represent the font characters.

The *font strike* consists of a bit image of fRectHeight pixels high by rowWords * 16 pixels wide. It is expressed as a series of bits, row by row, with a drawn pixel being indicated by a bit of 1 (see Figure 13-9). The

Figure 13-9
Font strike

characters in the font strike are placed in the bit image one after the other, without any space between characters. At the end of the font strike is an extra character, known as the *missing symbol.* This is the character drawn whenever an application requests the drawing of a character that is not defined in the font.

The font strike is followed by the location table (locTable). Each word-length value in this table is a value that specifies where that particular character begins in the font strike. The first value in the table is the first defined character, the second value is the second defined character, and so forth. The next-to-the-last value in the table is the location of the missing character. The last value in the table is the total width of the font strike in pixels, ignoring any padding that is added to the end of the font strike to make it end on a word boundary.

The location table can also be used to return the image width for any character by subtracting the locTable value for that character from the locTable value for the next character. An undefined character that is greater than firstChar and less than lastChar is given the same value as the next defined character in the table, resulting in an image width of 0.

The location table is followed by the offset/width table (owTable). This table contains the other width value for each character in the lower byte for each word, the character width. The higher byte is the character offset of this character. This value is added to kernMax, resulting in the horizontal distance in pixels from the character origin to the left edge of the character image. A negative value shows the character origin is to the right of the image's left edge, resulting in a character that kerns left.

Function Name	Function Number	CharExtra	CStringPtr	FGRecPtr	FIRecPtr	FontFlags	FontHandle	FontID	MaxFBRExten	MaxFontHt
Parameter Size		L	L	L	L	W	L	L	W	W
Parameter Type		F	P	P	P	BA	H	V	V	V
CharBounds	172									
CharWidth	168									
CStringBounds	174		I1							
CStringWidth	170		I1							
DrawChar	164									
DrawCString	166		I1							
DrawString	165									
DrawText	167									
ForceBufDims	204								I3	I2
GetCharExtra	213	O1								
GetFGSize	207									
GetFont	149						O1			
GetFontFlags	153					O1				
GetFontGlobals	151			I1						
GetFontID	209							O1		
GetFontInfo	150				I1					
GetSpaceExtra	159									
GetSysFont	179						O1			
GetTextFace	155									
GetTextMode	157									
RestoreBufDims	206								I3	I2
SaveBufDims	205									
SetBufDims	203								I3	I2
SetCharExtra	212	I1								
SetFont	148						I1			

Table 13-6

Quickdraw II Text Routines

MaxWidth	RectPtr	Size	SizeInfoPtr	SpaceExtra	StringPtr	TextFace	TextLen	TextMode	TextPtr	theChar	width	In Mac QDraw
W	L	W	L	L	L	W	W	W	L	W	W	
V	P	V	P	F	P	BA	V	V	P	C	V	
	I2									I1		
										I1	O1	X
	I2										O1	
											O1	
										I1		X
					I1							X
							I2		I1			X
I1												
		O1										
				O1								X
						O1						
								O1		O1		
I1												
			I1									
I1												
												I

Function Name	Function Number	CharExtra	CStringPtr	FGRecPtr	FIRecPtr	FontFlags	FontHandle	FontID	MaxFBRExten	MaxFontHt
SetFontFlags	152					I1				
SetFontID	208							I1		
SetSpaceExtra	158									
SetSysFont	178						I1			
SetTextFace	154									
SetTextMode	156									
StringBounds	173									
StringWidth	169									
TextBounds	175									
TextWidth	171									

Notes:

Parameter Size:

- L Long-word (32 bits)
- W Word (16 bits)

Parameter Type:

- BA Bit array
- C Character (only lower byte significant)
- F Fixed point value
- H Handle
- P Pointer
- V Value

Table 13-6

Quickdraw II Text Routines (continued)

There is one exception to the meaning of the values in the owTable. A missing character is indicated by a value of −1 ($FFFF) in the owTable. Thus, the maximum value for either width or offset is 254 ($FE) to avoid an ambiguity between a character with an offset and width of 255 each ($FFFF) and the missing character ($FFFF).

The next-to-the-last entry in the owTable is for the missing symbol. The final entry, marking the end of the table, is a value of $FFFF.

When Quickdraw II draws text, it first places the pixel image into an area of memory called the *text buffer,* which is a 1-bit-per-pixel buffer. When transferring the bits from the text buffer to the actual pixel image,

MaxWidth	RectPtr	Size	SizeInfoPtr	SpaceExtra	StringPtr	TextFace	TextLen	TextMode	TextPtr	theChar	width	In Mac QDraw
I1												
				I1								4
						I1						2
								I1				3
I2					I1						O1	X
					I1						O1	X
I3				I2			I2		I1			
							I2		I1		O1	

Macintosh Quickdraw Cross Reference

1 Called TextFont
2 Called TextFace
3 Called TextMode
4 Called SpaceExtra
X Present and with same name

the pixels are changed into the 2- (640 mode) or 4- (320 mode) bits-per-pixel values.

Quickdraw II normally sets up a text buffer of default size sufficiently large to handle most text drawing. While decreasing the size of the text buffer may result in some saving of memory, resizing the text buffer can take some time to clear it. And if the text buffer is too small, text drawing can have unpredictable consequences. Your application need be concerned about the text buffer size only if memory saving is very important, or if it uses very unusual fonts.

Several functions handle text buffer sizing. They are SetBufDims,

ForceBufDims, SaveBufDims, and RestoreBufDims. The sizing of the text buffer is not discussed further in this chapter. The reader who needs assistance on this advanced subject should refer to the Quickdraw II section in the *Apple IIGS Toolbox Reference Manual* from Apple.

Table 13-6 is a listing of the various text-related functions in Quickdraw II, together with the parameters expected by each and an indication whether the function has an equivalent in the Macintosh implementation of Quickdraw.

ScrapBootInit	Called at load time to initialize the Scrap Manager.
ScrapStartup	Called by the application before making Scrap Manager calls.
ScrapShutdown	Called by the application before shutting down if the Scrap Manager has been started.
ScrapVersion	Returns the version number of the Scrap Manager.
ScrapReset	Called by the system on reset.
ScrapActive	Always returns true because the Scrap Manager is always active.
UnloadScrap	Writes the scrap to the scrap disk file and clears memory (unless the scrap is already on the disk).
LoadScrap	Reads the scrap file into memory (unless the scrap is already in memory).
ZeroScrap	Clears the scrap, either in memory or on disk.
PutScrap	Appends data to the scrap data of the specified kind.
GetScrap	Copies the scrap data of the specified type to the memory location.
GetScrapCount	Returns the count of the scrap.
GetScrapState	Returns zero if the scrap is on disk and nonzero if it is in memory.
GetScrapHandle	Returns the handle to the scrap.
GetScrapSize	Returns the size of the scrap of the specified type.
GetScrapPath	Returns a pointer to the pathname used for the scrap file (clipboard) on disk.
SetScrapPath	Sets the pathname to be used for the scrap file (clipboard) on disk.

Table 13-7

Scrap Manager Routines

THE SCRAP MANAGER

Technically the Scrap Manager is a tool set that works with any kind of pixel image or data, not merely text. The Scrap Manager handles the clipboard, the memory area (either in the IIGS's RAM or on disk) that holds information being transferred either within an application or from one application to another (including new desk accessories).

The Scrap Manager was designed to handle only relatively small amounts of information. If a very large amount of information is attempted to be transferred, the Scrap Manager may fail because of lack of memory.

While there is only one clipboard holding scrap information, the information in that clipboard may be in several different formats. For example, word processing text may be in both text form and in pixel-image form. Or, a database may handle information in internal-representation form and in text form.

The two types of public scrap types are text (type = 0) and picture (type = 1). Your application must be able to write information to the clipboard in at least one of these types and must be able to read information from the clipboard in both formats.

Table 13-7 gives a description of the Scrap Manager routines, while Table 13-8 gives a list of the parameters expected by the routines and indicates which routines are also present on the Macintosh Scrap Manager.

LINEEDIT

Another tool set closely related to text and Quickdraw II is LineEdit. It allows for displaying a line or block of text and, in the case of a line of text, provides for editing the text by inserting characters, deleting characters by backspacing, selecting text with mouse or key activity, and cutting, copying, and moving text.

LineEdit supports all the standard editing features in the Apple Human Interface Guidelines (discussed in Chapter 2). Some of the advanced features of these guidelines are not supported by LineEdit, including

- □ More than 256 characters per line (except with LETextBox)
- □ Line wrap (except with LETextBox)

Function Name	Function Number	DataPtr	Destination	Length	PathPtr	Result	ScrapCount	ScrapHandle	ScrapState	ScrapType	Size	Version	InMacScrapMgr
Parameter Size		L	L	L	L	W	W	W	W	W	L	W	
Parameter Type		P	H	V	P	B	V	H	B	V	V	V	
ScrapBootInit	1												
ScrapStartup	2												
ScrapShutdown	3												
ScrapVersion	4											O1	
ScrapReset	5												
ScrapStatus	6					O1							
UnloadScrap	9												X
LoadScrap	10												X
ZeroScrap	11												X
PutScrap	12	I3		I1						I2			X
GetScrap	13		I1							I2			X
GetScrapCount	18						O1						
GetScrapState	19								O1				
GetScrapHandle	14							O1		I1			
GetScrapSize	15									I1	O1		
GetScrapPath	16				O1								
SetScrapPath	17				I1								

Notes:

Parameter Size:

- L Long-word (32 bits)
- W Word (16 bits)

Parameter Type:

- B Boolean
- H Handle
- P Pointer
- V Value

Table 13-8

Scrap Manager Parameters

- □ Centered or right-justified text (except with LETextBox)
- □ Fill-justified text
- □ Scrolling
- □ More than one font or style per line
- □ Intelligent cut and paste
- □ Tabs

LineEdit works with its editing environment stored in an edit record. LENew creates an edit record based on the data passed to it, including a destination rectangle and a view rectangle. Both of these rectangles are expressed in local coordinates. The maximum text length (1-256) is also passed to the routine. LENew then returns a handle to the edit record that is referred to in other LineEdit calls.

The structure of the edit record is shown in Table 13-9. The records fields should be changed not directly, but only through the various LineEdit routines. The format of the record is subject to change in the future.

Using LineEdit consists of initializing it after first initializing (in this order) Memory Manager, Quickdraw II, Event Manager, and Window Manager. When your application needs an edit record, it should call LENew to allocate the record and call LEDispose to dispose of the record when it is done with it.

To cause the caret to blink at the insertion point, your application should call LEIdle at least once through the main loop (longer if the main loop takes a large amount of processing time).

Events occurring in the LineEdit view rectangle are handled by the following routines.

Mouse-down events are handled by LEClick to allow for text selection with the mouse, alone or in combination with the SHIFT key.

Key events are handled by LEKey, which inserts characters, deletes characters backspaced over, adjusts the selection range according to the arrow keys, and handles CONTROL-F (delete character to the right of the insertion point), CONTROL-X (delete selection or entire line), or CONTROL-Y (delete selection or delete from the insertion point to end of line).

Byte	Name	Size	Use
0	TextHandle	Long	Handle to the text to be edited
4	Length	Word	Current text length
6	MaxLength	Word	Maximum text length
8	DestRect	Rect	Rectangle in which text is drawn
16	ViewRect	Rect	Rectangle within which text is visible
24	PortPtr	Long	Pointer to the Grafport
28	LineHite	Word	Height of line for caret or highlighting of text (leading + ascent + descent)
30	BaseHite	Word	Distance between top of DestRect and baseline of text (leading + ascent)
32	SelStart	Word	Character number at start of selection range
34	SelEnd	Word	Character number after end of selection range
36	ActFlag	Word	Private use
38	CarAct	Word	Private use
40	CarOn	Word	Private Use
42	CarTime	Long	Private use
46	HiliteHook	Long	Pointer to routine to be used for highlighting text (set to $00000000 on initialization to use default invert routine). Changed with LESetHilite.
50	CaretHook	Long	Pointer to routine to be used to draw the caret (set to $00000000 on initialization to use default line caret). Changed with LESetCaret.

Table 13-9
Edit Record Structure

LECut transfers selected text to the private LineEdit scrap, removing it from the text.

LEPaste inserts the contents of the private LineEdit scrap into the text at the insertion point.

LECopy transfers selected text to the private LineEdit scrap without removing it from the text.

LEDelete deletes the selected text without transferring it to the scrap. It can be used both to carry out the clear command and help carry out the undo and redo command.

LEInsert inserts specified text. It is useful to help carry out the undo and redo command.

Activate and deactive events for the text editing window are handled by LEActivate and LEDeactivate. Update events are handled by the following sequence of calls:

- BeginUpdate (in Window Manager—see Chapter 16)
- EraseRect (in Quickdraw II—see Chapter 12)
- LEUpdate
- EndUpdate (in Window Manager—see Chapter 16)

If needed by your application, the selection range of the text can be modified without user specification by use of the LESelSelect command.

Two routines transfer text between the private LineEdit scrap and the public scrap. LEFromScrap moves text from the public scrap. LEToScrap moves text to the public scrap. The handle to the LineEdit private scrap can be determined using LEScrapHandle. The current length of the scrap is determined by LEGetScrapLen and changed with LESetScrapLen.

The text within an edit record can be changed, without the need for a new edit record, by using LESetText.

The final LineEdit routine, LETexpBox, allows your application to display text in a given rectangle in multiple lines and in centered, left-, or right-justified form. The length of the displayed text can be up to 32,767 characters.

Table 13-10 gives a list of the parameters expected by each of the LineEdit routines. Table 13-11 is a comparison of the LineEdit routines on the IIGS and the routines available on the similar Macintosh tool, TextEdit.

Function Name	Function Number	BoxRectPtr	DestRectPtr	EventPtr	handle	Just	Key	Length	MaxTextLen
Parameter Size		L	L	L	L	W	W	W	W
Parameter Type		P	P	P	H	V	V	V	V
LEActivate	15				I1				
LEBootInit	1								
LEClick	13			I1	I2				
LECopy	19				I1				
LECut	18				I1				
LEDeactivate	16				I1				
LEDelete	21				I1				
LEDispose	10				I1				
LEFromScrap	25								
LEGetScrapLen	28							O1	
LEIdle	12				I1				
LEInsert	22				I3			I2	
LEKey	17				I3		I1		
LENew	9		I1		O1				I3
LEPaste	20				I1				
LEReset	5								
LEScrapHandle	27								
LESetCaret	31								
LESetHilite	30								
LESetScrapLen	29							I1	
LESetSelect	14				I3				
LESetText	11				I3			I2	
LEShutDown	3								
LEStartUp	2								
LEStatus	6								

Table 13-10

LineEdit Routines and Parameters

Modifiers	ProgramID	RoutineAdrs	ScrapHndl	SelEnd	SelStart	Status	TextPtr	Version	ViewRectPtr	ZeroPageAdrs
W	W	L	L	W	W	W	L	W	L	W
BA	V	P	H	V	V	B	P	V	P	P
							I1			
I2										
									I2	
			O1							
		I1								
		I1								
				I2	I1					
							I1			
	I2									I1
						O1				

Function Name	Function Number	BoxRectPtr	DestRectPtr	EventPtr	handle	Just	Key	Length	MaxTextLen
LETextBOX	24	I3				I4		I2	
LEToSCRAP	26								
LEUpdate	23				I1				
LEVersion	4								

Notes:

Parameter Size:

- L Long-word (32 bits)
- W Word (16 bits)

Parameter Type:

- B Boolean
- BA Bit array
- H Handle
- P Pointer
- V Value

Table 13-10

LineEdit Routines and Parameters (continued)

Modifiers	ProgramID	RoutineAdrs	ScrapHndl	SelEnd	SelStart	Status	TextPtr	Version	ViewRectPtr	ZeroPageAdrs
							I1			
								O1		

Apple IIGS	Macintosh
LEBootInit	
LEStartUp	TEInit
LEShutDown	
LEVersion	
LEReset	
LEStatus	
LENew	TENew
LEDispose	TEDispose
LESetText	TESetText
LEIdle	TEIdle
LEClick	TEClick
LESetSelect	TESetSelect
LEActivate	TEActivate
LEDeactivate	TEDeactivate
LEKey	TEKey
LECut	TECut
LECopy	TECopy
LEPaste	TEPaste
LEDelete	TEDelete
LEInsert	TEInsert
LEUpdate	TEUpdate
LETextBox	TextBox
LEFromScrap	TEFromScrap
LEToScrap	TEToScrap
LEScrapHandle	TEScrapHandle
LEGetScrapLen	TEGetScrapLen
LESetScrapLen	TESetScrapLen
LESetHilite	
LESetCaret	
	TEGetText
	TESetJust
	TEScroll
	SetWordBreak
	SetClikLoop
	TECalText

Table 13-11
Comparison of Apple IIGS LineEdit with Macintosh TextEdit

CHAPTER 14

Sound

The S in Apple IIGS stands for sound, and the IIGS comes with great sound capabilities. It has a 5503 Digital Oscillator Chip (DOC) made by Ensoniq and used in the Mirage and other professional-level music synthesizers made by that company. The DOC has 32 digital sampling oscillators that can be paired to form voice generators. Though there are 16 potential pairs, oscillators 30 and 31 are reserved for timing applications. This leaves the DOC with the ability to generate 15 different voices.

The Ensoniq chip also has an 8-bit analog-to-digital converter that can be used for digitizing input sound, volume control, and other control registers. A list of the various internal registers in the DOC is given in Table 14-1. Several of the registers contain a series of bits that use a pattern to convey information. Table 14-2 shows the meaning of the bit pattern for the control register, and Table 14-3 contains the bit pattern for the oscillator functions.

Each oscillator has an address generator that determines what value to take from the waveform table and pass to the Digital-to-Analog Output Converter in the DOC. The oscillator functions by taking the 24-bit value in its accumulator and adding to it a 16-bit frequency control register value. The result is truncated to 24 bits and stored back in the accumulator.

Up to 16 of the 24 bits in the accumulator can be used in determining the final address. The resolution register, discussed in Table 14-3, determines which 16 of the 24 bits are used. The address pointer register ($80-9F) contains an 8-bit address value. These bits in these two values are combined according to the size of the table to form a final address as shown in Table 14-4.

Programming the DOC chip to generate sound consists of building a sound wave table in the Sound RAM of the IIGS. The discussion of sound synthesis technique (whether noise, music, speech, or other sounds) is beyond the scope of this chapter. Indeed, whole books are written on the subject. The information in this chapter is designed for users who are already familiar with these techniques.

SOUND GLU AND RAM

The DOC is only part of the sound system built into the IIGS. The DOC has 64K of RAM dedicated for its use. It also has a sound general logic unit (Sound GLU) that serves as an interface between the DOC and the rest of the IIGS. The GLU provides the means for the DOC to continue to function and generate sound without the need for much intervention from the 65816 microprocessor. It also provides the means for passing values to the Sound RAM.

The Sound GLU sound control register is found at $E1/C03C. It is a multiple-function register with different functions indicated by the bit

Register Number	Use
$00-1F	Frequency Control Low. These 32 different registers are each mapped to one of the 32 oscillators. This forms the low byte of the increment value that is used to determine the output frequency of the oscillator.
$20-3F	Frequency Control High. These 32 different registers are each mapped to one of the 32 oscillators. This forms the high byte of the increment value that is used to determine the output frequency of the oscillator.
$40-5F	Volume. These 32 different registers are used by each oscillator to determine the final output volume from that oscillator. This register is not used when the oscillator is in self-enveloping mode.
$60-7F	Data Sample. These 32 registers, mapped to each oscillator, are read-only. They contain the last table read for the waveform table for the particular oscillator.
$80-9F	Address Pointer. These registers are used to determine where the waveform table for the particular oscillator begins in the dedicated 64K of RAM memory.
$A0-BF	Control Register. These registers control the channel assignment, oscillator mode, and halt bit for each oscillator in the form of a bit array. The meaning of each bit position is given in Table 14-2.
$C0-DF	Waveform Table Size - Resolution - Bank Select. These registers are an array of bits that are used to control three different oscillator functions. The meaning of each bit position is given in Table 14-3.
$E0	Oscillator Interrupt Register. Bits 1-5 contain the oscillator number of any oscillator generating an interrupt. Bit 7 shows if an oscillator is generating an interrupt. Bits 0 and 6 are always set to 1.
$E1	Oscillator Enable. This register contains the number of oscillators times 2 that are active in the DOC. There is always at least one oscillator active.
$E2	A/D Converter. This register contains the value of the A/D converter. A read begins the analog-to-digital conversion, which takes 26 machine cycles.

Table 14-1

Ensoniq DOC Registers

Bit Number	Use
0	Halt Bit. Set when an oscillator has been halted either by the DOC or otherwise.
1-2	Mode. The value in these two bits sets the oscillating mode as follows: 0 Free Run—Oscillator runs in a continuous loop, repeating the waveform until halted or until there is a 0 in the waveform table. 1 One Shot—Oscillator moves through the waveform table once and then halts. 2 Sync/AM—If lower oscillator is odd-numbered, it is used to amplitude modulate the even oscillator. If lower oscillator is even, the higher oscillator syncs to the lower one. 3 Swap—Uses a pair of oscillators (lower even and upper odd) in which the two oscillators swap off waveforms.
3	Interrupt Enable. If set, interrupt passed to the oscillator interrupt register when the oscillator completes the cycle.
4	Set to route output to channel 0 of an external analog multiplexer.
5	Set to route output to channel 1 of an external analog multiplexer.
6	Set to route output to channel 2 of an external analog multiplexer.
7	Set to route output to channel 3 of an external analog multiplexer.

Table 14-2

Control Register Bit Meaning

Bit Number	Use
0-2	Resolution register. Determines which of the 24 bits of the oscillator accumulator are used to determine the final address into the waveform table as follows: 0 Bits 1-16 1 Bits 2-17 2 Bits 3-18 3 Bits 4-19 4 Bits 5-20 5 Bits 6-21 6 Bits 7-22 7 Bits 8-23
3-5	Specify size of waveform table as follows: 0 256 bytes 1 512 bytes 2 1024 bytes 3 2048 bytes 4 4096 bytes 5 8192 bytes 6 16384 bytes 7 32768 bytes
6	Extend the addressing range of the DOC with address range beginning at 65536 if bit is 1.
7	Not used.

Table 14-3
Multiple-Function Bit Meaning

Table Size	Pointer Register Bits	Accumulator Bits
256 bytes	0-7	9-16
512 bytes	1-7	8-16
1024 bytes	2-7	7-16
2048 bytes	3-7	6-16
4096 bytes	4-7	5-16
8192 bytes	5-7	4-16
16384 bytes	6-7	3-16
32768 bytes	7	2-16

Notes:

Pointer register bits always form the most significant bits in the address.

The accumulator bits are numbered based on the remaining 16 bits after calculation with the resolution register, not the original bit number position.

Table 14-4

Final Address Calculation

Bit Number	Use
0-3	Volume control
4	Reserved
5	Enable auto increment addressing
6	Select access either to dedicated 64K Sound RAM or DOC Register
7	Busy flag

Table 14-5

Meaning of Sound Control Register Bits

patterns in the register. Table 14-5 shows the meaning of the various bits in this register.

The address register of the Sound GLU is located at $C03E-C03F. If the application is accessing the dedicated Sound RAM, these registers combine to form a 16-bit address. If the application is accessing a DOC register, the lower byte ($C03E) contains the register number. The data themselves are in $C03D.

The Sound GLU helps control both the DOC and the Sound RAM. The DOC can also access the Sound RAM. Output from the DOC is fed to an audio amplifier. The amplified signal is then fed to the following four locations:

- The built-in speaker in the IIGS
- The external speaker jack, which consists of stereo connectors wired together for mono sound (capable of driving a 600-ohm load)
- The sound line in the RGB output connector (capable of driving a 600-ohm load)
- The sound expansion connector, a 7-pin molex connector on the IIGS motherboard labeled J22

Figure 14-1 is a block diagram of the layout of the sound components.

The 7-pin connector provides different signals for use of peripheral equipment for both sound input and sound output.The use of each pin is given in Table 14-6.

The Apple IIGS comes with a number of ROM- and RAM-based sound tool sets. The Sound Manager, tool set 8, is located in ROM. The Note Synthesizer, tool set 25, and Note Sequencer, tool set 26, are located in RAM. At the time this book was written, no information was available

Pin Number	Use
1	Analog-to-digital input. This pin carries input to the 8-bit analog-to-digital converter that is part of the DOC. The input range is from 0 to 2.5 volts. Conversion to a digital value takes 31 microseconds.
2	Analog ground. This pin connects to the IIGS system ground.
3	Waveform out. This pin contains the waveform signal output by the DOC.
4	Channel address 0.
5	Channel address 1.
6	Channel address strobe.
7	Channel address 2.

Note:

The channel address output is used to group the output of the voices of the DOC or to create stereo output. See discussion of bits 4-7 in Table 14-2.

Table 14-6

Use of Sound Connector Pins

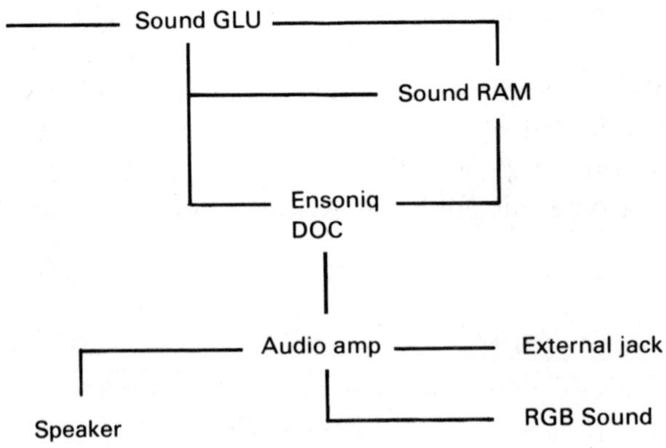

Figure 14-1

Sound block diagram

about the Note Sequencer. An instrument generator and, possibly, a speech synthesizer, may also be available in the future.

SOUND MANAGER

The purpose of the Sound Manager, and indeed the other sound tools, is to give the programmer access to the Ensoniq chip without needing to know the hardware input/output routines. The Sound Manager differs from the other IIGS tools in that it consists both of standard tool set type calls and a small set of low-level commands that are called in an atypical manner.

The Sound Manager also differs from the other IIGS tools in the manner in which it handles errors. The normal method of indicating an error (accumulator nonzero and carry flag set) is still followed. But the error number in the accumulator has its upper byte set to zero. Because the Sound Manager is tool set 8, it needs to return errors of the type $08xx. Therefore, any error code should be ORed with $0800 in order for the error code returned to be valid.

Many of the Sound Manager routines refer to generators. A *generator* is a pair (sometimes called a *swap pair*) of oscillators in swap mode.

A list of the various standard Sound Manager routines, together with a discussion of their functions, appears in Table 14-7. A list of the parameters expected by each routine appears in Table 14-8, and a list of error codes and the tool functions that can return each type of error appears in Table 14-9.

In addition to the standard type of Sound Tool functions, there are six low-level routines. These routines give your application the ability to read and write to the Sound RAM and the DOC registers, and to adjust the volume of the DOC. Parameters are passed through registers, not the stack, and the routines are entered by a JSL instruction. The routines return with an RTL call.

The addresses for the low-level routines are found in the jump table, whose address is obtained by the GetTableAddress function. The layout of the table is shown in Table 14-10. Each of these addresses is a 4-byte address with the least significant byte first and the most significant byte set to 0. The routines are entered by performing a JSL to the address contained in the jump table.

Tool	Description
SoundBootInit	Called by system at bootup time to initialize the Sound Manager. Should not be called by an application.
SoundStartup	Called by an application to set up a direct bank work area for use of the tool.
SoundShutdown	Shuts down the Sound Manager and frees memory allocated for the Sound Manager.
SoundVersion	Returns the version number of the Sound Manager.
SoundReset	Stops all generators from making sound. Should not be made by an application.
SoundToolStatus	Indicates whether Sound Manager is active.
WriteRamBlock	Writes a specified number of bytes from IIGS regular RAM into the dedicated Sound RAM.
ReadRamBlock	Reads a specified number of bytes from the dedicated Sound RAM into the normal IIGS RAM.
GetTableAddress	Returns the address of the jump table for the low-level routines.
GetSoundVolume	Returns the volume setting for a specified generator.
SetSoundVolume	Sets the volume for one or more specified generators or for the entire system.
FFStartSound	Begins to generate free-form waves on a particular generator.
FFStopSound	Stops the sound from one or more specified generators.
FFSoundStatus	Determines if each of the 15 generators is active.
FFGeneratorStatus	Returns the first word of a generator control block, indicating the following: Bits 0-3: Generator number ($00-0E) Bits 4-7: Channel number ($00-0F) Bits 8-11: 0=generator available; 1=generator doing free-form synthesis; 2=generator doing note synthesis Bits 12-14: Reserved; must be 0 Bit 15: Set to 1 when the last block of the waveform has been loaded.

Table 14-7

List of Sound Manager Tools

SetSoundMIRQV	Places the specified interrupt handling routine's address in the Master Sound IRQ Vector. This routine handles interrupts generated by the DOC.
SetUserSoundIRQV	Makes the specified routine used for a user-defined synthesizer interrupt handler. The older vector is returned and must be preserved as part of a chain. When this interrupt occurs, control is passed to the handler by a JSL with control passed back through an RTL.
FFSoundDoneStatus	Returns a boolean value indicating whether the specified generator is currently playing a waveform (result = \$0000) or not (result = \$FFFF).
GetTableAddress	Returns the address of the jump table for use in the low-level routines.

Table 14-7
List of Sound Manager Tools (continued)

Function Name	Function Number	Count	DestPtr	DOCStart	FFSynthMode	GenMask	GenNumber
Parameter Size		W	L	W	B	W	W
Parameter Type		V	P	A	01	BA	V
FFGeneratorStatus	$11						I1
FFSoundDone	$14						I1
FFSoundStatus	$10						
FFStartSound	$0E				I2		I1
FFStopSound	$0F					I1	
GetSoundVolume	$0C						I1
GetTableAddress	$0B						
ReadRAMBlock	$0A	I3	I1	I2			
SetSoundMIRQV	$12						
SetSoundVolume	$0D						I2
SetUserSoundIRQV	$13						
SoundBootInit	$01						
SoundReset	$05						
SoundShutDown	$03						
SoundStartup	$02						
SoundToolStatus	$06						
SoundVersion	$04						
WriteRAMBlock	$09	I3		I2			

Notes:

Parameter Size:
- B Byte (8 bits)
- L Long-word (32 bits)
- W Word (16 bits)

Parameter Type:
- 01 Always set to 1
- A Address
- B Boolean
- BA Bit array
- P Pointer
- V Value

Table 14-8

Sound Manager Functions and Parameters

GenStatus	JumpTable	MasterIRQVec	NewIRQVec	OldIRQVec	ParamBlockPtr	SourcePtr	ToolStatus	Version	VolSetting	WAPT
W	L	L	L	L	L	L	W	W	W	W
BA*	P	A	A	A	P	P	B	V	V	A
O1										
O1										
O1										
					I3					
									O1	
	O1									
		I1								
									I1	
			I1	O1						
										I1
							O1			
						I1		O1		
								I1		

*The meaning of the bit array is:

For FFGeneratorStatus — see discussion in Table 14-7.

For FFSoundDoneStatus — value is a boolean showing sound done ($0000) or currently playing ($FFFF).

For FFSoundStatus — bit number is set if generator with that number is not free.

Function	Error Codes 04	10	12	13	14	15	17	18
FFGeneratorStatus								
FFSoundDone				X				
FFSoundStatus								
FFStartSound			X	X	X	X	X	
FFStopSound								
GetSoundVolume								
GetTableAddress								
ReadRAMBlock	X							
SetSoundMIRQV								
SetSoundVolume								
SetUserSoundIRQV								
SoundBootInit								
SoundReset								
SoundShutDown								
SoundStartup	X							X
SoundToolStatus								
SoundVersion								
WriteRAMBlock	X							

Note:

Meaning of Error Codes

04	DOC address range error
10	No DOC chip found
12	No SoundStartup call made
13	Invalid generator number
14	Synthesizer mode error
15	Generator busy
17	Master IRQ not assigned
18	Sound tools already started

Table 14-9

Sound Error Codes by Function

The purpose of each of these routines is shown in Table 14-11, together with the registers used to pass parameters. Note that in all cases the 65816 emulation bit must be set to 0 (native mode), the memory and accumulator

Routine Name	Jump Table Byte Offset
Read Register	$00
Write Register	$04
Read RAM	$08
Write RAM	$0C
Read Next	$10
Write Next	$14

Table 14-10

Location of Entry for Low-Level Routines

Read Register	Pass the number of the DOC register to be read in the X register. The contents of that register are returned in the low byte of the accumulator.
Write Register	Pass the number of the DOC register to be written in the X register and the value to be written to that register in the low byte of the accumulator.
Read RAM	Pass the 16-bit address of the Sound RAM to be read in the X register. The contents of that address are returned in the low byte of the accumulator.
Write RAM	Pass the 16-bit address of the Sound RAM to be written in the X register and the value to be written in the low byte of the accumulator.
Read Next	The value of the next register or Sound RAM address location is returned in the low byte of the accumulator. (Must be preceded by a Read/Write Register, a Read/Write RAM, or a Read/Write Next call.)
Write Next	The value in the low byte of the accumulator is written to the next register or Sound RAM address location. (Must be preceded by a Read/Write Register, a Read/Write RAM, or a Read/Write Next call.)

Table 14-11

Low-Level Routines

width bit must be set to 1 (8-bit accumulator and memory), and the index register width bit be set to 0 (16-bit index registers).

The jump table also contains the address of three conversion tables. The location and use of each of these tables is shown in Table 14-12.

Byte Offset	Name	Use
$18	Oscillator Table	Table that takes oscillator values and returns the generator of which that oscillator is a part
$1C	Generator Table	Table that takes a generator and returns the lower of the two oscillators that make up that generator
$20	GCB Address Table	Table that returns the address of the Generator Control Block for the specified generator

Table 14-12

Jump Table Conversions

Byte	Name	Size (in bytes)
0	Envelope	24
24	ReleaseSegment	1
25	PriorityIncrement	1
26	PitchBendRange	1
27	VibratoDepth	1
28	VibratoSpeed	1
29	Reserved	1
30	AWaveCount	1
31	BWaveCount	1
32	AWaveList	6 × AWaveCount
*	BWaveList	6 × BWaveCount

* = (6 × AWaveCount) + 32

Table 14-13

Instrument Data Structure

NOTE SYNTHESIZER

The Note Synthesizer provides a method of creating musical sounds using the Ensoniq DOC. Your application first calls the Note Synthesizer to start it up. It then allocates a sound generator (oscillator pair), passes the generator a note to play, and turns off the note when it should be off.

Central to the working of the Note Synthesizer is the concept of an *instrument*. The instrument is a data structure that contains information concerning the various attributes of the particular note. The structure of the instrument record is shown in Table 14-13.

The *envelope* is divided into eight 3-byte segments composed of a 1-byte breakpoint and a 2-byte increment. While the particular envelope segment is active, the volume of the note increases by the increment 100 times each second until the breakpoint is reached. The breakpoint is a logarithmic scale sound level, with each 16 steps representing a 6-decibel change in amplitude.

The increment is a 2-byte fixed-point number. The upper byte represents an unsigned integer value between 0 and 255. The lower byte represents a binary fraction. The meaning of each fraction bit in this value is shown in Figure 14-2.

The envelope volume starts at 0. The first increment value is used to increase from this level to the first breakpoint value. Then the second increment value is used to increase to the second breakpoint value, and so on.

If the envelope has a sustain level (at which it maintains a set volume level), this level is created by setting the increment level to 0 for the segment that follows the segment whose breakpoint is the desired sustain level.

Bit Number	7	6	5	4	3	2	1	0
Value	1/2	1/4	1/8	1/16	1/32	1/64	1/128	1/256

Figure 14-2
Meaning of fraction bits in increment value

When an instrument is at the sustain level, it maintains that level until it enters the release stage by receiving the NoteOff command. At that point the release segment increment value is used to decrement the volume value until it reaches that breakpoint when it passes control to the next segment. The final breakpoint value should always be 0.

The PriorityIncrement value is discussed later under the generator priorities.

The PitchBendRange is a value of 1, 2, or 4, which is the number of semitones the pitch should be raised when the pitchwheel reaches a value of 127. VibratoDepth is the initial fixed depth of vibrato and ranges in value from 0 (vibrato off) to 127. The VibratoSpeed is the frequency rate of the vibrato.

A *wavelist* is a record structure that is part of the instrument record. It contains from 1 to 255 records, known as *waveforms,* each of which has 6 bytes. The waveform has the following parts:

- TopKey, a byte value that represents the highest MIDI semitone that will be played by the waveform. The items in the wavelist should be in increasing TopKey value order with the last TopKey being 127.
- WaveAddress is the high byte of the waveform address.
- WaveSize is a single-byte, combined wavetable size and frequency resolution.
- DOC mode is a byte value placed into the mode register (except for the value of the interrupt enable bit).
- RelPitch is a word value that is used to tune the waveform. The value is a signed fixed point value similar to that of the envelope increment value but represents semitones.

Each generator used by the Note Synthesizer has a Generator Control Block (GCB) associated with it. This is a 16-byte record used not only by the Note Synthesizer, but also by the other sound tools. The GCB contains a value of 2 in its first byte, which identifies it as a Note Synthesizer generator. The generator number is stored in the second byte. The semitone value passed as a parameter when the generator is called by NoteOn is stored in the third byte, while the volume passed by NoteOn is stored in the fourth byte. The pitchbend value (with 64 indicating no bend) is stored in the fifth byte, and the vibrato depth, as specified in the instrument associated with the generator, is stored in the sixth byte. The remaining 10 bytes are for the use of the Note Synthesizer.

The Note Synthesizer uses the largest number of generators of any of the sound tools. In order to prevent a generator from being used for a new note when that would be inappropriate, the Note Synthesizer has a priority scheme that allows it to take an in-use generator only when the priority is sufficient.

Each generator has a priority value of 0 to 128. A 0 priority indicates a free generator. A priority of 128 indicates the generator is locked. The generator-allocation routine (AllocGen) includes a specified priority value. The Note Synthesizer will allocate a generator with the lowest priority value, provided the priority value is less than or equal to the priority passed to AllocGen.

The Note Synthesizer changes the priority of a generator as it plays a tone. When the envelope reaches the sustain segment, the value of the priority increment field of the instrument record is subtracted from the generator's priority. When the release segment is reached, the priority of the envelope is halved. When the note stops, the priority of the generator is returned to 0.

The priority of each generator is also decremented by 1 each time a new generator is allocated. This procedure will generally cause the generators playing the older notes to be allocated for new notes when the AllocGen call is made.

There are three main calls in the Note Synthesizer. AllocGen requests a note generator with a specified priority. If a generator is available, it is allocated and its number is returned. If no generator is available, an error code of $1921 is returned. The priority of the generator is initially set to the value of the requested priority passed to AllocGen.

NoteOn is a command to a specified generator to begin playing a note. The values passed to the routine include:

- □ Generator number (from 0-14)
- □ Semitone in MIDI format (value of 0-127, with middle C being 60)

Function Name	Function Number	GenNum	InstrumentPtr	RequestPriority	Semitone	Status	UserRate	UserUpdateRtn	Version	Volume	ErrorNumber1901	ErrorNumber1902	ErrorNumber1921	ErrorNumber1922	ErrorNumber1923	ErrorNumber1924
Parameter Size		W	L	W	W	W	W	L	W	W						
Parameter Type		V	P	V	V	B	V	P	V	V						
AllNotesOff	0D															
AllocGen	09	O1		I1									X			
DeallocGen	0A	I1												X		
NoteOff	0C	I1			I2											
NoteOn	0B	I1	I4		I2					I3						X
NSBootInit	01															
NSReset	05															
NSShutdown	03														X	
NSStartup	02						I1	I2			X	X				
NSStatus	06					O1										
NSVersion	04								O1							

Notes:

Parameter Size:
- L Long-word (32 bits)
- W Word (16 bits)

Parameter Type:
- B Boolean
- P Pointer
- V Value

Error Codes:
- 1901 Already initialized
- 1902 Sound Tools not initialized
- 1921 No generator available
- 1922 Bad generator number
- 1923 Note Synthesizer not initialized
- 1924 Note already on

Table 14-14

Note Synthesizer Functions

- Volume ranging from 0 to 127, which is functionally equivalent to MIDI velocity
- Pointer to the instrument record

NoteOff is passed a generator number and a semitone. It causes the specified generator to stop playing. It is passed both a generator and a semitone because another note may have taken that generator. Both the generator and the semitone must match for NoteOff to work.

The other Note Synthesizer functions, besides the standard tool functions, are

- DeallocGen, which sets the specified generator's priority to 0
- AllNotesOff, which turns off all Note Synthesizer generators and sets their priorities to 0 (generators used by other sound tools are not affected)

The startup routine varies somewhat from a typical tool set startup function. NSStartup should be called only after the Sound Tools have been started because it shares a direct page with Sound Tools. The update rate is the rate at which envelopes are generated and the rate at which the user update routine is called, in values of 0.4 Hz. A lower update rate requires less system overhead, and a higher rate provides for smoother sound envelopes.

The user update routine is called on every timer interrupt. It is intended to be used by a sequencer program. A value of 0 provides that no update routine will be called.

A list of the Note Synthesizer routines, the parameters expected by each, and the error codes for each are shown in Table 14-14.

PART IV

Managing User Input/Output

CHAPTER

15

The Keyboard, Mouse, and Apple Desktop Bus

The Apple Desktop Bus (ADB) is a serial interface used to connect certain input devices—such as a keyboard, mouse, graphics tablet, or joystick—to the IIGS. The bus can handle data at a rate of about 500 characters per second (approximately 5000 baud).

Pin	Signal
1	Data line—bidirectional
2	Reserved
3	+5 volts
4	Ground

Table 15-1
ADB Connector Signals

The ADB supports multiple devices in a daisy chain. Up to 16 devices can be connected to this chain at one time. The basic Apple IIGS comes with two devices on the chain—a detached keyboard and a mouse.

The ADB devices are connected to the bus by a Circular-4 connector using four lines. The use of each of the lines is given in Table 15-1.

Communication between the ADB and the IIGS is handled by the Single-chip Microprocessor Keyboard Interface (SKI). The KeyGLU manages communications between the SKI and the IIGS.

KEYGLU

The KeyGLU has a number of internal data registers that are displayed in the softswitch and register area beginning at $E0/C000. These include

- □ Mouse data register ($C024)
- □ Modifier key register ($C025)
- □ Command/status register ($C026)
- □ Language select register ($C02B)

The KeyGLU also has two status registers: (1) a KeyGLU status register, with five read-only flags, located at $E0/C027, and (2) a system status register, which has eight flags (some of which are read-only and some of which are read/write). Table 15-2 shows the meaning of the bits in the two status registers.

Bit	Read-Only Status Register Purpose
0	1 = any key down
1-3	Always 0
4	1 = keyboard strobe set
5	1 = data register full
6	1 = command register full
7	1 = mouse X-axis register full

Bit	System Status Register Purpose
0	1 = command register full (read-only)
1	0 = mouse X-axis register available; 1 = mouse Y-axis register available (read-only)
2	1 = enable key data interrupt (read/write)
3	1 = key data full (read-only)
4	1 = data interrupt enable (read/write)
5	1 = data register full (read-only)
6	1 = mouse interrupt enable (read/write)
7	1 = mouse register full (read-only)

Table 15-2
KeyGLU Status Registers

SKI

The SKI performs the following three main functions:

1. Scans the standard keyboard for keyboard or keypad data.
2. Periodically polls the mouse.
3. Transmits commands to and data from other ADB devices.

The SKI can handle the keyboard in the following three different modes for use with 8-bit Apple II software:

1. Standard Apple II mode handles the keyboard in an unbuffered and asynchronous manner. Keyboard data are placed in $E0/C000 to be read by the program, and the keyboard strobe is cleared by the program by reading $E0/C010. The APPLE (corresponding to the OPEN-APPLE key on the Apple IIe and IIc) or the OPTION (corresponding to the CLOSED-APPLE key on Apple IIe and IIc) key status is displayed at $E0/C061 (APPLE) or $E0/C062 (OPTION).
2. Apple II mode with modifiers handles the keyboard in an unbuffered and asynchronous manner, but passes both keyboard data and key modifiers data.
3. Buffered Apple II mode saves keypresses and the modifier state for each keypress in a buffer, sending them to the key and modifier data registers after the keyboard strobe is cleared by the program. The buffer can be flushed by pressing CONTROL-APPLE-DELETE.

The modifier data register is a collection of bits indicating which, if any, of the modifier keys (SHIFT, CONTROL, CAPS LOCK, REPEAT, APPLE, and OPTION) was pressed by setting the appropriate bit equal to 1. In addition, one bit indicates if a key on the keypad was pressed and another bit (update) indicates if the modifier key information was generated in connection with or without a data key. The modifier register is updated without a data key being pressed only if the keyboard strobe is clear. The meaning of each bit in the modifier register is shown in Table 15-3.

Bit	Modifier
0	SHIFT key
1	CONTROL key
2	CAPS LOCK key
3	REPEAT key
4	Keypad key
5	Updated without keypress
6	OPTION key
7	APPLE key

Table 15-3

Meaning of Key Modifiers Data Byte

Commands can be sent over the ADB to the SKI. The ADB tool set, discussed next in this chapter, is used for transmitting these commands. A list of the SKI commands is given in Table 15-4.

Number	Command
$01	Abort—flushes any active commands
$02	Reset SKI—software reset by jump to power-on reset routine
$03	Flush keyboard type-ahead buffer
$04	Set modes according to the mode byte Mode Byte Bits 0 Auto-poll of ADB keyboard disabled 1 Auto-poll of ADD mouse disabled 2 Include spacebar and delete as dual speed keys 3 Dual speed keys go at four times normal repeat 4 Keyboard in buffered mode 5 ADB keyboard layout equivalent to IIe layout 6 Shift caps and lowercase in caps lock 7 Reset with reset only (no control needed)
$05	Clear modes according to the mode byte shown under command $04
$06	Set configuration using the next three bytes as follows: Byte 1: Low nibble—ADB keyboard address High nibble—ADB mouse address Byte 2: Low nibble—Keyboard language layout US—0 UK—1 FR—2 DN—3 SP—4 IT—5 GR—6 SW—7 DV—8 CN—9 High nibble—Character set with most significant bit set if keypad . swapped with keypad , Byte 3: Low nibble—auto-repeat rate (keys/second) 40 (0) 30 (1) 24 (2) 20 (3) 15 (4) 11 (5) 8 (6) 4 (7)

Table 15-4
SKI Commands

Number	Command
	High nibble—repeat delay rate (seconds) .25 (0) .5 (1) .75 (2) 1.0 (3) No repeat (4)
$07	Synch. Clear modes (using mode byte discussed in $04), set configuration (using configuration bytes discussed in $06), reset to internal power-up state, and then reset FDB devices
$08	Write. Place data in second byte into SKI RAM address ($00-5F) in first byte
$09	Read. Transfer data from address in next two bytes to data register in KeyGLU. Address can be either SKI RAM ($0000-005F) or SKI ROM ($1400-1FFF)
$0A	Read modes byte (discussed in command $04)
$0B	Read configuration bytes (discussed in command $06)
$0C	Read and clear ADB error byte whose bits have the following meaning: 0-1 Reserved 2 More than 8 data bytes received 3 Device sent pulse too long 4 Device sent pulse too short 5 Bus low when it should be high 6 SRQ more than 550 microseconds 7 Fatal (nonrecoverable) error
$0D	Return version number in low nybble of data latch
$0E	Read character sets available (number of bytes and data)
$0F	Read layouts available (number of bytes and data)
$10	Reset system
$11	Send ADB keycode in next byte
$40	Reset ADB
$48	Send command in next byte and then send back data
%01001nnn	Send command in next byte followed by nnn+1 data bytes that also follow command
%0101nnnn	Enable SRQ on ADB device at address nnnn
%0110nnnn	Flush buffer on ADB device at address nnnn
%0111nnnn	Disable SRQ on ADB device at address nnnn
%10rraaaa	Transmit two bytes from address aaaa to register rr using ADB listen command
%11rraaaa	Receive data (number of bytes followed by data) from address aaaa in register rr using ADB talk command

Table 15-4

SKI Commands (continued)

ADB KEYBOARD

Every printable character in the IIGS has a specific code assigned to it. In 8-bit Apple II text mode, there is a fixed relationship between these codes and the character that cannot be changed without changing the entire display layout, and then only in accordance with specified alternative layouts. These are all discussed in Chapter 8.

In IIGS super-resolution graphics text display, the relationship between codes and the character displayed depends on the characteristics of the particular font (discussed in Chapter 13).

In general, the 8-bit Apple II text code and the IIGS Quickdraw II text code conform to the ASCII code. The keycode returned to the key data register when a key is pressed is generally the ASCII code for that code. But the Apple IIGS ADB keyboard is capable of determining more about the keys pressed than a simple ASCII code. It returns a single code for each key pressed, without regard to the condition of the modifier key (which also has a code). These codes are listed in Table 15-5. Normally the codes will be changed to their ASCII equivalents, taking into account the modifier keys (such as SHIFT, CONTROL, and CAPS LOCK), before being used by your application.

ADB TOOL SET

Generally, if your application is using only the keyboard and mouse for input, it will rarely need to concern itself with the ADB or communicating with it. The Event Manager (discussed in Chapter 20) handles both mouse and key events and reports them back to your application.

If you are creating a device for use on the ADB, or planning to support devices on the ADB other than the keyboard and mouse, then your application may need to use the ADB tool set.

The ADB tool set is a ROM-based tool set, similar to the other Apple IIGS tools. It contains the standard functions found on all the tool sets, as well as specific functions used to send commands and data between the SKI and the IIGS. Commands can be used to control activity on the ADB, as well as other functions.

The ADB tool set differs in some respects from the other IIGS tools. Five of the tool functions contain a parameter known as the *command word,* a value that is passed to the function. Depending on the command chosen, the ADB tool performs a variety of functions. Also, the data passed to the routine or received from the routine vary, depending on the

Code	Key	Code	Key	Code	Key	Code	Key
0	A	24	=	48	TAB	72	DOWN ARROW
1	S	25	9	49	SPACEBAR	73	,
2	D	26	7	50	`	74	SPACE
3	F	27	-	51	DELETE	75	/
4	H	28	8	52	RETURN	76	RETURN
5	G	29	0	53	ESCAPE	77	UP ARROW
6	Z	30	]	54	CONTROL	78	-
7	X	31	O	55	APPLE	79	(
8	C	32	U	56	SHIFT	80	)
9	V	33	[	57	LOCK	81	=
10	Int. 10	34	I	58	OPTION	82	0
11	B	35	P	59	LEFT ARROW	83	1
12	Q	36	RETURN	60	RIGHT ARROW	84	2
13	W	37	L	61	DOWN ARROW	85	3
14	E	38	J	62	UP ARROW	86	4
15	R	39	'	63	Int. 63	87	5
16	Y	40	K	64	DELETE	88	6
17	T	41	;	65	.	89	7
18	1	42	\	66	RIGHT ARROW	90	ESCAPE
19	2	43	,	67	*	91	8
20	3	44	/	68	?	92	9
21	4	45	N	69	+		
22	5	46	M	70	LEFT ARROW		
23	6	47	.	71	CONTROL-X		

Notes: Codes above 63 are keypad codes.
Codes above 92 are passed through to keylatch directly.
Reset up is $FFFF and reset down is $7F7F.

Table 15-5
ADB Keycodes

command. The ADB tool set uses a data pointer to point to a data structure in calling the function so that the number of bytes pushed on the stack is always the same.

The SEND command (function $09) can use 1 of 16 subcommands. These subcommands differ in the number of data bytes that are transferred to the ADB SKI. The first word pushed on the stack before calling the SEND command contains the number of data bytes to be transmitted,

Command Number	Name	Number of bytes
$01	Abort	0
$02	Reset keyboard SKI	0
$03	Flush keyboard	0
$04	Set Modes Input — Modes (See Table 15-4)	1
$05	Clear Modes Input — Modes (See Table 15-4)	1
$06	Set Configuration Input — Configuration bytes (See Table 15-4)	3
$07	Synch Input — Modes and Configurations bytes (See Table 15-4)	4
$08	Write Memory Input — Zero page memory address (1 byte) Input — Data byte (1 byte)	2
$10	Reset system	0
$11	Send ADB Keycode Input — Keycode (1 byte)	1
$40	Reset ADB	0
$4y	Transmit ADB bytes y = 7 + n (number of bytes to transmit) Input — ADB command (1 byte) Data bytes (2-8 bytes)	n+1
$5x	Enable SRQ	0
$6x	Flush buffer	0
$7x	Disable SRQ	0
$8r	Transmit 2 ADB bytes r = ADB address Input — Data bytes 1 and 2 (1 byte each)	2

Note: x is ADB address in low nibble

Table 15-6

ADB Tool Function SEND — Subcommands and Data Structures

followed by a pointer to the data to be transmitted, followed by the subcommand. This information is shown in Table 15-6.

Command Number	Name	Number of bytes
$0A	Read Modes Output — Modes (See Table 15-4)	1
$0B	Read Configuration Output — Configuration bytes (See Table 15-4)	3
$0C	Read ADB Error Byte Output — Error code	1
$0D	Read Version Number Output — Version number	1

Table 15-7
ADB Tool Function RCV — Subcommands and Data Structures

The RCV (receive) command (function $0A) is similar to the SEND command except in the number and type of subcommands (four subcommands) and except that the data are being received, not sent, by the IIGS. The information concerning the subcommands for the RCV command is shown in Table 15-7.

The RDMem (read memory) command (function $0B), while similar in structure to the SEND and RCV commands, has only one command ($09), no number of bytes value, and both a datain and a dataout pointer. The input data consists of two bytes: low-memory address followed by high-memory address. The output byte consists of the data read.

Two commands are used in transmitting commands to an ADB device in order to receive data back from it. ADBPoll is generally used when the command type is talk (data to be sent to IIGS from device). ADBrcv is used if the command type is not talk. In both cases the command, address, and register are all sent as part of the command word. These two routines also have a completion vector that calls a routine (created as part of your application) that takes data from the buffer created by the routine and places it in your buffer. The format of the completion vector routine is

```
* Completion vector for ADB Poll or ADB Receive Routine
* 65816 will be in 8-bit native mode (e=0, m=1, x=1)
CompVect  START
          PHD         ;Save current direct register on stack
          TSC         ;And make stack new direct page
          TCD
* Address of data is 6 deep in stack -- 3 bytes for RTL address
```

```
* and 2 bytes for saved direct register
          LDA [6]   ;Length byte from buffer
          BEQ Done  ;If 0, no data returned
          TAY       ;Index with Y register
Loop      LDA [6],Y ;Get first byte
          STA BUF,Y ;into our buffer
          DEY       ;Set for next byte
          BPL Loop  ;and get it if not done
Done      PLD       ;Restore old direct register
          RTL       ;and back to application
          END
```

The SRQPL is similar to the ADBPoll and ADBrcv commands in that it also uses a completion vector. The routine passes an address of an ADB device, which will be added to the list of ADB devices to be polled when a service request (SRQ) has been asserted on the bus. The system will call the completion vector when an SRQ is asserted and data are transferred. The format of this completion vector is slightly different because the SRQ list handler leaves three extra bytes on the stack. The listing is

```
* Completion vector for SRQPL Routine 65816 will be in 8-bit native
* mode (e=0, m=1, x=1)
SRCpVect  START
          PHD       ;Save current direct register on stack
          TSC       ;And make stack new direct page
          TCD
* Address of data is 9 deep in stack -- 3 bytes for RTL address,
* 3 bytes for data left by SRQ list handler and 2 bytes for saved
* direct register
          LDA [9]   ;Length byte from buffer - will not be 0
          TAY       ;Index with Y register
Loop      LDA [6],Y ;Get first byte
          STA BUF,Y ;into our buffer
          DEY       ;Set for next byte
          BPL Loop  ;and get it if not done
Done      PLD       ;Restore old direct register
          RTL       ;and back to application
          END
```

Table 15-8 is a list of the other ADB tool set commands, while Table 15-9 is a list of all the commands, the parameters expected by each, and the potential error codes returned by each. Table 15-10 is a list of the ADB tool set error codes.

THE IIGS MOUSE

The Apple IIGS mouse, residing on the ADB, is mapped to the internal Slot 4. It somewhat resembles the Apple IIc mouse in the sense that the interface for the mouse is built into the IIGS—no card is needed.

But the IIGS mouse more closely resembles the Apple IIe mouse (running on an AppleMouse card) in the sense that it is under the control of a

Commands	Purpose
ABSON ($0F)	Enable automatic polling of an absolute device (default).
ABSOFF ($10)	Disable automatic polling of an absolute device.
RDABS ($11)	Determine if automatic polling of absolute device is enabled or disabled.
SCALE ($12)	Set up scaling for absolute devices. The datain buffer contains the following words: X-divide Y-divide X-offset Y-offset X-multiply (only lower byte significant) Y-multiply (only lower byte significant)
RDSCALE ($13)	Read the scaling values into the buffer. The data words are the same as in the SCALE ($12) command.
SRQRMV	Remove the device from the SRQ list.
CLRSRQTBL	Remove all devices from the SRQ list.

Table 15-8
Other ADB Tool Set Commands

separate microprocessor (in this case the ADB SKI), which permits it to run in a true passive mode. This relationship means that the mouse can update information about its movements and locations, but it cannot report the information until asked. Alternatively, it can interrupt the IIGS operation only during VBL cycles (60 times a second), thereby decreasing the amount of demands on the IIGS's 65816 microprocessor.

The status of the mouse can be obtained directly by using the KeyGLU status register at $E0/C027 in conjunction with the mouse data register at $E0/C024. Three bits in the KeyGLU status register affect mouse operations. These are shown in Table 15-11.

The mouse data are returned by the mouse firmware into the mouse data register located at $E0/C024. Each read of the mouse requires two bytes. These two bytes are transmitted one after the other. To get the full data, the values in $E0/C024 must be read twice.

Function Name	Function Number	ADBAddress	ADBCommand	Command	CompltnVctr	DatainPtr	DataoutPtr	HowMany	Status	Error $10	Error $82	Error $83	Error $84
Parameter Size		W	W	W	L	L	L	W	W				
Parameter Type		A	V	V	P	P	P	V	B				
SEND	09			I3			I2	I1		x			
RCV	0A			I3		I2		I1		x			
RDmem	0B			I3		I2	I1			x			
ADBpoll	0D			I2	I1					x	x		
ADBrcv	0E		I1	I3	I2					x	x		
ABSON	0F												
ABSOFF	10												
RDABS	11								O1				
SCALE	12					I1							
RDSCALE	13						I1						
SRQPL	14	I2			I1					x		x	x
SRQRMV		I1								x	x		
CLRSRQTBL													

Table 15-9

ADB Tool Set Functions and Parameters

Value	Meaning
$10	Command not completed
$82	Busy (command pending)
$83	Device not present at address
$84	SRQ list full

Table 15-10

ADB Tool Set Error Codes

Bit	Use	User Modifiable
1	0 = X position data available; 1 = Y position data available	No (read-only)
6	0 = mouse interrupts disabled; 1 = mouse interrupts enabled	Yes (read/write)
7	0 = mouse register not full; 1 = mouse register full	No (read-only)

Table 15-11
KeyGLU Status Register Mouse-Related Bits

To read the data, your application must first be sure that the data are valid. The data are valid if the following two conditions are met:

1. Bit 7 of $E0/C027 is 1 (mouse register full).
2. Bit 1 of $E0/C027 is 0 (X position available).

If Bit 7 is 0, the application must wait until the mouse firmware updates the information and fills the register. If bit 1 is 0, the X data has been lost and $E0/C024 holds the Y data (or just garbage). In the latter case, your application should read the data in $E0/C024 and throw it away.

If the data are valid, the data in the register are interpreted as shown in Table 15-12. The following routine accomplishes this:

```
* Routine to Check for Mouse Data and Read It If Valid Data
MouseRead START
          SEP #$30         ;8-bit mode
          STZ But0         ;Initialize buttons as up
          STZ But1
          PHB              ;Save current data bank register
          LDA #$E0         ;and change it to bank $E0
          PHA
          PLB
          LDA $C027        ;Get KeyGLU status
          BPL Exit         ;If bit 7 = 0, no data available
          AND #%00000010   ;Mask off bit 1
          BNE Corrupt      ;If bit 1 = 1 data is corrupted
          LDA $C024        ;X data
          BPL Up1          ;If bit 1 = 0, button 1 is still up
          INC But1         ;Otherwise show it is down
```

First Byte	Data
Bits 0-6	X (horizontal) relative mouse movement (signed value −64 to +63)
Bit 7	0 = button 1 up; 1 = button 1 down
Second Byte	**Data**
Bits 0-6	Y (vertical) relative mouse movement (signed value −64 to +63)
Bit 7	0 = button 0 up; 1 = button 0 down

Table 15-12
Meaning of Mouse Data

```
Up1      AND #%01111111 ;Mask off top bit
         STA DeltaX     ;And save value of X movement
         LDA $C024      ;Y data
         BPL Up0        ;If bit 1 = 0, button 0 is still up
         INC But0       ;Otherwise show it is down
Up0      AND #%01111111 ;Mask off top bit
         STA DeltaY     ;And save value of Y movement
Exit     PLB            ;Reset data bank register
         RTS            ;and back to routine
Corrupt  LDA $C024      ;Get rid of garbage byte
         BRA Exit       ;and leave
         END
```

When active, the mouse firmware uses the screen holes allocated to Slot 4 to store information about the mouse. Table 15-13 shows what data are stored in each location. The mouse firmware conforms to the Pascal 1.1 protocol for peripheral cards. It must be called from 65816 emulation mode with the data bank register equal to $00, the direct register equal to $0000, and text page 1 shadowing on. System speed can be either fast or slow. These routines function the same as the mouse firmware routines in the Apple IIc. They are nearly equivalent to the Apple IIe AppleMouse card routines except that the following AppleMouse card routines do nothing in the IIGS:

- □ Diagmouse
- □ Copyright

- Timedata
- SetVBLCnts
- OptMouse
- StartTimer

Table 15-14 lists the 8-bit Apple II mouse routines. They work the same as in the Apple IIe with an AppleMouse card or in an Apple IIc. For further information about these routines, see either the *Apple IIc Technical Reference Manual* or the *AppleMouse Card Manual.*

Location	Use	
$047C	Absolute X position—low byte	
$04FC	Absolute Y position—low byte	
$057C	Absolute X position—high byte	
$05FC	Absolute Y position—high byte	
$067C	Reserved for firmware use	
$06FC	Reserved for firmware use	
$077C	Button and interrupt status:	
	Bit 0	Button 1 was previously up (0) or down (1)
	Bit 1	Set if mouse movement interrupt
	Bit 2	Set if button 0/1 interrupt
	Bit 3	Set if VBL interrupt
	Bit 4	Button 1 current up (0) or down (1)
	Bit 5	Set if X or Y moved since last READMOUSE operation
	Bit 6	Button 0 was previously up (0) or down (1)
	Bit 7	Button 0 is currently up (0) or down (1)
$07FC	Mode byte	
	Bit 0	Mouse off (0) or on (1)
	Bit 1	Set to enable VBL interrupts on mouse movement
	Bit 2	Set to enable VBL interrupts on button down
	Bit 3	Set to enable VBL interrupts
	Bits 4-7	Reserved

Note: Screen holes are in main memory (bank $E0) and may be shadowed into bank $00.

Table 15-13

Use of Screen Holes

Offset Location	Name	Purpose
$C412	SetMouse	Set mouse mode as specified in accumulator
$C413	ServeMouse	Service mouse interrupt
$C414	ReadMouse	Read mouse position
$C415	ClearMouse	Clear mouse position to 0
$C416	PosMouse	Set mouse position to specified location
$C417	ClampMouse	Set mouse bounds
$C418	HomeMouse	Set mouse to upper-left corner of clamping area
$C419	InitMouse	Reset mouse clamps to default and position to 0,0

Note: Routines are found in bank $E0 and may be shadowed into bank $00.

Table 15-14

8-Bit Apple II Mode Mouse Routines

SetMouse ($19)

Input: Mode (word)

$0000	Turn off mouse
$0001	Set transparent mode
$0003	Set movement-interrupt mode
$0005	Set button-interrupt mode
$0007	Set button- or movement-interrupt mode
$0008	Turn mouse off, VBL interrupts active
$0009	Set transparent mode, VBL interrupts active
$000B	Set movement interrupt mode, VBL interrupts active
$000D	Set button-interrupt mode, VBL interupts active
$000F	Set button- or movement-interrupt mode, VBL interrupts active

ServeMouse ($1F)

Output: Interrupt status (in low byte of word)

ReadMouse ($17)

Output: High byte X position (byte)
Low byte X position (byte)

Table 15-15

Miscellaneous Tool Set Mouse Functions Corresponding to 8-Bit Apple II Mode Routines

High byte Y position (byte)
Low byte Y position (byte)
Mouse status (byte)
Mouse mode (byte)

ClearMouse ($1B)
No parameters

PosMouse ($1E)
Input: X axis position (word)
Y axis position (word)

ClampMouse ($1C)
Input: X axis minimum clamp value (word)
X axis maximum clamp value (word)
Y axis minimum clamp value (word)
Y axis maximum clamp value (word)

HomeMouse ($1A)
No parameters

InitMouse ($18)
Input: Mouse slot (word)
Must be either slot of mouse or $0000 to cause search for mouse slot

GetMouseClamp ($1D)
Output: X axis minimum clamp value (word)
X axis maximum clamp value (word)
Y axis minimum clamp value (word)
Y axis maximum clamp value (word)

Note: Routines are listed in 8-bit Apple II mode order.
GetMouseClamp is not available in the 8-bit Apple II mode functions.

Table 15-15
Miscellaneous Tool Set Mouse Functions Corresponding to 8-Bit Apple II Mode Routines (continued)

The Apple IIGS Miscellaneous Toolbox has a series of mouse tool functions that are designed for use with the IIGS in full 16-bit native mode. These routines generally mimic the 8-bit Apple II mode routines in the results, but handle data in a manner consistent with the Apple IIGS tools generally. These tools are listed in Table 15-15 together with their input and output parameters. These tools will work with either the ADB mouse or the AppleMouse card mouse. The InitMouse routine must be called before any other mouse function.

Reference	Data Length	Name
$000B	Byte	MouseSlot. If positive value, it indicates in what slot the mouse resides. If negative value, it indicates the mouse has not been initialized.
$000C	4 words	MouseClamps: X axis minimum clamp (word) Y axis minimum clamp (word) X axis maximum clamp (word) Y axis maximum clamp (word)
$000D	4 words	AbsClamps: X axis minimum clamp (word) Y axis mimimum clamp (word) X axis maximum clamp (word) Y axis maximum clamp (word)

Table 15-16

Mouse and Pointing-Device-Related Address

The GetAddr Miscellaneous tool function ($16) takes an input value specifying an address to be returned and returns with the address of a specified value. Three of the input values refer to items concerning mouse or other ADB pointing devices. The input value and the structure of the data at the specified address are listed in Table 15-16.

The absolute device clamps are provided for aid in working with an absolute pointing device attached to the ADB. The SetAbsClamp function ($2A) works just like the ClampMouse function except for an absolute device. The GetAbsClamp function ($2B) works just like the GetMouse-Clamp function except for an absolute device.

CHAPTER 16

Windows: The Environment

Programs written to take full advantage of the IIGS capabilities use windows to display program information. The full IIGS screen, minus any system menu bar across the top of the screen, is referred to as the *desktop* because it functions as an electronic desktop, holding all the material with which you are working. The desktop can have any number of different information displays on it.

These displays can be thought of as electronic file folders, each containing a set of organized information needed by an *application.* An application can have one or more such displays on the desktop at one time—some may contain information being processed by the application, some give warnings, and some seek additional information needed by the application. In addition, a desk accessory can also have one or more displays.

While the comparison to file folders is apt, these information displays are called *windows,* based on their display of a modifiable part of the entire data area. The display is similar to looking through a movable window over a part of the data area (see Figure 16-1). Indeed this ability to display serially a data area that is larger than the screen is the primary reason for use of windows.

CLASSIFICATIONS OF WINDOWS

There are several different classifications of windows. Windows that display the information with which the application is working are called *document windows* and are discussed in this chapter. Those that seek additional information needed by the application to perform a requested

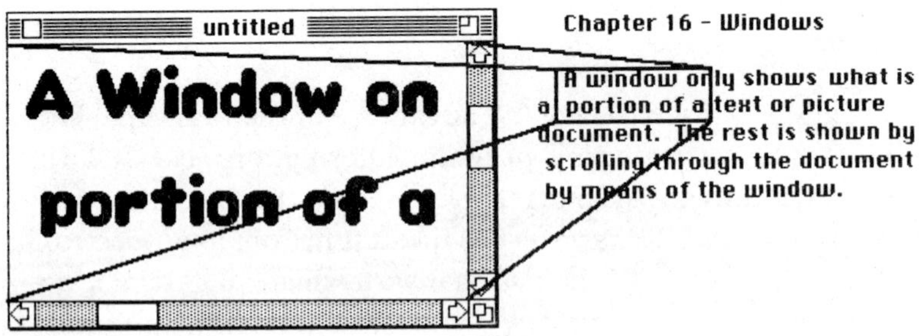

Figure 16-1
Sample window display

function are called *dialog windows* and are discussed in Chapter 19. Windows that warn about certain consequences of the action you are about to take, or tell you about a machine hardware or software malfunction, are called *alert windows* and are also discussed in Chapter 19. The distinction between document and alert windows, in addition to their function, is apparent from the different borders given the standard document and alert windows (see Figure 16-2).

Windows are also classified by the program that uses them. Applications, not surprisingly, use application windows. Desk accessories use system windows. The practical difference between these two types of

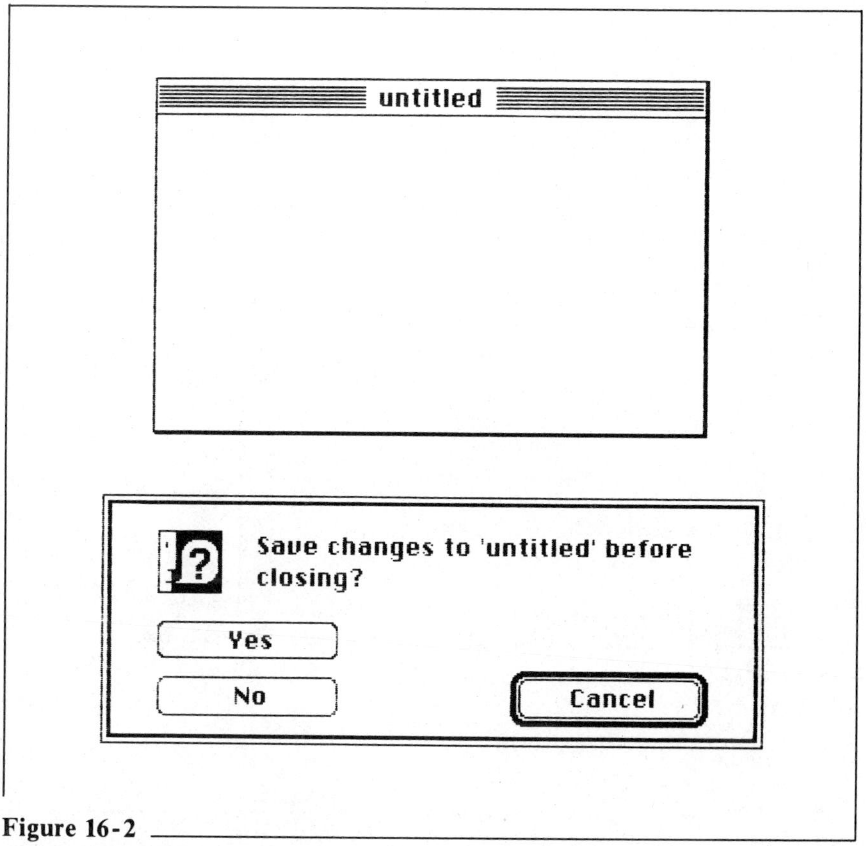

Figure 16-2
Borders for standard document and alert windows

windows is small from both the programmer's and user's points of view, although you must remember to use the right type of window when writing a program that uses the Window Manager.

STRUCTURE OF A WINDOW

A window consists of a content portion and a frame. These two portions of a window are Quickdraw II regions known as the Content Region and the Frame Region. Together they make up the Structure Region.

A window frame may have several additions to it, not all of which are present in every window (see Figure 16-3). These additions are collectively known as controls and are discussed in Chapter 18. A window may have all of these controls, some of them, or none of them, subject to the restriction that a title bar must be used if either a close box or a zoom box is desired.

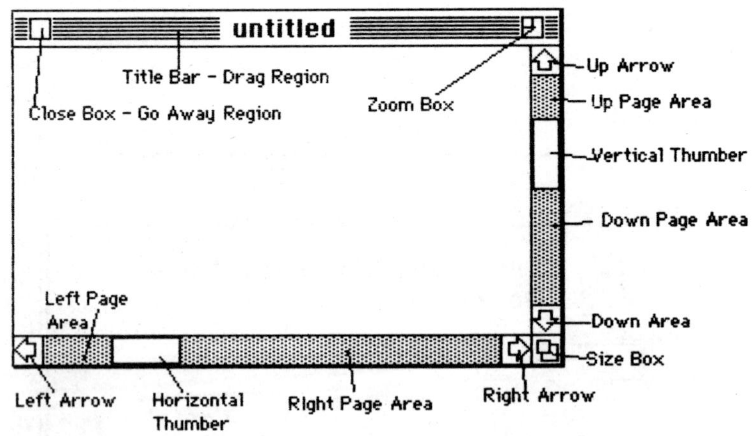

Figure 16-3
Window frame additions

The Frame Region of a window may be partially divided into other regions depending on the presence of certain controls. The *close box* represents the go-away region; the *grow box,* also known as the size box, represents the grow region; the *zoom box* represents the zoom region; the *title bar,* except for any close or zoom box, represents the drag region.

The stacking of windows on the desktop is accomplished so that each window occupies a logically separate vertical plane with the screen having imagined depth from front to back. Planes are numbered logically in a sequence with the first plane being in front (and normally holding the currently active and displayed window).

A highlighted window is displayed with the following: a specified frame color; title color (also used for the close and zoom boxes if present); title bar background color, pattern, and pattern color; grow box color; and an information bar that is the same color as the background color of the Content Region of the window. The recommended programming procedure is to highlight a window to show it is the active window. You can, however, highlight any and all windows on the desktop.

When a window is unhighlighted, the scroll bars are not displayed, but the location is outlined. The title is displayed in the specified inactive title color, and the title bar is displayed in the inactive title bar color without any specified pattern. The information bar, if present, is displayed in the specified inactive information bar interior color; the grow box, if present, is displayed in the specified inactive grow box interior color. (The method of specifying the various highlighted and unhighlighted colors is discussed later in this chapter.)

CHANGING WINDOWS

An existing open window can be visually removed from the desktop without closing it by making it invisible. You should probably do this procedure only with a window that is inactive, although you can theoretically make the active window invisible.

You can manipulate windows in a variety of ways. The portion of the data area being displayed can be changed (scrolling vertically or horizontally), the size of the display may be increased or decreased, the location of a window on the desktop may be changed, or an inactive window may be moved on top of the other windows and designated as the active window.

The various methods by which these operations are carried out, and the redrawing of the desktop display as windows are uncovered, recovered, made active, and made inactive, are all best done under the control of the Window Manager, a RAM-based IIGS toolset.

The various window events are all standard IIGS events. (Events are discussed in Chapter 20.) The Window Manager provides a variety of calls that help the programmer both in determining what the purpose of a particular event is and in providing the appropriate response to that event. Some of the major events, and the appropriate responses, include

- Moving the window when it is dragged to a new location by its title bar
- Closing a window when its close box is clicked
- Making a window active when the mouse is clicked in it
- Scrolling the window vertically or horizontally in response to clicks in its arrow or page-move areas or in response to movement of a scroll thumb
- Resizing a window when its size box is dragged to a new location
- Zooming a window either from its existing size to full size or from full size to its previous existing size when the zoom box is clicked

WINDOW RECORDS

The Window Manager makes use of several different tables and records in carrying out its functions. Each currently allocated window has a window record in RAM that consists of the window's Grafport plus additional information. (See Chapter 10 for a discussion of the Grafport.) When a new window is created, the program returns a pointer to the window's Grafport. This pointer is required by your program for later calls to the Window Manager so that it will know which window to manipulate.

The window record in the IIGS is only partially defined by Apple. The reason for only a partial definition is to discourage programmers from directly accessing the window record outside the Window Manager. Old-time Apple II programmers will remember that many programs written for that machine made direct access to the Apple II monitor ROM through locations that were not intended by Apple for use as entry points. This access resulted in problems when Apple sought to upgrade the monitor ROM—some programs would not run on the new ROMs and some portions of the ROM that should have been changed were not changed because too many programs used certain unauthorized access points.

Partially defining a record should help prevent direct access to the record. In addition, direct access is not required because programmers can modify the Window Manager itself. (See the discussion of modifying tools and the Tool Locator in Chapter 2.) Consequently we shall discuss only the supported portion of the Window Manager record.

Table 16-1 shows the defined portion of the IIGS window record. As you can see, a window record is part of a linked listof window records comprising all windows currently allocated. The first part of the record is a long-word pointer to the next window record. This is followed by the 186-byte Grafport for the window. Next come handles to various regions of the window, followed by a handle to the first item in the control list for that window. (Controls are discussed in Chapter 18.)

The last item in the defined part of the window record is a word-length

Byte Offset	Size	Title	Purpose
0	Long	wnext	Pointer to the next window in list
4	186 bytes	wport	Grafport for the window
190	Long	wstrucRgn	Handle to window's region (frame + content)
194	Long	wcontRgn	Handle to window's Content Region
198	Long	wupdateRgn	Handle to window's content portion that requires redrawing
202	Long	wcontrol	Handle to first control in the Content Region
206	Long	wFrameCtrl	Handle to frame's first control
210	Word	wframe	Frame attributes

Table 16-1
Window Record (Defined Portion)

collection of bits that describes various attributes of the window. Each bit and the attribute controlled by that bit are shown in Table 16-2.

When you create a new window, you pass a parameter to the New_Window routine pointing to the location of a five-word-long color table that is used in displaying the various parts of the table. If a zero is passed as the pointer, the Window Manager uses the default color table to draw the window. Table 16-3 shows the structure of the color table and the values used in the default color table.

The third major record structure used by the Window Manager is the TaskRecord. This is a record used only by the TaskMaster routine in the

Bit Number	Title	Purpose
0	F_Hilited	1 if window is highlighted
1	F_Zoomed	1 if window is at full size
2	F_Allocated	1 if record is allocated (that is, not provided by application)
3	F_Ctrl_Tie	1 if state of controls is independent of window being active or inactive
4	F_Info	1 if window has an information bar
5	F_Vis	1 if window is visible
6	F_QContent	1 to return wInContent from inactive window
7	F_Move	1 if window is movable
8	F_Zoom	1 if window has a zoom box
9	F_Flex	1 if grow and zoom don't change origin
10	F_Grow	1 if window has a grow (size) box
11	F_Bscrl	1 if window has a bottom scroll bar
12	F_Rscrl	1 if window has a right scroll bar
13	F_Alert	1 for alert typo frame
14	F_Close	1 if window has a close box
15	F_Title	1 if window has a title bar

Table 16-2

Frame Attributes Word

Window Manager, which we'll discuss in the next section. It consists of a standard event record (discussed in Chapter 20) with a long-word value appended to the end that contains any data that will be passed back to your routine by TaskMaster and a word-length bit array specifying what tasks TaskMaster is to handle.

TASKMASTER AND WINDOWS

Figure 16-4 is a flowchart illustrating the standard-type responses your application should make to events concerning windows when you use the Window Manager and certain other tools. As you can see, you can initiate

Word Number	Bit Numbers	Purpose
0	0-3	Unused
0	4-7	Outline color
0	8-15	Unused
1	0-3	Title, close and zoom box color, inactive
1	4-7	Title color, inactive
1	8-11	Title bar color, inactive
1	12-15	Unused
2	0-3	Background color
2	4-7	Pattern color
2	8-15	Pattern number
3	0-3	Interior color when selected
3	4-7	Interior color when not selected
3	8-15	Unused
4	0-3	Unused
4	4-7	Information bar interior color when not selected
4	8-15	Unused

Table 16-3
Window Color Table Structure

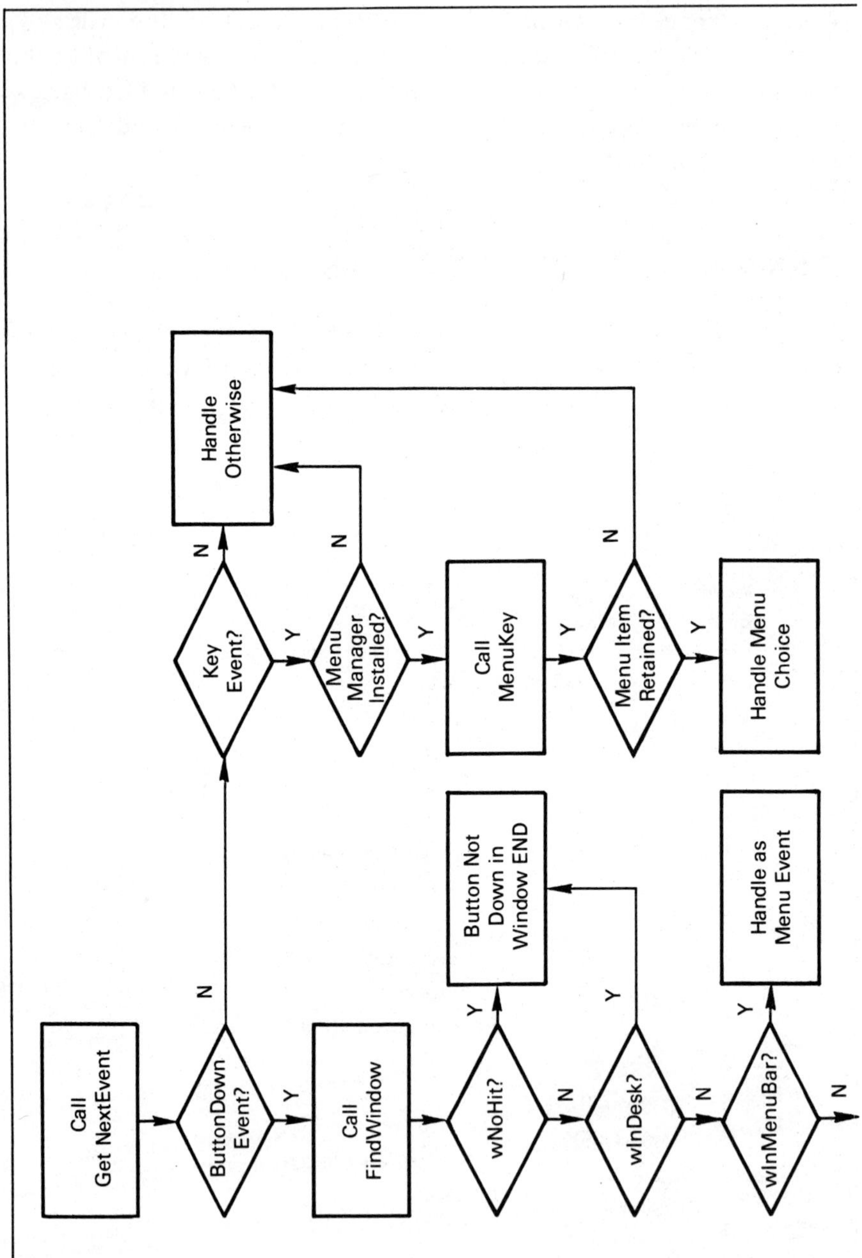

Figure 16-4

Flowchart of standard-type responses

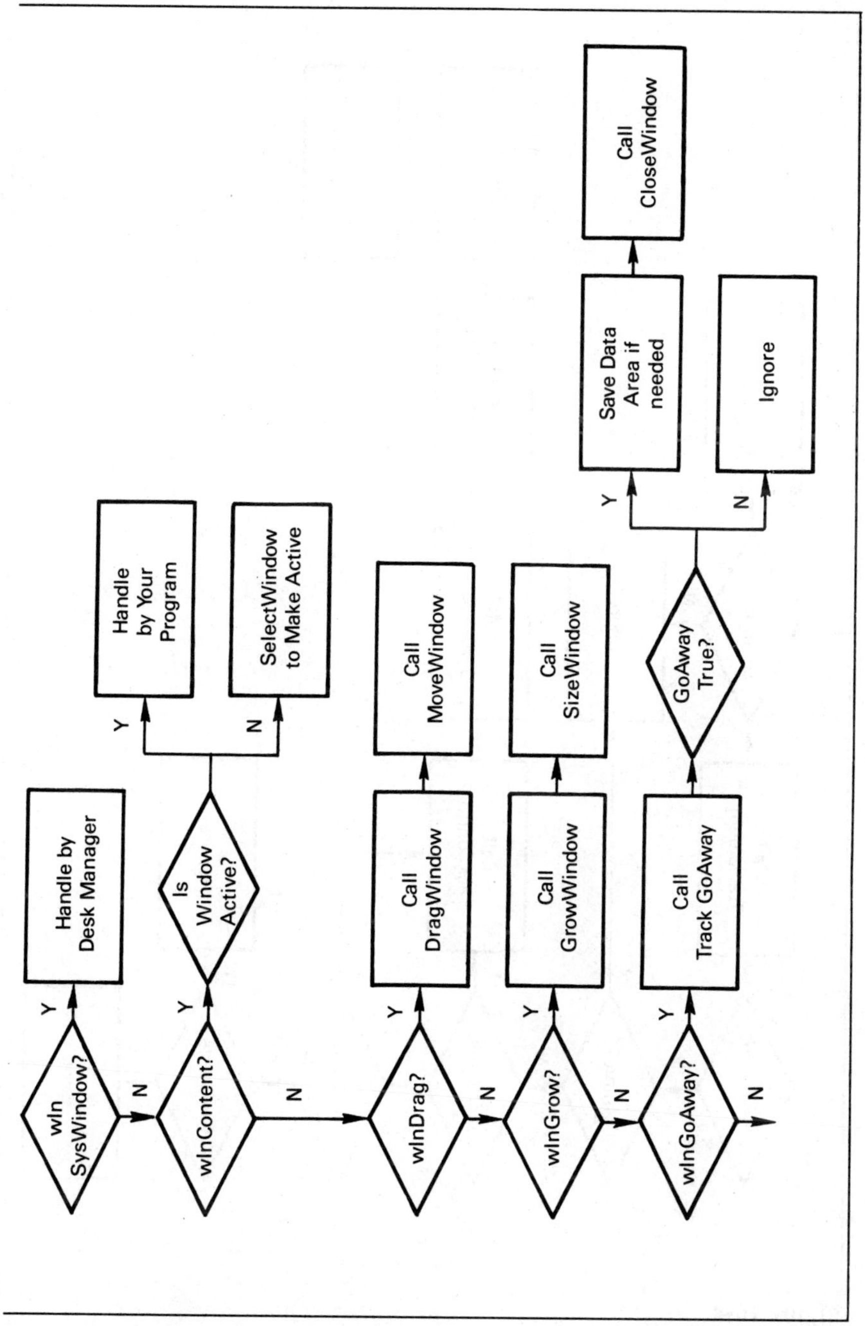
wIn SysWindow?
Y
Handle by Desk Manager
N
wInContent?
Y
Is Window Active?
Y
Handle by Your Program
N
SelectWindow to Make Active
N
wInDrag?
Y
Call DragWindow
Call MoveWindow
N
wInGrow?
Y
Call GrowWindow
Call SizeWindow
N
wInGoAway?
Y
Call Track GoAway
GoAway True?
Y
Save Data Area if needed
Call CloseWindow
N
Ignore
N

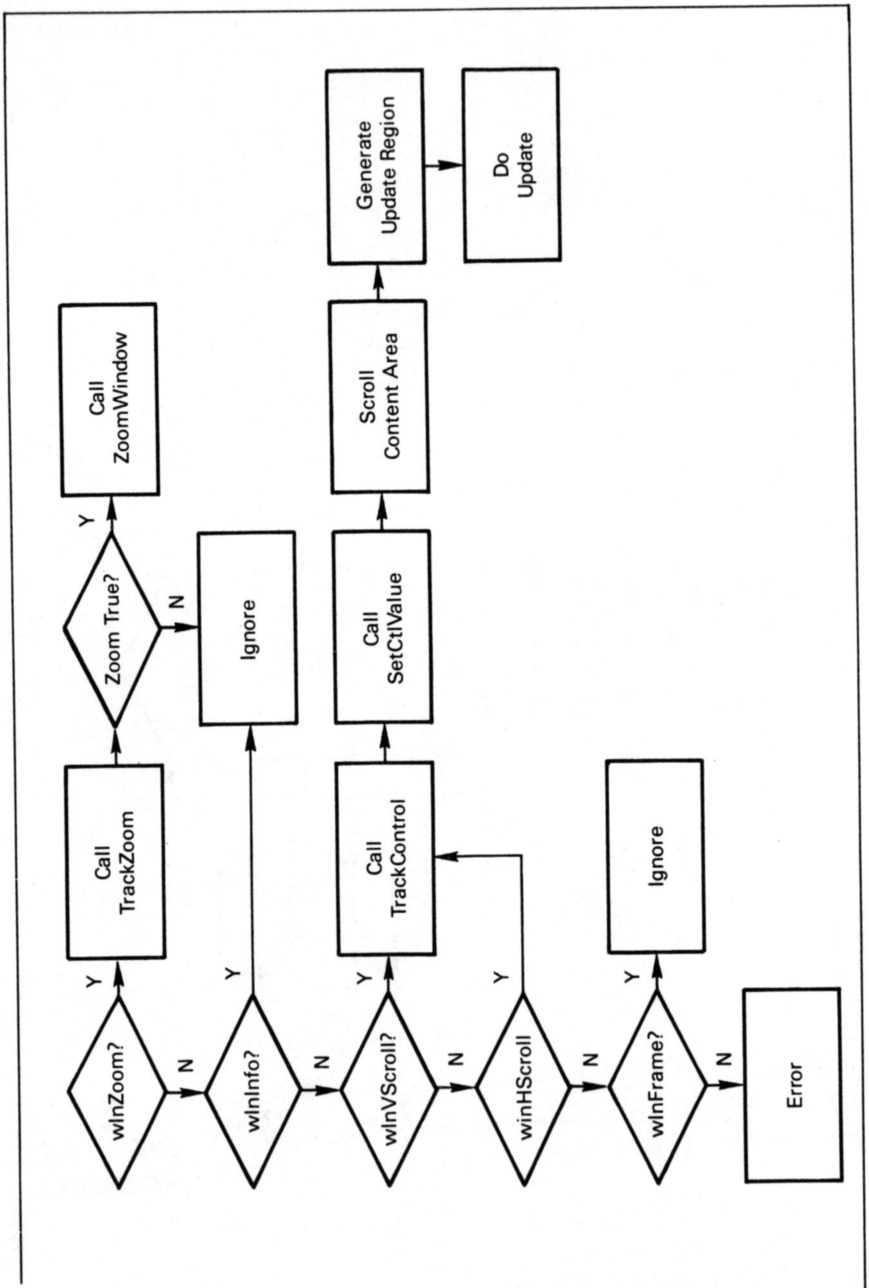

Figure 16-4

Flowchart of standard-type responses (continued)

a variety of different events that involve windows. Many of these events have a standardized response.

The Apple IIGS Window Manager has a function, known as the *Task-Master,* that is designed to make semiautomatic the responses to some of the window and menu events.

TaskMaster functions as an alternative call to the GetNextEvent call. (See discussion of this Event Manager function in Chapter 20.) It takes two inputs, a word EventMask identical to that used when calling GetNext-Event, and a long-word pointer to a TaskMaster record. TaskMaster calls GetNextEvent and takes a variety of actions depending on the event retrieved. TaskMaster returns data both in the TaskRecord and in the TaskCode, a word returned on the stack. A zero TaskCode indicates nothing further need be done by the application in regard to the event (that is, TaskMaster has handled everything).

Part of the task record used by TaskMaster is a task mask. If you want TaskMaster not to handle certain tasks, you merely clear (set to 0) the particular bit in that mask. (See Table 16-4 for a list of the functions that

Bit Number	Function
0	Menu key
1	Update handling
2	Find Window
3	Menu select
4	Open NDA
5	System Click
6	Drag Window
7	Select Window if wInContent
8	Track Go Away
9	Track Zoom
10	Grow Window
11	Scrolling
12	Handle special menu items
13-31	Must be zero

Table 16-4

Task Mask—Clear Bit to Disable Feature

can be disabled and the particular bit in the task mask to clear to disable that function.) Note that a value of $00001FFF will enable all functions. You must clear the highest 15 bits or TaskMaster will return an error.

The following are the events and responses handled by TaskMaster, if no tasks are disabled in the task mask:

- If there is a key event and Menu Manager is installed, TaskMaster will call MenuKey to determine if the key pressed refers to a menu item. (See discussion of menus and command keys in Chapter 17.) If the key is a menu command key with an ID number greater than 255, TaskMaster will exit with the menu identification number in the high word of the TaskData field of the TaskRecord, the item identification number in the low word of the TaskData field, and the return TaskCode of wInMenuBar. If the item ID number is less than 256, indicating a desk accessory item, TaskMaster calls Open NDA to open the desk accessory, unhighlights the menu using HiliteMenu, and returns a TaskCode of inNull.
- In all other key events TaskMaster returns a TaskCode of inKey with the event record part of TaskRecord set as by GetNextEvent.
- A button-down event in the menu bar that exits with a selected item will return with the menu identification number in the high word of the TaskData field of the TaskRecord, the item identification number in the low word of the TaskData field, and the return TaskCode of wInMenuBar.
- A button-down event in the menu bar that exits without a selected item will return with a TaskCode of zero. This is the typical action taken if MenuSelect returns with no item selected.
- A button-down event in the window drag region calls DragWindow, which calls MoveWindow to move the window to the new location. It returns a pointer to the window's Grafport in the TaskData field of TaskRecord and a TaskCode of zero.
- A button-down event in an inactive window's content area will result in a call to SelectWindow to make the window active and a TaskCode of zero.
- A button-down event in the active window's content area will result in a TaskCode of wInContent and the pointer to the window's Grafport in the TaskData field of TaskRecord.

- When there is a button-down event in the go-away box, TaskMaster monitors to see if the button is released in that box (using TrackGo-Away) and, if so, returns with a TaskCode of wInGoAway and a pointer to the window's port in the TaskData field of TaskRecord. Your application can then save any data from the data area as necessary and call CloseWindow.
- When there is a button-down event in the zoom box, TaskMaster monitors to see if the button is released in that box (using TrackZoom) and, if so, zooms the window (using ZoomWindow) before returning a TaskCode of zero.
- When there is a button-down event in the grow window, TaskMaster tracks the size to which the window should grow, using GrowWindow, and then changes the size of the window appropriately using SizeWindow. It returns a TaskCode of zero.
- When there is a button-down event in a scroll bar, TaskMaster calls TrackControl with its own action procedure, which performs scrolling and updates. The TaskCode returned is inNull.
- A button-down event in a system window (FindWindow value has a most significant bit set—that is, a negative value) results in a call to SystemClick and an exit with the result code from FindWindow. This is the limit of TaskMaster's capability with system windows.
- A button-down event elsewhere results in a TaskCode equal to the location's return value from FindWindow and the pointer to the window's Grafport (as returned from FindWindow) in the TaskData field of TaskRecord.
- Any event except a key or button-down event returns a TaskCode equal to the event code from the event record part of the TaskRecord.
- If the event is an update event, not disabled by the task mask, and the window needing updating has an update draw routine, TaskMaster will switch to the window's port, set origin as needed, call the window's update routine, return the window's origin to 0,0, restore the previous port, and return with a TaskCode of zero. Otherwise, it returns with a TaskCode of inUpdate.

As you can see, use of TaskMaster makes the work of programming the IIGS a lot easier. The procedure completely automates the following:

- □ Selecting a menu item by mouse or command key
- □ Activating a previously inactive window
- □ Zooming a window
- □ Growing a window
- □ Dragging a window

It partially automates the closing of a window; your application must call CloseWindow to complete.

TaskMaster serves several functions:

- □ It provides a simpler method for a beginning programmer to use the Window Manager and related tools.
- □ It permits the experienced programmer who wishes only standard responses to many window events to write more compact code.
- □ It functions as a "black box" that can be enhanced in system software updates. These updates will automatically be implemented on programs that use TaskMaster—the program itself will not need to be revised.

What if you wish to have the benefit of using TaskMaster, but you don't want to have one of the responses TaskMaster makes? In that case, you have two choices. The simplest way in most cases is simply to clear the appropriate bit in the TaskMask prior to calling TaskMaster. If the bit is clear, TaskMaster will not perform the specified function but, instead, will return values in TaskData and the TaskCode as shown in Table 16-5. Your application can then task whatever action is appropriate.

Another method of handling this situation is more useful when you want to mask not all but just some events of a particular type. The example used here is actually one that would call for the use of the TaskMask. It is presented here as a simple example of how to program, especially while still using TaskMaster.

Assume you wish to have the zoom box on the window function as a switch between a window displayed in color or monochrome. Your program should first call EventAvail in the Event Manager. This gets the next event but does not remove it from the head of the event queue. If the event

Bit	TaskData	TaskCode
0	—	inKey
1	—	inUpdate
2	—	inButtDwn
3	Low word = 0	wInMenuBar
4	Low word = Item ID High word = Menu ID	wInMenuBar
5	Window Ptr.	value from FindWindow
6	Window Ptr.	wInDrag
7	Window Ptr.	wInContent
8	Window Ptr.	wInGoAway
9	Window Ptr.	wInZoom
10	Window Ptr.	wInGrow
11	Window Ptr.	wInFrame

Table 16-5

Effect if Masked Operation Occurs in TaskMaster

is a button-down event, you can then call FindWindow to determine if the button was pressed in the zoom box. If FindWindow returns wInZoom, you should remove the event from the queue and perform your custom switch. Otherwise you should call TaskMaster as you normally would do. The code for performing this is

```
RSpace   DATA                    ;Record storage area
ERec     Anop                    ;This is the event record
Ewhat    DS 2                    ;Word for event code
Emessage DS 4                    ;Long word for event message
Ewhen    DS 4                    ;Long word - ticks since startup
Ewhere   DS 4                    ;Point where mouse located
Emods    DS 2                    ;Word (see Chapter 20 for details)
         END
ModTM    START                   ;Modified TaskMaster routine
         Pushword #$0000         ;Space for return word
         Pushword EventMask      ;Get event mask
         Pushlong #ERec          ;High word of event record address
```

```
         _EventAvail
         LDA Ewhat               ;Get type of event
         CMP #$0001              ;Was it a button-down event?
         BNE UseTM               ;No - use TaskMaster
*Let's call FindWindow to determine if button was down in
*zoom box
         PushLong #$00000000     ;Long word for window pointer
         PushWord Ewhere         ;Location of mouse onto stack
         _FindWindow             ;and let's see where it was
         PLA                     ;Location code is on stack
         CMP #$23                ;Is it wInZoom?
         BNE UseTM               ;No - use TaskMaster
*Since we are handling event, let's remove it from queue
*using GetNextEvent
         PushWord #0000          ;Space for return word
         PushWord EventMask      ;Get event mask onto stack
         PushLong #ERec          ;Event record address
         _GetNextEvent
         LDA Ewhat               ;Get type of event
         CMP #$0001              ;Let's hope it's same one
         BNE Oops                ;If not - put back in queue
*Further code checking, by recalling FindWindow, should go
*here; omitted from example for sake of brevity.
*Code that switches from monochrome to color display goes
*here
UseTM    . . .
*Code that uses TaskMaster normally goes here.
```

WINDOW MANAGER ROUTINES

The Window Manager has 76 different routines that can be divided into 8 different categories. The routines present in each category are listed in Table 16-6 with a brief description of their functions. Tables 16-7 to 16-16 list the routines in each category, and the input and output parameters used by each routine. Table 16-17 compares the Apple IIGS Window Manager commands with the Macintosh Window Manager commands.

In normal programming you will not need to use all or even a large fraction of the Window Manager routines. The rest of this chapter will discuss, from the programmer's viewpoint, some of the major routines. But, first, several of the routines in the tables require a bit more explanation.

The desktop refers, at least by default, to the entire IIGS screen with the exception of that area that is being used by the system menu bar. Since windows are considered a major component of the desktop area, the Window Manager has a command called, not surprisingly, desktop, which provides for a variety of operations on this area.

The desktop command always consists of a word-length input parameter that represents the desktop operation to be performed, a long-word input parameter that is the information needed for the operation, and a

Initialization and Termination Routines

WindBootInit	Called by system to initialize; do not use.
WindStartup	Called by your application to initialize Window Manager; clears any window list, sets default desktop pattern and color, creates Window Manager port and draws desktop; should be called once before using any other Window Manager routines.
WindShutDown	Called at the end of your application to free up memory allocated by the Window Manager.
WindVersion	Returns the version number of the Window Manager.
WindReset	Does nothing.
WindStatus	Does nothing.
WNewRes	Called when your application changes screen resolution; should be followed by a call to Refresh to redraw screen.
Desktop	Changes various aspects of, or returns various values of, the desktop.
NewWindow	Creates a new window, adding it to window list, allocating space for structure and content region of window, and calculating these regions; returns a pointer to the Grafport for the new window.
CloseWindow	Removes window from screen, deletes it from list, and releases memory used by window.

Window Record and Global Information Access Routines

GetWMgrPort	Returns a pointer to the Grafport for the Window Manager.
SetWMgrIcons	Changes or returns a handle to the icon font used to draw window controls.
SetWRefCon	Changes the application specified value that is part of the window record.
GetWRefCon	Returns the application specified value that is part of the window record.

Table 16-6

Window Manager Routine Descriptions

Window Record and Global Information Access Routines	
SetWTitle	Changes title of window.
GetWTitle	Returns title of window.
SetFrameColor	Changes window color table; to show window in new colors must do a HideWindow followed by a ShowWindow.
GetFrameColor	Returns a pointer to the window color table.
FrontWindow	Returns a pointer to Grafport of the first visible window in the window list, normally the active window; value is zero if there are no visible windows.
GetNextWindow	Returns a pointer to the Grafport of the window in the window list that follows the specified window.
GetWKind	Returns true if specified window is a system window and false if it is an application window.
GetWFrame	Returns the value of the window attributes word in the window record.
SetWFrame	Changes the value of the window attributes word in the window record.
GetStructRgn	Returns a handle to the window's Structure Region.
GetContRgn	Returns a handle to the window's Content Region.
GetUpdateRgn	Returns a handle to the window's Update Region.
GetDefProc	Returns a point to the routine that is used to draw and display a window (for custom-designed windows).
SetDefProc	Changes the address of the routine that is used to draw and display a window (for custom-designed windows).
GetWControls	Returns address of the first control in the window's control list (not the window frame's control list); value is zero if no controls.
GetFControls	Returns address of first control in the window frame's control list (not the window's control list); value is zero if no controls.
GetInfoRefCon	Returns value that is passed to the information bar draw routine when information bar is drawn on screen.
SetInfoRefCon	Changes value that is passed to the information bar draw routine when information bar is drawn on screen.

Table 16-6

Window Manager Routine Descriptions (continued)

Window Record and Global Information Access Routines	
GetFullRect	Returns pointer to the rectangle that will be used the next time the window's zoom box is clicked; this is the full size if the window is not currently zoomed and is the last size and position of the window prior to its last being zoomed if the window is currently zoomed.
SetFullRect	Sets rectangle that will be used the next time the window's zoom box is clicked; this is the full size if the window is not currently zoomed and is the last size and position of the window prior to its last being zoomed if the window is currently zoomed.
GetCOrigin	Returns the offset into the data area of the beginning of the displayed portion of the specified window; these values are also used to compute scroll bars and thumbs in the window frame.
SetCOrigin	Set the offset into the data area of the beginning of the displayed portion of the specified window; the application should generally redraw the window following this call, although an update event is not automatically generated.
SetOrgnMask	Used to force the origin for drawing purposes to certain horizontal positions if using dithering to produce more colors in 640 super-high-resolution mode. The TaskMaster ANDs the new horizontal origin with the origin mask. At startup the origin mask is $FFFF, which does not force any horizontal alignment.
StartDrawing	Used to make the specified window's Grafport the current Grafport and set its origin; if you are not using a standard document window with scroll bars, you should use SetPort (in Quickdraw II) instead.
GetDataSize	Returns the height and width of the data area of the specified window; this is the total amount of viewable data in the window, not just the amount that can be viewed in the window at one time.
SetDataSize	Sets the height and width of the data area of the specified window; this is the total amount of viewable data in the window, not just the amount that can be viewed in the window at one time; the application

Table 16-6
Window Manager Routine Descriptions (continued)

Window Record and Global Information Access Routines

	should update the window following this call because it does not automatically generate an update event or modify the scroll bars.
GetMaxGrow	Returns the value of the maximum height and width of the window's Content Region.
SetMaxGrow	Sets the maximum height and width of the window's Content Region.
GetScroll	Returns the number of horizontal and vertical pixels TaskMaster will scroll when a scroll bar arrow is selected.
SetScroll	Sets the number of horizontal and vertical pixels TaskMaster will scroll when a scroll bar arrow is selected.
GetPage	Returns the number of horizontal and vertical pixels TaskMaster will scroll when the page scroll region of the scroll bar is selected.
SetPage	Sets the number of horizontal and vertical pixels TaskMaster will scroll when the page scroll region of the scroll bar is selected.
GetCDraw	Returns the address of the routine that draws the window's Content Region; the drawing routine is that called by TaskMaster when it gets an update event for the window.
SetCDraw	Sets the address of the routine that draws the window's content region; the drawing routine is that called by TaskMaster when it gets an update event for the window.
GetSysWFlag	Returns true if window is system window.
SetSysWindow	Changes window to a system window.
GetInfoDraw	Returns the address of the routine that draws the window's information bar.
SetInfoDraw	Sets the address of the routine that draws the window's information bar.

Table 16-6
Window Manager Routine Descriptions (continued)

Window-Shuffling Routines	
SelectWindow	Makes the specified window the active window, bringing it in front of any other windows, highlighting it, and unhighlighting any other highlighted window.
GetRectInfo	Returns coordinates of any information bar rectangle.
HideWindow	Makes the window invisible; unhighlights it if previously active, bringing next window forward and highlighting it.
ShowWindow	Makes the window visible; draws the window if it was previously invisible.
ShowHide	Makes window visible or invisible as provided for in input value; does not affect whether window is highlighted, generate an activate event, or change ordering of windows; potentially dangerous if you hide an active window.
BringtoFront	Brings specified window to front of other windows and redraws as necessary; does not do highlighting; potentially dangerous if your application fails to highlight window as well.
SendBehind	Places the specified window behind the other specified window and redraws as necessary; highlights and unhighlights as needed and generates an activate event; use a value of $FFFFFFFE (-2) as behindWindow to place window at the end.

Window-Drawing Routines	
HiliteWindow	Highlights or unhighlights a window; potentially dangerous if you highlight an inactive window or unhighlight an active window; rarely used.
Refresh	Redraws entire desktop and all windows; takes more time than updating as needed but useful when updating is not sufficient.

Table 16-6

Window Manager Routine Descriptions (continued)

User Interaction Routines	
FindWindow	Tells whether specified point is in a window, which window, and which part of that window; value showing location is defined as shown in Table 16-7; not needed if using TaskMaster.
DragWindow	Moves window in reaction to user movement with mouse in window's title bar; not needed if using TaskMaster.
GrowWindow	Moves window size in reaction to user movement with mouse in window's grow or size box; not needed if using TaskMaster.
TrackGoAway	Checks, when button-down event in close box, if button-up also occurs while in close box; not needed if using TaskMaster.
TrackZoom	Checks, when button-down event in zoom box, if button-up also occurs while in zoom box; not needed if using TaskMaster.
TaskMaster	This routine is discussed in detail earlier in this chapter.

Window Sizing and Positioning Routines	
MoveWindow	Moves the window to another part of the screen, keeping its current size.
SizeWindow	Changes the width and height of a window as specified, by changing the portRect of the window's Grafport; redraws window frame and recenters and truncates title in title bar as needed.
ZoomWindow	Changes size and position of window from present (or last) size to full size and back again; this routine is a toggle.

Table 16-6

Window Manager Routine Descriptions (continued)

Update Region Maintenance Routines	
InvalRect	Adds the specified rectangle into the update region of the currently active window—that is, that window whose Grafport is the current port.
InvalRgn	Adds the specified region into the update region of the currently active window—that is, that window whose Grafport is the current port.
ValidRect	Removes the specified rectangle from the update region of the currently active window—that is, that window whose Grafport is the current port.
ValidRgn	Removes the specified region from the update region of the currently active window—that is, that window whose Grafport is the current port.
BeginUpdate	Used to bring sequence updating a window; followed by your drawing routine for that window; replaces visRgn of the window's Grafport with the intersection of the visRgn and the update region and then sets update region to an empty region.
EndUpdate	Used to end a sequence updating a window after your drawing routine has finished updating the content of the window; restores the normal visRgn of the window's Grafport, reversing the process of BeginUpdate.

Miscellaneous Routines	
PinRect	Returns the value of the point within the specified rectangle that is nearest the input point; value returned is as shown in Table 16-8.
CheckUpdate	Called by the Event Manager to determine if any visible windows exist with nonempty update regions—that is, any visible windows that need updating.
StartInfoDrawing	Set drawing rectangle to information bar.
EndInfoDrawing	Call after done drawing information bar.

Table 16-6

Window Manager Routine Descriptions (continued)

Value	Title	Meaning
$0000	wNoHit	Not in any window or desktop
$0010	wInDesk	On the desktop area
$0011	wInMenuBar	On the system menu bar
$0019	wInContent	In a window's Content Region
$0014	wInDrag	In a window's drag or title bar region
$0015	wInGrow	In a window's grow or size box
$0016	wInGoAway	In a window's go away or close box
$0017	wInZoom	In a window's zoom box
$0018	wInInfo	In a window's information bar
$001B	wInFrame	In a window but not any of the above areas

Note: If highest bit set, window is system window.

Table 16-7
Values Returned by FindWindow

	X < left	**X >= left + <= right**	**X > right**
Y < top	left	X	right − 1
	top	top	top
Y >= top + <= bottom	left	X	right − 1
	Y	Y	Y
Y > bottom	left	X	right − 1
	bottom−1	bottom − 1	bottom −1

Table 16-8
Results of PinRect Routine

Function Name	Function Number	userID	ParamList	theWindow	Operation	Param	wVersion	Status	RetParam
Size of Parameter		W	L	L	W	L	W	W	L
Type of Parameter		V	P	P	V	?	V	V	?
CloseWindow	11			I1					
Desktop	12				I1	I2			O1
NewWindow	9		I1	O1					
WindBootInit	1								
WindReset	5								
WindShutDown	3								
WindStartup	2	I1							
WindStatus	6							O1	
WindVersion	4						O1		
WNewRes	37								

Notes:
P= Pointer
V= Value
?= Variable

Table 16-9

Initialization and Termination Routines

Function Name	**Function Number**	**ControlList**	**FControlList**	**InfoDraw**	**InfoText**	**NextWindow**	**WContRgn**	**WDefProc**	**WStructRgn**	**WUpdateRgn**	**WindowKind**	**contDraw**	**dataHeight**	**dataSize**	**dataWidth**	**refCon**	**scroll**
Parameter Size		L	L	L	L	L	L	L	L	L	W	L	W	L	W	L	L
Parameter Type		A	A	A	V	P	H	P	H	H	B	A	V	2	V	V	3
FrontWindow	21																
GetCDraw	72											O1					
GetContRgn	47						O1										
GetCOrigin	62																
GetDataSize	64													O1			
GetDefProc	49							O1									
GetFControls	51		O1														
GetFrameColor	16																
GetFullRect	55																
GetInfoDraw	74			O1													
GetInfoRefCon	53															O1	
GetMaxGrow	66																
GetNextWindow	42					O1											
GetPage	70																
GetRectInfo	89																
GetScroll	68																O1
GetStructRgn	46								O1								
GetSysWFlag	87																
GetUpdateRgn	48									O1							
GetWControls	51	O1															
GetWFrame	44																
GetWKind	43										O1						
GetWMgrPort	32																
GetWRefCon	41													O1		O1	
GetWTitle	14																
SetCDraw	73											I1					
SetCOrigin	63																
SetDataSize	65												I2		I1		
SetDefProc	50							I1									
SetFrameColor	15																

Table 16-10

Window Record and Global Information Access Routines

hPage	hScroll	maxGrow	maxHeight	maxWidth	newColor	page	InfoRect	SysFlag	theWindow	title	vPage	VScroll	wFlag	wFullSize	wPort	xOrigin	xyOrigin	yOrigin	NewFont	OldFont	originMask
W	W	L	W	W	L	L	L	W	L	L	W	W	W	L	L	W	L	W	L	L	W
V	V	2	V	V	P	3	P	B	P	P	V	V	BA	P	P	V	1	V	H	H	V
									O1												
									I1												
									I1												
									I1								O1				
									I1												
									I1												
									I1												
					I1				I2												
									I1					O1							
									I1												
									I1												
		O1							I1												
									I1												
						O1			I1												
							I1		I2												
									I1												
									I1												
								O1	I1												
									I1												
									I1												
									I1				O1								
									I1												
															O1						
									I1												
									I1	O1											
									I2												
									I3							I1		I2			
									I3												
									I2												
					I1				I2												

	Function Number	ControlList	FControlList	InfoDraw	InfoText	NextWindow	WContRgn	WDefProc	WStructRgn	WUpdateRgn	WindowKind	contDraw	dataHeight	dataSize	dataWidth	refCon	scroll
SetFullRect	56																
SetInfoDraw	22			I1													
SetInfoRefCon	54															I1	
SetMaxGrow	67																
SetOrgMask	52																
SetPage	71																
SetScroll	69																
SetSysWindow	86																
SetWMgrIcons	88																
SetWFrame	45																
SetWRefCon	40															I1	
SetWTitle	13																
StartDrawing	77																

Notes:

A = Address
B = Boolean
BA = Bit array
H = Handle
P = Pointer
V = Value
1: low word = y origin; high word = x origin
2: low word = height; high word = width
3: low word = vertical amount; high word =4

Table 16-10

Window Record and Global Information Access Routines (continued)

hPage	hScroll	maxGrow	maxHeight	maxWidth	newColor	page	InfoRect	SysFlag	theWindow	title	vPage	VScroll	wFlag	wFullSize	wPort	xOrigin	xyOrigin	yOrigin	NewFont	OldFont	originMask
									I2					I1							
									I2												
									I2												
		I2	I1						I3												
									I2												I1
I1									I3		I2										
	I1								I3			I2							I1		
									I1												
																				O1	
									I2				I1								
									I2												
									I2	I1											
									I1												

Function Name	Routine Number	behindWindow	showFlag	theWindow
Size of Parameter		L	W	L
Type of Parameter		P	B	P
Select Window	17			I1
Hide Window	18			I1
Show Window	19			I1
ShowHide	35		I1	I2
BringToFront	36			I1
SendBehind	20	I1		I2

Notes:
B = Boolean
P = Pointer

Table 16-11
Window-Shuffling Routines

Function Name	Routine Number	Clobbered Rect	fHilite	theWindow
Size of Parameter		L	W	L
Type of Parameter		P	B	P
HiliteWindow	34		I1	I2
Refresh	57	I1		

Notes:
B = Boolean
P = Pointer

Table 16-12
Window-Drawing Routines

Function Name	Routine Number	BoundsRect	EventMask	GoAway	Location	TaskCode	TaskRec	Zoom	grace	grid	minHeight	minWidth	newSize	pointX	pointY	startX	startY	theWindow	whichWindow
Size of Parameter		L	W	W	W	L	W	W	W	W	W	W	L	W	W	W	W	L	L
Type of Parameter		P	BA	B	V	P	V	B	V	V	V	V	1	V	V	V	V	P	A
DragWindow	26	I5							I4	I1						I2	I3	I6	
FindWindow	23				O1									I2	I3				I1
GrowWindow	27										I2	I1	O1			I3	I4	I5	
TaskMaster	29		I1			I2	O1												
TrackGoAway	24			O1												I1	I2	I3	
TrackZoom	38							O1								I1	I2	I3	

Notes:

A = Address
B = Boolean
BA = Bit array
P = Pointer
V = Value
1: high word = new height; low word = new width

Table 16-13

User Interaction Routines

Function Name	Routine Number	newHeight	newWidth	newX	newY	theWindow
Size of Parameter		W	W	W	W	L
Type of Parameter		V	V	V	V	P
MoveWindow	25			I1	I2	I3
SizeWindow	28	I2	I1			I3
ZoomWindow	39					I1

Notes:
P = Pointer
V = Value

Table 16-14

Window-Sizing and Positioning Routines

Function Name	Routine Number	badRect	badRgn	goodRect	goodRgn	theWindow
Size of Parameter		L	L	L	L	L
Type of Parameter		P	H	P	H	P
BeginUpdate	30					I1
EndUpdate	31					I1
InvalRect	58	I1				
InvalRgn	59		I1			
ValidRect	60			I1		
ValidRgn	61				I1	

Notes:
H = Handle
P = Pointer

Table 16-15

Update Region Maintenance Routines

Function Name	Routine Number	Flag	pinned	theEvent	theRect	theXPt	theYPt	InfoRect	theWindow
Size of Parameter		W	L	L	R	W	W	L	L
Type of Parameter		B	Pt	P	R	V	V	P	P
CheckUpdate	10	O1		I1					
EndInfoDrawing	91								
PinRect	33		O1		I1	I2	I3		
StartInfoDrawing	90							I1	I2

Notes:

A = Address
B = Boolean
H = Handle
P = Pointer
Pt = Point
R = Rectangle
V = Value
1: high word = vertical delta; low word = horizontal delta

Table 16-16
Miscellaneous Routines

Routine	Macintosh	IIGS
BeginUpdate	x	x
BringToFront	x	x
CalcVis	x	
CalcVisBehind	x	
CheckUpdate	x	x
ClipAbove	x	
CloseWindow	x	x
Desktop		x
DisposeWindow	x	
DragGrayRgn	x	
DragWindow	x	x

Table 16-17
Comparison of IIGS and Macintosh Window Manager Routines

Routine	Macintosh	IIGS
DrawGrowIcon	x	
DrawNew	x	
EndInfoDrawing		x
EndUpdate	x	x
FindWindow	x	x
FrontWindow	x	x
GetCDraw		x
GetContRgn		x
GetCOrigin		x
GetDataSize		x
GetDefProc		x
GetFControls		x
GetFrameColor		x
GetFullRect		x
GetInfoDraw		x
GetInfoRefCon		x
GetMaxGrow		x
GetNewWindow	x	
GetNextWindow		x
GetPage		x
GetRectInfo		x
GetScroll		x
GetStructRgn		x
GetSysFlag		x
GetUpdateRgn		x
GetWControls		x
GetWFrame		x
GetWindowPic	x	
GetWKing		x
GetWMgrPort	x	x
GetWRefCon	x	x
GetWTitle	x	x
GrowWindow	x	x
HideWindow	x	x
HiliteWindow	x	x

Table 16-17

Comparison of IIGS and Macintosh Window Manager Routines (continued)

Routine	Macintosh	IIGS
InvalRect	x	x
InvalRgn	x	x
MoveWindow	x	x
NewWindow	x	x
PaintBehind	x	
PaintOne	x	
PinRect	x	x
Refresh		x
SaveOld	x	
SelectWindow	x	x
SendBehind	x	x
SetCDraw		x
SetCOrigin		x
SetDataSize		x
SetDefProc		x
SetFrameColor		x
SetFullRect		x
SetInfoDraw		x
SetInfoRefCon		x
SetMaxGrow		x
SetOrgMask		x
SetPage		x
SetScroll		x
SetSysWindow		x
SetWFrame		x
SetWindowPic	x	
SetWMgrIcons		x
SetWRefCon	x	x
SetWTitle	x	x
ShowHide	x	x
ShowWindow	x	x
SizeWindow	x	x
StartDrawing		x
StartInfoDrawing		x
TaskMaster		x

Table 16-17

Comparison of IIGS and Macintosh Window Manager Routines (continued)

Routine	Macintosh	IIGS
TrackGoAway	x	x
TrackZoom		x
ValidRect	x	x
ValidRgn	x	x
WindBootInit		x
WindReset		x
WindShutDown		x
WindStartup (InitWindows)	x	x
WindStatus		x
WindVersion		x
WNewRes		x
ZoomWindow		x

Table 16-17
Comparison of IIGS and Macintosh Window Manager Routines (continued)

long-word output parameter that is the information returned by the operation. If the operation does not require an input parameter, you should still push a long-word value of 0 on the stack. If the operation does not require an output parameter, you do not need to push room for the output on the stack. A summary of the various operations, the operation number, and necessary parameters is given in Table 16-18.

The desktop pattern parameter used by the GetDeskPat and SetDeskPat operations in desktop is a long-word parameter that has different meanings depending on whether it begins with a 0, 4, or 8.

If it begins with a 0, the remainder of the parameter should be a zero followed by the 3-byte address of whatever routine you have programmed to produce the desktop pattern. This routine should not require any inputs or outputs and should end with an RTL. It should also save and restore the current direct and data bank registers if it modifies these registers. The Window Manager will set the current port to the WindowManager port and the clipping region to the area needed to be drawn.

If it begins with a 4, the next two bytes are 00. These are followed by a 0 (indicating a solid pattern), a 1 (indicating a dithered pattern), or a 2 (indicating a horizontal striped pattern). The final byte consists of a

Operation Number	Operation Name	Function	Parameter	Returned Parameter
0	FromDesk	Subtract region from desktop	Handle of region to be subtracted	Not used
1	ToDesk	Add region to desktop	Handle of region to be added	Not used
2	GetDesktop	Get handle of desktop	Not used	Handle of desktop region
3	SetDesktop	Create handle for new desktop region	Handle of new desktop region	Handle of new desktop region
4	GetDeskPat	Get the current desktop pattern	Not used	Desktop pattern (See text)
5	SetDeskPat	Set a new desktop pattern	Desktop pattern (See text)	Not used
6	GetVisDesktop	Return desktop region less all visible windows	Handle of region to be set to desktop	Not used

Table 16-18
Desktop Routines

nibble indicating the foreground color of the pattern, followed by a nibble indicating the background color of the pattern.

If it begins with an 8, the next nibble is a 0, followed by the 3-byte address of the pattern to be used.

The Window Record and Global Access routines consist of a series of routines, many of which come in a Get and Set pair. The Get routine obtains the current program value, while the Set routine allows the application to change the value.

One pair of such routines is GetDefProc and SetDefProc. This routine is applicable only if you have provided for custom-designed windows in your application and have written your own routines. In most normal applications this will not be necessary. For more information about custom-designed windows, see the IIGS *Toolbox Reference* volume discussing the Window Manager.

PROGRAMMING WITH THE WINDOW MANAGER

Before the Window Manager can be used by your application, it needs to be started. A call toWindStartup accomplishes this goal. Before calling the WindStartup, you need to accomplish several other steps:

- □ Initialize the Tool Locator if not already done.
- □ Call the Memory Manager for a user-identification number because WindStartup requires this number.
- □ Initialize Quickdraw II because it is used to draw the windows.
- □ Initialize the Event Manager because the Window Manager calls the Event Manager.
- □ Initialize the Window Manager.
- □ Initialize the Control Manager if your windows will have controls. The following code accomplishes these steps:

```
Window_Init  START
             _Init_TL               ;Initialize Tool Locator
             Pushword #$0000        ;Space for Memory Manager ID value returned
             _MMAppInit             ;Initialize Memory Manager
             BCS Error_Rtn          ;Error occurred if carry set
             PLA                    ;Get ID returned by Memory Manager
             STA ID_Num             ;Save ID
;Save 5 pages for zero pages as required by the various tools.
             Pushlong#$00000000     ;Long-word handle returned by Memory Manager
             Pushlong #$00000500    ;Need to reserve five pages
             LDA ID_Num
             PHA                    ;Tell Memory Manager our program ID
             Pushword #$C001        ;Fixed bank, locked, fixed location
             Pushlong #$00000000    ;Fixed location address
             _NewHandle             ;Use Memory Manager to allocate space
             BCS Error_Rtn
             PLA                    ;Get handle to memory area
             STA Handle_Loc         ;And save it (on direct page)
             PLA                    ;Remember it's a long-word
             STA Handle_Loc+2
             LDA [Handle_Loc]
;Direct indirect long addressing gets values stored at address pointed to
;by Handle_Loc.  This gets actual address of memory reserved.  This
;technique is called dereferencing the handle.
             STA ZPAddress          ;Save actual address
             PHA                    ;Put zero page address on stack
             Pushword #Mode         ;Select desired Quickdraw mode
             Pushword #$0160        ;Scan line maximum size
```

```
               LDA ID_Num          ;Get identification number
               PHA                 ;Onto stack
               _QDInit             ;Initialize Quickdraw
               BCS Error_Rtn
               LDA ZPAddress       ;Get start of QD zero page
               CLC
               ADC $0200           ;Quickdraw takes two pages
               PHA                 ;Put Event Manager's zero page on stack
               Pushword #$0020     ;Size of event queue
               Pushword MinX       ;Minimum X mouse clamp
               Pushword MaxX       ;Maximum X mouse clamp
               Pushword MinY       ;Minimum Y mouse clamp
               Pushword MaxY       ;Maximum Y mouse clamp
               LDA ID_Num          ;Let Event Manager know ID number
               PHA
               _EMStartup          ;Initialize Event Manager
               BCS Error_Rtn
* Initialize the Window Manager
               LDA ID_Num          ;Let Window Manager know ID number
               PHA
               _Wind_Startup       ;and initialize Window Manager
* Control Manager needs to be initialized if controls are used
               LDA ZPage_Loc       ;Get Quickdraw zero pages start
               CLC                 ;Allow for use by Quickdraw and Event Manager
               ADC #$0300
               PHA                 ;And keep on stack
               _CtrlMStartup       ;Initialize Control Manager
```

Subsequently, your application should allocate a window or windows as needed for your application. This requires two steps. First, set up a parameter list somewhere in memory, preferably as a data structure that is part of the data portion of your program. Second, call the NewWindow function, which allocates the window by performing the following steps:

- □ Creates a window record including its Grafport
- □ Allocates space for the window's Structure and Content regions
- □ Calculates the Structure and Content Regions
- □ Adds the window record to the window list
- □ Places a pointer to the new window's Grafport on the stack

The first parameter passed to the NewWindow routine is a word value with the number of bytes used in the parameter list, including the byte count value. The second value in the list is the window frame type. This collection of bits is nearly identical to the wFrame word that forms part of the window record. Indeed, it is used to form that part of the record. The bits in the wFrame word that are not included in the window frame type are those bits that are controlled directly by calls to Window Manager routines. These bits show whether the window is currently zoomed (bit 1) and whether the window is currently highlighted (bit 0).

The method used in the program example for setting the window frame type uses the fact that each bit in the frame represents a numeric hexadecimal value. The various bits are accumulated by ORing their values, which results in each bit being properly allocated. While it would be easier for the programmer merely to compute the initial value needed for window frame type, the method chosen not only makes its purpose more clear but also simplifies code modification.

The portion of a program that allocates a new window is

```
WindData      Data
*************************************************************
*Window Frame Type Bit Position Values
*************************************************************
F_Title       EQU $8000          ;Title bar present
F_Close       EQU $4000          ;Close box present
F_Bscrl       EQU $1000          ;Bottom scroll bar present
F_Rscrl       EQU $0800          ;Right scroll bar present
F_Grow        EQU $0400          ;Grow box present
F_Zoom        EQU $0100          ;Zoom box present
F_MoveT       EQU $0080          ;Allow move by dragging title bar
F_Vis         EQU $0020          ;Window is visible
F_Info        EQU $0010          ;Information bar is present
;
*************************************************************************
*
*Next set up parameter list for a window with a title bar, close box, right
*scroll bar, movable and visible.
*
*************************************************************************
NBytes EQU RecLoc +4 -*
DC I 'NBytes ;Total bytes in parameter list
WindParm
F_Type        DC I'F_Title.OR.F_Close.OR.F_Rscrl.OR F_MoveT.OR.F_Vis'
TPtr          DC I4'W_Title'        ;Pointer to window title text
;RefValue is an application defined reference -- its value can be anything
;helpful to the application
RefValu       DC I4'12345678'
ContRec       DC I8'0'              ;Zero for default RECT (entire screen)
ColTab        DC I4'00000000'       ;Zero for default color table
VContOrig     DC I'0000'            ;Vertical offset into Content Region
HContOrig     DC I'0000'            ;Horizontal offset into Content Region
DataHt        DC I'1024'            ;Height of data area
DataWd        DC I'0000'            ;Zero; not using horizontal control bars
MaxCHt        DC I'0000'            ;Zero because no grow box
MaxCWd        DC I'0000'            ;Zero because no grow box
VArrowPix     DC I'0001'            ;Move 1 pixel for rt ctrl bar arrow
HArrowPix     DC I'0000'            ;Zero because no bottom scroll box
VPagePix      DC I'0040'            ;Move $40 (64) pixels for rt pg ctrl area
HPagePix      DC I'0000'            ;Zero because no bottom scroll box
IBRtn         DC I4'00000000'       ;Not using information bar
IBHt          DC I2'0000'           ;Not using information bar
WindDefProc   DC I4'00000000'       ;Standard document window; 0 value
IBDraw        DC I4'00000000'       ;Not using information bar
UpdateRtn     DC I4'Updt_Wind'      ;Routine that draws Content Region
*
*Updt_Wind is the starting address of your program routine that
*actually draws the window contents; it is a routine using Quickdraw II
*calls, among others.
*
PortRect      DC I'20,20,190,300' ;Size of Content Region
Behind        DC I4'FFFFFFFF'       ;Make topmost window
RecLoc        DC I'00000000'        ;Permit standard record allocation
*
*The window title must be preceded by length byte, that is, a value
*showing the number of characters in the title
*
W_Title       DC I1'13'
              DC C'Sample Window'
```

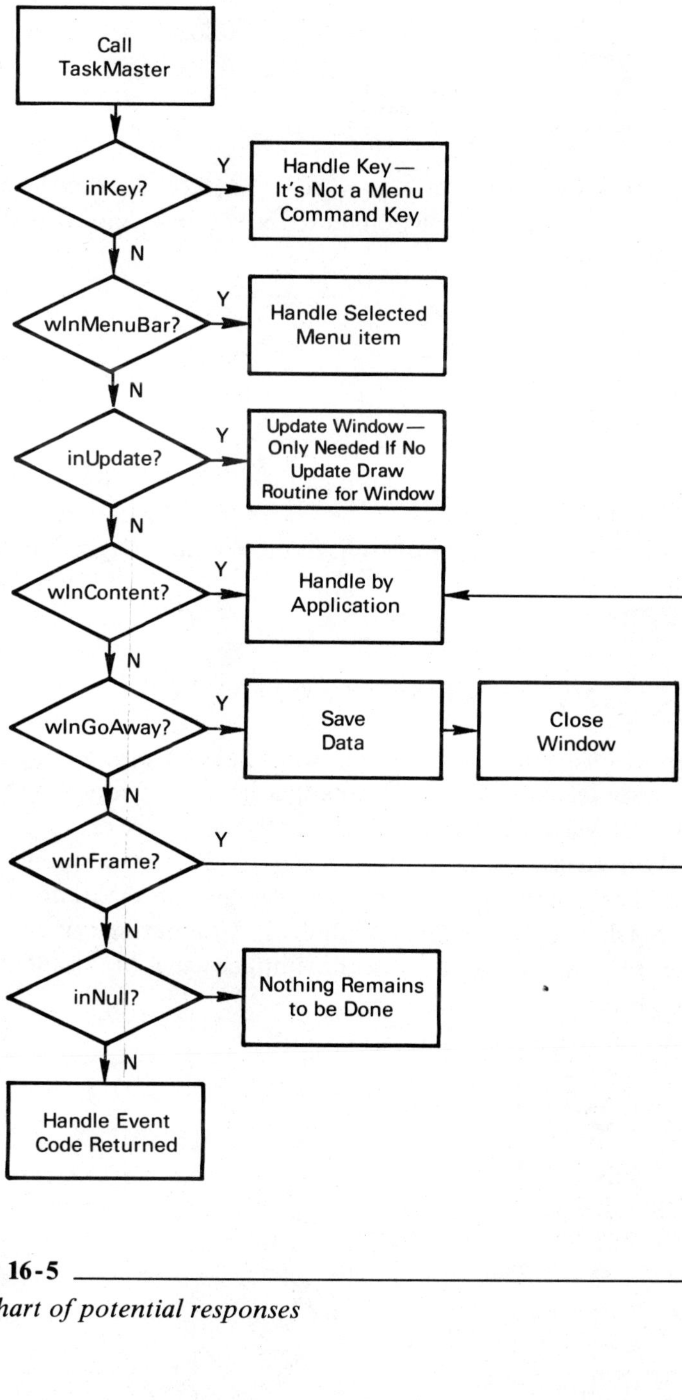

Figure 16-5
Flowchart of potential responses

```
            END
MakeWind    START
            Using WindData
            PushLong #$00000000 ;Make space for window port pointer
            PushLong WindParm   ;Long pointer to window parameter list
            _NewWindow
            PLA                 ;Get pointer to window port
            STA WPort           ;and save it
            PLA                 ;both words
            STA WPort+2
```

After creating a window, you can make it the active window by calling SelectWindow after pushing the pointer to the window's port on the stack as follows:

```
LDA WPort+2
PHA
LDA WPort
PHA
_SelectWindow
```

The same code, except for the macro call itself, can be used with other Window Manager routines such as CloseWindow, StartDrawing, HideWindow, ShowWindow, BringtoFront, ZoomWindow, BeginUpdate, and EndUpdate.

PROGRAMMING WITH TASKMASTER

As noted previously, the TaskMaster routine makes programming significantly easier in tracking various events that involve windows. Programming with TaskMaster consists of setting up a data record area for the task record, calling TaskMaster, and responding to the return code and record data. A flowchart of the potential responses is given in Figure 16-5, based on a TaskMask of $0FFF (all tasks handled). Comparing this chart with that in Figure 16-4 will demonstrate the simplicity that can result with the use of TaskMaster.

The code for use of TaskMaster is

```
*Data space for the TaskMaster record*
TaskRecord      Data
TaskWhat        DS 2
TaskMessage     DS 4
TastWhen        DS 4
TaskWhere       DS 4
TaskModifiers   DS 2
TaskData        DS 4
TaskMask        DS 2
                END
```

```
 * Equates for return codes*
 inNull          EQU 0
 inKey           EQU ????
 inUpdate        EQU ????
 wInMenuBar      EQU 17
 wInContent      EQU 19
 wInGoAway       EQU 22
 wInFrame        EQU 27
 *Program segment using TaskMaster
                 Using TaskRecord
                 Pushword Mask          ;Event Mask - See Chapter 20
                 Pushlong #TaskRecord
                 LDA #$0FFF             ;Task Mask - all tasks
                 STA TaskData
                 _TaskMaster
                 PHA                    ;Return code
                 CMP #wInMenuBar        ;Menu selection?
                 BNE N1                 ;No - continue
                 LDA TaskData           ;Get item number
                 ASL A                  ;Multiply as index
                 JSR (Table,X)          ;And perform function
                 Pushword #$0000        ;Push false word (0)
                 Pushword TaskData+2    ;and menu number
                 _HiliteMenu            ;and unhighlight menu
                 BRA Loop               ;Continue
N1               CMP #inKey             ;Is it a key event?
                 BEQ DoKey              ;Yes - handle as key event
*If in content, or frame, treat as button event
                 CMP #wInContent
                 BEQ DoButton
                 CMP #wInFrame
                 BEQ DoButton
                 CMP #wInGoAway         ;Was close box selected
                 BNE N2                 ;No - continue checking
                 JSR SaveData           ;Yes - so first save data
                 Pushlong TaskData      ;Put window's handle on stack
                 _CloseWindow           ;close window
                 BRA Loop               ;and continue
N2               CMP #wInUpdate         ;Is updating of window needed?
*This section only needed if there is
*no defined update routine for window
                 BNE N3                 ;no - continue checking
                 Pushlong TaskData      ;Yes - put window's handle on stac
                 _BeginUpdate           ;Prepare for update
*Update routine goes here
                 Pushlong TaskData      ;Once more handle of window on sta
                 _EndUpdate             ;to conclude update
                 BRA Loop               ;and continue
N3               CMP #inNull
                 BEQ Loop               ;Nothing further needed
*Remainder of program continues from here
```

CHAPTER 17

Menus: One Method of Choosing

Menus are the prime method of showing a IIGS program what you want to do.

A menu in a restaurant tells you what dishes the restaurant serves. You select from the list and inform the waitress or waiter of your choice. In the kitchen the required ingredients are combined according to a recipe, and, finally, your meal is served.

A IIGS menu also presents you with a list of functions that the current program can perform. You select an item from that menu; the program then performs the function and awaits your next response.

Sometimes an item on a restaurant's menu is out of season, so that you cannot order it. Likewise, you may not be able to use an item on the program's menu at a particular time, such as deleting text when no text has been selected to be deleted. The IIGS menus have a special means of showing you that a menu item may not be chosen. The item still appears on the menu but in dimmed type. This *disabled* item cannot be selected.

A restaurant may have several menus—a lunch menu, a dinner menu, a dessert menu, and a wine list. Each menu has several choices. Similarly, a IIGS program presents a list of menus in a *menu bar,* a section of the display screen in which the various titles of the menus appear (see Figure 17-1). When you want to make a selection from that menu, you move the mouse pointer to the word representing the menu and press the mouse button. The various items in the menu then appear immediately below the menu name. You move the mouse down until the desired item is highlighted, and then you release the mouse button.

THE MENU MANAGER

The various work entailed in menus—displaying the menus and items, determining if an item has been selected, highlighting a selected item, and determining which item was selected—is handled by a RAM-based tool called the Menu Manager. There are 52 different function calls as part of the Menu Manager. For purposes of discussion they are divided into eight different categories.

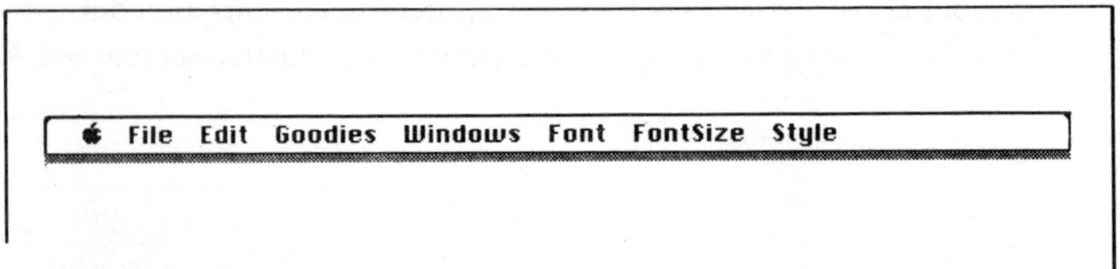

Figure 17-1
Menu bar

Like the treatment of the other IIGS tools, the discussion of the Menu Manager focuses on the most typical areas and on particularly problematic areas. Further discussion can be found in the IIGS *Technical Reference Series,* especially the IIGS *Toolbox Reference* volumes.

Menu Bars

There are two basic types of menu bars. A system menu bar is always present and appears at the top of the display screen (desktop). An application window can use either the system menu bar or its own window menu bar, which appears at the top of the window.

Care should be taken not to confuse the title system menu bar with the type of menus that can be found in the bar. The currently active program can control which menu titles appear in the system menu bar. As a general rule you should use the system menu bar rather than a separate window menu bar. Using one menu bar conserves both memory and desktop space. Several of the Menu Manager calls are easier to use if made using the system menu. Finally, applications may have several windows that are opened and closed during the course of a program, disturbing any window menu bars.

Menu Lines and Item Lines

Menus are defined by means of a list of menu lines and item lines that are passed to the Menu Manager. Each menu appearing on the menu bar consists of a string in the list that begins with a user-specified character. This character is the first character on the first line of the list. Following the menu-denoting character is a place-holding character and the title of the menu, which will be placed in the menu bar by the Menu Manager. The menu title may be followed by zero or more special characters and terminated by a carriage return or hexadecimal $00. The place-holding character will be replaced by NewMenu with the title string length.

The items appearing under each menu follow the menu line in the menu list. Each item line begins with the item-specification character, which is the first character in the first line following a menu line. This character is different from the menu-specification character. It should also be followed by a space-holding character.

Use a specific character to denote menu lines and another specific character to denote item lines. Change these characters only when you need to use them in the item or menu title. In addition, to ensure consistent use, the space-holding character should be the same as the menu or item line denoting character.

As an example, assume that you have developed a program that draws a picture of an animal on the screen and makes the sound of that animal through the speaker. You have divided the animals into three groups—barnyard, pets, and forest and stream. The list is shown in Table 17-1.

The menu bar for the program will include the three animal group names. When you select one of the three group names, that menu will pull down to reveal the names of the particular animals under that menu. See Figure 17-2 for a sample menu bar with the pets menu pulled down.

The menu list for this program would appear like this:

```
++Barnyard\N1
<<Cow\N256
<<Sheep\N257
<<Rooster\N258
<<Turkey\N259
|
++Pets\N2
<<Dog\N260
<<Cat\N261
<<Parrot\N262
<<Canary\N263
|
++Forest and Stream\N3
<<Owl\N264
<<Frog\N265
<<Coyote\N266
<<Crow\N267
|
```

Barnyard
Cow
Sheep
Rooster
Turkey
Pets
Dog
Cat
Parrot
Canary
Forest and Stream
Owl
Frog
Coyote
Crow

Table 17-1
List of Animals

Figure 17-2
Sample menu bar with pets menu pulled down

In this sample menu list the + character is used to designate a menu line (and hold space for length), and the < character is used to designate an item line (and hold space). The | symbol at the end of the list is known as the terminating character. It can be any character that appears first in the line and is different from the item line indicator. It can be the same as the menu line indicator (+).

Both the menu and item lines in the example list have their titles followed by a backslash (\), the letter N, and a decimal number. This number is the identification number, which must be attached to every menu and item (its value must be between 1 and 65535). The backslash character indicates the end of the title name and the beginning of special characters. The N symbol indicates a decimal, ASCII format.

Alternatively, you can use the letter H and a 2-byte hexadecimal, non-ASCII format identification number. The hexadecimal value must be low byte first.

The difference between ASCII and non-ASCII format refers to how the value is stored in memory. For example, ASCII format 1234 is stored in memory as 31 32 33 34. In non-ASCII format the hexadecimal value $1234 is stored in memory as 34 12. The following two item lines are equivalent functionally. They are listed as hexadecimal bytes stored in memory and the ASCII equivalent.

```
3C 3C 4F 77 6C 5C 4E 32 36 34 13  = <<Owl\N264 [Carriage return]

3C 3C 4F 77 6C 5C 48 08 01 13     = <<Owl\H0108 [Carriage return]
```

The 08 01 in the second line is the low-byte-first representation of the hexadecimal value $0108, which is equivalent to the decimal value 264.

The use of hexadecimal values in place of decimal values will result in a shorter menu or item line in every case with a decimal value over 99 (1 byte saved between 100 and 999, 2 bytes saved between 1000 and 9999, and 3 bytes saved between 10000 and 65535). The use of decimal values will result in a 1-byte-shorter menu or item line in cases of a decimal value between 1 and 9.

To enter the first form of the line in memory, using the IIGS assembler, you would use the code

```
DC C '<<Owl\N264'
DC H '13'
```

To enter the second form of the line in memory, you would use the code

```
DC C '<<Owl\H'
DC H '08 01 13'
```

You must adhere to the following rules when you apply menu and item numbers to menus and items:

- Menu numbers may be any value between 0 and 65535.
- Item numbers may be any value between 256 and 65534, except for desk accessory items, which must be between 1 and 255.
- A menu may have the same number as an item.
- Menus must each have a different number.
- Items should each have a different number from every other item on the menu bar, except that permanently disabled items, such as dividing lines, can have the same number as other permanently disabled items.

If items are numbered consecutively from 256 up, the item number can be used to index to a table of the addresses of routines implementing each item. Consider again the example of an animals menu with items numbered as follows:

256. Cow	257. Sheep	258. Rooster
259. Turkey	260. Dog	261. Cat
262. Parrot	263. Canary	264. Owl
265. Frog	266. Coyote	267. Crow

Each routine is given a label in the assembler with the name of the animal plus the suffix _Do. A table of the routines would thus appear as

```
Animal_Table  DC A 'Cow_Do'
              DC A 'Sheep_Do'
              DC A 'Rooster_Do'
              DC A 'Turkey_Do'
              DC A 'Dog_Do'
              DC A 'Cat_Do'
              DC A 'Parrot_Do'
              DC A 'Canary_Do'
              DC A 'Owl_Do'
              DC A 'Frog_Do'
              DC A 'Coyote_Do'
              DC A 'Crow_Do'
```

The code using this table would then take the following form:

```
* Assume Item #ID number is on the stack following routines
* to determine which menu item was selected
        PHA
        SEC                     ;Get set to subtract
        SBC 256                 ;Lowest item number is 256
        ASL A                   ;Multiply by 2 to use as index
        TAX                     ;Transfer to index register
        JSR (Animal_Table,X)
* Rest of code continues from here.
```

Another method of handling item numbers is to give each item a number corresponding to the low-order word of the routine that performs the action associated with that item. In this method you merely perform a JSR to the item number. The code to accomplish this is

```
* Assume Item ID number is on the stack following routines
* to determine which menu item was selected
        PHA
        STA  Jump_Loc
* We must use absolute indexed indirect addressing since
* there is no absolute indirect form of JSR command.  To do
* so, we simulate later form by setting X register to 0
* doing JSR.
        LDX #$0000
        JSR (Jump_Loc,X)
* Rest of code continues from here
```

You can change menu numbers using the SetMenuID routines, and you can change item numbers using the SetItemID routine. Menu names assigned to a given number can be obtained using GetMenuTitle and changed using SetMenuTitle. The same routines for item names are SetItem and GetItem.

Menu and item titles can appear with other attributes in the menu bar or menu. Either a menu or item title can be dimmed, in which case it is not selectable. To dim a menu or item initially, place the letter D in the special-character section of that line.

Item titles, but not menu titles, can also be displayed in bold text (B in special characters), italicized (I in special characters), and underscored (U in special characters).

Menu titles appear on the menu bar in an application-specified color, with an application-specified background color, and with an application-specified color used to produce outline shapes on the menu. Figure 17-3 shows where these various items appear in a menu. The colors with which

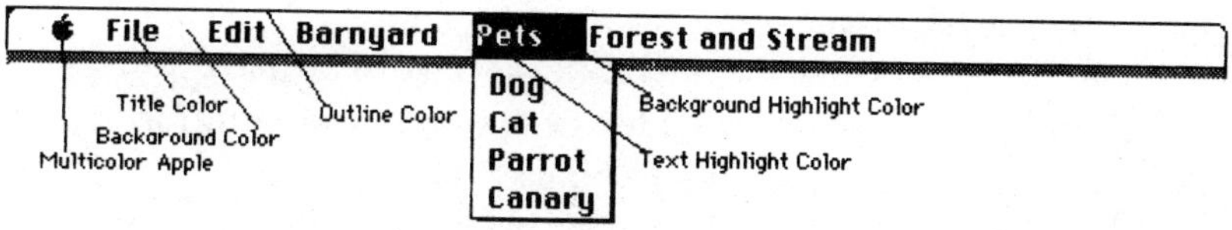

Figure 17-3

Sample menu titles

to replace both the background and text of a title when highlighted, if color highlighting is used, are also application-specified.

The selection of a menu and of an item in a menu is indicated by the highlighting of that menu or item name. The IIGS provides two methods of highlighting. The normal, or default, method of highlighting is XOR (exclusive OR). This method performs an exclusive OR of the title display with $FFFF, resulting in a reversal of the title display (dark becomes light and light becomes dark).

The second supported method of highlighting is color-replace highlighting. In this method, whenever a menu title or item is highlighted, a specified color replaces the text color and another specified color replaces the background color. Color-replace highlighting can be used in any menu or item by including an "X" in the special characters portion of the menu or item line. Color-replace highlighting is mandatory for use with the Apple (desk accessory and information) menu discussed next.

The current method of highlighting for a particular item can be obtained by the GetItemFlag routine. The second word on the stack is a 0 if color redrawing is used for highlighting and a 1 if XOR highlighting is used. The current method of highlighting can be changed by the SetItemFlag routine. The first word pushed on the stack should be a $0020 to enable XOR highlighting and a $FFDF to enable color-redrawing highlighting.

The Apple Menu

In addition to the menus you define yourself, the IIGS has a special, built-in, multicolor Apple menu you can specify to be placed on the menu bar. This menu is normally used for desk accessories and for basic program information, although it can be used for any other information as well. Do not use it for anything except the suggested uses, however. The IIGS user interface guidelines encourage consistent use of menus.

The Apple menu is specified by placing an "at sign" (@) as the menu title text string. This should be the first menu declared by your program and should appear first in the menu bar. Again, the Apple menu must have an "X" (to show color-replace highlighting) as part of its special characters.

It is common to indicate an item in a menu has been selected or turned on by placing a checkmark to the left of the item in the menu. You can also permanently, or initially, place a checkmark (or other character) next to an item by placing a C in the item's special characters followed by the character to be used as the checkmark.

The CheckItem routine will place a checkmark character or remove one from a given item. The first word on the stack should be true to place a checkmark and false to remove one. The current mark used as a checkmark can be obtained with the GetItemMark routine. The word returned on the stack is the character used to mark the item. SetItemMark changes the character used to mark an item. In both cases a zero indicates no mark will be used.

Many programs use keyboard equivalents for some menu items so that the user can use the mouse to select that item. (See also the discussion in Chapter 2.) This alternative is especially appropriate in keyboard-intensive programs such as word processing. To indicate a keyboard equivalent for an item, place an asterisk (*) in the list of special characters for that item followed by two characters that will be the keyboard equivalents for that item. To invoke the keyboard equivalent, press the APPLE key in conjunction with that character.

The preferred specification of keyboard equivalents is to use the uppercase and lowercase versions of a letter as the equivalents. If you wish only one keyboard equivalent, use a space as a filler for the second character. Because the first character is displayed following the item name in the menu, you should consistently use either the uppercase or lowercase equivalent first in the list. Apple's guidelines suggest the use of the uppercase character first.

Keyboard equivalents can be useful if they are carefully planned. For example, a paint program that is very mouse-intensive does not require many keyboard equivalents because the user is already using the mouse to draw. Its text functions, if any, would appear to be the one place where keyboard equivalents would be helpful.

By contrast, a text-oriented database program would benefit from more keyboard equivalents because the user is more likely to be using the keyboard when selecting an item from a menu.

Avoid making too many menu items with keyboard equivalents. The best keyboard equivalents are those with the same initial letter as the item, such as B for bold or I for italics. Obviously the more equivalents there are, the more tortured some of the connections between the keyboard equivalent and the menu item will be. For example, if you have chosen U for undo, you may have to use L instead of U for underline.

A keyboard equivalent that is difficult to remember will not be used much. Carefully consider which items are most often used when the user is typing at the keyboard and restrict your keyboard equivalents to no more than those ten or so items.

Each item in the menu takes up a separate line. For purposes of clarity of presentation, your application can have some form of division between two groups of related items in a menu. The Menu Manager provides three methods of delineating between the items in a menu.

□ The underscore can be specified as a special character (U) in defining an item and the item will then appear in the menu with a line directly under it, extending clear across the menu. This method of separating items has the advantage of requiring less space, in terms of both data storage and menu display. Underscoring of an item is accomplished by SetItemStyle with a ChStyle of $0004 or by SetItemFlag with a NewValue of $0040. Removal of underscoring is accomplished by SetItemFlag with a NewValue of $FFBF. The current underscore status can be obtained by GetItemStyle (ChStyle returned of $0004 indicates underscored) or by GetItemFlag (Divide word returned of 1 indicates underlining).

□ A dividing line can be placed under an item, without using a separate item, by placing a V in that item's special characters.

□ A dividing line as a separate item in the menu can be selected by making the item title a single dash (-). Specify, too, that the line be disabled or dimmed (D). This method of separating items has the advantage of producing a cleaner-looking menu with better visual appeal. A comparison of the menu produced with these three techniques is shown in Figure 17-4.

Table 17-2 lists the special modifying characters used in menu and item lists and indicates whether the character can be used in both lists or only item lists.

MENU RECORDS

Several different records are used by the Menu Manager. The overall record for any menu bar is a menu bar record. This record contains a pointer to another record, the color table. It also contains an array of

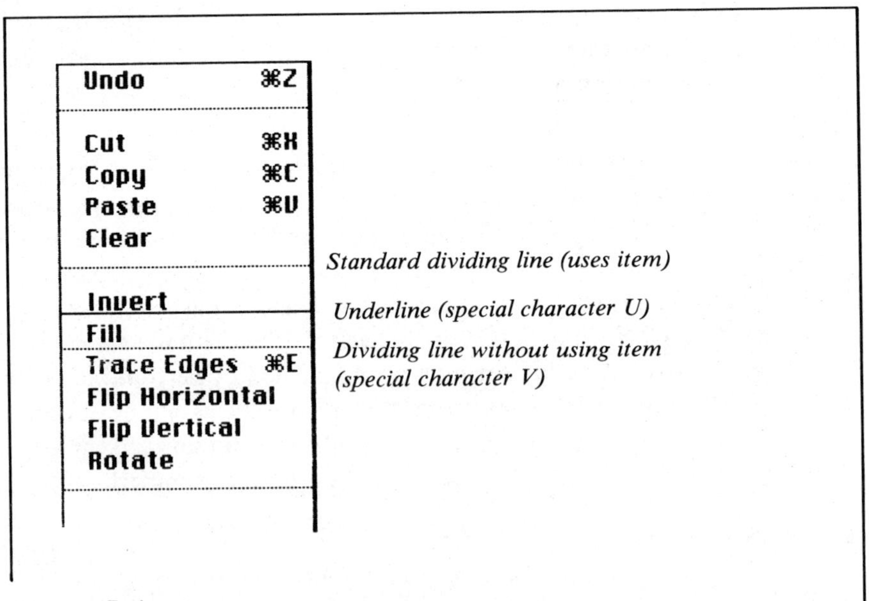

Figure 17-4
Two methods of delineating between items in a menu

Character	Meaning	Used in Menus	Used in Items
|	Beginning of special characters	x	x
*	Keyboard equivalents		x
B	Boldface text		x
C	Mark with character		x
D	Dim (disable)	x	x
H	Hexadecimal, non-ASCII ID follows	x	x
I	Italicize text		x
N	Decimal, ASCII ID follows	x	x
U	Underscore text		x
V	Dividing line under item		x
X	Use color-replace highlighting	x	x

Table 17-2
List of Modifying Characters in Menu and Item Lists

handles to the menu records. The menu records further contain references to the individual item records.

The menu bar record and color table are both fully defined. The beginning part of the menu record is defined, while the remainder is not. The item record, for a standard menu, is not defined at all.

Apple has chosen not to document the menu record fully, and not to document the item record at all, in order to preserve the ability to modify the records subsequently as the need arises. If the format of the record were fully documented, various programs might attempt to make specific use of portions of the record, preventing the subsequent modification of the record structure without rendering the program inoperative.

Apple has chosen instead to permit access to the record structure, as needed, through the various commands of the Menu Manager. This RAM-based manager can then be modified to access any modified structure. Calls to the new Menu Manager made by existing programs will function as they did with the old Menu Manager. The only effect will be that the old application will not be able to utilize any new features of the Menu Manager without being rewritten.

Byte Number	Name	Size	Purpose
0	NextCtrl	Long	Handle of next control in list
4	CtrlOwner	Long	Window number menu appears in; zero if a system menu bar
8	CtrlRect	Rect	Global rectangle coordinates of menu bar
10	CtrlFlag	Word	Attributes of menu
12	CtrlValue	Word	Must be zero — unused
14	CtrlProc	Long	$0A000000
18	CtrlAction	Long	True if system window, false if application window
1C	CtrlData	Long	Reserved
20	CtrlRefCon	Long	Field reserved for use by application; can be any value
24	CtrlColor	Long	Pointer to color table
28	MenuList[1]	Long	Handle of first menu record
2C	MenuList[2]	Long	Handle of second menu record
2C+nn*4	MenuList[n]	Long	Handle of nth (and last) menu record
30+nn*4	End	Long	$00000000

Note: The array of handles to the menu records is terminated by a zero item.

Table 17-3

Format of Menu Bar Record

Bits	Meaning
0-7	Menu number of highlighted menu, if any
8-13	Starting position of titles, in number of pixels from left side*
14	System (1) or Application (0) window menu bar
15	Invisible (1) or visible (0) menu

*This value may be obtained by using GetTitleStart. It may be changed by SetTitleStart.

Table 17-4

Menu Bar Record Control Flag

The menu bar record is a standard control record (see discussion of the Control Manager in Chapter 18). The layout of this record when used as a menu bar record is given in Table 17-3.

One of the items in the menu bar record is the control flag. This word-length item consists of a series of bits that indicate various aspects about the particular menu bar. The items included in this word are shown in Table 17-4.

The color table pointed to by the menu bar record indicates what colors are to be used for highlighted and unhighlighted text, highlighted and unhighlighted background, and the outline. The color table consists of a three-word record. Its layout is shown in Table 17-5.

The color table is set initially to default values when the menu is first created. Its current values may be found by the use of GetBarColors. The current color values may be changed by use of SetBarColors.

Only the first ten items in a menu record are defined. The remaining part of the record is accessible only through the various commands of the Menu Manager. The layout of the first part of the menu record is shown in Table 17-6. The meaning of the various bits in the MenuFlag portion of the menu record is shown in Table 17-7.

The current value of a menu flag can be obtained by using GetMenu-Flag. The value of certain bits in the menu flag may be changed by use of

Word	Bits	Meaning
0	0-3	Unhighlighted text color
0	4-7	Unhighlighted background color
0	8-15	Unused
1	0-3	Highlighted text color
1	4-7	Highlighted background color
1	8-15	Unused
2	0-3	Unused
2	4-7	Outline color
2	8-15	Unused

Table 17-5
Menu Bar Color Table Record

Byte Offset	Name	Size	Meaning
0	MenuID	Word	Identification number of menu
2	MenuWidth	Word	Width of menu in pixels
4	MenuHeight	Word	Height of menu in pixels
6	MenuProc	Long	Pointer to menu definition procedure; 0 for standard menus
A	MenuFlag	Byte	Attributes of menu
B	MenuRes	Byte	Reserved
C	FirstItem	Byte	Reserved
D	NumOfItems	Byte	Reserved
E	TitleWidth	Word	Width of title area of menu in pixels; selectable area of menu
1	TitleName*	Long	Pointer to title text. First byte of text is the number of characters in the title

*Title of menu may be obtained by GetMenuTitle and changed by SetMenuTitle.

Table 17-6

Menu Record (Defined Portion)

Bit	Meaning
0	Reserved
1	Reserved
2	Visible (0) or invisible (1) menu
3	Reserved
4	Standard (0) or custom (1) menu
5	Invert color (0) or XOR (1) highlighting
6	Normal (0) or inverted (1) menu title
7	Enabled (0) or disabled (1) menu

Table 17-7

Meaning of Menu Flag

NewValue	Result
FF7F	Menu enabled
0080	Menu disabled
0040	Normal menu title
FFDF	Color-redraw highlighting
0020	XOR highlighting
FFE7	Standard menu
0010	Custom menu

Table 17-8
Setting of NewValue in SetMenuFlag

SetMenuFlag. This routine requires placing three word values on the stack. The first value is NewValue and the second is the menu identification number of the desired menu. The setting of NewValue depends on what action you wish to accomplish. Table 17-8 shows the various settings depending on the desired result.

PROGRAMMING WITH THE MENU MANAGER

The first step in creating a menu is to set up the menu and item lines somewhere in your program. If you use the IIGS Assembler, the following code would set up the menu and item lines for the barnyard section of the animals menu discussed earlier in the chapter.

```
BarnMenu  DC C'++Barnyard\N1' H'13'
ICow      DC C'<<Cow\N256' H'13'
ISheep    DC C'<<Sheep\N257' H'13'
IRooster  DC C'<<Rooster\N258' H'13'
ITurkey   DC C'<<Turkey\N259' H'13'
          DC C'|'
```

Once the menu lists are defined, you should initialize the Menu Manager in the program initialization section using MenuStartup. This routine should be called after memory, for the zero pages needed by Quickdraw II, the Window Manager, and the Menu Manager have already been provided for, and the Memory Manager, Quickdraw II, and the Window Manager have already been initialized.

If your program is going to use only a system menu bar, you do not have to create it. Otherwise you will have to call the NewMenuBar routine. This routine is also called by MenuStartup—if you are using this initially created menu bar, you don't need to create another.

The next procedure is to pass a pointer to the NewMenu routine, which creates the space for the menu and its items, and insert the menu in the menu bar. The code for this procedure is

```
Pushlong $00000000       ;Space for long word MenuHandle returned
Pushlong FarmMenu        ;Handle of Barnyard Menu list
_NewMenu                 ;Call NewMenu via IIGS Assembler Macro
Pushword #$0000          ;Insert menu at front
_InsertMenu              ;Handle of menu still on stack
```

The next step is to insert each item in the menu. This is handled best by working from bottom to top—each new item can then be placed in the front of the previous ones. The code for this routine is

```
Pushlong ITurkey         ;Last item first
Pushword #$0000          ;Add item to front of list
Pushword #$0001          ;Add item to first menu
_InsertItem
Pushlong IRooster        ;Long address of item line
Pushword #$0000          ;Add item to front of list
Pushword $0001           ;Add item to first menu
_InsertItem
Pushlong ISheep          ;Long address of item line
Pushword #$0000          ;Add item to front of list
Pushword #$0001          ;Add item to first menu
_InsertItem
Pushlong ICow            ;Long address of item line
Pushword #$0000          ;Add item to front of list
Pushword #$0001          ;Add item to first menu
_InsertItem
```

This routine needs to be repeated for each menu and item list.

If you do not want the default menu colors, you must specify the new colors using SetBarColors. The default menu colors set upon initialization are black text on a white background and a black outline. The final step is to display the menu bar you have just finished creating. Such a display is accomplished simply by a call to the routine DrawMenuBar. This routine has no input or output.

Most tasks involving user interaction with the menus are made considerably easier if you use the TaskMaster routine in the Window Manager. (This routine is described more fully in Chapter 16.) If you are using TaskMaster, you merely need to respond to the selected item number by performing the process called for by the item number and then unhighlighting the item selected. This is done by calling the HiliteMenu and setting the first word on the stack (Hilite) to false to remove highlighting from the menu.

As you get more adept at using menus in your IIGS programs, you may want to use some of the other features of the Menu Manager. You even have the facility to define your own menu display and layout. The different Menu Manager routines and categories are listed by category, with a short description of each routine, in Table 17-9. The parameters required by each routine appear by category of routines in Tables 17-10 through 17-17. Table 17-18 contains a comparison of the Menu Manager routines in the IIGS and Macintosh.

Several of the routines in the tables require a bit more explanation.

CalcMenuSize calculates the menu width by finding the widest item in the menu and adds room for a mark and a command key; it then sets the entire menu width to that width. The routine uses a specified default value if the menu does not contain any item text. The routine will calculate either the menu height or width if the input value is zero. Otherwise it will set the height or width to the specified input value.

MenuSelect requires a pointer to a TaskRecord identical to that used by TaskMaster. (This Window Manager routine is discussed in Chapter 16.) The same is true of MenuKey. These routines return data, not via the stack, but in the TaskData field of the TaskRecord.

If Hilite is called with Hilite false, it will draw a normal title. If Hilite is true, the routine will draw a highlighted title.

When InsertMenu is called with an InsertAfter value of zero, the new menu is inserted at the front of the bar. Thus, if you continually call InsertMenu with InsertAfter set to zero, you can insert the menu titles into the bar from back to front. The same is true with InsertItem.

The menu size may need to be recalculated after an item is added via InsertItem or deleted via DeleteItem. Call CalcMenuSize to recalculate the menu size.

Initialization and Termination Routines	
MenuBootInit	Initialization of Menu Manager by system at boot time.
MenuStartup	Initialization of Menu Manager by application. Performs the following steps: 1. Initializes system menu bar with no menus 2. Makes system menu bar current menu bar 3. Reserves space for menu bar (via Desktop in Window Manager) 4. Opens a Grafport 5. Draws empty system menu bar via DrawMenuBar.
MenuShutDown	Deallocation of Menu Manager by application.
MenuVersion	Returns Menu Manager's version.
MenuReset	No action.
NewMenuBar	Creates default menu bar with no menus (menu height is 13 pixels, visible, black text on white background).
NewMenu	Allocates space for menu and associated items and returns handle to menu.
DisposeMenu	Deallocates space for menu, freeing up memory.
FixMenuBar	Determines height (using tallest font of menu title fonts) for menu bar.
CalcMenuSize	Determines width or height for menu bar.

User Interaction Routines	
MenuSelect	Determines selection, if any, when button-down event occurs in MenuBar (not needed with TaskMaster—see Chapter 17).
MenuKey	Determines if command key combination pressed is a menu keyboard equivalent and, if so, the applicable item ID number.
MenuRefresh	Calls the redraw routine when the Menu Manager cannot restore the screen under a menu that has been pulled down and released. Not needed if using Window Manager.

Table 17-9

Categories of Menu Manager Routines

Drawing Routines	
DrawMenuBar	Draws current menu bar together with all menu titles.
HiliteMenu	Draws applicable menu title in either highlighted or normal color as specified.
FlashMenuBar	Redraws menu bar in highlighted color and then in normal color.

Menu and Item Shuffling Routines	
InsertMenu	Add a specified menu handle to current menu bar; does not redraw new menu bar.
DeleteMenu	Removes menu with specified ID number from current menu bar; menu not deallocated; menu bar not redrawn.
InsertItem	Adds item to specified menu.
DeleteItem	Removes item from current menu bar.

Menu Bar Access Routines	
SetSysBar	Makes specified system menu bar current menu bar.
GetSysBar	Returns handle of current system menu bar.
SetMenuBar	Makes specified menu bar (system or otherwise) current menu bar.
GetMenuBar	Returns the handle or current (system or otherwise) menu bar
CountMItems	Returns the number of items, including any dividing lines, in specified menu.
SetBarColors	Changes colors used to draw menu bar.
GetBarColors	Returns colors used to draw menu bar.
SetTitleStart	Specifies starting point, in pixels, from left side of menu bar for title.
GetTitleStart	Returns starting point, in pixels, from left side of menu bar for title.

Table 17-9

Categories of Menu Manager Routines (continued)

Menu Record Access Routines	
GetMHandle	Returns the handle of the menu with the specified menu identification number.
SetTitleWidth	Specifies the width of a menu title (the area when a menu will be selected and the area that is highlighted along with the menu title text).
GetTitleWidth	Returns the width of a menu title (the area when a menu will be selected and the area that is highlighted along with the menu title text).
SetMenuFlag	Used to change menu flag values; see Table 17-8 for more details.
GetMenuFlag	Returns menu flag value.
SetMenuTitle	Changes the string that forms the specified menu title.
GetMenuTitle	Returns a pointer to the specified menu title.
SetMenuID	Changes the ID number of the specified menu.

Item Record Access Routines	
SetItem	Changes the string that forms the specified item name.
GetItem	Returns a pointer to the specified item.
EnableItem	Makes the specified item appear in normal text and be selectable.
DisableItem	Makes the specified item appear in dimmed text and not be selectable.
CheckItem	Place or remove a checkmark to the left of the specified item's text.
SetItemMark	Change the mark that will be used for checking an item.
GetItemMark	Returns the character that is used for checking an item.
SetItemStyle	Change the text style for a specified item as follows, depending on setting of ChStyle: 0001 Bold 0002 Italic 0004 Underscore

Table 17-9

Categories of Menu Manager Routines (continued)

Item Record Access Routines		
GetItemStyle	Returns the text style for a specified item, in ChStyle, as follows:	
	0001	Bold
	0002	Italic
	0004	Underscore
SetItemFlag	Sets the item flag to perform following functions:	
	Underline	0040
	No underline	FFBF
	Use XOR highlighting	0020
	Use color-replace highlighting	FFDF
GetItemFlag	Returns the underline and XOR highlight status values (1 = true).	
SetItemID	Changes the item ID number of the specified item.	
SetItemBlink	Specifies number of times an item blinks to show it is selected (normally set through Control Panel).	
Miscellaneous Routines		
GetMenuMgrPort	Returns pointer to Menu Manager's Grafport.	
MNewRes	Redraws current system menu bar to adjust for changed screen resolution	
InitPalette	Reinitialize color palettes as needed for the color Apple logo in the system menu bar after a change in the color palettes.	

Table 17-9

Categories of Menu Manager Routines (continued)

Function Name	Function Number	User ID	Zeropg	Version	theWindow	BarHandle	MenuString	MenuHandle	MenuHeight	MenuWidth	NewHeight	MenuNum
Size of Parameter		W	W	W	L	L	L	L	W	W	W	W
Type of Parameter		V	V	V	P	H	P	H	V	V	V	V
MenuBootInit	01											
MenuStartup	02	I1	I2									
MenuShutDown	03											
MenuVersion	04			O1								
MenuReset	05											
NewMenuBar	15				I1	O1						
NewMenu	2D						I1	O1				
DisposeMenu	2E							I1				
FixMenuBar	13								O1			
CalcMenuSize	1C									I1	I2	I3

Size codes:
L = Long-word (32 bits) W = Word (16 bits)

Parameter type codes:
H = Handle P = Pointer V = Value

Table 17-10

Initialization and Termination Routines

Function Name	Function Number	TaskRec	BarHandle	RedrawRoutine
Parameter Size		L	L	L
Parameter Type		P	H	P
MenuSelect	2B	I1	I2	
MenuKey	09	I1	I2	
MenuRefresh	0B			I1

Size codes:
L = Long-word (32 bits)

Parameter type codes:
H = Handle P = Pointer

Table 17-11

User Interaction Routines

Function Name	Function Number	Hilite	MenuNum
Size of Parameter		W	W
Type of Parameter		B	V
DrawMenuBar	24		
HiliteMenu	2C	I1	I2
FlashMenuBar	0C		

Size codes:
W = Word (16 bits)

Parameter type codes:
B = Boolean V = Value

Table 17-12
Drawing Routines

Function Name	Function Number	AddMenu	InsertAfter	MenuNum	AddItem	ItemNum
Size of Parameter		L	W	W	L	W
Type of Parameter		H	V	V	P	V
InsertMenu	0D	I1	I2			
DeleteMenu	0E			I1		
InsertItem	0F		I2	I3	I1	
DeleteItem	10					I1

Size codes:
L = Long-word (32 bits)
W = Word (16 bits)

Parameter type codes:
H = Handle
P = Pointer
V = Value

Table 17-13
Menu and Item Shuffling Routines

Function Name	Function Number	BarHandle	MenuNum	NumOfItems	NewBarColor	NewInvertColor	NewOutColor	Colors	XStart
Size of Parameter		L	W	W	W	W	W	L	W
Type of Parameter		H	V	V	BA	BA	BA	BA	V
SetSysBar	12	I1							
GetSysBar	11	O1							
SetMenuBar	39	I1							
GetMenuBar	OA	O1							
CountMItems	14		I1	O1					
SetBarColors	17				I1	I2	I3		
GetBarColors	18							O1	
SetTitleStart	19								I1
GetTitleStart	1A								O1

Notes:

Size:

L = Long-word (32 bits)
W = Word (16 bits)

Type:

BA = Bit array
H = Handle
V = Value

Table 17-14

Menu Bar Access Routines

Function Name	Function Number	NewWidth	NewState	FlagMask	NewString	NewID	MenuNum	TheWidth	MenuState	TheTitle	MenuHandle
Size		W	W	W	L	W	W	W	W	L	L
Type		V	BA	BA	P	V	V	V	BA	P	H
GetMHandle	16						I1				O1
SetTitleWidth	1D	I1					I2				
GetTitleWidth	1E						I1	O1			
SetMenuFlag	1F		I1	I2			I3				
GetMenuFlag	20						I1		O1		
SetMenuTitle	21				I1		I2				
GetMenuTitle	22						I1			O1	
SetMenuID	37					I1	I2				

Size codes:
- L = Long-word (32 bits)
- W = Word (16 bits)

Parameter type codes:
- BA = Bit array
- H = Handle
- P = Pointer
- V = Value

Table 17-15

Menu Record Access Routines

Function Name	Function Number	NewValue	NewStrg	Checked	Mark	ChStyle	NewID	ItemNum	ItemStrg	Divide	XOR	Count
Size of Parameter		W	L	W	W	W	W	W	L	W	W	W
Type of Parameter		BA	P	B	CH	BA	V	V	P	B	B	V
SetItem	24		I1					I2				
GetItem	25							I1	O1			
EnableItem	30							I1				
DisableItem	31							I1				
CheckItem	32			I1				I2				
SetItemMark	33				I1			I2				
GetItemMark	34				O1			I1				
SetItemStyle	35					I1		I2				
GetItemStyle	36					O1		I1				
SetItemFlag	26	I1						I2				
GetItemFlag	27							I1		O1	O2	
SetItemID	38						I1	I2				
SetItemBlink	28											I1

Size codes:
- L = Long-word (32 bits)
- W = Word (16 bits)

Parameter type codes:
- B = Boolean
- BA = Bit array
- Ch = Character
- P = Pointer
- V = Value

Table 17-16

Item Record Access Routines

Function Name	Function Number	Menu MgrPtr
Size of Parameter		L
Type of Parameter		P
GetMenuMgrPort	1B	01
MNewRes	29	
InitPalette	2F	

Notes:
Size:
L = Long-word (32 bits)

Type:
P = Pointer

Table 17-17
Miscellaneous Routines

Routine	Macintosh	IIGS
AddResMenu	x	
AppendMenu	x	
CalcMenuSize	x	x
CheckItem	x	x
ClearMenuBar	x	
CountMItems	x	x
DeleteItem		x
DeleteMenu	x	x
DisableItem	x	x
DisposeMenu	x	x
DrawMenuBar	x	x
EnableItem	x	x
FixMenuBar		x
FlashMenuBar	x	x

Table 17-18
Comparison of IIGS and Macintosh New Manager Routines

Routine	Macintosh	IIGS
GetBarColors		x
GetItem	x	x
GetItemFlag		x
GetItemIcon	x	
GetItemMark	x	x
GetItemStyle	x	x
GetMenu	x	
GetMenuBar	x	x
GetMenuFlag		x
GetMenuMgrPort		x
GetMenuTitle		x
GetMHandle	x	x
GetNewMBar	x	
GetSysBar		x
GetTitleStart		x
GetTitleWidth		x
HiliteMenu	x	x
InitPalette		x
InsertItem		x
InsertMenu	x	x
InsertResMenu	x	
MenuBootInit		x
MenuKey	x	x
MenuRefresh		x
MenuReset		x
MenuSelect	x	x
MenuShutDown		x
MenuStartup (InitMenus)	x	x
MenuVersion		x
MNewRes		x
NewMenu	x	x
NewMenuBar		x

Table 17-18

Comparison of IIGS and Macintosh New Manager Routines (continued)

Routine	Macintosh	IIGS
SetBarColors		x
SetItem	x	x
SetItemBlink		x
SetItemFlag		x
SetItemIcon	x	
SetItemID		x
SetItemMark	x	x
SetItemStyle	x	x
SetMenuBar	x	x
SetMenuFlag		x
SetMenuFlash	x	
SetMenuID		x
SetMenuTitle		x
SetSysBar		x
SetTitleStart		x
SetTitleWidth		x

Table 17-18
Comparison of IIGS and Macintosh New Manager Routines (continued)

Bar colors passed to SetBarColors consist of three words as follows:

NewBarColor contains

- □ Unhighlighted text color (bits 0-3)
- □ Unhighlighted background color (bits 4-7)
- □ Zero (bits 8-15)

NewInvertColor contains

- □ Highlighted text color (bits 0-3)
- □ Highlighted background color (bits 4-7)
- □ Zero (bits 8-15)

NewOutColor contains

- □ Color of menu bar outline, menu outline, underlines, and dividing lines (bits 4-7)
- □ Zero (bits 0-3 and 8-15)

To change only some colors selectively, call SetBarColors with the word containing the colors you do not wish to change set to a negative value (bit 15 = 1).

The value returned by GetBarColors is not the same record structure of that used by SetBarColors. Instead it is a long value with the following structure:

- □ Bits 0-3 unhighlighted text color
- □ Bits 4-7 unhighlighted background color
- □ Bits 8-11 highlighted text color
- □ Bits 12-15 highlighted background color
- □ Bits 16-19 zero
- □ Bits 20-23 menu bar outline, menu outline, underline, and dividing line color
- □ Bits 24-31 zero

Setting Checked to zero in CheckItem will remove the checkmark. Setting Mark to zero in SetItemMark will cause the mark not to appear. If Mark in GetItemMark is zero, that item is not marked.

CHAPTER 18

Controls: Another Method of Choosing

As discussed in Chapter 2, the typical IIGS application program should be circular in design, waiting for input from the user in various forms and responding appropriately, and then returning for more input. The last chapter looked at the primary method of selecting the various operating modes in the IIGS—menus. This chapter will explore another method of making choices with the IIGS—the control.

As a general rule, a menu bar nearly always is accessible to the application user who can switch from one type of operation to another through the menu. Controls are more restrictive. Most of them are not always present on the IIGS screen. Sometimes when they are present, the user is required to make a selection from them before doing anything else.

Controls in the IIGS do not exist in a vacuum. They always belong to a particular window. If you wish to write an application that has the same set of controls in two different windows, you must have two sets of controls.

TYPES OF CONTROLS

The two basic types of controls are *buttons* and *dials.* Each of these types has a variety of subtypes.

Buttons

Figure 18-1 shows some of the more common (and predefined) button-type controls. These include the *pushbutton,* the *checkbox,* and the *radio button.*

Pushbuttons (sometimes referred to merely as buttons) consist of a text title centered in a rounded rectangle. A pushbutton is selected by pressing down the mouse button when the mouse cursor is within the rounded rectangle of that pushbutton. Depending on how your application is programmed, selecting a pushbutton can cause one of the following two actions:

- □ Some pushbuttons begin a function when the mouse button is first pressed down and continue until the mouse button is released.
- □ Other pushbuttons take action only when the mouse button is both pressed and released while the mouse cursor is within the button.

An example of the use of the first type of a pushbutton is a scroll bar arrow that increases the red portion of a color as long as the pushbutton is selected. An example of the second type of pushbutton is opening a file when the open pushbutton is activated after a file is selected.

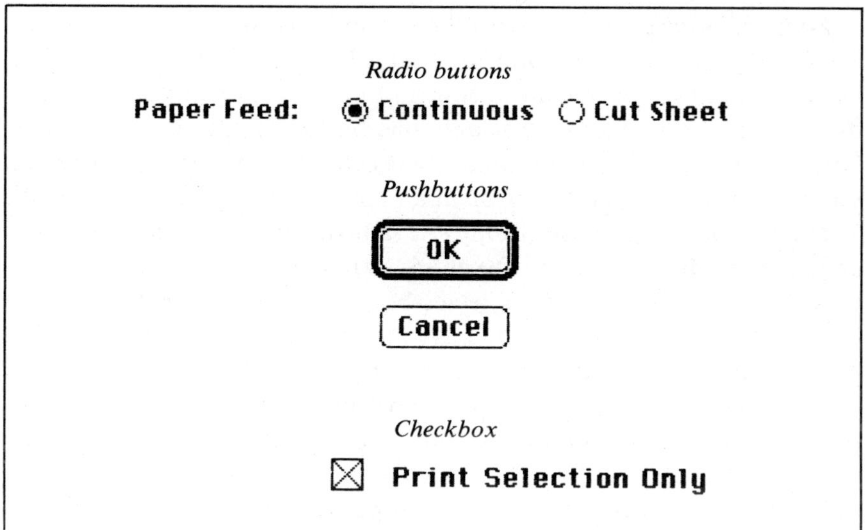

Figure 18-1
Display of common button-type controls

Obviously, if the activity being controlled is an incremental one, the first type of pushbutton is called for. (In many of these cases a dial type of control may be more appropriate.) If it is a one-shot type of activity, the second type of pushbutton is what is needed.

A *checkbox* consists of a small square followed by text. The text indicates what activity the checkbox controls. The square can be either empty, indicating that the checkbox is not selected, or it can have an "x" in it, indicating that the checkbox is selected.

A checkbox's status as either selected or not selected is changed each time the mouse is clicked on the box itself or on the text title next to the box. Both these parts are considered the control. If the box was previously checked, clicking will make it not checked; if the box was not checked, clicking will make it checked. This type of activity is referred to as a *toggle*.

Activities controlled by checkboxes typically do not start the moment the checkbox is selected. Rather, a checkbox affects the future processing of the application. An example of an activity that might be controlled by a checkbox is determining whether a screen image is to be sent to a printer, a disk file, or both.

Radio buttons consist of a small circle followed by text indicating the activity the radio button controls. Radio buttons are similar to checkboxes in that they both tend to control future processing activity. They differ from checkboxes in that only one button in any set of the radio buttons can be selected at one time. There can, of course, be more than one set of radio buttons on the screen at a time.

This attribute of permitting only one radio button of a set to be selected at one time is the basis for the rather odd name, "radio" button, applied to these controls. The name was selected because the response of a set of the buttons is similar to that of the pushbuttons on old car radios—if one button is pressed, all the other buttons are released.

The Control Manager on the Macintosh does not automatically ensure that a selection of one radio button in a set "deselects" all the others. In fact, the Macintosh Control Manager does not know which radio buttons belong to the same set. It is up to the application to do this.

By contrast, the IIGS Control Manager not only keeps track of which radio buttons belong to which set, it ensures that the selection of one radio button in the set will result in the "deselection" of all other radio buttons in the same set. While this frees up your application from the need to keep track of the radio buttons, you should be sure that you use radio buttons only when you want just one of a group of items to be selected.

An example of the use of radio buttons is determining whether output to a printer should be in draft, intermediate, or high-quality mode. Only one setting at any time is appropriate in this case.

Dials

The other major type of control is the dial. The most familiar form of this type of control is the *window scroll bar.* The dial differs from the button in that it is generally used to select from among a range of values, while the button is used to select in an either-or situation.

While the scroll bar is the only predefined form of the dial control, it is not the only type of dial available. Other dials can be defined and used by your application. Defining such custom controls is discussed at length in the Apple IIGS *Toolbox Reference Manual.* In its discussion of dials, the remainder of this chapter focuses on the scroll bar.

A scroll bar is a single control with a number of different parts, which are illustrated in Figure 18-2. Each part is given a particular number that

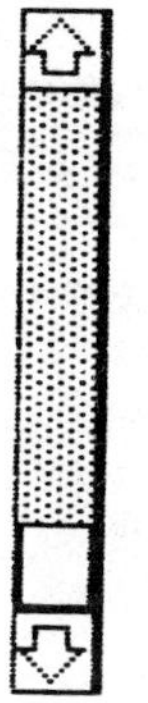

Figure 18-2
Scroll bar

is used by the Control Manager. The various other controls also have part numbers. When defining your own control, you also define parts of the control and give number values to them. A list of predefined and available part numbers is given in Table 18-1.

The IIGS uses a special method to draw the various parts of the standard controls. It defines a special character font, called the Control Manager Icon Font, which contains 17 characters used, in part, to draw the standard controls. A list of these characters is given in Table 18-2.

Each part of the scroll bar causes a different type of action to take place when it is selected. The scroll bar parts and the standard action taken when each is selected are given in Table 18-3. Note that both the arrow and page parts of the scroll bar function like a continuous-action pushbutton control—as long as it is pressed, it continues to scroll the window, a line or screen at a time.

The *thumber* part of the scroll bar is the true dial-type control part of the scroll bar. It is moved by dragging it with the mouse, much like a window is moved on the desktop. As the thumber is moved, an outline of it shows where it would be placed if the mouse button were released at that particular time. The amount of area on either side of the thumber indicates the relative position of the window in the entire data area. The size of the thumber indicates the size of the window display area relative to the entire data area.

0	No part
1	Reserved
2	Simple button
3	Check box
4	Radio button
5	Up arrow
6	Down arrow
7	Page up
8	Page down
9	Reserved
10	Grow box
11-31	Reserved
32-127	Application use (not for dial indicators)
128	Reserved
129	Thumb
130-159	Reserved
160-253	Application use (dial indicators)
254-255	Reserved

Table 18-1
Part Numbers

If you use the other control parts in the scroll bar to scroll the window display, the thumber moves up or down in the scroll bar to display continually the relative position of the window display to the entire data area. This is typical of the recommended behavior and display of dial-type controls.

ACTIVE AND INACTIVE CONTROLS

Controls, like windows, can be either active or inactive.The user can select an *active control,* which causes certain action to be taken by the application (or causes future settings to be changed). An *inactive control* cannot be selected. If the mouse is clicked on an inactive control, the Control Manager does not indicate that a control was selected.

A control, like a window, can also be either visible or hidden. A *visible control* is either shown on the screen or would be shown if it were not

No.	Part type	On/Off	Highlighted
0	Checkbox	Off	No
1	Checkbox	Off	Yes
2	Checkbox	On	No
3	Checkbox	On	Yes
4	Radio button	Off	No
5	Radio button	Off	Yes
6	Radio button	On	No
7	Radio button	On	Yes
8	RIGHT ARROW	—	No
9	RIGHT ARROW	—	Yes
10	LEFT ARROW	—	No
11	LEFT ARROW	—	Yes
12	UP ARROW	—	No
13	UP ARROW	—	Yes
14	DOWN ARROW	—	No
15	DOWN ARROW	—	Yes
16	Grow icon	—	—

Table 18-2

Control Manager Icon Font Characters

UP ARROW	Move window display one line up in data area
LEFT ARROW	Move window display one column left in data area
DOWN ARROW	Move window display one line down in data area
RIGHT ARROW	Move window display one column right in data area
PAGE UP	Move window display one screen up in data area
PAGE LEFT	Move window display one screen left in data area
PAGE DOWN	Move window display one screen down in data area
PAGE RIGHT	Move window display one screen right in data area
THUMBER	Change window display to show relative area as shown by final position of thumber

Table 18-3

Scroll Bar Parts and Action

covered up by other windows. A *hidden control,* by contrast, is not shown even when its window is the top window on the desktop.

Several methods can be used to make a control inactive. If the window (of which the control is a part) is either hidden or made inactive, the control follows along and becomes inactive. A hidden control is also inactive even if its window is not. And a control can be made inactive while still displayed by means of a command to the Control Manager.

When a button control is inactive, its title is displayed in dimmed text, as is the rounded rectangle, checkbox, or circle connected with it (see Figure 18-3). A scroll bar is shown as inactive in one of the following two ways, depending on the reason for its being inactive:

- □ If the scroll bar is inactive because the window display area is greater than or equal to the data area, the scroll bar is displayed without a thumber or page up/down/left/right area. There are still up/down/left/right arrows, although they do not function (see Figure 18-4).
- □ If the scroll bar is inactive for any other reason, it is shown merely as an empty rectangle (see Figure 18-5).

The method of displaying an inactive custom-designed control depends on how you define the control.

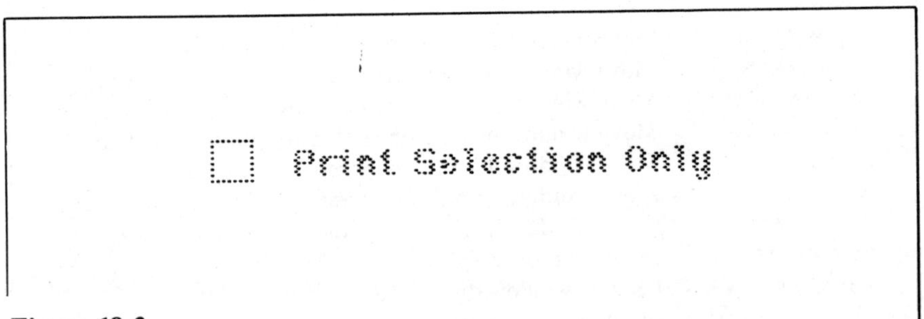

Figure 18-3
Display of dimmed button control

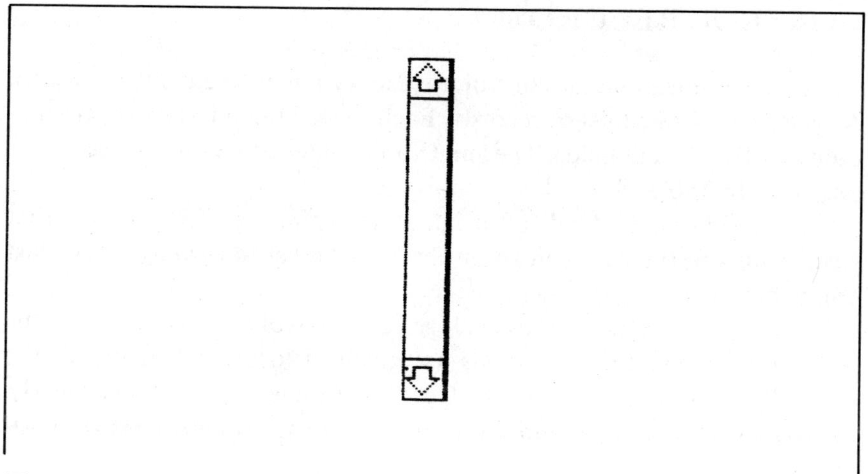

Figure 18-4
Display of inactive scroll bar

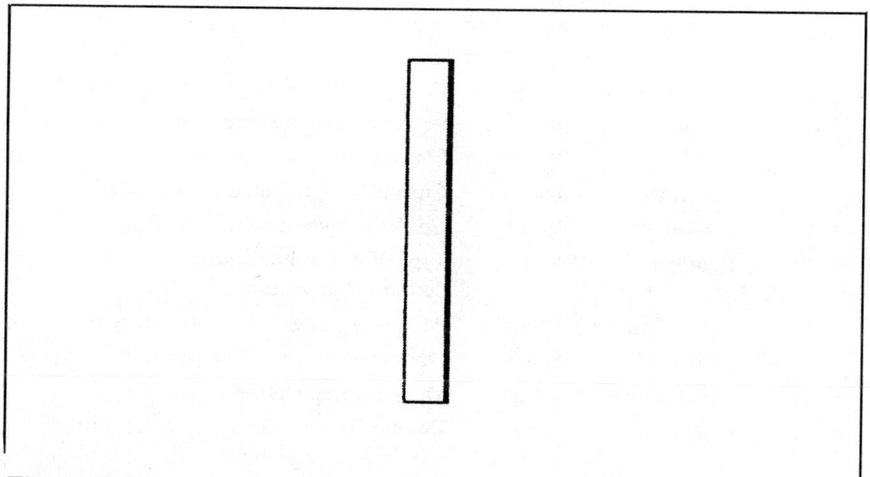

Figure 18-5
Scroll bar displayed as empty rectangle

CONTROL RECORDS

The information about the controls for each window is kept by the Control Manager in a linked list of records. Each record has a fixed portion that contains 11 different fields. The length and contents of each of these fields are given in Table 18-4.

New controls are added to the list at its beginning. CtrlNext, the first field, points to the next control in the list or is set to zero if it is the last control in the list.

CtrlRect is a rectangle that encloses the control and is used when the control is drawn. Its dimensions are given in local coordinates of the control's window. In order for the Control Manager to function properly, the top-left corner of the window's Grafport rectport must be set to local

Byte Offset	Field Name	Field Length	Field Use
0	CtrlNext	Long	Handle to next control; zero if last in list
4	CtrlOwner	Long	Pointer to window that owns control
8	CtrlRect	Rect	Rectangle that encloses control
16	CtrlFlag	Byte	Flags defining the control
17	CtrlHilite	Byte	Currently highlighted part, if any
18	CtrlValue	Word	Current value of control setting
20	CtrlProc	Long	Type of control or address of definition procedure
24	CtrlAction	Long	Address of control's action procedure
28	CtrlData	Long	Date used by definition procedure
32	CtrlRefCon	Long	Value for application use
36	CtrlColor	Long	Pointer to control's color table; zero to use default color table

Table 18-4
Format of Standard Part of Control Record

coordinates 0,0. If the coordinates are anything else, use SetOrigin to change them to 0,0 before using the Control Manager and then change them back after the routine.

CtrlFlag is a byte-length value that contains different flags based on the type of control. In all cases, if bit 7 = 1, the control is invisible; if bit 7 = 0, the control is visible. The other uses of this flag, depending on the type of control, are shown in Table 18-5.

The CtrlHilite field controls whether the control is active or inactive and, if active, what part (if any) is highlighted. If this field contains the value 0, the control is active with no highlighted parts. If the value is between 1 and 254, the part corresponding to that part of the code is highlighted. If the value is 255, the control is inactive.

CtrlValue represents the value of the control's setting. For checkboxes and radio buttons, 0 means the control is off and any other value means it is on (selected). For dials, the value represents where the start of the displayed window is in the data area. Its value thus ranges between 0 and the data size minus the window size. This value can be used by any custom-designed controls in any way appropriate to that use.

Bit Number	Used by	Meaning
0	Push button	1=bold outline (default button); 0=regular outline
0-6	Radio button	Family number (related radio buttons)
0	Scroll bar	1=up arrow present
1	Scroll bar	1=down arrow present
2	Scroll bar	1=left arrow present
3	Scroll bar	1=right arrow present
4	Scroll bar	1=vertical scroll bar; 0=horizontal scroll bar

Table 18-5
Uses of CtrlFlag

$00	Simple button
$02	Checkbox
$04	Radio button
$06	Scroll bar

Table 18-6
Meaning of High Byte of CtrlProc for Standard Controls

CtrlProc is either an indication of a standard control (if the lowest three bytes are 0) or the address of the customized control definition procedure for that control. In the case of a standard control, the highest byte indicates the type of control. The meaning of this byte of CtrlProc is shown in Table 18-6.

CtrlAction is the address of the action procedure of the control. This value, if positive, is the address of the routine to be called when the control is selected by the mouse and TrackHilite is called. If this field is zero, it is a signal to TrackHilite to do nothing when the control is selected. If the value is negative (bit 31 = 1), the definition procedure of the control is used as the action procedure.

The value in CtrlData varies depending on the type of control. For all standard buttons (pushbutton, checkbox, or radio button) the value is a pointer to the title of the button. For a standard scroll bar, the lower word of the value is the size of the window display, and the upper word is the size of the entire data area. For custom-designed controls, the value depends on your definition procedure.

CtrlRefCon is a reference value field that can be set by your application to any value, changed as appropriate, and read whenever desired.

CtrlColor is a pointer to the color table used when the definition procedure draws the control. The color table consists of up to eight colors (expressed as 16-bit values) depending on the type of control used. The record format of the color tables for the various types of controls are given in Tables 18-7 through 18-9.

In addition to the data fields just discussed, a control record can have additional data that appears after the standard fields. The standard pushbutton, checkbox, and radio button records do not have any additional data. The standard scroll bar record has two rectangle data fields following the standard data: Thumb (the rectangle enclosing the thumber) and

Color Number	Use
1	Normal outline color
2	Normal interior color
3	Interior color when selected (highlighted)
4	Normal text color
5	Text color when selected (highlighted)
6	Special highlight color
7	Thick outline color

Table 18-7

Color Table Format for Pushbutton

Color Number	Use
1	Not used
2	Normal color of checkbox/radio button
3	Highlighted color of checkbox/radio button
4	Title color

Table 18-8

Color Table Format for Checkbox/Radio Button

Color Number	Use
1	Outline color
2	Normal arrow color
3	Highlighted arrow color
4	Arrow box interior color
5	Normal thumber interior color
6	Highlighted thumber interior color
7	Page region's color (low nibble = background color)
8	Inactive color

Table 18-9

Color Table Format for Scroll Bar

PageRegion (the rectangle enclosing the page region—that rectangle in which the thumber can move). Note that although the data field is called PageRegion, it is a rectangle, not a region.

PROGRAMMING WITH THE CONTROL MANAGER

The first step in using a control is to create it. The NewControl routine provides that facility. The following code will create a set of radio buttons marked "Draft," "Middle," and "High" for use in setting the print output quality. See Figure 18-6 for an illustration of how these radio buttons will look. (Only the code for the first button is given here.)

```
         Pushlong #$00000000 ;Result space
         Pushlong #Window    ;Address of window pointer onto stack
         Pushlong #B1Rect    ;Address of control's rectangle onto stack
         Pushlong #B1Title   ;Title for button ('Draft') onto stack
         Pushword #$0000     ;Visible button, family #0
         PEA $0000           ;Radio buttons have no values here
         PEA $0000
         PEA $0000
         Pushlong #$00000400 ;Definition procedure; $04 makes it a radio button
         Pushlong #$00000000 ;No initial reference value for buttons
         Pushlong #$00000000 ;Use default color table
         _NewControl         ;Create control
         PLA                 ;Get handle to it
         STA B1Han           ;and save it
         PLA                 ;Long-word value
         STA B1Han+2
         . . .
B1Title  DC 5C'Draft'        ;Title of button
```

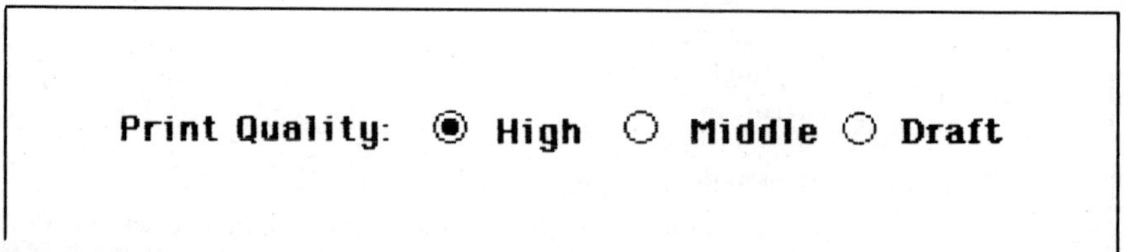

Figure 18-6
Set of radio buttons

The next step is to display the control. The Control Manager has two routines that cause the control to be shown. DrawControls is used to draw all the currently visible controls in a specified window. This does not make a currently invisible control visible, but it does draw all the controls. By contrast, ShowControl draws only the specified control. If the control was previously invisible (such as by a call to HideControl), ShowControl also makes the control visible.

To display the control you merely pass its handle to the ShowControl routine as follows:

```
PushLong B1Han          ;Button 1's handle onto stack
_ShowControl            ;and display it
```

When the Event Manager (see Chapter 20) or TaskMaster in the Window Manager (see Chapter 16) returns a mouse-down-and-up event with a value of wInContent, this indicates that the user pressed and released the mouse button while in the content area of a window. The content area includes controls associated with that window. Your application should then call FindControl to determine if the mouse button was pressed on a particular radio button. You then call HiliteControl, which results in the selection of that particular radio button and the concomitant "deselection" of the previously active one. The following code accomplishes this:

```
PEA $0000               ;Return space
PushLong #HanStore      ;Where to store control's handle
Pushword Where          ;X location from event record
Pushword Where+2        ;Y location from event record
Pushword WPtr           ;Pointer to active window
_FindControl
PLA                     ;Get part number
CMP #$0004              ;Was it a radio button?
BNE NoRadio             ;No - go elsewhere
PHA                     ;Radio button number back on stack
PushLong HanStore       ;and handle of control
_HiliteControl
```

A better way of dealing with a mouse-down event in a window content area is not to wait for the mouse-up event from the Event Manager. Instead, if the mouse is down in a control (found using FindControl), track the action of the mouse using TrackControl.

ActionProc	CtrlAction	Action taken
0	——	No additional action
Address	——	Use procedure at <address>
Negative	0	No additional action
Negative	Negative	Use control's definition procedure
Negative	Address	Use procedure at <address>

Table 18-10
Summary of Action Based on Values in ActionProc and CtrlAction

Note that if we were dealing with a dial indicator or a pushbutton that takes action as long as it was being pressed, the use of TrackControl is necessary, not just desirable. It allows your application to follow the mouse as long as the mouse is down in the control. The application can take appropriate action, using the action routine, while the button is down. The value passed to TrackControl in the actionProc parameter determines, in conjunction with the CtrlAction field of the control's record, what action will be taken. A summary appears in Table 18-10.

The Control Manager has 29 different routines, which are listed by type in Table 18-11. Following that table is a listing of each routine and the parameters it expects in Tables 18-12 through 18-17, with a separate table for each group of commands. Table 18-18 compares the IIGS Control Manager with the Macintosh Control Manager.

Initialization and Termination Routines	
CtrlBootInit	Called by system when initialized. Not called by your application.
CtrlVersion	Returns version number of the Control Manager.
CtrlReset	Called when system is reset, by system, not your application.
CtrlStatus	Returns true if the Control Manager is active and false if it is not active.
CtrlStartup	Called by your application to activate the Control Manager. If zeroPage is page aligned (address ends in $00), operation of the Control Manager will be faster.
CtrlShutDown	Called by your application to deactivate the Control Manager. Should be called only after the Window Manager has been shut down.
CtrlNewRes	Adjusts the display of control for changes in resolution after changing between 640 and 320 super-high-resolution modes.
NewControl	Creates a new control (but does not display it).
DisposeControl	Deallocates a control and releases associated memory and data structures.
KillControls	Deallocates all controls associated with a window. CloseWindow in Window Manager will do the same when deallocating a window.
Control Display	
SetCTitle	Changes the control's title, redrawing it in the process.
GetCTitle	Returns a pointer to title of control.
HideControl	Makes the control invisible.
ShowControl	Makes the control visible, drawing it in its window to the extent not obscured by other windows or objects.
DrawControls	Redraws all controls in the window in reverse order of creation.
HiliteControl	Highlights or unhighlights specified part of control. A hiliteState value of 0 unhighlights all parts of control and, if control was inactive, activates and redraws it. A hiliteState value of 255 makes control inactive.

Table 18-11

Summary of Control Manager Routines

Mouse Location	
FindControl	Returns part, if any, of control in which mouse was pressed. Should be called only if FindWindow returns a value of wInContent.
TestControl	Returns part of control in which specified point exists. Does not need to be called by your routine; use FindControl or TrackControl instead.
TrackControl	Follows mouse down movement in a control, taking care of highlighting and calling action procedure as appropriate.

Control Moving and Sizing	
MoveControl	Moves a control to a new location in local coordinates.
DragControl	Pulls dotted outline of control around screen until mouse button is released. Before exiting, calls MoveControl to move control to its new location.
SizeControl	Changes size of control by changing size of its enclosing rectangle.
SetCtlValue	Sets value of control's setting to specified value and redraws control as appropriate to show new value.
GetCtlValue	Returns value of control's current setting.
SetCtlParams	Resets values of scroll bar's extra parameters; param1 is view size and param2 is data size. Pass a -1 value for either parameter if you do not wish to change its value.
GetCtlParams	Returns values of scroll bar's parameters view size (high word of long-word) and data size (low word of long-word).

Miscellaneous Routines	
DragRect	Drags a dotted outline of specified rectangle around the screen in response to mouse movements as long as mouse button is down.
GetCtrlZPage	Called by Dialog Manager to get value of shared direct page.
SetCMgrIcons	Returns handle of current icon font before any changed value by calling this routine. If newFont is negative, no new font will be set.

Table 18-11

Summary of Control Manager Routines (continued)

Function Name	Function Number	ControlHandle	Version	boundsRect	colorTable	defProc	flag	param1	param2	ref Con	status	theControl	theWindow	title	value	yourID	zeroPage
Parameter Size		L	W	L	L	L	W	W	W	L	W	L	L	L	W	W	W
Parameter Type		H	V	P	P	P	BA	V	V	V	?	H	P	P	V	V	A
CtrlBootInit	1																
CtrlNewRes	18																
CtrlReset	5																
CtrlShutDown	3																
CtrlStartup	2															I1	I2
CtrlStatus	6										O1						
CtrlVersion	4		O1														
DisposeControl	10											I1					
KillControls	11												I1				
NewControl	9	O1		I2	I10	I8	I4	I6	I7	I9			I1	I3	I5		

Notes:

Size code

L = Long-word (32 bits)
W = Word (16 bits)

Type code

A = Address
BA = Bit array
H = Handle
P = Pointer
V = Value

Table 18-12

Initialization and Termination Routines

Function Name	Function Number	hiliteState	theControl	theWindow	title
Parameter Size		W	L	L	L
Parameter Type		V	H	P	P
DrawControls	16			I1	
GetCTitle	13		I1		O1
HideControl	14		I1		
HiliteControl	17	I1	I2		
SetCTitle	12		I2		I1
ShowControl	15		I1		

Notes:

Size code
L = Long-word (32 bits)
W = Word (16 bits)

Type code
H = Handle
P = Pointer
V = Value

Table 18-13

Control Display Routines

Function Name	Function Number	FoundCtrl	FoundPart	PartCode	actionProc	startX	startY	theControl	theWindow	xPoint	yPoint
Parameter Size		L	W	W	L	W	W	L	L	W	W
Parameter Type		P	V	V	P	V	V	H	P	V	V
FindControl	19	I1	O1						I4	I2	I3
TestControl	20			O1				I3		I1	I2
TrackControl	21			O1	I3	I1	I2	I4			

Notes:

Size code
L = Long-word (32 bits)
W = Word (16 bits)

Type code
H = Handle
P = Pointer
V = Value

Table 18-14

Mouse Location Routines

Function Name	Function Number	NewHeight	NewWidth	NewX	NewY	axis	limitRect	slopRect	startX	startY	theControl
Parameter Size		W	W	W	W	W	L	L	W	W	L
Parameter Type		V	V	V	V	V	P	P	V	V	H
DragControl	23					I5	I3	I4	I1	I2	I6
MoveControl	22			I1	I2						I3
SizeControl	24	I2	I1								I3

Notes:

Size code
L = Long-word (32 bits)
W = Word (16 bits)

Type code
H = Handle
P = Pointer
V = Value

Table 18-15
Control Moving and Sizing Routines

Function Name	Function Number	CurValue	param1	param2	params	theControl
Parameter Size		W	W	W	L	L
Parameter Type		V	V	V	V	H
GetCtlParams	28				O1	I1
GetCtlValue	26	O1				I1
SetCtlParams	27		I2	I1		I3
SetCtlValue	25	I1				I2

Notes:

Size code
L = Long-word (32 bits)
W = Word (16 bits)

Type code
H = Handle
V = Value

Table 18-16
Control Record Access Routines

Function Name	Function Number	CtrlZPage	MoveDelta	actionProc	axis	dragPattern	dragRect	limitRect	newFont	oldFont	slopRect	startX	startY
Parameter Size		W	L	L	W	L	L	L	L	L	L	W	W
Parameter Type		A	V	P	V	P	P	P	H	H	P	V	V
DragRect	29		O1	I1	I8	I2	I5	I6			I7	I3	I4
GetCtrlZPage	31	O1											
SetCMgrIcons	32								I1	O1			

Notes:

Size code
L = Long-word (32 bits)
W = Word (16 bits)

Type code
A = Address
H = Handle
P = Pointer
V = Value

Table 18-17
Miscellaneous Routines

Routine	IIGS	Macintosh
CtrlBootInit	x	
CtrlVersion	x	
CtrlReset	x	
CtrlStatus	x	
CtrlStartup	x	
CtrlShutDown	x	
CtrlNewRes	x	
NewControl	x	x
GetNewControl		x
DisposeControl	x	x
KillControls	x	x
SetCTitle	x	x
GetCTitle	x	x
HideControl	x	x
ShowControl	x	x
DrawControls	x	x
HiliteControl	x	x
FindControl	x	x
TestControl	x	x
TrackControl	x	x
MoveControl	x	x
DragControl	x	x
SizeControl	x	x
SetCtlValue	x	x
GetCtlValue	x	x
SetCtlParams	x	
GetCtlParams	x	
SetCtlMin		x
GetCtlMin		x
SetCtlMax		x
GetCtlMax		x
SetCRefCon		x
GetCRefCon		x
SetCtlAction		x
GetCtlAction		x
DragRect	x	
GetCtlZPage	x	
SetCMgrIcons	x	

Table 18-18

Comparison of IIGS and Macintosh Control Managers

CHAPTER 19

Dialogs: Refining the Choice

A *dialog* is a message placed on the Apple IIGS screen in its own window. This message gives information to, and seeks further information from, the user. A dialog window normally appears below the main (or system) menu bar. With a width somewhat shorter than full-screen width, the dialog window is typically displayed centered from left to right.

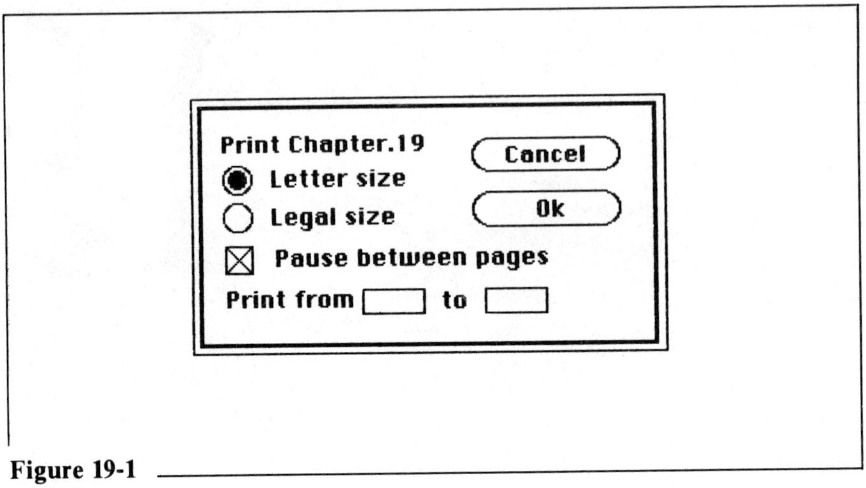

Figure 19-1
Modal dialog box

The dialog comes in two forms. A *modal dialog* puts the application into a particular operation mode. A selection must be from the modal dialog, or it must be dismissed, before the application can otherwise continue. A *modeless dialog,* by contrast, does not put the user in a mode. Either the dialog window or another window (application or system) may be used. The other functions of the application are ordinarily available when the modeless dialog is active.

A *modal dialog box* is a rectangular window with a heavier border inside a lighter border. It does not contain a title bar, a close box, a grow icon, a zoom icon, or similar controls. Such a box cannot be moved around the screen (see Figure 19-1).

A *modeless dialog box*, on the other hand, is a rectangular window with a title bar, close box, and usually a zoom box. Its border consists of a thin line. This box can be moved around the screen (see Figure 19-2).

A dialog box most often appears in response to a user initiated event. In many cases, choices from a menu require further information that is requested by a dialog box. If a menu selection requires additional information by means of a dialog, it should have three ellipsis points (. . .) as part of its displayed title.

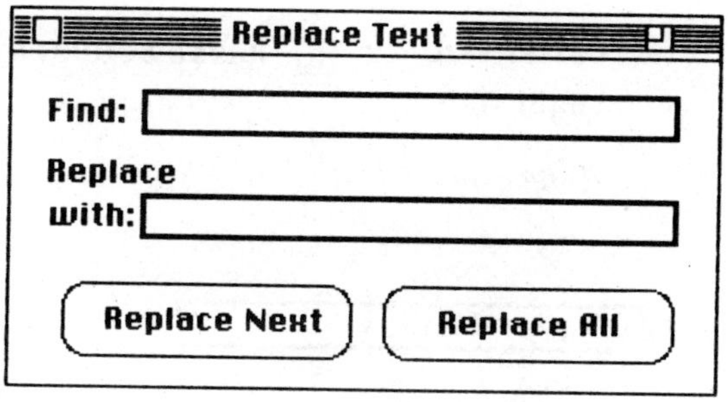

Figure 19-2
Modeless dialog box

The contents of the dialog window consist of different *items*. Many of these items are controls (discussed in Chapter 18). The items that can appear in a dialog window are listed in Table 19-1 by name, use, and numeric value, and are illustrated in Figure 19-3.

Any item can be disabled, but it is not displayed differently from an enabled item. (Compare this with the effect of making a control active or inactive, discussed in Chapter 18.) When an item is disabled, the Dialog Manager does not report events involving this item, and the item value is $8000 plus the value show in Table 19-1.

An *alert* is a specialized form of dialog with its own particular structure and commands that are part of the Dialog Manager. It should be used primarily to report erroneous action by the user, or to give warnings about the consequences of the selected action. The alert is similar in appearance and response to a modal dialog box but has several differences:

- The alert box is placed slightly below the normal placement of a dialog box.
- It normally provides the user with one or two choices, commonly known as OK and Cancel.

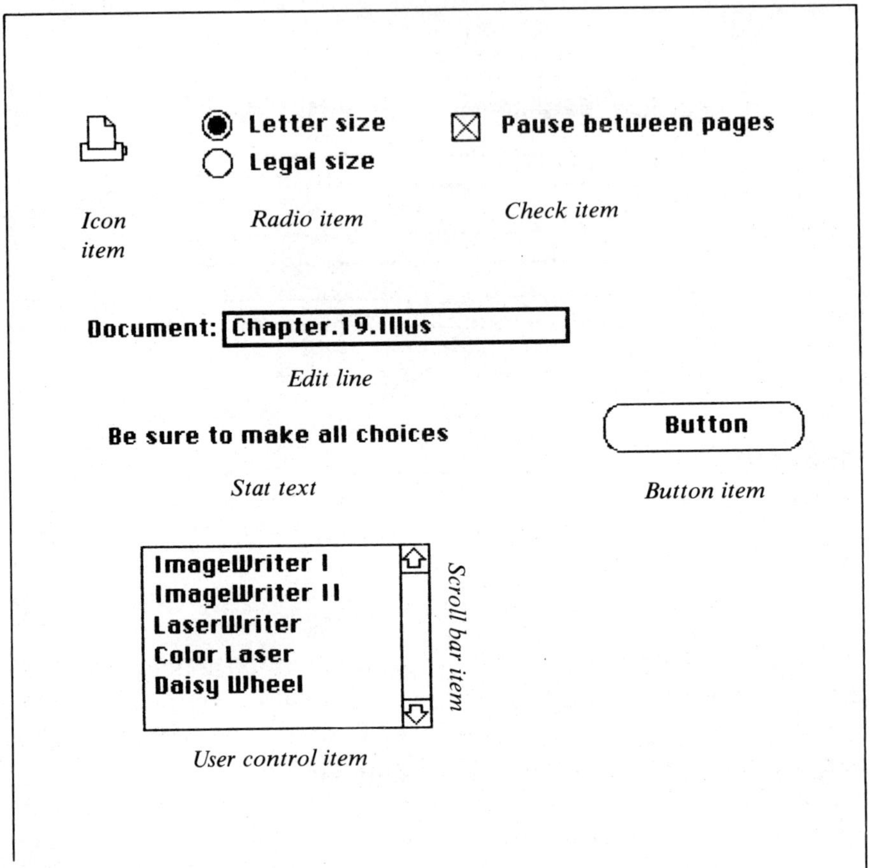

Figure 19-3
Items in dialog window

- □ The items in an alert consist of an icon showing the type of alert, static text containing the alert message, and one or two pushbuttons.
- □ The preferred, or safest, choice in an alert is the default choice, selected by pressing the RETURN key. It is outlined with a heavier, rounded rectangle.
- □ The alert can appear with a sound signal as well.

Name	Value	Use
ButtonItem	0010	Pushbutton control
CheckItem	0011	Checkbox control
RadioItem	0012	Radio button control
ScrollBarItem	0013	Special dialog-style scroll bar
UserCtlItem	0014	Custom-designed control
StatText	0015	Static (noneditable) text (up to 255 characters)
LongStatText	0016	Static (noneditable) text (up to 32,767 characters)
EditLine	0017	Editable, modifiable text (one line)
IconItem	0018	Icon (any size as long as it is a square with a pixel size that is a multiple of 8)
PicItem	0019	Quickdraw II picture
UserItem	0020	Custom-designed item

Table 19-1
Item Types

The four standard alerts are known as Stop, Note, Caution, and Talk. Associated with each is a particular icon that appears in the top-left corner of the alert box (see Figure 19-4). In addition, there is a general alert that has no icon in its top-left corner.

Other than the icon, no difference exists between the various forms of three of the alerts from an operational standpoint. Your application should differentiate between them depending on the seriousness of the situation. Informational alerts should use the Note format. Warnings about the seriousness of planned action, or the degree of danger in certain steps, can be shown from least detrimental (Note alert), through moderately detrimental (Caution alert), to potentially disastrous (Stop alert). The Talk alert is designed for use with speech synthesis.

An alert has four separate stages that correspond to the number of consecutive times the alert is called. The first time an alert is called, it

Figure 19-4
Alerts in top-left of alert box (courtesy Apple Computer, Inc.)

executes the action associated with its first stage. Subsequent consecutive calls to the alert result in second-, third-, or fourth-stage action. (Consecutive calls to an alert past the fourth time result in a fourth-stage alert.)

The stage of an alert controls the following three aspects of the alert:

- □ Whether the alert box is displayed
- □ Which sound should be emitted
- □ Which button (OK or Cancel) is the default button

Typically the first stage of an alert results in a single beep of the IIGS speaker and no display of the alert box. Subsequent stages result in display of the alert box and more beeps of the speaker. Your application may vary from this standard method, although it is recommended that you follow a consistent approach to alert stages in your application.

RECORD AND TEMPLATE STRUCTURES

Modal dialogs on the Macintosh are sometimes created from a *resource,* a specialized data structure not available on the IIGS. As a result, creating a modal dialog with the IIGS, in some cases, uses a substitute structure called a *template.* The structure of the modal dialog template on the IIGS is shown in Table 19-2.

Byte Offset	Item Name	Item Type	Item Size
0	BoundsRect	Rectangle	8 bytes
8	Visible	Word	2 bytes
10	Refcon	Long-word	4 bytes
14	Item1Ptr	Long-word	4 bytes

Note: There is a list of item pointers for each item in the dialog. Following the pointer to the last item is a terminating pointer of value $00000000.

Table 19-2
Modal Dialog Template

The BoundsRect for the dialog should be the bounds rectangle for the window displaying the dialog. (See Chapter 16 for a discussion of the bounds rectangle.) The visible word value determines if the dialog is initially visible (value does not equal $0000) or invisible (value of $0000). Refcon is a value for the use of the application. It can be used for whatever purposes best suit your program. The remainder of the template consists of a list of pointers to the item list for each item in the dialog. The end of the item list is shown by a pointer with a value of $00000000.

When a dialog is first created, the information required by it is passed either in the form of a template, discussed previously, or by parameters on the stack. The Dialog Manager makes this information into a record. The record structure is not defined and is not available to your application. Rather, different Dialog Manager routines access the various parts of this record. The only information needed to use the record structure is the pointer to the Grafport for the dialog, a value returned by the Dialog Manager when the dialog is first created.

As discussed in relation to the dialog template, the dialog needs pointers to its various items. All items are contained in an *item list* (see Table 19-3). Each item in the application should have a unique identifying number, which is used when calling that item with the Dialog Manager.

The *item type* is one of the types from Table 19-1. If the type is disabled, any events involving this item are handled by the Dialog Manager without reporting the event to your application. Disabling an item can be particularly useful for a scroll bar with a scroll routine. The Dialog Manager can handle the scrolling of the display without any need for intervention by your application. Note that a disabled item is still usable—the difference is whether your application knows about it being used. By contrast, clicking on an inactive control is similar to clicking on nothing.

Byte Offset	Item Name	Item Type	Item Size
0	ItemID	Word	2 bytes
2	ItemRectPtr	Long-word	4 bytes
6	ItemType	Word	2 bytes
8	ItemDescr	Long-word	4 bytes
12	ItemValue	Word	2 bytes
14	ItemFlag*	Word	2 bytes
16	ColorPtr*	Long-word	4 bytes

Note: Items marked with an asterisk (*) are optional parts of the item list.

Table 19-3

Item List

Item Type	Item Descriptor
ButtonItem	Pointer to title string for the pushbutton
CheckItem	Pointer to title string for the checkbox
RadioItem	Pointer to the title string for the radio button
ScrollBarItem	Pointer to dialog scroll bar action procedure
UserCtlItem	Pointer to control-definition procedure
StatText	Pointer to the static string (length byte)
LongStatText	Pointer to the beginning of the text
EditLine	Pointer to the default string
IconItem	Handle to the icon
PicItem	Handle to the picture
UserItem	Pointer to item-definition procedure

Table 19-4

Item Descriptors

The *descriptor of an item* varies depending on the type of item involved. Table 19-4 shows the purpose of the item descriptor for each type of item. Note that the descriptor is always either a pointer or a handle.

The text pointer that constitutes the descriptor of a text item points to either a Pascal-type string (that is, the first byte of the string contains the number of characters in the string) for a StatText or EditLine item, or to the first character of text for a LongStatText item. Several lines of text can be created for either a StatText or LongStatText item by placing a carriage return character (ASCII value is $0D) in the text.

The display rectangle for the item is applied somewhat differently depending on the particular type of item involved. Table 19-5 shows the application of the display rectangle for each type of item involved.

The use of the *item value* differs depending on the type of item involved. Table 19-6 indicates the use of the item value for each type of item.

The *item flag* is employed in the same manner as other control flags discussed in Chapter 18. The control flag should not be used to indicate which button is the default button, because the Dialog Manager, not the Control Manager, should handle this operation. The item flag is not a required part of the item record.

The *color table* refers to the specific color table for drawing the particular item. If the color table is not specified, or its value is 0, the default color table is used.

Item Type	Use of Display Rectangle
ButtonItem	Enclosing rectangle of pushbutton
CheckItem	Enclosing rectangle of checkbox
RadioItem	Enclosing rectangle of radio button
ScrollBarItem	Enclosing rectangle of scroll bar
UserCtlItem	Enclosing rectangle of user control
StatText	View rectangle for text
LongStatText	View rectangle for text
EditLine	View-and-frame rectangle for text
IconItem	Scale-and-clip rectangle for icon
PicItem	Scale-and-clip rectangle for icon
UserItem	Clip rectangle for drawing

Table 19-5
Use of Display Rectangle

Item Type	Use of Item Value
ButtonItem	Initial value of the pushbutton
CheckItem	Initial value of the checkbox
RadioItem	Initial value of the radio button
ScrollBarItem	Default value if action procedure = 0; otherwise 0
UserCtlItem	Initial value of the user control
StatText	As needed by the application
LongStatText	Length of text (0-32,767)
EditLine	Maximum length allowed for text (0-255)
IconItem	As needed by the application
PicItem	As needed by the application
UserItem	As needed by the application

Note: values used as needed by the application are not used by the Dialog Manager.

Table 19-6
Use of Item Value

Byte Offset	Item Name	Item Type	Item Size
0	BoundsRect	Rectangle	8 bytes
8	AlertID	Word	2 bytes
10	Stage1	Byte	1 byte
11	Stage2	Byte	1 byte
12	Stage3	Byte	1 byte
13	Stage4	Byte	1 byte
14	Item1Ptr	Long-word	4 bytes

Table 19-7
Alert Template

An alert uses an *alert template,* which is similar in structure to a dialog template. Table 19-7 identifies the structure of an alert template. The main difference between the two templates lies in the existence of the byte value known as *stage* in the alert template. This value describes the various

Bits	Use
0-1	Sound number for this state (0 to 3)
2-5	Unused
6	Default button minus 1 (0 or 1 representing button 1 or 2)
7	Draw alert flag (0-don't draw alert; 1-draw alert)

Table 19-8
Stage Byte Use

actions taken by an alert at each stage of that alert. The purpose of each bit in the stage byte value is shown in Table 19-8.

USING THE DIALOG MANAGER

The Dialog Manager relies on several other Apple IIGS managers, each of which must have been loaded into memory (if RAM-based) and initialized prior to the initialization of the Dialog Manager. The order of initializing other managers is important. Table 19-9 lists the managers that must be initialized in the proper order of initialization.

The next step is to start up the Dialog Manager by calling the Dialog-Startup routine. This routine installs the standard sound procedure for sound alerts, sets the substitutable text strings to empty strings, sets the display font for dialogs and alerts to the system font, and sets the alert stage to 1 (lowest).

The Dialog Manager does not need a direct page allocated to it because it shares the direct page used by the Control Manager. Thus the Control Manager must be present and initialized prior to the initialization of the Dialog Manager, even if you are not using controls in your dialog.

If you want to use a font other than the system font for the text displayed in dialogs and alerts, your application must change the font by calling SetDAFont. Note that this routine changes the font used in dialogs and alerts only after the routine is called. Thus, if you create a dialog, then call SetDAFont to change the font, and then create another dialog, the first dialog will use the system font and the second one will use the font specified by SetDAFont.

Memory Manager
Quickdraw II
Event Manager
Window Manager
Control Manager
LineEdit

Table 19-9
Initialization Order of Managers for Use of Dialog Manager

CREATING A MODELESS DIALOG

When your application requires a modeless dialog, it must first create the dialog by calling NewModelessDialog. The parameters that must be passed to the routine include the following:

- □ A pointer to the bounds rectangle for the dialog's window
- □ A pointer to the text of the title, if any, of the dialog
- □ A value specifying the window behind which the dialog window should appear
- □ A word-length bit array describing the frame of the dialog's window (see discussion in Chapter 16)
- □ Any long-word value that your application can use in association with the dialog
- □ A pointer to the rectangle for the zoomed size of the dialog's window

The following code creates a modeless dialog based on values previously stored in the data segment shown:

```
DialogData      DATA
MLess1Rect      DC I2'Top,Left,Bottom,Right'       ;Bounds rect of dialog
MLess1Title     DC C'Modeless Dialog #1'           ;Title of dialog
MLess1Pos       DC H'FFFFFFFF'                     ;Window in front
* CloseZoom (next line) has been defined as code for a window with both a
* close box and a zoom box.
MLess1Flag      DC I2'CloseZoom'                   ;Close and zoom boxes
MLess1Full      DC I2'FTop,FLeft,FBottom,FRight' ;Full rectangle when zoomed
                . . .
                END
```

```
MakeMLess1Diag START
               USING DialogData
               PushLong #$00000000        ;Space for returned value
               PushLong #MLess1Rect       ;Pointer to bounds rect
               PushLong #MLess1Title      ;Pointer to title of dialog
               PushLong MLess1Pos         ;Position on desktop
               Pushword MLess1Flag        ;Frame of dialog
               PushLong #$00000000        ;No reference value
               PushLong #MLess1Full1      ;Pointer to zoomed rectangle
               _NewModelessDialog         ;Create the dialog
               PLA                        ;Store pointer to the port
               STA ML1DiagPtr             ;of the dialog
               PLA                        ;It's a long word so get both
               STA ML1DiagPtr+2           ;parts of it
               . . .
               END
```

Following the call to NewModelessDialog, the top of the stack contains the pointer to the Grafport of the dialog created. Although the dialog and its Grafport (and window) now exist, there are no items in the dialog.

CREATING A MODAL DIALOG

There are two methods of creating a modal dialog. One method resembles creating a modeless dialog, except that certain values are not used. The routine NewModalDialog works in a manner similar to NewModelessDialog. This routine, though, has only three parameters passed to it on the stack: the bounds rectangle for the content window, whether the dialog is initially visible, and any associated reference value. The other items passed to the NewModelessDialog routine are not needed because they are not used in a modal dialog. The routine returns a long-word pointer to the dialog's Grafport. The dialog, like the modeless dialog created in the previous example, is empty of items.

The second method of creating a modal dialog uses a dialog template, located somewhere in memory, to pass the values to the modal dialog as well as the items in the dialog. The following code segment will create a modal dialog with two items in it. Note that the dialog template contains pointers to the item templates. The item templates are not shown in this code segment, but they are discussed later in this chapter in the section "Creating Items."

```
MdlDiag1Data   DATA
Md1DiagRect    DC I2'Top,Left,Botton,Right'   ;Bounds rect of dialog
Md1DiagVis     DC I2'0000'                    ;Dialog initially not visible
RefCon         DC I4'00000000'                ;No dialog reference value
Item1Ptr       DC I4'Item1Template'           ;Pointer to item 1 template
Item2Ptr       DC I4'Item2Template'           ;Pointer to item 2 template
Terminator     DC I4'00000000'                ;Long zero to terminate items
               . . .
```

```
                END
MakeMDDiag1     START
                USING MdDiag1Data
                PushLong #$00000000            ;Space for result
                PushLong #Md1DiagRect          ;Ptr to beginning of template
                _GetNewModalDialog             ;Create the dialog
                . . .
                END
```

Whether your application uses the first or second method of creating a modal dialog depends on whether the template has already been stored in memory. A dialog that is either reused or relatively fixed at program-creation time, and that has its items present in a template, is a good candidate for a template and thus GetNewModalDialog. A dialog that is likely to vary considerably from one running of the program to another, particularly as to items, is a better candidate for NewModalDialog and no template. Once the dialog and items are created, the method of creation is irrelevant.

CREATING ITEMS

Two routines exist for creating an item that can be used in either a modal or a modeless dialog. (Items are also used in alerts, although they are created as part of the alert template, not separately.)

NewDItem creates an item and places it in a dialog. To use NewDItem, your application must first pass the parameters describing the action, via the stack, to the routine. The following code creates an item of static text, reading "Apple IIGS Sample Item," which is made a part of the dialog created in the previous code segment:

```
Item1Data       DATA
I1Rect          DC I2'Top+2,Left+2,Top+2+Height,Left+2+Length'
* The text will start two pixels below and two pixels to the left
* of the origin of the content rectangle of the dialog
ItemType        DC I2'StatText'                  ;StatText = 15
ItemText        DC I1'TextEnd-ItemText-1         ;Length of Text
                DC C'Apple IIGS Sample Item'     ;Text content
TextEnd         ANOP
                . . .
                END
MakeItem1       START
                Using Item1Data
                PushLong ML1DiagPtr              ;Pointer to dialog
                LDA #$0001                       ;Item ID #1
```

```
PHA
Pushlong #I1Rect                ;Display rectangle
Pushword ItemType               ;Type of item
Pushlong #ItemText              ;Pointer to text of item
Pushlong #$00000000             ;No reference value
Pushword #$0000                 ;Default flag
Pushlong #$00000000             ;Default color table
_NewDItem                       ;Create the item
. . .
END
```

The alternative way of creating an item is to use GetNewDItem. This routine works much like NewDItem except that it requires only a pointer to the dialog's Grafport and a pointer to an item template. The following code segment creates the same type of item as the previous code segment but uses GetNewDItem instead of NewDItem:

```
Item1Data       DATA
Item1ID         DC I2'0001'                     ;Item ID #1
Item1Rect       DC I2'Top+2,Left+2,Top+2+Height,Left+2+Length'
* The text will start two pixels below and two pixels to the left
* of the origin of the content rectangle of the dialog
ItemType        DC I2'StatText'                 ;StatText = 15
ItemDescr       DC I4'ItemText'                 ;Pointer to text
ItemValue       DC I2'0000'                     ;No reference value
ItemFlag        DC I2'0000'                     ;Default flag
ItemColor       DC I2'0000'                     ;Default color table
ItemText        DC I1'TextEnd-ItemText-1        ;Length of Text
                DC C'Apple IIGS Sample Item'    ;Text content
TextEnd         ANOP
                . . .
                END
MakeItem1       START
                Using Item1Data
                Pushlong ML1DiagPtr             ;Pointer to dialog
                Pushlong #Item1ID               ;Beginning of item template
                _GetNewDItem                    ;Create the item
```

MANIPULATING ITEMS

Once items have been placed in a dialog, your application can still change various aspects of them. One of the most important changes you can make is the language used in static text items. For example, suppose when a user attempts to close a document, you want the program to check whether the changes made to the document should be saved. The text could read, "Save changes to document before closing?" However, in the case of an application with multiple open documents, this message would be ambiguous. And in all cases, a message giving the document name is better than merely referring to it as "document."

The Dialog Manager enables your application to set up an item of static text with one to four locations in the text where words can be substituted. To continue with the previous example, your application should create the static text item to read, "Save changes to ^0 before closing?" (Any number from 0 to 3 can appear after the caret.) When the application is ready to use the item, it substitutes the actual text for the ^0 placeholder by calling ParamText. This routine requires four long-word pointers to text to be used as a substitute. The first pointer points to the ^0 text, the second to the ^1 text, and so forth.

Several aspects of an item can be changed by the application and the current value of the aspect can be determined. The static or editable text of an item may be manipulated with GetIText and SetItext. SetlIText also allows your application to have the dialog appear with part or all of the EditText already selected.

The item type can be determined by GetItemType and it can be changed with SetItemType. The latter routine creates a significant problem if the structure of the changed item type is different from the original item type. In that case you should delete an existing item with RemoveItem and create a new one.

The display rectangle of an item may be determined with GetItemBox and changed with SetItemBox. If the rectangle is changed, the item must be redrawn before the changed display is shown. One way to handle this operation is by using HideDItem to hide the item before it is changed, change the item, and then use ShowDItem to redisplay the changed item. The following code segment accomplishes this:

```
ChangeBox      START
               . . .
               Pushlong #Dialog          ;Pointer to dialog
               Pushword ItemNum          ;Item to hide
               _HideDItem                ;Hide the item
               Pushlong #Dialog          ;Pointer to dialog
               Pushword ItemNum          ;Item to change
               Pushlong #Newbox          ;Pointer to new rectangle
               _SetItemBox               ;And change the item
               Pushlong #Dialog          ;Pointer to dialog
               Pushword ItemNum          ;Item number
               _ShowDItem                ;And redisplay it
               . . .
               END
```

In addition to making items visible and invisible with ShowDItem and HideDItem, you can enable or disable any item. DisableDItem disables the item while EnableDItem enables it. See the discussion earlier in this chapter concerning disabled items and contrasting a disabled item with a deactivated one.

The items in a dialog can be determined by using GetFirstItem, which returns the ID number of the first item in the dialog, followed by repeated calls to GetNextItem, which returns the ID number of the item in the dialog after the specified item. GetNextItem returns a value of zero when there are no more items in the dialog.

The item value setting, as shown in Table 19-6, can be determined with GetItemValue and modified with SetItemValue.

EVENTS INVOLVING DIALOGS

Events involving modal dialogs are possible once your application has created a modal dialog and made the dialog's window the front window on the desktop. A modal dialog event is handled by the ModalDialog routine. This routine first checks to see if the front window is a modal dialog window (immediately returning with a value of zero if not). ModalDialog then calls GetNextEvent in the Event Manager (see Chapter 20) to check events concerning the modal dialog.

Any mouse-down event that is outside the dialog's content region receives the response of sound 1 (a single beep by default). If the event involves an enabled item, ModalDialog handles the event and returns the ID number of the item to your application. The action of ModalDialog is somewhat similar to that of TaskMaster (discussed in Chapter 16).

Before any event is actually handled, it is filtered using either the standard filtering procedure or your custom procedure. The standard-filter procedure causes ModalDialog to return the default button (normally button 1) to be the hit item if the RETURN key is pressed, and permits use of the Apple-X, Apple-C, and Apple-V commands for cut-copy-paste editing operations inside the dialog.

A custom-filter procedure takes three input pointers: to the dialog Grafport, to the event record, and to the itemHit ID. It returns a boolean word result, which is true if the filter procedure handled the event and false if not. Before returning a true result, the filter procedure should also set itemHit to the value that should be returned by ModalDialog.

When the filter procedure returns true, ModalDialog returns control to your application. When it returns false, ModalDialog handles the event. If you want to have your filter procedure handle an event instead of having ModalDialog do so (but without returning control from ModalDialog to the application), the filter procedure should handle the event, change the What field of the event record to indicate a null event, and return to ModalDialog with a value of false.

The pointer to the custom-filter procedure, passed to ModalDialog, also indicates if the functions of the standard-filter procedure should be used in addition to the custom-filter procedure. If bit 31 (the highest bit) of the pointer is set to 1, the standard-filter procedure will be used in addition to the custom-filter procedure. This permits your application to have the use of the default-RETURN key and cut-copy-paste functions as well as a custom-filter routine without having to rewrite the standard routines.

The handling of modeless dialog events is not as automated as the handling of modal dialog events. If a modeless dialog is displayed, your application should first call GetNextEvent in the Event Manager (see Chapter 20) or TaskMaster in the Window Manager (see Chapter 16) and then pass the pointer to the event record to IsDialogEvent.

IsDialogEvent returns with a true result if the event is a modeless-dialog-related event. This category includes an activate or update event for a modeless dialog window, a mouse-down event in the Content Region of an active modeless dialog window, or other event type when a modeless dialog window is active. If IsDialogEvent returns false, your application should handle it as a nondialog-related event. If IsDialogEvent returns true, your application should pass the event to DialogSelect to handle.

DialogSelect is passed three parameters: a pointer to the event record, a pointer to a location to store the dialog pointer, and a pointer to a location to store the value of the item number hit. DialogSelect returns true if the event involved an enabled item (placing the dialog pointer and item number in the appropriate locations); otherwise, it returns false. It also handles the various events as follows:

- □ If the event is an activate or update event for the dialog window, DialogSelect activates or updates the window and then returns false.
- □ If the event is a key event in conjunction with the APPLE key, DialogSelect returns false.

- □ If the event is a mouse-down event in an EditLine item, DialogSelect displays an insertion point or selects text.
- □ If the event is a key event without the APPLE key and there is an EditLine item, text entry and editing are handled, and DialogSelect returns true if the EditLine item is enabled or false if disabled.
- □ If the event is a key event and there is no EditLine item, DialogSelect returns false.
- □ If the event is a mouse-down event in a control, DialogSelect calls TrackControl (see Chapter 18) to determine if the control is selected (in which case DialogSelect returns true) or not (in which case DialogSelect returns false).
- □ If the event is a mouse-down event in any other enabled item, DialogSelect returns true.
- □ If the event is a mouse-down event in a disabled item or no item, DialogSelect returns false.
- □ If the event is any other event, DialogSelect returns false.

DrawDialog is used in cases where there is a dialog box displayed for information, without requiring or permitting the user to do anything with the dialog. An example would be a dialog telling the user that the particular operation currently being performed will take some time. Other cases involving the drawing of a dialog box are handled by DialogSelect and ModalDialog.

HANDLING ALERTS

The four routines involving alerts are functionally similar. Alert, which is the generic routine, has an alert with no special icon in the upper-left corner. StopAlert is the same routine except that it uses a Stop icon. Likewise, NoteAlert and CautionAlert are the same routines as Alert, but use, respectively, a Note icon and a Caution icon.

The Alert routine requires two pointers as input parameters. The first is a pointer to the alert template, discussed in Table 19-7. The second is a pointer to the filter procedure identical to that used by ModalDialog.

Alert calls the current sound procedure for the particular stage of the alert and, if appropriate, draws the alert box for this state. If no box is to be drawn, the routine returns a result of -1 ($FFFF).

If the alert box is drawn, Alert retrieves and handles events in the alert window until an enabled item is clicked, at which time it returns with the ID number of the item clicked. Before returning control to your application, Alert removes the alert box from the screen.

The current stage of the alert is maintained by the Dialog Manager and it can be obtained by calling GetAlertStage. When your application changes the alert being used, it should also reset the alert stage to the first stage using ResetAlertStage.

Function Name	Function Number	AlertStage	AlertTemplate	dBehind	dBoundsRect	DefButID	dFlag	dFullSize	dRefCon	dTemplate	dTitle	dVersion	dVisible	EndSel	FilterProc	FirstItem	FontHandle	Itembox
Parameter Size		W	L	L	L	W	W	L	L	L	L	W	W	W	L	W	L	L
Parameter Type		V	P	P	P	V	BA	P	V	P	P	V	B	V	P	V	H	P
Alert	23		I1												I2			
CautionAlert	26		I1												I2			
CloseDialog	12																	
DefaultFilter	54																	
DialogBootInit	1																	
DialogReset	5																	
DialogSelect	17																	
DialogShutDown	3																	
DialogStartup	2																	
DialogStatus	6																	
DialogVersion	4											O1						
DisableDItem	57																	
DlgCopy	19																	
DlgCut	18																	
DlgDelete	21																	
DlgPaste	20																	
DrawDialog	22																	
EnableDItem	58																	

Table 19-10

Dialog Manager Routines Summary

OTHER PROCEDURES

The Dialog Manager also contains other routines not discussed in this chapter. However, most of these routines are not as commonly used as the ones discussed here. Table 19-10 is a list of all Dialog Manager routines with a list of the input and output parameters expected by each. Table 19-11 compares the Dialog Manager routines on the Apple IIGS with those in the Dialog Manager on the Macintosh.

ItemColor	ItemDescr	ItemFlag	ItemHit	ItemID	ItemRect	ItemTemplate	ItemType	ItemValue	nextItem	Param0	Param1	Param2	Param3	ProgramID	result	SoundProc	StartSel	Status	the Control	theDialog	theEvent	thePoint	theString	UpdateRgn
L	L	W	WL	W	L	L	W	W	W	L	L	L	L	W	W	L	W	W	L	L	L	L	L	L
P	M	V	VP	V	P	P	V	M	V	P	P	P	P	V	B	P	V	B	H	P	P	Pt	P	H
			O1																					
			O1																					
																				O1				
			I3												O1					I1	I2			
			I3												O1					I2	I1			
														I1										
																	O1							
				I2																I1				
																				I1				
																				I1				
																				I1				
																				I1				
																				I1				
			I2																	I1				

Function Name	Function Number	AlertStage	AlertTemplate	dBehind	dBoundsRect	DefButID	dFlag	dFullSize	dRefCon	dTemplate	dTitle	dVersion	dVisible	EndSel	FilterProc	FirstItem	FontHandle	Itembox
ErrorSound	7																	
FindDItem	36																	
GetAlertStage	52	O1																
GetControlItem	30																	
GetDefButton	55					O1												
GetFirstItem	42															O1		
GetItemBox	40																	I3
GetItemType	38																	
GetItemValue	46																	
GetIText	31																	
GetNewDItem	51																	
GetNewModalDialog	50									I1								
GetNextItem	43																	
HideDItem	34																	
IsDialogEvent	16																	
ModalDialog	15														I1			
NewDItem	13																	
NewModalDialog	10				I1				I3				I2					
NewModelessDialog	11			I3	I1		I4	I6	I5		I2							
NoteAlert	25		I1												I2			
ParamText	27																	
RemoveItem	14																	
ResetAlertStage	53																	
SelIText	33													I4				
SetDAFont	8																I1	
SetDefButton	56					I1												
SetItemBox	41																	I3
SetItemType	39																	
SetItemValue	47																	
SetIText	32																	

Table 19-10

Dialog Manager Routines Summary (continued)

ItemColor	ItemDescr	ItemFlag	ItemHit	ItemID	ItemRect	ItemTemplate	ItemType	ItemValue	nextItem	Param0	Param1	Param2	Param3	ProgramID	result	SoundProc	StartSel	Status	the Control	theDialog	theEvent	thePoint	theString	UpdateRgn
																I1								
				I2																I1				
				I2															O1	I1				
																				I1				
																				I1				
				I2																I1				
				I2			O1													I1				
				I2				O1												I1				
				I2											O1					I1			I3	
						I2														I1				
																				O1				
				I2					O1											I1				
				I2																I1				
															O1						I1			
			O1																					
I8	I5	I7		I2	I3		I4	I6												I1				
																				O1				
																				O1				
			O1																					
										I1	I2	I3	I4											
				I2																I1				
				I2													I3			I1				
																				I1				
				I2																I1				
				I3			I1													I2				
				I3				I1												I2				
				I2																I1			I3	

Function Name	Function Number	AlertStage	AlertTemplate	dBehind	dBoundsRect	DefButID	dFlag	dFullSize	dRefCon	dTemplate	dTitle	dVersion	dVisible	EndSel	FilterProc	FirstItem	FontHandle	Itembox
ShowDItem	35																	
StopAlert	24	I1													I2			
UpdateDialog	37																	

Notes:

Size: L Long-word (32 bits)
W Word (16 bits)

Type: B Boolean
BA Bit array
H Handle
M Miscellaneous (varies)
P Pointer
P Pointer
V Value
itemHit is a long-word pointer only in DialogSelect

Table 19-10

Dialog Manager Routines Summary (continued)

ItemColor	ItemDescr	ItemFlag	ItemHit	ItemID	ItemRect	ItemTemplate	ItemType	ItemValue	nextItem	Param0	Param1	Param2	Param3	ProgramID	result	SoundProc	StartSel	Status	the Control	theDialog	theEvent	thePoint	theString	UpdateRgn
				I2																I1				
			O1																					
																				I1				I2

Routine Name	Apple IIGS	Macintosh
Alert	X	X
CautionAlert	X	X
CloseDialog	X	X
CouldAlert		X
CouldDialog		X
DefaultFilter	X	
DialogBootInit	X	
DialogReset	X	
DialogSelect	X	X
DialogShutDown	X	
DialogStartup	X	
DialogStatus	X	
DialogVersion	X	

Table 19-11

Comparison of Apple IIGS Dialog Manager with Macintosh Dialog Manager

Routine Name	Apple IIGS	Macintosh
DisableDItem	X	
DisposeDialog		X
DlgCopy	X	X
DlgCut	X	X
DlgDelete	X	X
DlgPaste	X	X
DrawDialog	X	X
EnableDItem	X	
ErrorSound	X	X
FindDItem	X	
FreeAlert		X
FreeDialog		X
GetAlertStage	X	X
GetControlItem	X	
GetDefButton	X	
GetDItem		X
GetFirstItem	X	
GetItemBox	X	
GetItemType	X	
GetItemValue	X	
GetIText	X	X
GetNewDialog		X
GetNewDItem	X	
GetNewModalDialog	X	
GetNextItem	X	
HideDItem	X	
InitDialogs		X
IsDialogEvent	X	X
ModalDialog	X	X
NewDialog		X
NewDItem	X	
NewModalDialog	X	
NewModelessDialog	X	
NoteAlert	X	X
ParamText	X	X
RemoveItem	X	

Table 19-11

Comparison of Apple IIGS Dialog Manager with Macintosh Dialog Manager (continued)

Routine Name	Apple IIGS	Macintosh
ResetAlertStage	X	X
SellText	X	X
SetDAFont	X	X
SetDefButton	X	
SetDItem		X
SetItemBox	X	
SetItemType	X	
SetItemValue	X	
SetIText	X	X
ShowDItem	X	
StopAlert	X	X
UpdateDialog	X	

Table 19-11

Comparison of Apple IIGS Dialog Manager with Macintosh Dialog Manager (continued)

CHAPTER 20

Events

An *event* is an occurrence during a computer program— a signal from the user, the operating system, or the computer— that may require some action by the application. As discussed in Chapter 2, IIGS programs are event driven (that is, an application, after initialization, waits for an event to occur and then responds to that event). It continues to wait for another event and responds to that event until an event occurs that causes it to exit.

Events can come from a wide variety of sources, including the keyboard, mouse, peripherals, and other managers. The purpose of the Event Manager is to collect these events, organize them by importance and time of occurrence, and pass them onto the application one at a time as requested.

TYPES OF EVENTS AND RESPONSES TO EACH

The Event Manager classifies events into 14 categories.These are listed in Table 20-1 together with the code assigned to each and the potential or typical response your application may make to that type of event.

The various event types can be grouped into the following four categories:

□ *Mouse events* refer not so much to the movement of the mouse itself, but to activity concerning the button on the mouse. Of course, the location of the mouse is noted as part of the report of each event.

Mouse events should more properly be called *button events* because they refer to events that take place in response to movement of the mouse button, and because they can also refer to action taken to a button on a pointing device used alternatively to the mouse. (Alternative pointing devices are discussed later in this chapter.)

There are two types of mouse events. A *mouse-down event* results from the user pressing down the button on the mouse or alternative pointing device. A *mouse-up event* results from the user releasing the button. Though the IIGS mouse has but one button, the Event Manager can differentiate mouse-up and mouse-down events involving two buttons. Alternative pointing devices can have either one or two buttons.

□ *Keyboard events*, not surprisingly, refer to events that result from the user pressing a key on the IIGS keyboard or keypad. Pressing most keys results in a keyboard event. A few keys do not generate their own keyboard events but, rather, affect one of the modifier flags in the Event Record. (A discussion of the modifier flags appears later in this chapter.) The keys that do not generate their own keyboard events are listed in Table 20-2.

Event Code	Event Type	Typical Response
0	Null	
1	Mouse down	Determine location and respond accordingly
2	Mouse up	Determine time between mouse up and mouse down to detect double-click
3	Key down	Check modifiers for possible menu selection; else respond according to location of mouse
4	Undefined	
5	Auto-key	Basically respond as to key-down event
6	Update	Update contents of application window
7	Undefined	
8	Activate	Window probably already highlighted; show or hide scroll bar; highlight or unhighlight a selection
9	Switch	Call Switcher to change to next application
10	Desk accessory	Handled by Desk Manager
11	Device driver	Service device driver as needed
12	Application 1	Handle as appropriate to application
13	Application 2	Handle as appropriate to application
14	Application 3	Handle as appropriate to application
15	Application 4	Handle as appropriate to application

Table 20-1

Types of Events, Event Code, and Typical Response

Keys
CONTROL
OPTION
APPLE (COMMAND)
CAPS LOCK
SHIFT

Table 20-2

Keys Not Generating Keyboard Events

The initial pressing of a key results in a *key-down event*. If a key is pressed down and held long enough, it can result in an *auto-key event,* a fancy name for a repeating key. On the IIGS all keys that can generate a key-down event can cause an auto-key event if the key is continuously held down.

As discussed in Chapter 3, the time a key must be held down before it begins to repeat (repeat delay) and the rate at which it repeats (repeat speed) are both set by the Control Panel Options screen. The only distinction the Event Manager makes between a key-down and an auto-key event is simply the different code for the two types of events. Otherwise they return the exact type of information.

□ *Window events* refer to events generated by the Window Manager (discussed in Chapter 16) that signal your application to take some action to control properly the displays in windows on the screen. The first type of window event is called an *activate event,* although it is generated both when a window becomes active and when a window becomes inactive. Normally activate events come in two's — one window becomes active while another becomes inactive.

The second type of window event is an *update event,* generated by the Window Manager whenever it determines that the contents of a window need to be drawn (or redrawn) on the screen. Update events generally occur because a window has been uncovered, opened, activated, sized, or scrolled.

□ Other events are generated from a variety of different situations. The firmware on a device driver can be programmed to generate an event under certain circumstances. A situation involving a device driver that requires immediate attention will generate an interrupt request for servicing. A less-immediate situation, including passing noncritical information from a device driver to an application, may result in an event being posted. This permits the application or the user running the application to decide when or whether to respond to the device driver. (A noninterrupting device will use events to pass all information.)

The Control Manager (discussed in Chapter 18) generates a *switch event* when a button-down event occurs on the switch control. This is a signal that the present application should halt processing and transfer control to the next application. The application should call the Switcher, which saves the current state of the application before passing control to the next application.

A *desk accessory event* is generated when the desk accessory call is given (by pressing CONTROL-APPLE-ESCAPE). This action presents the menu, allowing the user to select from the active classic desk accessories. The event is automatically handled by the Desk Manager (see discussion in Chapter 24).

The four application events are defined as desired by you in creating an application. They can be used for any purpose. It is up to your application to post these events in the event queue (using PostEvent) and to respond to these events when they are returned by the Event Manager.

The final type of event is the *null event*. This event is not truly an event but rather a report by the Event Manager that it has no event in its queue. However, it is treated as an event by the Event Manager and even has an event record associated with it.

EVENT MANAGER RECORD STRUCTURE

The information about each event is maintained by the Event Manager in a data structure known as an event record. The structure of the event record is shown in Table 20-3.

Byte Number	Field Name	Field Type	Field Use
0	What	Integer	Contains event code showing type of event
2	Message	Long integer	Variable data depending on event type; see Table 20-4
6	When	Long integer	Number of ticks (1/60 second) since system was last started
10	Where	Point	Location of mouse (global coordinates) at time of event
14	Modifiers	Integer	Collection of flags; see Table 20-5

Table 20-3
Event Record Structure

The first field in the record is known as the *what field* because it tells what event occurred. It is a word length (16-bit) value between 0 and 15. Thus only the lower nibble of the lower byte is significant. Several of the codes between 0 and 15 are undefined and reserved for future expansion.

The second field in the event record is the *message field*. This is a multipurpose field whose exact use depends on the type of event being reported (see Table 20-4). In three types of events (switch, desk accessory, and null) this field is not used. In two others (device driver and application) the use of this field is defined by and interpreted by the program resulting in the posting of the event.

In the case of window events, the message field contains a long-word pointer (with the highest byte set to zero) to the Grafport of the particular window involved in the event. In the case of a mouse event, the lowest bit in the long-word is the only significant one. It contains a 0 if button 0 (or the only mouse button) is involved, and contains a 1 if button 1 (in the case of an alternative pointing device) is being pressed or released.

The ASCII code for the particular key being pressed in a keyboard event is placed in the lowest byte of the message field. This code is in

Event	Type	Contents of Message Field
0	Null	Undefined
1	Mouse down	Button number (0 or 1) in lower word
2	Mouse up	Button number (0 or 1) in lower word
3	Key down	Positive ASCII code of key pressed in lowest byte
5	Auto key	Positive ASCII code of key pressed in lowest byte
6	Update	Pointer to window needed updating
8	Activate	Pointer to window activate/deactivated
9	Switch	Undefined
10	Desk acc.	Undefined
11	Device	Defined by device driver
12	Applic.	Defined by application
13	Applic.	Defined by application
14	Applic.	Defined by application
15	Applic.	Defined by application

Table 20-4

Contents of Event Record Message Field Based on Type of Event

positive ASCII (that is, the high bit of the byte is set to zero). Note that the ASCII code may be affected by a modifier key. Thus the letter c, when pressed by itself, results in an ASCII code of $63. If pressed in combination with either the SHIFT key or the CAPS LOCK key, it results in an ASCII code of $43. This effect on the ASCII code is in addition to the proper setting of the modifier flags (discussed next). However, the use of the modifier flags permit different treatment of an uppercase letter key depending on whether it was generated in combination with the SHIFT key or the CAPS LOCK key. The following code makes this determination:

```
EventRec        Data
What            DS 2                ;Event code - word
Message         DS 4                ;Event message - long word
When            DS 4                ;Ticks since startup - long word
Where           DS 4                ;Mouse location - global coordinates
Modifiers       DS 2                ;Modifier flags - word
                END
                . . .
WhichMod        START
                Using EventRec
Capslock        EQU 1024            ;Bit 10 in flags
Shiftkey        EQU 512             ;Bit 9 in flags
Lowercase       EQU 'a'             ;First lowercase letter
                . . .
                LDA Message         ;Get ASCII code for key pressed
                AND #$00FF          ;Clear upper byte
                CMP Lowercase       ;An uppercase letter?
                BGE NotUpper        ;No - continue
                LDA Modifiers       ;Get flags
                AND #Capslock       ;Is CAPSLOCK pressed?
                BNE ByCapslock      ;Yes - process accordingly
                LDA Modifiers       ;Get flags
                AND #Shiftkey       ;Is SHIFT key pressed?
                BNE ByShiftKey      ;Yes - process accordingly
                . . .
```

When the IIGS is first started up, it begins counting ticks, each of which is approximately 1/60 of a second. The current number of ticks is maintained and updated by the IIGS as part of the system clock. This clock is initialized to zero each time the IIGS is started.

Do not confuse this clock with the battery backed-up clock and calendar in the IIGS that maintains the actual time of day and date. The two clocks function independently of each other. Ticks are measured by the system clock, not the time-of-day clock.

The time each event occurred is maintained as the *when field* of each event record. This time is always given in ticks since the system was started and is thus based on the system clock. The following routine will determine the length of time between when a particular event occurred and when it was reported out of the queue by the Event Manager.

```
TTimeGap        Start
                Using EventRec
                PushLong #$00000000 ;Long word for result
                _TickCount
                PLA                 ;Low word of system time
                SEC
                SBC When            ;Low word of event time
                STA Different
                PLA                 ;High word of system time
                SBC When+2          ;High word of event time
                STA Diff+2
*Diff now holds long-word value of number of ticks difference between
*time event occurred and present time when processed.
```

When the mouse is moved, it does not generate a mouse event. Instead the Quickdraw II cursor-handling routines continually update the location of the cursor on the screen to coordinate with movements of the

Bit Number	Name	Meaning
0	ActiveFlag	1=window being activated; 0=window being deactivated
1	ChangeFlag	1=active window changing from application window to system window or vice versa; 0= active window not changing type
2-5	Reserved	
6	Btn1State	1=button 1 of mouse/alternative device is up; 0=button 1 of mouse/alternative device is down
7	Btn0State	1=button 0 of mouse/alternative device is up; 0=button 0 of mouse/alternative device is down
8	AppleKey	1=APPLE key is down; 0=APPLE key is up
9	ShiftKey	1=SHIFT key is down; 0=SHIFT key is up
10	CapsLock	1=CAPS LOCK key is down; 0=CAPS LOCK key is up
11	OptionKey	1=OPTION key is down; 0=OPTION key is up
12	ControlKey	1=CONTROL key is down; 0=CONTROL key is up
13	KeyPad	1=key pressed on keypad; 0=key pressed on keyboard
14-15	Reserved	

Table 20-5
Modifier Flags

mouse. Nonetheless, the position of the mouse cursor is often quite important when dealing with events. Thus a part of every event record is the *where field,* which gives the location of the mouse cursor when the particular event occurred. The location is in the form of a point given in global coordinates.

The where field of the event record can be quite useful in determining where the action reported in a key record should take place.

The final part of the event record is the *modifiers field.* This is a word-length (16-bit) collection of bit flags that indicates the state of certain keys and buttons when an event occurred. It also indicates further information about the type of event in the case of a window event. The meaning and location of each of the flags are given in Table 20-5.

Special care should be taken in determining whether one of the modifier keys (CONTROL, OPTION, CAPS LOCK, SHIFT, and APPLE) is down and whether one of the buttons (0 or 1) is down. The modifier flags for the buttons are set to 0 to show the button is down (pressed) and are set to 1 to show the button is up (released). The modifier flags for the modified keys are just the opposite. They are set to 1 to show the key is down (pressed) and to 0 to show the key is up (released). This arrangement is contrary to how the same information is treated in the Macintosh world.

MOUSE EVENTS AND ALTERNATIVE POINTING DEVICES

On the IIGS, one of the main methods of informing the application of the user's desire is through use of the mouse. As discussed previously, the position of the mouse is always kept as part of every event record so the application can determine where the mouse was when the particular event occurred. (Although this discussion is in relation to the "mouse position," the term actually refers to the location on the screen, in global coordinates, of the cursor, whose movement is controlled by the mouse.)

In most applications, moving the mouse is not enough to make a choice. The button on the mouse must also be pressed. When the button is pressed down, the Event Manager interprets the action as a button-down event and makes an appropriate event record. When the button is released, the Event Manager interprets it as a button-up event and places an appropriate record in the queue.

The Event Manager's treatment of the keyboard and keypad keys is different from its treatment of the mouse button. Only key-down events are reported. The releasing of a key is not considered an event on the IIGS. (This is different from Macintosh Event Manager, which treats a key-up event as a reportable event.)

One of the reasons the IIGS Event Manager reports button-up events is to aid in determining if the mouse button has been double-clicked. Double-clicking on an icon or file name is often permitted as an alternative to clicking on that item and then selecting the open command. And double-clicking on a word in a word processing document is an alternative to selecting the entire word.

The Event Manager does not detect and report double-clicks. It is up to your application to do so (as it is up to your application whether to make special use of double-clicks). The Event Manager does, however, provide some routines that aid in determining whether a double-click has occurred.

The GetDblTime function is the recommended maximum number of ticks that should be permitted to occur between a mouse-up event and a mouse-down event in order for the two clicks to be considered a double-click. This value is set and modified by means of the Control Panel (see Chapter 3). Your application should also check to see that the difference in location between the mouse-up and mouse-down events be sufficiently close. What is sufficiently close depends on the particular application and the desire to trap unintentional double-clicks while the mouse is being moved rapidly. The desirability of trapping spurious double-clicks is, in part, dependent on the difficulty of undoing the action initiated by the double-click.

The following code determines whether a double-click has occurred and, if so, whether the two events occurred within ten screen pixels of each other. If so, the two events are treated as a double-click.

```
DblClick        Start
                Using EventRec
BDownMask       EQU $0002               ;Gets only button-down events
BUpMask         EQU $0004               ;Gets only button-up events
                PEA $0000               ;Result space
                Pushword #BUpMask       ;Set mask for only button-up
                Pushlong #What          ;Event record address
                _GetNextEvent
                PLA                     ;Get result
                CMP #False              ;Any button-up event?
                BEQ NoEvent             ;No - skip rest
                MoveLong When,SWhen     ;Save when mouse up occurred
                MoveLong Where,SWhere   ;Save where mouse up occurred
                PEA $0000               ;Result space
                Pushword #BDownMask     ;Set mask for only button-down
                Pushlong #What          ;Event record address
                _GetNextEvent
```

```
               PLA                     ;Get result
               CMP #False              ;Any button-down event?
               BEQ NoEvent             ;No - skip rest
               PEA $0000               ;Result space
               PEA $0000               ;long-word length
               _GetDblTime             ;Ticks for double-click
               PLA                     ;Get result
               STA SDTime              ;and save it
               PLA                     ;Long-word value
               STA SDTime+2
*Compare if two events within recommended number of ticks for a
*double-click
               LDA When
               SEC
               SBC SWhen
               STA SWhen
               LDA When+2
               SBC SWhen+2
               STA SWhen+2
*SWhen now holds difference in ticks between the two events
               CMP SDTIme+2            ;Compare two higher words
               BLT DClick1             ;May still be a double-click
               BEQ CheckLower          ;If higher words equal, check lower words
               BRA NoDbl               ;Else not a double-click
CheckLower     LDA SWhen
               CMP SDTime
               BLT DClick1             ;May still be a double-click
               BEQ DClick1             ;Even if equal
               BRA NoDbl
DClick1        LDA Where               ;Compare X locations
               SEC
               SBC SWhere
               BPL NoComp1             ;Adjust if negative
               EOR #$FFFF              ;by doing two's complement
               INC A
NoComp1        CMP #11                 ;Within 10 pixels?
               BGE NoDbl               ;No - not a double-click
               LDA Where+2             ;Compare Y locations
               SEC
               SBC SWhere+2
               BPL NoComp2             ;Adjust if negative
               EOR #$FFFF              ;by doing two's complement
               INC A
NoComp2        CMP #11                 ;Within 10 pixels?
               BGE NoDbl               ;No - not a double-click
*It's a double-click
```

One of the costs of having the Event Manager report mouse-up events (and thus have the capability to detect double-clicks) is the need to process many mouse-up events to determine if it is part of a double-click. In many cases the mouse-up event will just be the result of the selection process made by pressing and releasing the mouse button. Your application will not necessarily need to process every mouse-up event. If double-clicking is not permitted as part of a certain selection process, your application can safely ignore the mouse-up event that follows a mouse-down event that makes a selection.

Several other Event Manager routines report on the state of the mouse button.

The Button function reports if the mouse button is currently down. It does not note if the button has been released since it was originally detected down.

StillDown checks the event queue to see if there are any mouse events in the queue. It is usually called after a mouse-down event, and it returns true if there are no mouse events pending. Note that this is a true indication of whether the mouse button remains down. If it were released and pressed down again, there would be two mouse events in the queue—a mouse-down and a mouse-up event.

The final mouse routine is WaitMouseUp. It differs from StillDown in only one respect. When the mouse button has been released, resulting in a mouse-up event, WaitMouseUp and StillDown both return a False result. WaitMouseUp removes the mouse-up event from the event queue, while StillDown leaves it in the queue.

The IIGS supports the use of pointing devices other than the AppleMouse. Each device should transmit data showing an X-Y location in response to some action taken with the device and should also have at least one button that may be pressed in simulation of the mouse button. The IIGS supports the use of two buttons if your device has two buttons and is capable of differentiating between them. Examples of alternative pointing devices include a graphics tablet, a trackball, a light pen, and a joystick.

When an alternative pointing device has been properly installed with a correct driver program, its use is transparent to your application. Indeed the IIGS may have several pointing devices active at the same time. In this case the device currently moving or changing state is the one whose location is reported to the Event Manager. If no device is currently moving or changing state, the location of the device that last moved or changed state is used.

Devices may be physically connected to the IIGS through a separate interface card in an expansion slot, through either of the two serial ports, or through the Apple Desktop Bus (see Chapter 15). The device driver itself is installed in memory as part of a startup program. The startup program should take the following steps:

- □ Determine the slot number (if a card device), port number (if a serial port device), or the address number (if an Apple Desktop Bus device) and store that number in the device driver header described in the next few steps.

- Initialize the device (if a separate card or a serial device).
- Take the following action depending on the type of device. If it is an Apple Desktop Bus device, install the device in the firmware SRQ list completion vector and enable SRQ for that device (see discussion in Chapter 15). If it is a serial device, install the device in the serial firmware's completion vector and turn on buffering for that port. If it is a separate card device that does not interrupt, install the driver into the heartbeat queue (see Chapter 25). If it is a separate card device that does interrupt, install the driver into the IRQ_Other interrupt vector (see Chapter 25).
- Place the device driver itself in memory as part of the installation process described in the previous step.

The device driver itself consists of a program with a 6-byte header. (In the case of a driver installed in the heartbeat queue, the device driver header is preceded by the Heartbeat Task header discussed in Chapter 25.) This header takes the following form:

```
BRA  Realstart
DC   2H '$FF Deviceinfo'        ;Device-specific information
DC   2H '$8989'                 ;Device driver signature
```

Deviceinfo is an 8-bit value that describes the device. Information includes whether the device is a *relative* or *absolute device* (that is, whether the movement values returned by the device refer to actual global screen coordinates or whether they refer to movement relative to the previous location). Other information describes how the device communicates with the IIGS. The meaning of each bit of this value is given in Table 20-6.

The third byte of the header (initially set to $FF by the assembler) should be modified by the installation program as follows:

- If the device is a card device, replace with the slot number (1-7) in which the card is located as determined by the startup program.
- If the device is a serial device, replace with the port number (1-2) to which the device is connected as determined by the startup program.
- If the device is an Apple Desktop Bus device, replace with the address number assigned to the device by the Apple Desktop Bus firmware.

Bit Number	Meaning
0	1=device has own card and does not generate interrupts
1	1=device has own card and does generate interrupts
2	1=device communicates through a serial port
3	1=device communicates through Apple Desktop Bus
4-5	Reserved
6	1=device is a relative device
7	1=device is an absolute device

Table 20-6
Device Information Byte for Alternative Pointing Device Driver

The device driver itself should perform the following steps:

1. Entry to the drive must be in native 8-bit mode.
2. Switch to 16-bit mode to use the Miscellaneous Tool Set to get the address of the relative or absolute clamp values. This address should be saved so this call is not needed after the first use of the device driver.
3. If the driver is a Heartbeat task, reset task counter.
4. Take one of the following steps, depending on the type of device:
   - □ If the device is a card device, obtain its current location and button state(s). (The code for this depends on the device's characteristics.)
   - □ If the device is a serial device, read the serial input queue for the device's location and button state(s).
   - □ If the device is an Apple Desktop Bus device, read the data buffer for the device's location and button state(s).
5. Compare the current location and button state(s) of the device with the previous (stored) location and button state(s).
6. If the location and button state(s) have not changed, exit from the routine, being sure the 65816 is in native 16-bit mode.
7. If either the location or button state(s) or both have changed, set up the stack for the FakeMouse call as follows:

- □ Push a word with bit 0 = 0 if the location of the device has not changed and bit 0 = 1 if the location has changed. Set bit 1 = 1 if the button state has changed and = 0 if the button state has not changed (see Table 20-7 for a list of values to use with each combination of conditions).
- □ Change to 8-bit native mode (if not already in that mode).
- □ Read address $C025 and push its value on stack.
- □ Push $00 (1 byte only) on stack.
- □ Change to 16-bit native mode.
- □ Obtain absolute X (horizontal) position (calculating from relative position if necessary).
- □ Get X clamps, clamp the X position, and push word value on stack.
- □ Obtain absolute Y (vertical) position (calculating from relative position if necessary).
- □ Get Y clamps, clamp the Y position, and push word value on stack.
- □ Push word on stack, showing the button state(s) as follows (0=button up; 1=button down):

  Bit 8—Previous state of button 1
  Bit 12—Current state of button 1
  Bit 14—Previous state of button 0
  Bit 15—Current state of button 0 (the values to use for each combination of events are shown in Table 20-8)

		Button State	
		changed	unchanged
Location State	Changed	$0003	$0001
	Unchanged	$0002	$0000

Table 20-7
Value to Push for Button State and Location State

Button 0 Previous	Current	Button 1 Previous	Current	Value
up	up	up	up	$0000
up	up	up	down	$1000
up	up	down	up	$0100
up	up	down	down	$1100
up	down	up	up	$8000
up	down	up	down	$9000
up	down	down	up	$8100
up	down	down	down	$9100
down	up	up	up	$4000
down	up	up	down	$5000
down	up	down	up	$4100
down	up	down	down	$5100
down	down	up	up	$C000
down	down	up	down	$D000
down	down	down	up	$C100
down	down	down	down	$D100

Table 20-8
Effect of Button State on FakeMouse ButtonStatus Value

8. Call the FakeMouse routine.
9. Change to 8-bit native mode.
10. Exit from the driver using an RTL (return from subroutine long).

EVENT QUEUE

As discussed briefly in other parts of this chapter, the Event Manager keeps information about many of the different events in an *event queue,* a list of the various events that have occurred. The size of the queue is determined upon startup of the Event Manager by your application. The queue size can be any value between 1 and 3639. An attempt to use a queue size larger than that will result in a startup error. Specifying a queue size of 0 will cause the default queue size of 20 to be used.

Since the Event Manager requires memory storage space for its queue, the larger the queue size, the more memory is required by the Event Manager. Too small a queue size can also create a problem. When the queue is full, the Event Manager stores new items in the queue and discards the oldest existing item in the queue.

The proper queue size to produce the right trade-off between preserving memory and not losing events is obviously dependent on your application. An application that is likely to have many events backed up, awaiting processing, will require a larger event queue in order to prevent losing events. Apple suggests that for most normal applications a queue size of 20 is sufficient.

Not every event is placed into the event queue. Particularly, window and switch events are not handled through the event queue. The Event Manager handles events outside the queue by assigning them a priority based on the type of events. Events placed in the queue all have the same priority and are retrieved in first-in, first-out (FIFO) order.

The highest priority event is the activate window event. This event, not actually placed in the queue, usually occurs in pairs. When one window needs to be activated, another usually needs to be deactivated. Because the previously active window is deactivated before the new window is activated, there can never be more than one pair of activate events pending at any one time.

A switch event is the second highest priority and is also not placed in the queue. A switch event is generated by the Control Manager and is a signal that the present application should be halted and a new application started up. If there is a pending switch event, the Event Manager will first check that all update events are handled (that is, that all windows needing updating are updated). It does this by holding back the switch event until it has passed all pending update events to the application and the application has handled them. It then passes the switch event to the application, which closes itself down and transfers control to the next application. By definition, only one switch event can be pending at a time.

The third priority of events are all those events that are placed in the event queue. This include mouse events (mouse-down and mouse-up), key events (key-down and auto-key), device driver events, desk accessory events, and application-defined events. The various events in the event queue are all given the same priority and are handled in FIFO order.

The lowest priority of the actual events are the update events. Like the other window events, update events are not placed in the event queue. Instead, the Event Manager checks for update events in two circumstances:

- When a switch event has occurred, before the switch event itself is passed onto the application
- When no higher priority event is pending (that is, no activate event and the event queue is empty).

Update events are not technically generated when a window needs updating. Rather, when the Event Manager has no higher priority event to report (or is checking for update events following a switch event), it checks each window to see if it has anything in its Update Region. Windows are checked and updated in front-to-back order (see Chapter 16).

The lowest priority event is the null event. It is returned whenever the Event Manager has no other event to return.

EVENT MASKS

The type of event returned by a call to the Event Manager can be specified by the application by means of an *event mask*. This is a word-length value in which each bit location corresponds to a particular type of event. The bit location in the word for each event corresponds to its event number as shown in Table 20-1. The event mask contains a 1 in those bit locations corresponding to events the application is interested in receiving, and contains a 0 in the other locations.

Those calls that use the event mask to restrict events returned include GetNextEvent, EventAvail, FlushEvents (removes specified types of events from the event queue), GetOSEvent, and OSEventAvail.

Up to this point the Event Manager has been discussed as though it were one tool, and technically it is. But for conceptual and programming purposes there are really two managers, the Tool Box Event Manager (TBEM) and the Operating System Event Manager (OSEM).

The OSEM detects the keystrokes and button activity that constitute events and posts the events and the information about them in the queue. It also permits the application to post events in the queue or to remove them. The TBEM is the application's main Event Manager. It retrieves events from the queue, using the OSEM, and reports window and switch events. It also contains routines permitting direct reading of the current mouse button state and location.

Just as there are two Event Managers, event masks have two uses. The toolbox use of an event mask retrieves events with GetNextEvent and EventAvail as well as removes events with FlushEvents (technically an OSEM routine).

Two OSEM routines also use the event mask in a manner similar to that of the TBEM. GetOSEvent uses the mask to determine which event to report from the event queue. It functions similarly to GetNextEvent, except that it does not first call the Desk Manager to see if the system wants to respond to the event and it works only on events in the queue, not on window or switch events. OSEventAvail, like EventAvail, works like GetOSEvent, except that it does not remove the event from the queue.

The OSEM also has a routine that makes a different use of the event mask. SetEventMask sets the system mask to permit the posting in the queue of only those events whose types are set in event mask. (The routine has no effect on the nonqueue window or switch events.) You should be particularly careful in screening out events using SetEventMask. A desk accessory may be set to respond to a particular type of event. If your application sets the system event mask to avoid posting of this type of event, the desk accessory will not function properly.

In addition to the automatic posting of events in the event queue and removal of events from the queue that is accomplished by the Event Manager, your application may also post and remove events. Posting an event requires only a call to the PostEvent routine. The most common use of this routine is for an application or device driver to post its own type of event in the event queue. The current system time, mouse location, and state of the modifier keys are placed in the queue together with the event type and event message as specified by the routine parameters.

Another use sometimes made of PostEvent is to replace an event in the queue that was removed with GetNextEvent or GetOSEvent. This action is useful only if the system time, mouse location, and state of the modifier keys are not important for that event as it is changed from its original state by PostEvent.

There is no way to remove any selected event from the event queue using the Event Manager. The next event of a specified type can be removed from the queue using GetNextEvent or GetOSEvent with the event mask set to the specified type. And the FlushEvents routine can be used to remove any event in the queue of a specific type or types up to the first occurrence of an event of another type or types.

JOURNALING

Journaling is defined as the record of a series of keystrokes, mouse movements, and button presses in order to permit the playing back of these events at a later time. Journaling is not completely implemented in the IIGS Event Manager. Rather, "hooks" are present that permit you to write your own journaling device driver and connect it to the Event Manager without great difficulty.

Journaling is designed to record both the call to and the results from five different Event Manager calls: GetNextEvent, EventAvail, GetMouse, Button, and TickCount. When journaling is active, these routines will push information onto the stack and then do a JSL (jump to subroutine long) to the journaling device driver. The address of the device driver must be placed at $E1/00E9. The device driver should record the information on the stack and then remove that information before returning to the Event Manager.

The information placed on the stack consists of that shown in Table 20-9. Table 20-10 shows the journal code, the routine calling the journal device, and the type of data returned.

The control of journaling is done by way of the value of the journalflag, located at $E1/00E7. If the value of this flag is 0, journaling is not active. If the value is positive ($0001-7FFF), journaling recording mode is active. If

Name	Length	Purpose
journalflag	Word	Current value of journal flag that is stored at $E1/00E7
journalcode	Word	Code for the routine that initiated the journaling call (see Table 20-10 for details)
resultpointer	Long-word	Pointer to the actual data returned by the routine (see Table 20-10 for details)

Table 20-9

Journaling Information Pushed on Stack (in Order of Pushing)

the value is negative ($8000-FFFF), journaling playback mode is active.

More information on journaling is available in the Apple IIGS *Toolbox Reference Manual.*

EVENT MANAGER ROUTINES

Table 20-11 gives a list of each Event Manager routine and a brief description of each routine. They are divided into Tool Box Event Manager and Operating System Event Manager routines. Table 20-12 presents a summary of the TBEM routines, the input and output parameters used by each routine, and potential error codes. Table 20-13 presents the same information for the OSEM routines. Table 20-14 is a listing of the Event Manager error codes. Finally, Table 20-15 briefly compares the Apple IIGS Event Manager routines with those found in the Macintosh Event Manager.

As described in Chapter 16 on windows, the use of the TaskMaster routine in the Window Manager makes the use of the GetNextEvent routine in the Event Manager unnecessary as TaskMaster itself calls GetNextEvent to determine what event to respond to. Your application will need to call the Event Manager routine GetNextEvent or EventAvail directly only if you are not using TaskMaster.

Journal Code	Routine Calling	Type of Data Returned
0	TickCount	Long-word — number of ticks
1	GetMouse	Point — mouse location
2	Button	Boolean
3	GetNextEvent	Event record
4	EventAvail	Event record

Table 20-10

Journal Code and Returned Data

Tool Box Event Manager (TBEM) Routines

Routine	Description
EMBootInit	Called at boot time, not by your application.
EMStartUp	Initializes the Event Manager, provides direct page for use of Event Manager and queue size. Should be called once by your application before using other Event Manager routines.
EMShutDown	Shuts down the Event Manager and deallocates any memory assigned to it.
EMVersion	Returns the version number for the Event Manager.
EMReset	Returns an error (#0602) if Event Manager is active and does nothing otherwise.
EMActive	Returns true (nonzero) if Event Manager is active and false (zero) if not.
DoWindows	Called by Window Manager when it is initialized to allow sharing of direct page area. Should not be called by your application. Event Manager should be initialized before Window Manager.
GetNextEvent	Places event record of next event in location pointed to, removing it from queue if in queue. Returns a false value if either a null event returned or if Desk Manager is responding to event, else a true value (meaning your application should handle the event). The Desk Manager responds to the following events: desk accessory events, activate and update events involving desk accessory windows, and mouse and keyboard events if the current active window is a desk accessory window.
EventAvail	Performs same function as GetNextEvent except that the event is not removed from the queue.
GetMouse	Places the current mouse location, in the local coordinates of the current Grafport (usually the currently active window), in the point pointed to by MouseLocPtr.
Button	Returns true (not zero) if specified button is currently pressed and false (zero) if not. Button number can be either 0 or 1.
StillDown	Returns true (not zero) if the specified button is currently pressed and no more mouse events for that button are in the queue. Button number can be either 0 or 1.
WaitMouseUp	Works like StillDown except if returning false, it removes the preceding mouse-up event from the queue first.

Table 20-11

List of Event Manager Routines

Tool Box Event Manager (TBEM) Routines	
TickCount	Returns number of system ticks (1/60th of a second) since system last started up.
GetDblTime	Returns the suggested maximum difference in ticks for a double-click.
GetCaretTime	Returns the number of ticks between blinks of insert caret in modifiable text. This value is user-selectable by means of the Control Panel. This routine is needed only if your application is not using LineEdit or TextEdit, as these tools cause the caret to blink properly.
SetSwitch	Called by the Control Manager to inform the Event Manager of a pending switch event. Your application should never call this routine itself.

Operating System Event Manager (OSEM) Routines	
PostEvent	This places an event of the specified type in the event queue using the current system time (ticks), mouse location, and modifier key status. It returns a 0 if the event was posted and a 1 if the event was not posted because the event type is not permitted by the system event mask.
FlushEvents	Removes events from the event queue. It removes all events of the type(s) specified by EventMask, stopping at the first event of the type(s) specified by StopMask. Result is 0, if all events of the specified type(s) were removed, or the number of the event type that stopped removal of events.
GetOSEvent	Returns an event in a manner similar to GetNextEvent except that (1) only events in the event queue are returned, and (2) the Desk Manager is not permitted to intercept and handle the event.
OSEventAvail	Works like GetOSEvent except that the event is not removed from the event queue.
SetEventMask	Set the system event mask to a specified value, permitting the posting of only those types of events whose bits are set in the mask. This routine is potentially dangerous if not used carefully.
FakeMouse	Used to permit an alternative pointing device, with a properly installed device driver, to function in place of or in addition to the mouse.

Table 20-11

List of Event Manager Routines (continued)

Function Name	Function Number	ActiveFlag	ButtonNum	Count	EventMask	EventPtr	MaxTicks	MouseLocPtr	NumTicks
Parameter Size		W	W	L	W	L	L	L	L
Parameter Type		B	V	V	V	P	V	P	V
Button	13		I1						
DoWindows	9								
EMActive	6	O1							
EMBootInit	1								
EMReset	5								
EMShutDown	3								
EMStartUp	2								
EMVersion	4								
EventAvail	11				I1	I2			
GetCaretTime	18								O1
GetDblTime	17						O1		
GetMouse	12							I1	
GetNextEvent	10				I1	I2			
SetSwitch	19								
StillDown	14		I1						
TickCount	16			O1					O1
WaitMouseUp	15		I1						

Notes:

For parameter size:
- L = Long-word (32-bit value)
- W = Word (16-bit value)

For parameter type:
- A = Address (16-bit)
- B = Boolean
- P = Pointer (32-bit; highest byte zero)
- V = Value

Table 20-12

Tool Box Event Manager Summary

ProgramID	QueueSize	Result	VersionInfo	XMaxClamp	XMinClamp	YMaxClamp	YMinClamp	ZeroPageAdrs	0601	0602	0603	0605	0606	0607
W	W	W	W	W	W	W	W	W						
V	V	B	V	V	V	V	V	A						
		O1									X	X		
											X			
										X		X	X	X
											X			
I7	I2			I4	I3	I6	I5	I1	X					
			O1								X			
		O1									X			
											X			
											X			
											X			
		O1									X			
											X			
		O1									X			
											X	X		
		O1									X			

Function Name	Function Number	ButtonStatus	ChangedFlag	EventCode	EventMask	EventMsg	EventPtr	ModLatch	Padding	Result V	Result B	StopMask	TheMask	XPosition	YPosition	0603	0604
Parameter Size		W	W	W	W	L	L	B	B	W	W	W	W	W	W		
Parameter Type		BA	BA	V	V	V	P	V	Z	V	B	V	V	V	V		
FakeMouse	25	I6	I1					I2	I3					I4	I5	X	
FlushEvents	21				I1					O1		I2				X	
GetOsEvent	22				I1		I2				O1					X	
OSEvent Avail	23				I1		I2				O1					X	
PostEvent	20			I1		I2					O1					X	X
SetEvent Mask	24												I1			X	

Notes:

For parameter size:
- B = Byte (8-bit value)
- L = Long-Word (32-bit value)
- W = Word (16-bit value)

For parameter type:
- BA = Bit array
- B = Boolean
- P = Pointer (32-bit; highest byte zero)
- V = Value
- Z = Zero

Table 20-13

Operating System Event Manager Routine Summary

Code	Meaning
0601	Duplicate EMStartUp call was issued
0602	Reset error
0603	Event Manager is not active
0604	Illegal event code given (not 0-F)
0605	Illegal button number given (not 0 or 1)
0607	Not enough memory available to set up specified size of event queue
0681	Event queue damaged (fatal system error)
0682	Queue handle damaged (fatal system error)

Table 20-14

Event Manager Error Codes

Routine	IIGS	Macintosh
EMBootInit	x	
EMStartUp	x	
EMShutDown	x	
EMVersion	x	
EMReset	x	
EMActive	x	
DoWindows	x	
GetNextEvent	x	x
EventAvail	x	x
GetMouse	x	x
Button	x	x
StillDown	x	x
WaitMouseUp	x	x
GetKeys		x
TickCount	x	x
GetDblTime	x	x
GetCaretTime	x	x
SetSwitch	x	
PostEvent	x	x
FlushEvents	x	x
GetOSEvent	x	x
OSEventAvail	x	x
SetEventMask	x	x
FakeMouse	x	
GetEvQHdr		x

Table 20-15
Comparison of IIGS and Macintosh Event Managers

PART V

Disk Input/Output

CHAPTER 21

Smartport, IWM, and Diskport

The Smartport consists of firmware built into the IIGS. It serves as a communications link between the computer and one or more devices connected to the Diskport connector, either directly or in a daisy chain through other devices, to which data may be written or from which data may be read. Data may be read or written either in blocks of 512 bytes or in characters.

For a peripheral device to be connected to the Smartport, it must adhere to certain requirements and respond to certain commands. Devices that can be connected to the Smartport include the Apple Disk 3.5, the UniDisk 3.5, a RAM or ROM card, and hard disks that adhere to the Smartport standards. Future devices that may be included on the Smartport are a network, a modem, or a printer.

Each device connected to the Smartport must have another connector on its back to which another device may be connected in a daisy chain. The exception to this last condition is a Disk II, an Apple 5 1/4-inch or a DuoDisk unit which, because it lacks a connector and the appropriate hardware, must be the last unit in the chain. Note that a special adaptor is needed to connect a Disk II-type unit to the end of the chain. This adaptor is not available from Apple, and Apple recommends against using them.

The theoretical limit on the number of units that may be attached to the Smartport is 127. This number is subject to several limiting considerations, though:

- No more than two Apple 3.5 disks may be attached to the Smartport, and they must be the first two units in the chain.
- Only one RAM card, one ROM card, or one combination RAM/ROM card may be attached to the Smartport, and this attachment must be done through the memory expansion slot.
- The power consumption of the various devices may not exceed the specifications made available by the IIGS power supply, taking into consideration the power demands of other devices.
- A maximum of two 5 1/4-inch drives may be connected to the chain. (This can include a Disk II, a Disk II clone, an Apple 5 1/4-inch drive, or a DuoDisk.) Because these units are not Smartport devices, they must be the last unit on the chain. Since the connector for many Disk II-type devices is not compatible with the connector for most Smartport devices, a converter assembly of some kind is usually needed.

The firmware for the Smartport on the IIGS is mapped to Slots 5 and 6. In the Control Panel, the choice for Slot 5 is either a Smartport or your own card (see discussion of the Control Panel in Chapter 3).

The Smartport is an extension of the Protocol Converter on some Apple IIe and IIc units. The Protocol Converter firmware is built into the Apple IIc (with 32K ROMs) and in those earlier Apple IIc's that have been upgraded for the UniDisk 3.5. The Protocol Converter is also a part of the UniDisk 3.5 Interface Card and the Apple Memory Expansion Card for the Apple IIe, which goes into one of the numbered slots. (It is not part of the Apple IIe extended 80-column card or similar units that go into the Aux slot on the IIe.)

The main difference between the Protocol Converter and the Smartport is that the Smartport supports both regular Protocol Converter devices and extended devices. An extended device differs from a regular device in that the parameter list for its commands can be placed anywhere in memory. The parameter list for a standard device must be within bank zero ($00/0000-$00/FFFF).

Several aspects of the Smartport are included in its specifications but are not implemented on the IIGS at present. These include

- *Interrupts.* The Smartport supports devices that may interrupt the computer through the Smartport.
- *Character devices.* Devices on the Smartport are either block devices or character devices. Block devices read and write data one 512-byte block at a time. Character devices read and write data one character or byte at a time. The UniDisk and Apple 3.5 can read and write a nonstandard size chunk of data using the character read and write commands.

One of the major components of the Diskport hardware is an integrated circuit known as the *IWM* (or Integrated Woz Machine). This unit first appeared on the Macintosh. It is named after Steve Wozniak, designer of the original Apple II and the Disk II system, the first disk drive for the Apple II.

HOW THE SMARTPORT WORKS

Data are sent out over the Smartport in the form of packets. When data are to be written to a device on the Smartport bus, they are sent to the Smartport in normal fashion. The Smartport then converts the data into the proper packet form with the correct additional information needed by the particular device for which the data are intended. The packet is then sent out over the Smartport bus line and received by the appropriate device. When data are being read from a Smartport device, that device sends them in packet form. The Smartport then decodes the packet and places it in an appropriate memory location in standard format.

The format of the data packet is shown in Table 21-1. Note that the high bit of each byte is always set to one. This is because of the requirements of the IWM part of the Smartport system.

The standard bootup routine of the IIGS, when the Control Panel is set to scan, searches the various slots for a bootable disk beginning with the highest numbered slot. Assuming you have bootable disks only in drives connected to the Diskport, the Smartport first checks whether there is a Disk II-type unit connected to the chain, as this is mapped to Slot 6.

If Smartport finds a 5 1/4-inch unit, it attempts to boot a disk in that drive. If there is no disk in that drive, or the drive door is open, Smartport then checks for the first 3.5 drive connected in the chain on the Diskport.

If you have both a 3.5 drive and a 5 1/4-inch drive connected to your IIGS Diskport, you can easily select which unit to boot. Set the Control Panel startup option to scan and follow these steps:

- □ Place a bootable 5 1/4-inch disk in your 5 1/4-inch drive to have it booted.
- □ Leave the door to your 5 1/4-inch drive open (or remove any disk) and place a bootable 3 1/2-inch disk in your 3 1/2-inch drive.

Or, you may set the Control Panel startup option as follows:

- □ Slot 6 to boot the 5 1/4-inch unit
- □ Slot 5 to boot the 3 1/2-inch unit

USING THE SMARTPORT

Using the Smartport can be broken down into two parts: (1) finding its location and characteristics, and (2) giving it appropriate commands.

The Smartport, or a nonextended Protocol Converter device, can be recognized by the existence of four signature bytes in its peripheral ROM

Byte Number	Values	Function
0	C3	Packet beginning mark
1	80-FF	Destination device identifier + 80. 00+80 = Smartport itself
2	80-FF	Source device identifier + 80. 00+80 = Smartport itself
3	80-82	Packet type. Command = 80; status = 81; data = 82
4	80, C0	Auxiliary type. Regular call = 80; extended call = C0
5		Status byte. Error code for read/write operations
6		Number of "odd" bytes (content bytes MOD 7) + 80
7		Number of "group bytes" (full groups of 7 content bytes — INT [content bytes/7]) + 80
8-o		"Odd" content bytes — send as 0 to 7 bytes as 7 in 8 encoded form
o+1−g		"Group bytes" — 8 bytes for each group of 7, sent as 7 in 8 encoded form
g+1		Checksum, even bits. (Bits 0, 2, 4, and 6, separated by 1's.) Checksum is an 8-bit exclusive OR of all information sent except for Packet beginning and ending marks
g+2		Checksum, odd bits. (Bits 1, 3, 5, and 7, separated by 1's.) Checksum is an 8-bit exclusive OR of all information sent except for Packet beginning and ending marks
g+3	C8	Packet ending mark

Table 21-1

Format of Protocol Converter Packet

space. This space is located for each device at memory addresses $Cn00-CnFF in bank $E0, where n represents the slot number. Thus the normal Smartport in the IIGS is found in Slot 5. Its peripheral ROM space is, thus, located at $E0/C500-C5FF.

The four signature bytes for the Smartport are at $Cn01 (value = $20), $Cn03 (value = $00), $Cn05 (value = $03), and $Cn07 (value = $00). Any device with these values in its peripheral ROM is supposed to be a Protocol Converter-type device.

Finding the Smartport or a nonextended Protocol Converter, then, consists of merely checking the four signature byte values for Slots 7 through 1 until there is either a match or no more slots. While the search can take place either beginning with Slot 7 or Slot 1, the Apple II standard search method is to start with the highest number slot and work down. A sample scan routine is

```
         PEA $C700         ;Push slot 7 start on stack
         SEP #$20          ;Byte width accumulator
TryAgain LDY #$0001        ;Find byte at Cn01
         LDA ($01,S),Y
         CMP #$20          ;First signature byte matches?
         BNE Nextslot      ;No - try next slot
         INY
         INY
         LDA ($01,S),Y     ;Second signature byte zero?
         BNE Nextslot      ;No - try next slot
         INY
         INY
         LDA ($01,S),Y     ;Cn05
         CMP #$03          ;Signature 3 valid?
         BNE Nextslot      ;No - try next slot
         INY
         INY
         LDA ($01,S),Y     ;Signature 4 byte zero?
         BNE Nextslot      ;No - try next slot
         LDA $02,S         ;Get Cn
         STA CnSlot        ;and save it
         PHA
         PHA               ;Restore stack
         REP #$20          ;back to 16-bit mode
* Rest of program goes here
         . . .
Nextslot LDA $02,S         ;Get CN
         DEC A             ;Move down one slot
         CMP #$C0          ;All slots done?
         BNE Tryagain      ;No - keep checking
*Routine showing no Smartport devices found goes here
```

When the Protocol Converter-type device is located, the next step is to determine what flavor of converter we have found. Every such device has, at location $CnFB, a code indicating what it is. This 1-byte value has 3 bits that indicate whether it is an extended device or Smartport (bit 7=1), a SCSI (Small Computer Standard Interface) device (bit 1=1), or a RAM-

0	1	2	3	4	5	6	7
RC	S	R	R	R	R	R	E

E = *Extended device* (*1=extended*)
R = *Reserved*
RC = *RamCard* (*1=RAMCard*)
S = *SCSI Device* (*1=SCSI Device*)

Figure 21-1
Smartport identification type

card (bit 0=1) (see Figure 21-1). A sample routine for determining the type of device is

```
            . . .
            STZ SCSI         ;Initialize to no SCSI device
            STZ Extended     ;and not extended device
            STZ Ramcard      ;and not a RAMcard
            SEP #$20         ;8-bit accumulator
            LDA CnSlot       ;Get Cn
            PHA              ;Put on stack
            LDA #$FB         ;Get set for CnFB
            PHA              ;Stack now has CnFB
            LDY #$0000       ;Initialize Y to zero
            LDA ($00,S),Y    ;Get type byte from CnFB
            BPL Notext       ;Bit 7 = 0, not extended
            INC Extended     ;Bit 7 = 1, is extended
Notext      ROR A            ;Push bit 0 into carry
            BCC NotRAM       ;Bit 0 = 0, not a RAMcard
            INC Ramcard      ;Bit 0 = 1, is a RAMcard
NotRAM      ROR A            ;Push bit 1 into carry
            BCC NotSCSI      ;Bit 1 = 0, not a SCSI device
            INC SCSI         ;Bit 1 = 1, is a SCSI device
NotSCSI     REP #$20         ;16-bit accumulator
            . . .            ;continue with program
```

The final step in getting ready to use the Smartport consists in determining the proper entry point for the device. This is the memory address to which a jump to subroutine should be made as part of the command process.

Each extended Smartport has two entry points—one for the ProDOS/16 operating system and one for the Smartport command system. The ProDOS/16 entry point can be determined by adding the value $Cn00 to the value found at $CnFF. The Smartport entry point is 3 bytes higher. Thus, if a Smartport device is found in Slot 5, and the value at $C5FF is $DC, the ProDOS/16 entry point is $C5DF and the Smartport entry point is $C5DC. A sample program for determining these values is

```
          . . .
          SEP #$20          ;8-bit accumulator
          LDA CnSlot        ;Get Cn
          PHA               ;Put on stack
          LDA #$FF          ;together with FF for entry point
          PHA
          LDY #$0000
          LDA ($00,S),Y     ;Get value at $CnFF
          STA CnSlot-1      ;and save ProDOS/16 entry point
          CLC
          ADC #$03          ;Smartport entry is 3 higher
          STA CnSlot+1      ;Save Smartport entry
          LDA CnSlot        ;Get CN
          STA CnSlot+2      ;and copy
*CnSlot-1 now holds, low byte first, ProDOS/16 entry point
*CnSlot+1 now holds, low byte first, Smartport (Protocol
*Converter) entry point.
```

The various Smartport commands with a brief description of each are listed in Table 21-2. Table 21-3 shows device status bytes, Table 21-4 shows the Smartport device status bytes, and Table 21-5 shows a device information block. Table 21-6 lists the command number, the number of parameters, the actual parameters and their sizes for each command. Table 21-7 lists the error codes that each command can return. Using a command consists of setting up a parameter list in memory (bank $00 for a nonextended call) and issuing a JSR (for standard Smartport) or JSL (for extended Smartport) to the command dispatches whose address has previously been located. Following that command, your codes should contain a byte of data specifying the command number, and a word pointer (long-word pointer in the case of an extended command) to the parameter list. The command dispatcher returns to the location in your code following the parameter list pointer.

Command	Description	
Status	Returns various information about the Smartport or devices on it as follows:	
	Code 00	Device status in 4 bytes as shown in Table 21-3.
	Code 00 with unit 00	Device status of Smartport in 8 bytes as shown in Table 21-4.
	Code 01	Device control block for unit—device-dependent.
	Code 02	Newline status (presently undefined).
	Code 03	Device information block in 25 bytes as shown Table 21-5.
Read block	Reads a 512-byte block of data into data buffer.	
Write block	Writes a 512-byte block of data from data buffer.	
Format	Formats a block device but does not put any operating system-specific information on disk.	
Control	Provides control over functions as follows:	
	Code 00	Soft reset of device to default values.
	Code 00 with unit 00	Enable interrupts (not available on IIGS).
	Code 01	Set device control byte.
	Code 01 with unit 00	Disable interrupts (not available on IIGS).
Init	Resets Smartport.	
Open	Prepares a character device for reading or writing.	
Close	Takes a character device out of readiness for reading or writing.	
Read	Reads specified number of bytes from character (or some block) devices.	
Write	Writes specified number of bytes from character (or some block) devices.	

Table 21-2
Smartport Commands

Byte 0	General status byte
Bit 0	1 if (character) device currently open
Bit 1	1 if device currently interrupting (not available on IIGS)
Bit 2	1 if media write protected (block device)
Bit 3	1 if formatting allowed
Bit 4	1 if device is on line (including disk in drive)
Bit 5	1 if read allowed
Bit 6	1 if write allowed
Bit 7	1 if block device; 0 if character device
Bytes 1-3	Size of block device in 512K blocks (0 if character device). Maximum size is $FFFFFF block, which is approximately 8 gigabytes (billion bytes).

Table 21-3
Device Status Bytes

Byte 0	Number of devices
Byte 1	Interrupt status (bit 7 clear = no interrupt)
Bytes 2-7	Reserved

Table 21-4
Smartport Device Status Bytes

Bytes 0-3	Same as device status bytes
Byte 4	Length of device name in bytes (maximum = 16)
Bytes 5-20	Device name (uppercase positive ASCII, blank padded)
Byte 21	Device type
Byte 22	Device subtype—if negative, supports extended calls
Bytes 23-24	Firmware version number

Table 21-5
Device Information Block

Command Name	Command Number	Number Parameter	Unit Number	Stat List Parameter	Buffer Parameter	Block Number	Control List Parameter	Stat Code	Control Code	Byte Count	Address Parameter
Status	00	3	x	xx				x			
Read Block	01	3	x		xx	xxx					
Write Block	02	3	x		xx	xxx					
Format	03	1	x								
Control	04	3	x				xx		x		
Init	05	1	x								
Open	06	1	x								
Close	07	1	x								
Read	08	4	x		xx					xx	xxx
Write	09	4	x		xx					xx	xxx
*Status	40	3	x	xxxx				x			
*Read Block	41	3	x		xxxx	xxxx					
*Write Block	42	3	x		xxxx	xxxx					
*Format	43	1	x								
*Control	44	3	x				xxxx		x		
*Init	45	1	x								
*Open	46	1	x								
*Close	47	1	x								
*Read	48	4	x		xxxx					xx	xxxx
*Write	49	4	x		xxxx					xx	xxxx

Notes:

Each "x" in a column indicates 1 byte in length for that parameter.

Parameters are listed in order to be passed to the Smartport.

The number of other parameters is the first parameter to be passed to the Smartport

Command names prefixed with an * are extended commands.

Table 21-6

Smartport Command Parameter Listing

Command Name	Command Number	01	04	06	11	21	22	27	28	2B	2D	2F	30-3F
		ERROR CODES											
Status	00		x	x	x	x							x
Read Block	01		x	x	x			x	x		x	x	
Write Block	02		x	x	x			x	x	x	x	x	
Format	03		x	x	x			x	x	x		x	
Control	04		x	x	x	x	x						x
Init	05		x	x	x				x				
Open	06	x	x	x	x				x				
Close	07	x	x	x	x				x				
Read	08		x	x	x			x	x	x	x	x	
Write	09		x	x	x			x	x	x	x	x	
EStatus	40		x	x	x	x						x	
ERead Block	41		x	x	x			x	x		x	x	
EWrite Block	42		x	x	x			x	x	x	x	x	
EFormat	43		x	x	x			x	x	x		x	
EControl	44		x	x	x	x	x						x
EInit	45		x	x	x				x				
EOpen	46	x	x	x	x				x				
EClose	47	x	x	x	x				x				
ERead	48		x	x	x			x	x	x	x	x	
EWrite	49		x	x	x			x	x	x	x	x	

Error codes:

01	BADCMD	Nonexistent command issued
04	BADPCNT	Bad call parameter count
06	BUSERR	Bus error
11	BADUNIT	Invalid unit number
21	BADCTL	Code given is not permitted by the device
22	BADCTLPARM	Invalid information in control list
27	IOERROR	Input/output error
28	NODRIVE	Device not connected
2D	BADBLOCK	No such block number on device
2F	OFFLINE	Device off-line or no disk in disk drive
30-3F	DEVSPEC	Device-specific error codes

Table 21-7

Smartport Commands—Potential Errors

At this point you can check for an error by seeing if the carry bit is set. If the carry is set, there was an error and the accumulator contains the error code. Calls should be made with the decimal flag clear. Following a call, the following registers or flags may be changed:

- Sign (N) bit
- Overflow (V) bit
- Zero (Z) bit
- X register (shows the number of bytes transferred from device if no error)
- Y register (shows the number of bytes transfered from device if no error)
- Program counter (increment to point to next instruction)

Following a Smartport call, the following registers or flags have the following values:

- Decimal (D) flag = 0.
- Interrupt disable (I) flag is unchanged.
- Carry flag shows error state (0 = no error; 1 = error).
- Accumulator contains zero if no error, or the error code if there is an error.
- The stack pointer is unchanged. (Note that although the stack pointer is left unchanged after returning from a Smartport call, the firmware uses up to 35 bytes of stack space. Be sure the stack will permit this much usage.)

For example, the following code reads block $4A7 from device #2 into a data buffer located at memory address $12/A456 (using extended read).

```
Parm_List DATA
          DC I1 '3'           ;Number of parameters
          DC I1 '2'           ;Unit number 2
          DC I4 '$0012A456' ;Pointer to data buffer
          DC I4 '$000004A7' ;Block number to read
          END
          . . .
Readblock START
          Using Parm_List
          . . .
          JSR Dispatch        ;Smartport entry point
          DC I1 '$41'         ;Extended read block command
          DC I2 'Parm_List' ;Pointer to parameter
          DC I2 '^Parm_List'
          BCS Error_Handler
* Rest of code goes here
```

Device-specific drivers obtain their parameters from the Smartport through fixed, absolute zero page memory locations. These locations are shown in Table 21-8. Smartport saves the previous contents of locations $00/0040-0062 prior to using them and restores the location after using the device-specific driver.

The Apple Disk 3.5, RAMdisk, and ROMdisk all pass error codes and the number of bytes transferred to the host (if any) through the memory locations shown in Table 21-9. The RAMdisk is a IIGS tool, and calls are made using the RAMdisk tool set.

Up to eight banks of the IIGS ROM space may be used for a ROMdisk ($F0/0000-F7/FFFF). This provides for 0.5 MB for ROM files, less any space taken up by the ROMdisk driver. A ROMdisk driver must begin at memory address $F0/0000 and must contain the ASCII string "ROMDISK" as the first 7 bytes. (The characters must be in negative ASCII—that is, the high bit of each byte must be set.) The ROMdisk entry point is at $F0/0007.

A ROMdisk is one of the two main uses that can be made of the expansion ROM space in the IIGS. The other use is for extensions to the IIGS tools. The expansion ROM area can be divided between ROMdisk space (including a driver) and tool extensions. In this case the ROMdisk drive should include, as part of its initialization routine, a call to the Tool Locator to install the ROM tool extensions. This eliminates the necessity of downloading the tool extensions to RAM for use by the Tool Locator.

Byte	Parameters	Calls That Use
$42	Buffer address (bits 0-7)	All
$43	Buffer address (bits 8-15)	All
$44	Buffer address (bits 16-23)	All
$45	Command number	All
$46	Number of parameters	All
$47	Buffer address (bits 24-31)	All
$48	Extended block (bits 0-7)	ReadBlock & WriteBlock
	Status or Control Code	Status & Control
	Byte count (bits 0-7)	Read & Write
$49	Extended block (bits 8-15)	ReadBlock & WriteBlock
	Byte count (bits 8-15)	Read & Write
$4A	Extended block (bits 16-23)	ReadBlock & WriteBlock
	Address pointer (bits 0-7)	Read & Write
$4B	Extended block (bits 24-31)	ReadBlock & WriteBlock
	Address pointer (bits 8-15)	Read & Write
$4C	Address pointer (bits 16-23)	Read & Write
$4D	Address pointer (bits 24-31)	Read & Write

Table 21-8

Use of Absolute Zero Page by Device-Specific Drivers

	Unified	RAMdisk	ROMdisk
Error code	00/0050	00/0050	00/0050
Low byte of bytes transferred	E1/0FB4	00/0051	00/0051
High byte of bytes transferred	E1/0FB5	00/0052	00/0052

Table 21-9

Transfer Points for Apple Disk 3.5, RAMdisk, and ROMdisk Drivers

At bootup, the IIGS checks addresses $F0/0000-0006 for the negative ASCII string "ROMDISK." If the IIGS finds the string, the IIGS issues an initialization call through the ROMdisk entry point at $F0/0007. If there is no error on return from that call, the ROMdisk driver is included in the Smartport chain of devices.

When the Smartport originally assigns devices during initializations, it numbers any RAMdisk first, followed by any ROMdisk, then all Apple 3.5 Disk units, and finally any UniDisk 3.5 units. This sequence can create a problem because all these devices are mapped to Slot 5 and the Smartport can boot only the first device in the chain. Thus, if a device is specified as a boot device that is not the first device in the chain (for example, a ROMdisk when a RAMdisk is present or an Apple 3.5 Disk or UniDisk 3.5 when either a RAM or ROMdisk is present), the Smartport reassigns the device numbers so that the proper device is the first unit in the chain. (Note that Smartport does not reassign a UniDisk 3.5 unit ahead of an Apple 3.5 Disk unit, and you cannot specify between the two types of units as a boot device. From a programming point of view, any 3.5-inch drive behaves the same; the only difference is which unit must be connected first and how many of each unit can be connected.)

CHAPTER 22

The Loader and Standard File Operations

The Apple IIGS comes with two disk-handling utilities that were not present on earlier Apple II's — the Loader and Standard File Operations. Both systems work in the ProDOS/16 environment only.

SYSTEM LOADER

The System Loader takes a file that is a ProDOS/16 load file (discussed in Chapter 23) and places all or part of the file into memory, performing any needed relocation along the way.

Each load file consists of one or more *segments.* Segments, in turn, consist of *records.* The precise format of the segments and their individual records do not need to be known to the application that uses the Loader or segmented files. In fact, generally the Apple IIGS Programmer's Workshop handles the necessary segmenting and creating of records based on the instructions given the linker. For further information on this subject, see the *Apple IIGS Programmer's Workshop Reference.* For more information on record, segment, and load file format, see the *Apple IIGS ProDOS/16 Reference.*

Load file segments can be classified into three major types, depending on how they are loaded into memory and maintained there. A *static load segment* is loaded into memory when the program is first loaded and relocated if necessary; it stays in memory as long as the program is running. A *dynamic load segment* is loaded into memory only when it is needed by the program, and is kept in memory only for as long as needed. It can also be relocated, if necessary, by the Loader. A *position-independent load segment* can be either a static or dynamic load segment, but it need not be relocated when moved to a different memory location. (For more information on writing position-independent code, see Chapter 14 of Fischer, *65816/65802 Assembly Language Programming,* Osborne/McGraw-Hill, 1986.)

The System Loader works with only some of the types of segments that are part of the Apple IIGS Object File Format (discussed in Chapter 23). Generally these segments include

- Relocatable code segments
- Absolute bank segments
- Fixed code segments
- Relocatable data segments
- Jump table segments
- Pathname segments

□ Initialization segments

□ Direct page/stack segments

A *relocatable code segment* contains executable program code. While it may not be position-independent, it contains a relocation dictionary as part of its record structure that enables the Loader to place the code anywhere in memory and make necessary code adjustments to allow the code to run properly. By contrast, a *fixed code segment* contains executed program code that can be loaded only in a particular memory location. Given the power of the Apple IIGS Assembler and Programmer's Workshop, there is little need for code segments to be fixed.

A special type of relocatable code segment is an *absolute bank segment.* This consists of program code that can be relocated but only within a specified bank.

Data segments within the IIGS Programmer's Workshop environment are always relocatable. These data segments can be thought of as a rough approximation of the data resource in the Macintosh.

A *jump table* is the means by which the System Loader maintains communication between the static program segments and the dynamic segments. It is the means by which the Loader determines if the dynamic segment being jumped to is already in memory (and, if so, where). If the segment is not in memory, it will then be loaded into memory.

A *pathname segment* contains information about the various load files that are used by a particular application. Since a program may make use of run-time libraries, for instance, the pathname segment lets the Loader know where to find these libraries when they are needed.

An *initialization segment* is a specialized form of code segment. If present, it is loaded and executed first when the application is begun. Only after it has finished execution, with control being transferred back to the Loader by the RTL command at the end of the routine, are the other needed program segments loaded.

Another type of special segment is the *direct page/stack segment.* This segment is used to determine the size and location of the direct page and stack used by the application. The direct page for the application begins at the starting address for this segment. The top of the stack is set to the end of this segment.

Nearly all of the memory management work done by the System Loader is handled by calls made by the Loader to the Memory Manager. By

Routine	Description
LoaderInit	Called by the system at system initialization time. All tables are cleared. Should not be called by your application.
LoaderStartup	Does nothing; does not need to be called.
LoaderShutdown	Does nothing; does not need to be called.
LoaderVersion	Returns the version number of the Loader.
LoaderReset	Does nothing; does not need to be called.
LoaderStatus	Always returns true since Loader is always initialized at system initialization.
InitialLoad	Called by a controlling program (such as ProDOS or the Finder) to perform the initial loading of an application before transferring control to the application.
Restart	Called by a controlling program (such as ProDOS or the Finder) to restart certain applications.
LoadSegNum	Loads a specified segment into memory.
UnloadSegNum	Makes a specified, memory-resident program segment purgeable.
LoadSegName	Loads a named segment into memory.
UnloadSeg	Makes a program segment encompassing a specified address purgeable.
GetLoadSegInfo	Returns the segment entry in the Memory Segment Table.
GetUserID	Returns the UserID for a specified file pathname.
GetPathname	Returns the pathname for a specified UserID and File number.
UserShutdown	Closes down an application that has completed its operation.
JumpTableLoad	Internal routine used by the Loader to load a dynamic segment.
CleanupRoutine	Internal routine used by the Loader to free memory by cleaning up internal tables.

Table 22-1
Description of Loader Routines

properly setting attribute calls to the Memory Manager (see discussion in Chapter 5), the System Loader can handle fixed memory locations for segments, locked or movable locations, purgeable (dynamic) and non-purgeable (static) segments, and page or bank alignment. The exact method of handling these operations is not discussed in this chapter, but it is described in the Apple IIGS *ProDOS/16 Reference*.

Table 22-1 lists the functions present in the Loader. These routines are called in the same manner as other tool functions. Table 22-2 lists the parameters expected by each of the Loader functions. Table 22-3 is a list of Loader error codes.

Function Name	**Function Number**	**DirectPageAdd**	**DirectPageSze**	**FileNum**	**LFileName**	**LFileNum**	**LSegName**	**LSegNum**	**LSegOffset**	**Pathname**	**RestartFlag**	**SegmentAdd**	**SpecMemFlag**	**StartAdd**	**Status**	**UserBuffer**	**UserID**	**Version**
Parameter Size		W	W	W	L	W	L	W	L	L	W	L	W	L	W	L	W	W
Parameter Type		P	V	V	P	V	P	V	P	R	B	P	B	P	B	P	V	V
CleanupRoutine	NA																I2	
GetLoadSegInfo	0F					I2		I3								I4	I1	
GetPathname	11			I2						O1							I1	
GetUserID	10									I1							O1	
InitialLoad	09	O3	O4		I2								I3	O2			IO1	
JumpTableLoad	NA					I2		I3	I4								I1	
LoaderInit	01																	
LoaderReset	05																	
LoaderShutdown	03																	
LoaderStartup	02																	
LoaderStatus	06														O1			
LoaderVersion	04																	O1
LoadSegName	0D				I2	O2	I3	O3				O1					I1	
LoadSegNum	0B					I2		I3				O1					I1	
Restart	0A	O3	O4												O2		IO1	
UnloadSeg	0E					O2		O3				I1					O1	
UnloadSegNum	0C					I2		I3									I1	
UserShutdown	12										I2						IO1	

Table 22-2

Loader Routines and Parameters

$01	Segment, application, or entry not found
$04	File is not a load file
$05	Loader is busy
$07	File version error
$08	User ID error
$09	Segment number out of sequence
$0A	Illegal load record found
$0B	Segment is foreign

Table 22-3
Loader Error Codes

As with some of the other tools in the Apple IIGS toolbox, most applications use the Loader for just a few functions.

An application is first started by a controlling program when the controlling program calls InitialLoad to perform the initial load of that application. This function loads the static load segments of the specified application into memory, after first obtaining memory for this from the Memory Manager. If it loads an initialization segment, it will transfer control to that segment to run, regaining control upon termination of the initialization segment.

If InitialLoad handles a direct page/stack segment, it returns the address of the direct page/stack buffer (that is, the direct-page starting location for that application) and the length of the buffer. The controlling program should set the direct register to the direct-page starting location before passing control to the program. Likewise it should set the stack pointer to the direct register value plus the size of the buffer.

Transfer of control can then be given to the starting address returned by InitialLoad. This address is the address of the first noninitialization load segment, normally the beginning of the application.

When a program is running, it can call the Loader to load into memory dynamic load segments when needed. LoadSegNum loads the specified segment number from the specified file number. It returns the starting address of the loaded segment. The Loader first checks to see if the requested segment is already in memory. If so, it returns without performing the unnecessary load.

When a dynamic segment is in memory but no longer needed, the application can call UnloadSegNum. This routine makes the specified load segment purgeable. If both the load file number and load segment number are nonzero, the segment will be made purgeable whether that segment is static or dynamic. (An application cannot be restarted if a static segment is unloaded.) If either the file or segment number is zero, only a dynamic segment will be unloaded.

When an application is completed, the controlling program can call UserShutdown to shut down the application. This shutdown can result in an application that cannot be restarted if the restartable flag is false because the Loader calls Cleanup to purge its internal tables.

If the restartable flag is true, the dynamic segments of the program are purged, using the Memory Manager, and the static segments are made purgeable. This application is in what is called a "zombie" state. It can be restarted by the Loader quickly if no static segments are purged.

The restart command restarts a program in a "zombie" state. In order to be restartable, the program must initialize its variables rather than expect them to be preset at load time.

STANDARD FILE OPERATIONS

The Apple IIGS Standard File Operations tool set is a small set of tools that make it easy for your application to use a standard dialog format when the user requests the loading or saving of a file. The standard dialog box is shown in Figure 22-1.

The Standard File Operations functions are described in Table 22-4. A list of the parameters required by each function is given in Table 22-5.

There are only five functions in this tool set, in addition to the standard tool set functions. Two of the functions provide a dialog box for use when saving a file, and two provide a dialog box for use when loading a file. The difference between the two routines that perform the same function is that one provides a set dialog format, and the other permits you to use a customized format. In either case, the function takes care of the ProDOS/16 calls.

The following get-file routines provide two methods of determining what files will be displayed in the dialog box:

1. The FilterProc is a routine called by Standard File Operations with the 65816 in full native mode. The stack has space for a word result and a long-word pointer to the 27-byte directory entry for the particular file.

The filter procedure must process the file entry and decide whether to: (1) not display the file (result of $0000); (2) display the file but not have it selectable (result of $0001); or (3) display the file and have it selectable (result of $0002). Like tool functions, the filter procedure must remove the input parameter from the stack before returning control to the tool.

2. The TypeListPtr points to a record containing a series of bytes representing the ProDOS/16 file types that can be displayed. The record begins with a 1-byte value defining the number of file types included in the list.

The WhereX and WhereY parameters passed to the four routines determine where the dialog box is placed (in screen coordinates). The

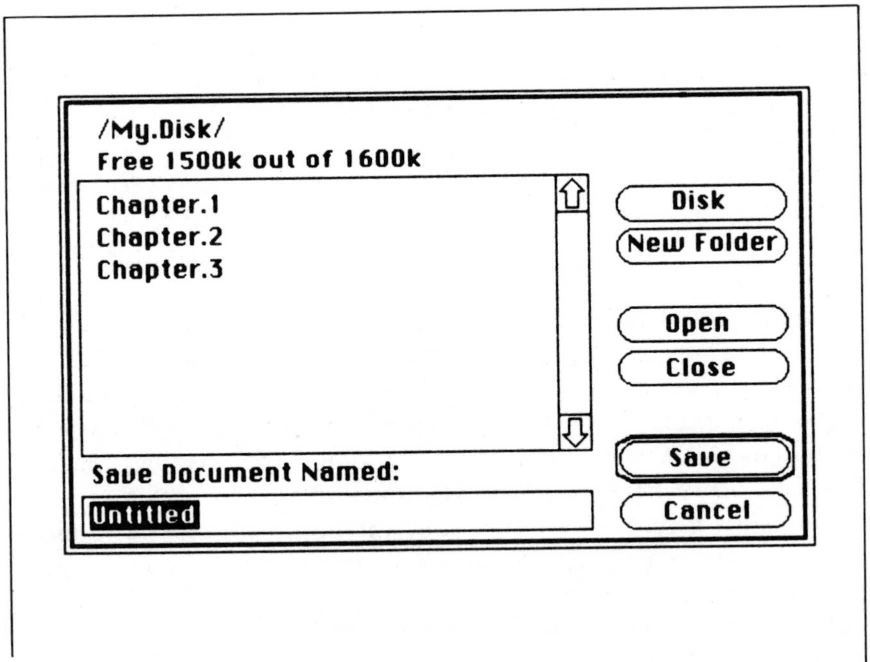

Figure 22-1
Standard dialog box

PromptPtr points to a standard ProDOS string (that is, a length byte) that is displayed at the top of the dialog box.

The put routines have several parameters that the get routines do not. The OrigNamePtr is a pointer to a string that holds the default file name that will appear in the dialog box. MaxLen is the maximum number of characters a user may type. Since a ProDOS/16 file name cannot exceed 15 characters, this value should never be more than 15. If your application is going to append a prefix or suffix to the file name, the maximum user-entered length should be shortened accordingly.

If your application is using one of the customized dialog routines (SFPGetFile or SFPPutFile), it needs to pass two other parameters to the routine. DialogPtr points to a dialog template (discussed in Chapter 19).

Routine	Description
SFBootInit	Called at load time for initialization.
SFStartup	Called by your application before using Standard File Operations.
SFShutdown	Called by your application after it is through using Standard File Operations.
SFVersion	Returns the version number.
SFReset	Called when CONTROL-RESET is pressed.
SFStatus	Returns whether Standard File Operations is active.
SFGetFile	Returns the file pathname selected by the user.
SFPutFile	Returns the file pathname for the file being saved by the user.
SFPGetFile	Returns the file pathname selected by the user using a customized dialog box.
SFPPutFile	Returns the file pathname for the file being saved by the user using a customized dialog box.
SFAllCaps	Permits a file name to be either all uppercase letters or only initial uppercase letters.

Table 22-4

Description of Standard File Operations Routines

Function Name	Function Number	CapsFlag	DialogHookPtr	DialogPtr	FilterProcPtr	IDNum	MaxLen	OrigNamePtr	PromptPtr	ReplyPtr	Status	TypeListPtr	Version	WhereX	WhereY	ZPAddress
Parameter Size		W	L	L	L	W	W	L	L	L	W	L	W	W	W	W
Parameter Type		B	P	P	P	V	V	P	P	P	B	P	V	V	V	P
SFAllCaps	13	I1														
SFBootInit	01															
SFGetFile	09				I4				I3	I6		I5		I1	I2	
SFPGetFile	11		I7	I6	I4				I3	I8		I5		I1	I2	
SFPPutFile	12		I7	I6			I5	I4	I3	I8				I1	I2	
SFPutFile	10						I5	I4	I3	I6				I1	I2	
SFReset	05															
SFShutdown	03															
SFStartup	02					I1										I2
SFStatus	06										O1					
SFVersion	04												O1			

Table 22-5

Standard File Operations Routines

Several items must be included in the dialog template. These items are shown in Table 22-6. In addition, the DialogHookPtr is a routine that filters the item hit in the dialog. It is passed the address of the dialog's Grafport and the address of item hit, both as long-words. On termination, the DialogHookPtr must strip the 8 bytes of input parameter. It should leave the value of item hit alone if it wants the SFPGet or SFPPut routine to handle the item, and it should place a zero value in item hit if it has handled the item.

When creating a custom dialog, be careful to leave sufficient space in the Files User Item to display an adequate number of files. The bounding rectangle needs to be 10 pixels high for each file to be displayed (plus 2 pixels for "housekeeping").

The following dialog template is used for the standard get-file operation:

```
StdFileTemplate     Data
                    DC I'0,0,114,400'        ;Bounds rectangle
                    DC I'-1'                 ;Visible
                    DC I4'0'                 ;RefCon
                    DC I4'It1, It2, It3, It4'
                    DC I4'It5, It6, It7, It8'
                    DC I4'0'
It1                 DC I'1'                  ;Item ID
                    DC I'54,265,66,375'      ;Item rectangle
                    DC I'ButtonItem'         ;Item type
                    DC I4'StrBut1'           ;Item descriptor
                    DC I'0'                  ;Value
                    DC I'0'                  ;Flag
                    DC I4'0'                 ;Color
It2                 DC I'2'                  ;Item ID
                    DC I'72,265,84,375'      ;Item rectangle
                    DC I'ButtonItem'         ;Item type
                    DC I4'StrBut2'           ;Item descriptor
                    DC I'0'                  ;Value
                    DC I'0'                  ;Flag
                    DC I4'0'                 ;Color
It3                 DC I'3'                  ;Item ID
                    DC I'28,265,40,375'      ;Item rectangle
                    DC I'ButtonItem'         ;Item type
                    DC I4'StrBut3'           ;Item descriptor
                    DC I'0'                  ;Value
                    DC I'0'                  ;Flag
                    DC I4'0'                 ;Color
It4                 DC I'4'                  ;Item ID
                    DC I'98,265,110,375'     ;Item rectangle
                    DC I'ButtonItem'         ;Item type
                    DC I4'StrBut4'           ;Item descriptor
                    DC I'0'                  ;Value
                    DC I'0'                  ;Flag
                    DC I4'0'                 ;Color
It5                 DC I'5'                  ;Item ID
                    DC I'28,214,119,239'     ;Scroll Bar rectangle
                    DC I'ScrollBarItem'      ;Item type
                    DC I4'0'                 ;Filled by GetFile
                    DC I'0'                  ;Garbage
                    DC I'03'                 ;Flag
                    DC I4'0'                 ;Color
It6                 DC I'6'                  ;Item ID
                    DC I'12,15,24,395'       ;Path rectangle
                    DC I'UserItem'           ;Item type
                    DC I4'0'                 ;Filled by GetFile
                    DC I'0'                  ;Value
                    DC I'0'                  ;Flag
                    DC I4'0'                 ;Color
It7                 DC I'7'                  ;Item ID
                    DC I'28,15,110,215'      ;Files rectangle
                    DC I'UserItem'           ;Item type
                    DC I4'0'                 ;Filled by GetFile
                    DC I'0'                  ;Garbage
                    DC I'0'                  ;Flag
                    DC I4'0'                 ;Color
It8                 DC I'8'                  ;Item ID
                    DC I'0,15,12,395'        ;Prompt rectangle
                    DC I'UserItem'           ;Item type
                    DC I4'0'                 ;Filled by GetFile
                    DC I'0'                  ;Value
                    DC I'0'                  ;Flag
                    DC I4'0'                 ;Color
StrBut1             STR 'Open'
StrBut2             STR 'Close'
StrBut3             STR 'Disk'
StrBut4             STR 'Cancel'
                    END
```

This template is presented for assistance in determining how to modify the template for your own use.

Item	Type	ID
Save button	Button	1
Open button	Button	2
Close button	Button	3
Next button	Button	4
Cancel button	Button	5
ScrollBar	Scroll Bar	6
Path	UserItem	7
Files	UserItem	8
Prompt	UserItem	9
FileName	EditItem	10
FreeSpace	UserItem	11
CreateButton	Button	12

Table 22-6

Required Items in Customized Standard File Dialog Template

Byte Offset	Length	Type	Name	Use
0	2	Boolean	Good	True if open pressed; false if cancel pressed
2	2	Value	File type	ProDOS file type
4	2	Value	Aux type	ProDOS aux file type
6	15	String	Filename	Name of the file in prefix 0
21	128	String	Pathname	Full pathname of selected file

Table 22-7

Standard File Operations Reply Record

The four procedures all return their data in the form of a reply record. Your application must pass a pointer to this record as an input parameter. The format of this record is shown in Table 22-7, together with the meaning of each item in the record.

CHAPTER

23

Programming with ProDOS/16

The main operating system for the Apple IIGS is the ProDOS/16, which is an enhanced version of ProDOS that has been available on the Apple II family since 1983. This chapter discusses ProDOS/16 from the standpoint of one who has some familiarity with the 8-bit version of ProDOS. Readers wishing more familiarity with that system should consult the *Apple ProDOS Technical Reference Manual* (Addison-Wesley).

Much of the literature about ProDOS refers to the 8-bit version of ProDOS as just ProDOS, or by the various version numbers such as ProDOS 1.0, 1.1, or 1.1.1. The 8-bit version of ProDOS for the Apple IIGS is referred to variously as ProDOS/8 or ProDOS 1.2. This chapter will use the term ProDOS/8 when referring to this operating system. The major difference between ProDOS/8 and ProDOS 1.1.1 is the support for the Apple IIGS clock in ProDOS/8. Table 23-1 is a comparison of ProDOS/8 with ProDOS/16.

This chapter discusses version 1.0 of ProDOS/16. A newer version (2.0) of ProDOS/16 is expected to be available in the near future. It will differ from version 1.0 in the following respects:

- The program has completely new code, optimized for 16-bit operation on the 65816. Version 1.0 is a shell built around ProDOS/8 and uses mainly 8-bit code designed for use on the 6502.
- An unlimited number of files may be open, not just the eight open files permitted in version 1.0.

ProDOS/8	ProDOS/16
Works in 8-bit mode only.	Works in 8- or 16-bit mode.
Calls made only from bank $00.	Calls made from anywhere in memory.
Manages memory with a global page bit map.	Manages memory with the IIGS Memory Manager.
Manages variables, buffers, and date using the system global page.	Uses Toolbox calls to manage variables, buffers, and date information. Does not have a system global page.
Does not support named devices.	Supports named devices.
Does not support user-definable prefixes.	Suports user-definable prefixes.
Uses a hierarchical file system.	Uses a hierarchical file system.
Runs on all Apple II's.	Runs on Apple IIGS only.

Table 23-1

Comparison of ProDOS/8 and ProDOS/16

- An unlimited number of devices may be on-line, not just the 14 permitted in version 1.0.
- A minimum of three block device protocols are supported, not just the one supported by version 1.0.
- Named devices are supported in a variety of calls, not just Volume and Get_Dev_Num as in version 1.0.
- There is a volume mount function.
- There is a format command that can format a device.

Version 2.0 will also have six commands not available in version 1.0. These commands are listed in Table 23-2.

ProDOS/8 calls are known as MLI calls (for Machine Language Interface). The calls are the standard method of calling ProDOS/8 routines from any language except Applesoft BASIC. The standard method of calling a ProDOS/8 command uses the following code:

```
JSR PRODOS8             ;Call the ProDOS/8 MLI
DC I1'Command'          ;ProDOS/8 command number
DC I'Parmtable'         ;Pointer to parameter table in bank $00
BCS Error               ;Carry is set if error occurred
```

ProDOS/16 calls are known as *system calls*. The adjective "system" refers to the entire operating system, including individual files, not just calls directly affecting the operating system parameters. It is equivalent to

Get_DIB	Returns the device information block
Get_Entry	Returns an ASCII string with directory information
Restore_State	Restores the previous system state on return to an application
Save_State	Saves the current system state on exit from an application
Set_Int_Mode	Sets a method for handling unclaimed interrupts
Write_Protect	Returns the write-protect status of a volume

Table 23-2
Added Calls in ProDOS/16 Version 2.0

the ProDOS/8 MLI call except that it uses a 16-bit command number (with the higher byte set to 0) and a 32-bit parameter table address pointer (with the highest byte set to 0), resulting in a parameter table that can be anywhere in the memory of the IIGS. The code for a ProDOS/16 system call is

```
JSL PRODOS16            ;Call the ProDOS/16 entry point
DC I2'Command'          ;ProDOS/16 command - upper byte $00
DC I4'Parmtable'        ;Pointer to parameter table anywhere
BCS Error               ;Carry is set if error occurred
```

ProDOS uses certain memory locations in bank $E1. The entry location for ProDOS/16 is $E1/00A8-AB. Locations $E1/00AC-B9 are reserved. Two bytes of guaranteed zeroes are at $E1/00BA-BB. If the current operating system is ProDOS/8, there is a $00 at $E1/00BC (ProDOS/16 places a $01 there). The same values at $E1/00BD show what operating system was initially booted. The active flag location is discussed later in this chapter.

PRODOS BOOT PROCESS

The boot process of ProDOS has been changed to accommodate ProDOS/16 files. Any ProDOS disk must contain a file on it called PRODOS and of type $FF (SYS). The boot loader loads this file into memory at $00/2000 and executes it. The operation performed by this file will vary in the following ways:

- If the disk is meant to be operated on an 8-bit Apple II, the PRODOS file should be ProDOS/8. The standard boot process used in 8-bit ProDOS will then occur.
- If the disk is meant to be operated on a IIGS, PRODOS should be an operating system loader.

The ProDOS operating system loader and application selector will not run on an 8-bit Apple II. On the IIGS, it performs the following steps:

1. Relocates the PQUIT code (discussed later in this chapter) to a new permanent location.

2. Loads the file named P16 (type $F9) in the system subdirectory.
3. Loads the ProDOS loader.
4. Executes any needed set-up routines by checking the System.Setup subdirectory of the System subdirectory. It will execute any set-up specified by the Tool.Setup first and then any other available set-up. A set-up file is of type $B6 (start-up load file or STR). Each set-up file is called with a JSL and must return with an RTL command. After the machine returns from the set-up file, it unloads that file.
5. Searches for the application to actually run as follows:
   - □ Looks for a file of type $B3 (S16) called START. This file will normally be a finder or launcher.
   - □ If no START file is present, it looks for the first system-type (type $FF or SYS, suffix .SYSTEM) or system/16-type (type $B3 or S16, suffix .SYS16) file.
   - □ If a system ($FF) file is found, it will load in P8 and transfer control to that file.
   - □ If a system ($FF) file is found, but P8 is not present, it will look for a system/16 ($B3) file.
   - □ If the first file found is a system/16 ($B3) file, it will transfer control to the PQUIT routine to load and run the program.

These steps are shown in Figure 23-1.

In order to function properly as a system/16 program, any application you write must

- □ Be executable machine code.
- □ Be in IIGS Object Module Format (discussed later in this chapter).
- □ Be type $B3 (S16) or $B6 (STR).
- □ Use the PQUIT call properly.
- □ Use the Memory Manager to obtain memory.
- □ Have a suffix of .SYS16 if it is to be automatically loaded and executed at boot time.

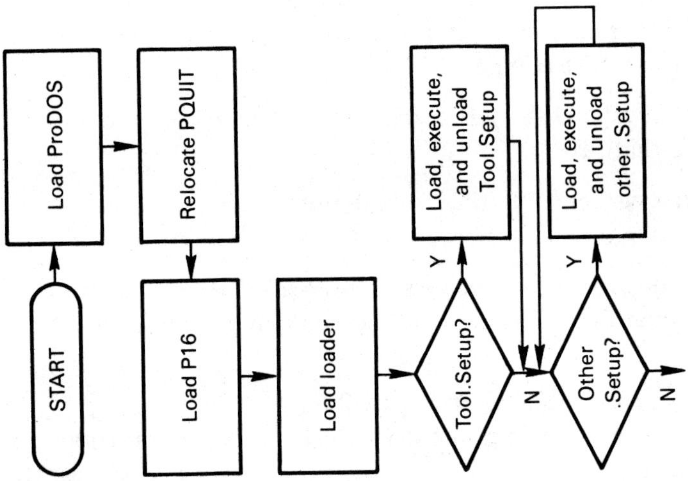

Figure 23-1

Steps performed by ProDOS operating system loader and application selector

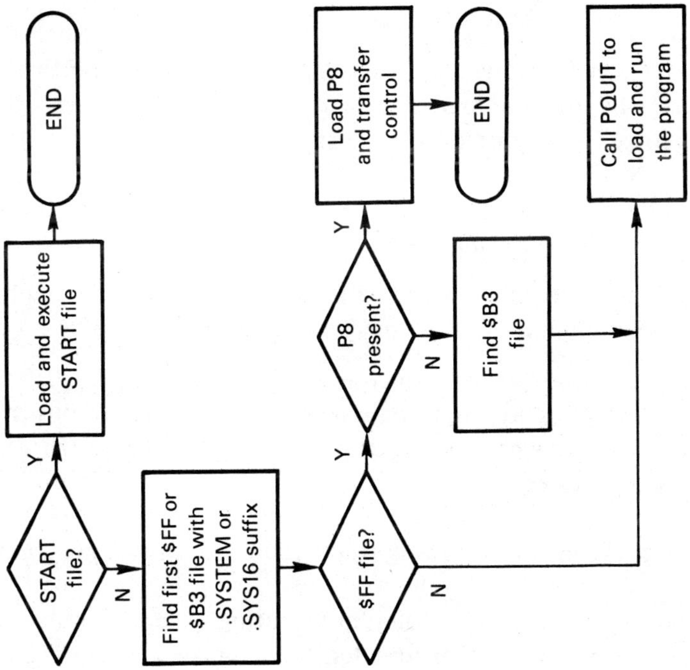
START file?
Y
N
Load and execute START file
END
Find first $FF or $B3 file with .SYSTEM or .SYS16 suffix
$FF file?
Y
N
P8 present?
Y
N
Load P8 and transfer control
END
Find $B3 file
Call PQUIT to load and run the program

ProDOS/16 is loaded into memory of the IIGS at $00/D100-FFFF and $01/D100-FFFF including both parts of bank-switched memory in banks $00 and $01. ProDOS/16 also calls the Memory Manager to reserve RAM for its input/output buffers, interface tables, and other code. The memory is located in the area of $00/9000-BFFF.

PQUIT ROUTINE

The PQUIT routine is the ProDOS program dispatcher and ProDOS/8 loader. PQUIT uses the loader to load ProDOS/16 programs. PQUIT supports these three types of quit calls:

1. The standard ProDOS/8 quit call documented in the *Apple ProDOS Technical Reference Manual.*
2. An enhanced ProDOS/8 quit call, which can contain a pointer to the string containing the pathname of the next program to be executed.
3. The ProDOS/16 quit call, which supports a pointer to the pathname of the next program and optionally permits the system to return to the calling program when the called program is completed. These return calls can be nested.

PQUIT performs the following steps when executing a program:

1. If the new program uses a different operating system, it shuts down the current operating system and loads in the new operating system, freeing up and allocating memory as needed by means of the Memory Manager.
2. If the new program is a ProDOS/8 program, PQUIT allocates all special memory in the IIGS (discussed in Chapter 5) for the use of the application.
3. If the previous program was a ProDOS/16 program, it calls the application shutdown routine in the Loader to put the application into a zombie state (discussed in Chapter 22).
4. It loads the program either directly (if the program is a ProDOS/8 program) or through the System Loader (if the program is a ProDOS/16 program).

5. It assigns a direct register (and thus a direct page) and a stack pointer (ProDOS/16 only) to the application and passes these values to the application.

These steps are shown in Figure 23-2.

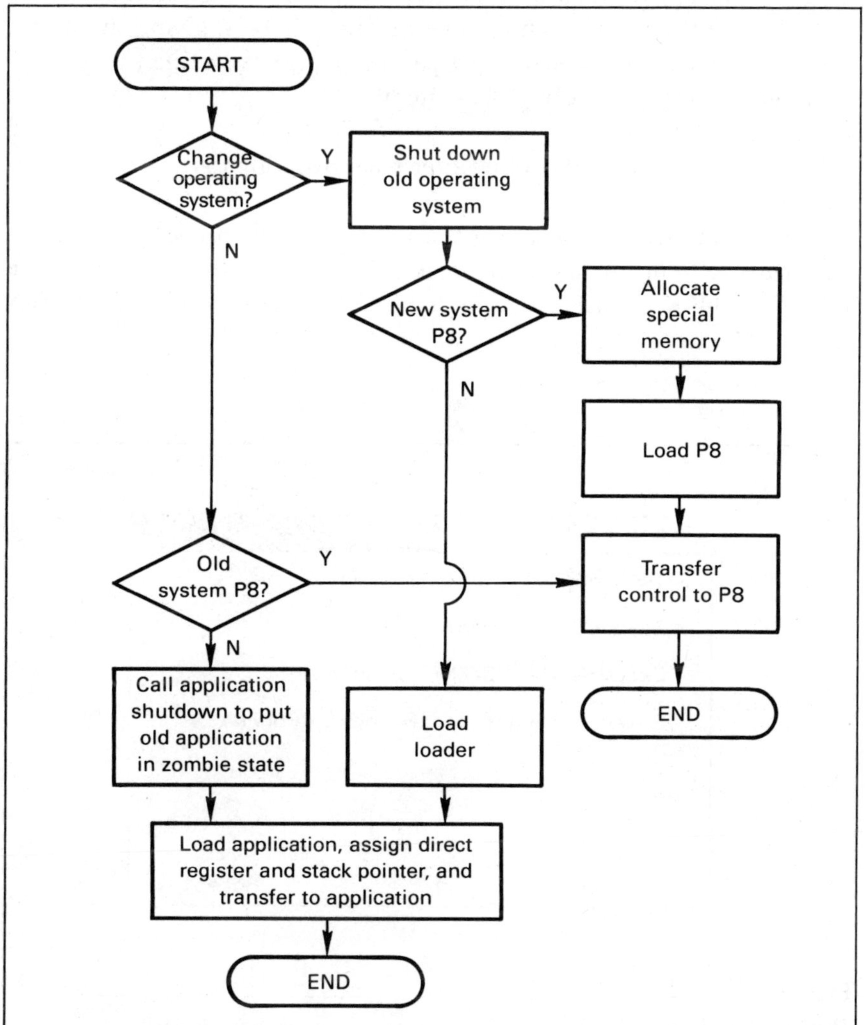

Figure 23-2
Steps performed by PQUIT

PQUIT uses the following series of steps to determine which program to load and run:

1. If a pathname is specified, that program is used.
2. If no pathname is specified, PQUIT checks whether there are any calling programs that need to be returned to.
3. If there is no pathname specified, and no return program, it displays a dialog on the text screen (shown in Figure 23-3), giving the user a choice between (1) specifying a pathname, (2) executing the START program, or (3) rebooting the system.

The steps that are used to determine what program to run are shown in Figure 23-4.

The various steps concerning the boot and quit process mandate a certain disk arrangement for boot disks. The necessary files normally take more than 140K of disk space, thus requiring the use of 3.5-inch disks

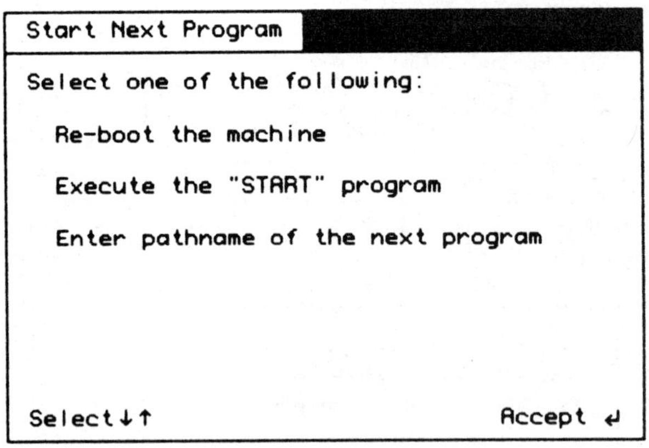

Figure 23-3
Dialog box display with no pathname and no return program

(holding 800K) instead of 5 1/4-inch disks (holding 140K). The files that can appear on a system disk, and their uses, are listed in Table 23-3.

ProDOS/8 supports one prefix that can be added to a partial pathname to create the complete pathname. Only one prefix is available at one time—changing the prefix for one use changes it for all uses.

ProDOS/16 has nine different prefixes. Each prefix is maintained separately, and changing one prefix does not change any of the others. The prefixes are numbered from 0 to 7, plus the system prefix of */. The system prefix */ can be found by the GetBootVol call. To specify a pathname with prefix 3, for example, the partial pathname should be "3/<partial pathname>".

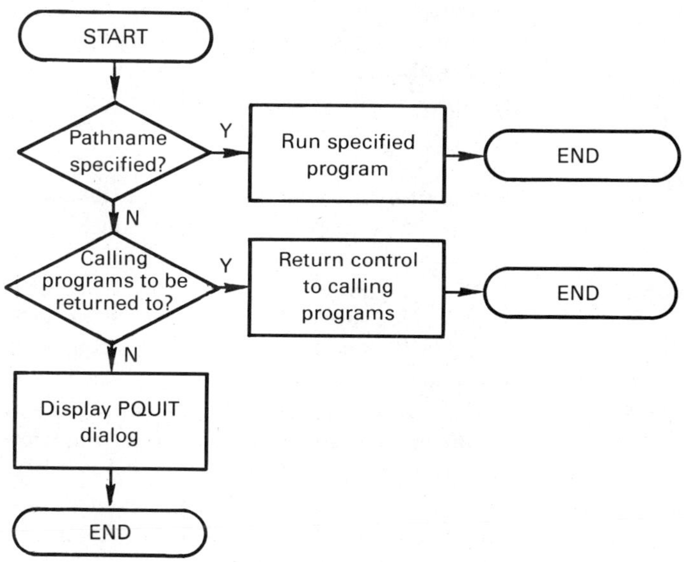

Figure 23-4
Steps performed by PQUIT to determine what program to run

File	Use
PRODOS	Required file. Loads the proper operating system and the selected application (type $FF or SYS).
SYSTEM	Required subdirectory. Holds various files needed to set up operating system.
P8	In System subdirectory. Contains ProDOS/8 kernal and loader. Needed if a ProDOS/8-based application is used (type $FF or SYS).
P16	In System subdirectory. Required if a ProDOS/16-based application is used (type $F9).
LOADER	In System subdirectory. ProDOS/16 loader. Required if a ProDOS/16-based application is used.
START	In System subdirectory. Normally contains the Finder. Required only if an application uses it (type $B3 or S16).
LIBS	Subdirectory in System subdirectory. Holds the standard libraries. Required only if used by the application.
TOOLS	Subdirectory in System subdirectory. Holds the RAM tools and RAM patches to ROM tools. Required only if used by the application (tools type $BA).
FONTS	Subdirectory in System subdirectory. Holds the fonts used by an application. Required only if used by the application.
DESK.ACCS	Subdirectory in System subdirectory. Holds any classic and new desk accessories (CDAs of type $B8; NDAs of type $B9).
SYSTEM.SETUP	Subdirectory in System subdirectory. Holds any set-up load files (set-up load files of type $B6 or STR if not removed after execution, and type $B7 if removed after execution).
TOOL.SETUP	Set-up load file in System.Setup subdirectory in System subdirectory. Load file that loads ROM tool patches and installer (type $B6 or STR).
BASIC.SYSTEM	Applesoft interface to ProDOS. Required only if the application is written in Applesoft BASIC (type $FF or SYS).

Table 23-3
Boot Disk Files

Four of the nine prefixes are used for special purposes:

1. Prefix * is the system prefix. It is assigned at boot time as the volume name of the start-up disk and cannot be changed.
2. Prefix 0 is often the boot volume name, although it can also be used for other purposes.
3. Prefix 1 is the Application subdirectory prefix. It is the pathname of the subdirectory containing the currently running application.
4. Prefix 2 is the System Library subdirectory prefix. It is the pathname of the subdirectory containing the library modules used by the current system program.

Prefixes 3-7 can be defined by the application as needed.

INTERRUPTS

Like ProDOS/8, ProDOS/16 not only allows, but actively supports, interrupts. Interrupts are initially vectored to $00/03FE. This is a 2-byte pointer to another location in bank zero. That location contains a 3-byte address that passes control to the ProDOS/16 interrupt dispatcher.

The dispatcher begins by switching the 65816 to full, 16-bit native mode. It then polls the various interrupt handlers, including the 16 potential user-installed handlers.

These handlers should be written to expect the emulation, memory width, and index register width bits set to 0 and the interrupt disable and carry bits set to 1. System speed is fast (2.5 MHz). On exit from the interrupt handler, by means of an RTL, these various bits should be set as they are on entry, except for the carry bit. The carry bit is set to 1 if the interrupt was not serviced by the particular handler and set to 0 if the interrupt was serviced. Because ProDOS is not re-entrant, the interrupt handler should take special care in making ProDOS calls.

Table 23-4 contains a list of the ProDOS/16 interrupt control calls. Like all the call tables in this chapter, it lists both the ProDOS/16 and ProDOS/8 command numbers and the parameters expected by each call. The numbers under each parameter specify the order in which the

	ProDOS/16 Number	ProDOS/8 Number	Interrupt Number	Interrupt Code
Parameter Size			W*	L*
Parameter Type			V	P
AllocInterrupt	31	40	I1	I2
DeallocInterrupt	32	41	I1	

Notes:

Parameter Size:
L = Long-word (32 bits)
W = Word (16 bits)
* shows top byte of parameter not used (must be 0)

Parameter Type:
P = Pointer
V = Value

Table 23-4
Interrupt Control Calls

parameters appear in the parameter list. An I indicates that the parameter is input to the command. An O indicates that the result is placed by the call either in the parameter list itself or in the location pointed by the parameter.

ProDOS/16 sets bit 15 of the word at $E1/00BE-BF to 1 to show it is active (currently executing a call) and clears it to 0 when it is inactive. Though checking this flag can help prevent the return of a busy error, the only sure method is to use the Scheduler (discussed in Chapter 25). ProDOS/16 increments the busy flag before it starts a task and decrements that flag when it completes the task.

SYSTEM CALLS

ProDOS/16 has added certain calls that do not exist under ProDOS/8. These are listed in Table 23-5. Also, certain MLI calls in ProDOS/8 have been eliminated or changed in ProDOS/16. These are listed in Table 23-6.

Call	Use
Change_Path	Expanded version of the ProDOS/8 Change_Path call, which can move a file from one subdirectory to another.
Clear_Backup_Bit	Changes the back-up bit in the specified file's access byte to 0 if not already 0. Should be used only by a disk back-up program.
Get_Boot_Vol	Returns the pathname of the volume from which ProDOS/16 was last loaded.
Get_Dev_Num	Returns the device number associated with the specified device name.
Get_Level	Returns the current system file level value. This value determines which files will be closed or flushed by a multiple-file close or flush call.
Get_Pathname	Returns the pathname of the currently running system program.
Get_Version	Returns the version number of ProDOS/16.
Set_Level	Changes the current system file level value. This value determines which files will be closed or flushed by a multiple-file close or flush call.

Table 23-5

System Calls Added by ProDOS/16

Call	Disposition
Rename	Now part of expanded Change_Path
Get_Time	Use the time routines in the Miscellaneous Toolset
Set_Buf	Memory management is handled by the Memory Manager
Get_Buf	The Open command returns a handle
Online	Now part of the Volume command

Table 23-6

ProDOS/8 Calls Not Available or Changed in ProDOS/16

Function Name	ProDOS/16 Number	ProDOS/8 Number	Access	AuxType	BlocksUsed	CreateDate	CreateTime	DevName	FileSysID
Parameter Size			W*	L*	L	W	W	L*	W*
Parameter Type			BA	V	V	D	T	P	V
ChangePath	04	C2††							
ClearBackupBit	0B	—							
Create	01	C0	I2	I4		I6	I7		
Destroy	02	C1							
GetFileInfo**	06	C4	O2	O4	O1	O6	O7		
GetPrefix**	0A	C7							
SetFileInfo**	05	C3	I2	I4		I6	I7		
SetPrefix**	09	C6							
Volume**	08	C5††						I1	O5

Notes:

Parameter Size:

L = Long-word (32 bits)
W = Word (16 bits)
* shows top byte of parameter not used (must be 0)

Parameter Type:

BA = Bit array
D = ProDOS packed date format
P = Pointer
T = ProDOS packed time format
V = Value

Other Notes:

** = Parameter layout in ProDOS/8 does not match ProDOS/16
† = If call is for Volume directory, returns total blocks
†† = ProDOS/8 equivalent call has different name

Table 23-7

ProDOS/16 File Housekeeping Calls

Field								|				
Filetype	W*	V			I3		O3	|		I3		
FreeBlocks	L*	V						|				O4
ModDate	W	D					O8	|		I8		
ModTime	W	T					O9	|		I9		
NewPathname	L*	P	I2					|				
NullField	W	V						|		I5		
Pathname	L*	P	I1	I1	I1	I1	I1	|		I1		
Prefix	L*	P						|	O2		I2	
PrefixNum	W*	V						|	I1		I1	
StorageType	W*	V			I5		O5	|				
TotalBlocks	L*	V					O4†	|				O3
VolName	L*	P						|				O2

The ProDOS/16 system call preserves the X, Y, direct, data bank, and program bank registers, and the stack pointer. The accumulator is zero if the system call is successful and contains the error number if the call is not successful. The memory register width, index register width, decimal, interrupt disable, and emulation bits in the processor status register are preserved. The sign, overflow, and zero bits are undefined. The carry bit is set if the call returned an error and is clear if the call was successful. Note that this is different from ProDOS/8, where the sign and zero bits are set according to the value in the accumulator.

ProDOS/16 calls can be made from either native or emulation mode. Because the call is made with a JSL, it can be made from anywhere in memory. The calls all use long addressing where needed so that parameter blocks can be anywhere in memory, pointers can point to anywhere in memory, and data can be transferred anywhere in memory.

Any currently running program can make ProDOS/16 calls, including the current application, a classic or new desk accessory, or an interrupt handler.

Every parameter is an even number of bytes. If it needs an odd number of bytes, the unused byte is set to $00. Some of the parameter lists in ProDOS/16 are arranged differently from the similar list in ProDOS/8. Similar parameter lists are used across calls in ProDOS/16. This permits a list in memory to be reused.

ProDOS/16 parameter lists also vary from ProDOS/8 lists in regard to the first parameter in the list. ProDOS/8 requires that the first parameter be a single byte containing the number of other parameters in the list. ProDOS/16 does not have this parameter count in its list.

The various ProDOS/16 system calls can be broken down into logical categories. The calls are listed in tables according to their category as follows: housekeeping calls (Table 23-7), file access calls (Table 23-8), device calls (Table 23-9), and environment calls (Table 23-10).

Several of the housekeeping calls use special format parameters. The file creation or modification date is stored in a special packed word-length format shown in Table 23-11. The file creation or modification time is stored in a special packed word-length format shown in Table 23-12. The access code is a word-length array of bits. The meaning of each bit position is shown in Table 23-13.

Each of the ProDOS/16 system calls can return one or more errors. As discussed previously, the code for each error is returned as a value in the

Function Name	ProDOS/16 Number	ProDOS/8 Number	DataBuffer	EnableMask	EOF	I/O Buffer	Level	NewlineChar	Pathname	Position	RefNum	RequestCount	TransferCount
Parameter Size			L*	W*	L*	L*	W*	W*	L*	L*	W*	L*	L*
Parameter Type			P	M	V	H	V	C	P	V	V	V	V
Close	14	CC									I1		
Flush	15	CD									I1		
GetEOF	19	D1			O2						I1		
GetLevel	1B	—					O1						
GetMark	17	CF								O2	I1		
Newline	11	C9		I2				I3			I1		
Open"	10	C8				I3			I2		O1		
Read	12	CA	I2								I1	I3	O4
SetEOF	18	D0			I2						I1		
SetLevel	1A	—					I1						
SetMark	16	CE								I2	I1		
Write	13	CB	I2								I1	I3	O4

Notes:

Parameter Size:

L = Long-word (32 bits)
W = Word (16 bits)
* shows top byte of parameter not used (must be 0)

Parameter Type:

C = Character
H = Handle
M = Mask
P = Pointer
V = Value

Other notes:

" = Parameter layout in ProDOS/8 does not match ProDOS/16

Table 23-8

ProDOS/16 File Access Calls

Function Name	ProDOS/16 Number	ProDOS/8 Number	BlockNum	DataBuffer	DevName	DevNum
Parameter Size			L*	L*	L*	W*
Parameter Type			V	P	P	V
GetDevNum	20	—			I1	O2
ReadBlock	22	80	I3	I2		I1
WriteBlock	23	81	I3	I2		I1

Notes:

Parameter Size:

L = Long-word (32 bits)
W = Word (16 bits)
* shows top byte of parameter not used (must be 0)

Parameter Type:

P = Pointer
V = Value

Table 23-9

ProDOS/16 Device Calls

Function Name	ProDOS/16 Number	ProDOS/8 Number	ChainPath	NullField	Pathname	ReturnFlag	Version
Parameter Size			L*	L	L*	W	W
Parameter Type			P	V	P	B	Vn
GetBootVol	28	—			O1		
GetName@	27	—			O1		
GetVersion	2A	—					O1
Quit"	29	65	I1	I3		I2	

Notes:

Parameter Size:

L = Long-word (32 bits)
W = Word (16 bits)
* shows top byte of parameter not used (must be 0)

Parameter Type:

B = Boolean
P = Pointer
V = Value
Vn = Version number

Other notes:

" = Parameter layout in ProDOS/8 does not match ProDOS/16
@ = Returns not full pathname but just file name

Table 23-10

Environment Calls

Bits	Use	Range
9-15	Year	00-99
5-8	Month	1-12
0-4	Day	1-31

Table 23-11

Layout of ProDOS Packed Date Format (Word Value)

Bits	Use	Range
13-15	Unused	Always 0
8-12	Hours	00-23
6-7	Unused	Always 0
0-5	Minutes	00-59

Table 23-12

Layout of ProDOS Packed Time Format (Word Value)

Bit	Use
8-15	Unused
7	Destroy
6	Rename
5	Backup needed
2-4	Reserved
1	Write
0	Read

Notes:

Bit is 1 if use is enabled and 0 if disabled
Unused and reserved bits must be 0

Table 23-13

Access Code Bit Meanings

accumulator. Only the lower byte of the accumulator is significant in this process. Table 23-14 shows the possible error codes that can be returned for each system call. Table 23-15 shows the meaning for each of the potential error codes.

While there are potentially several methods to create a parameter list, the simplest method is to place the list in your program code. Using this method results in a somewhat faster program execution. It may also result in a slightly greater amount of disk storage depending on the application. The following code calls Get_File_Info and sets up the parameter block for the routine:

```
GetInfo   START
          Using InfoData
          JSL PRODOS16          ;Call the ProDOS/16 entry point
          DC I2'0006'           ;GetFileInfo command
          DC I4'FileInfo'       ;Pointer to parameter list
          BCS FIError           ;Error-handling routine
          . . .                 ;Rest of code goes here
FIError   . . .                 ;Error-handling routine goes here
          END

InfoData  DATA
FileInfo  DC I4'Path'           ;Pointer to pathname
Access    DS 2                  ;Access byte will go here
Filetype  DS 2                  ;File type will go here
Auxtype   DS 4                  ;Auxiliary type will go here
Storage   DS 2                  ;Storage type will go here
CreateD   DS 2                  ;Creation date will go here
CreateT   DS 2                  ;Creation time will go here
ModDate   DS 2                  ;Modification time will go here
ModTime   DS 2                  ;Modification time will go here
Blocks    DS 4                  ;Number of blocks will go here
Path      DC I1 'PEnd-Path+1'   ;Length byte for pathname
Name      DC C'1/Filename'      ;Name of file with prefix
PEnd      ANOP
          END
```

Unless your application has some special need, this method of setting up a parameter list is the preferred style, particularly in view of its ease of operation.

ProDOS/16 is, technically speaking, not one of the IIGS tools. Nonetheless it does have a set of macros for it on the Apple Programmers Workshop disk. Each macro consists of the name of the particular ProDOS/16 system call. The name should be followed by the address of the parameter, as follows:

```
_GetFileInfo InfoData
```

This macro call takes as an input parameter the address of the parameter list required by the call.

ProDOS Call	05	06	10	11	25	27	28	2B	2E	40	42	43	44	45
	Error Codes													
AllocInterrupt	x	x			x									
ChangePath	x	x				x		x		x			x	x
ClearBackupBit	x	x								x			x	x
Close	x	x				x		x				x		
Create	x	x	x			x		x		x			x	x
DeallocInterrupt	x	x												
Destroy	x	x	x			x		x		x			x	x
Flush	x	x				x		x				x		
GetBootVol	x	x												
GetDevNum	x	x	x											
GetEOF	x	x										x		
GetFileInfo	x	x				x				x			x	x
GetLevel	x	x												
GetMark	x	x										x		
GetPathname	x	x				x				x			x	x
GetPrefix	x	x				x				x			x	x
GetVersion	x	x												
Newline	x	x										x		
Open	x	x				x				x	x		x	x
Quit	x												x	
Read	x	x				x						x		
ReadBlock	x	x		x		x	x							
SetEOF	x	x				x						x		
SetFileInfo	x	x				x		x		x			x	x
SetLevel	x	x												
SetMark	x	x				x						x		
SetPrefix	x	x	x			x				x			x	x
Volume	x	x	x			x			x					x
Write	x	x				x		x				x		
WriteBlock	x	x		x		x	x	x						

Table 23-14

ProDOS/16 Error Codes for Each Call

Error Codes

46	47	48	49	4A	4B	4C	4D	4E	50	52	53	54	55	57	58	59	5A	5B	5C
											X								
X	X			X	X			X	X	X				X	X				
X				X						X					X				
																	X		
X	X	X	X		X					X	X				X		X		
											X								
X				X	X			X	X	X					X		X		
		X															X		
X				X	X					X	X				X				
X				X	X														
X				X						X					X				X
X				X	X			X	X	X		X		X					
X												X							X
						X		X											
							X	X								X			
X				X	X		X			X	X				X				
																X			
							X										X		
				X	X						X	X			X				
				X							X		X	X	X				
		X																	
						X		X									X		

Code (Hex)	Meaning
01	Invalid call number (nonexistent command number)
05	Pointer to parameter block is out of permissible range
06	ProDOS is busy with another call
10	No device on the line with the given name
11	Device number given is not in list of active devices
25	Maximum number (16) of user-defined interrupt handlers already installed
27	Hardware input/output error
28	No device connected as specified by device number
2B	Volume is write-protected
2E	Disk switched when file open (works only on calls that check the volume name)
30-3F	Code defined and used by individual device driver
40	Pathname contains illegal characters
42	Table of file-control blocks is full because maximum number (8) of files are open
43	File reference number does not match any currently open file
44	Subdirectory in pathname does not exist
45	Volume in pathname does not exist
46	File name does not exist
47	New pathname already exists
48	Volume full
49	Volume directory full (maximum of 51 entries in version 1.0)
4A	File format version incompatible with existing operating system
4B	File storage organization unknown
4C	End-of-file mark found during read
4D	Mark position is greater than end of file
4E	Attempted type of access not allowed
50	Illegal operation attempted on open file
51	Directory structure damaged (number of directory entries not equal to number of entries expected)
52	Not a ProDOS/16, ProDOS/8, or SOS disk
53	Value of a parameter is out of range
54	Out of memory

Table 23-15

ProDOS/16 Error Codes and Meaning

Code (Hex)	Meaning
55	Maximum number of on-line volumes (8) reached (volume control block table full)
57	More than one volume on-line with the same volume name
58	Access attempt made to nonblock device
59	Value for system file level is out of range
5A	Block number out of range—disk directory damaged
5B	Attempt to change pathname to different volume
5C	Attempt to execute nonexecutable system file (file type must be $B3 [.S16] or FF [.SYS])

Table 23-15

ProDOS/16 Error Codes and Meaning (continued)

OBJECT MODULE FORMAT

Under ProDOS/8, executable program code is in a file that is loaded in a specified memory location. Generally the code is written to be run at that specified location and will not run if loaded into another location unless special techniques are used to make the code position-independent.

Under ProDOS/16, all executable code is in a file that can be loaded into a variety of memory locations and can be run at those locations. Each code file contains information that permits the code to be located at different addresses. This information is known as *relocatable information.*

The Apple Programmers Workshop automatically creates the relocatable object files when it links and assembles or compiles your source code. Generally, you need not concern yourself about the actual file contents. Actually, more than just executable code files follow the ProDOS/16 Object Module Format specification. The particular files that use the Object Module Format are listed in Table 23-16. Each object module file contains one or more segments, of the types listed in Table 23-17.

The creation and use of the various forms of segments are generally handled by the Apple IIGS Programmer's Workshop Assembler, Compilers, and Linker. For more information about this function, consult the *Apple IIGS Programmer's Workshop Reference Manual.* Many of these segments are used by the Loader, which is discussed in Chapter 22.

File Type	Use
Source ($B0 - SRC)	Source code for assembler or compiler.
Object ($B1 - OBJ)	Contains the output from the assembler or compiler and serves as the input to the linker.
Library ($B2 - LIB)	General object type code segments that can be be used by the linker.
Load ($B3 - S16)	Common type of executable code files.
Run Time Library ($B4 - RTL)	General utilities that can be shared by applications and that contain executable code segments.
Shell Loader ($B5 - EXE)	Load-type file that can be run from a system shell.
Startup Load ($B6 - STR) (Permanent)	Load-type file that is meant to be executed once at system start-up, returning to the system when it is done. Generally contains initialization code. Stays in memory when done.
Startup Load ($B7) (Removable)	Load-type file that is meant to be executed once at system start-up, returning to the system when it is done. Generally contains initialization code. Removed from memory when done.
Classic Desk Accessory ($B8 - CDA)	Contains executable code for a Classic Desk Accessory.
New Desk Accessory ($B9 - NDA)	Contains executable code for a New Desk Accessory.
Tools ($BA)	RAM-based tools and RAM patches to ROM-based tools.

Table 23-16

File Types Using the Object Module Format

Segment Type	Use
Jump Table	Provides the means for memory-resident segments to cause nonresident segments to be loaded into memory
Pathname	Contains the pathnames of used load files
Initialization	Contains code that is to be executed at load time and before the loading of other segments
Absolute Bank	Segment relocatable only within a specified bank
Direct Page/Stack	Defines the applications direct page and stack requirement

Table 23-17

Object Module Format Segment Types (for Load Files)

PART VI

Interrupts

CHAPTER 24

Desk Accessories

The Apple IIGS has two kinds of desk accessories — classic desk accessories (CDA) and new desk accessories (NDA). This chapter discusses both kinds of accessories, explains how to program a desk accessory, and describes the use of the Desk Manager with the accessories.

CLASSIC DESK ACCESSORIES

Two of the CDAs come in ROM and are present in every Apple IIGS program as long as interrupts are not disabled. These desk accessories are available by pressing the APPLE, CONTROL, and ESCAPE keys simultaneously. The two built-in CDAs are the Control Panel (discussed in Chapter 3) and the Alternate Display Mode.

The Alternate Display Mode is available for compatibility with certain pre-Apple IIGS programs that used Page 2 of text or low-resolution graphics (located at $E0/0800-0C00). Page 2 is not shadowed into bank $00 under normal circumstances. If the Alternate Display Mode is active, it periodically moves screen data from Text Page 2 in bank $00, where the 8-bit Apple II program places it, to the Text Page 2 area of bank $E0, which results in it being displayed.

A CDA does not normally operate in a window on the desktop. Rather, it interrupts the running of the application and takes full control of the Apple IIGS during its operation. The accessory is responsible for its own input/output as well as for the protection of the memory used by the interrupted application. It is normally not event-driven.

Up to 13 CDAs can be on the menu at one time. In order to have the system load a CDA onto the desk accessory menu, the desk accessory code must be in the DESK.ACCS subdirectory of the System directory on the boot (system) disk. These files must have a file type of $B9 (which appears in the ProDOS/16 directory as type CDA). This is a load-type file (see Chapters 22 and 23).

The selection of a CDA is made from the CDA menu. An illustration of that menu appears in Figure 24-1.

The CDA file must have an identification section at its beginning as follows:

```
CDA_Start       START
                Str 'CDA Name'         ;Name of CDA preceded by length byte
                DC I4'CodeStart'       ;Pointer to start of code
                DC I4'Shutdown'        ;Pointer to shutdown routine
                END
CodeStart       START
* Main program code goes here
                . . .
                END
Shutdown        START
* Shutdown code goes here
                . . .
                END
```

The main code of the CDA is similar to any program. It can freely use the space used by text pages in banks $00, 01, E0, and E1, since this space is

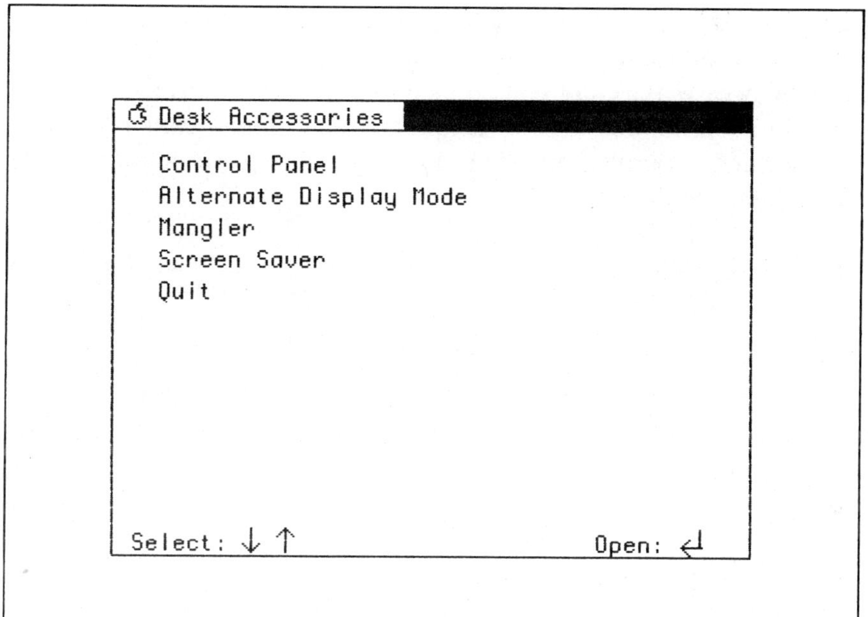

Figure 24-1
CDA menu

saved by the Desk Manager before it passes control to the CDA. Note that the Desk Manager also restores this space at the conclusion of the operation of the CDA so that memory variables stored in these locations are not saved in between calls to the CDA.

The CDA may freely use Page 0 in bank $00 and may also use the stack as long as it does not at any time remove more bytes from the stack than it has placed on the stack. The CDA must request any other memory from Memory Manager (discussed in Chapter 5). The program should be written so that the CDA does not require memory in bank $00 and $01 because this memory may not be available.

The shutdown routine is called whenever the Desk Manager DeskShutdown call is made. This call must be made by any application that supports new desk accessories before shutting down, and it is also made by ProDOS when it switches between ProDOS/8 and ProDOS/16 in either order. The shutdown routine should ensure that the desk accessory has been turned off and has restored any changes it has made to the operating system. In most cases this shutdown routine need merely be an RTL (long return from subroutine) instruction.

In many cases the CDA code should first save the current value in the data bank register and then set it equal to the program bank register so that data and program code can use 16-bit addressing. The following code will accomplish this:

```
PHB                     ;Save data bank register on stack
PHK                     ;Transfer program bank register
PLB                     ;into data bank register
```

The end of the CDA code should perform an RTL back to the Desk Manager. If the data bank register has been modified, it should be restored before the return. The following code will accomplish this:

```
* Assumes the stack has been cut back so that only the saved data bank
* register remains on the stack from the data placed on the stack by the
* CDA
            PLB                 ;Restore data bank register
            RTL                 ;and return to Desk Manager
            END
```

The Desk Manager contains several routines that it uses in working with CDAs. With the exception of two, none of these routines need be called by your application—and, indeed, they should not be called. The Desk Manager handles the work for you.

The routines not to be called by your application include the following:

□ SaveScrn is used to save the text screens in banks $00, 01, E0, and E1 when a CDA is called.

□ RestScrn is used to restore the text screens in banks $00, 01, E0, and E1 when a CDA has completed its operation.

□ SaveAll saves the variables preserved by the Desk Manager when the CDA is called.

□ RestAll restores the variables preserved by the Desk Manager when the CDA is called.

□ InstallCDA is used to install each CDA found in the DESK.ACCS subdirectory of the System subdirectory.

□ ChooseCDA activates the Desk Manager and displays the CDA menu. (This occurs when the user presses the APPLE-CONTROL-ESCAPE key combination.)

The Desk Manager contains a routine that permits your application to modify the CDA menu to provide for different text. The primary use of this routine is for display in languages other than English. This routine, SetDAStrPtr, also permits you to modify the Alternate Display Mode desk accessory to be anything you wish.

The SetDAStrPtr takes two inputs. The first is a long-word handle to the Alternate Display desk accessory. The second is a long-word pointer to the table of strings in the CDA menu.

The table of strings contains four pointers to the actual text of the four preset lines in the CDA menu. The title line consists of the outline Apple symbol, the words "Desk Accessories," and 18 inverse spaces. The code for this string is

```
TitleStr        DC H'5A A0 41 A0'
                DC C'Desk Accessories '
                DC 18H'20'
                DC H'5F 00'
```

The number of characters in the line must remain constant. Therefore, if you change the title string, you must adjust the number of inverse spaces ($20), initially set at 18.

The second line in the table of strings is the title of the Control Panel. This title is preset to "Control Panel" (followed by a hexadecimal $00 to show the end of the string, as is true of all the strings in the table of strings). The title can be changed to any item as long as it is less than 34 characters.

The third line in the table of strings is the title of the Quit command. This line may not necessarily be the third line in the CDA menu if other items have been added to the menu by the Desk Manager. The line is still the third preset line in the CDA menu. The present value of the string is "Quit." It can be changed to any item as long as it is less than 34 characters.

The final line is the select string. This line normally reads "Select: ", followed by an up and down arrow and "Open: ", followed by the return arrow symbol. The code for this string is

```
SelectStr           DC C' Select: '
                    DC H'4A A0 4B'
                    DC 17H'A0'
                    DC C'Open: '
                    DC H'4D A0 A0 5F 00'
```

The number of characters in the line must remain constant. A good way of accomplishing this is to change the number of space characters, initially set at 17 by the line "17H'A0'."

The pointer to the current table of strings can be obtained by means of the GetDAStrPtr function.This function returns a long-word pointer to the table of strings.

NEW DESK ACCESSORIES

A new desk accessory (NDA) is similar in use to a Macintosh desk accessory. It is available only with applications running in Apple IIGS mode on a window-desktop environment and with the Apple menu available on the menu bar.

An NDA is a load file that, like the CDA, is kept in the DESK.ACCS subdirectory of the System subdirectory of the boot disk. Its file type differs from that of the CDA. The value of the file type is $B8, and it appears in ProDOS/16 directories as NDA.

An NDA consists of a program with a special header required for an NDA, and four parts or entry points. The entry points are known as open, close, action, and init. When control is passed to the NDA, the 65816 is in native mode with 16-bit registers and memory. The NDA does not have a direct page assigned to it, although it can temporarily use the stack for its direct page by means of the following code:

```
PHD              ;Save direct register on stack
TSC              ;Transfer stack pointer through accumulator
TCD              ;into direct register
```

When programming an NDA, you should assume the following tools are loaded and initialized and, thus, available to your application:

- □ Control Manager
- □ Dialog Manager
- □ Event Manager

□ Line Edit

□ Menu Manager

□ Quickdraw II

□ Scrap Manager

□ Window Manager.

The NDA can check for the availability of other tools and request them if needed.

Whenever your NDA does any drawing or uses its Grafport, it should be sure first to save the previous Grafport and restore that Grafport on exit. This step can be accomplished by the following code:

```
                PushLong #$0000          ;Space for result
                _GetPort                 ;Save current Grafport on stack
                PushLong NDAPort         ;NDA's port
                _SetPort                 ;now the current port
                . . .
*Code using port goes here
                . . .
                _SetPort                 ;Restores old port
```

The old port is restored at the end of the routine by using the SetPort command without pushing the old port's pointer, since its pointer is already on the top of the stack by means of the GetPort command issued at the beginning of the segment.

The header of an NDA contains pointers to the four routines (open, close, init, and action), a value specifying the number of ticks (1/60th of a second) between run commands being passed to the NDA, a mask specifying the events that should be passed to the NDA, and a specification of the Apple menu item text for that NDA. The code appears as the following:

```
NDAHeader     START
              DC I4'OpenNDA'          ;Pointer to the open routine
              DC I4'CloseNDA'         ;Pointer to the close routine
              DC I4'NDAAction'        ;Pointer to the action routine
              DC I4'InitNDA'          ;Pointer to the init routine
              DC I2'NumTicks'         ;Number of ticks between run commands
              DC I2'EventMask'        ;Mask showing which events handled
              DC C'  Title\H**'       ;Menu item text line
```

The Event Mask is the same as the Event Mask used in the discussion of the Event Manager (see Chapter 20).

The four entry points to the NDA perform four different functions and are called by the Desk Manager at different times. The open routine is called by the Desk Manager function OpenNDA. This routine should check if the NDA is already active and return without any action if it is. Otherwise the routine should create a new window, making it a system window, change the NDA variable to show that it is active, and return with the pointer to the new window's Grafport on top of the stack. The following code segment performs this action. It assumes that the data segment containing the window parameters required by NewWindow are also part of the NDA.

```
OpenNDA         START
                Using NDAData
                LDA >NDAActive              ;Is NDA already active?
                BNE AlreadyOpen             ;Yes - don't open again
                PushLong #$0000             ;Space for result
                PushLong #NDAWindParms      ;Pointer to window parameters
                _NewWindow                  ;Create the new window
                PLX                         ;Low word of window pointer
                PLA                         ;High word of window pointer
                STA 6,S                     ;Save on stack for return from open
                STA >NDAWindPtr+2           ;and within NDA for NDA's reference
                TXA                         ;Get low word of window pointer
                STA 4,S                     ;Save on stack for return from open
                STA >NDAWindPtr             ;and within NDA for NDA's reference
                PushLong NDAWindPtr         ;Window pointer on stack
                _SetSysWindow               ;Make window a system window
                LDA #$8000
                STA >NDAActive              ;Make active flag true
AlreadyOpen     RTL                         ;Back to Desk Manager
                END
```

The close routine should shut down the desk accessory when it is open. It should also work, without creating an error situation, if it is called when the desk accessory is not open. A typical close routine should check the active flag to see if the NDA is active. If the NDA is active, it should close the window and return. If the NDA is already closed, the routine should just return. The following code accomplishes this, using the NDAActive flag set up in the previous code segment:

```
CloseNDA        START
                Using NDAData
                LDA >NDAActive              ;Is NDA already open?
                BEQ NotOpen                 ;No - so don't close
                PushLong NDAWindPtr         ;Window pointer on stack
                _CloseWindow                ;Close the NDA's window
                STZ >NDAactive              ;Make active flag false
NotOpen         RTL                         ;Back to Desk Manager
                END
```

The init routine is called when DeskStartup or DeskShutdown is called by the application to initialize and shut down all NDAs. The Desk Manager puts a value in the accumulator to show whether the call is a startup (nonzero value) or a shutdown (zero value) call. Your NDA should determine whether it is receiving an initialization or a shutdown command by testing the accumulator and then perform any necessary initialization or shutdown work. The following code accomplishes this:

```
InitNDA         START
                CMP #$0000              ;Initialire or shutdown?
                BEQ Shutdown            ;Zero is a shutdown
* Initialization code goes here
Init            . . .
                RTL
* Shutdown code goes here
Shutdown        . . .
                RTL
```

The action routine is the routine that does the real work in an NDA after it has been opened and before it is closed. This routine handles all user action involving the NDA as well as the periodic action that some desk accessories require. The action routine is actually a preprocessor for nine different potential actions that the desk accessory should be able to perform. These commands are listed in Table 24-1, together with the code applied to each command and the meaning of the command.

The command code is received by your NDA in the accumulator. For command codes 1 (Event) and 4 (Menu), additional information is passed in the X and Y registers. For Event, the additional information is a pointer (low word in the X register) to the event record. For Menu, the additional information is the MenuID of the selected menu in the X register and the ItemID of the selected item in the Y register. The action routine should

Code	Command	Meaning
1	Event	Event being passed to NDA
2	Run	Specified time has passed
3	Cursor	NDA is front window and SystemTask called
4	Menu	Item from system menu selected
5	Undo	Undo edit menu command selected
6	Cut	Cut edit menu command selected
7	Copy	Copy edit menu command selected
8	Paste	Paste edit menu command selected
9	Clear	Clear edit menu command selected

Table 24-1
List of Action Routine Commands and Codes

save these values and then dispatch control to the proper routine to handle the particular type of command. The following code shows the general framework of this action:

```
NDAAction       START
                Using NDAData
                PHY                     ;Save Y register and
                PHX                     ;X register on stack
                ASL A                   ;Make action code into index
                TAX                     ;and transfer to X register for use
                JSR (Action,X)          ;Use jump table to direct action
                PLA                     ;Remove X and Y registers from stack
                PLA                     ;so stack is left the same
                RTL                     ;and back to routine
Action          DC I'Nothing'           ;0 code shouldn't be used
                DC I'DoEvent'           ;Pointer to event code routine
                DC I'DoRun'             ;Pointer to run code routine
                DC I'DoCursor'          ;Pointer to cursor code routine
                DC I'DoMenu'            ;Pointer to menu code routine
                DC I'DoUndo'            ;Pointer to undo code routine
                DC I'DoCut'             ;Pointer to cut code routine
                DC I'DoCopy'            ;Pointer to copy code routine
                DC I'DoPaste'           ;Pointer to paste code routine
                DC I'DoClear'           ;Pointer to clear code routine
                . . .
                END
```

This code example makes use of the absolute indexed indirect form of addressing permitted for the JSR command on the 65816 microprocessor.

The steps taken by each of the action routines, of course, depend on what your NDA is designed to accomplish. When an event is passed to your NDA, it must first determine what the event was and then take appropriate action. This procedure requires yet another dispatch-type of routine in your code, similar to that used in handling the action event code. The following segment will perform this action:

```
DoEvent         START
                Using NDAData
DirSave         EQU 1                   ;Stack loc. of saved direct register
ReturnAddr      EQU DirSave+2           ;Stack loc. of RTS return address
EventPtr        EQU ReturnAddr+2        ;Stack loc. of saved X & Y registers
                PHD                     ;Save direct register on stack
                TSC                     ;And make the stack pointer
                TCD                     ;into the direct register as well
                LDA [EventPtr]          ;Get type of event
                ASL A                   ;Make into index
                TAX                     ;used by X register
                JSR (Events,X)          ;And select routine for event type
                PLD                     ;Restore direct register
                RTS                     ;and return to main NDA action
Events          DC I'Nothing'           ;Null event
                DC I'DoMDown'           ;Location of button-down routine
                DC I'DoMUp'             ;Location of button-up routine
                DC I'DoKey'             ;Location of key-press routine
                DC I'Nothing'           ;Undefined event code
                DC I'DoAutoKey'         ;Location of auto key routine
                DC I'DoUpdate'          ;Location of update routine
                DC I'Nothing'           ;Undefined event code
                DC I'DoActivate'        ;Location of activate routine
                DC I'DoSwitch'          ;Location of switch routine
                . . .
                END
```

The Desk Manager routines for NDAs provide a method for your application to work with any NDAs that are active. If your application is using TaskMaster (discussed in Chapter 16), it will need to use only three commands of the Desk Manager. These three commands are the following:

1. DeskStartup is called at the beginning of the program to initialize the Desk Manager. This call takes no parameters. It should be called only after the various conditions required for using NDAs are present: (1) required tools are loaded; (2) tools are initialized; (3) menu bar is present; and (4) menu bar has edit menu. The call results in the initialization of all NDAs that are installed.
2. FixAppleMenu places the various installed NDAs in the menu bar. The routine must be passed the identification number of the menu to which the NDAs should be added. Typically this is the Apple menu.
3. DeskShutdown is called at the end of the application. It takes no parameters. This command causes a shutdown call to be made to all desk accessories (NDAs and CDAs). It should be made before the application is shut down and before any of the tools needed by an NDA are shut down.

Other Desk Manager routines are necessary if your application is not using TaskMaster. (If it is used, TaskMaster makes these calls for your application.) These calls include the following:

- OpenNDA is called when the user has selected an NDA from the menu (normally the Apple menu). It requires an input word consisting of the item ID returned by the Menu Manager. A word value, used to refer to that NDA, is returned by the routine.
- SystemTask should be called at least once each time your application goes through its main event loop. If the loop takes a significant time to run, you should consider calling SystemTask more often. This routine, which takes no parameters, checks if the time has passed for giving the NDA a run command and, if so, transfers control to the NDA with a run command.
- SystemClick should be called whenever your application reports a button-down event in a system window (value returned by Find-Window, discussed in Chapter 16). It takes three inputs: a long-word

Edit Type	Edit Value
Undo	1
Cut	2
Copy	3
Paste	4
Clear	5

Table 24-2
Value of Edit Types Passed by SystemEdit

pointer to the EventRecord containing the button-down event; a long-word pointer to the Grafport of the system window in which the button-down event occurred; and the pointer returned by FindWindow disclosing where in the window the button went down. This routine transfers control to the appropriate NDA, giving it an event command.

□ SystemEdit should be called when the user has selected a menu edit item. The routine takes an input parameter of the edit type (shown in Table 24-2) and returns a boolean value, showing whether the edit was meant for system window (that is, if the top window is a system window). If the top window is a system window, the Desk Manager passes the command on to the NDA, using the appropriate edit command. If the top window is not a system window, SystemEdit will return false and your application should handle the edit item for itself.

□ CloseNDA closes the specified NDA (reference number passed as a parameter). This routine is rarely needed because SystemClick will normally handle a close command from the user given by means of a click in the NDA's close box.

□ CloseNDAbyWinPtr is an alternate method of closing an NDA. It is likely to be used when the user chose to close the NDA by selecting

Routine	Function
CloseAllNDAs	Closes all open NDAs. Requires no input or output parameters.
GetNumNDAs	Returns a word value containing the number of NDAs currently installed.
SystemEvent	The routine by which the Event Manager passes events to the Desk Manager. Requires as input the event type (word), event message (long-word), event time (long-word), event location (long-word), and the event modifier flags (word). Returns a boolean value if the event was processed by a desk accessory and false if it is to be processed by your application.

Table 24-3

Rarely (or Internally) Used Desk Manager Routines

close from the file menu rather than clicking in the close box. When close is selected from the file menu, your application should call FrontWindow (in the Window Manager) to determine the Grafport of the front (active) window. If this is a system window, the application should push the pointer to the Grafport on the stack and call this routine. Otherwise your application should handle the close as one of its commands.

Several other Desk Manager calls are used either internally by the Desk Manager or, in an unusual case, by your application. These are summarized in Table 24-3.

Table 24-4 is a list of all Desk Manager calls, showing their function numbers and the input and output parameters required by each. Table 24-5 is a comparison of the Apple IIGS and Macintosh Desk Manager routines.

Function Name	Function Number	AllDispDA	CDAHandle	DAID	EditType	EventLoc	EventMesg	EventModF	EventPtr
Parameter Size		L	L	W	W	L	L	W	L
Parameter Type		H	H	V	V	Pt	V	BA	P
ChooseCDA	17								
Close NDA	22								
CloseAllNDAs	29								
CloseNDAByWinPtr	28								
DeskBootInit	1								
DeskReset	5								
DeskShutdown	3								
DeskStartup	2								
DeskStatus	6								
DeskVersion	4								
FixAppleMenu	30								
GetDAStrPtr	20			I1					
GetNumNDAs	27								
InstallCDA	15		I1						
InstallNDA	14								
OpenNDA	21								
RestAll	12								
RestScrn	10								
SaveAll	11								
SaveScrn	9								

Table 24-4

Summary of Desk Manager Routines

EventTime	EventType	MenuID	NDAHandle	NDARefNum	NumNDAs	Processed	Result	StringTable	Version	WindowLoc	WindowPtr
L	W	W	L	W	W	W	W	L	W	L	L
V	V	V	H	V	V	B	B	P	V	Pt	P
				I1							
											I1
							O1				
									O1		
		I1									
								O1			
					O1						
			I1								
		I1		O1							

Function Name	Function Number	AllDispDA	CDAHandle	DAID	EditType	EventLoc	EventMesg	EventModF	EventPtr
SetDAStrPtr	19	I1							
SystemClick	23								I1
SystemEdit	24				I1				
SystemEvent	26					I4	I2	I5	
SystemTask	25								

Notes:

Size: L long-word (32 bits)
W word (16 bits)

Type: B Boolean
BA Bit array
H Handle
P Pointer
Pt Point
V Value

Table 24-4

Summary of Desk Manager Routines (continued)

EventTime	EventType	MenuID	NDAHandle	NDARefNum	NumNDAs	Processed	Result	StringTable	Version	WindowLoc	WindowPtr
								I2			
										I3	I2
						O1					
I3	I1					O1					

Routine	Apple IIGS	Macintosh	Macintosh Name If Different
ChooseCDA	X		
Close NDA	X	X	CloseDeskAcc
CloseAllNDAs	X		
CloseNDAByWinPtr	X		
DeskBootInit	X		
DeskReset	X		
DeskShutdown	X		
DeskStartup	X		
DeskStatus	X		
DeskVersion	X		
FixAppleMenu	X		
GetDAStrPtr	X		
GetNumNDAs	X		
InstallCDA	X		
InstallNDA	X		
OpenNDA	X	X	OpenDeskAcc
RestAll	X		
RestScrn	X		
SaveAll	X		
SaveScrn	X		
SetDAStrPtr	X		
SystemClick	X	X	
SystemEdit	X	X	
SystemEvent	X	X	
SystemTask	X	X	
SystemMenu		X	

Table 24-5

Comparison of Apple IIGS and Macintosh Desk Manager Routines

CHAPTER

25

Other Interrupts

The Apple IIGS is the most interrupt-driven Apple II ever. Not only do many of the functions of the IIGS depend on interrupts (for example, Classic Desk Accessories discussed in Chapter 24), but the machine has a number of built-in facilities for handling interrupts. Interrupts can occur on the IIGS in a number of different ways. This chapter will discuss some of these sources of interrupts and methods of dealing with them.

TYPES OF INTERRUPTS

The Apple II family of computers has not always been able to work with interrupts. The initial disk operating system for the Apple II, DOS, had no provisions for interrupts. Presently, however, ProDOS/8 and ProDOS/16 both have extensive facilities for working with interrupts. So does the other major operating system for the IIGS, Pascal 1.3.

An *interrupt* is defined as a signal to the microprocessor, generated either in hardware or software, that causes the microprocessor to stop its present operation temporarily and begin to execute a special program called an *interrupt-handling routine.* Typically the interrupt-handling routine disables further interrupts, saves the values in the machine register, determines the cause of the interrupt and services it appropriately, restores the registers to prior values, and resumes the interrupted operation.

The use of interrupts in the IIGS should be of concern to you as an application programmer in the following two ways:

1. Your application, whenever possible, should be coded in re-entrant format so that values used by the application are not lost during the interrupt. A re-entrant routine is one that can be interrupted, run a second time by the interrupt handler, and re-entered on the first run without losing variable values, even if the re-entered routine has also been run as part of the interrupt-handling routine. Re-entrant programming using the 65816 microprocessor is discussed in Chapter 13 of Fischer, *65816 Assembly Language Programming,* Osborne/McGraw-Hill, 1986.
2. Your application may need to make use of some of the interrupt capabilities of the IIGS or the interrupt routines may make your programming task easier.

The 65816 has four forms of hardware interrupts and two forms of software interrupts. Each of these interrupts is vectored to a particular location, depending on the type of interrupt and whether the interrupt occurred in native or emulation mode. These interrupts, their vectors, and the routine pointed to by the vectors in the IIGS are listed in Table 25-1.

Interrupt	Native Vector (and Pointer)	Emulation Vector (and Pointer)	Hardware/Software
Abort	$FFE8-9 ($C079)	$FFF8-9 ($C079)	Hardware—pin 3
BReaK	$FFE6-7 ($C074)	$FFFE-F ($C074)	Software
COProcessor	$FFE4-5 ($C07B)	$FFF4-5 ($C07B)	Software
IRQ	$FFEE-F ($C074)	$FFFE-F ($C074)	Hardware—pin 4
NMI	$FFEA-B ($03FB)	$FFFA-B ($03FB)	Hardware—pin 6
Reset	$FFFC-D ($FA62)	$FFFC-D ($FA62)	Hardware—pin 40

Table 25-1

65816 Interrupts and Their Vectors

INTERRUPT MANAGER

The many different IIGS interrupts all fall under one of these six types of 65816 interrupts. In most cases the interrupts are of the IRQ type. Sorting out these various interrupts is the job of the Interrupt Manager.

Unlike the previous managers discussed for the Apple IIGS, the Interrupt Manager is not a toolbox tool set. It does not need to be called by your application to handle interrupts. Rather, it functions transparently to your application unless you wish to make some change to it.

The Break and IRQ vectors both point to $FF/C074 for the interrupt handler. An examination of the code at this location shows two instructions:

```
CLV                     ;Clear the overflow bit
JMP $E1/0010            ;Jump to the interrupt RAM vector
```

The instruction found at memory location $E1/0010, following a normal system boot, is

```
JMP $FF/B673
```

This is the address of the default ROM-based Interrupt Manager.

Note that the interrupt-handling routine does not jump immediately to $FF/B673, but jumps through $E1/0010. It does this so that your application can modify the jump instruction at $E1/0010 to point to a custom-designed Interrupt Manager instead. If you do create a custom Interrupt Manager, you should be sure that you at least perform the housekeeping chores done by the default Interrupt Manager. These chores include

```
CLC
XCE                     ;Be sure we're in native mode
REP #$30                ;with 16-bit registers and memory
PHP                     ;Save processor status register on stack
PHB                     ;and data bank register
PEA $E1E1               ;Set data bank register
PLB                     ;to bank $E1
STA $0108               ;Save accumulator in $E1/0108
LDA $C035               ;Shadow register
STA $0119               ;saved in $E1/0119
ORA #$8000              ;and adjust shadowing
AND #$9F1E
STA $C035
STX $010A               ;Save X register in $E1/010A
STY $010C               ;Save Y register in $E1/010C
TDC                     ;Save direct register, through accumulator
STA $0110               ;in $E1/0110
LDA #$0000              ;and make direct register point to
TCD                     ;absolute page zero
SEP #$30                ;Go into 8-bit mode
. . .                   ;and handle interrupt
```

When you change the Interrupt Handler vector, you do not directly adjust the values at $E1/0011-12. While this is the current location of that vector, future ROM revisions in the IIGS may move it. To guarantee future compatibility with possible revisions, use the appropriate tool function in the Miscellaneous Tool Set to change the vector.

To change an interrupt vector, you use SetVector. This routine requires you to push a word value that represents the particular interrupt vector desired to be changed, followed by a long-word value containing the new vector address. The values for each adjustable interrupt vector are listed in Table 25-2, together with the vector pointed to by each on initialization.

The default routine for some of the interrupts given in Table 25-2, $B498, does essentially nothing when called. It is a dummy routine used when an actual routine has not been activated. The code at $B498 consists of the following:

```
SEC
RTL
```

The current value of any interrupt vector can be obtained with the GetVector function. To use this function, your application should push the word-value code of the interrupt vector desired. The long-word address of the vector is returned on top of the stack.

Many of the interrupts specified in Table 25-2 can be enabled or disabled as sources of interrupts. The IntSource function performs this function depending on a word value passed to the function. The meaning of the various values passed is shown in Table 25-3.

Interrupt Type	Vector Value	Vector Pointer
Interrupt Manager	$0004	$FF/B673
COP Manager	$0005	$FF/B665
Abort Manager	$0006	$FF/B665
System Death Manager	$0007	$FF/A474
SCC Interrupt Handler	$0009	$FF/B498
Scan Line Interrupt Handler	$000A	$FE/4385
Sound Interrupt Handler	$000B	$FF/B498
Vertical Blanking Interrupt Handler	$000C	$FE/98EE
Mouse Interrupt Handler	$000D	$FE/C65A
Quarter-Second Interrupt Handler	$000E	$FF/B498
Keyboard Interrupt Handler	$000F	$FE/C6F1
ADB Response Byte Interrupt Handler	$0010	$FF/8492
ADB SRQ Interrupt Handler	$0011	$FF/8192
Keyboard Micro Interrupt Handler	$0014	$FF/B540
One-Second Interrupt Handler	$0015	$FF/B498
External VGC Interrupt Handler	$0016	$FF/B498
Other Unspecified Interrupt Handler	$0017	$FF/B498
Increment Busy Flag	$0019	$FE/C8E4
Decrement Busy Flag	$001A	$FE/C881

Table 25-2
Interrupt Vector Values and Initialization Vectors

Interrupt Type	Enable	Disable
Keyboard interrupts	$0000	$0001
Vertical blanking interrupts	$0002	$0003
Quarter-second interrupts	$0004	$0005
One-second interrupts	$0006	$0007
ADB data interrupts	$000A	$000B
Scan line interrupts	$000C	$000D
External VGC interrupts	$000E	$000F

Table 25-3

Values Passed to IntSource to Enable or Disable an Interrupt

Bit Number	Meaning
0	External VGC interrupts enabled
1	Scan line interrupts enabled
2	ADB data interrupts enabled
3	Reserved
4	One-second interrupts enabled
5	Quarter-second interrupts enabled
6	Vertical-blanking interrupts enabled
7	Keyboard interrupts enabled
8-15	Undefined

Table 25-4

Meaning of Bits in Interrupt Enable State Word

Your application can also check if certain interrupts have been enabled by calling GetIRQenbl, a routine that returns a word value specifying the interrupt enable state. The meaning of this value is shown in Table 25-4.

SYSTEM DEATH MANAGER

One of the special interrupt routines on the IIGS is the System Death Manager. This somewhat draconian routine does just what it is advertised to do—it causes the death of the current operating system, requiring a rebooting of the IIGS. The routine can be called by several of the IIGS toolbox managers or by your application. If your application calls System Death, it must be done via the SysDeathMgr function in the Miscellaneous Tool Set. The routine expects two values—a word value indicating the error code and a long-word pointer to an ASCII string constituting the system death message.

The System Death Manager displays the system death message followed by a dash and the error code. It then displays a sliding solid Apple below the message. There is no return from the routine.

If your application is to use the default system death message ("Fatal System Error"), it need only pass a value of zero for the ASCII string pointer. If it is using a custom message, the string should start with a byte containing the number of characters in the string, followed by the string with each byte having the most significant bit off (positive ASCII). The message can have up to 255 characters. The meaning of the error codes shown by the System Death Manager is listed in Table 25-5.

THE SCHEDULER

The Scheduler is a special tool that deals with interrupts, particularly those involving desk accessories. A variable known as the busy flag is located at $E1/00FF. Although this is the current location of the flag, its location is not guaranteed in future versions of the IIGS. The flag should be accessed only through the routines provided for it.

Whenever the busy flag has a nonzero value, interrupts that access the Scheduler are placed in a queue rather than executed immediately. When the busy flag is decremented to a zero value, the items in the queue are then called in the order in which they were placed in the queue.

Incrementing the busy flag is done by a JSL to INCBUSYFLG when the 65816 is in full native mode. The location of INCBUSYFLG can be found through the GetVector tool function. The routine disables interrupts,

Code	Meaning
$0001	ProDOS/16—unclaimed interrupt
$0004	Attempted division by zero
$000A	ProDOS/16—volume control block unusable
$000B	ProDOS/16—file control block unusable
$000C	ProDOS/16—block zero allocated illegally
$000D	ProDOS/16—interrupt occurred with I/O shadowing off
$0015	Segment loader error
$0017-24	Cannot load a package
$0025	Out of memory
$0026	Segment loader error
$0027	File map trashed
$0028	Stack overflow error
$0030	File Manager alert—please insert disk
$0032-53	Memory Manager errors
$0100	Cannot mount system startup volume

Note: Errors above $0100 contain tool set number reporting error in high byte and error code for tool in low byte (value other than $00).

Table 25-5
System Death Manager Error Codes

increments the flag, and then returns after restoring whatever value was in the interrupt disable bit and the accumulator.

If your application needs to prevent interruptions, it should call INCBUSYFLG when needed and then call DECBUSYFLG when it is done. DECBUSYFLG decrements the busy flag, being careful to check that the value of the flag is not decremented below zero. If the flag is decremented to zero, the routine also calls the various items in the Scheduler queue.

To place an item in the Scheduler queue, you need to call SchAddTask, which contains a long-word pointer to the start of the task being placed in the queue. The routine returns a nonzero word value if the task was added to the queue and a zero value if the task was not added to the queue. Only

Call	Number	Inputs	Outputs
SchBootInit	1	None	None
SchAppInit	2	None	None
SchAppTerm	3	None	None
SchVersion	4	None	Version
SchReset	5	None	None
SchActive	6	None	ActiveFlag
SchAddTask	9	TaskPointer	AddedFlag
SchFlush	10	None	None

Table 25-6
Scheduler Tool Set

four items may be placed in the queue at one time. Items in the queue are called with a JSL with the 65816 in full native mode and the data bank register set to $E0.

The Scheduler tool set also contains a SchFlush function, which removes all items from the Scheduler queue. The full Scheduler Tool Set is listed in Table 25-6.

HEARTBEAT INTERRUPT HANDLER

A final, somewhat unusual, interrupt-driven routine is the HeartBeat Interrupt Handler. It is installed by the Event Manager. The handler is called 60 times a second, whenever there is a vertical blanking interrupt. Its main function is maintaining the Tick Counter, although it also can be used for other purposes.

Every time the HeartBeat Interrupt Handler is called, it checks each routine in its queue. If the task count value for a routine is not zero, the HeartBeat Interrupt Handler decrements the value. If the value is decremented to zero, the routine is called.

Any routine and any number of routines may be installed in the HeartBeat Interrupt Queue, although it is recommended that the queue be used for fairly short routines only. Otherwise the counting of ticks could be adversely affected, as could the ability to run the main application.

A routine installed in the queue must have a special header in the following form:

```
HBTaskLink      DS 4            ;Long-word space for link to next item in queue
TaskCount       DC I'60'        ;Place whatever value you want here
ID              DC H'A55A'      ;Signature of $A5A5 required
                . . .           ;Rest of code goes here
```

When the routine is called by the HeartBeat Interrupt Handler, the 65816 is in native mode with 8-bit memory and registers. If your routine is going to be called periodically, rather than just once, the task count value must be reset. The HeartBeat Interrupt Handler ignores routines with a zero task count. Finally, the routine must end with an RTL. The following is a code skeleton for a HeartBeat Interrupt Queue task:

```
* Note: routine assumes it already has header that appeared in previous
* listing
TaskCode        BEGIN
                REP #$30        ;If desire 16-bit registers and memory
                LDA #60         ;Reset counter
                STA TaskCount
                . . .           ;Code for routine goes here
                RTL
                END
```

An item is placed in the HeartBeat Interrupt Queue by the Miscellaneous Tool Set function SetHeartBeat. This function requires an input of a long-word pointer to the address of the routine to be installed. Similarly the DelHeartBeat function, with a long-word input pointer to the address of a routine, deletes the specified routine from the queue. The entire queue can be cleared by ClrHeartBeat.

PART VII

Math: Computing with the Apple IIGS

CHAPTER 26

Computing on the IIGS: Integer Math and SANE

With all the focus on the graphics and sound of the Apple IIGS, it is easy to forget that one of the things computers do best is to compute. Besides the basic mathematical capabilities of the 65816 microprocessor, the Apple IIGS contains many routines, either in RAM or ROM, that provide significant mathematical functions. Some of these routines, such as the floating-point routines that are part of the Applesoft Interpreter, have been available since the 8-bit Apple II days. This book will not discuss those routines. However, two new sources of math capability have been added to the Apple IIGS—"integer" math tools, and support for the Standard Apple Numerics Environment (SANE).

INTEGER MATH

The Integer Math Tool Set on the IIGS is designed for use by the other tools when they need to make "integer" calculations. It is partially derived from similar routines found on the Macintosh. The name of the tool set is a misnomer because it supports several different types of numbers, both integer and fractional. For instance, it supports multiplication, division, and transcendental functions, as well as conversion between the various types of numbers support, plus ASCII representation of numbers and conversion to the SANE extended numeric format.

Integer Math Types

The four types of numbers supported by the Integer Math routines are listed in Table 26-1. The *integer value* is a standard signed word-length value. The highest bit is the sign bit, and is clear (=0) if the number is positive and is set (=1) if the number is negative. The value, given in the lower 15 bits, is in standard binary format if the number is positive and in

Name	Size	Type	Range
Integer	16 bits	Signed integer	+/− 32767
Long integer	32 bits	Signed integer	+/− 2.145 billion
Fixed	32 bits	Signed w/ 16 bits frac	+/− 32767
Frac	32 bits	Signed w/ 30 bits frac	+/− 3

Table 26-1

Number Types Supported by Integer Math

two's complement if the number is negative. (Number format, including two's complement, is discussed in Fischer, *65816/65802 Assembly Language Programming,* Osborne/McGraw-Hill.) The 32-bit *long-integer* is similar in structure except its sign bit is bit number 31 and its value is contained in the lower 31 bits.

A *fixed value* is a 32-bit value containing three parts. The sign is bit 31, and bits 16 to 30 contain the integer portion of the value. Note that the integer value is the same whether the value is positive or negative—there is no two's complement representation. The lower 16 bits of the number is the fraction part of the value. Each bit represents a binary fraction such that the first bit is 1/2, the second bit is 1/4(1/ [2^2]), the third bit is 1/8 (1/[2^3]), and so forth (see Figure 26-1 for an illustration of this). Note that the maximum value that can be represented by the fraction part of the number is always less than 1. The conversion from a decimal fraction value to binary is often inexact because of the inability of the binary system to represent decimal values within the 16 bits allotted for this.

The *frac value* consists of a 32-bit value divided into three parts in a manner similar to the fixed value. The main difference is the number of bits allotted for each function. In the frac value there is 1 bit for the sign, 1 bit for the integer portion, and 30 bits for the fraction portion. This allocation results in a much smaller range than a fixed value (approximately +/−32767 for the fixed value versus approximately +/− 3 for the frac value). The advantage is that the frac value can represent fractional value in much greater precision.

Bit Number:	15	14	13	12	11	10	9	8
Value:	$\frac{1}{2}$	$\frac{1}{4}$	$\frac{1}{8}$	$\frac{1}{16}$	$\frac{1}{32}$	$\frac{1}{64}$	$\frac{1}{128}$	$\frac{1}{256}$
Bit Number:	7	6	5	4	3	2	1	0
Value:	$\frac{1}{512}$	$\frac{1}{1024}$	$\frac{1}{2048}$	$\frac{1}{4096}$	$\frac{1}{8192}$	$\frac{1}{16384}$	$\frac{1}{32768}$	$\frac{1}{65536}$

Figure 26-1
Fraction part of fixed value

Integer Multiplication and Division

The Integer Math Tool Set provides multiplication and division routines using any of the four types of numbers supported by the tool set. Multiplication of integers results in a long-integer result. Multiplication of long integers results in a 64-bit (four-word) result.

Multiplication of either fixed or frac values returns a rounded fixed or frac value. If the result exceeds the maximum value for the fixed or frac type, the routine outputs the most positive or most negative fixed or frac value, depending on whether the input values were the same (most positive) or different (most negative).

The four multiplication routines are used similarly. Space for the result is first pushed on the stack. Then the multiplicand is pushed on the stack. Finally, the multiplier is pushed on the stack. The routine is then called, and the product is left on the stack following the return from the routine. The four multiplication routines are summarized in Table 26-2.

Note that in the case of integer or long-integer multiplication, the product result space on the stack must be twice the size of the multiplier or multiplicand input space.

The integer routines also provide for multiplication of either signed or unsigned values. Because of the way signed integers work, any 16-bit value can be considered either as a full 16-bit unsigned integer or as a signed, 15-bit integer (in two's complement form). The Multiply and LongMul routines do not care which type of value they receive. If the values are signed integers, the signed result is returned in the lower half of the result. If the values are unsigned integers, the unsigned result is returned in the full result.

Routine Name	Function Number	Input Size	Output Size	Unsigned or Signed	Value Type
Multiply	$09	16 bits	32 bits	Either	Integer
LongMul	$0C	32 bits	64 bits	Either	Long-integer
FixMul	$0F	32 bits	32 bits	Signed	Fixed
FracMul	$10	32 bits	32 bits	Signed	Frac

Table 26-2

Integer Math Multiplication Routines

The division routines are not an exact mirror of the multiplication routines, either in the size of the value used or in the type of inputs supported. The routines are summarized in Table 26-3.

When integer or long-integer values are used for dividing, resulting in integer or long-integer results, two values are returned by the routine. The first value is the integer or long-integer quotient, and the second is the integer or long-integer remainder. There is also a routine (called Ratio) that returns a single, signed, fixed result to the division of two integer values. Dividing of long-integer values is restricted to unsigned numbers.

The fixed and frac division routines return only one value. This is the quotient expressed as either a fixed or frac value, depending on the type of input values. In either case, the result is signed and is rounded to the nearest possible representation of the value. If the result is either too large or too small to be expressed in fixed or frac format, the result is set to either the most-positive or most-negative possible value. The most-positive value is used if the signs of the input values are the same, and the most-negative value is used if the signs of the input values are different.

Integer Transcendental Functions

The Integer Math Tool Set provides a limited set of transcendental functions, providing for square root, cosine, sine, and arctangent. Only a limited number of types of input values can be used with these functions. They are summarized in Table 26-4.

Routine Name	Function Number	Input Type	Output Type	Signed or Unsigned
SDivide	$0A	Integer	Integer	Signed
UDivide	$0B	Integer	Integer	Unsigned
LongDivide	$0D	Long	Long	Unsigned
FixRatio	$0E	Integer	Fixed	Signed
FixDiv	$11	Fixed	Fixed	Signed
FracDiv	$12	Frac	Frac	Signed

Table 26-3

Integer Math Division Routines

Function Number	Name	Function Type	Input Type	Output Type
14	FracSqrt	Square root	Frac (unsigned)	Frac (rounded)
15	FracCos	Cosine	Fixed (radians)	Fixed
16	FracSin	Sine	Fixed (radians)	Fixed
17	FixATan2	Arctangent	Long, fixed, or frac (both of same type)	Fixed (radians)

Table 26-4
Integer Math Transcendental Function Routines

The square root function simply returns a rounded frac square root for the frac value passed as input. The input value is considered unsigned. That is, the first two bits of the value are considered to be binary integers permitting a range of nearly 0 to 4.

The cosine and sine functions both work with fixed input and output values. The input value should be in radians, not degrees. The arctangent function takes inputs of any long-word type (long, fixed, or frac), although both inputs must be of the same type. The two inputs represent the length of the sides, and the output is the fixed arctangent expressed in radians.

Integer Math Conversion

The various integer math types can be converted to other integer math types as well as to certain other types of number formats. Some types cannot be converted to certain other types. For example, the fixed type can be converted only to the other integer math types, the frac type can be converted only to the fixed type, the long-integer type can be converted only to the frac type, and the integer type cannot be converted to any other integer math type.

Note that a frac type can still be converted to an integer or long integer by first being converted to a fixed value and then having that fixed value converted. Similarly a long integer can be converted to a frac, the frac can be converted to a fixed, and the fixed can be converted to an integer.

The integer and long integer can also be converted to ASCII representation. This representation can be either decimal or hexadecimal. Note that the ASCII representation of a value is not the same as the value itself. For example, the number "1" is represented in ASCII as the value $31. The hexadecimal value $1234, then, is the numeric equivalent of the ASCII string $34 33 32 31 (from the lowest to the highest memory location).

Each hexadecimal nibble requires 1 byte for its ASCII representation. Thus, an integer value—2 bytes or 4 nibbles—requires a 4-byte ASCII string to represent its hexadecimal value. A long-integer value requires 8 bytes for its ASCII string.

When the hexadecimal value is converted to an ASCII decimal string, it may require even more bytes. The largest unsigned value that can be represented by an integer is 65,535, which requires 5 bytes for its ASCII decimal representation. The largest unsigned value that can be represented by a long integer is 4,294,967,295, which requires 10 bytes for its ASCII decimal representation.

Conversion routines also exist to change the fixed and frac values into the extended format used by SANE, which is discussed later in this chapter. Other routines convert from extended format into fixed and frac.

The format of values passed for the conversion routines is fairly simple. As with the IIGS toolbox, space for any output first must be pushed on the stack. This space is followed by the input value. The input value in all cases, except ASCII strings or extended format values, is passed directly on the stack. Extended values and ASCII strings are passed by means of a pointer to the actual value or, in the case of output, the location where the value is to be placed.

ASCII strings also have placed on the stack a word value that represents the length of the string being input or the length of the output string to be created. Note that since your application specifies the length of the output string, you can have too short a string to represent the value being converted. This is especially likely if you fail to consider the space used by any sign.

Conversion of ASCII decimal strings also requires consideration of whether the hexadecimal value is to be considered signed or unsigned. The signed flag, input to these routines, is set to a value other than zero to show that a signed value is being used. The signed flag also is used in routines converting from an ASCII decimal string to a hexadecimal value. An error will occur if your application tells the Integer Math routines to expect an unsigned value while you input a signed decimal string.

CONVERSION FROM \ CONVERSION TO	ASCII Decimal[3]	ASCII Hexadecimal[3,4]	Extended (SANE)	Fixed	Frac	Integer	Long Integer
ASCII Decimal[1]	—					$28	$29
ASCII Hexadecimal[1]		—				$24	$25
Extended (SANE)[2]			—	$20*	$21*		
Fixed			$1E	—	$1C	$13*	$1B*
Frac			$1F	$1D*	—		
Integer	$26	$22/2A				—	
Long Integer	$27	$23			$1A		—

Notes:

* Value is rounded.

1. Input string is right-justified and padded on the left with blanks or zeros. High bit of each byte can be set (negative ASCII) or clear (positive ASCII). Overflow error returned if value too large.
2. Overflows, NaNs, and Infinities return the most positive or negative value based on the sign of the input value.
3. Output is right-justified and padded on the left with blanks. The high bit of each byte is clear (positive ASCII).
4. The $2A function returns a 4-byte string in all cases.

Table 26-5

Integer Math Conversion Routines

Table 26-5 is a cross-reference of the various conversion routines showing which values can be converted into which other values.

Table 26-6 is a listing of all the Integer Math routines together with the function number assigned to each routine and the input and output values used by that routine.

STANDARD APPLE NUMERICS ENVIRONMENT (SANE)

The other built-in mathematics tool set in the Apple IIGS is the Standard Apple Numerics Environment, known as SANE. This tool set is similar to the one available on the Macintosh and also is available for the 65C02-based Apple II family. It provides extended-precision mathematic functions conforming to the IEEE Standard 754-1985, Standard for Binary Floating-Point Arithmetic.

This standard includes data types, mathematical operations, conversion, and tools for cases involving exceptions like division by zero, infinities, and overflows. It also contains extensions to the standard such as scientific and financial functions, as well as a data type especially created for accounting functions.

SANE includes the following:

- Single (32-bit), double (64-bit), and extended (80-bit) floating-point number types as specified by the IEEE standard
- A special 64-bit integer value used for applications requiring exact matching values (such as accounting)
- Standard operations such as addition, subtraction, multiplication, division, square root, remainder (modulo), and comparison
- Higher math functions such as logarithms, trigonometric functions, exponentials, compounding, and annuity
- Random-number generation
- Type conversions as well as conversion between binary and decimal format

This chapter summarizes only the basics of the SANE system. For a full treatment, including the handling of exceptional cases, special results, and the entire SANE environment, see the *Apple Numerics Manual,* Addison-Wesley, 1985.

Function Name	Functioh Number	Angle	ATSide1	ATSide2	Cosine	Dividend	Divisor	ExtendedPtr	Fixed	Frac	HexString	Integer
Parameter Size		L	L	L	L	V	V	L	L	L	L	W
Parameter Type		C	A	A	X	V	V	P	X	F	S	I
Dec2Int	40											O1
Dec2Long	41											
Fix2Frac	28								I1	O1		
Fix2Long	27								I1			
Fix2X	30							O1	I1			
FixATan2	23	O1	I1	I2								
FixDiv	17					I1X	I2X					
FixMul	15											
FixRatio	14					I1W	I2W					
FixRound	19								I1			O1
Frac2Fix	29								O1	I1		
Frac2X	31							O1		I1		
FracCos	21	I1			O1							
FracDiv	18					I1F	I2F					
FracMul	16											
FracSin	22	I1										
FracSqrt	20									I1		
Hex2Int	36											O1
Hex2Long	37											
HexIt	42										O1	
HiWord	24											
IMActive	6											
IMBootInit	1											
IMReset	5											
IMShutDown	3											

Table 26-6

All Integer Math Routines

LongInteger	LongWord	Multiplicand	Multiplier	Product	Quotient	Remainder	Result	SignedFlag	Sine	SquareRoot	StringLen	StringPtr	Version	Word
L	L	V	V	V	V	V	W	W	L	L	W	L	W	W
L	V	V	V	V	V	V	B	B	X	F	V	P	V	V
								I3			I2	I1		
O1								I3			I2	I1		
O1														
		I1X	I2X	O1X										
					O1X									
		I1F	I2F	O1F	O1F									
									O1					
										O1				
											I2	I1		
O1											I2	I1		
	I1													O1
	I1													O1
						O1								

Function Name	Function Number	Angle	ATSide1	ATSide2	Cosine	Dividend	Divisor	ExtendedPtr	Fixed	Frac	HexString	Integer
Parameter Size		L	L	L	L	V	V	L	L	L	L	W
Parameter Type		C	A	A	X	V	V	P	X	F	S	I
IMStartup	2											
IMVersion	4											
Int2Dec	38											I1
Int2Hex	34											I1
Long2Dec	39											
Long2Fix	26								O1			
Long2Hex	35											
LongDivide	13					I1L	I2L					
LongMul	12											
LoWord	25											
Multiply	9											
SDivide	10					I1W	I2W					
UDivide	11					I1W	I2W					
X2Fix	32							I1	O1			
X2Frac	33							I1		O1		

Notes:

Size: L Long-word (32-bits)
V Varies with routine (indicated in chart)
W Word (16-bit)

Type: A Any of fixed, frac, or long-integer
B Boolean
F Frac
I Integer
L Long integer
P Pointer
S String
V Value
X Fixed
* 64-bit value

Table 26-6

All Integer Math Routines (continued)

LongInteger	LongWord	Multiplicand	Multiplier	Product	Quotient	Remainder	Result	SignedFlag	Sine	SquareRoot	StringLen	StringPtr	Version	Word
L	L	V	V	V	V	V	W	W	L	L	W	L	W	W
L	V	V	V	V	V	V	B	B	X	F	V	P	V	V
													O1	
							I4				I3	I2		
											I3	I2		
I1							I4				I3	I2		
I1														
I1											I3	I2		
					O2L	O1L								
		I1L	I2L	O1*										
	I1													O1
		I1W	I2W	O1L										
					O2W	O1W								
					O2W	O1W								

SANE can support six numeric types, and also supports a decimal format ASCII record.

The Single type is a 32-bit value, with a 23-bit mantissa, an 8-bit exponent, and a sign bit, as follows:

- □ *Bits 0-22* Mantissa normally presumed to be preceded by a value of 1 plus a binary point
- □ *Bits 23-30* Exponent whose actual value is 127 less than the value shown
- □ *Bit 31* Sign bit (set to show negative)

Thus the Single value %1001 0111 0111 0010 1110 1101 0000 1001 is evaluated as follows:

Bits 0-22 = 111 0010 1110 1101 0000 1001 =

(Implied 1) + 1/2 + 1/4 + 1/8 + 0/16 + 0/32 + 1/64 + 0/128 + 1/256 + 1/512 + 1/1024 + 0/2048 + 1/4096 + 1/8192 + 0/16384 + 1/32768 . . .

Bits 23-30 = 001 0111 0 = 0010 1110 = $2E = 46

Exponent = 46−127 = −81

Sign = 1 so value is negative

The Double type is similar to the Single except that its mantissa is 52 bits (bits 0-51), its exponent is 11 bits (bits 52-62) with a true exponent value being the exponent value minus 1023, and its sign bit is bit 63.

The Comp type is used for applications in which it is important to have exact results without the minor differences caused by conversion of a fractional value from binary to decimal or from decimal to binary. This is an all-integer value comprised of 64 bits. Bits 0-62 are the representation of the number, in two's complement form, if the value is negative. Bit 63 is the sign bit and is set to 1 if the value is negative.

The Extended type is used for nearly all computations within the SANE system. Since it is larger that the Single, Double, or Comp form, most values are converted to Single, Double, or Comp form for purposes of storage, thus saving storage space. A Single, Double, or Comp value may be converted to an Extended type without any loss of precision. An Extended type may lose some precision when converted to a Single, Double, or Comp type and may overflow or underflow.

The Extended type is 80 bits in size. It has 64 bits of mantissa, 15 bits of exponent, and a sign bit as follows:

- *Bits 0-62* Mantissa portion following the binary point
- *Bit 63* Mantissa portion preceding the binary point
- *Bits 64-78* Exponent whose actual value is 16383 less than the value shown
- *Bit 79* Sign bit (set to show negative)

SANE also supports a standard integer (16 bits, bit 15 is sign bit, two's complement representation) and a long integer (32 bits, bit 31 is sign bit, two's complement representation) value.

SANE also supports a decimal record for holding a numeric value in modified decimal string format. The SANE scanner can convert a decimal ASCII string into a decimal record. The record consists of the following three parts:

1. A word indicating the sign, set to 0 for positive and to 1 for negative
2. A word indicating the value of the exponent
3. A Pascal-type string (the first byte contains the string length) of 18 or less characters containing the mantissa with a decimal point

When a value is converted from a SANE value-type into an ASCII decimal string, the form of representation depends on a record passed to the conversion routine known as a Decform (for decimal string format) record. This record contains two word-length fields as follows:

1. A word containing a 0 if the format is floating-point and a 1 if the format is fixed-point
2. A word showing the number of significant digits if the style is floating-point and showing the number of digits (positive or negative) to the right of the decimal point if the style is fixed-point

Superficially, the SANE tool set seems like many of the other tool sets on the Apple IIGS. It has the five standard functions present in each tool

Name	Function Number
SANEBootInit	1
SANEStartup	2
SANEShutDown	3
SANEVersion	4
SANEReset	5
FPNum	9
DecStrNum	A
ElemNum	B

Table 26-7
SANE Tool Set Functions

set as well as a few other tools, all shown in Table 26-7. But the tools are not called in the normal Apple IIGS fashion. As seen in Table 26-7, the SANE tool set contains only three calls other than the normal tool set housekeeping functions. The FPNum command performs all of the standard arithmetic operations, comparisons, conversions, and environmental control operations available in the SANE tool set. The DecStrNum function handles the string scanning and formatting operations. The ElemNum function handles the various logarithmic, trigonometic, and accounting functions.

The SANE operations work normally with either one or two input values and place the output in one of the input values. The output value that is also used as an input value is called the destination, or DST, value and, for most operations, is of Extended type. The other input value for operations that take two operands, called source or SRC, is of any of the various SANE types. Exceptions to this method are discussed with the description of the operation.

When performing a SANE operation, your application first pushes the address of the source operand, if any, on the stack. This is a long-word value. (In a few cases the actual value, rather than the address of the value, is pushed on the stack. This is indicated in the tables.) Next, the address of the destination operand is pushed on the stack. Finally, the macro using the name of the SANE operation is invoked. When this macro is expanded, it first pushes the opword for this operation on the stack and then calls the appropriate SANE tool function through the standard tool locator call. The macro thus appears like the following:

```
Pushword OpWord
LDX #SANETSNum + FuncNum * 256
JSL $E10000
```

Note that this macro contains one more line than the standard tool set macros, the Pushword OpWord instruction. Thus, to invoke the SANE function that adds two extended format numbers, your application should use the following code:

```
SANEData  DATA
SRC       DS 10             ;Space for extended number source
DST       DS 10             ;Space for extended number destination
          END
          . . .
Addem     START
          USING SANEData
          PushLong #SRC ;Address of source value on stack
          PushLong #DST ;Address of destination value on stack
          _FADDX        ;SANE Macro: DST = SRC + DST
          . . .
          END
```

Because of the way SANE functions, it does not return values on the stack, with the exception of the SANEVersion call. SANE may use as much as 50 bytes on the stack while it is functioning, but it always returns the stack with no return values and any input values removed.

When your application starts SANE with the SANEStartup call, it must pass a 2-byte address, in bank zero, that SANE can use as a direct page. This 256-byte chunk of memory must have been obtained previously from the Memory Manager. Bytes $18-1D of this direct page must be preserved in between calls to SANE. When your application is finished using SANE, it may call SANEShutdown, although that function presently does not do anything. The application should call the Memory Manager to deallocate the direct page used by SANE.

The SANE basic math functions (addition, subtraction, multiplication, division, remainder, and copy-sign) all work with each of the six SANE value types as the source value, placing the result in the extended destination value. The name of the macro setting up the routine consists of the

Operation	Root of Macro Name
Addition	FADD
Subtraction	FSUB
Multiplication	FMUL
Division	FDIV
Remainder	FREM
Copy-sign	FCPYSGN

Table 26-8
SANE Basic Math Functions

Value Type	Suffix
Extended	X
Double	D
Single	S
Comp	C
Integer	I
Long-integer	L

Table 26-9
SANE Value Types and Suffix Used

root shown in Table 26-8, followed by the one-letter suffix representing the value type, shown in Table 26-9.

The remainder routine not only returns the remainder in the destination value, it also returns the integer quotient as well. The absolute values of the quotient are returned in the low 7 bits of the X register. The sign of the quotient is returned in bits 7 and 15 of the X register, as well as the sign bit of the 65816 processor status register.

The other SANE math functions are listed in Table 26-10 together with the macro used to call each one—whether the routine is a unary routine (only uses the DST operand) or a binary routine (uses both SRC and DST operands)—and the type of value(s) involved.

The SANE tool set also provides for conversion of any type of value either to or from an extended type of value. A decimal record also can be

Operation Type	Name	Unary or Binary	Value Type DST	SRC
Square root	FSQRTX	Unary	X	
Round to integer	FRINTX	Unary	X	
Truncate to integer	FTINTX	Unary	X	
Binary log	FLOGBX	Unary	X	
Binary scale[1]	FSCALBX	Binary	X	I
Negate	FNEGX	Unary	X	
Absolute value	FABSX	Unary	X	
Next-After[2]	FNEXTX	Binary	X	X
	FNEXTD	Binary	D	D
	FNEXTS	Binary	S	S
Log to Base e	FLNX	Unary	X	
Log to Base 2	FLOG2X	Unary	X	
Log1 to Base e	FLN1X	Unary	X	
Log1 to Base 2	FLOG21X	Unary	X	
Base e exponential	FEXPX	Unary	X	
Base 2 exponential	FEXP2X	Unary	X	
Base e exp1	FEXP1X	Unary	X	
Base 2 exp2	FEXP21X	Unary	X	
Integer exponent[3]	FXPWR1	Binary	X	I
General exponent[3]	FXPWRY	Binary	X	X
Compound interest[4]	FCOMPOUND	Three	X	X X
Annuity[4]	FANNUITY	Three	X	X X
Arctangent	ATANX	Unary	X	
Sine	FSINX	Unary	X	
Cosine	FCOSX	Unary	X	
Tangent	FTANX	Unary	X	
Random	FRANDX	Unary	X	

Notes:

1. Operation is X * 2^I.
2. Operation is next value after DST toward SRC.
3. Operation is DST^SRC.
4. Operation uses DST as principal, SRC as number of periods, and SRC2 as rate.

Table 26-10

Other SANE Math Operations

converted to an extended number or converted from an extended number. In the case of conversion from an extended number to a decimal record, the Decform record is used to determine the format of the decimal value. Table 26-11 summarizes these operations.

SANE provides routines that permit you to compare two values. In addition to the standard less-than, equal-to, and greater-than comparison results, SANE also provides a result of unordered. This is the result when at least one of the values is the special SANE type NaN (not a number).

Operation Name	Source	Destination Type	Type of Conversion
FX2X	X	X	Binary to binary
FX2D	X	D	Binary to binary
FX2S	X	S	Binary to binary
FX2C	X	C	Binary to binary
FX2I	X	I	Binary to binary
FX2L	X	L	Binary to binary
FD2X	D	X	Binary to binary
FS2X	S	X	Binary to binary
FC2X	C	X	Binary to binary
FI2X	I	X	Binary to binary
FL2X	L	X	Binary to binary
FX2DEC	X	DecRecord	Binary to decimal*
FD2DEC	D	DecRecord	Binary to decimal*
FS2DEC	S	DecRecord	Binary to decimal*
FC2DEC	C	DecRecord	Binary to decimal*
FI2DEC	I	DecRecord	Binary to decimal*
FL2DEC	L	DecRecord	Binary to decimal*
FDEC2X	DecRecord	X	Decimal to binary
FDEC2D	DecRecord	D	Decimal to binary
FDEC2S	DecRecord	S	Decimal to binary
FDEC2C	DecRecord	C	Decimal to binary
FDEC2I	DecRecord	I	Decimal to binary
FDEC2L	DecRecord	L	Decimal to binary

Note:

* The address of a Decform record is pushed first; the destination record is formatted based on this record.

Table 26-11

SANE Conversion Routines

Performing a comparison involves testing the source value (type X, D, S, C, I, or L) with the destination value (always type X). Two different sets of routines are available. FCMP + <source type suffix> is used when your application does not wish to have SANE signal an invalid comparison if the values are unordered. FCPX + <source type suffix> is used when your application does want to have unordered values signaled invalid. (Signaling is a special aspect of the SANE system and is discussed in the *Apple Numerics Manual.*)

The result of the comparison is passed back to your application in the 65816 status, X, and Y registers as shown in Table 26-12. Note that the 65816 results are treated slightly differently from the 6502 results, as discussed in the *Apple Numerics Manual.*

A final aspect of SANE that has been changed somewhat by the 65816 version on the Apple IIGS is the halt mechanism. This routine lets your application transfer program control to a special handling routine, pointed to by the halt vector, when certain exceptions occur during number processing. (For further details on halt itself, see the *Apple Numerics Manual.*)

The halt vector is stored as a 4-byte address. SetHaltVector requires that this address be placed on the stack before it is called. GetHaltVector returns the address in the X and Y registers, as shown in Figure 26-2. Note that byte 2 is repeated in the two registers and byte 4, which is always $00, is not returned.

The contents of the SANE direct page, on entry to the halt routine, are shown in Figure 26-3. The 'C' address is the address of DST in the case of unary and binary functions, and the address of the Decform record in

	Status Register				
Relationship	**Z**	**N**	**V**	**X register**	**Y register**
SRC > DST	0	0	1	4040	??40
SRC < DST	0	1	0	8080	??80
SRC = DST	1	0	0	0002	??00
Unordered	0	0	0	0101	??01

Note: ?? indicates the value is variable.

Table 26-12
Result of SANE Comparisons

Y Reg Hi	Y Reg Lo	X Reg Hi	X Reg Lo
Byte 3	Byte 2	Byte 2	Byte 1

Figure 26-2
Format of halt vector returned by GetHaltVector

Offset from Bottom of Page	Use	Length
0	RTL #1	3 bytes
3	RTL #2	3 bytes
6	Application's direct page	2 bytes
8	Application's data bank	2 bytes
10	Current opword	2 bytes
12	'C' address	4 bytes
16	'B' address	4 bytes
20	'A' address	4 bytes
24	Halt vector address	4 bytes
28	Environment word	2 bytes
30	Pending exceptions word	2 bytes
32	Pending X register lo	1 byte
33	Pending X register hi and Y register lo	1 byte
34	Pending Y register hi	1 byte

Figure 26-3
SANE direct page on entry to halt routine

binary-to-decimal conversions. The 'B' address is the address of SRC in the case of binary functions and the address of the binary value in binary-to-decimal conversions. The 'A' address is the address of the decimal record in binary-to-decimal conversions.

On return from the halt routine, the accumulator should contain the value of pending exceptions. This can be assured by including, at the end of the halt routine, the LDA PendingExceptions command. Unpredictable results may occur if the accumulator is not so adjusted.

APPENDIX

A

Apple IIGS Keyboard Layouts*

*The material in this appendix is courtesy of Apple Computer, Inc.

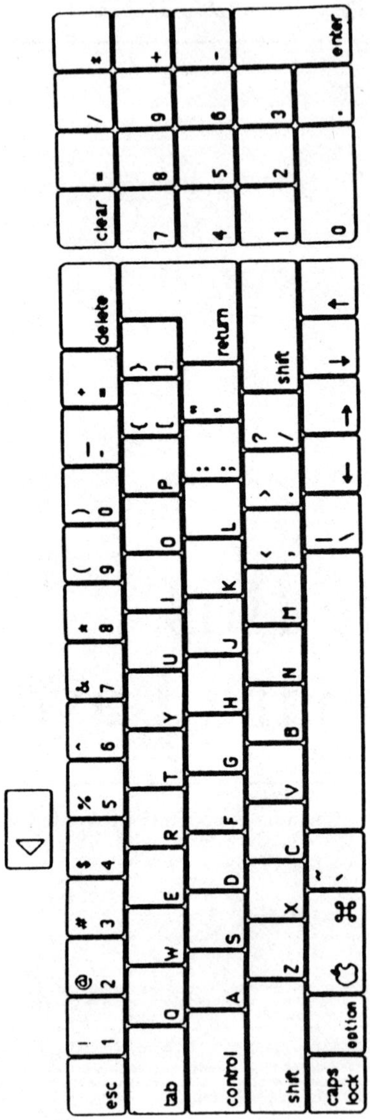

Figure A-1

U.S.A. English keyboard

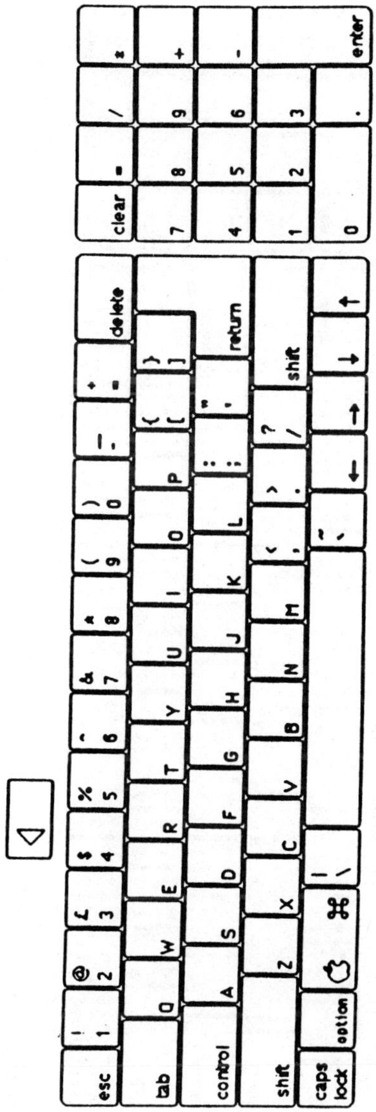

Figure A-2
U.K. English keyboard

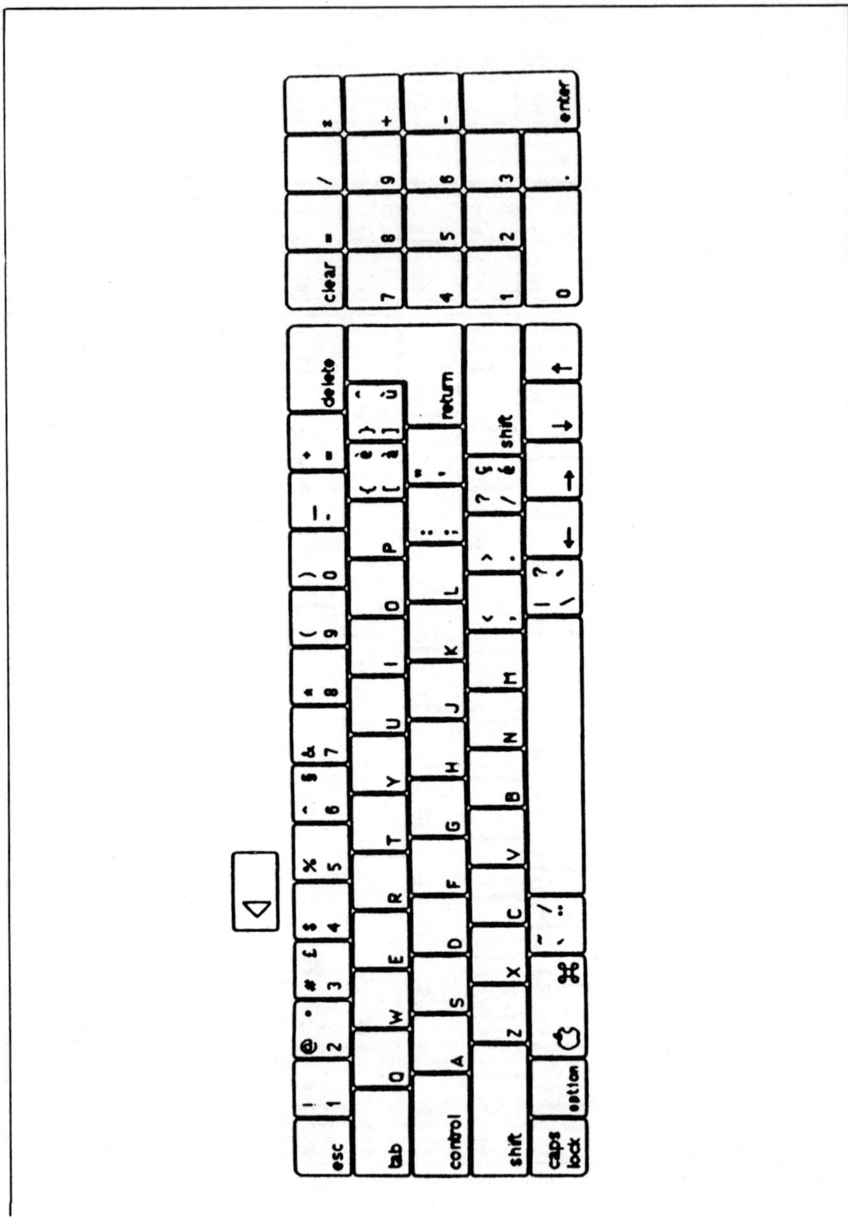

Figure A-3

Canadian keyboard

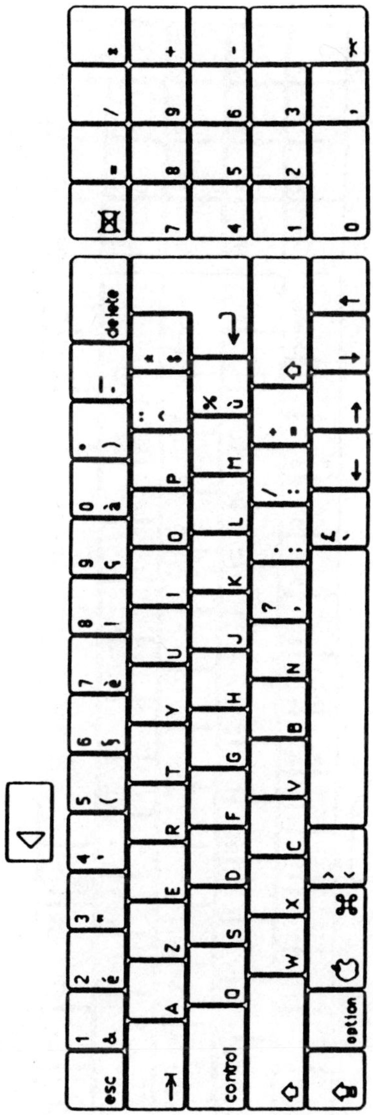

Figure A-4
French keyboard

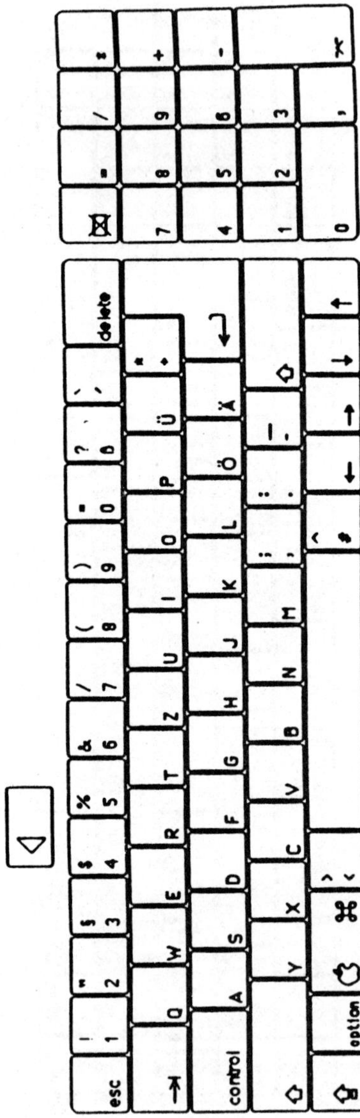

Figure A-5
German keyboard

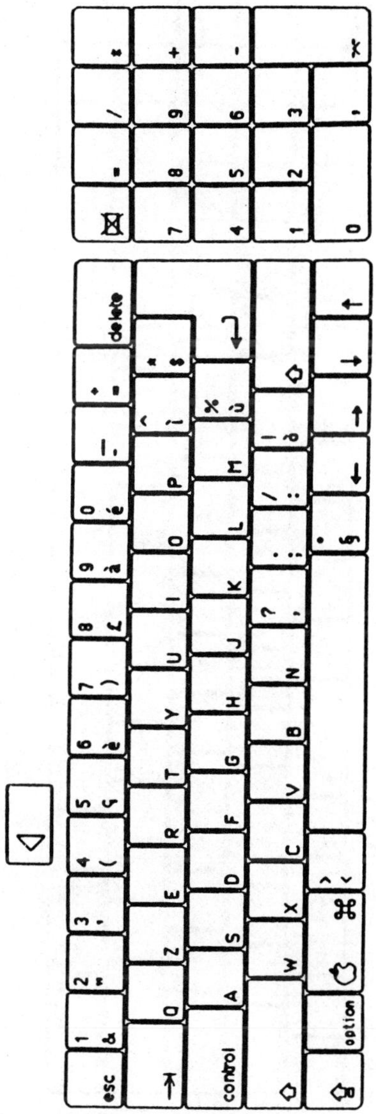

Figure A-6
Italian keyboard

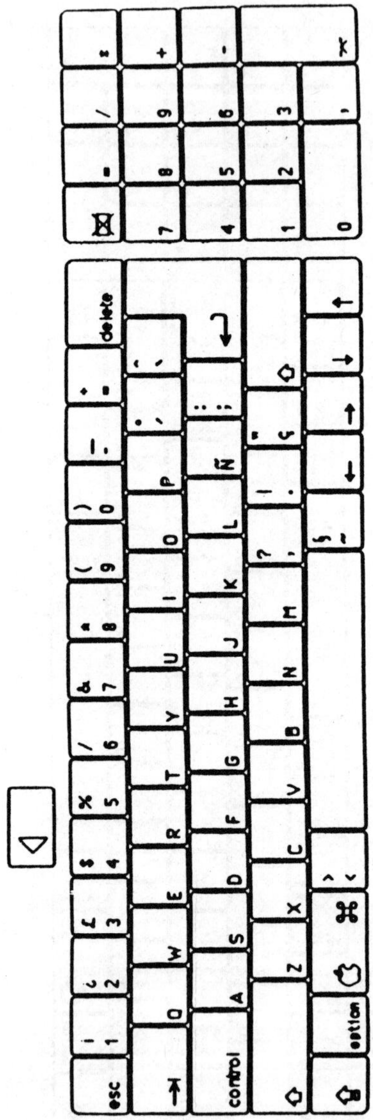

Figure A-7
Spanish keyboard

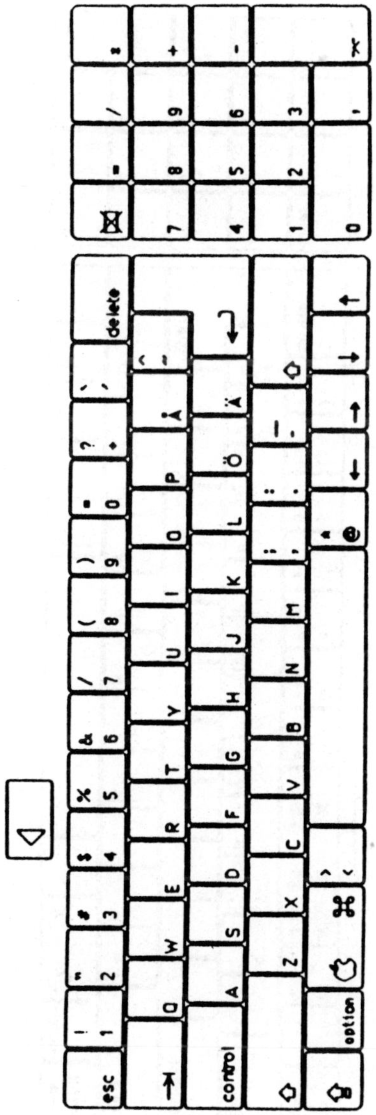

Figure A-8
Swedish keyboard

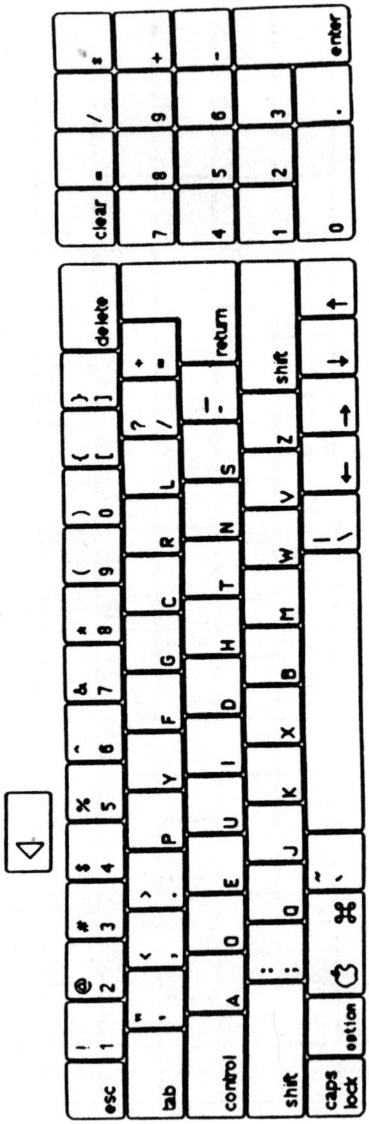

Figure A-9

U.S.A. Dvorak keyboard

APPENDIX

B

65816 Opcodes and Addressing Modes

Code	Mode	Operand Size
#	immediate	one to two bytes
a	absolute	two bytes
a,x	absolute indexed (with X register)	two bytes
a,y	absolute indexed (with Y register	two bytes
al	absolute long	three bytes
al,x	absolute long indexed (with X register)	three bytes
(a)	absolute indirect	two bytes
(a,x)	absolute indexed (with X register) indirect	two bytes
Acc	accumulator	none
d	direct	one byte
d,x	direct indexed (with X register)	one byte
d,y	direct indexed (with Y register)	one byte
(d)	direct indirect	one byte
(d),y	direct indirect indexed (with Y register)	one byte
(d,x)	direct indexed (with X register) indirect	one byte
[d]	direct indirect long	one byte
[d],y	direct indirect indexed (with Y register) long	one byte
i	implied	zero to one byte
r	program counter relative	one byte
r,s	stack relative	one byte
(r,s),y	stack relative indirect indexed (with Y register)	one byte
rl	program counter relative long	two bytes
s	stack	zero to two bytes
xya	block move	two bytes

Table B-1

65816 Addressing Modes Code

Opcode	Addressing Modes
ADC	# a a,x a,y al al,x d d,x (d) (d),y (d,x) [d] [d],y r,s (r,s),Y
AND	# a a,x a,y al al,x d d,x (d) (d),y (d,x) [d] [d],y r,s (r,s),Y
ASL	a a,x ACC d d,x
BCC	r
BCS	r
BEQ	r
BIT	# a a,x d d,x
BMI	r
BNE	r
BPL	r
BRA	r
BRK	i
BRL	rl
BVC	r
BVS	r
CLC	i
CLD	i
CLI	i
CLV	i
CMP	# a a,x a,y al al,x d d,x (d) (d),y (d,x) [d] [d],y r,s (r,s),Y
COP	i
CPX	# a d
CPY	# a d
DEC	a a,x ACC d d,x
DEX	i
DEY	i

Table B-2

Addressing Modes Applicable to Each Opcode

Opcode	Addressing Modes
EOR	# a a,x a,y al al,x d d,x (d) (d),y (d,x) [d] [d],y r,s (r,s),Y
INC	a a,x ACC d d,x
INX	i
INY	i
JML	(a)
JMP	a al (a) (a,x)
JSL	al
JSR	a (a,x)
LDA	# a a,x a,y al al,x d d,x (d) (d),y (d,x) [d] [d],y r,s (r,s),Y
LDX	# a a,y d d,y
LDY	# a a,x d d,x
LSR	a a,x ACC d d,x
MVN	xya
MVP	xya
NOP	i
ORA	# a a,x a,y al al,x d d,x (d) (d),y (d,x) [d] [d],y r,s (r,s),Y
PEA	s
PEI	s
PER	s
PHA	s
PHB	s
PHD	s
PHK	s
PHP	s
PHX	s
PHY	s
PLA	s
PLB	s
PLD	s

Table B-2

Addressing Modes Applicable to Each Opcode (continued)

Opcode	Addressing Modes
PLP	s
PLX	s
PLY	s
REP	#
ROL	a a,x ACC d d,x
ROR	a a,x ACC d d,x
RTI	s
RTL	s
RTS	s
SBC	# a a,x a,y al al,x d d,x (d) (d),y (d,x) [d] [d],y r,s (r,s),Y
SEC	i
SED	i
SEI	i
SEP	#
STA	a a,x a,y al al,x d d,x (d) (d),y (d,x) [d] [d],y r,s (r,s),Y
STP	i
STX	a d d,y
STY	a d d,x
STZ	a a,x d d,x
TAX	i
TAY	i
TCD	i
TCS	i
TDC	i
TRB	a d
TSB	a d
TSC	i
TSX	i
TXA	i
TXS	i
TXY	i

Table B-2

Addressing Modes Applicable to Each Opcode (continued)

Opcode	Addressing Modes
TYA	i
TYX	i
WAI	i
WDB	i
XBA	i
XCE	i

Table B-2
Addressing Modes Applicable to Each Opcode (continued)

TRADEMARKS

The following names are trademarked products of the corresponding companies.

Apple®	Apple Computer, Inc.
AppleColor™ RGB monitor	Apple Computer, Inc.
Apple Desktop Bus™	Apple Computer, Inc.
AppleMouse™	Apple Computer, Inc.
Applesoft™	Apple Computer, Inc.
AppleTalk™	Apple Computer, Inc.
Apple II™	Apple Computer, Inc.
Apple IIc™	Apple Computer, Inc.
Apple IIe™	Apple Computer, Inc.
Apple IIGS™	Apple Computer, Inc.
Apple® II Plus	Apple Computer, Inc.
Ensoniq®	Ensoniq Corporation
ImageWriter II™	Apple Computer, Inc.
Lisa®	Apple Computer, Inc.
Macintosh™	Apple Computer, Inc.
Macintosh™ Plus	Apple Computer, Inc.
Motorola® 68000	Motorola Corporation
ProDOS®/16	Apple Computer, Inc.

I N D E X

B

C

H

I

X

Y

Z

The manuscript for this book was prepared and submitted to Osborne/McGraw-Hill in electronic form.

The acquisitions editor for this project was Cynthia Hudson. The technical reviewer was Jim Mensch, of Apple Computer, Inc. Lyn Cordell was the project editor.

Text design is by Pamela Webster using Times Roman for text and display.

Cover art is by Bay Graphics Design Associates. Cover supplier is Phoenix Color Corporation. This book was printed and bound by R.R. Donnelley & Sons Company, Crawfordsville, Indiana.

Other related Osborne/McGraw-Hill titles include:

AppleWorks™ Made Easy, Second Edition

by Carole B. Matthews

Osborne's top-selling title has been revised and expanded to cover the new AppleWorks™ version 2.0 as well as the original version. Apple's integrated software that combines database, spreadsheet, and word processing capabilities now runs on the Apple® IIGS and on the Apple II, IIc, and IIe. Whether you're a first-time user or an experienced one, *AppleWorks™ Made Easy* offers you outstanding business solutions that you can apply directly to your work. Matthews shows you how to create basic solutions such as form letters, a name/address database, and an accounts receivable invoice, before advancing to more sophisticated solutions such as a business plan, an inventory database, and budgets. Numerous examples and exercises help you take full control of all three AppleWorks components so you can use them separately or integrate them for greater power. With this "hands-on" approach you'll quickly master all the new AppleWorks features, including the Mail Merge capability. An excellent teaching guide, *AppleWorks™ Made Easy* is designed to make the time you spend "AppleWorking" more efficient and profitable.

$18.95p

0-07-881260-7, 400 pp., 7³/₈ x 9¹/₄

AVAILABLE: 3/87

AppleWorks™ Tips & Traps

by Dick Andersen, Janet McBeen, and Janice M. Gessin

Every AppleWorks™ user will find helpful tips and trap solutions in this book that are guaranteed to save hours of frustration and computing time on the Apple® II Plus, IIe, and IIc. *AppleWorks™ Tips & Traps* shows you how to gain maximum benefit from each AppleWorks environment—database, spreadsheet, and word processing. You'll find practical information on handling files and disks, integrating data in different files, setting up useful home and office applications, and transferring data from other programs into AppleWorks. Like all the books in the *Tips & Traps* series, this is an indispensable dictionary of shortcuts to your software.

$16.95p

0-07-881207-0, 250 pp., 7³/₈ x 9¹/₄

capabilities, setting up printing formats, and integrating WordPerfect™ with other products, such as Lotus® 1-2-3,® dBASE III,® Sidekick,® and ProKey.™ *Advanced WordPerfect®* is the source for ambitious users who want information that exceeds the documentation.

$16.95p
0-07-881239-9, 300 pp., 7³/₈ x 9¹/₄

AppleWriter™ II Made Easy
by Leah Freiwald

This step-by-step tutorial teaches you how to use AppleWriter™ II, the best-selling, powerful word processing system for your Apple® IIe and IIc computer. Written to include AppleWriter II, version 2.0, *AppleWriter™ II Made Easy* provides you with hands-on experience you need to produce business letters, sales reports, memos, and much more. Application exercises show you how to use specific features of AppleWriter II to develop glossaries and handle mail merge. Complete explanations of system commands, helpful screen displays, and convenient appendixes guide you smoothly through the program and make this book the perfect complement to your AppleWriter II package.

$16.95p
0-07-881166-X, 210 pp., 7³/₈ x 9¹/₄

Apple® II User's Guide For Apple® II Plus and Apple® IIe, Third Edition
by Lon Poole, Martin McNiff and Steven Cook

The all-time best-selling *Apple® II User's Guide*, with more than 500,000 copies in print, is now available in a third edition. Apple expert Lon Poole has revised the text to show you how to use the enhanced Apple® IIe, as well as the Apple II, Apple II Plus, Apple IIe, and all peripherals. You'll also find complete instructions for using the ProDOS® and DOS 3.3 operating systems. With Poole's easy-to-follow tutorials in BASIC programming, you'll learn how to utilize all the sound and graphics capabilities of your Apple, including the double high-resolution feature of the enhanced Apple IIe. As a handy reference for years of computing with your Apple, the *Apple® II User's Guide* is an undisputed classic.

$18.95p
0-07-881176-7, 512 pp., 6⁷/₈ x 9¹/₄

Apple® IIc User's Guide
by Lon Poole

The top-selling Osborne/McGraw-Hill title, *Apple® II User's Guide*, has been adapted by Lon Poole for the Apple IIc computer. Following the original easy-to-use format, the *Apple IIc User's Guide* introduces you to the computer and its peripherals. A comprehensive tutorial on Applesoft® BASIC is provided, along with instructions for using your Apple IIc's color graphics and sound features. You'll find the most up-to-date information on ProDOS,® Apple's latest operating system. In addition, helpful appendixes provide convenient summaries and tables for long-term reference. The *Apple IIc User's Guide* is an extensive hands-on resource book for all Apple IIc users.

$18.95p
0-07-881156-2, 480 pp., 6½ x 9¼

Project Management Using Microcomputers
by Harvey A. Levine

Business professionals in all fields can make informed decisions about the best project management software available for their specific needs with the essential information in this guide. Levine discusses state-of-the-art project management techniques that can be applied to every business and to most computer systems. Beginning with an overview of project management, Levine considers the role of the microcomputer in this application. Various capabilities of project management software are then discussed: resource and cost planning, reporting and graphing, scheduling, and tracking. To give you a better idea of how project management software can be used, Levine divides applications into elementary, intermediate, custom designed, and mass-market categories. Every category offers project management examples, each contributed by an industry expert who discusses the reasons and methods behind the application.

$18.95p
0-07-881221-6, 350 pp., 7⅜ x 9¼